ANNUAL REVIEW OF
POLITICAL SCIENCE

ANNUAL REVIEW OF POLITICAL SCIENCE

VOLUME 6, 2003

NELSON W. POLSBY, *Editor*
University of California, Berkeley

www.annualreviews.org   science@annualreviews.org   650-493-4400

ANNUAL REVIEWS
4139 El Camino Way • P.O. Box 10139 • Palo Alto, California 94303-0139

ANNUAL REVIEWS
Palo Alto, California, USA

International Standard Serial Number: 1094-2939
International Standard Book Number: 0-8243-3306-3

TYPESET BY TECHBOOKS, FAIRFAX, VA
PRINTED AND BOUND BY MALLOY INCORPORATED, ANN ARBOR, MI

PREFACE

All academic disciplines arise from the creative endeavors of individuals who are bound together by the sharing of certain life experiences. These occur as the result of graduate training, cohabitation in university departments, exposure to a common range of ideas, and adherence to special norms of discourse. Political science is no exception. Under the best of circumstances, these institutional forces interact with the stuff of politics to stimulate individuals to do the work on which *Annual Reviews* report. This year we have bagged, among other things, accounts of three exemplary scholarly lives that over the last half-century or so have brought great distinction to our part of the intellectual terrain, and have meaningfully shaped the agendas of the rest of us.

Herbert Simon died in 2001 at age 84. He created a body of scholarship devoted to exploring decision-making in its many manifestations. His long, fruitful intellectual journey carried him from the framing and testing of proverbs and principles of public administration to the co-invention of the study of artificial intelligence and the discipline of cognitive science. Richard Neustadt's thoughtful work illustrates what can be made out of a sustained encounter with the lore arising from the operational codes of actors who practice politics at the highest level. Their slightly senior contemporary, Robert Dahl, still active and productive, has greatly refreshed a field of inquiry we now call democratic theory, combining the penetrating consideration of classic texts with a broad critical attention to findings of modern social science. The result has been an especially graceful, original, and illuminating career-long contribution to the appraisal of the ways in which political systems around the world—and organizations within these systems—uphold, or compromise, or undermine, core human values.

From the standpoint of an editor, this is all wonderful stuff: interesting minds at work on interesting problems. I like to think that these scholars, and others similarly occupied, define who we are as an intellectual community. We are indebted to Jonathan Bendor, Charles O. Jones, the team of David Braybrooke and Michael Bailey, and Sergio Fabbrini for their appreciations of some of the achievements of these notable political scientists.

There is more, of course, to this volume, as the table of contents discloses. We try to keep up with the literature as it emerges from the steady—or unsteady—march of history (as in articles about the literature of the Cold War, the Vietnam War, and terrorism). We attempt to keep an eye on significant political institutions (the news media, the Supreme Court) and on great books and their authors (Sammy Finer, John Rawls, Jurgen Habermas) and on the latest new thinking about political processes (electoral fraud, international trade, health policy, ethnic conflict) and about emerging or re-emerging topics of special scholarly concern (feminism, individualism, etc.). No single *Annual Review* can capture everything that goes on in a lively discipline like political science, but as we look back over the six volumes we have produced so far, and peer into the mists ahead, we think we can discern the outlines of a portrait that begins to do justice to our ongoing enterprise.

—Nelson W. Polsby
Editor

Annual Review of Political Science
Volume 6, 2003

CONTENTS

ERRATA
  An online log of corrections to *Annual Review of Political Science*
  chapters (if any have yet been occasioned, 1998 to the present) may be
  found at http://polisci.annualreviews.org/

RELATED ARTICLES

From the *Annual Review of Anthropology*, Volume 32 (2003)

Sustainable Governance of Common-Pool Resources: Context, Methods, and Politics, Arun Agrawal

Urbanization and the Global Perspective, Alan Smart and Josephina Smart

Maddening States: On the Imaginary of Power, Begona Aretxaga

The Anthropology of Welfare "Reform": New Perspectives on U.S. Urban Poverty in the Post-Welfare Era, Sandra L. Morgen and Jeff Maskovsky

Urban Violence and Street Gangs, James Diego Vigil

From the *Annual Review of Psychology*, Volume 54 (2003)

Implicit Measures in Social Cognition Research: Their Meaning and Use, Russell H. Fazio and Michael A. Olson

Personality, Culture, and Subjective Well-Being: Emotional and Cognitive Evaluations of Life, Ed Diener, Shigehiro Oishi, and Richard E. Lucas

Community Contexts of Human Welfare, Marybeth Shinn and Siobhan M. Toohey

Qualitative and Quantitative Analyses of Historical Data, Dean Keith Simonton

From the *Annual Review of Sociology*, Volume 29 (2003)

Beyond Rational Choice Theory, Raymond Boudon

The Changing Picture of Max Weber's Sociology, Richard Swedberg

The Science of Asking Questions, Nora Cate Schaeffer, Stanley Presser

Covert Political Conflict in Organizations: Challenges from Below, Calvin Morrill, Mayer N. Zald, and Hayagreeva Rao

Associations and Democracy: Between Theories, Hopes, and Realities, Archon Fung

The Lopsided Continent: Inequality in Latin America, Kelly Hoffman and Miguel Angel Centeno

The Dynamics of Racial Residential Segregation, Camille Zubrinsky Charles

The African American "Great Migration" and Beyond, Stewart E. Tolnay

Welfare-State Regress in Western Europe: Politics, Institutions, Globalization, and Europeanization, Walter Korpi

Annu. Rev. Polit. Sci. 2003. 6:1–22
doi: 10.1146/annurev.polisci.6.121901.085848
First published online as a Review in Advance on Dec. 18, 2002

RICHARD E. NEUSTADT: Public Servant as Scholar

Charles O. Jones

*Department of Political Science, University of Wisconsin-Madison, North Hall,
Bascom Mall, Madison, Wisconsin 53706; email: cjones@polisci.wisc.edu*

Key Words   President, Presidency, presidential power, executive, politics

■ **Abstract**   Richard E. Neustadt is the author of one of the most influential books
ever written about political leadership. Headed for a career as a political-level bureaucrat, he "drifted" to academia after the 1952 election brought a Republican to the White
House. He observed a disconnect between what he had experienced in the executive
branch in Washington and what was then written about the Presidency. He decided to
write a book that would close this gap and, in doing so, contribute to political science.
Presidential Power was the product of this effort, a book that continues to dominate
the thinking about leadership in the White House. This essay focuses on the career
and writings of Neustadt, including an analysis of his critics and his responses. It
incorporates the results of two interviews with Neustadt.

INTRODUCTION

> I really am a political-level bureaucrat who drifted back to academia, where
> I had never been except as a graduate student. Once I was in academia, it
> was clear that I couldn't get anywhere if I wasn't serious. I had to convince
> my academic colleagues that I was serious about their business. The first
> thing they gave me to do at Columbia was teaching a course on American
> politics with some emphasis on the Presidency. In 1954–55, when I had to
> read all [of what] had been written in the twelve years since I had taken
> my general exams, just to keep ahead of my students, the descriptions, par-
> ticularly about the Presidency, seemed to be very remote from what I had
> experienced. The effort to get that straight is what underlies *Presidential
> Power.*
>
> *Presidential Power* was an effort to fill the gap between the academic liter-
> ature that existed in the middle '50s on the Presidency and my experience of
> it. Also, at that time in academia, if one could fill that gap, the political scientists

would think it a contribution. I don't suppose the political scientists would think that was a contribution now. But they did then.[1]

Thus does Richard E. Neustadt identify his motivations as a scholar and mark changes that have occurred from his generation to the present generation. He explains further why his academic environment was accommodating to what he wrote.

As colleagues, I had David Truman on the one side and Wallace Sayre on the other, and we were a very close little combine. And due to both of them and to their colleagues, Columbia was a very compatible place in those years. To them, it did seem that what I had done did not just fill a gap between my understanding and the literature but added something important to the literature. Pendleton Herring and Arthur Holcombe [of Harvard] would have agreed with them, the people who trained me in political science. But I don't think many departments would think that was so now.

Neustadt's observations about his career and writings justify this essay. He moved to political science from a remarkably fast-paced rise in public and political service. He was, as he describes it, a "political-level bureaucrat" who rather quickly ran out of his politics in Washington and needed a job (see below). As with us all, his background and experiences helped to shape his purposes. As a scholar, he wanted his research and writing to be useful to practitioners, while contributing to political science. As a teacher, he wanted to train others to be like him, to start, perhaps to finish, as public servants. The purpose of this essay is to describe, analyze, and, candidly, promote the Neustadt career as a role model, perhaps even as a corrective to the distance that Neustadt observes between old and new purposes of the discipline.

Among other goals, I hope to create an altered basis for evaluating Neustadt's work. For it is my contention that his motivations have not been those attributed to him by his critics. Often the commentaries appear to be based on the interests and purposes the critic would have pursued if he or she had written *Presidential Power*. Neustadt's questions are not strikingly different from those of more contemporary scholars of the Presidency. He asks: What have I seen? What have others seen? What does it mean? Does it square with what has been written? Whom might I help? What differs is the location and time of the sightings, that which is being viewed, the context within which meaning is sought, and the groups or clients being served.

---

[1]Personal interview with Richard E. Neustadt, November 1, 2001, at the Reform Club, London, England. A second interview was conducted on April 20, 2002, in Cross Plains, Wisconsin. Subsequent quotations not otherwise attributed are taken from these interviews. Transcripts of the interviews will be available in time at the Miller Center of Public Affairs, University of Virginia.

THE MAKING OF A PUBLIC SERVANT

Dick Neustadt was headed for a career in government. He identifies several "accidents" that redirected him into academia. But his start, which we are assured is critical to life's path, was in government service. According to Neustadt, it all began with his father: "My father was a youngster in the Teddy Roosevelt era, the Progressive era. He was a Democrat, at least from Wilson's time, but he was greatly influenced by Teddy." After college, Neustadt's father had a fellowship at South End House, a settlement house in Boston, and then went to New York to serve as secretary of the Governor's Commission on Widows and Orphans. He moved back and forth between the public and private sectors over the next two decades. "The minute the Depression set in seriously and the opportunity afforded, he dived back into public service with enthusiasm . . . which he didn't leave thereafter."

> This meant, among other things, that I was in Washington all through high school from '33 to '36. And that in a way is the first part of my public service. People do not believe me when I say that no one walked on the sidewalk in Washington in 1934; they floated six inches above it. At night you could stand in Lafayette Park and look over at the White House and see that halo. So having a father with Teddy Roosevelt's ideals about public service and then being there during this glorious period: That did it.

Upon receiving his B.A. at the University of California at Berkeley in 1939, Neustadt assumed he would "go on to academia." He was interested in studying nationalism and went to Harvard to study with Rupert Emerson. Once there, and Emerson having left for a post in Washington, Pendleton Herring convinced Neustadt to take a joint degree in Political Economy and Government. He worked with Herring, Arthur Holcombe, Edward Mason, and young economists (including John Dunlop, who served later as Secretary of Labor in the Ford Administration).

Military service was inevitable after Pearl Harbor and so Neustadt applied for a commission in the Navy. He was assigned to the Supply Corps but was told that he would not be called up for six months. Having taken the civil service examination earlier, he "rustled . . . up a job in the Rent Control division of the Office of Price Administration for six months." Thereafter, Neustadt served in the Aleutian Islands, the supply center in Oakland, California, and back in Washington at the end of the war. "So I was in Washington, about to get married. I contemplated going back to Harvard to write my thesis. I just couldn't stand the thought. I'd been active for four years. It just seemed intolerable."

Instead, with the help of a Harvard friend, Neustadt got a job with the Bureau of the Budget. He was aided in this quest by his having passed the civil service examination and taken a job prior to war service. The 1930s and 1940s encouraged a government-service orientation in academia, at least that part of it familiar to Neustadt.

At Harvard . . . numbers of people in both economics and government departments were very much interested in what was going on in Washington. It was
a time when the Keynesians were just raising their heads in economics and
were very much policy-oriented. Also [it was a time] when public administration questions were new and exciting to key people in political science. That
experience did nothing to dim my enthusiasm and directed it.

It seemed that Neustadt was destined to serve in the national government by reason
of his upbringing, training, Washington base, period away from academia, and the
rising status of such service. But there was more. He was, by his own account,
being fitted into the higher-level Washington policy world.

So there I was in the Budget Bureau . . . an exciting institution. Partly because
of my father, who knew an awful lot of people in the New Deal, and partly
again accidents, my wife and I got picked up socially by numbers of people
with far more experience than I in places like the Office of War Mobilization,
and people like Jim Rowe, who was back in the practice of law but had been
at the White House through the '30s. They sort of undertook to educate this
youngster.

An estimates analyst, Neustadt worked for Elmer Staats and was given responsibility for units of the Executive Office of the President. "Instead of taking [these
estimates] literally in budgetary terms, I took them in policy and political terms. So
they decided to promote me . . . to make me staff assistant to the Budget Director,
Jim Webb." Neustadt was then in a key spot for observing the Truman Administration. The new Administration "was getting its staffing feet under itself but the
issue of its direction, liberal or conservative, was being fought for." Webb and
Clark Clifford were more liberal; John Steelman and Secretary of the Treasury
John Snyder more conservative. "So for a youngster, this was all very interesting
and illuminating."

At the end of 1947, Neustadt was assigned to the Legislative Reference Division
of the Budget Bureau, soon working immediately under its Director, Roger Jones.
He was responsible for bills of special interest to the White House, and therefore to
Clark Clifford, serving as Special Counsel. The acquaintanceship with Jones came
to be important for Neustadt's career as an academic. Jones' own ambitions for
a doctorate had been thwarted by the Depression. He urged Neustadt not to pass
up the opportunity. After all, Dewey might win, and Neustadt was too oriented to
Democratic objectives to serve a Republican administration.

Persuaded by Jones, Neustadt approached Merle Fainsod at Harvard with the
suggestion that a dissertation be written on the clearance function of the Legislative
Reference Division, drawing from the files of the Budget Bureau.[2] Fainsod agreed
and Neustadt produced the dissertation, never actually leaving Washington for
Cambridge. "Lo and behold," as the dissertation was being written, "Truman won."

---

[2]Later a Russian scholar, Fainsod was interested in American public administration when
Neustadt was doing graduate work.

In 1950, Neustadt shifted to the White House, working for Clifford's successor, Charles S. Murphy, as a junior staff person. Here he was very much at the center of the action.

> I did all kinds of things, you know, policy things, some political things. I had a large hand in screwing up the steel seizure. I remember that well. In June 1950, I was the guy who had to organize the departments on war legislation . . . for the management of the economy in the Korean outbreak because there was no department that could do that. In the summer of '52 I was the guy who wrote the White House version of the Democratic platform . . . . Then during the campaign I inherited the job that George Elsey had done in '48. Truman ran a separate campaign for Stevenson, 26,000 miles by rail, whistle stops galore. And I wrote all the "extemporaneous" whistle stop speeches . . . there were 300-odd speeches. I could never write speeches again.

The election of Eisenhower in 1952 presented Neustadt with a career decision, one that ultimately confirmed the wisdom of Roger Jones' advice to complete the doctorate. Neustadt's Washington career had moved him into increasingly important political positions, identifying him with partisan policy commitments. Had Adlai Stevenson won in 1952, Neustadt undoubtedly would have stayed in Washington, probably as a high-level political bureaucrat. His career then would have been in government, not the academy. "It would have been inconceivable to turn to academia that late [after a Stevenson Administration]. I would have been priced out of the academic marketplace. Whatever I would have done, it would not have been in academia."

But, of course, Stevenson did not win, not even close. Republicans even won majorities in the House and Senate. Now with a wife and two children, Neustadt needed a job.

> What was I going to do? The Administration was coming to an end . . . I'd never thought of the Republicans being elected. It was sort of against nature . . . I mean, my first knowledge of Washington was '33 . . . .
>
> I was very clear. I didn't want to stay in Washington. I'd been at the White House. I'd been at the center. I could have gone up on the Hill. I could have gone to the National Committee. I didn't want to do that. It just seemed like living on the fringes. I wanted to get out of there. But the only things that occurred to me to do were to go to a foundation or a university.

THE MAKING OF A SCHOLAR

Neustadt approached the Ford Foundation but decided that was not a world in which he wanted to work. His first academic job was at Cornell University in the newly formed School of Business and Public Administration, "a combination in which I did not believe." He stayed one year. He was then hired as an assistant professor for a year at Columbia University. He was kept on the two following years and then was tenured. His first publications were drawn from his dissertation on legislative clearance: two articles in the *American Political Science Review* (Neustadt 1954a, 1955) and one in *Public Policy* (Neustadt 1954b).[3] His career as an academic was launched.

Looking back, it is apparent that he had an almost instinctive bent toward participant observation. His first stop was Washington and the White House, with no immediate intention of writing a correction to the prevailing literature. A conceptualizer and note taker, he formed an idea of how politics worked at the highest levels of government. His next stop was the academy with its classrooms and political science faculty. Given that most academic learning in the social sciences then was a combination of reading and listening, it followed that the literature and lectures ought to be right, real, and synchronous. He found what had been written on the Presidency "to be very remote from what I had experienced" and therefore unlikely to be in sync with his lectures. And so he wrote what he knew so others might know. Thus it was that *Presidential Power* (Neustadt 1960) came into being.

Additionally, he had a preference for career-oriented teaching. He thought that students should learn about government as preparation for working there, or at least for being good citizens. "I always thought that political science—how was I to know better?—had among its roles service to government. None of the people who trained me, or my colleagues, told me that was untrue. I think they would say now: 'Oh, it's not true.' " Given his understanding of the discipline's applied mission at that time, it was not in the least surprising that, when given the chance, Neustadt would design and develop a school of public service. Harvard offered that opportunity and he moved there in 1965.

Neustadt and Don K. Price started the Kennedy School of Government at Harvard, with its Institute of Politics. "We did it because we wanted to train public servants, not political scientists. In fact, we were not interested in political science per se. I remember saying to myself in the middle '60s, I don't want to have to think about 'whither political science' ever again. It was a boring subject as far as I was concerned. Here [we] were trying to train people to work in the world, not people to work as academic scholars." Neustadt served as the Director of the Institute and Associate Dean of the School.

Creating a separate faculty was crucial for the success of the Kennedy School, and Neustadt and Price made a substantial effort to achieve that goal. The Dean of the Woodrow Wilson School at Princeton, Marver Bernstein, "impressed on me the horrors of not having one's own faculty." Hiring a separate faculty was a struggle, as it often is in the creation of most schools, centers, and institutes. Neustadt is not entirely satisfied that sufficient separation was achieved or that the faculty is as dedicated to public service as he and Price intended.

---

[3]Neustadt tried to get the dissertation published, but the judgment was that few would be interested, given that Eisenhower had won in 1952 and the original source material preceded the 1952 election.

The internal politics at Harvard are interesting in their own right, but what is relevant for present purposes is Neustadt's motivation for engaging in them. What was emerging for him at Harvard was an opportunity to realize his conception of purposeful training in government and politics. The Kennedy School offered a means by which he could remain in academia, be true to his own convictions, and prepare students for the kind of career in government he might have had. Understanding that he prefers public service to political science is central to analyzing his contributions to both. It is also pertinent that he judges political science to have moved in a direction of ever decreasing relevance to his own concerns and purposes.

Anthony King of the University of Essex identifies a different, but related, aspect of Neustadt's interests. "He is not interested in process for its own sake, rather in how the substance of policy interacts with process. He doesn't see them as separate things at all. They are intimately related, as they are, of course, in the life of a real-world person. Only academics think that a distinction like that one is useful."[4] This observation too goes to the very essence of Neustadt's written work, consistently motivated as it is by policy issues: how they are dealt with, what they teach us, and how those lessons might be applied in the future. It so happens that political scientists have learned important lessons about process from these treatments. Often they then evaluate Neustadt's contributions as though teaching about process had been his central purpose.

NEUSTADT'S PUBLISHED WORK

Several political scientists flew to Atlanta, on to Columbus, Georgia, then drove to Americus and Plains in October 1982, to interview former President Jimmy Carter.[5] We met him in his mother's house, which was being used as a headquarters for his staff. Each of us was introduced to President Carter. As he met Richard E. Neustadt, my recollection is that Carter said something like: "Oh yes, I read your book on the Presidency. I should have learned more."

Presidential Power achieved almost immediate fame when President-elect John F. Kennedy read it. By Schlesinger's account, Neustadt gave him the book, suggesting he read Chapters 3 and 7. Kennedy read it all. "When he did, he found an abundance of evidence and analysis to support his predilections toward a fluid Presidency" (Schlesinger 1965, p. 126). Some even believed that Kennedy meant to fashion a *Presidential Power* Presidency, a conclusion the new President wished to dispel, according to Schlesinger (1965, pp. 678–79): "He [Kennedy] was fond of Richard Neustadt but a little annoyed by the notion that he was modeling his Presidency on the doctrines of *Presidential Power*. He once remarked that Neustadt 'makes everything a President does seem too premeditated.' " Sorensen

---

[4]Personal interview with Anthony King, Wakes Colne, England, November 4, 2001.
[5]The interview was part of an oral history project on the Carter Presidency, sponsored by the Miller Center of Public Affairs, University of Virginia.

(1965, p. 389) also confirms Kennedy's annoyance but adds, "Neustadt would be the first to agree that John Fitzgerald Kennedy, a third-generation practitioner of political power, already knew its nature without being obsessed by either its burdens or its glories" (Sorensen 1965, p. 389).

Recognition of the book's contribution was not limited to Presidents and the Washington political elite. In 1961, *Presidential Power* won the American Political Science Association's Woodrow Wilson Foundation Award as the best book published in 1960 on government, politics, or international affairs. This is the most prestigious award given out by the APSA. The book clearly met the author's goals of having an impact in the public service sphere and, by his own declaration, of convincing his academic colleagues that he "was serious about their business."

Presidential Power is presently in its fourth enlarged revision (Neustadt 1968, 1976, 1980, and 1990). It has sold over one million copies throughout the world (now translated into several languages), arguably the greatest number in history for a book on a single political institution. Published over 40 years ago, it is still assigned in undergraduate and graduate courses. Why? Possibly because it is a good, persuasive, and enduring book that reads well. It defies standard political science classification, yet compels political scientists' notice. No one had written a book like it then. No one has since.

What is so special about Neustadt's work? Nearly all of his books and articles are a result of his varied personal experiences in government and in teaching to govern. His first articles on legislative clearance were drawn from a dissertation written from the files of the Bureau of the Budget, many of them his own. *Presidential Power* (1960) was the product of comparing his White House and Bureau of the Budget experiences in Washington with what was then written about the Presidency. Revisions as expansions (the original work was not altered) were based on personal experiences in working for Presidents Kennedy, Johnson, and Carter and conversations with his contacts in Washington (many of whom were former students). *Alliance Politics* (Neustadt 1970) grew out of an assignment for President Kennedy to report on U.S. and British decision making in regard to the Skybolt missile system. Much later the report itself was published, along with Neustadt's subsequent reflections and a frequently cited paper comparing White House and Whitehall decision making (Neustadt 1999).

In 1977, Neustadt and his former student Harvey V. Fineberg, M.D., were asked by Secretary of Health, Education, and Welfare Joseph Califano to write a report on the controversial swine flu vaccine decisions. Califano had read and was impressed by Neustadt's Skybolt study while serving at the Pentagon in the Kennedy Administration. The report for Califano was published by the Department in 1978; it was later published by a commercial publisher in 1983 with the title *The Epidemic That Never Was* (Neustadt & Fineberg 1983). Both the Skybolt and swine flu cases provided Neustadt with instances of the complexity and importance of thinking ahead. *Thinking In Time* (Neustadt & May 1986), written with Harvard historian Ernest R. May, is a series of stories about policies and decisions that formed the basis of a Kennedy School course on the "Uses of History." Students were mostly mid-career and senior officials in the government. And Neustadt had direct involvement or close acquaintance with many of the stories.

The most recent book at this writing, *Preparing to be President* (Jones 2000), is a collection of memoranda that Neustadt prepared for President-elect Kennedy in 1960 and, later, for others associated with the transition planning of presidential candidates Dukakis and Clinton and President-elect Reagan. Neustadt wrote a new essay, "Advising the Advisers," for this volume. The Kennedy memos in particular represent a direct application of many of the lessons of *Presidential Power*. After all, Neustadt had just completed the book. But the advice to Reagan, actually addressed to his Chief of Staff, James Baker, is wholly consistent with the perspective on presidential power defined in the 1960 book.

These several works share other features in addition to being wrought from the direct knowledge of the author. They are directed to a broader audience, not just to political scientists or the classroom. "This book is addressed to those who govern" is the opening sentence of *Thinking in Time* (Neustadt & May 1986, p. xi). "My interest is in what a President can do to make his own will felt within his own Administration" is the statement of purpose of *Presidential Power* (Neustadt 1960, p. vii). Action, too, is a stated purpose of *Alliance Politics* (Neustadt 1970, p. x): "This book is meant to open issues, to stir argument, to spur research in spheres far wider than its self-selected limits." These messages were from the trenches, not from the planning tents behind the lines.

Integral to this applied purpose is a writing style that is forthright, certain, and clear. The narrative is progressive, with what follows dependent on an understanding of what went before. Word use is explicit and purposeful. Neustadt's books are memoranda writ large for a broad audience. Bear in mind that his successes in government were a consequence of his clear, weighty, and cogent reports and memos. He was also a speechwriter for a President renowned for speaking clearly and bluntly, Harry S. Truman. "I learned to write [a speech] in Anglo Saxon, the way Truman spoke. I had to learn how to do that, otherwise he wouldn't deliver it."

The Neustadt style contrasts sharply with that of contemporary social science, which, understandably, is theory sensitive and data bound. Neustadt is assertive; social scientists tend not to be. Neustadt takes what he knows as far as he believes necessary for his purposes to be served. Modern social scientists are constrained by the canons of proof and the mission of science. Why then pay any attention to him? Because he achieves what he recommends for Presidents. He is persuasive for reasons we cannot exactly specify. That makes us wary and encourages criticisms based on our own methods, even as those methods change. And still he won't go away. Seemingly his insights cannot be resisted.

Neustadt himself is not preoccupied with method. He was in a position to observe major power holders, he understood what he saw, he participated in important policy processes and decisions, and he had reason to believe that his work was consequential. He drew on these experiences in writing about the Presidency and decision making. One critic observed that *"Presidential Power* is written more in the manner of the humanities than the social sciences" (Greenstein 2000, p. 253). Others have repeated that opinion. In response, Neustadt recalls the time in which the book was written. "Social science was much less self conscious when I went to the government in 1942 or when I came to Columbia in 1954 than it has since become." He points out further that when *Presidential Power* was published in 1960 it "was hailed as behavioralism, which was on the cutting edge of social science . . . . I was being bracketed as a behavioralist. I didn't really understand what that meant."

This essay's remaining commentary on Neustadt's published work concentrates on *Presidential Power*, referencing the other major works to illustrate and support the points made. The comments are organized into two topics: (*a*) the book itself— its structure, concepts and purposes; and (*b*) critical analyses of the book and Neustadt's reactions to them. A final section summarizes this man's contribution and his special place in political science.

THE BOOK

Purchased now, *Presidential Power* is more than one book, although faithful to one argument. The reader will find the eight chapters of the original book intact. "Revising the original text struck me as inappropriate, a bit Orwellian. Books should stand where they first saw the light of day, expressive of their setting and confined by it" (Neustadt 1990, p. xv). This choice was in keeping with Neustadt's fidelity to the original exposition and design. "The book remains now what it was originally, one man's argument . . . " (Neustadt 1990, p. xxvii). What changed was the addition of new material with each new edition, as well as the title in 1990, *Presidential Power and the Modern Presidents*. A chapter on Kennedy was added in 1968, one on Johnson and Nixon in 1976, one on Carter in 1980, and the final two on Reagan and a revised consideration of Eisenhower and Kennedy in 1990. Accordingly, one's assessment of the book's scope and supporting cases may vary depending on when one read it during its 40-plus years of life.

The argument of *Presidential Power* begins with an absolutely fundamental distinction between "power" and "powers." Failure to grasp this difference prevents a full understanding of the author's mission and invites mistaken evaluation of his contribution. These errors of omission or misreadings may also help to explain why, despite its popularity, *Presidential Power* has spawned so few empirical tests. Neustadt himself remains puzzled that there has been so little appreciation of the distinction.

> It's like this wonderful fellow [cites a critic] who pays no attention to the distinction between power and powers . . . . The whole profession balked at that distinction. As far as I know, nobody applies it. Yet it's the essential piece of shorthand that I thought would keep the analysis on track. Well, if everybody ignores it, it sure as hell doesn't keep the analysis on track. What

have I done wrong? There isn't a single political scientist who is meticulous about distinguishing personal influence from constituted authority.

Power, for Neustadt, is personal influence. It is what a President can do to get his way in governing. Powers are the collected delegations of authority assigned to the President by the Constitution, Congress, or custom. Making this authority work for the President is the problem Neustadt seeks to address. Having duly constituted powers is no guarantee of an effective wielding of power. The constitutional separation of powers explains why because, in practice, it is a "separation of institutions *sharing* powers" (Neustadt 1990, p. 29). This formulation has become a cliché, with its full implications not necessarily integrated into the thinking of scholars as they design and execute their research.

Having others legitimately sharing, even competing for, the powers of the President is a significant contextual feature of the political landscape. How can the President prevail and stay on top? Neustadt wrestles with that question. "My interest is in what a President can do . . ." (1990, p. xx). In fact, in response to my question regarding a broader theme for his work, he wrote:

> My fundamental question remains the same throughout, namely how best to think about the possible effects of one's own choices on one's own prospects for personal influence within the institutional setting of a given office—using something or other as clues to spur thought. This amounts to seeking the essence of thinking politically, an endless search since that is so much an instinctive, intuitive process. "Power stakes" are the something-or-other drawn from Chapters 6–8 of *Presidential Power*. By light of Johnson and Nixon, this is lamely amended in Chapter 10, with "backward mapping" offered as one supplement among others. *Thinking in Time*, a decade later, sets out an array of clues from history to be derived by shorthand means. Four years after that, Chapter 13 of *Presidential Power* highlighted personal experience and also stresses "Nancy" as a source of clues to future Ronald Reagans. Meanwhile, *Alliance Politics* has opened up the problem of two or more simultaneous choice-makers, while the swine flu and Skybolt stories illustrate the choice-maker's dilemmas in depth, with respect to uncertainty and ambiguity, and also with respect to staff. And my Seattle lecture, "Presidents, Politics and Analysis" (1986), illustrates "thinking politically" with respect to Reagan's deficits, assuming his rationality.[6]

It is vital that the reader not confuse the emphasis on the President as person with the personal Presidency, a label never used by Neustadt. The President as person does not extend to personal staff, the Executive Office of the President, or the Cabinet. Rather the term applies to the man (someday woman) in the Oval Office. These others are others. Even as they serve the President, they serve themselves. Neustadt spoke bluntly on this point. "The institutions that surround the President

---

[6]From a personal letter to the author, May 20, 2002.

are, in their way, the usurpers and enemies. It doesn't matter whether it's the cabinet or the staff. These people have separate agendas because of separate institutions sharing and competing for powers and they're not immune from that."

For their own protection, Presidents need to be wary of staff persons or other loyalists who are "holier than the Pope." Their uncontrolled actions, too, can adversely affect the President's power (see Chapter 10). Delegation must be tempered by an awareness of limits, which, if exceeded, may reduce presidential power to make prudent choices in the future. Insuring that personal staff possess the knowledge and skills to identify what is in the best interests of protecting a President's power is a significant challenge. It explains why a President typically surrounds himself with those who have lived his political experiences first-hand up to the point of entering the Oval Office.

Critical also to the Neustadt formulation is the continuous calculation of the effects of a particular choice on personal influence for making the next and succeeding choices. "Advance calculations of the consequences" are central to preserving one's options. "The history you know, the experiences you've had are critical. How useful it is if you've had it and how difficult it is to apply if it isn't your history." These comments by Neustadt clarify the problems faced by Presidents who are newcomers to Washington or to high executive positions. Among other hazards for the neophyte are those related to relying on others to interpret and apply someone else's history. "The Presidency is no place for amateurs" (Neustadt 1990, p. 151).

What are a President's advantages? What must he protect to be effective? No review of the Neustadt formulation of presidential power can omit this summary (Neustadt 1990, p. 150):

> Effective influence . . . stems from three related sources: first are the bargaining advantages inherent in his job with which to persuade other men that what he wants of them is what their own responsibilities require them to do. Second are the expectations of those other men regarding his ability and will to use the various advantages they think he has. Third are those men's estimates of how his public views him and of how their publics may view them if they do what he wants. In short, his power is the product of his vantage points in government, together with his reputation in the Washington community and his prestige outside.

The three sources are understood to be variable. The President's place in the separated system may not always grant the same bargaining advantages. Institutional status may change, possibly altering what is inherited, a point fixed on by the group of scholars referred to as the "new institutionalists." Reputations differ among Presidents and with one President over time. Prestige, too, can fluctuate, both as a measure of performance and as a set of estimates by power holders of the President's status (Clinton serves as a recent example of moderately high job ratings and substantially lower estimates). In Chapter 10, "Reappraising Power," Neustadt wrote of changes that affected prestige and reputation as sources of power. "In the aftermath of Watergate . . . we have seen occasions where distinctions between reputation and prestige seemed to dissolve, where Washingtonians seemed quite like members of the general public, reacting to a President in almost the same terms, conducting themselves accordingly" (Neustadt 1990, p. 186). Under these circumstances, legitimacy itself is undermined and, with it, the advantage of formal powers.

The variability among and within vantage points does not alter the central problem addressed by Neustadt, only the results. For his part, Neustadt remains extraordinarily focused and disciplined, even dogged. "I'm constantly in pursuit of *Presidential Power*." And so he persistently settles into the head of the President so as to evaluate what is best for him, accepting who that President is and what his advantages are. Neustadt's pursuit is aimed at an understanding of how present choices can be approached so as to improve prospects for power. But it is also targeted at Presidents themselves so that they might know how to be effective in a political system designed as much to constrain as to hearten them.

Thus it was that in advising the soon-to-be-elected President in late October 1960, Neustadt consistently urged Kennedy to identify and define what was best for him. In his transition memo labeled "Staffing the President-Elect," Neustadt's recommendations were tempered with statements such as the following: "Define in your own mind the staff jobs for which you feel a concrete, immediate need in the weeks ahead." "Do not let me or anyone else talk you into anything." "At this stage, I urge you to consider only needs of the first sort—your own" (Jones 2000, p. 6). These suggestions were right out of the "self-help" construct in *Presidential Power*.

Thinking prospectively is crucial to the realization and preservation of presidential power. This undertaking may well be the most difficult of all, especially in a separated system. A President's formal powers may provide him with the authority to capture the day, but at what cost? Neustadt discusses cases of command (Chapter 2) and specifies the features of the self-executing order. However, the President needs to think prospectively even in cases of command—"looking down the line and around corners" (Neustadt 1990, p. xviii). It is also vital to understand that the effect of failure, i.e., serious loss of influence, is not restricted to the President and his status. Failure may well have serious consequences for the political system and the public. "That is my crowning point. Not the President alone but everyone who cares about our government's performance has a stake in his concern for his own influence prospectively" (Neustadt 1990, p. xviii).

These are the basics, illustrated throughout with policy and decision-making stories. "I've always felt that you must illustrate every proposition. . . . Illustration is not proof but illustration makes it possible to seek other illustrations so you and others may eventually pile up something that passes for proof." The concern, however, is that readers will miss or forget the purpose of the illustration or mistakenly believe that Neustadt's propositions are not testable because he himself only illustrates and does not prove them.

THE CRITIQUES

Among the earliest and most comprehensive critiques of *Presidential Power* was "Bargaining and Overload," an essay by Sperlich (1969). His overview of the book is attentive to Neustadt's concepts and purposes. He models choice making for a Neustadt Presidency, linking it to "guarding power prospects" and thence to bargaining success (Sperlich 1969, p. 177). He encourages more rigorous testing of the manifold propositions in the book, as suggested by his modeling exercise. His principal criticism is that a Neustadt President is overloaded. He judges: "An immense and consistent overloading of [the President's] physical and mental apparatus will produce a breakdown in short order" (Sperlich 1969, p. 192). According to Sperlich, such strain is unnecessary and over-reliant on bargaining. The President does not have to do it all. He can rely on loyal staff who view him as their constituent and he can strive to create an organizational ideology supportive of presidential goals.[7] Thus, a Sperlich President would concentrate on personnel and "supportive norms and ideologies." "Mobilization of 'ecological control' will permit a President to employ strategies of influence less expensive of his personal resources than bargaining" (Sperlich 1969, p. 190). The solution, in brief, is to make the personal more institutional.

Many have joined Sperlich in criticizing Neustadt for concentrating too heavily on the President as a person (see below). But, of course, Neustadt is well aware of his intentions. For him, there is just one person on top, not a committee, a staff, or an ideology. And the problems he seeks favorably to resolve are those associated with staying on top in the face of constant threats to that status. It is likely that Neustadt's dedicated and unrelenting focus invites the criticism he has received. For he does not give way. Comparisons with Machiavelli's *The Prince* only add to the discomfort of some readers and subtract from an understanding of the larger separated institutional setting within which a President must try to lead. Neustadt's formula for success also may appear to be nonideological when it is mostly nonpartisan. Presidents of either party face the challenges outlined by Neustadt and can profit from his advice. *Presidential Power* is democratic, constitutional, political, and practical. I would expect Neustadt to agree with Sperlich that the President cannot do everything. But he is unlikely to concede that physical and mental limitations should prevent the President from fully comprehending the demands of effectively exercising power in a separated system. Once a President understands his status at the top, he may then be able to structure staff and promote organizational ideology to serve his purposes, ever attentive to the effects of his contrivances. Placing Sperlich's points in that context is useful. Designing supporting structures without the focus and lessons of *Presidential Power*, however, would be difficult because of the lack of orienting rationale.

At a conference on presidential research at the University of Pittsburgh in 1990, Terry Moe offered a status report on *Presidential Power*. Moe acknowledged the book's impact as having "brought the behavioral revolution to the study of the presidency . . ." (1993, p. 338). It was Moe's judgment, however, that the "personal

---

[7]Also see Rockman (2000), in regard to Neustadt's concept of staff in relation to the President's exercise of power, and Moe (1993, p. 368).

At root is this view: "Presidential behavior can no longer be understood, if it ever was, in mainly personal terms" (Jacobs & Shapiro 2000, p. 492). Government is increasingly complex, more people act in the name of the President, Congress structures presidential and executive choices, processes become entrenched from one Presidency to the next, and demands on the President have become routinized, thus reducing presidential options. Overlaying these developments is an attachment among rational choice scholars to a principal-agent construct that places the President in a more dependent position than they judge Neustadt allows (even though presidential weakness is a persistent theme for Neustadt's analysis of power).

Much of this reaction is puzzling to Neustadt, primarily because he is, in his view, explicit about his analytical location. He is writing about presidential power as he defines it—"the capacity of the President to have his way." At no point does he dismiss any one of the developments said to be contributing to the institutionalization of the Presidency and the greater dependency of the President. But let us hear from him directly:

> If you choose to look at the power issue as the issue of the individual with nominal authority (or *powers* as I use that term) trying to put his own impact on the actions of the organizations or the system, then he's doing it at any time within the institutional setting and if he is going to think about his prospects for effectiveness next time, he has to think about everything that has to be influenced then. He has to.
>
> At any point of institutional development the Presidency can say more things to more people outside, can represent itself, but whether that is the President is always a question. It isn't any less a question because the institutional enlarges . . . .
>
> It seems to me that if you are pursuing what I regard as a President-focused perspective, you have to take very careful account of the institutional context as it will present itself in the future that you are thinking about. You can't talk about power as I use the term and the institutional Presidency in the same breath, even though the one is affected by the other, because power is the capacity of the President to have his way. It's not the capacity of the entire aggregation. So I get stuck. I make this distinction in my head but nobody [else] seems to make it.

One can appreciate Neustadt's frustration, believing as he does that he has sited his inquiry and defined his terms. Let us suppose, then, that those promoting a principal-agent relationship have it right. Is it not useful to direct attention to the agent's power and the effects of how it is exercised? Would such work not be relevant as well for understanding the role of the principal? As it is, however, Neustadt does not accept the agency characterization. "I don't acknowledge that the Presidency is an agent of Congress. That is Whiggery carried too far. I'm not a Whig in that respect. I'm a Jacksonian."

Toward the end of their concluding chapter, Jacobs & Shapiro (2000, pp. 499–500) make this point: "What must be avoided is the tendency to replace one extremism—one that gives nearly exclusive emphasis to the personality of individual presidents—with another (one in which institutions dictate presidential behavior). Presidential studies must avoid the false dichotomy between institutions and presidential personality." This appears to be a call to move from the personal Presidency to the institutional Presidency, and thence to an incorporation of both (Jacobs & Shapiro 2000, p. 501). But the "personal Presidency" is a tag line invented by others, not Neustadt. His is a study of presidential power as clearly defined by him. It most assuredly is not confined to or dominated by personality. And Neustadt's presidential power can and typically does incorporate constitutional, institutional, political, and policy changes (see his quoted statement above). In fact, he regards as "cuckoo" the notion that analysis of personal power perforce ignores institutional change.

The third type of criticism is most closely identified with Skowronek (1993). Skowronek's comments are directed to a point that was more important for his own purpose than for Neustadt's intent. Skowronek produced an exceptional historical, conceptual, and comparative study, rightly described by one reviewer as "a milestone in the study of the presidency" (Young 1995, p. 188). At the start, he reads a great deal into Neustadt's having located his analysis at the "mid-century" and his observation that whereas in the past a President could enlarge his role, "nowadays he cannot be as small as he might like" (Neustadt 1990, p. 6). Skowronek viewed this as periodization between modern and premodern contexts, which he judged to be so "simple" as to "impose severe limits on the analysis of leadership." Indeed, such a judgment comparing the past and present "is no more than the conceit of modern times" (Skowronek 1993, p. 5).

Skowronek's point is well taken and certainly relevant to his own effort to establish patterns by which Presidents have accommodated to their historical place. Using what Neustadt wrote is, however, somewhat contrived in that Neustadt explicitly stated that it was not his purpose to compare historical periods (1990, p. xxi). Nevertheless, he did offer an assertion with important implications for comparison: "Power [recall his definition] problems vary with the scope and scale of government, the state of politics, the progress of technology, the pace of world relationships" (Neustadt 1990, p. 4). He also explained that his attention would be directed to the postwar Presidents at the time of his completing the book: Eisenhower, Truman, and "the shadow of another," Roosevelt—Presidents at the mid-century (Neustadt 1956). As it happened, he was urged by a colleague at Columbia to include these demarcations.

> I wrote that I was only dealing with the mid-century Presidency because I didn't think that power, that is, personal influence, was exercised in the same way under all circumstances. These [Eisenhower and Truman] were the only ones I was prepared to write about now. I remember very well that I put that in on Dave Truman's advice. He said otherwise you are going to get killed by people who'll say you're being too presumptuous about generalizations

and hypotheses on too narrow a band. So [Truman advised] say it to begin with—your band is narrow and then you'll be out in the clear. Good advice. It was intended to be modest. Instead, it got interpreted as an assertion that the modern Presidency was different from all others. And people have written whole books to show that isn't so. I don't think you can win.

There are other criticisms too of *Presidential Power* as scholars seek to shake loose from its hold (Neustadt's reactions are in parentheses). The book is said to be

- Too enamored with Roosevelt ("He was the most sophisticated character in my immediate background.")
- Too unappreciative of Eisenhower ("I didn't fully appreciate how clever Ike had been before his heart attack in legitimating his Presidency by seeming to be above the struggle while organizing a hidden Presidency. So I made up for it in Chapter 13.")
- "Subjective and nonformulaic" (Rockman 2000, p. 163). ("I think that is probably right, though I am not sure I understand 'nonformulaic'.")
- More interested in advising Presidents than in contributing to political science analysis ("What was political science analysis when this came out in 1960? But the ground clearing . . . first five chapters sure as hell contributed to political science analysis if [they] turned 'separated institutions sharing powers' into a cliché.")

On a note of personal privilege, my book, *The Presidency in a Separated System* (Jones 1994), has been identified by some as offering a contradictory perspective to that of Neustadt. One reviewer even referred to him as my "old nemesis." This is a good opportunity to set the record straight. Neither of us understands how the two books can be read as anything but complementary. Both accept the "separated institutions sharing powers" cliché; Neustadt now includes my "and competing for" addendum. His focus is exclusively on the President and his exercise of power; mine is more broadly attentive to the President and Congress. He is ever sensitive to the constraints challenging, sometimes defeating, Presidents; I describe the source of many of those constraints. I seek to widen the lens and he narrows the focus within that broader field, mindful of threatening motion. I can state categorically that at no time in the research and writing of my book did I believe I was defying the lessons of *Presidential Power*, nor was there any such indication in Neustadt's extensive comments as a reader of the manuscript prior to publication.

CONCLUDING COMMENTS

Few scholars have had a greater impact on the study of any institution than Richard E. Neustadt has had on the study of the Presidency. The explanation lies in the circumstances of his knowledge, the motivation of his effort, the timing of the publication, the style of his telling, and the scope of his teaching. The first circumstance was that Neustadt experienced the subject of his eventual book. He had a catbird's perch for observing the exercise of power (influence) as framed by powers (authority). The next circumstance, Stevenson's defeat in 1952, led to his exiting Washington and entering academic life, his head full of what he had observed.

The motivation to write was driven by two imperatives. First was his understanding that success as an academic required being taken seriously as a scholar. That meant writing good books. Second was his discovery that the books on the subject of his experience, and now his teaching, were out of sync with or failed to address what he had learned on site. He sought to make that right and set about writing *Presidential Power*. He likened it to "leaning on an open door." "I was really trying to come to grips with the essence of political thinking, looking ahead, trying to anticipate, [and] hold onto what you have and improve on it."

The timing was exquisite. The book was published in an election year and the winner in 1960 was the first President born in the twentieth century. Just as the book turned a page in presidential studies, the new young President represented dramatic change in the White House. Further, President Kennedy read and liked the book, giving it a cachet seldom accorded to academic literature.

Neustadt's narrative style is spare, yet illustrative. He is precise in locating his analysis and defining terms. Comprehending what follows depends heavily on what went on before. The cases are stories with a purpose, which derives from Neustadt's vantage point ("from over the President's shoulder") and his interest in being there (to "explore the power problem"). Hence, *Presidential Power* is not a book to be read out of chapter sequence or even skipping the Preface. The narrative builds, one concept and story at a time, toward an integrated perspective. It is a fair criticism that the chapters added over a period of 22 years, 1968–1990, are challenging for the reader. Those chapters too must be incorporated into the original framework. Yet in places the writing is less spare and the connections more intricate. Neustadt writes in the 1990 Preface, "My intent in the new chapters is to strengthen it [the original book]." (1990, p. xv). And so they do, but only if the reader is facile enough to carry the original forward into the supporting argument and illustrations, making the suitable modifications.

Also reasonable is the worry that the stories were selected to make the case; other stories might portray a different Presidency. Case studies have often been criticized as an insufficient basis for generalization. Yet they served a purpose much valued by Neustadt—they offered the types of real-life experiences that stimulated his thinking in the first place. There are other ways to blend the real and the imagined (see Edwards et al. 1993, especially essays by Miller, Moe, and King). At the very least, *Presidential Power* is an invitation to experiment with these other methods. No one effort has yet succeeded in matching its impact, however.

Finally, the book is noteworthy for the scope of its teaching. The original subtitle was "The Politics of Leadership." Attention was directed to presidential power, to be sure. But it is Neustadt's own belief that endemic to political leaders is the problem of "how to be on top in fact as well as name" (1990, p. xx). He was "charmed when I got a letter from the Chancellor of UCLA after the book came out saying: 'It was eye opening. I learned so much about my job from it.' "

Neustadt meant for the book to be read by a broad audience—journalists, politicians, administrators, educators, and, of course, students. He is puzzled by an impression that "readers with government experience follow my argument more easily than do some of those for whom it remains theoretical" (Neustadt 1990, p. xv). Perhaps the answer lies in the story of the book's creation. An author with government experience wrote about what he had observed and did so in a framework designed to meet the demands of an academic discipline. As it happened, the practitioners were able to adapt to the framework more easily than the theorists were able to absorb an altered perspective. It is relevant to this essay that neither group has yet put the book away, nor is likely to—at least not until another equally shrewd political-level bureaucrat drifts back to academia, motivated to "get it straight."

The *Annual Review of Political Science* is online at
http://polisci.annualreviews.org

LITERATURE CITED

Edwards GE. 2000. Neustadt's power approach to the presidency. See Shapiro et al. 2000, pp. 9–15

Edwards GE, Kessel JH, Rockman BA, eds. 1993. *Researching the Presidency: Vital Questions, New Approaches.* Pittsburgh: Univ. Pittsburgh Press

Greenstein FI. 2000. *The Presidential Difference: Leadership Style From FDR to Clinton.* New York: Free

Gunnell JG. 2000. Richard Neustadt in the history of American political science. See Shapiro et al. 2000, pp. 16–27

Jacobs LR, Shapiro RY. 2000. Conclusion: presidential power, institutions, and democracy. See Shapiro et al. 2000, pp. 489–508

Jones CO. 1994. *The Presidency in a Separated System.* Washington, DC: Brookings Inst.

Jones CO. 2000. *Preparing to be President: The Memos of Richard E. Neustadt.* Washington, DC: AEI Press

Jones CO. 2001. Professional reputation and the Neustadt formulation. *Pres. Stud. Q.* 31:281–95

Moe TM. 1993. Presidents, institutions, and theory. See Edwards et al. 1993, pp. 337–86

Neustadt RE. 1954a. Presidency and legislation: the growth of central clearance. *Am. Polit. Sci. Rev.* 4:641–71

Neustadt RE. 1954b. Congress and the Fair Deal: a legislative balance sheet. *Public Policy* 5:349–81

Neustadt RE. 1955. Presidency and legislation: planning the President's program. *Am. Polit. Sci. Rev.* 49:980–96

Neustadt RE. 1956. The Presidency at midcentury. *Law Contemp. Prob.* 21:609–45

Neustadt RE. 1960. *Presidential Power: The Politics of Leadership.* New York: Wiley. 2nd ed. 1968

Neustadt RE. 1970. *Alliance Politics.* New York: Columbia Univ. Press

Neustadt RE. 1976. *Presidential Power: The Politics of Leadership with Reflections on Johnson and Nixon.* New York: Wiley

Neustadt RE. 1980. *Presidential Power: The Politics of Leadership from FDR to Carter.* New York: Wiley

Neustadt RE, Fineberg HV. 1983. *The Epidemic That Never Was.* New York: Vintage Books

Neustadt RE. 1986. *Presidents, politics and analysis.* Presented at Graduate School of Public Affairs, University of Washington, Seattle

Neustadt RE, May ER. 1986. *Thinking in Time: The Uses of History for Decision Makers.* New York: Free

Neustadt RE. 1990. *Presidential Power and the Modern Presidents: The Politics of Leadership from Roosevelt to Reagan.* New York: Free

Neustadt RE. 1999. *Report to JFK: The Skybolt Crisis in Perspective.* Ithaca, NY: Cornell Univ. Press

Neustadt RE. 2000. A preachment from retirement. See Shapiro et al. 2000, pp. 459–67

Peterson MA. 2000. Presidential power and the potential for leadership. See Shapiro et al. 2000, pp. 363–79

Ragsdale L. 2000. Personal power and presidents. See Shapiro et al. 2000, pp. 31–46

Rockman BR. 2000. Staffing and organizing the presidency. See Shapiro et al. 2000, pp. 159–77

Schlesinger AM Jr. 1965. *A Thousand Days: John F. Kennedy in the White House.* Boston: Houghton Mifflin

Shapiro RY, Kumar MJ, Jacobs LR, eds. 2000. *Presidential Power: Forging the Presidency for the Twenty-First Century.* New York: Columbia Univ. Press

Skowronek S. 1993. *The Politics Presidents Make: Leadership from John Adams to George Bush.* Cambridge, UK: Belknap

Sorensen TE. 1965. *Kennedy.* New York: Harper & Row

Sperlich PW. 1969. Bargaining and overload: an essay on *Presidential Power.* In *The Presidency*, ed. A Wildavsky, pp. 168–192. Boston: Little, Brown

Young JS. 1995. Thinking about the purposes of presidential power. *Miller Center J.* 2:179–88

Annu. Rev. Polit. Sci. 2003. 6:23–40
doi: 10.1146/annurev.polisci.6.121901.085530
First published online as a Review in Advance on Dec. 6, 2002

GOVERNMENT TERMINATION

Michael Laver

*Department of Political Science, Trinity College, University of Dublin, Dublin 2, Ireland;
email: mlaver@tcd.ie*

Key Words   government stability, coalitions, cabinets, early elections, shocks

■ **Abstract**   This paper reviews a range of approaches to the analysis of government termination, by any account a very important substantive concern for political science. One essential preliminary matter is the distinction between government duration and government durability—the former an essentially empirical concept, the latter essentially theoretical. It is also important to note that empirical research into government termination is heavily conditioned by the precise definition of what marks the end of one government and the beginning of the next. Approaches to analyzing government termination can be divided into those that are fundamentally empirical and those based on a priori modeling. Both research traditions are reviewed. The empiricist approach has evolved into a body of work that applies increasingly sophisticated event-history models to a dataset that has become to a large extent common within the profession. The a priori approach has developed within the traditions of noncooperative game theory to model the responses of key actors to new information, for example, about the likely results of an election that might be called if the government were to fall. There is clearly unfulfilled potential to merge these two research traditions into a single more comprehensive account of government termination.

1. INTRODUCTION

How long will the government last? What might happen to bring it down? When we talk to the wider community about the relevance of political science, we find that such questions interest people from many different walks of life. Although these questions have surprisingly not been at the very forefront of the research agenda for political science, political scientists have had some success at answering them since the first systematic studies of government durability, which we can date to the early 1970s.

Political historians have long been concerned with the death, as well as with the life, of governments, but I do not deal here with descriptions of the fate of individual governments within the methodological traditions of contemporary history. In what follows, I discuss systematic theoretical or comparative empirical accounts of government termination within the political science literature. The bulk of the work on this subject has been conducted in the style of empirical comparative politics, but recently those with expertise in a priori formal models have also explored the area. Before considering this work, however, it is necessary to clear away some conceptual undergrowth, addressing first an often-elided distinction between the durability and the duration of governments, and second the surprisingly tricky issue of defining when, exactly, a government has terminated.

2. GOVERNMENT DURABILITY AND GOVERNMENT DURATION

The distinction between government durability and government duration is to a large extent a distinction between theoretical modeling and empirical research on government termination. For this reason, it is a distinction that throws light on a number of important matters. The duration of a past government is in principle a simple observable quantity—a straightforward empirical record of the elapsed time between the formation of a government and its termination. Notwithstanding operational niggles to which I return below, this is not in itself a complicated idea. However, apart from generating tables for textbooks, why should we be interested in the durations of past governments? We are interested because we want to know what makes some governments last longer than others. This in turn is important because we seek generalizations that allow us to say something about how long present or future governments with particular characteristics are likely to last, or about how long past governments might have lasted in different circumstances.

How long a present or future government is likely to last, or how long a past government might have lasted, are of course unobservable quantities. Crucially, they only have meaning in the context of some model of government termination that identifies a range of key parameters associated with any given government, parameters that are not only observable but are also associated by the model with a forecast of the government's potential duration. The model may be an a priori theoretical model, or it may be a statistical model fitted to observations of the durations of past governments. But only in terms of an explicit model of government termination can anyone justify a statement such as "other things being equal, Government X is likely to last longer than Government Y." This is in effect a statement that Government X is more durable than Government Y.

Of course other things are never equal in the real world, where Government Y may far outlive more durable Government X. The healthiest person in the world can be hit by a bus tomorrow, while someone who is a total physical wreck can limp on to a ripe old age. The fact that some government lasts only a few weeks does not in itself imply that the government was not a strong (and durable) one. It might simply have been overwhelmed by an irresistible disaster. However, although the durability of any government—past, present, or future—is not directly observable and has meaning only in the context of an explicit model of government termination, it is precisely the durability of governments that interests both political scientists and the world at large. The concept of durability allows us to make interesting statements about past governments such as "Government X would have lasted much longer if the Minister for Finance hadn't been caught with his hands in the till." It also allows us to make statements about present or potential governments such as "Government Y has very little chance of running a full term." Apart from its value to train-spotters who like to collect government terminations and file them away in big books, the topic of government termination is important to those who seek to make well-grounded statements about the unobservable yet intriguing attribute of government durability. And to do this we need a model, whether a priori or statistical, formal or informal.

3. DEFINING THE BIRTH AND DEATH OF GOVERNMENTS

Defining what we take to be the birth and the death of a government is an altogether more prosaic matter. But it is important and surprisingly difficult nonetheless, particularly if we want to engage in comparative empirical research, either to fit a statistical model or to test a theoretical one.

The problem arises in large part because every sovereign state has different constitutional conventions that determine both what it takes to put a government in office and what it takes to remove one. It also arises because every state that elects its governments has constitutional requirements for regular elections. And regular elections may or may not result in the return of precisely the same government to office. There is finally a stubborn grey area that cannot be airbrushed away, in which, for example, the Prime Minister resigns because of old age or ill health and is replaced in an orderly way by another notable from the same party, while nothing else changes. For the empirical researcher, the situation is compounded by the fact that different countries have different conventions about naming their own governments. Some declare, for example, that the government has not changed when an election is held and the incumbent government effectively continues in office with the same Prime Minister, party composition, and cabinet ministers, whereas other countries declare in identical circumstances that a new government has been formed.

These problems have been compounded in the political science literature by a tendency to engage in separate discussions of how to define government formation and government termination. In terms of constitutional law, of course, this does not make sense, since constitutions in parliamentary democracies invariably go to great pains to ensure that there is always an incumbent government, that government buildings are never left empty with their doors swinging in the breeze. Constitutionally, therefore, the death of an old government and the birth of a new one are always two sides of the same coin.

It may happen that a government has been defeated in a confidence vote or has resigned, but has not been replaced with an alternative. To use a helpfully concise French term, the government is then *démissionné*, in the sense that it has lost its constitutional mandate to continue to govern indefinitely, but nonetheless does continue to fulfil the key functions of government in what is typically referred to as a "caretaker" capacity. Legally, a *gouvernement démissionné* is still a government.

Laver & Shepsle (1994, pp. 291–92) provide a comparative overview of the powers of caretaker governments in different European states and show that in some countries, such as Ireland, a caretaker government can and does use the full range of powers of any normal government. In other countries, such as Denmark, a caretaker government is very strictly constrained by constitutional conventions to do only what is absolutely necessary to keep the ship of state afloat.

Put all of this together and you find that in a piece of empirical research on government termination, the precise definition of an old government's end and a new one's beginning is not a given; it depends on substantive choices made by the researcher that may well have a significant effect on results. And these choices will inevitably be conditioned by the theoretical concerns of the analyst.

Government termination may be defined in various ways (see Lijphart 1999 for a review), but the definition used by Browne and various coauthors (Browne et al. 1984a,b; 1986) has become reasonably widely accepted in the profession. By this definition, a government falls when any one of the following happens: There is an election; the Prime Minister changes; the partisan composition of the cabinet changes; the government voluntarily or involuntarily resigns and the head of state subsequently accepts this resignation. A similar definition is used by Strom (1985), King et al. (1990), Alt & King (1994), and Mershon (1996, 1999, 2001). Warwick (1994), in his book-length study of government terminations, works with more or less the same definition, modifying it to include all government resignations, whether or not accepted by the head of state. Certainly, no graduate student will be taken out and shot for using this definition and backing it up with appropriate citations of well-known authors.

But why should we consider a new government to have formed simply because, for example, an election has been held but nothing else has changed? There has indeed been a change in the bargaining environment; this is the usual justification for considering the pre-election government to have terminated. But do the authors who use this definition consider a new government to have formed when two opposition parties merge between elections? They do not, even though this also creates a change in the bargaining environment. Why is the accidental death of a Prime Minister a sign that the government has changed? Why should a government's attempt to resign, followed by unsuccessful attempts to replace it and a continuation of the incumbent government in office, be considered a government termination? None of the answers is as obvious as it might seem at first sight. In each of these cases, one perfectly reasonable view is that a government that was in equilibrium confronted a perturbation in the external environment and survived. It is not at all self-evident that these should be treated as cases of government termination.

All of this might seem complicated enough, but we must also consider that, if what we are really interested in is the stability of governments, then the very notion of government termination may be misleading. Political systems with frequent government terminations may turn out to be much more stable than they appear at first sight, once we take into account the actual turnover of parties in power and the ministers who hold important cabinet portfolios. For example, Mershon

(1996, 1999, 2001) points out that for most of the postwar period, despite average government durations very much shorter than the European norm, Italy had the lowest rate of partisan turnover of any European country because the large Christian Democratic party almost always dominated the government. (She explains this in terms of the ability of the parties to "lower the costs" of making and breaking governments.)

Conversely, a government with the same partisan composition and Prime Minister can undergo a comprehensive reshuffle that changes the holder of every single cabinet portfolio. Nearly all conventional studies of government termination would treat this as a continuation of the same government, although the portfolio-allocation model of the making and breaking of governments (Laver & Shepsle 1996) treats any reallocation of key cabinet portfolios between parties as in effect a new government. In short, we should be very careful before we conclude that political systems in which governments tend to have relatively short durations, according to some operational definition, are for this reason relatively unstable.

If the truth be told, the definition of government termination used in many pieces of empirical work on the subject is driven as much by easily available data sources as it is by carefully argued theory. Recent work has made much use of Woldendorp et al. (1993, 1998), for example, who consider the outgoing government to terminate immediately before the incoming government takes office, but who also reserve a special category for caretaker governments in certain countries, which are *démissionné* outgoing governments deemed to form after an election and to remain in power until ongoing formation negotiations have installed a new government. This reliance on standard datasets is understandable, because to create a comparative dataset using theoretically well-justified but nonstandard definitions would require a painstaking return to primary sources for every single case. But it is important to remember that much of the work on government termination discussed below is influenced by the availability of convenient datasets, which come with built-in definitions of government termination that are themselves driven by raw data availability rather than by well-crafted theoretical arguments. In one sense, many of those writing on government termination in recent years have been picking over the entrails of essentially the same dataset.

4. EMPIRICAL STUDIES OF GOVERNMENT TERMINATION

The Government Survival Debates

Warwick (1994), in the first and as yet the only book-length study within the political science literature on the subject of government termination, provides a very helpful review of the literature published up to the early 1990s on what he calls "the government survival debates." Following a controversy in the *American Political Science Review* between Strom (1988) and Browne et al. (1988), these debates were cast at the time Warwick was writing as being between "attributes" and "events" approaches to studying government termination.

Early empirical studies of government termination identified a series of cabinet attributes—essentially independent variables—that were statistically related to observed government durations. Commonly cited are Taylor & Herman (1971), Laver (1974), Dodd (1976), Sanders & Herman (1977), Warwick (1979), and Strom (1985). These studies identified the following attributes as prolonging government life: majority status (Sanders & Herman 1977); minimal winning status (Laver 1974, Dodd 1976); ideological compactness [Warwick 1979—see also theoretical work by Axelrod (1970) and de Swaan (1973)]; low party system fragmentation (Taylor & Herman 1971, Sanders & Herman 1977); and formal investiture procedures (Strom 1985). Thus, a government that is ideologically compact, with a single-party majority cabinet or minimum winning coalition, in a party system with low fragmentation and subject to a formal investiture requirement is predicted to last a longer than an ideologically diverse minority coalition in a fragmented party system with no investiture requirement. This literature was characterized as the "attributes" approach by Strom (1988) because it identified properties of either the government or its political environment that were presumed to be related deterministically to government duration. Although they were not derived as observable implications of any coherent theory of government termination, the particular attributes that were identified did appear to make good intuitive sense.

Late in the period when this research was taking place, Browne and coauthors began working on what seemed a completely different research program (Browne et al. 1984a,b, 1986; Frendreis et al. 1986; see also Cioffi-Revilla 1984). Their approach looked different because it was essentially stochastic. The grounding assumption, also very plausible, was that governments exist in a world of "critical events"—scandals, international conflicts, financial and monetary crises, the deaths and illnesses of key personalities—each of which poses a threat to the life of the incumbent administration. Browne et al. showed that the pattern of observed frequencies of government terminations does indeed resemble the Poisson distribution that would arise if governments were terminated by random events. For Browne et al., however, the "hazard rate" of governments—essentially the probability of termination—was not a function of the type of government attributes under investigation in the alternative research tradition.

It was this that lay at the root of the debate between the "attributes" and "events" schools of thought (Strom 1988, Browne et al. 1988). It made intuitive sense to regard some governments as having attributes that made them more durable than others—albeit in terms of some rather vague and implicit model of government formation. But it also made sense to see governments as being terminated by one of a continuous stream of critical events to which every government is subjected. The trouble was that neither school of thought was taking account of the concerns of the other.

One part of this discussion can in retrospect be viewed, not as a debate about the substance of the government termination process, but as a by-product of the transition to the more appropriate event-history methodology for analyzing data on government durations, discussed below. All early published empirical work on government termination used a linear ordinary least squares (OLS) regression methodology that we now know was very unsuited to the problem at hand; for example, it was quite capable of predicting governments with negative durations on the basis of plausible values of independent variables. The event-history models of government duration that emerged in the early 1990s as a result of this debate effectively subsumed many of its arguments in a more encompassing methodology; they have now become *de rigeur* in the field. Nonetheless, as is so often the case, rerunning the earlier models on the same data with better methodology showed that the originals were not too wide of the mark in terms of substantive results. No stunning new discoveries were made, even if graduate students *would* now be taken out and shot for using simple OLS regressions to analyze government durations.

The other part of the debate ran much deeper, as it was essentially about the appropriate epistemological approach for understanding the durability of governments. Unfortunately, this epistemological debate has been rather neglected in the wake of the success of event-history models in resolving methodological issues. I reopen this discussion when discussing theoretical models of government termination.

The Rise and Rise of Event-History Methodology

The resolution of the debate between "events" and "attributes" theorists came with the publication by King et al. (1990) of an event-history method for analyzing government durations. They proposed an essentially stochastic approach that nonetheless made the hazard rate of governments a function of a range of independent variables—most of these being attributes of particular governments. They developed a statistical model based on appropriate assumptions about the distribution of government durations, and this event-history methodology, subsequently refined and developed (Warwick & Easton 1992; Warwick 1992a, 1994; Alt & King 1994; Diermeier & Stevenson 1999, 2000; Diermeier & Merlo 2000), is now the standard way to analyze government terminations. It takes account of the fact that the observed pattern of terminations implies a Poisson process—thus the dependent variable, government duration, is not (as with OLS regression) assumed to be a normally distributed random variable but is given an appropriate functional form. At the same time, the probability of a government termination at any time is made a function of those independent variables that interest the analyst. Substantively, this work confirmed many of the earlier findings, but on a much sounder methodological basis.

King et al. (1990, p. 863) showed that observed government durations were related to:

- the majority status of the government. Every empirical study of the matter has found that majority governments last longer.

- party system fractionalization. More fractionalized party systems have more frequent terminations.

- the existence of an investiture requirement. Countries with an investiture requirement have less frequent terminations, presumably because at least some potentially less long-lived governments are weeded out by the need to pass an investiture test.

- the polarisation of the opposition. Where there is greater support for "extremist" opposition parties there are more frequent terminations.

- the number of "formation attempts" made when the government was put together. This number is taken as an indicator of the difficulty of the bargaining environments within which governments find themselves; more formation attempts imply more frequent terminations.

Warwick (1994), now working within this methodological tradition, added further variables to the analysis. He found that governments with a high level of ideological diversity run a higher risk of termination (see also Warwick 1992c) and that economic variables, such as the inflation rate and changes in the unemployment rate, also have a significant effect, with rising inflation and unemployment rates implying higher risks of government termination (see also Warwick 1992b). Warwick argued that his measure of the ideological diversity of the government effectively subsumed the impact of party system fragmentation on government termination that had been found in earlier studies. In theoretical terms, this can be seen as an argument that what has an important impact on government durations is the type of coalition generated in a more complex party system, not the complexity of the party system in itself.

This is certainly an interesting point. However, the difficulty in coming to firm conclusions about it on the basis of the empirical evidence offered is that, within this very empiricist tradition of modeling, the addition of new variables to the model always opens up the possibility that the analyst may be forced to reevaluate previous causal inferences. What is clearly needed at this juncture is a well-grounded and coherent theoretical model generating observable implications that can be tested. This would be in stark contrast to almost all reported empirical work on government termination, which has tended to assemble a portfolio of independent variables gleaned from previous published work and the author's own ideas, each given a brief ad hoc "theoretical" justification in its own terms. But the set of independent variables taken as a whole does not amount to the empirical elaboration of a coherent theoretical model of government termination.

Analyzing Government Terminations in Anticipation of Scheduled Elections

As well as unifying what appeared to be two quite different approaches to the study of government terminations, event-history methodology solved a methodological problem that had long plagued empirical analyses in this area. Many observed government durations are in a sense artificially terminated, at least under standard definitions of government termination (see above), by the calling of a constitutionally mandated election. The empirical pattern of government durations—graphed for the first time by King et al. (1990)—shows a sharp increase in terminations as a constitutionally mandated election approaches, lending support to the idea that it can be an exogenous election, not any inherent weakness in the government, that generates a termination. We now see why it is so important to maintain a careful distinction between the duration and durability of a government. Although the ostensible empirical task was to model the pattern of observed government durations, the existence of a constitutionally determined maximum interelectoral period left most analysts feeling that observed durations were in some sense misleading. This must have been because analysts were interested not only in the observed durations but also in the unobservable durability of governments. It is only in the context of durability that we can make statements like "this government would have lasted x months longer if there had not been an election."

King et al. (1990) set out to solve this problem by introducing a "censoring" mechanism into their approach to estimation. This divides the data on government durations into two categories. In one category are the durations of governments assumed to have fallen apart under their own steam. These are defined (using the pattern of observed frequency distributions of terminations referred to above) as governments terminating up to one year before a constitutionally mandated election. The life-spans of these governments are treated as observed durations. In the other category are governments terminating in the year prior to a constitutionally mandated election, whose durations are assumed to have been possibly truncated by the upcoming election. Technically, they are treated as "censored" observations, in the sense that the "real" duration (as might be predicted from the durability of the government) is at least the observed duration but quite possibly longer. The event-history model, when corrected for this censoring effect, permits the analyst to make intriguing estimates of how long governments would have lasted without the intervention of constitutionally mandated elections. This allowed King et al. (1990, Table 3) to estimate that constitutionally mandated elections cut the life of a typical British or Canadian government in half, for example, and that they have also played a big part in shortening the life of governments in countries such as Iceland, Ireland, and Sweden. In countries such as Italy and France, where governments have tended to be short-lived over the postwar period as a whole, the need for scheduled elections seems to have played little part in "premature" government terminations.

Do the Risks of Government Terminations Rise as Governments Age?

Another important matter made accessible by event-history methodology has to do with the hazard rates of governments—the probabilities that they will terminate at any given time. The original King et al. (1990) specification retained the assumption made by Browne and coauthors of a constant hazard rate; in other words, King et al. assumed that a government's underlying risk of collapse does not rise or fall throughout its life. Certainly many popular commentators, however, hold the view that governments can become "tired" or at least more vulnerable as they get older—in the sense of being more accident-prone and hence more likely to collapse when faced with a given event. The popular intuition is that hazard rates rise during the lifetimes of governments.

Following preliminary work by Warwick & Easton (1992), Warwick (1994) conducted an exhaustive exploration of this possibility and found that the underlying hazard rate of governments does indeed tend to rise throughout their lives—that longer-lived governments face a higher rate of termination than shorter-lived ones. Delving deeper, he found that this effect was largely explained by an increasing impact of higher inflation on hazard rates during the lives of governments. Speaking intuitively, we might explain this by saying that governments are better able to survive relatively high inflation rates that they inherit, but are under increasing threat from inflation rates that rise during their stewardship of the economy. Alt & King (1994) reanalyzed the original King et al. (1990) dataset in search of rising hazard rates and found limited evidence of these, confirming what does appear to be a consistent pattern in the data but also finding that the original conclusions about the effects of the key independent variables were not substantively affected by this pattern.

The issue of whether the underlying risk of government termination increases with the duration of the government was largely resolved by Diermeier & Stevenson (1999), who analyzed essentially the same dataset as King et al. and Warwick but did this within a methodological framework of what they called "competing risks." This involved rethinking the approach to censoring observations of government terminations in the run-up to scheduled elections that was used by both King et al. and Warwick. Rather than censoring all observations within 12 months of a constitutionally mandated election, they divided government terminations into "replacements" (where a government termination was followed by another government without an election) and "dissolutions" (where a government termination was followed by the dissolution of the legislature and an early election). Only governments that ran to the very end of the constitutionally mandated interelection period (which are rare) were treated as censored observations. The logic of this approach is that both replacements and dissolutions represent government terminations that arise from the voluntary decisions of key actors (whether or not in anticipation of scheduled elections), whereas only governments that run right into the buffers of a constitutionally mandated election are in a strict sense involuntary terminations. Obviously, early dissolutions may well occur in anticipation of an approaching constitutionally mandated election, and the more imminent this election is, the higher the probability of an early dissolution (Lupia & Strom 1995— see below). But the competing-risks approach allows separate hazard rates to be estimated for replacement and dissolution terminations and thus enables investigation of the possibility that, although the hazard rate for replacement terminations remains constant over time, the hazard rate for dissolution terminations rises with the approach of a constitutionally mandated election.

The results of Diermeier & Stevenson's (1999) competing-risks analysis were clear-cut. They found that hazard rates for replacement terminations were essentially flat, whereas hazard rates for dissolution terminations did rise significantly over time. These findings neatly reconciled the earlier empirical results of King et al. (1990) and Warwick (1994) by highlighting what appear to be two distinct processes. One is what we might think of as a "baseline" process in which governments are continually exposed to critical events; their ability to withstand these depends on various attributes of the governments, but the underlying risk of government termination remains constant. Superimposed on this is a process generated by the constitutionally mandated cycle of regular elections, with a government's incentives to cut and run, and hence the underlying risk of government termination, increasing significantly as a scheduled election approaches. Diermeier & Stevenson's results suggest that these two processes are quite different in character.

These findings show the considerable power of the event-history method in analyzing government terminations and account for its near-universal acceptance in the field. This type of analysis has been extended to cover the termination of political leadership more generally (Alt & King 1994), a somewhat different matter that will not be explored here. The acceptance of this method of data analysis opens up the possibility of a period during which scholars interested in the empirical analysis of government termination roll up their sleeves and get on with the business of finding the statistical model that best fits observations of government durations. However, with existing standard datasets effectively mined out, the progress of normal science in this area will depend to a large extent on the willingness of researchers to take on the relatively unglamorous tasks associated with the more rigorous definition of variables and collection of data, discussed in Section 3.

5. A PRIORI MODELS OF GOVERNMENT TERMINATION

Although there is a long tradition of a priori models of party competition and government formation, a priori models of government termination have been much thinner on the ground. The main reason for this has been that many a priori models of party competition and government formation are deterministic. There is an old joke about the game theorist who refuses to cross the road to pick up a hundred-dollar bill lying on the sidewalk because, if it were in fact a hundred-dollar bill, someone would have already picked it up. As far as government termination is concerned, this way of thinking has the effect that all anticipatable events unfolding during the life of the government are assumed to be impounded, appropriately discounted, at the time of government formation in the calculations of the actors, and hence in the government equilibrium. Essentially, therefore, most a priori models in this area are static rather than dynamic, which tends to have the effect that the termination of governments is explained, often implicitly, in terms of unanticipated shocks. Absent a shock, there is no reason for an equilibrium government to fall in a static model.

This does not mean that static government formation models need have nothing to say about government termination. For one thing, the very concept of an equilibrium government is defined in terms of government termination—a government is in equilibrium as long as no actor with the ability to replace it with some alternative also has the incentive to do so (Laver & Shepsle 1996, p. 61). This of course implies that either the abilities or the incentives of key political actors have to change in unanticipated ways if a government that is in equilibrium according to a static model is to be replaced. One of the crucial properties of any equilibrium is its robustness in the face of shocks or perturbations, however, and it is this that provides a way for static a priori models to say interesting things about government termination. The robustness of a government equilibrium is no more and no less than the durability of the government involved.

It would be fair to say that, with the exceptions discussed below, the robustness of particular government equilibria has not been a matter of passionate concern to many a priori theorists of party competition and government formation, but the relationship between this and the important matter of government durability shows why it should interest them very much. Furthermore, the notion of a government equilibrium subjected to a stream of shocks and perturbations comes quite close to the epistemological position of the original "events" theorists. The main difference is that the original events theorists had no model explaining why any government was in equilibrium in the first place. Thus, the events theorists' view of the world was in effect "Government X forms; it is then subjected to shocks that may or may not bring it down." The a priori modelers' approach at least has the potential to be "Government X, according to Model Y, was in equilibrium given a set Z of particular parameter values; these values are then subjected to shocks, which, if sufficiently large (in ways made explicit by the model), destroy the equilibrium position."

This does not in any way imply a prediction that governments that are in equilibrium according to some model will be of longer duration than governments that are not. Because the model predicts no out-of-equilibrium governments, it has nothing whatsoever to say about their durability—except perhaps in terms of mistakes made by key actors that are subsequently identified and corrected in some unmodeled way. Of course, any government that actually forms must be in equilibrium in some sense. If it is not the equilibrium outcome of some modeled process, then it is the outcome of some unspecified process that we cannot understand or model. But if we cannot understand why some government formed, then it is hard to see how we can understand why it should terminate (Laver & Shepsle 1998, pp. 44–45). Thus, the very advantages that an explicit model provides in helping to analyze the robustness of equilibrium governments mean that we cannot use this model to analyze the robustness of out-of-equilibrium governments. This point was the subject of a brisk controversy in the *British Journal of Political Science* in 1999 (Warwick 1999a,b; Laver & Shepsle 1999a,b), in a debate that trenched fundamentally on the relative advantages of a priori and empirical modeling in the analysis of government terminations.

The first explicit model of government termination within this tradition, developed by Lupia & Strom (1995), made use of an important constitutional asymmetry between government and opposition in most parliamentary democracies—that the government (typically the Prime Minister) can dissolve the legislature and call new elections, but the opposition cannot. (Countries, such as Norway, with fixed-term parliaments are the exception to this rule; for a statement of the position in each European country, see Gallagher et al. 2001.) This implies that a majority government can terminate itself if it expects this to be worthwhile in the long run, but the opposition cannot unilaterally bring down a government that still commands a legislative majority. Lupia & Strom's objective, therefore, was to model the circumstances in which "equilibrium" governments might find it worthwhile to terminate themselves and call an election.

This constitutional asymmetry means that, for the government, essentially two legislatures are in play at any given time. One is the actual legislature in its present state. The other is the legislature anticipated to arise if the existing legislature were to be dissolved and new elections held. If this anticipated new legislature would put the government in a better position than the extant legislature, then there might be an incentive for the government to bring itself down and realize anticipated electoral gains. In coalition governments, the incentive to withdraw and bring the government down (if this is expected to force new elections) may arise for any of the government parties. There are important variations between countries in the likelihood of new elections following the fall of a government. In some countries, such as Italy, it is common for the fall of one government to be followed by the rise of another without an intervening election. In others, such as Ireland, such an event is extremely rare. This is important because, although the power to force new elections rests constitutionally with the Prime Minister, it may reside de facto with other parties who pull out of a government coalition.

What might make the members of an equilibrium government want to bring that government down? Lupia & Strom's (1995) answer is that a critical event may change the electoral expectations of key actors. We might think of this as an "opinion poll shock" since, generically, it is unanticipated opinion poll findings that are likely to change the electoral expectations, and hence incentives, of key actors. Of course, bringing down a sitting government has serious costs for its members. There are opportunity costs—since the sitting government has to forgo the remainder of its term of office in order to cash in with new elections. And there are the transaction costs of both campaigning in new elections and negotiating a new government. In the Lupia-Strom model of government termination, these costs mean that it is often more rational for the beneficiaries of opinion poll shocks to renegotiate the existing coalition deal—perhaps getting more cabinet portfolios or a better deal on government policy—than it is to attempt to realize opinion poll gains by forcing an election. According to Lupia & Strom, contrary to the intuitive argument advanced earlier by Grofman & van Roozendaal (1994), coalition members may not always bring down governments when they anticipate electoral gains.

In addition to the possibility that shocks provoke a renegotiation of the coalition deal rather than a government termination, the Lupia-Strom model has the intriguing implication that the probability of government terminations should increase steadily throughout the lifetime of a government, in line with the empirical evidence of rising hazard rates discussed in the previous section. This is because, although the transaction costs of bringing down the government remain constant, the opportunity costs of losing the residual term in office decline with every day of a government's life. Thus, the prediction of rising hazard rates can be derived from a formal model as well as from informal intuition. It is worth noting for the purposes of future empirical analysis, as Diermeier & Stevenson (2000) subsequently pointed out, that the probability of terminations should increase, not as the age of the government increases, but as the time before the next scheduled election decreases. This is because opportunity costs are driven by the unexpired term of office; two governments with the same unexpired term may be of different ages.

Lupia & Strom's theoretical results, though interesting, were proved only for three-party legislatures—which are of course almost nonexistent in the real world— and were not subjected to extensive empirical analysis. The problem of empirical analysis was tackled by Diermeier & Stevenson (2000). As noted in Section 4, Diermeier & Stevenson (1999) had earlier distinguished between "replacement" and "dissolution" government terminations and estimated different hazard rates for these. The logic of the Lupia-Strom model applies explicitly to "dissolution" terminations rather than to government terminations more generally. Thus, Diermeier & Stevenson (2000) first recast the Lupia-Strom model in a stochastic rather than its original deterministic form (again for three parties) and then subjected the prediction of rising dissolution hazard rates to empirical testing, finding strong support for this. It is worth noting that, even though their model applies strictly only to three-party systems, Diermeier & Stevenson tested it using data from party systems of widely varying sizes. There is, however, no intuitive reason to suppose that the prediction of rising dissolution hazard rates would not be a feature of Lupia-Strom–style models of government termination in larger party systems, if these could be specified and solved.

A somewhat different direction was taken by Laver & Shepsle (1998), who built on their earlier model of government formation and the progress made by Lupia & Strom to provide an account of government termination. Laver & Shepsle proposed a way to investigate government durability by exploring the robustness of the government equilibria identified by their model. This involves simulating a real-world event-history environment by subjecting key parameters of equilibrium governments to a stream of random perturbations and observing the relative frequencies with which these perturbations destroy the equilibria identified by the model. The more easily government equilibria are destroyed by streams of random shocks of a given amplitude, the less robust these equilibria, and the less durable the corresponding governments.

The key parameters used to generate equilibrium predictions in the Laver-Shepsle model are the distribution of seats between legislative parties, the positions of each party on key policy dimensions, the party-specific salience of these policy dimensions, and the decision rule—typically majority voting in the legislature. Shocks to the distribution of seats between parties correspond closely to the type of public opinion shock explored by Lupia & Strom (1995). Shocks to party policy positions, not considered by Lupia & Strom, were interpreted by Laver & Shepsle as "policy shocks"—unanticipated events that force the parties to take policy positions on matters they had not considered before—possibly rearranging the spatial configuration of parties. Shocks to the party-specific salience of policy dimensions were interpreted as "agenda shocks"—unanticipated events that push some issue, on which parties already have stated positions, significantly up or down the policy agenda. These new types of shock considerably generalize the Lupia-Strom approach. Many of them are not tied to the dissolution of the legislature, in the manner of public opinion shocks, and are thus likely to feed into baseline hazard rates for government replacement, as well the (rising) hazard rates specifically linked to dissolution.

By applying simulated shock streams to real-world governments identified as equilibria by their model, Laver & Shepsle were able to make inferences about the relative vulnerability of different real-world governments to different types of shock. However, they did not subject their approach to exhaustive empirical testing. This would be a daunting task, since it would involve first identifying every government in the dataset that was in equilibrium according to the Laver-Shepsle model and then subjecting each one to an extensive series of simulations to derive some estimate of equilibrium robustness that could be compared with observed cabinet duration. Although conceptually very simple, this would in practice be a very time-consuming business.

6. WHAT IS TO BE DONE?

The empirical and a priori modeling approaches to the analysis of government termination have to a large extent developed along completely separate tracks, although recent methodologically sophisticated work by Diermeier & Stevenson (1999, 2000) has taken a step toward bringing them together.

As far as empirical modeling is concerned, most of the recent intellectual action has been devoted to developing and refining a methodology suited to the statistical analysis of government durations. Huge strides have certainly been made. In rather paradoxical contrast to these methodological advances, substantive empirical work has tended to involve the application of ever more sophisticated techniques to the continuous analysis and reanalysis of more or less the same dataset. Although new independent variables have been regularly added to it, typically justified on an ad hoc basis, very little serious thought has been devoted to the units of analysis, operational definitions, and raw data sources that underlie the entire structure of this dataset. The main reason for this is that the essential research task has been seen as one of fitting data, of refining descriptions of by now rather well-known empirical regularities rather than evaluating some model that has been carefully developed on an a priori theoretical basis.

Returning to the key distinction that I emphasized at the beginning of the paper, the empiricist tradition in studying government terminations has ultimately been much more concerned with the empirical pattern of observed durations than with the underlying durability of governments. Yet, from the perspectives of both academic and lay observers of the cut and thrust of real politics, the pattern of observed durations is intrinsically less interesting and important than the matter of what makes some governments more durable than others.

As far as a priori theorizing is concerned, the profession is only now beginning to take a serious interest in modeling the processes that lead to government terminations. Existing a priori models are essentially static and thus in some sense will always struggle as they attempt to explain the inherently dynamic processes of the life and death of governments. Yet serious dynamic modeling has made almost no inroads into mainstream political science, so these static models are currently all that is on offer.

Existing a priori models have also not been subjected to systematic empirical testing—with the sole exception of Diermeier & Stevenson's (2000) test of one important observable implication of the Lupia-Strom (1995) model. The indications suggest that such empirical testing will involve a lot of unglamorous work. Neither the Lupia-Strom nor the Laver-Shepsle approaches, for example, can be properly operationalized in terms of current datasets. The core Lupia-Strom result deals with renegotiations of existing coalition arrangements in the face of unanticipated shocks. Conducting systematic empirical research on this matter will require a very carefully thought-through research design—involving not least an operational definition of an unanticipated shock and a control group strategy that will allow valid inferences about cause and effect. It will also require the collection of a completely new dataset from primary sources with information on shocks and renegotiations as well as terminations, a dataset for which the fundamental unit of analysis is not immediately obvious. The Laver-Shepsle model certainly redefines the unit of empirical analysis, since any reallocation of key cabinet portfolios defines a new government equilibrium and effectively triggers a new case, whereas a continuation of the same allocation of key portfolios implies the same government equilibrium and arguably the same case. Once again, a return to primary sources will be needed to construct the dataset that is tailored to testing this approach exhaustively.

It is of course conventional at the end of a review to call for a closer integration of theoretical and empirical work. Nonetheless, the need for such integration is nowhere more evident than in the analysis of government terminations. The empirical tradition has developed a powerful methodological tool, but, with the exception of Diermeier & Stevenson (2000), this has been applied to at best quarter-baked theoretical propositions using recycled data. The tradition of a priori theoretical modeling is at last beginning to tackle the problem of government termination, but so far with very little empirical underpinning. If ever there were two groups of researchers who ought to put their heads together, it is these.

The *Annual Review of Political Science* is online at
http://polisci.annualreviews.org

LITERATURE CITED

Alt J, King G. 1994. Transfers of governmental power: the meaning of time dependence. *Comp. Polit. Stud.* 27:190–210

Axelrod R. 1970. *Conflict of Interest*. Chicago: Markham

Browne EC, Frendreis JP, Gleiber D. 1984a. An "events" approach to the problem of cabinet stability. *Comp. Polit. Stud.* 17:167–97

Browne EC, Frendreis JP, Gleiber D. 1986. The process of cabinet dissolution: an exponential model of duration and stability in western democracies. *Am. J. Polit. Sci.* 30:628–50

Browne EC, Frendreis JP, Gleiber D. 1988. Contending models of cabinet stability: a rejoinder. *Am. Polit. Sci. Rev.* 82:930–41

Browne EC, Gleiber D, Mashoba C. 1984b. Evaluating conflict of interest theory: Western European cabinet coalitions. *Br. J. Polit. Sci.* 14:1–32

Cioffi-Revilla C. 1984. The political reliability of Italian governments: an exponential survival model. *Am. Polit. Sci. Rev.* 78:318–37

Diermeier D, Merlo A. 2000. Government turnover in parliamentary democracies. *J. Econ. Theory* 94:46–79

Diermeier D, Stevenson R. 1999. Cabinet survival and competing risks. *Am. J. Polit. Sci.* 43:1051–98

Diermeier D, Stevenson R. 2000. Cabinet terminations and critical events. *Am. Polit. Sci. Rev.* 94:627–40

De Swaan A. 1973. *Coalition Theories and Cabinet Formation*. Amsterdam: Elsevier

Dodd LC. 1976. *Coalitions in Parliamentary Government*. Princeton, NJ: Princeton Univ. Press

Frendreis JP, Gleiber D. Browne EC. 1986. The study of cabinet dissolutions in parliamentary democracies. *Leg. Stud. Q.* 11:619–28

Gallagher M, Laver M, Mair P. 2001. *Representative Government in Modern Europe*. New York: McGraw-Hill. 3rd ed.

Grofman B, van Roozendaal P. 1994. Toward a theoretical explanation of premature cabinet termination: with application to post-war cabinets in the Netherlands. *Eur. J. Polit. Res.* 26:155–70

King G, Alt J, Burns NR, Laver M. 1990. A unified model of cabinet dissolution in parliamentary democracies. *Am. J. Polit. Sci.* 34:846–71

Laver M. 1974. Dynamic factors in government coalition formation. *Eur. J. Polit. Res.* 2:259–70

Laver M, Shepsle KA. 1994. *Cabinet Ministers and Parliamentary Government*. New York: Cambridge Univ. Press

Laver M, Shepsle KA. 1996. *Making and Breaking Governments*. New York: Cambridge Univ. Press.

Laver M, Shepsle KA. 1998. Events, equilibria and government survival. *Am. J. Polit. Sci.* 42:28–54

Laver M, Shepsle KA. 1999a. Understanding government survival: empirical exploration or analytical models? *Br. J. Polit. Sci.* 29:395–401

Laver M, Shepsle KA. 1999b. Government formation and survival: a rejoinder to Warwick's reply. *Br. J. Polit. Sci.* 29:412–15

Lijphart A. 1999. *Patterns of Democracy: Government Forms and Performance in Thirty-Six Countries*. New Haven, CT: Yale Univ. Press

Lupia A, Strom K. 1995. Coalition termination

and the strategic timing of legislative elections. *Am. Polit. Sci. Rev.* 89:648–65

Mershon C. 1996. The costs of coalition: coalition theories and Italian governments. *Am. Polit. Sci. Rev.* 90:534–54

Mershon C. 1999. The costs of coalition: a five-nation comparison. In *Party Cohesion, Party Discipline, and the Organization of Parliaments,* ed. S Bowler, DM Farrell, RS Katz. Columbus: Ohio State Univ. Press

Mershon C. 2001. Party factions and coalition government: portfolio allocation in Italian Christian democracy. *Elect. Stud.* 20(4):509–27

Sanders D, Herman V. 1977. The stability and survival of governments in western democracies. *Acta Polit.* 12:346–77

Strom K. 1985. Party goals and government performance in parliamentary democracies. *Am. Polit. Sci. Rev.* 79:738–54

Strom K. 1988. Contending models of cabinet stability. *Am. Polit. Sci. Rev.* 82:923–30

Taylor M, Herman V. 1971. Party systems and government stability. *Am. Polit. Sci. Rev.* 65:28–37

Warwick P. 1979. The durability of coalition governments in parliamentary democracies. *Comp. Polit. Stud.* 11:465–98

Warwick P. 1992a. Rising hazards: an under-lying dynamic in parliamentary government. *Am. J. Polit. Sci.* 36:857–76

Warwick P. 1992b. Economic trends and government survival in West European parliamentary democracies. *Am. Polit. Sci. Rev.* 86:875–87

Warwick P. 1992c. Ideological diversity and government survival in Western European parliamentary democracies. *Comp. Polit. Stud.* 25:332–61

Warwick P. 1994. *Government Survival in Parliamentary Democracies.* Cambridge, UK: Cambridge Univ. Press

Warwick P. 1999a. Ministerial autonomy or ministerial accommodation? Contested bases of government survival in parliamentary democracies. *Br. J. Polit. Sci.* 29:369–94

Warwick P. 1999b. Getting the assumptions right: a reply to Laver and Shepsle. *Br. J. Polit. Sci.* 29:402–12

Warwick P, Easton S. 1992. The cabinet stability controversy. New perspectives on a classic problem. *Am. J. Polit. Sci.* 36:122–46

Woldendorp J, Keman H, Budge I. 1993. Party government in 20 democracies. *Eur. J. Polit. Res.* 24:1–119

Woldendorp J, Keman H, Budge I. 1998. Party government in 20 democracies: an update. *Eur. J. Polit. Res.* 33:125–64

Annu. Rev. Polit. Sci. 2003. 6:41–54
doi: 10.1146/annurev.polisci.6.121901.085740

POLITICAL SCIENCE ON THE PERIPHERY: Sweden

Olof Ruin

*Department of Political Science, Stockholm University, SE-10691 Stockholm, Sweden;
email: olof.ruin.statsvet.su.se*

Key Words   domestic politics, international influences, surrounding society

■ **Abstract**   Swedish political science has a long pedigree. The Johan Skytte professorship of discourse and politics was established at Uppsala University in 1622, although political science teaching and research did not begin until the 1860s. Today, the discipline is represented at all 10 Swedish universities and at a number of other centers for higher education. Early Swedish political science gravitated toward constitutional law, history, and philosophy. In principle, the discipline today deals with all possible aspects of politics; as far as domestic politics research is concerned, special emphasis has been given to analysis of ideas, local politics, interest organizations, and political parties, as well as public administration and public policy. Contacts with the outside world have been close; different worldwide theories and methods have successively been incorporated. The relations between the discipline and the surrounding Swedish society have also been close and the reputation and visibility of the discipline fairly high.

INTRODUCTION

Today, at the beginning of the twenty-first century, it is proper and legitimate to characterize Swedish political science as being situated on the periphery of the worldwide political science community. The main reasons are that Swedish political science is pursued in a country with no more than nine million inhabitants and that a substantial part of the research produced is written in a language understood by hardly more than 20 million (taking into account all those who understand Swedish in the entire Scandinavian region).

This situation was preceded by a time when Sweden almost appeared to be one of the world centers of the discipline. Academic study of politics was established in Sweden earlier than in many other Western countries. The memory of this history left its marks on the development of Swedish political science during the latter part of twentieth century in parallel with an increasing awareness of the more peripheral position of today (Ruin 1986). The tensions between these two perspectives are visible in the following analysis of this development.

Recently, Swedish political science has been the object of a systematic international evaluation. The evaluating group consisted of three political science professors working at universities outside of Sweden and having the common

1094-2939/03/0615-0041$14.00

qualification that they all understood Swedish. They were Göran Hydén at the University of Florida, Ellen M. Immergut at the University of Konstanz, and Arild Underdal at the University of Oslo; I myself was also part of this group in the sense that I was asked to present a historical overview (Swedish Research Council 2002).

THE PEDIGREE

Swedish political science came formally into existence in the seventeenth century. In 1622, the Johan Skytte professorship of discourse and politics was established at the University of Uppsala. The scholars holding this chair did however primarily concentrate on the study of rhetoric and Latin for more than 200 years. In a more real sense, therefore, academic studies of politics in Sweden began when Wilhelm Erik Svedelius, the holder of the chair during the years 1862–1881, explicitly taught and researched constitutional history and constitutional law (Falkemark 1992). Since then, in one sense or another, all the Skytte professors have been oriented toward the study of politics (Leif Lewin is today the holder of this old chair). A birth of political science teaching and research in the 1860s rather than in the 1620s still constitutes a comparatively early birth.

Gradually political science as an independent discipline was established at the other main Swedish universities. This spread is documented by the dates of researchers taking office of chairs devoted to the study of politics. At the University of Lund a historian, Martin Weibull, received a chair in "political science and history" in 1877; he was succeeded by Pontus Fahlbeck, who can be classified as a political scientist. In 1902, this chair was renamed "political science and statistics," and in 1926, finally, only in "political science." At the University of Gothenburg, Rudolf Kjellén, an internationally well-known representative of the geopolitical tradition, received a chair in "political science and statistics" in 1901; statistics as part of the title of the chair was deleted as late as 1952, although the holders of the chair had already previously concentrated on the study of politics. At Stockholm University in 1935, Herbert Tingsten, the internationally known author of *Political Behavior*, became the holder of a new chair exclusively devoted to the study of politics, The Lars Hierta professorship in Government (Falkemark 1992, Ruin 1978). Thereby political science as an independent university subject was well established before the Second World War at all four universities existing in Sweden at that time.

One more sign of the fairly early establishment of this discipline in Swedish academia is that a scholarly periodical, *Statsvetenskaplig tidskrift*, exclusively oriented toward political science, began to appear as early as 1897. This review has continued to appear—in principle with four issues yearly—always published in Lund and supported by a special foundation, The Fahlbeck Foundation.

A further expansion of Swedish political science took place during the latter part of the twentieth century in parallel with the general expansion of academic teaching and research in Sweden as well as in the rest of the Western world. Six new universities were added: Umeå University in the 1960s, Linköping University in the 1970s, and universities in Luleå, Karlstad, Växiö, and Örebro in the 1990s. Today, political science is represented in Sweden not only at these ten universities but also at a number of other centers for higher education. Still, however, the four oldest departments—those in Gothenburg, Lund, Stockholm, and Uppsala—have remained the largest ones in terms of enrollment (Swedish Research Council 2002).

Naturally enough, the Swedish political science faculty has expanded in parallel with the increase in number of places where the subject is taught and the number of students enrolled. This faculty, as well as faculties generally in Swedish academia, consists of several different categories. The most important ones are those classified as professors (mainly involved in research and supervision of graduate students) and university lecturers (mainly involved in undergraduate teaching). The production of PhD dissertations in political science has also been fairly intense; from 1976 through 1996, for example, 212 PhD theses in the discipline were presented at the universities in Gothenburg, Lund, Stockholm, Umeå, and Uppsala (Larheden 1999).

Why the Early Start?

The early start of Swedish political science is due to many factors. The Skytte chair itself was originally established in order to improve the education of government officials to serve the emerging great power of Sweden. The most important explanation for the early growth of the discipline is probably the very respect that the constitutional system—traditionally a central object of study of the political science discipline—enjoyed in Swedish cultural life. Sweden had a long constitutional tradition with its roots in the so-called provincial laws of the 1300s. A parliament divided into four estates began to meet from the middle of the 1400s; there had been a succession of formal written constitutions since the first part of the 1600s; a system in which royal powers were strictly circumscribed and in which there were clear elements of parliamentarism was established during the so-called Period of Liberty, 1720–1772; and in 1809 a constitution, which regulated the political life of Sweden until the mid-1970s, was adopted. In a country with such a long constitutional tradition, constitutional history appeared to be both a natural and an important field of study.

An aspect of this history that for a long time received particular attention was the question of the sources of the long-lasting 1809 constitution. One school of thought claimed that this constitution was primarily shaped by constitutional discussions in Europe in general at the time of its ratification, especially by Montesquieu. Another school of thought claimed that this constitution was primarily influenced by experiences particular to Sweden during the course of many centuries. Swedish history was said to be reflected in the very content and wordings of the clauses of the written constitution.

While Swedish political science remained close to constitutional law during the first part of the twentieth century, it also remained close to the disciplines of history and philosophy, which is a pattern of relations seen in other countries as well.

Increasingly, political events of the fairly recent past came to be analyzed with methods similar to those commonly used in historical research. An analysis restricted only to written law was no longer viewed as providing an adequate picture of the functioning of political institutions. At the center of this attention was the evolution of parliamentarism, primarily in Sweden but also in other countries. The express purpose was to elucidate the successive shifts in power in the relationships between the head of state, parliament, and the government.

In addition to history, early Swedish political science gravitated toward philosophy and the history of ideas. Classical political thought as well as modern ideologies were regarded as a major line of inquiry. Works were published on various bodies of ideas, their background and historical development, and the correctness of their appraisals of reality.

At the end of the Second World War, these lines of inquiry—constitutional law, history, and philosophy—were dominated by three central figures in Swedish academia: Fredrik Lagerroth, Axel Brusewitz, and Herbert Tingsten, respectively. Lagerroth, at the University of Lund, mainly concentrated on a study of written laws and their origins. Brusewitz was at the University of Uppsala, and among his accomplishments was an inspiring leadership of the extensive research on the evolution of parliamentarism. At the University of Stockholm there was Herbert Tingsten, the most dynamic of the three, whose major area of research was the analysis of ideas. Each of these three central scholars could be said to symbolize a particular line of inquiry, but at the same time they all showed an ability to fuse perspectives and ways of thinking found in law, history, and philosophy into a single study of the institutions and processes of central importance in political systems (Ruin 1978).

INWARDNESS

As in most countries, political science in Sweden during the latter part of the twentieth century contained tendencies toward "inwardness." One type of inwardness, generally accepted in the discipline as a whole, is the research emphasis on domestic politics. The other type, generally criticized, is simple ethnocentricity and neglect of scholarly trends in the international political science community. A tendency of this kind was far less visible in Sweden, although there were signs of it.

Domestic Politics Research

The domestic politics research, originally very much limited to institutional issues, came gradually to encompass all possible aspects of the Swedish political system. Data sources were excellent; Swedish society (political representatives as well as citizens) had a natural interest in an improved knowledge of their own affairs; money-allocating entities encouraged research in this area. Domestic politics thereby remained the most prominent field of the discipline throughout the whole of the twentieth century (Swedish Research Council 2002).

This research was in many ways influenced by tendencies from outside Sweden but also showed traits that appear somewhat special, compared to domestic politics research in other countries. I will limit myself to five such traits.

ANALYSIS OF IDEAS   Swedish political science was characterized by a continuous interest in the analysis of ideas. In this type of analysis, as well as in Swedish political science research generally, the distinction between normative and empirical statements was upheld with remarkable tenacity. The fundamental difference between propositions containing an evaluation and those containing a statement of reality was emphasized again and again. The latter can be verified but not the former, according to a philosophical tradition that has been very strong in Swedish intellectual life.

A remarkable number of studies of political debates were published. The purposes and focal points varied. One aim was simply to interpret and present the nuances in the content of a debate; another was to dissect the logical structures of debates and to examine the relationships between arguments; a third was to explain the behavior of actors participating in a debate through an analysis of arguments presented.

LOCAL POLITICS   Another trait of domestic politics research in Sweden was a sudden and intense attention to politics on a local level. The external reason for this was that local government in the country was in the midst of a dramatic transition during the first postwar decades. As a result of steady migration, three fourths of the population were already living in built-up areas. In parallel with this, local government had rapidly expanded and become more diversified; local government units had successively been merged into larger units. In the early 1950s, the number of local governments units, the communes, had been reduced from 2500 to l000; 20 years later, their number had declined to roughly 300.

Three large local-politics research projects were launched, the first and largest in the mid-1960s, encompassing all five political science departments existing at that time. The actual research in this project was largely done in the form of dissertations, which numbered close to 40. The result of this first project showed, not very surprisingly, that small cities scored higher as well-functioning democratic entities than large cities or sparsely populated country communes (Strömberg & Westerståhl 1984).

INTEREST ORGANIZATIONS AND POLITICAL PARTIES   A third trait concerned interest organizations and political parties. Of course, such actors have been studied everywhere in the political science community, but in the Swedish context the study was given a special emphasis.

In relation to research about interest organizations, a debate arose fairly early about corporativistic tendencies, a debate which later became common in political science generally (Heckscher 1946, Ruin 1974). In Sweden, all conceivable interests were well-organized and the rate of organization among potential members was high; moreover, these organizations had come to play an exceedingly important role in the political system. Gradually, they even came to be incorporated in formal governmental decision-making processes.

Within research about political parties, special attention was directed toward the strategies that the parties were assumed to employ in their ambition to maximize different goals. The fact that the country has a multiparty system—for a long time five parties were represented in the national parliament and now there are seven—evidently created an interest especially in party strategies (Sjöblom 1968).

PUBLIC ADMINISTRATION AND PUBLIC POLICY   A fourth trait of Swedish domestic politics research is the present strength of the field of public administration and public policy. The interest in public administration research has developed against the background of a rapid growth of the public sector in Sweden and of an intensified public debate about the governability of this sector. Several public-administration–oriented projects have been launched; several chairs in political science with a public adminstration profile have been established; several scholars in the field have received international recognition, among them Lennart Lundquist in Lund; and the public administration parts of the undergraduate curriculum have been strenghtened (Swedish Research Council 2002).

The present interest in public policy research has a special history in Sweden in the sense that the political system itself has a long tradition of producing policy-oriented studies of an academic nature. This tradition is due to the great number of commissions of inquiry that have played an important role in Swedish politics, which have tended to order policy studies from the universities as a background for their own policy proposals. However, from the 1970s onward, political science researchers in Sweden, as in many other countries, increasingly took the initiative in the analysis of contemporary policies, such as those concerning environment, housing, and higher education.

MICRO-ORIENTED RESEARCH   A fifth trait of Swedish political science research is that it was for a long time predominantly micro-oriented; studies that adopted broad perspectives and tried to analyze and describe the Swedish political system in toto were rare. In the 1980s, however, the Swedish government launched an extensive and clearly macro-oriented research project, led by Olof Petersson of Uppsala, which came to be called "*Maktutredningen*" (the power commission). The task of this project was to make a thorough investigation into the distribution of power in Swedish society and the general situation of Swedish democracy. Twenty monographs and a final report were published (Petersson 1991). The influence of this project has been extensive, both for the political science profession and for the public debate about the health of Swedish democracy.

The international evaluation of Swedish political science found a widespread and strong focus on democracy and its preconditions, both in the domestic politics research and in the research of the discipline generally (Swedish Research Council 2002).

Ethnocentricity

The risk that an interest in one's own society might turn into ethnocentricity seems to be a greater problem in large research communities than in smaller ones. The reason for this is simply that smaller communities are less self-sufficient, needing impulses from the outside for their own development. Swedish political science fits this pattern in its openness to influences from the outside world. But even in the Swedish case, there have been examples of an inwardness bordering on ethnocentricity.

One example is that Swedish political science was fairly slow in integrating political-behavior research, based on quantitative data and influenced by sociology-oriented theories. The slowness appears somewhat surprising considering that as early as 1937, Tingsten's *Political Behavior* analyzed correlations between election behavior and various traits in the population. In neighboring Denmark and Norway, where political science as an independent academic discipline was established much later than in Sweden, there was at first greater openness toward political-behavior approaches. The slowness on the Swedish side was primarily due to the fact that political science in this country already had a long tradition of its own with emphasis on legal, historical, and philosophical dimensions.

Political-behavior–oriented research was introduced to the Swedish political science community by the Gothenburg department. Jörgen Westerståhl, appointed professor there in the 1950s, gave this type of research a high profile in the department. Since the mid-1950s, voter surveys in conjunction with all parliamentary elections as well as referendums in the country have been carried out in cooperation with the Swedish National Central Bureau of Statistics. The Gothenburg series of election studies now represents one of the longest series of voter surveys in the world, and the department itself has sometimes been characterized as the "Michigan of Sweden" (Holmberg 2002).

Another example of an inwardness bordering on ethnocentricity was a lack of interest among Swedish political scientists in comparing findings about their own political system with those on other political systems. This lack was surprising because Swedish politics evoked considerable international interest during several decades in the latter part of the twentieth century. The country was looked on as one of the most advanced welfare states in the world and there was much talk about the "Swedish model." The political scientists who put this system in a comparative perspective tended to be foreign scholars and not Swedish. The international evaluation of Swedish political science offers an interesting explanation for this. It may be, the report states, "that the high international interest in Swedish politics and the 'Swedish model' has proved to be a 'false friend' in that Swedish scholars—like US scholars—have been under less pressure" to integrate the study of domestic politics within a comparative framework (Swedish Research Council 2002, p. 102). In this respect, Sweden, although a small country on the periphery of political science worldwide, is assumed to have fallen into the same trap as bigger research communities, namely the assumption that one's own system is unique.

OUTWARDNESS

Contacts between Swedish political science and the outside world have existed for a long time but increased dramatically during the latter part of the twentieth century. Swedish political scientists were drawn to various intellectual milieux, approaches, and methods, which they applied both to domestic politics and to other areas of investigation.

Input and Networks

Until the Second World War, German academia was the foreign intellectual milieu that primarily influenced Swedish academic disciplines, including political science. Germany was also one of the few countries where the academic field of political science existed, besides Sweden and the United States. The emphasis in German political science at this time, as well as in Sweden, was mainly on constitutional issues. Furthermore, it was not uncommon for Swedish political scientists during the prewar years to live abroad and conduct research on political institutions and practices in other countries. For example, Elis Håstad, who later became a professor at Stockholm University, wrote a voluminous dissertation—unfortunately not in German but in Swedish—on the Swiss political system, with its special combination of all-party governments and intensive use of referendums.

After the Second World War, the influence of American political science started to grow in Sweden, as elsewhere. The influence was intense from the 1960s onward. Theoretical frameworks worked out by American scholars were decisive in forming many research designs. For example, the first of the above-mentioned projects on Swedish local politics was heavily based on Easton's system theory, just as as the research on Swedish party strategies was strongly influenced by Downs' *An Economic Theory of Democracy*. These intensified contacts also meant that increasing numbers of Swedish political scientists spent time at American universities.

During the latter part of the twentieth century, Swedish political science also joined three formal international networks. One was the International Political Science Association (IPSA) founded in 1949, which was expected to have global membership but was for a long time dominated by American and Western European political scientists (Andrews 1982). The impact of this organization on Swedish political science has been limited, although the third of the IPSA world congresses took place in Stockholm. Sweden also joined two regional networks. In 1970, the European Consortium of Political Research (ECPR) was established with the aim of intensifying scholarly contacts across Western Europe. Early on, all the political science departments in Sweden joined the organization. Many Swedes became active, both in its scholarly and administrative activities; gradually more Swedish doctoral students have presented papers at the yearly workshop sessions that ECPR arranges. In 1975 the Nordic Political Science Association (NOPSA) was created, preceded by many years of different forms of internordic collaboration. Today the task of this organization is to publish a review, *Scandinavian Political Studies*, to organize Nordic congresses at regular intervals, and generally to initiate Nordic research with the aim of increasing cooperation among Nordic political scientists.

The existence of these international networks has not substantially diminished the influence of American political science on Sweden or on other countries. It can even be said that theoretically oriented American political science literature often serves as a common denominator in scholarly discussions taking place within these networks.

Integration of New Ideas

The increased contact between Swedish political scientists and the outside world has also meant that trends in the discipline, regardless of their country of origin, have come to influence the development of Swedish research. New perspectives, methods, and techniques en vogue have been discussed and to some extent even implemented. New problem areas and objects of attention have been incorporated.

The debates about new approaches and issues, and even their integration into the discipline, have often been surprisingly uncontroversial in the Swedish political science community. For example, the political-behavior approach gradually gained ground in the 1950s and 1960s at the expense of the history-law-philosophy tradition, without a major contest. In the 1970s, the wave of Marxist-inspired analyses that swept across the social sciences worldwide left few scars on Swedish political science. More recently, public choice theories, which have received some support in Sweden, have not been targets of such serious polemics here as in other countries.

This comparative calm is due to many factors. One is the consensual atmosphere generally prevailing in Swedish academia, although scholarly fields have also been torn by internal conflicts. Another factor might have been the hierarchical structure with only a few persons holding chairs, which for a long time characterized the political science discipline; these chairholders were on the whole able to maintain good personal relations with each other and were willing to establish cooperation between their departments both in the instruction of graduate students and in the execution of joint research projects. It might even be speculated that political science itself, with its emphasis on rules and institutions, tends to attract people less prone to getting involved in conflicts than people in many other academic fields.

This rather idyllic picture has to some extent been contradicted by a present-day trend in the international political science community which has also gained considerable support in Sweden, namely gender research. The international evaluation team emphasized that while Swedish gender research in political science has received favorable international attention, it has triggered a sharp debate in Sweden itself (Swedish Research Council 2002). The gender researchers have encountered barriers against getting recognition for their activity in mainstream political science; many of those outside the field have accused the gender researchers of not engaging in open dialogue with other political scientists and, furthermore, of subscribing to methods and theories that have little in common with those traditionally used in political science.

Fields of Research

The internationalization of Swedish political science has also meant that research on different aspects and areas of the world outside of Sweden has expanded while the domestic politics field has remained a central part of the discipline.

The study of international politics, which has a fairly long tradition in Sweden, has grown in volume. This field is now represented at most departments, although it has continued to be particularly strong in Lund and Stockholm. The array of topics covered has been large, and there has been considerable pluralism of theoretical approaches (Jönsson 1993). Some Swedish scholars in international politics, such as Christer Jönsson in Lund and Kjell Goldmann in Stockholm, have also obtained international recognition (Swedish Research Council 2002).

The study of politics in different foreign areas and countries has also expanded, although it has been somewhat sporadic in the choice of objects. At one time it even seemed as if political conditions in distant places evoked greater interest than those nearby (with the exception of the Nordic neighbors, similar to Sweden, which always tended to catch attention). For example, Africa was for many years particularly in focus, both because Swedish public opinion was committed to the black liberation struggle and because the continent was a major recipient of Swedish aid.

In this rather ad hoc character of the study of the world outside of Sweden, a change took place in the 1990s. Suddenly at least one nearby region, Europe as a whole, caught interest almost everywhere in the Swedish political science community. The explosion was triggered partly by intellectual curiosity about the substantive transformation that followed the Cold War, but mainly by the fact that Sweden joined the European Union in 1995. Groups were established at many Swedish political science departments with the general aim of studying European integration. This research has focused on topics such as the allocation of power between different levels in this emerging multilevel European governance, the relations between different institutions in a very complicated decision-making structure, and the difficulties of making authorities accountable for their decisions and promoting citizen involvement in European affairs. This interest in EU-connected matters is of course not unique to Swedish political science but characteristic of European political science generally. For example, the European University Institute in Florence, of which Sweden is now also part, has "europeanization" in all its different dimensions as its special research profile.

The comparative politics field, which gained in popularity worldwide in the 1960s and today is well-organized in many countries, has for a long time remained fairly weak in Sweden. In the recent international review of Swedish political science, it is even characterized as "the least developed" (Swedish Research Council 2002, p. 109). One reason for this state of affairs is probably the above-mentioned sporadic nature of the selection of areas and countries for closer examination. An improvement in this respect, however, seems to have occurred at the end of the twentieth century. The evaluators refer to several Swedish political scientists now engaged in comparative research, including Hadenius in Uppsala (*Democracy and Development*, 1992), Rothstein in Gothenburg (*Just Institutions Matter*, 1998), and Sainsbury in Stockholm (*Gender, Equality and Welfare States*, 1996).

The Swedish research that covers aspects and areas of the world outside of Sweden is naturally often written in English. As a whole, the internationalization of the discipline has meant that English is used more and more. In this respect, however, Swedish political science has not gone as far as many other social sciences in the country, particularly economics and psychology, where English has come to be the dominant tool of communication. One reason for still insisting on the use of Swedish is the discipline's awareness of having two different addressees: not only the international research community, but also its own society, which supports the discipline and hopefully also gains from studies produced. Furthermore, to express oneself in scholarly matters in a foreign language still constitutes a burden for many. This is one explanation for the fact that studies written in Swedish about particular Swedish phenomena have not been translated into English, which would enable them to become part of the international political science debate. In the international review of Swedish political science, researchers are urged to publish more in other tongues than their own (Swedish Research Council 2002).

The special features that have characterized the development of Swedish political science research during the latter part of the twentieth century do not imply that this development should have been essentially different from that of other Western countries. Gradually in Sweden most of the possible dimensions and subfields of the political science discipline have been covered: theoretically as well as empirically oriented research; ideas as well as institutions; the output of political processes as well as all the different segments into which these processes can be divided; national and international as well as local politics; and comparative studies as well as in-depth studies of one particular system, which mostly tended to be the Swedish system.

THE SURROUNDING SOCIETY

Foreign observers of Swedish political science have been struck by the close relations they perceive between this discipline and the surrounding society, including the state. Finnish political scientist Dag Anckar, for example, in an article about trends, roles, and approaches in Nordic political science, reported Swedish political scientists on the whole to be more integrated in society and more in agreement with the organization and norms of the political system than their colleagues in the other Nordic countries (Anckar 1991). The recent international evaluation makes a similar point concerning the mood that they find characteristic of the Swedish political science faculty. The research undertaken is said to be "inspired by basic values that constitute the normative foundation of the Swedish political system and of Swedish political culture, including ideals of . . . democratic governance, due procedure, and the solidarity norms of the welfare state" (Swedish Research Council 2002, p. 136). The evaluators state that the political science faculty does not include rebels that fundamentally question the very principles of the surrounding society; when criticism is expressed—the Swedish political science community is not written off as totally uncritical—it is often framed in support of the basic values of Swedish society.

Unquestionably, the relations between Swedish political science and the surrounding society have been close for a long time. The pattern in these relations has however changed somewhat over the decades. The very shaping of the research undertaken once reflected a greater distance than is apparent today. Several generations of Swedish political scientists were imbued with an ambition to make a clear distinction in their research between the analysis of political phenomena and an outright evaluation of them. In this outlook they were strongly influenced by Uppsala philosopher Axel Hägerström, who in several works strongly and explicitly emphasized the distinction between facts and values (Hägerström 1939). This intellectual tradition was maintained for a long time but began to be challenged during the last decades of the twentieth century.

One type of challenge was an increased awareness, partly influenced by postmodernistic thinking, of the difficulties involved in maintaining a clear distinction between facts and values. Another challenge lay in the form of public financing of academic research. Public money for research in Sweden has not only been in the hands of universities, research councils, foundations, etc., but lately also in the hands of public authorities with responsibility for specified public policy areas. The academic research funded by one of these authorities is expected to be valuable to the public sector served by that authority. This "sectoral research" (*sektorsforskning*) has also to some extent affected political science and thereby contributed to undermining the earlier ambition of keeping a clear borderline beween facts and values.

Despite the ambition to keep a clear distinction between analysis and evaluation of political phenomena, individual political scientists tended, perhaps paradoxically, to commute between universities and positions in the surrounding society. One form of such traffic was engagement in party politics. In the middle of the twentieth century, for example, three chairholders in the discipline—Georg Andrén in Gothenburg and Gunnar Heckscher and Elis Håstad in Stockholm—all served as representatives for the conservative party in parliament, in the Riksdag. In the 1940s, Georg Andrén had been a member of the Cabinet; in the 1960s, Heckscher was for a few years leader of his party. The present chairman of the Stockholm political science department, Daniel Tarschys, was earlier in his career a member of the Riksdag and for a short time he served as permanent secretary (*statssekreterare*) to a liberal Prime Minister. A number of university lecturers in political science have during the latter part of the twentieth century held seats in the Riksdag. Today, however, there is only one parlamentarian of this kind, namely the Social Democrat Björn von Sydow, who was appointed member of the Cabinet in 1996 and now serves as defense minister. Furthermore, members of the political science faculty have been assigned various tasks in the above-mentioned system of commissions of inquiry. Political scientists have most often served as experts in ongoing commission work, but occasionally they have chaired or been members of a commission.

The reputation of Swedish political science in the society seems historically to have been good and remains so today, although we do not have reliable data as to public evaluation of different social sciences. The visibility of political scientists is high, measured in terms of newspaper articles and interviews in mass media.

A difficult question is to what extent ideas based on political science research have directly influenced the development of the society. The fact that public authorities have begun to make use of the universities, including political science departments, as sources of information and advice does not necessarily mean a corresponding increase in direct influence. Probably the influence has continued to be mostly of an indirect character. Traditionally, Swedish political scientists have shown a reluctance, in their research as well as in their activities as experts or as contributors to the public debate, to give clear recommendations for action to be followed by politicians and administrators. Instead, the tendency for a long time has been only to formulate pros and cons. Today, however, there seems to be a trend among some Swedish political scientists to be openly normative in their conclusions.

The close relations between the Swedish political science community and the surrounding society have not been an object of much discussion in the profession itself, although complaints are always heard about the system and extent of the public financing of the discipline. The close relations can of course entail both disadvantages and advantages. A possible disadvantage might be that individual political scientists feel hampered in their analysis of domestic politics. A fear of jeopardizing existing relations might unnecessarily reduce their willingness to pose fundamental questions as to the political organization of the country. However, the continuing scholarly debate about the political system as such seems on the whole to be fairly unrestricted. A clear advantage, on the other hand, of the closeness is good access to central actors in society. Thereby the sources of Swedish domestic politics research have been expanded, and the insights into political processes have been improved. The advantages of the present relations seem in my opinion to outnumber possible disadvantages, although the dangers of too close relations between researchers and central political actors should not be overlooked.

Swedish political science research is in good health according to the recent international evaluation. The discipline is said to be solid, well-organized, and well-crafted. The evaluators, however, deliberately abstain from superlatives such as outstanding, cutting-edge, daringly innovative, etc. in their characterization.

Instead they say that Swedish political science, although doing reasonably well by international standards, could do even better (Swedish Research Council 2002). The state of affairs of Swedish political science today is of course a function of many different facts and circumstances, including the recruitment pattern of scholars, the organization of academic work, and the distribution of resources for research across a country that is large in area though small in population. But maybe this state of affairs can also to some extent be seen as a reflection of the surrounding society. As Swedish political science is said to be solid, well-organized, and well-crafted but lacking in daringly new initiatives, so in some ways is the society of which this discipline is an integral part.

The *Annual Review of Political Science* is online at http://polisci.annualreviews.org

LITERATURE CITED

Anckar D. 1991. Nordic political science: trends, roles, approaches. *Eur. J. Polit. Res.* (Spec. issue) 20:3–4

Andrews WG, ed. 1982. *International Handbook of Political Science*. West Point, CT: Greenwood

Falkemark G. 1992. *Statsvetarporträtt. Svenska statsvetare under 350 år*. Stockholm: SNS Förlag

Hadenius A. 1992. *Democracy and Development*. Cambridge, UK: Cambridge Univ. Press

Hägerström A. 1939. *Socialfilosofiska Uppsatser*. Stockholm: Bonniers

Heckscher G. 1946. *Staten och organisationerna*. Stockholm: KF:s bokförlag

Holmberg S. 1994. Election studies the Swedish way. *Eur. J. Polit. Res.* (Spec. issue) 25:3

Jönsson C. 1993. International politics: Scandinavian identity amidst American hegemony? *Scand. Polit. Stud.* 16:2

Larheden H. 1999. Trender och traditioner inom svensk statsvetenskap. *Statsvetenskaplig tidskrift* 102:1

Petersson O. 1991. *Makt En sammanfattning av maktutredningen*. Stockholm: Allmänna förlaget

Rothstein B. 1998. *Just Institutions Matter. The Moral and Political Logic of the Universal Welfare State*. Cambridge, UK: Cambridge Univ. Press

Ruin O. 1974. Participatory democracy and corporativism: the case of Sweden. *Scand. Polit. Stud. Yearb.* 9:171–84

Ruin O. 1978. Political science research in Sweden 1960–1975: an overview. *Scand. Polit. Stud. Yearb.* 12. Reprinted 1982 in *International Handbook of Political Science*, Sweden Research, ed. WG Andrews, pp. 299–319. London: Greenwood

Ruin O. 1986. Swedish political science: a periphery which was at one time almost a center. In *Political Life in Sweden,* No. 22, ed. Swedish Information Service, New York, pp. 1–10. Reprinted 1986 as "Political science in Sweden," *Politologen* 1986:1

Sainsbury D. 1996. *Gender, Equality and Welfare States*. Cambridge, UK: Cambridge Univ. Press

Sjöblom G. 1968. *Party Strategies in a Multiparty System*. Lund: Studentlitteratur

Strömberg L, Westerståhl J. 1984. *The New Swedish Communes. A Summary of Local Government Research*. Stockholm: Liber Distribution

Swedish Research Council. 2002. Swedish research in political science an evaluation 2002. *Rapport* 2002:1

Annu. Rev. Polit. Sci. 2003. 6:55–76
doi: 10.1146/annurev.polisci.6.121901.085542
First published online as a Review in Advance on Mar. 6, 2003

FOLIE RÉPUBLICAINE

Robert E. Goodin

*Social & Political Theory and Philosophy Programs, Research School of Social Sciences,
Australian National University, Canberra ACT 0200, Australia;
email: goodinb@coombs.anu.edu.au*

Key Words republican political theory, common good, civic virtue

■ **Abstract** Republican political theory has undergone a recent revival, first and
most strongly among historians, subsequently in a more limited way among lawyers,
philosophers, and political scientists. Surveying the many contexts in which republican
principles are invoked, I find that appeals to republicanism are often redundant (there
being other, probably better, ways of arguing for the same practices and outcomes)
and sometimes unfortunate (setting off, among "street-level republicans," resonances
with darker features of the older republican tradition that contemporary academic
theorists of republicanism would prefer to forget). Even the more attractive features of
the republican ideal—deliberative engagement in pursuit of the common good—can
invite communitarian excesses, and even the "liberal republican" versions that strive
to avoid that outcome are largely bereft of mechanisms for realizing their vision.

INTRODUCTION

Republican themes resonate differently in the domestic politics of various places
for various reasons. This essay considers real-world traditions of republicanism as
well as its academic theory.

Republicanism itself is of ancient vintage, of course. It originated with the
Roman Republic and exercised continuing influence on the Western consciousness
largely through the law. Roman law served as the default legal system throughout
Christendom for more than a millenium (Berman 1983). Well into the early modern
era, the works of Grotius, Pufendorf, and Coke are littered with references to the
Institutes of Gaius and Justinian.

As a more narrowly academic phenomenon, the "republican revival" is a relatively cohesive project with a relatively clear lineage. It dates to the work of two
remarkable intellectual historians, Skinner (1978) and Pocock (1975). Skinner
was interested in the the way ancient Roman ideals were picked up and represented in the city-states of Renaissance Italy. Pocock's work focused on the
way in which those ideals, in turn, were picked up and reworked by the "North
Atlantic republicans," primarily Harrington (1992) in England and the Founders in
America.

Over the past quarter century, historians have substantially rewritten the story of the American Founding in those republican terms. "An effect of the recent research," Pocock wrote as long ago as 1972, "has been to display the American revolution less as the first political act of revolutionary enlightenment than as the last great act of the Renaissance. In a variety of ways, we are now to see the Founding Fathers as the culminating generation of civic humanists and classical republicans . . . " (Pocock 1972, p. 124). That much-quoted summary judgment has proven ever more prescient with the passing years (Wood 1969; Shalhope 1972; Kramnick 1982; Appleby 1985, 1992; Rogers 1992). Locke is now seen as much less central than we were led to believe (Becker 1922, Hartz 1955), and North Atlantic republicans far more so (Herzog 1986).

Recalling the Founders' vision of a self-governing community of free and equal citizens, some lawyers, philosophers, and political theorists succumbed to the temptation to reappropriate the language of republicanism to describe their pre-ferred blend of "deliberative democracy" and "civic engagement" (Michelman 1986; Sunstein 1988, 1990, 1993a,b,c; Selznick 1992; Sandel 1996; Dagger 1997; Southwood 2002). Even if there are sharp breaks between the republicanism of the founding moments and subsequent American history (Sandel 1984, 1996), the thought was that republicanism of some form or another was still a viable ideal and a genuine force in contemporary politics.

Among political theorists as distinct from historians, however, this "republican revival" has been a relatively muted affair. Republicanism rates barely a mention in most teaching texts on political ideologies; in the first five years of the new *Journal of Political Ideologies*, only a couple of articles have been devoted to it. Among political theorists, as distinct from intellectual historians, the republican revival was largely an American phenomenon, albeit with distant echoes in Australia and (of course) France. In retrospect, the republican revival within political theory seems to have lasted a relatively brief moment, since many of the original major players now seem to have moved on. Still, it was an interesting moment, and it is well worth recording both why we collectively were tempted and why in the end we did not collectively succumb to the allures of republican rhetoric.

In key texts of this republican revival, references to "the republican ideal" often prove to be both allusive and elusive.[1] Often the real expository aim lies elsewhere: in explicating the ideas of Machiavelli or Harrington or Madison or Tocqueville or the Warren Court or the malaise of contemporary American politics. Although republicanism is a useful lens through which to view all those things, the object in view is rarely republicanism itself (cf. Pettit 1997a).

Theorizations of the republican ideal inevitably loom large in any assessment of republican political theory. But it is equally important to explore the wider

---

[1]Indeed, as Michelman (1986, p. 17) writes, "Republicanism is not a well-defined . . . doctrine. As a 'tradition' in political thought, it figures less as canon than ethos, less as blueprint than as conceptual grip, less as settled institutional fact than as semantic field for normative debate and constructive imagination."

ways in which republican traditions might resonate in many of the darker corners of our political communities. Those resonances are typically unintended in those academic texts; few of the scholars I cite here would endorse many of the practices peculiar to this "street-level republicanism." Those wider resonances, however, are at least as important as any academic text in deciding, socially and politically, whether we really want to recommend republicanism as a preferred political self-conception.

REASONS TO BE TEMPTED, PART I

Historically, republics served as alternatives to empires. In the classical model to which republicans repeatedly hark back, the republic in question is the Roman Republic, before Julius's and Octavian's Caesarian ambitions.

Empire, in turn, has two aspects, one foreign and the other domestic. Republicanism repudiates imperial pretensions in both dimensions—though not uniquely so, as this essay shows. There are many perfectly good grounds for repudiating imperialism without turning to republicanism.

Self-Rule

Throughout the modern era, "republicanism" has most commonly served as a rallying cry for those who would (metaphorically or otherwise) behead a foreign king. The republican revival among the Italian city-states amounted to an assertion of independence from the Holy Roman Emperor and the Holy See. The Dutch Republic represented a rebellion among the burgers of the United Provinces against the Spanish crown (van Gelderen 1993). The American Republic was proclaimed to replace the British crown, as was the Irish Republic and as one day will be the Australian (Turnbull 1993; cf. Francis 2001).

In sloughing off claims of a distant empire and a foreign crown, republicanism is not the only option, however. Virtually all of the great decolonizing crusades of the twentieth century adopted the rhetoric of nationalism rather than republicanism (Geertz 1973, 1977). Despite sitting adjacent to a notorious co-Celtic hotbed of republicanism, even Scots dub their home-rule campaign "nationalist" rather than "republican" (if only perhaps strategically, to avoid old Jacobin specters).

From a moral point of view, many of us prefer nationalism to be tempered by liberalism (Tamir 1993).[2] The republican variation on that theme is to wish for patriotism to manifest itself as republican pride in good political institutions rather than ethnic or other tribal identities (Viroli 1995). Such wishes are particularly fervent where notions of democratic self-rule are otherwise likely to succumb to anxieties over the composition of the "demos" (Dahl 1979), and thence to "ethnic cleansing."

---

[2]One might wish republicanism to be tempered by liberalism, as well (Sunstein 1988, Dagger 1999), more of which below.

Republican wishes along those lines are, however, largely in vain. Pride in one's political institutions is a peculiar attitude. Only 3% of Italians and 7% of Germans manifested it, by Almond & Verba's count (1963, p. 64).[3] If good institutions were all that mattered to our patriotic pride, we would have no reason to get all worked up about replacing Westminster-style institutions imposed by a Colonial Office with Westminster-style institutions all our own. Colonial peoples demanding home rule have always wanted more. They are concerned much less with institutional forms than with the nationality of the placeholders within them. Even if they were to be ruled by autocrats, better their *own* autocrats (Geertz 1973, 1977).

While some republicans hope to distance themselves from nationalism (Viroli 1995), others hope to make common cause with it. Sandel (1996, p. 344), for example, supposes that the nation-state provides a potentially important republican "link between identity and self-rule." Sandel's idea is that the nation-state has served as the "unit that gave expression to the collective identity of a people defined by a common history, language or tradition." But that is simply not how nationalism has worked, in the bulk of self-styled nationalist campaigns for home rule in the modern world. The initial "primordial sentiments" have invariably been of a more tribal than national sort. The whole point of nation-building has traditionally been to subsume those primordial sentiments under some newly constructed national ideals and identities (Geertz 1963).

Nation-building has historically been more a matter of inventing commonalities than aligning political institutions with pre-existing commonalities. The story is broadly the same from Third-Republic France (Weber 1976) to postcolonial Africa (Mazrui 1972). Accidents of history or whims of colonial cartographers had joined together a grab bag of peoples with almost nothing in common: no language, no religion, no ancestors. In the fullness of time, all going well, shared traditions might be invented and new identities concocted (Hobsbawm & Ranger 1972; Pocock 1957; 1973, ch. 7). But decolonizing campaigns were for *home* rule, in the first instance. They were far less concerned about the self-government of a self-consciously unified people than about the politics of a self-governing *place* (Barry 1989, ch. 6).

Thus, self-government—understood as the rejection of foreign crowns and imperial apron strings—can be, and has been, defended on many different grounds. Republicanism is one. But historically (and certainly in contemporary history) it has been a distinctly minor theme—and understandably so.

---

[3]The German results presumably cannot be explained away as translation error, compelling though MacIntyre's (1972, pp. 10–11) commentary on the Italian case might be: "The notion of pride in Italian culture is still inexorably linked, especially in the South but also in the North, to the notion of honour. What one takes pride in is what touches on one's honour. If asked to list the subjects which touched upon their honour, many Italians would spontaneously place the chastity of their immediate female relatives high on the list. . . . Hence we cannot hope to compare an Italian's attitude to his government's acts with an Englishman's in respect of the pride each takes. . . . "

Mixed Constitution

Republicans of old not only resisted rule by foreign princes but renounced the sovereignty of any prince, foreign or domestic. The difference between republics and their imperial successors, recall from Roman history (or Star Wars), was historically the power of the Senate, which in an Empire is displaced by an Emperor. When Schlesinger (1973) inveighed against the *Imperial Presidency* of Richard Nixon, he was merely echoing this ancient theme.

The balanced powers of the old Roman constitution served as a model for Montesquieu and thence for republicans across the North Atlantic. In this tradition, evident even in the concillarism of the medieval Church (Black 1997), republicanism is equated with non-tyranny—self-government by a band of equals rather than the tyrannical rule of any one central authority.

Of course, historically, that band of coequals was small. It was formally limited to literally a handful of officials. Informally, they represented and responded to an only slightly larger handful of influentials. The vast majority of ordinary people—all women and slaves, all peasants and parishioners, all artisans and workmen—were officially excluded, both as representatives and represented. So the "checking and balancing" done by these early republican institutions was in the service of a very narrowly circumscribed public.

Strongly associated though republicanism historically was with the "mixed constitution" and balancing of powers within, however, there is nothing uniquely republican about those institutional arrangements. They are found in Plato's *Laws* and Aristotle's *Politics*. They are as much in evidence in liberal Locke's *Second Treatise* as in republican Montesquieu's *Spirit of the Laws*. There are numerous connections between liberalism and republicanism more generally (Dagger 1999).

In our own day, Rawls (2001, p. 144) professes to see no incompatibility between his liberalism and "classical republicanism." The latter he characterizes as

> the view that the safety of democratic liberties, including the liberties of nonpolitical life . . . , requires the active participation of citizens who have the political virtues needed to sustain a constitutional regime . . . The idea is that unless there is widespread participation in democratic politics by a vigorous and informed citizen body moved in good part by a concern for political justice and public good, even the best-designed political institutions will eventually fall into the hands of those who hunger for power and military glory, or pursue narrow class and economic interests, to the exclusion of almost everything else.

Rawls goes on to say,

> Between classical republicanism, so understood, and the liberalism represented by Constant and Berlin, there is no fundamental opposition . . . . [T]he question is [just] to what degree citizens' engaging in politics is needed

for the safety of basic liberties, and how the requisite participation is best achieved . . . . [T]his is . . . . a matter of political sociology and institutional design . . . . [C]lassical republicanism . . . is . . . fully compatible with political liberalism, and with justice as fairness as a form thereof.

Unaccustomed though I am to accepting such *ex cathedra* pronouncements as gospel, I see no reason to demur from that particular judgment.

Republican Freedom

Searching for something that is distinctive in the republican theory of self-rule, some influential commentators attempt to isolate an identifiably republican conception of freedom (Skinner 1984, 1985). Built on the Roman legal notion of *dominium*—being one's own man (rather than another's servant)—this notion migrates through medieval notions of "the freedom of the city" to analytic reconstructions of a notion of "resilient liberty" (Pettit 1989; 1996; 1997a, esp. ch. 2; 1997b; 1999).

The root idea underlying the concept of resilient liberty that it is not enough to merely to *be* free. It is not enough to be free to whistle while you work, for example, just because your employer does not mind your whistling. Instead, you want to be secure in your freedom against arbitrary interventions by others. You want your freedom to be resilient, capable of withstanding any change in others' preferences or predilections. In the grand language of the Preamble to the U.S. Constitution, you want "to *secure* these liberties." In the trivial example just given, you are not really (resiliently) free to whistle unless you are free to keep on whistling even if your boss decides she does not like your whistling.

Neo-republicans commend republicanism on the ground that it, and it alone, secures resilient liberty. The failure of other social arrangements to secure that value, while republicanism succeeds, distinguishes it from them and makes it uniquely superior among them. Or so neo-republicans would say.

Those analyses err, however, in their assertion (and their need to assert, to differentiate republicanism from liberalism) that this resilient liberty is a different *kind* of liberty, distinct from all the other familiar forms. It is not. Rather, it is merely an aspect of any of the other more familiar forms. Furthermore, it is an aspect that anyone who cares about any other form of liberty would value. If you care about X as a good, then it follows that you care about the security of your enjoyment of X. You do not have two separate concerns, one about security and the other about X. Caring about X and caring about securely retaining X are part and parcel of a single concern.

This sort of argument is familiar from the analysis of many other second-order values. Time is one. If I think X is good, then enjoying X for a longer time rather than a shorter time must be good. That does not mean I value two separate things (time and X), nor does it mean that I value X in some special temporally extended way. It is merely in the nature of valuing X that more of X is better than less, and that more time with X is better than less.[4]

Efficiency is another second-order value. As that term is technically understood by economists, it means getting to the "production possibility frontier" in tradeoffs between two goods, X and Y; it merely means never settling for a situation in which you get less of both of those goods than you could have had through some other choice. Is efficiency an independent value, then? Of course not. Its value is purely derivative from the value we assign to X and Y. What makes efficiency good—what makes it desirable not to settle for less X than we can get, for any quantity we choose of Y—is simply the value we attach to X (Goodin 1988, ch. 8; Le Grand 1990; Barry 1990, p. xxxix–xl).

The value of resilient republican liberty, understood as security in the enjoyment of our liberty, is a second-order value of the same sort. We value security in our liberty only because we value our liberty. It need be no more complicated than that. Rhetorically distinctive though the republican emphasis on securing freedom against domination might have been, there is nothing analytically distinctive about it.

A liberal concern about one's freedom from interference should logically extend, equally, to a concern with the security of one's freedom from interference. Historically, liberals may have been negligent (or worse) on this score. But logically, liberals can (and, by the internal logic of their own principles, should) be as concerned with the resilience of the liberty that they champion as is any republican.

REASONS TO BE WARY

From Status to Contract, and Back Again

A defining feature of the movement from premodern to modern social forms is the movement "from status to contract" (Maine 1901). That republican notion of freedom as dominion—the status of being "a freeman"—is quintessentially a status concept. Republicanism, understood as non-domination, thus constitutes a movement back to a status society of a strikingly premodern form.

In older republics, both ancient and early modern, rights of citizenship were tightly circumscribed. Modern democrats wary of republicanism recall these traces well. "Historically," Dryzek (1996, pp. 64–65) reminds us,

---

[4]A similar argument can be made with respect to the familiar old argument between positive and negative liberty. Rawls (1971, p. 204) suggests that positive liberty is not really liberty but rather represents the "worth of liberty"; but then anyone who values liberty (understood in its purest negative form) must then also value positive liberty on that construal, since no one who values liberty could value worthless liberty.

an emphasis on exclusion for civic benefit has been central to the theory and practice of republicanism. Republics . . . could flourish as a result of their exclusion and exploitation of slaves, noncitizens and women. Republican citizenship and public freedom for the few was bought at the expense of excluding the many. In the republican tradition, exclusion benefited only those who were included in the state, which was the only recognized venue for politics.

Whereas ancient and early modern republics were layered, hierarchical status orders, contemporary republicans want their new republics to be single-status status communities (Sunstein 1988, pp. 1541, 1552–55; Sandel 1996, pp. 318–19; Pettit 1997a, pp. 190–94). In the current republican vision, everyone is supposed to be a citizen like any other, equally able to look every other in the eye. Therein lies the appeal of the image of a "republic of science": a world of no hierarchy, no aristocracy; each man is as good as his Jack; communication is free and open; and so on.[5]

Still, the equality envisaged by even contemporary republicans is purely an equality of status, the status of citizen. And that is as empty a form of equality as is the equality of all who are of noble birth. Some nobles may be rich whereas others are down at heel; but all are equally noble. Such is the way with status equality as well.

That is why many republicans often seem relatively indifferent to broader distributional questions. For republicans,

> what is vital to the status of person or citizen establishes a minimum equality of entitlement . . . . Equal protection speaks above all to membership, and membership presumes that all who belong share a core identity. This identity is wholly compatible with rich diversity so long as that diversity does not undermine equality of membership. (Selznick 1992, pp. 484, 189)

Selznick, an advocate, regards that as a plus. Others, mindful of Marx's fulminations "On the Jewish Question," see more clearly that pure status equality is an almost empty formalism (Isaac 1988, p. 357).

To be sure, republicans might have instrumental reasons for favoring more equality of resources (or opportunities or even of material outcomes), because equality in all those respects feeds causally into the fundamental equality of political status that is of signal concern to them.[6] Sunstein (1988, pp. 152–53, 1576–78), for example, builds a powerful case for campaign finance reform in the United States on these premises. But at the end of the day it is equality of political status, and that alone, which really matters to them. Equalities in all those other dimensions

---

[5]Polanyi's (1962) own version of it has more disciplinary authority than that. The real world of contemporary science, however, may be further removed from Polanyi's extended gentleman's club (the Royal Society sits in the heart of St. James clubland, after all) and nearer the vision of Churchill, who famously mused, "Scientists don't have to have good manners, they just have to be right."

[6]Or, less plausibly, into a strong sense of community attachment (Sandel 1996, pp. 330–31).

are of no republican value in and of themselves. They are of value only as they impinge on the enjoyment of political status.

Traditionally, only persons who have sufficient independent means not to be dependent on (and hence subservient to) any other person were deemed fit for republican citizenship (Goodin 1988, pp. 171–72; 1993; Isaac 1988, 365 ff.; James 1992).[7] A qualified case for equality of material circumstances might today be constructed by reversing that relationship, giving everyone whom (on whatever other grounds) we think we would like to include as citizens sufficient material resources that they can qualify for that status by republican standards (Pettit 1997a, pp. 158–63).[8] However, the principle by which we decide whom we want to qualify for citizenship must of course be determined outside republican principles.

To criticize republicanism as essentially a status society is not to say that we should go from those status concerns back to unqualified ideals of freedom of contract again. That ideology, too, has well and truly run its course (Atiyah 1979). Its follies are familiar, their remedies likewise. But the remedies in question are of a more robustly egalitarian sort—ranging across opportunities, resources, and outcomes—than republicanism can easily accommodate. What we need is to move from status to contract and beyond, not back.

Shame Societies

Republicanism thus marks a return to a status culture, albeit in single-status form. If there is only one status, why does it matter that it is a "status culture" at all? What difference can it make? Well, perhaps it cannot make the standard difference of *Homo hierarchicus* (Dumont 1980). But it does make an important difference in terms of what is at stake in political and social life, and what is an appropriate way of pursuing it.

Status societies, even single-status ones, are driven by notions of honor and shame, dignity and embarrassment. The saga of *Romeo and Juliet* could only occur in its particularly perverse form among families driven by republican conceptions of pride and honor. So too could Bernstein's *West Side Story*. So too could the Sicilian mafia and its "men of honor" (Gambetta 1993, Lyttleton 1995).

The nice thing about republican honor is that people at least internalize social norms of some sort. You can call on them to act in the name of those higher

---

[7]Drawing on materials from Stoics, who were also central in classical republicanism, Slote (1993) considers self-sufficiency a prime political virtue. So does Galston (1988), by an ostensibly more liberal route.

[8]But as Pettit (1997a, p. 161) goes on to say, "the policy is almost certain to fall short of strict material egalitarianism, however interpreted." Elsewhere, Pettit (1997b, pp. 125–28) argues that republican "freedom as non-domination" is compatible with redistribution, in a way that liberal "freedom as non-interference" is not. But again, to say that his conception is not opposed to redistributive interventions is not to say it positively requires them; and liberals post-Rawls have dozens of ways of being more egalitarian than a strict Hayekian commitment to "freedom as non-interference" would allow.

norms rather than always providing some sordidly self-interested reason for acting (Braithwaite & Pettit 1990; Brennan & Pettit 1993, 2000; Pettit 1997a, pp. 253–60).

The nasty thing about republican honor is that it is so terribly precious. Although it is not self-interest in any crass material sense, it is nonetheless *amour propre* in a fairly robust sense. The question always is, "How I will come out of this looking (in the eyes of those whose opinion matters to me)?" Internalizing concerns with one's image differs importantly from internalizing morality as such (Barry 1989, ch. 12)—particularly when the guardians of the image themselves internalize merely a code of image-based honor, rather than a substantive code of morality as such.

Republics grounded in this sort of honor are quintessentially dueling societies. There, honor must be satisfied and courage manifested in the craziest and cruelest of ways.[9] Dueling itself may have died out, but its lineal descendents are to be found in the street code of the American ghetto, where "dissing" someone—showing them disrespect—remains a reliable path to an early grave (Stone 1995).

Codes of Honor and Their Limits

A code of honor binds members of a republican community. But it binds them alone. In its most traditional form, it bound members of the republican oligarchy: No one was traditionally obliged to accept a challenge to duel from one below his station, because those of lesser social standing simply have no capacity to impugn the honor of those above them (Wyatt-Brown 1982, p. 349–61). Even today, archaic societies that run on an honor code (notoriously including military academies), are plagued with problems arising from the fact that the honor code gives rise to a stronger sense of obligation to one's fellows than to anyone outside, leading to cover-ups to protect the band of brothers rather than respect for the code as such. It is not an external code but an internal one. It is less a morality than a mutual assistance pact, often amounting to a conspiracy against the outside world.

Now, where the brotherhood has been expanded (as contemporary republicans would expand it) to all members of the republican community, those problems would be ameliorated. But they would not be eliminated. At the margins there would always be problems of defining the boundaries of the community. Whether immigrants and aliens are to be counted as members is very much queried today in the Republic of France (Balibar & Wallerstein 1988, Brubaker 1992, Favell 1998), not least by the self-styled "Front Républicain" (Fennema & Maussen 2000).

There will always be some people beyond the borders, however generously construed. Toward them republicans suppose no honorable performances are owed. Think of the profound cynicism of the Republic of France in sending official agents to sink a Greenpeace ship moored in another country's harbor. Republicanism thus constitutes a particularly vicious form of closed communitarianism, a collective attitude of "We're all right, Jacques."

---

[9]Recall that one of the authors of the *Federalist Papers*, Alexander Hamilton, died in a duel (at the hands of Vice President Aaron Burr, no less).

A further problem with a code of honor, alluded to above, is that it tends to be a code—a "list morality." Scrupulously adhering to the items on the list, you can do plenty of damage to the spirit of the listing. (Think of the military academies, once again.)

The items on the republicans' moral list ostensibly add up to "civic virtue." Republicans hope that its "civic" nature might rescue their virtue ethic from the complaints ordinarily lodged against the narcissistic personalism that typifies a preoccupation with virtue.[10] But republican virtue, like all virtue, must at root be an attribute of character.[11] Republicans propose civic-oriented standards against which to assess one's character, but the unit to be assessed remains one's character rather than one's performances.

That inevitable fixation on character renders republicanism's virtue ethic vulnerable to all the familiar objections to virtue ethics. The virtue in view is a distinctly circumscribed one: Its application is limited to one's dealing with one's fellow citizens. The virtue in view is (as I have said) precious, focusing on "how will I come out of this looking?" And the virtue in view is indifferent (as most virtue ethics or list moralities are) to the consequences of its preciousness on others.

Civic Virtue with a Martial Twist

Among republicanism's many odd resonances, here is perhaps the oddest: Benjamin Franklin's description of the United States as "a republic, if you can keep it" (rather than a vulgar democracy) is quoted repeatedly by right-wing opponents of central state authority—indeed of government seemingly in any form. It is the catch-cry, *in extremis*, of the Minutemen and the Montana Militia (Wills 1995).

Upon reflection, there is nothing odd about that fact. It is fully in keeping with older republican traditions, as today's republicans are acutely embarrassed to recall (Sunstein 1988, p. 1539–40, 1564; Pettit 1997a, pp. 150–53). The Roman Republic was famously secured by legions of citizens, enlisted by military commanders acting on commission from the Senate. The city republics of the Italian Renaissance were singularly martial affairs, as any reader of Machiavelli knows well. The cities of the Dutch Republic were chockablock with "companies of the guard," the most famous of which is today the Company of Franz Croq, immortalized in Rembrandt's *Nightwatch*.

---

[10]Sunstein (1988, pp. 1550–51), for example, wants to deny that "the appeal to civic virtue is designed to improve individual character." Important though he acknowledges that theme to have been in classical republican thought, "modern republicans invoke civic virtue primarily in order to promote deliberation in the service of social justice, not to elevate the characters of the citizenry." See also Morrow (1991) and Dagger (1997).

[11]As Sandel (1996, p. 25), for example, writes, "republican theory . . . seeks . . . to cultivate in citizens the qualities of character necessary to the common good of self-government. Insofar as certain dispositions, attachments and commitments are essential to the realization of self-government, republican politics regards moral character as a public, not a private, concern."

Classically, it was thought that martial virtue should extend throughout the entire community. "No standing armies" and "no professional soldiers" were central principles of republics from the earliest days. And these emphases were nowise mitigated as republicanism migrated north. In Harrington's *Oceana*, "county assemblies are at once assemblies of the electorate and musters of the militia"—a proposition that Pocock (1973, p. 114) regards as Harrington's "chief gift to eighteenth-century political thought." And as in fictional republics, so too in real ones of the period. The key texts bequeathed us by Cromwell's Commonwealth are the Putney debates within the General Council of the Army over the New Model Army (Woodhouse 1974, Sharp 1998).

Against that background, it is neither odd nor inappropriate that the Irish Republicans should form an Army. Neither is it odd that Australian Republicans should adopt, as their ensign, the banner of fighters at the vanquished Eureka stockade. Neither, in that context, is it odd that the self-styled militias of the United States profess allegiance to what they see as an embattled Republic.

Academic republicans may no longer welcome the martial implications of the model with quite such gusto. Nonetheless, the republican ideal still clearly remains the sturdy man of honor, relying only on the strength of his own arms (Slote 1993); and that easily shades over into armaments as well. That resonance remains strong among "street-level republicans," even if it is now largely suppressed within republicanism as an academic-cum-literary tradition.

REASONS TO BE TEMPTED, PART II

Public Deliberation

After those false starts and real worries, let us now return to the question of what can be attractive about republics. They are self-governing communities, deliberative bodies without any fixed heads. Traditionally, they were a club of burgers, notables, or landed gentry who had overthrown a monarch and proposed to govern themselves. Now that the model has been extended to include everyone on the same footing, it looks like everyone has the run of the same clubhouse and boardroom.

Of course, throwing the boardroom thrown open to the hordes can hardly be expected to result in the gentlemanly deliberations of a handful of business-like Netherlandish city fathers. The boardroom model of deliberation is simply inappropriate—certainly once the membership extends to all and sundry, and maybe even before (Dryzek 2000, ch. 3).

But it is not merely one particular model of deliberation that is undermined by size. Deliberation more generally is supposed to be a matter of giving reasons rather than merely weighing interests or taking votes. It is rule by reason rather than rule by the numbers. But outside of teledemocracy fantasies or focus-group–style equivalents, how can reasons rule in a populous republic except by the force of numbers? Taking a vote in the Governing Body of an Oxford college is admission of breakdown of ordinary norms of those self-governing communities. But taking a vote in the Congregation of Oxford University—the governing body of governing bodies, as it were—is the standard way of doing business.

Already two centuries ago the Founders of the American republic were facing up to the problems posed by a widespread and numerous republic. Their solution—what made their creation a "republic," in their eyes, as distinct from a populist democracy—was the establishment of representative institutions staffed (they hoped) by the "better sort" (Madison 1961 [1787], pp. 62–64). Charged as trustees, the new American republic's representatives were supposed to do our deliberating for us.[12]

Many republicans remain attracted to that model. Courts, as reason-giving institutions par excellence, are often regarded as paradigmatic deliberators (Rawls 1993, pp. 235–40; Pettit 1999, pp. 180 ff.); and many of today's most distinguished republicans are constitutional lawyers writing political theory at least partly with a view to judicial implementation [Michelman 1986, 1988; Sunstein 1988 (esp. pp. 1579–86), 1990, 1991, 1993a,b,c; 2001]. One of the hallmarks of the "liberal republican" model (as distinct from the "populist republican" one) is that deliberation is done substantially, if not exclusively, within and between branches of government—courts, bicameral legislatures, the legislature and the executive, and so on—rather than among the population as a whole.

Even liberal republicans, however, would also like to find some way to extend deliberative prerogatives to the citizenry more broadly. Even liberal republicans hanker for deliberative modes of mass decision, and the free and equal political communication governing them. "The underlying vision of 'republican' politics," says Sunstein (1991, p. 4), "is one of frequent participation and deliberation in the service of decision, by the citizenry, about the sorts of values according to which the nation will operate." So say virtually all contemporary republicans of virtually all stripes.[13]

But deliberation classically presupposes small numbers of people in a "face to face society" (Laslett 1956). Modern polities are far larger than that, and it is unclear how traditional models of deliberation can be adapted to those new circumstances

---

[12]As Roger Sherman said to the first federal Congress, "When the people have chosen a representative, it is his duty to meet others from the different parts of the Union, and consult, and agree with them to such acts as are for the general benefit of the whole community. If they were to be guided by instructions, there would be no use in deliberation" (quoted in Sunstein 1993a, p. 242).

[13]Michelman (1988, p. 1503), for example, writes that "in the strongest versions of republicanism, citizenship—participation as an equal in public affairs, in pursuit of a common good—appears as a primary, indeed constitutive, interest of the person." Stone et al. (1991, p. 20) write, "In all its forms, republicanism appears to prize democratic self-government; to emphasize deliberative politics; to see citizenship as a good; and to believe in the possibility of settling at least some disputes with substantively right answers." See also Elkin (1994, pp. 128–34) and Sandel (1996, pp. 348–49).

(Goodin 2000). The "populist republican" deliberative ideal is simply infeasible when the populace is too populous. That commonplace is generally accepted by contemporary republicans, much though they may rue it and strive to re-empower local institutions.[14]

What contemporary republicans are therefore left with is little more than the Founders' oligarchic model of representative deliberation. Contemporary republicans continue to pay obeisance to mass deliberative ideals, all the more so perhaps because they have no particularly good ideas how to implement them in a genuinely mass society.

All this is simply a report of positions that republicans have staked out, of propositions that they would hope to sustain. Those are generally aspirations in search of an argument and a mechanism. Still, aspirations must surely count for something in political theory.

Republicans are far from unique in these aspirations, however. They share their advocacy of public deliberation and reason-giving in politics with theorists of many other stripes, who reach those same conclusions without recourse to republican rhetoric of any form.

Here is one telling exercise: Scan the indices of all the major recent works on "deliberative democracy." Notice that the term republicanism is missing from virtually all of them. It is nowhere employed positively in Habermas' *Between Facts and Norms* (1996); and it is nowhere to be found in Rawls's "Idea of Public Reason Revisited" (1997), nowhere in Gutmann & Thompson's *Democracy and Disagreement* (1996), nowhere in Young's *Inclusion and Democracy* (2000), nowhere in Dryzek's *Deliberative Democracy and Beyond* (2000).

This is not the place to trace the intricate differences among all these alternative models and how they contrast with the republican vision (Habermas 1994; Bohman 1996, esp. ch. 6; Dryzek 1996, pp. 64–65; Southwood 2002). Suffice it to say that republican models are not the only ones that appeal to those virtues. There are

---

[14]Sandel (1984, p. 94; see similarly 1996, pp. 339–40), for example, writes, "If a virtuous republic of small-scale, democratic communities was no longer a possibility, a national republic seemed democracy's next best hope .... But this project failed .... Except for extraordinary moments, such as war, the nation proved too vast a scale across which to cultivate the shared self-understandings necessary to community in the formative, or constitutive sense. And so the gradual shift, in our practices and institutions, from a public philosophy of common purposes to one of fair procedures, from a politics of good to a politics of right, from the national republic to the procedural republic." Sandel's (1996, p. 345) proposals for "dispersing sovereignty ... [to] a multiplicity of communities and political bodies—some more, some less extensive than nations" will clearly not help reduce the number of others (other individuals in the former case, other groups in either case) with whom we have to deliberate. Contemporary republicans still harbor localist yearnings, though, as is clear in Sandel's (1996, pp. 333–35) praise of Community Development Corporations and of local shops over national chain stores, or Sunstein's (1988, p. 1578) praise of "'reconstitutive law' reforms that allow state and local flexibility by restructuring markets" and of "proposals to loosen restrictions in federal grant programs."

many ways to endorse the deliberative democratic ideal without wrapping oneself in republican rhetoric, and many ways to pursue that ideal without encumbering oneself with all the other "street-level republican" baggage.

Common Good

Republicans—again, in company with many others—count on public deliberation to alter people's preferences, helping them to transcend narrow self-interest or sectional interest and concentrate on the common good of the community as a whole.

Contemporary republicans see this as an important contrast between politics and markets, between high (common-good) and low (private-interest) models of politics. Republicans view the "political processes not as an aggregation of purely private interests, but as a deliberative effort to promote the common good .... On the republican account, self-interest ... must be translated into some broader conception of the public interest" (Sunstein 1990, p. 12). Republican laws and public policies reflect, in consequence, "not the preferences that [people] hold as private consumers, but instead ... collective judgments, ... aspirations or considered reflections" (Sunstein 1991, p. 14; see similarly Sunstein 1988, pp. 1548–49; 1993a,b,c).

This distinction between superior public preferences and inferior private ones has several important consequences. It justifies democracy in overriding markets, for republicans as well as many others (Sunstein 1991, 1997). It justifies courts in ignoring the pushing and hauling of pluralist private interests, self-consciously pursuing instead the public interest through some form of "juridical democracy" (Sunstein 1988, pp. 1543–45; 1993a; cf. Lowi 1969, ch. 10). It justifies legislatures in taking various measures to promote as well as protect free speech, including public financing of elections and policies to promote social mixing, even on the internet (Sunstein 1991, 1993b, 2001). And so on.

All these seem eminently sensible policy proposals, defensible from many different perspectives. They are not uniquely commendable, either separately or as a package, on republican grounds alone. Still, if those policy proposals constituted the core of republicanism, it would be an unexceptionable (if perhaps unexceptional) model.

What is more exceptional and exceptionable about republicanism is that its strong prioritization of the public over the private risks undercutting the autonomy (and indeed independence) of individual judgment. That would be an ironic result, given republicans' historical emphasis on the importance of sturdy independence among the citizenry.

Prioritizing the public over the private has been a recurring republican theme since classical times. Classical republicanism, in the words of Ptolemy of Lucca (often falsely attributed to Aquinas), "puts not the private things before those held in common, but the things held in common before those of the private" (quoted in Viroli 1995, p. 22). In our own day, Pettit (2000, p. 197) describes what he sees as the legitimate scope of republican government in similar terms:

> Common interests will be matters that people are capable of recognizing . . . in the course of discussion and reflection . . . Government ought to be oriented toward the satisfaction of [those] common, recognizable interests of the people governed . . . . [T]hose are the only factors that it ought to take its ultimate guidance from. Government ought to countenance no other master.

One possible reading of those texts is innocuous, indeed laudatory, from a liberal Enlightenment perspective. We start with autonomous individuals (manifesting the "sturdy independence" traditionally associated with republican virtue), and working with inputs from each autonomous individual, we somehow adduce a notion of the "public interest," which (because they internalize republican "civic virtue" as well as republican "sturdy independence") all those individuals are motivated to pursue collectively, in preference to their private interests. That might be a broadly "liberal republican" reading of how the republican quest for the common good is supposed to work (Sunstein 1988, Dagger 1999).

Some authors, however, come to their republicanism by way of communitarianism (Sandel 1984; 1996, pp. 290 ff.; Selznick 1992). They prioritize the public over the private as part of their program of deprioritizing rights and restoring public duty and responsibility to the center of the political stage.[15] Sometimes this communitarian republicanism amounts to virtual "soulcraft" (Will 1983; Sandel 1996, p. 319).

Seeing individuals as being so deeply embedded in "communities of subsumption" that they cease to be autonomous sources of value at all would, of course, be anathema from a liberal-Enlightenment perspective (Goodin 1998). But there are forebodings of it in various republican writings. Benjamin Rush, a signer of the American Declaration of Independence, explicitly aspired "to convert men into republican machines," teaching each citizen that "he does not belong to himself, but that he is public property."[16]

Modern versions of "communitarian republicanism" say similarly that "political community depends on the narratives by which people make sense of their condition and interpret the common life they share"—and, tellingly, conversely. As Sandel (1996, pp. 350–51) goes on to remark,

> [W]hen the narrative resources of civil life are . . . strained . . . it becomes increasingly difficult to tell the tales that order our lives. There is a growing

---

[15]Even Sunstein (1990, p. 246, n. 1), who bemoans the "false . . . conflict between liberalism and republicanism" and resists "converting republicanism into a nightmarish, totalist vision that rejects rights altogether," tellingly entitles his book *After the Rights Revolution* and takes as its central task justifying a "regulatory state" in pursuit of common, if not collectivist, projects.

[16]This passage is quoted by Herzog (1986, pp. 483 ff.), who goes on to detail some of Rush's grander schemes for homogenizing the American public by, among other things, soaking blacks' skins in unripe peach juice. The same passage is quoted by Sandel (1996, p. 319), who in fairness wants to distance himself from this position (though in my view not nearly enough). On the Founders on these issues more generally, see Wood (1969, pp. 57-8).

danger that, individually and collectively, we will find ourselves slipping into a fragmented, storyless condition . . . . [That would lead to] the ultimate disempowering of the human subject, for without narrative there is no continuity between present and past . . . .

In short, communitarian republicans maintain that individual agency is a function of collective identity.

Habermas (1994, p. 4) rightly resists this reduction of politics "to a hermeneutical process of self-explication of a shared form of life or collective identity. Political questions may not be reduced to the type of ethical questions where we, as members of a community, ask ourselves who we are and who we would like to be." Instead Habermas insists that "the democratic will-formation does not draw its legitimating force from a previous convergence of settled ethical convictions, but from both the communicative presuppositions that allow the better arguments to come into play . . . and from the procedures that secure fair bargaining processes."

Republicans of a more liberal sort would concur. They would want to retain their emphasis on the fact that preference formation is, and ought to be, endogenous within the collective decision process: people's preferences are, and ought to be, shaped and reshaped in the course of public conversations (Sunstein 1991). But while holding on to that central republican theme, liberal republicans also envisage citizens as coming to those conversations with divergent prior and private views. Indeed, they suppose that that is precisely what citizens exchange with one another in their public encounters. The liberal republican view thus hopes to preserve individuals as autonomous sources of value, who then find they have things in common, rather than postulating some "unanimity . . . secured in advance by a substantive ethical consensus" (Habermas 1994, p. 4).

Some (perhaps many) republicans do therefore want to prevent their preoccupation with the public from sliding into communitarian excess. Their challenge is to identify some way to do that, some method whereby the common good can be discerned among individuals whose identities are not assumed to be (or reconstructed to be) wholly constituted by their membership in the collectivity.

The American Founders experimented with various mechanistic models whereby the separation of powers in a mixed constitution was supposed to supply this magic. Others following broadly in their footsteps recommend institutionalized vetoes of various sorts. Alas, those mechanisms prove to be thoroughly unreliable (Barry 1989, chs. 4–5; 1990, chs. 14–15; Goodin 1996; Pettit 1999, pp. 178–79; 2001, p. 157n). Granting the right to appeal one's case to an impartial tribunal (Pettit 1999, pp. 180–83) or allowing courts to conduct a "rationality review" of legislation (Sunstein 1988, p. 1579) provides a negative mechanism for blocking policies that are not in the common interest, rather than any guarantee of policies that are in the common interest.

To ensure the positive pursuit of such policies, contemporary republicans most often place their faith in deliberation and the interplay of free public reason. That is fine among small groups (courts or maybe even legislatures). But, as argued above, no credible mechanism has yet been offered whereby the whole of a large political community can be simultaneously party to such deliberations (Goodin 2000).

Civic republicans place their faith in small and dispersed communities. "In the age of NAFTA," Sandel (1996, p. 346) says, "the politics of neighborhood matters more, not less." For Sandel (1996, p. 347), what differentiates "Tocqueville's republicanism from Rousseau's . . . [is] sovereignty dispersed and citizenship formed across multiple sites of civic engagement."[17] But although public-spirited attitudes might be more easily evoked within those smaller groups, the public to which those attitudes attach is smaller as well (Dahl & Tufte 1973). This is no solution to the problem of size, understood as the problem of how to get people to internalize the common good of the whole community rather than just their own particular parts of it.

Note well: The problem does not lie in any analytic difficulties with the notion of "public interest" or "common good." Conceptually, those terms make perfectly good sense and can be given various relative, precise meanings (Barry 1964; 1989, ch. 20; 1990, ch. 11; Goodin 1996). The difficulty with these concepts is operational, a problem of finding some reliable way politically to determine their content and to harness political action effectively in their service. In the absence of any credible political mechanism for doing that, republican injunctions to "seek the common good" are empty exhortations to virtue, devoid of substantive content or political punch. To echo Bohman's (1996, p. 29) summary judgment, "Civic republicans either presuppose such overlapping virtues and values that democracy is unnecessary, or they offer us no assistance in specifying how to resolve conflicts and disagreements about values."

CONCLUSION

Why were we political theorists collectively briefly tempted by the republican ideal, and why in the end did we not collectively succumb?

As for the temptation, let me interject a note of realpolitik. American historians have largely come around to the view that the Constitution is essentially republican. Judges attuned to the original intent of that document's authors regard that as a significant fact. It is only natural, therefore, that constitutional lawyers seeking to influence judicial outcomes should try, for the benefit of members of the bench who are so persuaded, to couch their arguments in republican terms.

Apart from such strategic gaming vis-à-vis the bench, however, I can see no good reason for framing our arguments in any deeply republican way. Many of republicanism's component propositions are independently attractive, but their attraction is independent of republicanism. There are plenty of other perfectly good ways of arguing for those propositions. All that is gained in assimilating

---

[17]In an ellipsed portion of the quotation, Sandel (1996, p. 347) says that this pluralism "saves the formative project from slipping into coercion." That seems a plausible and desirable consequence. My point here is merely that the noncoerciveness of these arrangements is bought at the price of rendering them ineffective as a means of pursuing the "common good" of the whole community that is supposed to be the republican's chief concern.

them with republicanism are the unfortunate further associations here described as "street-level republicanism."

Once again, the wisdom of the multitude has prevailed. Seductive though intellectual historians make republicanism as an account of various fascinating moments in political history, it does not represent a way forward for contemporary political theory. We were right to have a look—and we were right to reject.

ACKNOWLEDGMENTS

I am grateful for comments from John Dryzek, Dave Estlund, Nancy Rosenblum, Michael Smith, and Nic Southwood.

The *Annual Review of Political Science* is online at
http://polisci.annualreviews.org

LITERATURE CITED

Almond G, Verba S. 1963. *The Civic Culture.* Boston: Little, Brown

Appleby JO. 1985. Republicanism and ideology. *Am. Q.* 37:461–73

Appleby JO. 1992. *Liberalism and Republicanism in the Historical Imagination.* Cambridge, MA: Harvard Univ. Press

Atiyah PS. 1979. *The Rise and Fall of Freedom of Contract.* Oxford, UK: Clarendon

Balibar É, Wallerstein I. 1988. *Race, Nation, Classe.* Paris: Éd. Découverte

Barry B. 1964. The public interest. *Proc. Aristotelian Soc. (Suppl.)* 38:1–18

Barry B. 1989. *Democracy, Power and Justice.* Oxford, UK: Clarendon

Barry B. 1990. *Political Argument.* Berkeley: Univ. Calif. Press. Rev. ed.

Becker CL. 1922. *The Declaration of Independence: A Study in the History of Political Ideas.* New York: Vintage

Berman HJ. 1983. *Law and Revolution: The Formation of the Western Legal Tradition.* Cambridge, MA: Harvard Univ. Press

Black A. 1997. Christianity and republicanism: from St. Cyprian to Rousseau. *Am. Polit. Sci. Rev.* 91:647–56

Bohman J. 1996. *Public Deliberation.* Cambridge, MA: MIT Press

Braithwaite J, Pettit P. 1990. *Not Just Deserts: A Republican Theory of Criminal Justice.* Oxford, UK: Clarendon

Brennan G, Pettit P. 1993. Hands invisible and intangible. *Synthese* 94:191–225

Brennan G, Pettit P. 2000. The hidden economy of esteem. *Econ. Phil.* 16:77–98

Brubaker R. 1992. *Citizenship and Nationhood in France and Germany.* Cambridge, MA: Harvard Univ. Press

Dagger R. 1997. *Civic Virtues: Rights, Citizenship, and Republican Liberalism.* New York: Oxford Univ. Press

Dagger R. 1999. The Sandelian republic and the encumbered self. *Rev. Polit.* 61:181–217

Dahl RA. 1979. Procedural democracy. In *Philosophy, Politics and Society*, 5th ser., ed. P Laslett, J Fishkin, pp. 97–133. Oxford, UK: Blackwell

Dahl RA, Tufte ER. 1973. *Size and Democracy.* Stanford, CA: Stanford Univ. Press

Dryzek JS. 1996. *Democracy in Capitalist Times.* Oxford, UK: Oxford Univ. Press

Dryzek JS. 2000. *Deliberative Democracy and Beyond.* Oxford, UK: Oxford Univ. Press

Dumont L. 1980. *Homo Hierarchicus: The Caste System and its Implications.* Transl. M Sainsbury, L Dumont, B Gulati. Chicago: Univ. Chicago Press (From French)

Elkin SL. 1994. Business-state relations in the commercial republic. *J. Polit. Phil.* 2:115–39

Favell A. 1998. *Philosopies of Integration.* London: Macmillan

Fennema M, Maussen M. 2000. Dealing with extremists in public discussion: Front National and Front Républicain in France. *J. Polit. Phil.* 8:379–400

Francis M. 2001. Histories of Australian republicanism. *Hist. Polit. Thought* 22:351–62

Galston W. 1988. Liberal virtues. *Am. Polit. Sci. Rev.* 82:1277–90

Gambetta D. 1993. *The Sicilian Mafia: The Business of Private Protection.* Cambridge, MA: Harvard Univ. Press

Geertz C. 1963. The integrative revolution: primordial sentiments and civil politics in new states. In *Old Societies and New States: The Quest for Modernity in Asia and Africa*, ed. C Geertz, pp. 105–57. New York: Free

Geertz C. 1973. After the revolution: the fate of nationalism in the new states. In *The Interpretation of Cultures*, pp. 234–54. New York: Basic Books

Geertz C. 1977. The judging of nations. *Arch. Européenes de Sociologie* 18:245–61

Goodin RE. 1988. *Reasons for Welfare.* Princeton, NJ: Princeton Univ. Press

Goodin RE. 1993. Independence in democratic theory: a virtue? a necessity? both? neither? *J. Soc. Phil.* 24:50–57

Goodin RE. 1996. Institutionalizing the public interest: the defense of deadlock and beyond. *Am. Polit. Sci. Rev.* 90:331–43

Goodin RE. 1998. Communities of enlightenment. *Br. J. Polit. Sci.* 28:531–58

Goodin RE. 2000. Democratic deliberation within. *Phil. Public Aff.* 29:79–107

Gutmann A, Thompson D. 1996. *Democracy and Disagreement.* Cambridge, MA: Harvard Univ. Press

Habermas J. 1994. Three models of democracy. *Constellations* 1:1–10

Habermas J. 1996 [1992]. *Between Facts and Norms.* Transl. W Rehg. Oxford, UK: Polity (From German)

Harrington J. 1992. *Commonwealth of Oceana*, ed. JGA Pocock. Cambridge, UK: Cambridge Univ. Press

Hartz L. 1955. *The Liberal Tradition in America.* New York: Harcourt, Brace & World

Herzog D. 1986. Some questions for republicans. *Polit. Theory* 14:473–93

Hobsbawm E, Ranger T, eds. 1992. *The Invention of Tradition.* Cambridge, UK: Cambridge Univ. Press

Isaac JC. 1988. Republicanism vs. liberalism? a reconsideration. *Hist. Polit. Thought* 9:349–77

James S. 1992. The good-enough citizen: female citizenship and independence. In *Beyond Equality and Difference*, ed. G Bock, S James, pp. 48–65. London: Routledge

Kramnick I. 1982. Republican revisionism revisited. *Am. Hist. Rev.* 87:629–64

Laslett P. 1956. The face to face society. In *Philosophy, Politics and Society*, 1st ser., ed. P Laslett, pp. 157–84. Oxford, UK: Blackwell

Le Grand J. 1990. Equity versus equality: the elusive trade-off. *Ethics* 100:554–68

Lowi TJ. 1969. *The End of Liberalism.* New York: Norton

Lyttleton A. 1995. The crusade against the Cosa Nostra. *NY Rev. Books* 42 (15):51–56

MacIntyre A. 1972. Is a science of comparative politics possible? In *Philosophy, Politics and Society*, 4th ser., ed. P Laslett, WG Runciman, Q Skinner, pp. 8–26. Oxford, UK: Blackwell

Madison J. 1961 [1787]. Federalist # 10. In *The Federalist*, ed. JE Cooke, pp. 56–65. Middletown, CT: Wesleyan Univ. Press

Maine HS. 1901. *Ancient Law.* London: John Murray. 17th ed.

Mazrui AA. 1972. *Cultural Engineering and Nation-building in East Africa.* Evanston, IL: Northwestern Univ. Press

Michelman F. 1986. Traces of self-government. *Harvard Law Rev.* 100:4–77

Michelman F. 1988. Law's republic. *Yale Law J.* 97:1493–537

Morrow J. 1991. Republicanism and public virtue: William Godwin's "History of the Commonwealth of England." *Hist. J.* 34:645–64

Pettit P. 1989. The freedom of the city: a republican ideal. In *The Good Polity*, ed. A Hamlin, P Pettit, pp. 141–68. Oxford, UK: Blackwell

Pettit P. 1996. Freedom as antipower. *Ethics* 106:576–604

Pettit P. 1997a. *Republicanism.* Oxford, UK: Oxford Univ. Press

Pettit P. 1997b. Republican political theory. In *Political Theory: Tradition and Diversity*, ed. A Vincent, pp. 112–31. Cambridge, UK: Cambridge Univ. Press

Pettit P. 1999. Republican freedom and contestatory democratization. In *Democracy's Value*, ed. I Shapiro, C Hacker-Cordón, pp. 163–90. Cambridge, UK: Cambridge Univ. Press

Pettit P. 2000. Democracy, electoral and contestatory. In *Nomos XLII: Designing Democratic Institutions*, ed. I Shapiro, S Macedo, pp. 105–45. New York: NY Univ. Press

Pettit P. 2001. *A Theory of Freedom.* Oxford, UK: Polity

Pocock JGA. 1957. *The Ancient Constitution and the Feudal Law*. Cambridge, UK: Cambridge Univ. Press

Pocock JGA. 1972. Virtue and commerce in the eighteenth century. *J. Interdiscip. Hist.* 3:119–34

Pocock JGA. 1973. *Politics, Language and Time*. New York: Atheneum

Pocock JGA. 1975. *The Machiavellian Moment: Florentine Political Thought and the Atlantic Republican Tradition*. Princeton, NJ: Princeton Univ. Press

Polanyi M. 1962. The republic of science: its political and economic theory. *Minerva* 1:54–73

Rawls J. 1971. *A Theory of Justice*. Cambridge, MA: Harvard Univ. Press

Rawls J. 1993. *Political Liberalism*. New York: Columbia Univ. Press

Rawls J. 1997. The idea of public reason revisited. *Univ. Chicago Law Rev.* 94:765–807

Rawls J. 2001. *Justice as Fairness: A Restatement*. Cambridge, MA: Harvard Univ. Press

Rogers DT. 1992. Republicanism: the career of a concept. *J. Am. Hist.* 79:11–38

Sandel MJ. 1984. The procedural republic and the unencumbered self. *Polit. Theory* 12:81–96

Sandel MJ. 1996. *Democracy's Discontent: America in Search of a Public Philosophy*. Cambridge, MA: Harvard Univ. Press

Schlesinger AM Jr. 1973. *The Imperial Presidency*. Boston: Houghton Mifflin

Selznick P. 1992. *The Moral Commonwealth: Social Theory and the Promise of Community*. Berkeley: Univ. Calif. Press

Shalhope RE. 1972. Toward a republican synthesis: the emergence of an understanding of republicanism in American historiography. *William & Mary Q.* 29:49–80

Sharp A, ed. 1998. *The English Levellers*. Cambridge, UK: Cambridge Univ. Press

Skinner Q. 1978. *The Foundations of Modern Political Thought*. Cambridge, UK: Cambridge Univ. Press

Skinner Q. 1984. The idea of negative liberty. In *Philosophy in History*, ed. R Rorty, JB Schneewind, Q Skinner, pp. 193–221. Cambridge, UK: Cambridge Univ. Press

Skinner Q. 1985. The paradoxes of political liberty. *Tanner Lect. Hum. Values* 7:225–50; reprinted 1995 in *Equal Freedom*, ed. S Darwall, pp. 15–38. Ann Arbor: Univ. Mich. Press

Slote M. 1993. Virtue ethics and democratic values. *J. Soc. Phil.* 24:5–38

Southwood N. 2002. Beyond Pettit's neo-Roman republicanism: towards the deliberative republic. *CRISPP* 5: In press

Stone R. 1995. The sins of the fathers. *NY Rev. Books* #17, Nov. 2, p. 20

Stone GR, Seidman LM, Sunstein CR, Tushnet MV. 1991. *Constitutional Law*. Boston: Little, Brown. 2nd ed.

Sunstein CR. 1988. Beyond the republican revival. *Yale Law J.* 97:1539–90

Sunstein CR. 1990. *After the Rights Revolution: Reconceiving the Regulatory State*. Cambridge, MA: Harvard Univ. Press

Sunstein CR. 1991. Preferences and politics. *Phil. Public Aff.* 20:3–34

Sunstein CR. 1993a. *Democracy and the Problem of Free Speech*. New York: Free

Sunstein CR. 1993b. The enduring legacy of republicanism. In *A New Constitutionalism*, ed. SE Elkin, KE Soltan, pp. 174–206. Chicago: Univ. Chicago Press

Sunstein CR. 1993c. *A Partial Constitution.* Cambridge, MA: Harvard Univ. Press

Sunstein CR. 1997. *Free Markets and Social Justice.* New York: Oxford Univ. Press

Sunstein CR. 2001. *Republic.com.* Princeton, NJ: Princeton Univ. Press

Tamir Y. 1993. *Liberal Nationalism.* Princeton, NJ: Princeton Univ. Press

Turnbull M, chair. 1993. *An Australian Republic: The Options.* Rep. Repub. Advis. Comm. Canberra: Aust. Gov. Publ. Serv.

van Gelderen M, ed., transl. 1993. *The Dutch Revolt.* Cambridge, UK: Cambridge Univ. Press (From Dutch)

Viroli M. 1995. *For Love of Country.* Oxford, UK: Clarendon

Weber E. 1976. *Peasants into Frenchmen: The Modernization of Rural France, 1870–1914.* Stanford, CA: Stanford Univ. Press

Will GF. 1983. *Statecraft as Soulcraft: What Government Does.* New York: Simon & Schuster

Wills G. 1995. The new revolutionaries. *NY Rev. Books* 42 (13):50–55

Wood GS. 1969. *The Creation of the American Republic, 1776–1787.* Chapel Hill: Univ. N. Carol. Press

Woodhouse ASP, ed. 1974. *Puritanism and Liberty: Being the Army Debates (1647–9) from the Clarke Manuscripts with Supplementary Documents.* London: Dent. 2nd ed.

Wyatt-Brown B. 1982. *Southern Honor: Ethics and Behavior in the Old South.* Oxford, UK: Oxford Univ. Press

Young IM. 2000. *Inclusion and Democracy.* Oxford, UK: Oxford Univ. Press

Annu. Rev. Polit. Sci. 2003. 6:77–98
doi: 10.1146/annurev.polisci.6.121901.085556
First published online as a Review in Advance on Mar. 6, 2003

THE COLD WAR AS HISTORY

Jonathan Haslam

*Corpus Christi College, Cambridge University, Cambridge CB2 1RH, United Kingdom;
email: jgh1001@cam.ac.uk*

Key Words   Cold War origins, Stalin, Molotov, Khrushchev, Soviet Union

■ **Abstract**   The fall of Soviet Communism led to the release of top secret documents vital to our understanding of the Cold War. This material is, however, available to research only to a limited extent. The best access is to be obtained in the archives of the Warsaw Pact countries, including those in Berlin. In Moscow itself, secrecy still forestalls access to the most important documents, above all those relating to the origins of the Cold War under Stalin. It is therefore not surprising that the debate about Cold War origins is still with us, and without any notable improvement in the quality of evidence adduced in the debate. It is by no means clear, as historians such as Gaddis have asserted, that the origins can be laid merely at the door of one unreasonable and unreasoning man: Stalin. It is, however, equally unconvincing to hear from Trachtenberg that Stalin was merely doing what all statesmen do and did so entirely rationally. The complementary argument from Leffler that, given the rational nature of Russian decisions, the answer lies more with U.S. than with Russian policy makers begs as many questions as it seeks to answer. The wary reader is well advised that the jury is still out until both the prosecution and the defense actually have adequate access to the evidence.

INTRODUCTION

The Cold War fashioned and distorted our lives in a manner and to a degree that even now we scarcely suspect. Ended over a decade ago, it has always been easier to define than to explain. Whatever its causes, the Cold War fast became an all-encompassing ideological and geopolitical conflict between the Soviet Union (and its "satellites," as Stalin called them) and the United States (and its allies) by all means short of war.

It is usually assumed that, had the superpowers not possessed thermonuclear weapons, World War III would have been a certainty, and that for this reason the Cold War may be unique in the history of international relations. Instead of dissipating into the ether or culminating in widespread violence, the heightened accumulation of tensions that normally precipitate war was sustained over an extraordinarily lengthy period. Since steadfast endurance of such tension over an indefinite period proved too much, the Cold War inevitably fluctuated in intensity from 1947 until 1991—which meant that ennervated commentators who were either blasted by desperation or buoyed by hope blew the whistle prematurely,

1094-2939/03/0615-0077$14.00   **77** only for us to find that they had confused half-time with the end of the game. Despite well-intentioned illusions and efforts—the "end of ideology," "convergence," "détente"—the conflict never completely receded. No sooner was the corpse wheeled safely to the mortuary than it sprang to life to wreak further havoc; indeed, the late 1970s and early 1980s saw tension rise again on a scale comparable to the war scares in the previous two decades, and not merely in the traditional cockpit of Europe.

One key source of aggravation to the West was the extraordinary arsenal of weapons accumulated on the other side of Europe—to take just one instance, by 1989 Moscow possessed a total of some 56,000 tanks; yet these proved of no avail in the East-Central European revolutions of that year because the will to use them had gone. Another source was the Soviet Union's relentless meddling in the domestic affairs of NATO partners and assistance to revolution in the world beyond. The Soviet government did not drop support for national liberation movements in the Third World until 1987, and even under Mikhail Gorbachev, the Soviet Communist Party continued to fund fraternal parties even in Western Europe and the United States until the collapse of the regime in August 1991 (Riva 1999). But the conflict had long raged with little restraint on both sides. As far back as December 1948, the British government had, in common with the United States, set itself the task to eject the Soviet Union from Eastern Europe and to subvert the Soviet regime internally by "all available means short of war" (Foreign Office 1948).

DEBATING ORIGINS

The Cold War ended in the capitulation of the Soviet Union on all fronts. The temptation natural to the American historian and politician alike has been to declare victory and to assign all the causes of the conflict, both in origins and continuation, exclusively to the Russians; "to the victor belong the spoils," as Senator Marcy pointed out in 1832. Self-congratulation is, however, a poor guide to serious research, since we live still within the Cold War's long dark shadow. And lessons should be learned from our own errors as well as those, more publicized, of our former adversaries.

Since August 1991, top secret documents from East and West have cascaded into our hands. Yet, even with the full complement of evidence from both parties, it is most unlikely that a universal consensus will easily arise as to the origins or, indeed, the very purpose of the Cold War. At the time of writing, given the most recent publications on the subject, even a tentative and intermediate consonance of views seems still a distant dream. This is not least because any serious enquiry into the origins of the Cold War necessarily delves into the behavior of, and therefore judges, implicitly or explicitly, not just Soviet leaders but also our own statesmen. This is, after all, contemporary history—the most contentious and problematic history of all. We should not expect too much. It took over 100 years to obtain anything approaching an objective analysis of the French Revolution and what it represented. And only now are we reaching a more comprehensive understanding of the October Revolution.

For a long time, the history of the Cold War naturally formed the preeminent domain of voracious hunter-gatherers from political science, particularly those in the field of Soviet studies. Only very recently have farmer-historians homed in en masse to enclose this fertile pasture for exclusive cultivation. The massive windfall of formerly secret documents from the East has indeed driven a number of political scientists out. And they are not the only species threatened. The average student of postwar international history, unschooled in foreign languages and thus insufficiently equipped to compete, faces the bleak prospect of marginalization or, indeed, near extinction.

CONTENDING SCHOOLS OF THOUGHT

Initially the only top secret documents open to scholars since 1945 lay exclusively in U.S. national archives. Prior to disclosure, the predominant interpretation of the Cold War in the West placed the causes exclusively with Stalin and his regime. A classic based on privileged access is the semiofficial history by Feis (1957). Under Stalin, Feis concluded, "the Russian people . . . were trying not only to extend their boundaries and their control over neighboring states but also beginning to revert to their revolutionary effort throughout the world" (1957, p. 655). The opening of the first tranche of U.S. documents did not sustain the consensus, however, because the destructive burden of the war in Vietnam from 1964 sundered agreement about the origins of the Cold War, just as it severed the threads that had held together American society since the late 1940s. Hitherto only dissentient voices on the margin—Wisconsin's William Appleman Williams in particular—had uttered contrary views.

One group among historians of U.S. diplomacy enthusiastically identified themselves as revisionists. They split into two groups: those who argued that the Cold War was primarily attributable to the pressures toward empire from within the U.S. capitalist system (structure); and those who focused instead on the shift in presidential policy upon the demise of Franklin Roosevelt (intentionality). Both held firm against the orthodox interpretation, which laid responsibility entirely at the door of the Soviet Union. Their press was never good. In 1970, Maier issued a damning indictment, all the more harmful because it came from the Left: "In the end it is this attempt by the revisionists to analyze specific historical issues on the basis of a priori values about the political system that most strongly affects the controversies their writings have touched off. For their values cannot be derived from the mere amassment of historical data nor do they follow from strictly historical judgements, but rather underlie such judgements" (Maier 1970).

This is an interesting sally because it appears to be based on a particular view of historical method that sees the determination of causation as entirely reliant on documentation: a classic restatement of Baconian inductivism curiously at odds with the author's own subsequent work. Few would dispute the fact that we cannot determine causation without inductive research. But many might contest the assumption that the causes of events are to be found exclusively within the evidence adduced from that research, and many might argue that a priori values determine which forms of evidence are deemed more important than others. The long-term operations of an economic system with no single locus of decision making may have a determining effect on foreign policy and yet not be visible in an archive, since that system may affect decisions at the most discreet level of unwritten assumptions. Is the historian really to ignore such possible effects and to acknowledge no assumptions?

The drive to empire makes little sense if we are to rely exclusively on government archives. Under capitalism, government kept finding itself in a position where action was taken by a freebooting enterprise over which it had no control, but because their activities benefited the national treasury, government felt obliged to step in and protect it against all and sundry. Surely this is how a few states on the Atlantic seaboard extended across an entire subcontinent, leaving a trail of treaties broken with the Indian "nations." This was preeminently a market-driven foreign policy, less the product of deliberate intention than the outcome of disaggregated but purposeful individual decision. The invisible guiding hand was in this instance "Manifest Destiny."

Ironically, a more charitable assessment of the revisionist school came from the pen of Robert W. Tucker (1971), a conservative realist, who found the "evident strength of radical criticism" in "its insistence upon the self-interested character of American foreign policy. By contrast, the dominant historiography since World War II has found in American foreign policy a rather consistent disregard of self-interest." Or is Tucker also to be accused of reasoning purely a priori?

The bifurcation of historiography set in train by the revisionists shows its traces still in some U.S. history departments, where faculty of a certain generation remain unnaturally apart, segregated by seminar and divided by custom born of bitter debate. The reluctant and disorderly retreat from Vietnam that began under President Nixon in 1969 eventually enabled a healing of the wounds in U.S. society and was paralleled by an attempt to dissipate the fundamental differences that divided revisionist from orthodox. The cracks were papered over with post-revisionism: On the one hand was the claim that there prevailed a misunderstanding common to both the Soviet Union and the United States—they were inadvertently working at cross purposes—which made for conflict; on the other hand was the assertion that the United States and the Soviet Union were merely responding, as all great powers had done, to the dictates of the international states system. This interpretation coincided—unconsciously no doubt—with the emergence of détente and served as a comforting rationale for compromise between the superpowers. Simultaneously, explanations that depended on a systems-oriented approach to international relations inspired by Waltz (1979) acquired a certain vogue, arguing as they did that both superpowers merely competed in time-honored fashion for global predominance. Whereas post-revisionism diminished the role of ideology to a residual, systems-oriented explanations dismissed it altogether in favor of the mechanics of state interaction.

Encouraged, no doubt, in the belief that the Cold War could be wound down with the progress of détente, once-intensive interest in its origins appeared to drift out of fashion. At the same time, the nonstop process of chasing documentary declassification in the United States—which has generally operated on a rule of disclosure after the elapse of 30 years—lured researchers hungry for novelty to escape into the uncharted 1950s, the false promise of the "Thaw" and the paranoia of the "Bomber Gap." Moreover, the concurrent opening of British, French, German, and, more recently, Italian diplomatic archives made scarcely any impact on the disarray left after the chasm opened in U.S. historiography. It was not entirely wrong to assume that fundamental answers had to lie elsewhere. The sudden and dramatic end of the Cold War with the self-destruction of the Soviet regime in August 1991 thus raised expectations of a definitive resolution of uncertainty once Russian archives opened, even if few on either side of the Atlantic were equipped to read what they contained.

The Russians began to open foreign policy archives only grudgingly and hesitantly in January 1992—a process accelerated by the threat to the Foreign Ministry archive that its funding was to be axed. They have, however, unceremoniously closed important documents once declassified, and have without evident embarrassment refused to release the most informative that remain. Many hopes have thus been dashed. To borrow the memorable words of former Prime Minister Viktor Chernomyrdin: "We had hoped for the best, but things turned out as they usually do." What has been released, though a great advance on what preceded it, is of uneven quality and irregularly distributed down the years open to inspection. Here politics has inevitably played its part.

The irony is that we have more secret documents relating to the course of the Cold War than to its origins. Documents covering subsequent crises were declassified by the Russian Foreign Ministry for operational diplomatic reasons. In order to appease post-Communist Hungary, top-level material was released on the suppression of Hungary's tragic bid for liberty in October 1956; similarly, materials were made publicly accessible on the Warsaw Pact invasion of Czechoslovakia (August 1968), the Soviet decision against an invasion of Poland (November 1981), Moscow's direct involvement in and sponsorship of the invasion of South Korea (June 1950), and the means by which Nikita Khrushchev became entangled in and disentangled from the Cuban missile crisis (1962). Another reason Cold War documents are more available than materials revealing the origins of the Cold War is that a timely, well-funded, and otherwise pathbreaking initiative from the United States to press for declassification—the Cold War International History Project, inspired and pioneered by that most distinguished historian of postwar U.S. foreign policy, Gaddis—understandably but unfortunately chose to seek evidence on a scattered range of crises across the entire span of the Cold War, instead of a less sensational but more thorough unearthing of documents in sequence from the very beginning of the conflict. Some of us—the more old-fashioned, no doubt—were brought up to finish the first course before being allowed the second. Whether nonobservance of this rule is attributable to a belief that the origins of the Cold War no longer held any secrets or merely to popular demand for sheer novelty is a matter for conjecture.

We have not been entirely dependent on the whims of the Russian authorities. Collapse of the Soviet empire in Eastern-Central Europe in 1989 led to a hurried withdrawal from East Germany, which left in its wake a veritable treasure trove of classified material on East-West and East-East relations since the late 1940s. These are available in western Berlin at the *Bundesarchiv*. (These were formerly the archives of the Institut für Geschichte der Arbeiterbewegung—Zentrales Parteiarchiv.) In addition, some, but not all, East European governments have also opened up most of their top secret records relating to Soviet policy in the region. Regularly refused permission to join the Warsaw Pact, Castro's Cuba has now allowed selective access for a chosen few to some foreign policy files below top level. But lacunae are gaping: On the other side of the globe, Communist China still holds history's secrets close to its chest, as does Japan (which simultaneously obliges the United States to withold declassification on certain episodes embarrassing to Tokyo), allowing only limited release of declassified material to official historians and certainly not to foreigners. Fraternal but nongoverning Communist parties, such as the PCI in Italy, also received from Moscow copies of documents previously retained by their Russian godfather, the Communist Party of the Soviet Union (CPSU). These can be consulted at the Gramsci Institute in Rome. Yet none of these sources really takes us toward a better understanding of the origins of the Cold War.

A final judgment as to who or what caused the Cold War is thus not to be expected in the near future. This does not mean we are in a state of such ignorance that everything published on the subject is of equal value, a state we appeared to be in before archives were opened. Much of the literature on Cold War origins remains poor pickings—feebly researched, embarrassingly ethnocentric (equally so in Britain and the United States), of mere textbook quality, or only superficially complete. The persistence in U.S. universities of the long outdated and isolationist practice of teaching the history of international relations as a branch of the history of American foreign policy (i.e., from exclusively English-language sources) has not helped.

In these less than satisfactory circumstances, the reader should be wary of attempts by any author, however well regarded, to convey an impression of finality that may be misleading. Bear this in mind when judging the most prominent and most informative of recent publications, notably that of Gaddis, whose latest work carries the provocatively triumphalist title *We Now Know* (Gaddis 1997)—because we most certainly do not. Even Gaddis (1997, p. 294) accepts that his conclusions are based on "very incomplete evidence." This has since been qualified further: "at least, we know a good deal more than we once did" (Gaddis 2000, p. 27). The standard of measurement is, as the circumstances demand, properly relative.

Better informed of fact than the social scientist, but more naive, perhaps, with respect to method, the historian seldom reflects on the degree to which an apparently incontrovertible conclusion about the ultimate determinant of events is mediated by a particular philosophy of history. The most obvious dichotomy is between agency and structure, or intentionality and invisible forces—what Soviet writers usefully called subjective versus objective factors. And in their unconscious state, historians all the more fall victim to a philosophy that threatens the validity of their entire oeuvre. Rarely are the quantity and quality of information in the history of international relations sufficient to decide with any conviction which outlook provides the best explanation of any event. And certainly, given the paucity and unevenness of the documentary evidence available, we are in no position to expect more from existing work on the origins of the Cold War. Whereas the average social scientist, in search of constants that enable construction of a working model, somewhat grandly dispenses with the changes wrought by time under the convenient caveat "ceteris paribus," the historian regards change itself as a significant object of enquiry. This creates a conundrum that arises in starkest form with the renewed fashion for counterfactual history. Surely, it is asserted, choices lay out there in the past. Could all really have been foreordained? That cannot be proven. All we know for sure is that most of those making decisions at the time under study believed choices existed and thought they were exercising freedom of choice. Yet we cannot know for certain that the choices are or were real. We study the abstract. We are still in Plato's cave, seeing only reflections of the world outside. Counterfactualists propose that we stop the camera and rewind the film to a certain point and then introduce what might have happened. The problem here is critical for historians: Who chooses the point at which the film is rewound? As the Italian philosopher Benedetto Croce wisely pointed out, history is in movement. To write counterfactual history is necessarily to make an entirely arbitrary choice as to where to stop and divert the current. This leads us to a problem perennial to historians writing history proper. All historians, and not just those engaged in counterfactual speculation, choose the beginning and the end of the period under analysis, however much they may believe that this is dictated by the documents themselves. And periodization itself can determine the explanation of events. Examining the origins of the Cold War from 1947 puts Leffler (1992) in the position of placing much of the blame squarely on the United States. Taking 1945 as his point of departure may have prompted Gaddis to shift the blame entirely onto the Russians. By electing dates, each writer may, by accident or by design, predetermine the cast of explanation. The question is: How aware are they of the implications of what they have been doing?

AGENCY VERSUS STRUCTURE

With respect to agency and structure, Gaddis consciously opts for agency as the sum of his explanation. His position in *We Now Know* may be collapsed into the bold assertion that "there was going to be a Cold War whatever the west did" (Gaddis 1997, p. 294). This claim follows the reduction of the causes of the Cold

War solely to the person of Stalin: "as long as Stalin was running the Soviet Union a cold war was unavoidable" (Gaddis 1987, p. 292). The allegation is not a casual aside. It bears directly on a crucial assumption made by Gaddis. Not only does he reduce without qualification the source of the entire conflict to the agency of one statesman acting in defiance of the behavior of his counterparts abroad; but, adopting the stance long held by veteran Sovietologist Robert C. Tucker, he also maintains that Stalin's foreign policy was merely a direct extension of his domestic policies: "the more we learn, the less it makes sense to distinguish Stalin's foreign policies from his domestic practices or even his personal behavior" (Gaddis 1997, p. 293).

It has been pointed out that "even a crucially important person such as Stalin can be given too much importance" (Lundestad 2000). Indeed, in his own defense Stalin quoted the Russian proverb, "One man is not a warrior" (Petersen 1946). Much of what Gaddis has to say is alarmingly reminiscent of the references veteran Sovietologist Leonard Schapiro used to make in characterizing Moscow's conduct as "totalitarian foreign policy." Yet it is hard to see how one can translate behavior within a political system walled in by terror, and thereby subjected to passive and obsequious obedience, into behavior in a decentralized international states' system, where most of the levers of power lie all too often in the resolutely independent hands of others. All foreign policy is necessarily interactive whether the dictator likes it or not. And it does not take much research into the foreign policy conducted by Stalin in the 1930s and, indeed, during World War II, to see the enforced interplay—not completely unproductive—between Moscow and the other powers. Indeed, if Stalin liked cold wars so much, apparently for their own sake—Gaddis refers to a "personal propensity for cold wars" (1997, p. 294)—why did Soviet foreign policy veer so dramatically toward the democracies in the 1930s? Clearly, objective factors played their part. Some kind of threat assessment operated in the 1940s as in the 1930s. We have yet to see those documents.

One need not posit some artificial equality of responsibility for the origins of the Cold War to acknowledge that a more complicated equation may have been at work. Whether Stalin liked it or not, realities from abroad always impinged on the conduct of foreign policy by the Kremlin. The entire argument in favor of containment as U.S. policy toward the Soviet Union in 1946–1947 was surely based on this premise. The assumption had to be that, when confronted with a wall of resistance, Stalin and his successors could be restrained. The power of constraint as well as the power of purpose has to account for policy. We do not know to what degree Western conduct prior to the adoption of containment—not toughness (which the revisionist always assumes) but plain inconstancy and, at times, fear—determined Stalin's own thinking and planning. We are not obliged to supplant the intentionality of one party with the intentionality of another, to substitute Truman for Stalin as the sole agent causing the Cold War, as some revisionist historians have traditionally done. It is, indeed, entirely possible that the Cold War resulted at least in part from the unintended consequences of the actions of more than one party to the dispute. This was argued at the time with respect to the conflict that arose between Russia and the West as World War II came to a close.

Moreover, what are we to make of the tendency of Gaddis to dismiss the issue, consistently and repeatedly raised by the revisionists, of U.S. expansionism? He mentions that "*the United States and the Soviet Union built empires after World War II, although not of the same kind*" (Gaddis 1997, p. 284, italics in original), then drops the point in indecent but revealing haste. Does the behavior of some prominent and defiantly unilateralist figures in the current administration have no bearing on the origins of the Cold War? Is this attitude of mind merely the by-product of a transformation entirely wrought by the Cold War? Do they have no connection with a more distant past or the very dynamics that brought the United States center stage in world politics? As Warren Buffett never tires of reminding those who buy stocks, "It's only when the tide goes out that you learn who's been swimming naked."

Undeniably from 1945 the United States was a rising power that fast became a near-global power. Can all this be laid entirely at the door of the Soviet Union? Could not this process have been in the making regardless of Stalin's behavior? Were the Russians merely the unwitting catalysts to the global extension of American power? Here the less than distant past in U.S. foreign policy is hard to ignore, given similarities between the behavior of the United States in the Third World once the Cold War was under way and the pattern and purposes of its behavior in its own hemisphere and elsewhere since the annexation of Texas. Were the repetitious landings of marines in the Caribbean even under Franklin Roosevelt merely responses to the threat of Bolshevism? Did not the United States use its overwhelming presence in the Middle East Supply Center in British Egypt during the war to capture dominance over Saudi oil? Was the attempted emasculation of the British imperial preference system by the United States during the negotiations for the postwar loan in any conceivable sense a response to Stalin? Did the tearing away of Japanese territory correspond to concerns about the Russians in the Far East? Was the insistence that the U.S. Air Force remain in occupation of its base in Iceland, regardless of the wishes of the inhabitants, the act of a democracy in foreign policy? Some years later, was the enforced independence of the Dutch East Indies under the threat of withholding Marshall Plan aid from the Netherlands really an anti-Communist move?

The assumption of total U.S. passivity and naivete at the end of World War II is too big a pill to swallow, as Tucker himself points out. The United States did not then build a formal empire; Britain, too, had no formal empire in nineteenth-century Latin America and early twentieth-century China, yet to all intents and (commercial) purposes these were subject territories. But what the United States constructed was recognizably an empire all the same—a series of protectorates dominated by the power of the dollar, backed by the world's largest blue-water fleet and intercontinental air force. (Like Britain in its heyday, the United States never built a large standing army that would immediately jeopardize the balance of power in Europe.) Would Washington have built a kind of empire in Asia had communism been absent? This is certainly how it appeared at the time. As a memorandum from Britain's Foreign Secretary Ernest Bevin noted in November 1945: "The United States have long held, with our support, to the Monroe doctrine for the Western Hemisphere and there is no doubt now that, notwithstanding all the protestations, they are attempting to extend this principle financially and economically to the Far East to include China and Japan" (Bullock 1983, p. 193). Similarly, Bevin told U.S. ambassador to Moscow Averell Harriman several weeks later that "The United States already had their 'Monroe' on the American continent and were extending it to the Pacific" (Harriman 1945b). This is precisely the dynamic many British imperialists found themselves forced to accept, and why Stalin foolishly thought he could in the end rely on interimperialist contradictions to break the wartime axis between London and Washington.

Whether the United States unilaterally exerted its hegemony over Western Europe is another question. Lundestad (1986) insists that this was not so. If not, then this duality in U.S. foreign policy requires explanation. Was it entirely due to the greater residual power of West European countries relative to Latin American countries, for example? One could not tell merely by statements of policy. Look to the more distant past. The same high-minded Wilsonian statements of principle that had appeared to govern U.S. policy in Europe during the Paris peace conference back in 1919 had also justified military intervention to protect U.S. business interests against the Mexican revolution only a few years before. Lundestad's (1986) claim that what was forged in Europe after 1945 was merely "an empire by invitation" is not to be ruled out. But neither is it to be assumed that matters were quite so simple. We know that France, for one, would never have accepted German rearmament without imposition from the United States—certainly not by invitation. And was it really an empire by invitation that followed in the Third World—in Guatemala (1954), the Dominican Republic (1965), or, indeed, Chile (1973)? Furthermore, was U.S. power indifferent to financial self-interest? Certainly not in the Far East. And was it not diehard Republican Senator Taft who accused Truman of launching the Marshall Plan to forestall a recession in the United States (presumably to win the next election)?

In direct contrast to Gaddis, Trachtenberg (1999, p. 3) forcefully rejects one form of agency at the root of the Cold War, namely the assumption "that the conflict was ideological at its core." On Trachtenberg's reasoning, a "spheres of influence" agreement was reached and could have been sustained. "American policymakers, and Soviet leaders as well, were not prisoners of their own ideologies, and were perfectly capable of recognizing power realities and constructing their policies accordingly," he maintains (Trachtenberg 1999, p. 4). Similarly, "Stalin was not opting for a policy of confrontation with the west. What he wanted was to conduct foreign policy in classic pre-World War I fashion" (Trachtenberg 1999, p. 19). A greater contrast with Gaddis could scarcely be conceived, though both have had access to identical sources. The trusting reader can be forgiven for being confused.

Trachtenberg's formulation is, of course, no less speculative than that of Gaddis. By assuming "rational" decision making, Trachtenberg in a sense substitutes one intentionality for another. Whereas the Stalin of Gaddis is demonic and entirely self-determining, Trachtenberg's Stalin is fundamentally reasonable and reactive, very much reminiscent of A.J.P. Taylor's characterization of Hitler as another Stresemann in his *Origins of the Second World War*. The skeptical reader may well suspect that Trachtenberg's image of Stalin is at root a projection of the historian's rationality onto Stalin. We do not, on the other hand, have to assume with Gaddis that Stalin's policy was completely nonrational. It is perfectly plausible that his rationality was severely limited, incorporating distortions of ideology and personality both. On this view, Trachtenberg's image fails to come to grips with certain plausible essentials that may have to be factored in. For instance, it neglects the role of the Bolshevik Weltanschauung in filtering and counterfeiting the real world in the minds of the Soviet leadership. It leaves out the impact of the 1930s in international relations—beginning with the appeasement of the Nazis by Colonel Beck of Poland as well as Neville Chamberlain of Britain, and ending in the unceremonious ejection of the USSR from the League of Nations after it attacked Finland—on the Kremlin as a whole and not just Stalin. Trachtenberg does not consider Stalin's own extreme suspicion, which is demonstrated in foreign as well as domestic policy and which may have been only an extension of an attitude more general to the Kremlin, since only one of his successors has done much better. Finally, Trachtenberg's account omits the role of Soviet domestic requirements— not least the all-pervasive and not unfounded fear that opening the door to the world outside would bring down the regime—in forging foreign policy. In these desperate conditions, the slightest indication of U.S. ill will could easily be blown out of proportion. As the Russian proverb has it, "Fear has large eyes" (*U strakha glaza veliki*). The explanation offered by Trachtenberg is, in contrast, strikingly reminiscent of the systems interpretation of international relations underpinned by the balance of power. Subjective factors are, on this view, less determinant than objective factors, and the determining objective factors are international, not domestic. Agency gives way to structure, intention to force of circumstance.

Whereas Trachtenberg has, remarkably, emerged substantially unscathed, Gaddis was forcefully attacked from two corners of the revisionist camp: by Leffler (2000), whom we have already encountered, and Stephanson (1998). They represent the intentionalist (left liberal—Leffler) and the structuralist (Marxist— Stephanson) schools. Stephanson takes Gaddis to task for "retelling the familiar story of the Cold War as a struggle between good and evil" (Stephanson 1998,p. 121). He finds fault with the idea that Stalin, Mao, Khrushchev, and other Communist leaders were at root "romantics." On the contrary, he argues, "the object of action and decision was to preserve the Soviet Union and the Stalin regime. . . . About this project there was nothing romantic whatsoever" (Stephanson 1998, p. 122). He thus rejects the Gaddis proposition of a Manichean polarity between the Communist camp and the West. This, Stephanson argues, allows Gaddis "to explain why Stalin and the Soviet Union acted against its [sic] own interests; and it renders unnecessary any questions about the role of the United States in the proceedings" (Stephanson 1998, p. 123).

In contrast, the attack by Leffler is the more measured continuation of a long-running debate. Leffler (1996, p. 122) had asserted, "The Cold War was not a simple case of Soviet expansionism and American reaction. Realpolitik held sway in the Kremlin. . . . They [the Russians] were concerned mostly with configurations of power, with protecting their country's immediate periphery, ensuring its security, and preserving their rule." His position at that time thus differed little from that adopted by Trachtenberg more recently. In a recent review of Gaddis, however, Leffler (1999, p. 517) conceded on a core issue—the mediating role of ideology: "to say that Stalin was acting defensively to enhance the security of his state and his power does *not* mean that one should negate the influence of Marxist-Leninist ideology and Soviet culture." And, instead of insisting merely on realpolitik, he responds to Gaddis' emphasis on the importance of Stalinist thought by insisting that new historians of the Cold War "should follow the logic of their argument and look closely at the beliefs in Washington as well as in Moscow and Beijing" (Leffler 1999, p. 522). The reader may thus conclude that what once appeared crystal clear has now become distinctly murky. Not only do Trachtenberg and Gaddis disagree while working from the same sources, but Leffler disagrees with Gaddis and, implicitly, with arguments he himself made earlier.

At this point, we might turn directly to the new sources emerging from Russia that throw light on the issue of agency versus structure and, therein, the issue of intentionality as a product of realpolitik or ideology (Marxism-Leninism), since this is the crux of the debate over the origins of the Cold War on the Soviet side. For although direct documentary evidence has only trickled through, we do now have testimony from those directly involved in foreign policy formulation and execution; fortunately, there is yet more to come even on the Stalin period. Of those who served the Soviet regime, Vyacheslav Molotov (1890–1986) ranked second only to Stalin as Chairman of the Council of People's Commissars (1930–1941) and then as Commissar for Foreign Affairs (1939–1949) and First Deputy Chairman (1941–1953). It was long rumored and emphatically denied (by his son-in-law, with whom he lived) that he had been writing his memoirs. The denial was true but only technically so. In fact Molotov had been answering probing questions from friend and poet Feliks Chuev in regular meetings taped between 1969 and 1986, the last 17 years of a very long and eventful life. The sum totalled 140 conversations, 4–5 hours each. As a young secretary of the Party's Central Committee, Molotov had been among a handful who read Lenin's damaging testament, including his condemnation of Stalin's worst faults, with which he concurred. Yet during the battle for power that followed Lenin's death in January 1924, Molotov sided with Stalin, first against Trotsky and the United Opposition of the Left, then against Bukharin and the Right. Stalin was well aware that Molotov shared Lenin's judgment. But the collaboration between them grew ever closer, founded as it was on Stalin's confidence that Molotov, in striking contrast to almost everyone else, would air his disagreements only in close quarters; second, any disagreements would be contained within a strict boundary of loyalty to Stalin; and third, whatever the disagreement, Molotov would always ultimately defer to Stalin's judgment.

Chuev's edited version of the tapes was not published until 1991 (Chuev 1991). It was published in English as *Molotov Remembers*, and a second, expanded edition came out subsequently (Chuev 2000). The first contained 553 pages of Chuev's text, the second edition runs to 735 pages and contains more on foreign affairs than the original. As with all recollections, the scholar has to be careful. But where original documentation and complementary sources can be checked, Molotov's memory appears remarkably precise. And one significant area where this precision is so valuable is his differences with Stalin.

No one seriously disputes the fact that from 1929 Stalin had the last word on all questions of policy. But this did not rule out debate. We have direct evidence of this not only from the recollections of Marshal Zhukov (Haslam 1992, p. 17) but also from those of Oleg Troyanovsky (Troyanovsky 1997), who worked for Molotov. "Some of Stalin's views I criticised . . . and told him personally," Molotov recalled. "I consider that a Communist, a member of the Politburo, for thirty years, without an opinion is a chatterbox" (Chuev 2000, p. 442). On another occasion he commented, "I am not the kind of person who was riveted by what Stalin said [*Staliny v rot zaglyadyval*], I argued with him, I told him the truth!" (Chuev 2000, p. 362). Indeed, on a key issue of doctrine that had originally divided Stalin from Trotsky, Molotov and Stalin stood apart. This concerned the likelihood of world revolution and the possibility of establishing socialism in one country. It bears directly on the early Cold War, since it illustrates not only differences of expectation within the Kremlin but also Stalin's relentlessly negative views on the subject. On November 19, 1944—with the defeat of Germany still in prospect but with the French Communist Party spearheading at least half of the national resistance—Stalin punctured bloated expectations of a revolution in France, telling leader Maurice Thorez unequivocally that he wished "the Party did not exaggerate its strength. If enemies succeed in provoking the Party, it would be strangled. A leftist bloc has to be constructed gradually and with patience" (*Istochnik* 1995). Similarly, the Chinese Communists were told to come to terms with Chiang Kai-shek (Chen 2001, ch. 1). And when tension led to widespread rioting and storming of police stations, in December 1947 Italian Communists were told in no uncertain terms that Moscow did not want another Greece (civil war prompting British military intervention) (Secchia 1978).

These facts alone suggest that Stalin was none too keen on foreign revolutions, and this reticence went back a long way. In a speech to the XV Party Conference, at the height of the struggle with the United Opposition in 1926, Molotov announced, "The policy of our party is and remains a policy of the final triumph of socialism on a world scale. . . . " It had been the standard party line ever since 1917. Nonetheless, before publication he took the precaution of sending it to Stalin for comment. Typically, Stalin evaded any written comment (an alternative view leaked to the outside world would have publicized a politically fatal heresy). Instead he tackled Molotov in person. Do you wish to occupy mid-field between ourselves and Trotsky? He asked. Molotov acknowledges that Stalin had correctly understood him: His interpretation did stand at some distance from that of Stalin himself

(Chuev 2000). Stalin dismissed Molotov's words as mere prophecy. Instead he believed one could create socialism in one country. "I argued with him about it," Molotov remembers (Chuev 2000, p. 123). On a much later occasion the difference in outlook re-emerged when Molotov became argumentative at Stalin's insistence on attempting to seize the Dardanelles at the end of the war, a prize that Nicholas II had valued. Molotov was unimpressed. "In his last years Stalin began giving himself airs," Molotov tells us, "and in foreign policy the demand arose that Milyukov had raised: the Dardanelles! Stalin: 'Go ahead, pressure them! ... ' I told him: 'They won't give way.' 'But you make the demand!'" (Chuev 2000, p. 148). Observers noticed with interest that whereas Molotov invariably referred to his country as the Soviet Union, Stalin was wont to use the term Russia. It therefore becomes problematic to see Stalin as Gaddis sees him, as some kind of romantic revolutionary.

On the other hand, the assumption by Leffler (1996) and Trachtenberg (1999) that Stalin can be encased completely within Realpolitik does not easily fit with the new (or old) evidence either. As the great terror of the 1930s might have indicated, we are not here dealing with a fully rational mind. To take just one instance, in the gloomy depths of war, with Stalingrad under siege, Stalin wrote to ambassador Ivan Maisky in London: "All of us in Moscow are getting the impression that Churchill is sustaining a course towards the defeat of the USSR, in order to come to terms with the Germany of Hitler or Brüning at the expense of our country" (Gromyko 1983, p. 147). There is no evidence from the British archives of such intentions. That Stalin found them credible carries implications for the way we assess his outlook during the course of the Grand Alliance and thereafter. To impute a rationality that one would associate with the conduct of foreign policy within the predictable straitjacket of Reasons of State is unwise. Further to this line of thought, the reader should consider what happened during the London conference of Foreign Ministers that convened in September 1945. Those present included Molotov, Ernest Bevin (for Britain), and James Byrnes (for the United States). Byrnes proposed to Molotov a Four Power Pact (USA, USSR, Britain, and France) to guarantee against any future German aggression while winding down military occupation as Germany was demilitarized over the course of 20–25 years. Molotov recommended acceptance.

In a ciphered telegram rejecting the offer categorically, Stalin revealed his underlying concerns: "Byrnes' proposal has four aims: to distract our attention from the Far East, where America is behaving as the latter-day friend of Japan, and by that means creating the impression that in the Far East everything is fine; second, to receive from the USSR formal consent that the USA will play in the affairs of Europe the same role as the USSR, so as, later in a bloc with England, to take into its hands the fate of Europe; third, to devalue the treaties of alliance which the USSR has already concluded with states of Europe; fourth, to render pointless any future treaties of alliance between the USSR and Romania, Finland etc." (Pechatnov 1992, pp. 74–75). What Stalin demanded on these and other questions was "a policy of fortitude and endurance" (Pechatnov 1992, p. 85).

Several observations emerge from this episode. First, Stalin believed the Soviet Union should provide for its security unilaterally, buttressed by treaties of alliance with subordinate neighbors; second, he deeply resented the assertion of U.S. predominance in the Far East only too evident in MacArthur's complete control over Japan; third, he held the view that the United States should, in essence, stay out of Europe, as Roosevelt had indicated he would at the Teheran Conference in November 1943; and fourth, he suspected, from this apparent reversal of policy, U.S. ambitions to predominate in Europe as it was predominating in Asia. Further light is shed on Stalin's state of mind at the time by the record of his candid meeting with ambassador Averell Harriman on October 25 in Gagri. After protesting the exclusion of the Soviet government from the arrangements made in postwar Japan, Stalin pointed out that "For a long time the isolationists had been in power in the United States. He had never favored a policy of isolation, but perhaps now the Soviet Union should adopt such a policy. Perhaps in fact there was nothing wrong with it" (Harriman 1945a).

It was clear to Stalin that the United States was bent on global hegemony and that this ambition threatened Soviet security. If indeed this was Stalin's view, the question naturally arises: When did Stalin develop it? The second question is whether Stalin was in any sense justified in his belief. If so, then the revisionist case must also be answered.

In a wide-ranging conversation with Britain's newly appointed ambassador to Moscow Sir Maurice Petersen in May 1946, Stalin said that "the deterioration in relations . . . was due to an accumulation of facts antedating the return of the Labour Government to power [August 1945]" (Petersen 1946). Indeed, as early as June 4, Stalin expressed his belief that the division of Germany would lead to "America's unlimited domination" (Falin 1999, p. 53). Circumstantial evidence suggests that these suspicions began to crystalize well before the death of Roosevelt (April 1945) but after the visit to Moscow of Edvard Kardelj, representing the Yugoslav Communist Party, in November 1944. On this occasion Kardelj, in conversation with Deputy Commissar for Foreign Affairs Lozovsky, referred to the Americans as the future great power in Western Europe with whom they would all have to come to terms. He was, however, rapidly corrected. That was not how the Boss (Stalin) saw things: "he still thinks that England is the centre of world imperialism, the main enemy of the proletariat, and that America plays a secondary role. But here you are, saying that the United States is taking over from England as the centre of world imperialism" (Kardelj 1982, pp. 66–67). Stalin's assumption fit in with the assurances given to him and Winston Churchill by Franklin Roosevelt at Teheran a year before. It appeared also to square with the fact that it was Churchill, on a visit to Moscow in October, who had just negotiated a deal with Stalin dividing the Balkans into spheres of influence. The Americans had known yet stood back.

The waters broke on November 15, when *Voina i rabochii klass*, the sole informal mouthpiece of the Kremlin on foreign affairs, published a belated review of Joseph Jones' *A Modern Foreign Policy for the United States* (1944), which had appeared earlier that year. The delay is interesting, because the contents of the book had appeared in *Fortune* magazine prior to Teheran, in August, September, and October 1943. Evidently, someone of importance in Moscow discounted their significance until rather late in the day. Two other major works on the future of U.S. foreign policy had emerged in 1943—*America's Strategy in World Politics* by the Dutch-American Nicholas Spykman of Yale, whose influence was inevitably weakened by the fact that it had been completed before Pearl Harbor, and *U.S. Foreign Policy: Shield of the Republic* by the popular columnist Walter Lippmann—but neither contradicted what Roosevelt had said in private to Stalin about Europe; indeed, Lippmann effectively argued for what Stalin so desperately sought: the right to Eastern Europe as a sphere of influence/protectorate. What was unusual about Jones' work, on the other hand, was the peremptory assertion of American primacy—"no country but the United States is equal to the task of leadership in organizing world power for peace-keeping purposes" (Jones 1944, p. 7), the emphasis on the importance of "a living principle" for U.S. foreign policy (p. 14), and the link established between that principle ("freedom") and the need for "expanding markets" for the United States (p. 32). Indeed, the anonymous Soviet reviewer seizes on these ideas permeating the text, summed up in Jones' remark that "the moment is ours." Leadership would go to the United States above all because of its massive industrial and technological power and the colossal increase in its air force. The review concludes that "Jones' judgements about the 'leadership' of the United States, although in a less acute form, in essence reproduce the stance of those American circles which are very vociferously laying claim to the domination of the United States in the postwar world" (Petrov 1944).

Hostility born of a deep-seated fear was reinforced, at least among Stalin's immediate subordinates, through use of the atomic bomb by the United States to secure the surrender of Japan. Leaving aside whether deploying the bomb was intended to intimidate the Russians, it was certainly hoped in Washington that it would forestall the need for Russian military intervention against Japan, which would otherwise allow the Russians to collect on the extensive menu of promises handed over by Roosevelt at Yalta, including military bases in China and the annexation of territory from the Japanese home islands. And Stalin had suspected since February that the Americans might come to terms with Japan directly, thus cutting Moscow out of the picture. What is more, the Russians believed use of the bomb was, at least in part, designed to intimidate them; hence Stalin's determined sangfroid when Truman "casually" mentioned it at the Potsdam conference in August 1945. Stalin told Molotov, "They are killing the Japanese but they are intimidating us. Once again everything is being done in secret" (Gromyko 1997, p. 65). Andrei Gromyko, then ambassador to the United States and a close protégé of Molotov's, told his son that when news of the bomb reached their ears, "the military in our General Staff clutched their heads. The Soviet Union, having only just beaten fascist armies, was once again under threat of attack. . . . The Kremlin and the General Staff were in a state of nerves; mistrust of the allies quickly grew. The opinion was voiced in favour of maintaining a large land army, the establishment of control over great expanses as a counter-balance to possible losses from atomic bombardment" (Gromyko 1997, p. 65). It was Molotov who decided to adopt a pose that would reassure them (Chuev 2000, p. 112). Indeed, he foolishly stated that the Soviet Union would have the bomb and "something else." As he recalled, "Stalin later used this to restrict any talk of the fact that we were weak, at a time when we had nothing" (Chuev 2000, p. 113). If, then, the bomb was supposed to make the Russians more tractable about dominating Eastern Europe, it had precisely the reverse effect. It appears to have reinforced Stalin's instinct to grab what he could while it was freely available before a full confrontation in the form of war with the United States became a reality. George Kennan, whose accurate prognosis led to recall to Washington and promotion to policy making, noted in the summer of 1946 that "Security is probably their [the Russians'] basic motive, but they are so anxious and suspicious about it that the objective results are much the same as if the motive were aggression, indefinite expansion. They evidently seek to weaken all centers of power they cannot dominate, in order to reduce the danger from any possible rival" (Gaddis 1987, p. 39).

It would thus appear that logic was at work in Stalin's mind, but a logic resting on premises which, at least in terms of Western intentions, show signs of being baseless. One possible reason for the peculiarly mistrustful element in Stalin's character moving ever further to the fore was connected with his health. On seeing Stalin, British ambassador Petersen (1946) noted that he "looked a man who was far from well." Molotov himself attributes the mistrust Stalin began feeling toward him—beginning in the autumn of 1945, leading to the imprisonment of his wife, and culminating in frightening threats eight years later—not least to the encroachment of arteriosclerosis. With the war drawing to a close, Stalin had talked of retirement: "Let Vyacheslav [Molotov] do some work!" he declared (Chuev 2000, p. 116). Yet he was jealous when Molotov failed properly to consult him. As Molotov recalls, "in my opinion [in] the last years Stalin began to weaken . . . sclerosis comes to all with age to various degrees. . . . But in him it was noticeable" (Chuev 2000, p. 362). Indeed, having taken no holiday since 1936, Stalin now spent annually an increasing number of months secluded on the Black Sea, where deep introspection exacerbated by self-imposed isolation fed morose and, indeed, lethal suspicions. It was from here that he communicated with Molotov in London in the autumn of 1945.

BEYOND ORIGINS

It makes sense to ask whether the explanations given for the origins of the Cold War also account for its continuation. Some, most notably liberals Robert C. Tucker and Stephen Cohen, have always given the benefit of the doubt to the Soviet regime after Stalin but simultaneously regarded the Cold War as Stalin's responsibility. In contrast, anti-Communist diehards such as Richard Pipes have essentially seen no difference. Given the peculiarities of Stalin as dictator, one would not necessarily assume the explanation for the causes would also account for continuation—if the focus is on intentionality, that is. Were the answer to be sought in structure, the argument would follow equally that systemic determinants on the U.S. side and on the Soviet side could be expected to continue to operate. Thus, the reader might expect to find that Gaddis—who focuses exclusively on intentionality— would find an alternative explanation for the continuation of the Cold War than for its causes, whereas Trachtenberg—whose approach is only partly fixed on intentionality—could be expected to provide the same explanation for both causes and continuation. The reader would, however, be mistaken with respect to Gaddis because he provides the same explanation for Khrushchev's behavior as for Stalin's, and the same explanation for for U.S. policy vis-à-vis both: that all these Soviet leaders were subject to what he calls "authoritarian romanticism" (Gaddis 1997, p. 289).

The divergent consequences of the reasoning of Trachtenberg and Gaddis can be found in their respective treatments of the Cuban Missile Crisis, which has received a great deal of attention not least because it appears to have been the event that drew us all closest to the brink of annihilation, certainly in Europe. Many in the U.S. Air Force did not see that there was a problem. An interview with USAF Generals Curtis LeMay, Leon Johnson, David Burchinal, and Jack Catton makes alarming reading (to a European), since they grandly assert that because of overwhelming U.S. strategic superiority, Khrushchev had no choice but to back down. "We could have gotten not only the missiles out of Cuba," asserts LeMay, "we could have gotten the Communists out of Cuba at the time" (Kahn & Harahan 1988). Similarly, one senior official at the Pentagon assured the author in 1983, "We could have wiped them [the Russians] out." For those living in Western Europe under the shadow of vast numbers of Soviet medium-range ballistic missiles, the perspective was and is a little different.

The stationing of Soviet medium- and intermediate-range missiles (MRBMs and IRBMs) in Cuba through the summer and autumn of 1962 proved disastrous and was perhaps one of the most important foreign policy blunders that ultimately ejected Khrushchev from high offfice. As First Secretary of the CPSU, he made the decision essentially on his own and gave the Presidium (Politburo) little choice but to accept it, as was customary; that was how Soviet foreign policy was always made when the chief had made up his mind. The fact that, prior to this, President Anastas Mikoyan, a trusted foreign policy advisor of enormous experience and no little sagacity, had argued against the idea—as had the less wise and experienced Andrei Gromyko, then Foreign Minister, at least in name—meant nothing. So it is scarcely to be expected that Khrushchev's memoirs present an honest account of events; and they do not. They merely reiterate the official line at the time. Doubtless if Stalin had presented his explanation for the causes of the Cold War in his memoirs, few, if any, would have believed him. For some reason, Khrushchev is taken to be different when rationalizing his own blunders.

Contrary to what might naturally be assumed, the insertion of forward-based strategic missiles in Cuba did not necessarily bear any direct relationship with Soviet policy toward Havana. Trachtenberg sees the answer in the strategic imbalance between Moscow and Washington and links this with the outstand-ing crisis over the fate of West Berlin. He has always claimed, correctly, that the division of the city by the building of the Berlin Wall in August 1961 was a temporary expedient to stem the flood of migrants from the East, and that what Khrushchev needed was a proper resolution of the German problem—a peace treaty formalizing the division of Germany—of which West Berlin was but a sig-nificant symptom. Citing discussions between President Kennedy and his senior advisors, Trachtenberg argues that "it seemed that the point of the missile deploy-ment was to improve the Soviet strategic position quickly and cheaply, and thus to put the USSR in a better position to bring the Berlin Crisis to a head" (Trachtenberg 1999, p. 353). Trachtenberg thus reduces Soviet thinking entirely to the level of Reasons of State. This is not mere speculation. From the moment the Wall went up, the Russians relentlessly pressed for a solution to the German problem on their own terms. Lack of a solution undermined Soviet prestige and thereby weakened Khrushchev's own standing at home. This was a point noted by several witnesses (Sulzberger 1972, pp. 784, 799).

Gaddis, however, takes an altogether different tack. He accepts Khrushchev's assertion that the missiles were installed to protect Cuba. "The Soviet leader," he writes, "gave first priority to defending Cuba; the strategic balance was, for him, an important but secondary consideration" (Gaddis 1997, p. 265). No mention at all is made of Berlin. In his explanation for Khrushchev's motivation, Gaddis hauls in the same reasoning applied to Stalin: "Marxism-Leninism produced more romanticism than realism. It convinced Khrushchev that he should risk the security of the Soviet state to rescue an unruly gang of youthful revolutionaries in Havana, of all places" (Gaddis 1997, p. 266).

This explanation has always seemed somewhat implausible, for several reasons. First, the way to secure Cuba against American attack would have been to put in Soviet ground forces with or without tactical nuclear weapons. Indeed, Castro himself later said, "Really, deploying missiles in its territory wasn't absolutely necessary for Cuba's defense, because a military pact could have been entered into, and the Soviet Union could have said that an attack on Cuba was equiva-lent to an attack on the Soviet Union, as is stated in the pacts the United States has with practically everybody in the world, which are respected. Or a military agreement could have been entered into, and the purpose of Cuba's defense could have been served without the presence of the missiles" (Lechuga 1995, p. 36). Yet Khrushchev had actually cut Soviet military aid to Cuba after the Bay of Pigs invasion launched by the Americans. Moreover, Castro's requests for assistance—most notably surface-to-air missiles to defend Cuba from U.S. airpower—made in September 1961 were held up by the Russians until the late spring of 1962. No sense of urgency was apparent in Moscow about the defense of Cuba and its actions are scarcely indicative of overwhelming concerns in that direction. One reason was because Khrushchev disliked Castro's predilection for exporting rev-olution into the territory of his neighbors, a factor that did not change with the arrival of MRBMs and IRBMs.

Second, Khrushchev, a supposed "romantic," simultaneously sold Communists down the river elsewhere when their protection did not immediately suit Soviet interests (Laos, arguably Vietnam, and certainly Egypt, Syria, and Iraq, to name just a few major instances). His "revolutionary romanticism," if operative, was not infrequently suppressed for Reasons of State. Third, Khrushchev reached his decision before consulting Castro, which is a strange way of defending an ally. Fourth, Castro flatly contradicts the assertions made by Khrushchev, which in fact infuriated him. He says he was asked to take the missiles in order to "reinforce the socialist camp at a global level." "It was not," he added, "in order to assure our own defence, but above all to reinforce socialism at the international level. That is the truth even if other explanations are being provided elsewhere" (Julien 1963). And alternative reliance can scarcely be placed on the memoirs of Khrushchev's foreign policy adviser Oleg Troyanovsky. It is clear from the text that he was not directly privy to Khrushchev's reasoning—few advisers to the leader of the Party ever were, even under Gorbachev—since, in his memoirs, he is reduced to speculating with the rest of us as to the First Secretary's true motives (Troyanovsky 1997).

CONCLUSIONS

The space above is too limited to do justice to the wealth of new findings that have emerged on the Cold War. But even the sample we have dipped into highlights the fact that these new findings have as yet been insufficiently assimilated to satisfy the more demanding reader. For although this field is now energetically given over to historians, the latter seem still to operate largely within the framework created by their political scientist predecessors and to no greater advantage. Those categories of explanation—loosely summed up as ideology versus Realpolitik—though convenient as organizing principles, may be too unwieldy to do justice to the complexity of the evidence. Both appear to rest on an intentionality that bears little direct connection with the reality of the times. It is apparent, for example, that the notion of "revolutionary romanticism" does not fit with Stalin; probably not with Khrushchev either. Even with Lenin, the dose of realism was always too strong for a mixture that could merit such a label, as Carr's (1953) early analysis long ago demonstrated. And neither approach takes sufficiently seriously the lines of argument pressed on the profession by its dissentient college: those revisionists who focus on structure rather than intentionality. The merit of the latter approach is that most history is not satisfactorily explained purely in terms of intentions. Because diplomatic historians are trained to draw their explanations from state documents, they inevitably assume that the expressions of policy therein determine events. This is an inductivist fallacy, even if one takes seriously the documents created by bureaucrats and politicians. They have their place. At times they may even merit primacy of place. But they still have to be bridged and circumscribed by the unwritten assumptions that emerge from the society in which they were originally set.

This may be taken as a plea for a more nuanced appreciation of the origins of the Cold War and its continuation—a plea for, on the one side, a serious examination of those economic forces that were committing the United States to a global role regardless of the intentions of individual policy makers; and on the other side, further research into what set Stalin's mind in the pattern that developed toward the end of World War II. The role of personality here seems at least as important as ideology. And in regard to ideology, we are not speaking of the classic Old Bolshevik of the Leninist type but someone who is comfortable modeling himself on Ivan the Terrible while not completely divested of the negative features of the communist mindset. In his memoirs, Old Bolshevik Anastas Mikoyan, who, like Molotov, was destined for the scaffold had Stalin lived beyond April 1953, recalls one of Stalin's great qualities: the speed with which he could grasp the essence of things even where they extended beyond his range of knowledge. "But at times," he notes, "he became very strange. He was overtaken by some idée fixe or other, which would transform itself into a genuine fetish" (Mikoyan 1999, p. 523). The obsession with the danger of treachery from his allies abroad matched the obsession with betrayal even by his closest colleagues. Even with Khrushchev, the make-up of his post-revolutionary mind cannot be reduced to Leninist purity, if such a thing existed past 1917. Whereas the Old Bolshevik Mikoyan decisively rejected the overthrow of the regime in Hungary in 1956, Khrushchev acted as Stalin would have, in a tradition of unreflective Realpolitik worthy of their Tsarist predecessors. And whereas revolutionary Cuba was seeking actively to bring Marxist revolution to Latin America, under Khrushchev since 1957 the Russian regime had been stultifying these movements in favor of a constitutionalism that Lenin would have found pitiful. No one would deny that there was, too, in Khrushchev a purely whimsical element—such as planting the steppe with maize regardless of prevailing conditions—but this was not Marxist-Leninist ideology but the behavior of a despotic temperament traditional to Russia and only too visible in Stalin. It will take us more time and much greater immersion in twentieth-century Russia to make sense of all this. We have come a long way, but there is plenty of unexplored virgin land for the committed scholar in various archives, and not just in the United States.

The *Annual Review of Political Science* is online at
http://polisci.annualreviews.org

LITERATURE CITED

Bullock A. 1983. *Ernest Bevin: Foreign Secretary, 1945–1951*. Oxford: Oxford Univ. Press

Carr EH. 1953. *The Bolshevik Revolution*, Vol. 3. London: Macmillan

Chen J. 2001. *Mao's China and the Cold War*. Chapel Hill: Univ. North Carolina Press

Chuev F. 1991. *Sto sorok besed s Molotovym: iz dnevnika F. Chueva*. Moscow: Terra

Chuev F. 2000. *Molotov: Poluderzhavnyi vlastelin*. Moscow: Olma-Press

Falin V. 1999. *Bez Skidok na Obstoyatel'stva*. Moscow: Sovremennik

Feis H. 1957. *Roosevelt—Churchill—Stalin. The War They Waged and the Peace they Sought*. Princeton, NJ: Princeton Univ. Press

1948. *Foreign Office (FO)* 371/71632A.

Foreign Office archive: Public Record Office, Kew, UK

Gaddis J. 1987. *The Long Peace: Inquiries Into the History of the Cold War.* Oxford, UK: Oxford Univ. Press

Gaddis J. 1997. *We Now Know: Rethinking Cold War History.* Oxford, UK: Oxford Univ. Press

Gaddis J. 2000. On starting all over again: a naive approach to the study of the Cold War. In *Reviewing the Cold War: Approaches, Interpretations, Theory,* ed. O. Westad, pp. 27–42. London: Cass

Gromyko A. 1997. *Andrei Gromyko: V labirintakh Kremlya—Vospominaniya syna.* Moscow: Avtor

Gromyko A, ed. 1983. *Sovetsko—angliiskie otnosheniya vo vremya velikoi otechestvennoi voiny 1941–1945,* Vol. 1. Moscow: Politizdat

Harriman A. 1945a. *Harriman Papers* (Library of Congress): Box 183

Harriman A. 1945b. *Harriman Papers* (Library of Congress): Box 185

Haslam J. 1992. *The Soviet Union and the Threat from the East, 1933–41.* London: Macmillan

1995. Anglichane i Amerikantsy khotyat vezde sozdat' reaktsionnye pravitel'stva. *Istochnik* 4:152–58

Julien C. 1963. *Le Monde,* Mar. 22, p. 1

Kahn R, Harahan J. 1988. U.S. strategic air power, 1948–1962. *Int. Sec.* 4:93

Kardelj E. 1982. *Reminiscences: The Struggle for Recognition and Independence: The New Yugoslavia, 1944–1957,* pp. 66–67. London: Blond & Briggs

Lechuga C. 1995. *In the Eye of the Storm: Castro, Khrushchev, Kennedy and the Missile Crisis.* Victoria, Austr.: Ocean

Leffler M. 1992. *A Preponderance of Power: National Security, the Truman Administration, and the Cold War.* Stanford, CA: Stanford Univ. Press

Leffler M. 1996. Inside enemy archives: the Cold War reopened. *For. Aff.* 75:120–35

Leffler M. 1999. The Cold War: What do 'we now know'? *Am. Hist. Rev.* 104:501–24

Lundestad G. 1986. Empire by invitation? The United States and Western Europe, 1945–1952. *J. Peace Res.* 23:263–77

Lundestad G. 2000. How (not) to study the origins of the Cold War. In *Reviewing the Cold War: Approaches, Interpretations, Theory,* ed. O Westad, p. 74. London: Cass

Maier C. 1970. Revisionism and the Cold War. *Persp. Am. Hist.* IV:345

Mikoyan A. 1999. *Tak Bylo: Razmyshleniya o minuvshem.* Moscow: Vargius

Pechatnov V. 1992. "Soyuzniki nazhimayut na tebya dlya togo, shtoby slomit' u tebya volyu . . . " Perepiska Stalina s Molotovym i drugimi chlenami Politburo po vneshnepoliticheskim voprosam v sentyabre—dekabre 1945g. *Istochnik* 2:74–75

Petersen M. 1946. *Foreign Office (FO)* 371/56784. Foreign Office archive: Public Record Office, Kew, UK

Petrov D (nom de plume). 1944. Novaya kniga o vneshnei politike Soedinennykh Shtatov. *Voina i rabochii klass* 22:28–30. This journal later became *Novoe vremya (New Times)*

Riva V. 1999. *Oro da Mosca: i finanziamenti sovietici al PCI dalla Rivoluzione d'ottobre al crollo dell'URSS. Con 240 documenti inediti degli archivi moscoviti.* Milan: Mondadori

Secchia P. 1978. *Annali Fondazione Giangiacomo Feltrinelli. Archivio Secchia.* p. 611

Stephanson A. 1998. Rethinking Cold War history. *Rev. Int. Stud.* 24:119–24

Sulzberger C. *Last of the Giants.* London: Weidenfeld & Nicolson

Trachtenberg M. 1999. *A Constructed Peace: The Making of the European Settlement 1945–1963.* Princeton, NJ: Princeton Univ. Press

Troyanovsky O. 1997. *Cherez gody i rasstoyaniya.* Moscow: Vargius

Tucker RW. 1971. *The Radical Left and American Foreign Policy.* Baltimore, MD: Johns Hopkins Press. 19

Waltz K. 1979. *Theory of International Politics.* Reading, MA: Addison-Wesley

Annu. Rev. Polit. Sci. 2003. 6:99–118
doi: 10.1146/annurev.polisci.6.121901.085839
First published online as a Review in Advance on Dec. 6, 2002

ROBERT A. DAHL'S PHILOSOPHY OF DEMOCRACY, EXHIBITED IN HIS ESSAYS

Michael Bailey[1] and David Braybrooke[2]

[1]Department of Government, Berry College, Mount Berry, Georgia 30149;
email: mbailey@berry.edu; [2]Departments of Government and Philosophy, The University
of Texas at Austin, Austin, Texas 78712; email: braeburn@mail.la.utexas.edu

Key Words size of political societies, pluralism, capitalism, polyarchy, ruling-elite
model

■ **Abstract** Dahl's collected essays give more weight to his achievements as a
philosopher of democracy than to his empirical investigations. Nevertheless, they
clearly reflect his habit of working close to empirical facts, in particular the problems created for democratic practices by the size of modern political societies, their
pluralism, and their intricate involvement with capitalism. His trenchant account, under
the head of "polyarchy," of basic democracy, of the further criteria for full democracy,
and of the conditions for achieving democracy at both these levels has established the
current standard for discussing democratic theory. Moreover, he clears the way for
continuing hope for democracy by demolishing (by arguments supported by observations) the ruling-elite model and advances the prospects of democracy by championing
a variety of jurisdictional arrangements for citizens' participation.

INTRODUCTION

The two volumes of Dahl's collected essays, *Toward Democracy: A Journey*
(1997), offer an opportunity to appreciate and celebrate his life's work. The opportunity relates in particular to the achievements of Dahl the political philosopher,
reasoning about the nature and problems of democracy in a philosophical way.
His achievements as an empirical political scientist do not get full weight. For one
thing, one third of the 57 essays in the collection represent Dahl's work in the ten-
year period after his retirement in 1986, when he was doing little new empirical
work. Nothing in the collection directly parallels *Who Governs?* (1961), Dahl's
empirical inquiry into the applicability of the ruling-elite model in New Haven.
True, some brisk defenses of that study are present, as well as Dahl's searching
analysis of the theoretical issues posed by the ruling-elite model. There are also
important empirical studies of the Supreme Court and of the distribution of power
in Congress, and these make up to some extent for the relative absence here of his
empirical work in *Congress and Foreign Policy* (Dahl 1950) and, on comparative
politics, in *Size and Democracy* (Dahl & Tufte 1973) and *Polyarchy* (Dahl 1971).

(The collection, as we fully take into account below, does include a robust amount of theorizing about size.)

The fundamental political problem that preoccupies Dahl as a philosopher (and as an empirical political scientist as well) is the difficulty of self-governance in a complex, populous modern society. The qualifier "in modern society" is important because it sets Dahl apart from the other classic writers on democratic theory, in the nineteenth century and earlier, with whom we would rank him. Self-governance is always difficult. Dahl, more perhaps than any other writer, makes us fully aware of how much more difficult it has become in modern society. The impediments have strengthened and multiplied. It is with these impediments that he is preoccupied.

Dahl is no Hegelian. He does not believe that the impediments will inevitably be transcended and left behind. Neither does he argue, as did Tocqueville (1969 [1848]), that a mysterious fate precludes anything but a democratic future (for better or worse). Indeed, some critics (Pye 1990) have argued that Dahl is strangely pessimistic about the prospect of extending democratic governance. They can find a pretext for arguing this because of Dahl's preoccupation with impediments, both in nations that have never tried to practice democracy and in nations that have practiced some approximation of it for a long time. But Dahl does not indulge in pessimism when he calls for more effort at theoretical understanding ("The Problem of Civic Competence," Dahl 1997, p. 220).

Though our future is not fated, Dahl admits that politics has changed in ways that are irreversible for practical purposes. Sometime around the fifth century B.C., Greek society shifted from aristocracy (or tyranny) to democracy ("A Democratic Dilemma: System Effectiveness Versus Citizen Participation," Dahl 1997, p. 431). The fundamental democratic institution of that age was the city assembly, where free citizens conducted politics face to face. Centuries later the small city-state, revived sporadically in medieval Italy, was eclipsed by the nation-state, which in democratic instances ushered in changes that are familiar to twenty-first–century Americans: free political expression, representation, universal suffrage. Today, Dahl claims, a third transformation is taking place, the slow coalescence of smaller jurisdictions into larger ones and hence the expansion of "the boundaries of the decisions that significantly affect the fundamental interest of its citizens" ("A Democratic Dilemma: System Effectiveness Versus Citizen Participation," Dahl 1997, p. 432). The democracies of today, to stay relevant and effective, must cope not only with the realities of enormously populous societies and with social pluralism inside and outside national boundaries, but also with a globalizing modern market economy.

However, Dahl does not turn away from the past of democracy and democratic philosophy. Dahl as a political philosopher is steadily concerned with how much of democratic practice in ancient Athens—and democratic theory, especially Rousseau's—can be preserved for contemporary society, in particular for the United States in the second half of the twentieth century (and now). (He does notably insist on taking a view of the United Sates in which its politics is continually compared with other states, including the Scandinavian democracies.) So he is not inspired by Athens and by Rousseau simply in the sense of targeting them for reaction. He is inspired as a philosophical disciple to make the most of them, giving due attention to the broad empirical facts about current politics turned up often by many less theoretical investigators.

Indeed, he is more their disciple than he fully acknowledges. The persistent aim of his thinking is to find ways in which rank-and-file citizens can effectively participate, even when (as is now the case) they can exercise vanishingly little influence one by one as voters (or as participants in other ways). Can they even have an illusion of having influence when they share that influence with millions of other citizens? Yet Dahl, without fully acknowledging Rousseau on this point, is deeply attached to Rousseau's fundamental principle, that to be free a person must be governed only by laws of his own choosing. (Dahl would cheerfully read "his" as interchangeable with "her.")

How is this to be achieved in a modern society? Dahl has spent a lot of time making sure that the consequences for democracy of size, pluralism, and an industrial economy get and keep a prominent place on the agenda of democratic theory, both philosophical and empirical. Moreover, he has offered important findings, both philosophical and empirical, on all these points. We make a quick survey of these topics in the next section before we treat the most basic of Dahl's philosophical contributions—fully represented in these volumes—his theory of polyarchy as the basis for modern democracy.

SIZE, PLURALISM, AN INDUSTRIAL ECONOMY

Three grand complications for democracy in modern society arise from the large size of the society in almost every national state (not only there); from the various pluralistic aspects of the society in each case; and from the presence and growth of an industrial economy, in which a good deal of economic and political power is exercised by the executives of private corporations.

Dahl has focused, to a degree unprecedented in contemporary political science, on the singular importance of size in politics. Even today, despite Dahl's lead, the role of size in politics remains, in his own view, "overly neglected" ("Introduction to Section 5: Size and Democracy," Dahl 1997, p. 379). Both population size and geographical size demand attention, but also population density (holding geographical boundaries constant) and shifting boundaries (treating boundaries, including geographical ones, as variables).

One of the reasons size has become so critical in recent years is that the appropriate size for dealing with social problems is in flux. It is one thing to fix the boundaries of a political jurisdiction, quite another to have these boundaries demarcate an appropriate unit for effective self-governance. Military instability, environmental and ecological hazards, communicable diseases, communication networks, and economic instability are but a few of the problems too impolite to halt their advance at political boundaries. No jurisdiction—whether subnational or national—can be effectively sheltered from other jurisdictions' policies. The upshot of this interrelatedness is that one's life chances and deepest interests are significantly affected by political decisions made by outsiders. Political boundaries marking the scope of our political jurisdictions require constant revisiting, both in practice and in theory.

For Dahl, the most intractable problem that democracy has about size boils down to a trade-off between effective citizen participation and system effectiveness. Dahl accepts that a citizen in a complex, populous, modern society must renounce some personal influence (on the national scene, just about all of it) to have a government that is effective in dealing with macropolitical issues. "We may need different models of democracy for different kinds of units," he acknowledges ("The City in the Future of Democracy," Dahl 1997, p. 395). However, "the central theoretical problem," Dahl writes, "is no longer to find suitable rules, like the majority principle, to apply within a sovereign unit, but to find suitable rules to apply among a variety of units, none of which is sovereign" (Dahl & Tufte 1973, p. 135). Unfortunately, though he poses the question, he has little if anything to say about the interunit rules. Once again, we do best to think of the discussion of size offered in *Toward Democracy*, even in the substantial section devoted to them, as more an effort to place questions firmly on the agenda of democratic theory than an effort to answer the questions. (The answers, or at least a beginning of the answers, are rather to be found in Dahl & Tufte 1973.)

Yet on the point of citizen participation in particular, Dahl does advance toward some possible answers by exploring ways of saving or restoring participation and effective personal influence without complicating constitutional arrangements. He has taken a persistent interest in worker control of industrial enterprises, and in this and other respects he has been steadily unwilling to accept unquestioned leadership by the business elite. He has been interested, too, in neighborhood associations as scenes for realizing participation, and in statistically representative citizens' councils (chosen, in the ancient way, by lot) at various levels of government. This ingredient of his thought is summed up in the principle (the "Chinese boxes" principle) that jurisdictions should fit within one another so that every issue should be dealt with in the jurisdiction most appropriate for dealing with it effectively ("The City in the Future of Democracy," Dahl 1997, pp. 393–94, 404, 410).

On pluralism as well as size, it is best to think of Dahl as making a powerful case (this time not as a lonely pioneer) for keeping certain questions in an unmistakably important place on the agenda of democratic theory. The dangers of faction raised by social pluralism so troubled Rousseau that he thought democracy possible only in the most improbable of circumstances (Rousseau 1978 [1762]). Democratic society required in his view a small and homogeneous group of virtuous citizens whose virtue is bolstered by the rhetoric of civil religion. Madison, equally troubled by faction, attempted to deal with it by expanding the size of the nation, thereby multiplying the number of interest groups so that no single interest group could dominate.[1] Under Madison's scheme, "the principal task of modern legislation" would be the regulation of interest-based factions (Madison et al. 1961, p. 79). Implicit in Madison's idea is that since no group can dominate, all groups will learn over time to cooperate, to bargain, and to deliberate. They will learn the language of democratic policy making, work with a variety of allies, and translate their private interests into the language and reality of public interest. Groups that fail to learn these lessons will drop out for lack of influence. Though Dahl owes a great intellectual debt to Rousseau, on this point he adopts the realistic assumption offered by Madison, agreeing with Madison that pluralism is "an inevitable consequence of democracy on a *large* scale" ("Introduction to Section 4: Democracy, Pluralism, and the Public Good," Dahl 1997, p. 279).

On one question about pluralism, Dahl has not only taken an important lead, putting and keeping it on the agenda of democratic theory, but also presents a famous and thoroughly developed answer of his own. Are the elites who exercise power in the United States a unified set or a plurality, with different elites active in different connections? From *Who Governs?* (1961) to *Dilemmas of Pluralist Democracy* (1982), Dahl has attempted to lay bare the distribution of power in American politics. In *Toward Democracy*, the main theoretical effort lies in the essay "The Analysis of Influence in Local Communities" (Dahl 1997, pp. 877–96), which lays out the hypothetical alternatives for any political body, large or small; but several other essays contain brisk empirical defenses of Dahl's repudiation of the ruling-elite model. Is power concentrated in a few hands, or is it distributed among many discrete associations and actors? The problem is complex not only because it is notoriously difficult to measure power or influence but also because power is a complex concept to begin with. "The overarching concept, whether it be called power, influence, or something else, is a filing cabinet chock full of very different items" ("Power, Pluralism, and Democracy: A Modest Proposal," Dahl 1997, p. 296). Nor is policy making, the arena for the exercise of power, a simple subject to study; it too entails a number of complex variables: attitude formation, recruitment or entry into the political system, the rules of decision making, and the distribution of political resources.

Despite these complications, Dahl has steadily argued that power in American politics is pluralistic. This position has put him in the crosshairs of many left-leaning ideological critics (Bachrach 1967, Lukes 1974, Domhoff 1978, Gaventa 1980), who view his perception of American politics as naive. This impression arises largely from his findings in *Who Governs?*, which described minorities rule in New Haven, Connecticut. After 30 years, Dahl stands firm in his empirical findings. He argues, "There is a tendency to think that if you depart from equality at all, you must have domination. And if you don't have domination, then you must have equality. Now, we all know that's simply not true. You can have inequality, greater inequality, and lesser inequality" ("Rethinking *Who Governs?* New Haven

---

[1]Moving away from his ideal, Rousseau says the same thing: If there have to be associations in the state, let them be as numerous as possible (1978 [1762], p. 65).

Revisited," Dahl 1997, p. 926). Elite theories of American politics fail to recognize that the power of corporate leaders is not "solely a function of the 'size' of their resources" ("Equality and Power in American Society," Dahl 1997, p. 903). They also fail to see that minorities rule over "massive indifference" rather than angry majority opposition ("The Analysis of Influence in Local Communities," Dahl 1997, p. 895). Ironically, elite theories weaken the power of ordinary citizens by helping to persuade them that democracy can do little to influence the distribution of power, and that their voices will go unheard ("Who Really Rules?," Dahl 1997, p. 919). Inequalities do exist, and they often translate into political inequalities—but it does not follow that an elite or a set of elites call all the shots, nor that citizen participation is futile. Dahl argues that too often elite theorists form their pessimistic conclusions in the absence of "careful examination of a series of concrete decisions" ("A Critique of the Ruling Elite Model," 1997, p. 1001).

None of this is to say that Dahl finds American-style pluralism devoid of problems. He highlights how inequality of resources, strong differences in personal motivations, and profound differences in knowledge, information, and understanding can qualify the descriptive accuracy of pluralism and undermine its normative acceptability. Moreover, pluralism, like size, poses challenges to the ideal of citizen responsibility. These problems are so serious and intractable that "no altogether satisfactory solution seems yet to have been found" ("Pluralism Revisited," Dahl 1997, p. 311). Pluralism diminishes the importance, and even the possibility, of discovering the common good and giving it effect. As our identities splinter among competing associations, the particular goods of those associations get in the way of pursuing the common good, just as Rousseau expected (1978 [1762]). And because in a pluralist society policies typically hurt some groups even as they promote the interests of others, it becomes unclear whether any policy can unambiguously promote a common good. But if the common good is no longer identifiable, then public virtue, at least as defined as fidelity to the good of the public, cannot be known or taught. In pluralist societies, people who deny this and believe "that the public good is clear and self-evident" are not likely to adopt a helpful "spirit of civility" ("Is Civic Virtue a Relevant Ideal in a Pluralist Democracy?," Dahl 1997, p. 361). Their absolutism allows little room for tolerance, negotiation, or even listening.

Accordingly, Dahl promotes a citizen ethic appropriate to pluralist democracies that goes beyond self-interest but falls short of classical republican virtues (courage, self-sacrifice, moderation, readiness to take office). He calls this ethic "robust civility" ("Is Civic Virtue a Relevant Ideal in a Pluralist Democracy?," Dahl 1997, p. 372). Robust civility entails a commitment on the part of citizens to the process of democracy. The common good as a set of contentful propositions slowly disappears, like the Cheshire cat, with the diversification of society, but what must remain is the sense that the democratic process takes into account the interests of all persons without seeking to conflate them. Pluralist democracy is, in short, a risky departure from the position of Rousseau, but Dahl argues that the risks cannot be avoided—pluralism is inevitable and demands a strategy of tensions, trade-offs, and second-best solutions.

In addition to pluralism and large size, a third feature of modern democracy that Dahl fixes on for repeated treatment is democracy's place in a highly industrialized capitalist economy. Dahl's position is complex and defies easy categorization. One feature of his position is a readiness to believe that capitalism, broadly understood, supports democracy for two broad reasons. First, "a market-oriented capitalist system helps to create and sustain a considerable number of practices, structures, and attitudes that in turn help to sustain the political institutions" basic to democracy ("Introduction to Section 7: Economics, Politics, and Democracy," Dahl 1997, p. 548). The many private associations generated in a free economy and the large scope for personal freedom generally present, along with a widespread desire for autonomy, lead to welcoming (indeed insisting on) political freedom, representative government, and the rule of law. A second reason for holding that capitalism is favorable to democracy is that the alternatives to capitalism thus far tried have been grossly inefficient as well as incompatible with democratic norms and decentralization ("Introduction to Section 7: Economics, Politics, and Democracy," Dahl 1997, p. 548).

Yet all democracies regulate the economy for two inescapable reasons. First, and most obviously, unfettered free-market capitalism generates social disorders that can quickly become intolerable. Second, unregulated markets distort the political process. They undermine the legitimacy of democratic outcomes not only by enriching the war-chests of preferred candidates but also by dominating and biasing the information lawmakers need to make their choices. Left unregulated, corporations hold intolerable amounts of power over their workers and other persons as well. Indeed, Dahl urges his readers to take it as axiomatic that "every large corporation should be thought of as a political system, that is, an entity whose leaders exercise great power, influence, and control over other human beings" on the payroll and in the general public ("Governing the Giant Corporation," 1997, p. 630).

Even if one disagrees with Dahl's animadversions about corporations (which one of the present writers at least is far from doing), the analytical advances that he brings to the discussion compel admiration. Dahl carefully distinguishes between ownership and control, between centralized and decentralized decision making, between market and command economies, between personal private property and publicly created corporations, between efficiency taken narrowly and efficiency taken broadly, and between individual, cooperative, state, and social ownership of corporations. Dahl uses these distinctions to call for a corporate world that is responsive to market forces (and to the welfare of consumers) but that also places the good of its workers at the center of its decision making. Dahl would put decision making and—when possible—ownership in the hands of the workers. And if some decisions would be outside the competency of workers, the workers would have final say over who their surrogate decision makers are. Rather than responding to a far-away, unseen body of shareholders, managers would be responsive to other owners, the workers themselves.

Though still a pluralist, Dahl has shifted away from being reconciled in the main to the American system of government to being a radical critic of the system.

[Consider, by contrast, the position that he and Lindblom took in *Politics, Economics, and Welfare* (Dahl & Lindblom 1953), published at the high tide of the postwar consolidation of the welfare-state reforms of the New Deal; note the roseate concluding sentence of his *A Preface to Democratic Theory* (Dahl 1956) as well as the basic message of *Who Governs?* (Dahl 1961).] Or, rather, he has shifted back; as the biographical features of *Toward Democracy* make clear, Dahl began as a socialist. He is a radical critic, hampered, however, (*a*) by spurning the traditional socialist demand that the economy be nationalized under central planning, (*b*) by having no social movement to appeal to, (*c*) by his own work undermining the charges of radical elite theory, and (*d*) by his having brought with Lindblom the received issue of capitalism versus socialism effectively to an end by treating every politico-economic system as a mixture of market, hierarchy, bargaining, and polyarchy (Dahl & Lindblom 1953). The United States may still reasonably be thought to mix these things better than many other systems, including many self-described socialist systems. Dahl cannot perhaps acknowledge this without some discomfort. By arguing that democracy is "incompatible with a strictly free market economy" (because all democratic regimes have had to accept a mixed economy), Dahl takes on not only his libertarian critics but also, by implication, the very left-leaning critics with whom his sympathies most naturally lie ("Why All Democratic Countries Have Mixed Economies," Dahl 1997, p. 671).

POLYARCHY

Democracies today must solve their problems, so far as they can solve them, within the context of a large, pluralistic, capitalistic society. Participation, always problematic, has become almost intractably problematic. As a result, Dahl's career can be characterized, echoing his own words, as "an odyssey in search of adequate democratic theory," a theory that is simultaneously modern and democratic, just in respect to participation ("Introduction to Section 2: Democracy and Polyarchy: Theory," 1997, p. 52). The main theme of that odyssey, revisited repeatedly over the years, is his justly famous model of the basis for modern democracy: polyarchy. Offered in outline in *Politics, Economics, and Welfare* (Dahl & Lindblom 1953), in *A Preface to Democratic Theory* (Dahl 1956), and in *Polyarchy* (Dahl 1971), the fundamental dimensions have "pretty much remained unchanged" ("Introduction to Section 2: Democracy and Polyarchy: Theory," 1997, p. 48), though Dahl has continually elaborated and commented on them.

What is polyarchy? To begin with, polyarchy is not simply democracy, and certainly not democracy Athens-style or Rousseau-style. Like any fundamental political concept, polyarchy invites a number of interpretations. Dahl articulates five: polyarchy as a regime; as a product of democratizing nation states; as necessary to the democratic process; as a system of control by competition; and as a system of rights ("Polyarchy, Pluralism, and Scale," Dahl 1997, pp. 112–14). Each of these interpretations warrants a few words. First, compared to other kinds of regimes, polyarchy requires the presence of seven political institutions ("Polyarchy," Dahl 1997, pp. 94–95). At some cost to their impact, we simply list them here, omitting Dahl's immediate elaborations: elected officials, free and fair elections, inclusive suffrage, (an inclusive) right to run for office, freedom of expression, alternative sources of information (freedom of media), and associational autonomy (freedom of association).

The second interpretation of polyarchy associates it in particular with nation-states, of a size with which city-state democracy cannot cope ("Polyarchy, Pluralism, and Scale," Dahl 1997, p. 113). Polyarchy is not only a modern form of government but also a modern form of democracy. It did not exist in earlier eras because there was little need for it; different forms of democracy, which depended more on face-to-face interaction, prevailed. Our "occasional, intermittent, or part-time citizens" would hardly have been considered citizens at all in ancient city-state democracies ("The Problem of Civic Competence," Dahl 1997, p. 215). [Recall Rousseau's contention that for want of participation between elections, the British were not citizens between elections but slaves (1978, p. 102).]

A third perspective on polyarchy treats it as a necessary condition for the democratic process so far as this can be realized in the modern era. Democracy aims at complete self-governance for free and equal citizens. The institutions of polyarchy are necessary but not sufficient to achieve "the democratic process of government in a large scale system such as a nation state or a country" ("Polyarchy," Dahl 1997, p. 97). To be fully democratic, a state must also have effective participation, voting equality, opportunities for enlightened understanding (i.e., adequate opportunities for citizens to understand the issues facing them and the state), final control of the agenda by the citizenry, and inclusive citizenship. Polyarchy does not make sure of these things, though it does contribute to having them.

Dahl gives special attention to the problem of inclusive citizenship. The major part of "Procedural Democracy" (Dahl 1997, pp. 57–91) is devoted to a thorough, full-dress treatment of the subject, and he brings it up several other times. Historically, numbers, virtue, money, birth, and wisdom have all made claims to inclusion on a superior footing. Today the question of inclusion and rule has been answered for most of us; the people should rule. But the question remains: Which people are the people? This is a problem about which democratic theory has been surprisingly careless. Dahl warns us that our first impulse to allow a people to define itself is grievously mistaken. It suggests that "past might makes present right" ("The City in the Future of Democracy," Dahl 1997, p. 382). Even given a territory, allowing some of the people to exclude whomever they wish among the other inhabitants is a recipe for what we now call with disgust "ethnic cleansing," race crimes, and other forms of discrimination. The default position, according to Dahl, should reflect the assumption of citizen competence. All members of an association, except children, transients, and the mentally defective, should have their say ("Polyarchy," Dahl 1997, p. 97). Dahl firmly believes that the moral allure of democracy is so compelling that a strong burden of proof is placed on anyone who would defend or tolerate impediments to its full realization, including full inclusion. That full realization Dahl calls "full procedural democracy with respect to an agenda and in relation to its demos" ("Procedural Democracy," 1997, p. 65).

In a fourth perspective, polyarchy presents itself as "a system of control by competition" ("Polyarchy, Pluralism, and Scale," Dahl 1997, p. 113). Polyarchy is extraordinarily tolerant of opposition to the existing government and to the officials running it; and polyarchy provides ample opportunities for citizens to express that opposition. Citizens in a polyarchy may attempt with some hope of success to influence their government, and they may work successfully to some degree both to place their concerns on the policy agenda and to help determine the outcome of policy debate. Opposition parties—associations of all kinds—are therefore good and natural in polyarchy. So ingrained is the freedom of association in polyarchies that "it would be impossible to prevent relatively autonomous associations from existing in a modern society except by a very high level of coercion applied against them by the government of the state" ("Dilemmas of Pluralist Democracy: The Public Good of Which Public?," Dahl 1997, p. 346).

Last, Dahl interprets polyarchy as a system of rights. The rights that Dahl emphasizes are those necessary to protect and guarantee the institutions of polyarchy. In this approach, he departs quite radically from the standard liberal understanding of rights under the Constitution, which takes them to be personal protections (Held 1987, pp. 61–66). "Protective democracy" views government as a mechanism for protecting prepolitical (or private) interests, especially private property, against the claims of majoritarian rule. Against the view that rights can be antithetical to democracy, Dahl sees rights chiefly as establishing the conditions for good government to operate fairly, justly, and democratically. Rights are at root procedural, not sacred political attributes, not ontological features of persons. Free speech, for instance, is necessary to challenge government and to provide citizens not only with information but also with choices about their destiny. Dahl derives rights from democracy because he believes that the fundamental right is the procedural right of human beings to govern themselves ("Fundamental Rights in a Democratic Order," Dahl 1997, p. 208). And assuming for the moment that no one among us is a god, the basis for our self-governance ought to be the "equal consideration to the interests of all" ("Fundamental Rights in a Democratic Order," Dahl 1997, p. 207).

A superior, prepolitical right, then, is not simply a right against the state; it is a right against the democratic process (Dahl 1997, p. 207). Moreover, all experience shows that, contrary to the fears of anti-democrats, rights are best protected in nations with democratic governments. Though some democracies build into their systems protective devices, such as judicial review, aimed at protecting rights-holders against the encroachments of overbearing majorities, it is by no means clear that nations without such devices, such as Great Britain, have done any worse. Those protective devices, which always amount to Guardianship (governance by the experts) in one form or another, restrict the autonomy of citizens, which includes the freedom to disagree with experts and specialists. Though Dahl concedes that it would be "arbitrary and indefensible" to conclude that no right is ever superior to the democratic process, he makes a powerful case that recognizing such a right comes at a cost, namely Guardianship. Therefore "a heavy burden of proof" should be placed on those who would supplant the democratic process with Guardianship in any connection ("Fundamental Rights in a Democratic Order," Dahl 1997, p. 209).

Dahl takes great pains to distinguish polyarchy, in all its interpretations, from its alternatives. Not only is it distinguishable from many other regimes that do not get even this far toward democracy, it is also distinguishable from democracy in other forms. Given its emphasis on representative government, polyarchy cannot be associated with small-scale, directly participatory democracy. Neither is polyarchy to be confused with any utopian project. The presence of even a perfect democracy that confirms and supplements polyarchy by fulfilling the further criteria would not guarantee that decisions are made wisely, that the government is effective, or that the people are up to the task of solving the problems they face.

If polyarchy is not perfect or even the whole of democracy, it is at least good. How so? One of the deficiencies of *Toward Democracy* (1997) is that it largely omits Dahl's exploration of this question—secondary in concern in most of his works but something that he distinguishes for serious treatment in *Democracy and Its Critics* (1989) and *On Democracy* (1998). That being said, Dahl says enough in *Toward Democracy* for us to extract three defenses of democracy, and of polyarchy as a necessary condition and foundation of democracy. First, Dahl rejects alternatives to polyarchy because the alternatives to democracy are unacceptable. Dahl rejects Guardianship, in his mind the best of plausible alternatives to democracy, because Guardianship banks on what Dahl holds to be the indefensible proposition that some people are so much wiser and more virtuous than others that their rule can promote the good of all better than it can be promoted by giving everyone a voice. If we believe that all persons should be afforded equal consideration in government—Dahl's Equal Consideration criterion—then the state's "extraordinary influence, power, and authority, and the capacity of those who govern the state to control the resources, structures, agendas, and decisions of all other associations" make it extremely unwise for any portion of the sufficiently qualified adult population to abandon their voice and influence in government ("Procedural Democracy," Dahl 1997, p. 90).

A second reason for choosing democracy with polyarchy at its base is that democracy holds a superior moral vantage point to which we refer, if only unconsciously, even in justifying other regimes. If a nation were to choose any form of government from the ground up, so to speak, would it not have to do so democratically to have the choice ascribed to the nation? Moreover, the only way to determine whether the people want to maintain their nondemocratic government would be to consult them democratically ("From Personal History to Democratic Theory," Dahl 1997, pp. 9–10).

A third defense of democracy, hence of polyarchy, is that it protects or uniquely realizes genuine human goods. "The values that justify democracy are human, not parochial" (Dahl 1997, p. 9). These goods range from economic prosperity to peace with other democracies. But of all the goods generated by democracy, Dahl gives most weight to autonomy, the responsibility implied by autonomy, and reasonableness, especially deliberative reason. Indeed, democracy and reason are, finally, not fully separable for Dahl. Democracy itself is reasonable, at least at its best, because it affords the best political forum for genuine opposition, for argumentation, for the free exchange of ideas, for serious inquiry into alternative policies. Genuinely democratic decisions are not based on the authority of name, tradition, or money. Nor do genuinely democratic decisions express our raw, undeliberative preferences. They are genuinely democratic only when they reflect our considered judgments, developed in deliberation—reasoning together with other citizens, considering different points of view, and calling for information to reconcile the differences.

DEMOCRATIZATION: CHANCES OF SUCCESS AND SPECIAL PROBLEMS

To obtain democracy, further criteria must be met on top of polyarchy. But how, in the real world, is polyarchy itself to be obtained? What are the conditions that underlie its development and maintenance? What special problems does polyarchy contend with? Dahl addresses these questions extensively in his other works, especially *Polyarchy* (1971), *Dilemmas of Pluralist Democracy* (1982), *Democracy and its Critics* (1989), and *After the Revolution?* (1990). He is remarkably consistent in his answer, and what he says in *Toward Democracy* (1997) parallels what he says in those works. Though Dahl has been accused of unrealistic optimism about the contributions to social life that unimpeded democracy can offer (Ceaser 1986), it would be unfair to accuse him of being unduly confident about the possibility of democracy actually overcoming the real-world impediments that it faces. Dahl has tremendous faith in the capacity of ordinary persons to govern themselves, but he is also unflinching (given his behavioralist allegiance) in his determination to keep close to thorough observational data and in his acknowledgment of how far political practice falls short of the ideal in this respect. Dahl observes that the success of polyarchy (and, beyond, the other features of democracy) turns on the following:

1. *Democratic beliefs and culture.* A democracy can survive extremely challenging times—war, depression, and sharp ideological conflict—if its citizenry is deeply committed to democratic institutions. Data show, in fact, that it is *important* that ordinary citizens hold democratic opinions but *essential* that elites do (Dahl 1997, p. 468). Where those opinions are weak or challenged by nondemocratic beliefs, polyarchy has some difficulty in surviving. Cultural attitudes, which are transmitted intergenerationally, are extremely difficult to cultivate quickly, and so little can be expected in the way of quickly transforming nondemocratic regimes into thriving democratic regimes. Simple changes in constitutional form do not suffice.

    Even established polyarchies deal with the challenge, nowadays aggravated, of promoting enlightened understanding in citizens. Dahl does not

dismiss the importance of civic virtue in democracies; instead, he emphasizes that the virtues necessary and appropriate to democracies are not heroic.
The virtue that Dahl promotes, robust civility, stresses commitment to the
democratic process ("Is Civic Virtue a Relevant Ideal in a Pluralist Democracy?," 1997, p. 373). It requires translating our raw individual preferences
into public-regarding reasons. (On this point Dahl may be converging closer
than he realizes upon an objective common good.) A genuinely democratic
process requires that consequences be weighted, that deliberation be promoted, that decision making be truly public and transparent. It requires that
where people disagree about ends or outcomes, they work to identify and
put into use the fairest process for resolving debate. It requires them to stay
abreast, as much as possible, of current events and political developments.

   It is this last commitment that asks the most from citizens. The problem
of political ignorance grows more serious year by year. Not just information
but some theoretical understanding of events becomes more important as our
problems become increasingly complex and subject to rapid change ("The
Problem of Civic Competence," Dahl 1997, p. 220). Complexity in public
policy, ranging from stabilizing the ecosystem in the Florida Everglades to
projecting future revenues based on birth rates, not only makes it more difficult for ordinary citizens to solve problems, it also makes it more difficult for
them to understand, trust, or intelligently challenge their government ("The
Problem of Civic Competence," Dahl 1997, p. 217). None of us, experts
included, can understand, beyond the personal impacts of some policies,
more than the most general issues at any tolerable level of adequacy, and
in detail all of us are dependent upon experts other than ourselves to make
final decisions. Therefore, to an unprecedented degree, a serious problem is
simply deciding which surrogates of popular authority are trustworthy. The
result of the inevitable frustration induced by dealing with complex policy
issues is the tendency of politics as a meaningful activity to vanish from the
lives of more and more citizens. Over time, the alienation of citizens from
the democratic process undermines genuine self-government and autonomy.
Similarly, changes in scale erode the empathic understanding citizens have
for one another, a trait essential to making democracy work. That kind of
empathic understanding depends to a remarkable extent "on intimacy and
direct relationships, which in turn can exist only within small-scale groups"
("The Problem of Civic Competence," Dahl 1997, p. 221).

   The good news is that though the quality of democratic government cannot rise above the quality of the citizenry, the quality level of the citizenry
is not fixed. Humans respond, at least given encouragement, to the interests
of others. "The most fundamental and universal human feelings include not
only selfishness but also sympathy" ("Reflections on *A Preface to Democratic Theory*," Dahl 1997, p. 37).[2] Dahl repeatedly encourages experiments

_____

[2]On this point Dahl is allied with Hume (1888 [1739]).

with various democratic arrangements to improve understanding of problems, tolerance of others, and empathic understanding. Some of Dahl's proposed solutions are common fare among political scientists—for example, shifting, at least in the American case, to a parliamentary system based on multiple parties ("On Removing Certain Impediments to Democracy in the United States," Dahl 1997, p. 749). Another of his solutions involves fostering more face-to-face democracy. Dahl champions citizen assemblies, "minipopuluses," and similar devices such as the deliberative polls advocated by Fishkin (1995). Such devices offer innovative ways of discovering what citizens' opinion amounts to once it has been informed. The devices would increase both education and representation. They would not supplant Congress and other legislatures but would instead parallel the major standing committees of the legislatures in analyzing policy and making recommendations.

2. *Control of military and police*. The framers of the U.S. Constitution, both Federalists and anti-Federalists, were obsessed with the importance of keeping the military firmly under civilian control. Their fears were well founded. Dahl reminds us that on 50 occasions in the twentieth century, authoritarian regimes—some of them very repressive ones—replaced democracies, typically by military coups and dictatorships.

3. *Limits to heterogeneity*. As noted above, pluralism is "necessary, inevitable, and desirable" in a polyarchy ("Polyarchy, Pluralism, and Scale," Dahl 1997, p. 121). It is a natural product of freedom and is generally good for human beings. Diversity gives people more choice and leads to self-understanding. Where social cleavages are deep, however, and hinge on sharply differentiated subcultures based on religion, ideology, language, ethnic groups, and race, polyarchy falters. Special care must be taken in such situations, as in Switzerland and other consociational democracies, to reconcile the various groups peacefully.

   Polyarchies not only have difficulty accommodating extreme conflict, they may actually generate and exacerbate it. By allowing citizens to articulate their grievances freely and join associations to advance their causes, polyarchies place political weapons in the hands of people who may be culturally hostile to their fellow citizens. Unfortunately, in part because democratic theory offers little help in determining who a "people" is, civil war is always a possibility during times of extreme conflict, especially when what is at stake is the right of a subculture to participate in governance ("Polyarchy," Dahl 1997, p. 103).

   No easy solution exists to the problem of extreme cultural pluralism. However, Dahl believes that it is possible to learn "to tolerate differences that are not inherently conflictive, except in our minds, differences that do not reflect 'real' conflicts of interests, so to speak" ("Egoism, Altruism, and the Public Good," Dahl 1997, p. 340). Accordingly, Dahl views politics as most felicitous when driven by interests rather than ideology, identity, or religion. In this approach, Dahl agrees with Hume (1994 [1748]) that politics generally benefits to the extent that it is about interests rather than religion. Interest-based politics allows for bargaining and compromise, but a principle-based politics rests on honor, which does not easily admit of either. In taking this position, Dahl also follows Madison, who argues that "neither moral nor religious motives can be relied on as an adequate control" to factions (Madison et al. 1961, p. 81).

4. *Modern economic and social systems.* Market economies, with their attendant high levels of wealth, organizational pluralism, and widespread literacy and education, all contribute to the success of polyarchy. However, the correlation between capitalism and full democracy is not so encouraging. Dahl sums up his position as follows: "A market-oriented capitalist economy in a country has been favorable to democratization up to the level of polyarchy; but it is unfavorable to democratization beyond the level of polyarchy" ("Equality Versus Inequality," 1997, p. 147).

5. *Rule of law.* As one would expect, polyarchy flounders when arbitrary action rather than conformity to the rule of law prevails.

6. *Independence.* Obviously, even stable polyarchies can fall prey to stronger foreign powers hostile to polyarchy. However, the integrity of a nation's independence can be jeopardized by nonmilitary threats as well. Increasingly, the problem of internationalization has taken up much of Dahl's recent writings in, for example, *After the Revolution?* and *Democracy and Its Critics.* Internationalization also figures in *Toward Democracy*, but only fleetingly except in the essay "A Democratic Dilemma: System Effectiveness Versus Citizen Participation" (Dahl 1997, pp. 429–41). Nations are increasingly losing their autonomy as the problems they encounter become inescapably international. If democracy means self-governance, then the internationalization of political problems—whether they be military, economic, environmental, or cultural—deeply threatens the ability of any group of people, apart from every other people, to shape its collective destiny.

One of Dahl's most interesting and controversial positions regarding the success of polyarchies is the relatively light weight that he gives to constitutions (apart, we should say, from some basic set of procedural rights). He does strongly believe that the United States Constitution obstructs democracy to a significant degree ("Removing Certain Impediments to Democracy in the United States," Dahl 1997, pp. 733–36), but even the United States has had some success in realizing democracy. Not only do constitutional arrangements matter less in his view to the success of polyarchies than the criteria mentioned above, but their importance in shaping the quality of life even within established polyarchies is overrated. Dahl notes that among polyarchies, especially older ones, constitutional arrangements vary widely. They vary as to whether they are written; whether they contain a bill of rights; whether those rights, when recognized, are exclusively political or include economic or social rights; whether the government is federal or unitary; whether the legislature is unicameral or bicameral; whether judicial review is practiced; whether referenda are possible; and whether the government is presidential or parliamentarian. By most accounts, these differences are far from trivial. Dahl, however, boldly invites us to throw concerns about them to the winds. In stable democracies, "constitutional variations have no effect on the stability of basic democratic institutions" ("Thinking About Democratic Constitutions: Conclusions from Democratic Experience," Dahl 1997, p. 491).

Dahl should not be understood as saying that constitutions are never important. Where constitutions do seem to matter, however, American pride takes another hit. Dahl contends that parliamentary systems contribute to stability more than do presidential systems, at least for nations whose circumstances are not especially favorably suited to polyarchy. Taking his cue from Lijphart's (1984) work on consociational democracies, Dahl concludes that for nations with sharply divided societies, well-developed constitutional arrangements can provide stability, lead to transparency, and give a nation's various cultures a sense of political ownership.

EVALUATIVE DIALOGUE BETWEEN THE AUTHORS

DB: Michael, you took the lead in establishing the basic plan and content of our review of *Toward Democracy*. I think the review is accurate and well-balanced in what it makes of Dahl as a democratic theorist—though we could easily have used twice as much space. But might it not seem to others, even to us, that the points ascribed to Dahl are too familiar, even commonplace, to justify his reputation? Who, for example, would doubt that democracy requires free and fair elections?

MB: You're making myopically too much of an item-by-item review of the seven features of polyarchy, the further criteria for full democracy, and the conditions for democratization; and you're forgetting the controversial disdain for constitutions, the ambivalent judgment of capitalism, the special slant on rights, the powerful analysis and demolition of the ruling-elite model, and a number of other things. Separating the ideal of democracy from its basic institutional framework is, even today, a telling maneuver. You've also, for the moment, got things precisely backwards. We come to Dahl's work with our minds already formed by what he says. If the points that Dahl makes in assembling the features of polyarchy and of democracy beyond polyarchy seem familiar, that is because he has made them so or made them more so, in the course of assembling them and making them fully explicit. Not all of them were commonplaces to begin with (consider inclusive citizenship for one thing); and assembling the points, giving each a notably trenchant formulation, has been enormously useful.

DB: True; he is not for nothing the most prominent theorist steadily concerned with the basic dimensions of democracy. On this subject, his work is comparable in stature to what Rawls (1971) has done (also working in the spirit of democracy) on the neighboring subject of justice. Dahl has been very thorough in identifying the features of democracy that theory needs to treat and so trenchant in describing the features that his points have stuck. Furthermore, he has, in being trenchant, been a model of rigor—about as exact and rigorous as has any hope of winning widespread agreement in the present state of political science. In one essay ("The Concept of Power," Dahl 1997, pp. 849–75), he shows what he could do if he sought mathematical precision (at once with empirical application); but if he had sought that too often, might he not have become (as much of rational choice theory may have become) embroiled in futile controversy? Mathematical precision gives you some chance of being exactly—unsurpassedly exactly—right in your description of reality at the risk, a considerably greater risk, of being exactly wrong.

MB: Agreed. But Dahl too often for my taste sticks to the easily measurable at the cost of neglecting the bigger picture of how life is lived under democracy. His behavioralist methodology [described here in his famous essay, "The Behavioral Approach in Political Science: Epitaph for a Monument to a Successful Protest" (Dahl 1997, pp. 1089–109)], in other words, gets in the way of his developing the strengths that Tocqueville had in appreciating how politics affects persons. Dahl writes again and again about the institutions that constitute democracy, but he is almost silent about what democracy does to our souls (hearts, if you prefer). Family life, religion, friendship, art, and philosophy are all affected by the democratic ethos, but these subjects hardly show up on Dahl's intellectual radar screen. Dahl's writings clarify and discuss many trade-offs in political life, especially the trade-offs common within democracies, but strangely missing in Dahl is a full recognition of the trade-offs involved in adopting democracy itself. He is such a partisan of democracy that he hardly sees, as Tocqueville saw, that democracy itself (at least democracy pursued to its logical limits) may cost us some human goods. Democracy is desirable without qualification only when it is tempered to preserve other values such as stability, liberty, and deliberation, as well as the possibility of human greatness both in and out of public life. Isn't it revealing that Dahl, in the course of championing democracy, puts so much emphasis on participation? As Shaw says, "The problem with socialism is that it leaves you no free evenings."

DB: Dahl is sensitive to the possibility of demanding too much political activity from every citizen, though perhaps he is clearer about this, not in any of these essays, but in *After the Revolution?* (1990, pp. 40–56), where that possibility is checked by the Criterion of Economy, including economy of attention. But more important, and more doubtful, perhaps, is Dahl's reliance on multiplying jurisdictional arrangements (inside and outside politics strictly speaking) for increasing opportunities to participate. No doubt multiplying jurisdictional arrangements will increase the number of people taking part in deciding on the laws that are to govern them. More people will have a better sense of having effective influence. But does it get to the heart of the problem? Won't being just one participant among a thousand, not to speak of millions, preclude any real sense of effective personal influence? Or being just one among a hundred?

MB: But what, pray tell, can be done about that? And doesn't this conundrum prove that people are not altogether foolish to put their hearts into private life, where at least they can have some real say?

DB: Dahl, taking Rousseau again as a point of departure, might have modified the principle of being governed only by laws of one's own choosing on another line, which leads to putting a good deal of weight on a well-founded sense of vicarious participation. Would it not be important (and satisfying to a degree) to be able at least to say the law is one that I endorse? Suppose that endorsement has a footing both in my own political activity, including voting, and in the knowledge that (not accidentally) there were among the decision makers (or at least among the candidates for being decision makers) people who spoke for me and were listened to, even if they did not win any of the rounds? This vicarious participation is something that practical arrangements for legislation can provide more readily than they can a sense of effective personal influence. Moreover, it is something that can be strongly associated with citizens' responsibility in a democracy, not just to affirm their acceptance of its procedures by taking part in ceremonies like voting, but also to forego insincere and merely self-serving rejection of the results of those procedures, fairly carried out. Something like the idea of vicarious participation seems to hover on the threshold of Dahl's writings, though he does not capture it and pin it down. Moreover, Dahl's citizens' advisory councils can figure again here, offering a further footing for vicarious participation.

MB: You seem to have wandered away from the point about Dahl not giving enough weight to goods other than democracy and not necessarily embraced by it.

DB: Perhaps, though I would say that under both real and vicarious participation we may suppose that other goods would be at issue, including features of the common good like meeting basic needs that Dahl somewhat loosely leaves to the support of "enlightened" preferences. I think it must be admitted, however, that Dahl leaves the topic he refers to as "superior rights"—goods that may be at odds with democracy, at least at moments—in an unsatisfactory state. He does hold that it would be dangerous to assign the protection of superior rights to any agency not under the control of democratic procedures. This would be Guardianship, Platonic or Bolshevik. In one penetrating essay ("Decision Making in a Democracy: The Supreme Court as a National Policymaker," Dahl 1997, pp. 707–27) that we have not made much of, Dahl explodes the notion that a Supreme Court (the U.S. Supreme Court) can be relied on for a disinterested protection of basic rights. Would making sure that the Supreme Court was composed of sincere adherents to rights who continually took part in the give-and-take of jurisprudential discussions in a wider deliberative community, including academic lawyers as well as judges, make a difference? But how is one going to make sure of this? What test of intelligence and capacity to understand issues about rights would have kept Scalia off the Court? What is left? Nothing more than self-restraint on the part of the electorate. Can this be enough?

MB: Maybe not, as Dahl would have to admit. Yet it might be enough if, along with other elements of civic education, it is carefully cultivated, as Dahl would insist. Dahl is not only a democratic theorist, as everybody realizes. He is an un-remittingly radical democratic theorist who, like Dewey before him, believes that the cure to the problems of democracy is *more* democracy. But much of life is al-ready politicized, and certainly too much of life has fallen under micromanagment by the state.

DB: People don't like to be regulated, or to take time out of their lives to deal with regulators even if they have had some say in what the regulations are to be. But they also feel, most often quite reasonably, that they have not had enough say. This is just what Dahl wants to remedy. Remember, Dahl champions polyarchy and polyarchy improved by meeting further democratic conditions. It is a very firm ideal about democracy that he upholds, not just a cloud of democratic gas.

MB: I concede that Dahl takes important steps to oppose state imposition contrary to the preferences of the people, but more needs to be done in the way of delineating the appropriate use of power and authority given different social or institutional competencies. Dahl is typically sensitive to the many variations power and authority may take, but he cannot adequately explain what in life should *not* be subject to political control because he lacks a theory of how the several distinct social spheres relate one to another—though such a theory could be made out consistently with a robustly, if carefully circumscribed, democratic theory of the state. Dahl's omissions in this connection have important consequences, such as his relative tone-deafness on the problems and promises that religion, both in practice and thought, can pose in public life. For example, had Dahl tapped into the vast literature on subsidiarity, developed in recent decades mainly by Catholic thinkers, his principle of the "Chinese boxes" for nested jurisdictions could have been usefully amplified and elaborated.

DB: There may be room for religion in his perspective, but you're right, he has (like me, for one, and like Thomas Hobbes) little sympathy for religion in politics; or at least he expresses none. Religion has contributed to democracy at many times and in many places, for example, in the theory and practice of church governance and in humanitarian movements; but it has also assisted in the oppression of peoples and in the denial of rights—for example, to women. Does it not rely too much on mystery to be consistently controlled? Dahl is, besides being a radical democrat, a radical rationalist, not merely in respect to deliberation, but also in having no use for religious mysteries.

ACKNOWLEDGEMENT

Florian Bail of Dalhousie University did us the kindness of reading through a draft of this paper; and we have responded to his comments with a number of improving nuances.

The *Annual Review of Political Science* is online at
http://polisci.annualreviews.org

LITERATURE CITED

Bachrach P. 1967. *The Theory of Democratic Elitism: A Critique.* Boston: Little, Brown
Ceaser J. 1986. In defense of republican constitutionalism: a reply to Dahl. In *The Moral Foundations of the American Republic,* ed. RH Horwitz, pp. 253–91. Charlottesville: Univ. Press Va.

Dahl RA. 1950. *Congress and Foreign Policy.* Westport, CT: Greenwood

Dahl RA. 1956. *A Preface to Democratic Theory.* Chicago: Univ. Chicago Press

Dahl RA. 1961. *Who Governs?* New Haven, CT: Yale Univ. Press

Dahl RA. 1971. *Polyarchy.* New Haven, CT: Yale Univ. Press

Dahl RA, Tufte ER. 1973. *Size and Democracy.* Stanford, CA: Stanford Univ. Press

Dahl RA. 1982. *Dilemmas of Pluralist Democracy.* New Haven, CT: Yale Univ. Press

Dahl RA. 1989. *Democracy and Its Critics.* New Haven, CT: Yale Univ. Press

Dahl RA. 1990. *After the Revolution?* New Haven, CT: Yale Univ. Press

Dahl RA. 1997. *Toward Democracy—A Journey, Reflections: 1940–1997.* Berkeley, CA: Inst. Gov. Stud. Press

Dahl RA. 1998. *On Democracy.* New Haven, CT: Yale Univ. Press

Dahl RA, Lindblom CE. 1953. *Politics, Economics, and Welfare.* New York: Harper

Domhoff G. 1978. *Who Really Rules?* New Haven, CT: Yale Univ. Press

Fishkin J. 1995. *The Voice of the People: Public Opinion & Democracy.* New Haven, CT: Yale Univ. Press

Hamilton A, Madison J, Jay J. 1961 [1787–1788]. *The Federalist Papers,* ed. C Rossiter. New York: Mentor

Gaventa J. 1980. *Power and Powerlessness: Quiescence and Rebellion in an Appalachian Valley.* Chicago: Univ. Ill. Press

Held D. 1987. *Models of Democracy.* Stanford, CA: Stanford Univ. Press

Hume D. 1888 [1739]. *A Treatise of Human Nature,* ed. LA Selby-Bigge. Oxford, UK: Clarendon

Hume D. 1994 [1748]. Of parties in general. In *Hume: Political Essays,* ed. K Haakonssen, pp. 33–39. Cambridge, UK: Cambridge Univ. Press

Hume D. 1994 [1748]. Of the independency of Parliament. In *Hume: Political Essays,* ed. K Haakonssen, pp. 24–27. Cambridge, UK: Cambridge Univ. Press

Lijphart A. 1984. *Democracies: Patterns of Majoritarian and Consensus Government in Twenty-One Countries.* New Haven, CT: Yale Univ. Press

Lukes S. 1974. *Power: A Radical View.* London: Macmillan Educ.

Pye L. 1990. Review of *Democracy and Its Critics. Am. Polit. Sci. Rev.* 84:627–29

Rawls J. 1971. *A Theory of Justice.* Cambridge, MA: Harvard Univ. Press

Rousseau JJ. 1978 [1762]. *On the Social Contract.* New York: St. Martin's

Tocqueville A. 1969 [1848]. *Democracy in America,* ed. JP Mayer, transl. G Lawrence. New York: Harper/Perennial

Annu. Rev. Polit. Sci. 2003. 6:119–37
doi: 10.1146/annurev.polisci.6.010302.115514
First published online as a Review in Advance on Jan. 8, 2003

Bringing Robert A. Dahl's Theory of Democracy to Europe

Sergio Fabbrini

Department of Sociology and Social Research, Università degli Studi di Trento, via Verdi, 26, 38100 Trento, Italy; email: fabbrini@soc.unitn.it

Key Words   pluralism, separation of powers, judicial review, institutions

■ **Abstract**   The recent publication of all the essays and articles written by Robert A. Dahl between 1940 and 1997 is an occasion to note the capacity of Dahl's theory of democracy to address specific problems within specific democratic countries. This review draws the threads of Dahl's work together and then applies them to the European situation. Its aim is not only to give coherence to Dahl's lifelong research project but also to show that his theory may help identify the basic institutional and normative questions that the political development of European integration has to answer.

INTRODUCTION

Robert A. Dahl is universally considered one of the greatest living scholars of contemporary democracy and democratic theory (along with Giovanni Sartori and a few others). Although well-known among European political scientists, Dahl deserves to be regarded as a standard for reflection on politics by a broader European public. The decision by the Institute of Governmental Studies (IGS) of the University of California at Berkeley to collect, in two bulky volumes totaling 1157 pages, all the articles and essays published by Dahl during 1940–1997 (Dahl 1997) furnished an occasion to introduce him to a larger audience. With this undertaking, IGS has enabled the international community of political scientists to grasp the inner coherence of the research pursued by Dahl for half a century, and to appreciate the moral integrity of a scholar distinguished by his intellectual rigor and civic commitment.

Here, I draw together the threads of Dahl's work, keeping in mind some of the central issues in contemporary European politics. This accounts for the division of the article into four parts. The first concerns relationships between democracy and organizational pluralism; the second concerns relationships between institutional pluralism and separation of powers; the third concerns the relationship between citizens' rights and judicial system; and the fourth concerns the interpretation of the public good. The discussion of these topics brings out crucial and correlated components of Dahl's theory of democracy. My ambition is to show that Dahl's theory of democracy, as it is framed here, might be very helpful to scholars of European integration (and, if my method is appropriate, to scholars of European national democracies as well).

DEMOCRACY AND ORGANIZATIONAL PLURALISM

It was only after World War II that the relationship between democracy and the market once again became a central concern of scholars of democracy. This was largely the work of Dahl, who along with Charles Lindblom contributed decisively to the revival of political economy after the divorce of neoclassical economics from political science in the late nineteenth century. Like all divorces, this one had harmful aftereffects, primarily a widespread tendency by economists to despise politics and an equally widespread tendency by political scientists to ignore economics. Dahl attempted, with some success, to restore the tradition of political economy—with such celebrated scholars as Adam Smith, David Ricardo, and Karl Marx as its founders—to its former status. He did so by providing an original and innovative interpretation of the relationship between economics and politics.

It was original and innovative because although Dahl is a convinced defender of democracy, he has never gainsaid the contradictory nature of the relationship between democracy and the market. It is a relationship, one might say, with a twofold outcome, in that some features of the market foster the growth of democracy but others constrain it once it has begun. The fostering relationship is demonstrated by the fact that although there has never been a democratic regime in the absence of a capitalist market system, there have been several capitalist market systems that have not been associated with a democratic regime. The constraining relationship is demonstrated by the fact that although a democratic regime is safest in a capitalist market system, such market systems have nonetheless prevented democratic regimes from fully developing their potential.

It is this latter case that is of the greatest interest to Dahl. And it is precisely with reference to the market democracies that he (along with Lindblom) coined the term polyarchy. Polyarchies are democracies that, although well-consolidated, are not fully democratized. They are not fully democratized because their egalitarian promise has been impossible to fulfill in the conditions of a nonegalitarian economic order. Yet, although the market has historically hampered the growth of democracy, democracy has mitigated these inegalitarian effects by acting politically on the market. The result has been that as the market has interacted with democracy, it has become much less inegalitarian than it might have been or than it was at the beginning of its historical interaction with democracy. This outcome has both confounded capitalism's critics and disappointed its defenders, in the sense that the market democracies are less than the critics want but much more than the defenders are willing to concede.

For Dahl, a polyarchy springs from the pluralistic nature of the market and, especially, democracy. Polyarchy and organizational pluralism are mutually supportive;

indeed, one may say that pluralism is intrinsic to modern democracy. However, one must remember that pluralism is (theoretically and in practice) an American invention—an invention that owes a substantial amount to the distinctive religious experience at the origin of the "first new nation" in the West. [This is the now classic thesis advanced by Lipset (1976, 1996).] After all, a nation born from a plurality of communities made up of fugitive heretics from the Old World could not adopt a monistic model of religious organization. Not only the distinction between religion and state, but the very recognition of religious pluralism, derived from political necessity rather than from ideological choice. And naturally, once religious pluralism had been accepted, social, cultural, and political pluralism became easier to accept and to promote.

Nevertheless, Dahl is fully aware of the negative or undesired effects of pluralism on the functioning of democracy. Pluralism entails, in fact, the use of a resource—the organization—that is unequally distributed among interests and individuals. Thus, social groups with greater ability or opportunity for self-organization tend to exert greater influence on public decision making than do groups with less ability or opportunity. Consequently, once a particular trajectory has been imposed on public decisions, the well-organized groups will be able to preserve it to the detriment of the less well-organized.

Although freedom of association is normatively constitutive of democracy, its use has in practice become a factor in democracy's curtailment, in the sense that public policy tends to reflect the interests of well-organized groups. Such an outcome, however, cannot be neutralized by abolishing organizational pluralism. This would undermine democracy itself, rather than reduce inequality, because it would be necessary to abolish one of the freedoms—in this case freedom of association—that makes democracy possible. As Madison wrote in *Federalist* 10, "Liberty is to faction what air is to fire, an element without which it instantly expires. But it could not be less folly to abolish liberty, which is essential to political life, because it nourishes faction, than it would be to wish the annihilation of air, which is essential to animal life, because it imparts to fire its destructive energy" (quoted in Beard 1964, p. 69).

What is to be done? For Dahl, any solution must be subjected to empirical verification, given that by definition there is no universally satisfactory solution in a democracy. Moreover, no solution can be satisfactory unless it starts from the realization that pluralism is by nature inegalitarian, because some economic, social, and cultural interests have sufficient resources to bend public decisions to their own purposes, to the detriment of other interests without those resources. This realization is especially necessary in Europe, where pluralism is becoming the predominant mode of the policy-making process at the Community level. If neocorporatism has been the predominant mode of organization of the policy-making process at the level of the European nation-states, the European Union (EU) policy-making pattern is not structured around the bargaining between very few, encompassing and centralized associations and the representatives of governmental institutions. In the "disjointed and competitive setting of the EU," Schmitter writes (2000, p. 36),

"Euro-associations may not be preferred over more specialized ones. They must compete for influence with a wide variety of other units: national states, parastate corporations, subnational governments, large private firms, and even lobbyists and lawyers intervening on behalf of individual clients. The policy outcomes become less predictable. . . . The power of public coercion is blunted. . . . The most accurate appellation for this system of interest intermediation is *pluralism*." In sum, the EU is more similar to the United States than to the EU member states.

Unfamiliar with pluralism, EU officials and leaders seem to have undervalued its undesired implications. In order to address the criticism that the EU policy-making process is not sufficiently democratic (the so-called democratic deficit criticism), the EU institutions (and the Commission in particular) paradoxically reinforced that criticism by looking for the support (and the involvement) of a growing number of interest groups. Schmitter observes (2000, p. 81), "Especially since the signing of the Single European Act in 1985, Brussels has been literally invaded by 'Euro-lobbies'. . . . While all this pluralism (to use the American expression) is entirely appropriate in modern democracy, its highly skewed nature does raise some questions about whether these channels for the expression of particular interests are freely and fairly available to all citizens of Europe. So far, the evidence suggests a mobilization of bias in favor of business interests." This is not a novel experience for the United States, where the development of organizational pluralism has both impaired the individual basis of the democratic system—as Lowi (1969) argued—and institutionalized a pro-business bias in the policy-making process, although business interests never perceived the federal state as "their own" (Skocpol 1992).

Moreover, also at the level of the EU member states, new structural transformations are challenging old institutional solutions. In fact, once European leaders and publics recognized the impracticability (in a global economy) of the traditional strategies of nationalization and/or public control of the main economic sectors in order to tame the negative externalities of the market, then the democratic system appeared to lack barriers against the influences of market forces on the political process. For example, in Italy, after the traditional parties collapsed in the early 1990s, the best-organized interests were able to transfer their power directly from the market to the public institutions, from the economy to politics, without encountering regulatory or legislative constraints. A media tycoon has created a whole new political party out of his business organization that in a few years has become the country's largest party. Without giving up control of his media empire, Silvio Berlusconi was nominated Prime Minister twice, in 1974 and 2001. Not surprisingly, therefore, Italy still has no legislation on conflict of interest (intended to prevent the coincidence of economic and political interests). Nor does it have legislation to regulate the power of blackmail exerted by functional interest groups in order to increase their bargaining power, to the detriment of the rights of citizens. Nor, moreover, does it have legislation to favor full-fledged market competition and undermine monopolist or rent positions, and this lack encourages the interweaving of economic and financial monopolies with political interests. And this is true also for other European countries, especially Eastern ones.

Dahl's analysis thus provides valuable insights for Europeans who wish to introduce a democratic political economy, based on (*a*) regulating pressure groups' power in order to guarantee some influence to less-organized interests and (*b*) regulating conflict of interest in order to impede the private use of public authority.

INSTITUTIONAL PLURALISM AND SEPARATION OF POWERS

We should reflect more on pluralism, given its crucial importance in Dahl's view of democracy. Organizational pluralism is a distinctive feature of societies with differentiated interests, which results in different interpretations of the public or common good, defined by Dahl (1997, 1:277) as "the good of all, the good of the city." Only very small societies can embrace the unitary vision of the public good cultivated by the Athenians of the fifth century BC, and also by Jean Jacques Rousseau, who on the basis of ancient Athens maintained (with qualifications) that a democracy can remain a democracy only if it remains small. For the first time in history, this view was radically questioned during the debate at the Constitutional Convention of Philadelphia that led to the drafting of the (second) Constitution of the United States in 1787.

On that occasion, a veritable Copernican revolution was wrought in democratic political theory, and this revolution was mainly James Madison's work. Madison saw in small size exactly the opposite of what Rousseau and all other political thinkers had seen. Madison believed the small democracies had perished because they lacked effective treatments for the mortal disease of factionalism. This, Madison argued, was a disease that only a large-scale democracy could cure. As he put it in *Federalist* 10, in the large democracies the factionalism that arises on one side or the other can be diluted across a broader area, or at least counterbalanced by an opposing factionalism arising from some other part of that broad area. In sum, "extend the sphere, and you take in a greater variety of parties and interests; you make it less probable that a majority of the whole will have a common motive to invade the rights of other citizens; or if such a common motive exists, it will be more difficult for all who feel it to discover their own strength, and to act in unison with each other" (Madison quoted in Beard 1964, p. 74). Thus, in contrast to a post-1789 Europe still seeking to establish a monistic model of political organization (a "fusion of powers" system) stood a post-1787 America that established a pluralistic model (a "separation of powers" system). This model, along with other extraordinarily favorable circumstances, has helped protect American democracy against authoritarianism and totalitarianism, which the monistic model in Europe has failed to do.

However, Dahl argues, it is in the United States that institutional pluralism has revealed its defects. The absence of centralized authority fostered the conditions (also institutional) that gave rise to the bloody Civil War of 1861–1865. Thereafter, the institutionalization of pluralism in the form of a separation-of-powers system (that is, a system based on reciprocal electoral and institutional independence between the President, the two chambers of the Congress, and the judiciary) helped to preserve the inequalities of income, wealth, status, information, and opportunity produced by the market economy and the culture of racial segregation. Why? Because the American system, implying diffusion and fragmentation of power, tends to institutionalize multiple veto points. This happens in all power-sharing systems, where a decision can be made only through the consent of a large number of actors endowed with specific institutional resources that might be used to block or postpone an undesired policy outcome (Tsebelis 2002). This institutional context is (and was) a powerful barrier against choices not supported by a wide consensus. But this context is (and was) also a powerful aid to minorities interested in preventing any change that might challenge their social, economic, or political status or privileges. Indeed, even today, American institutional pluralism penalizes blacks, minorities, women, and the poor, all of whom have fewer resources with which to join the "pluralistic game" (see Shklar 1991 for an historical analysis of the problem).

Consequently, while American separation of powers has prevented the tyranny of (diffused) majorities it has facilitated domination by (concentrated) minorities. It has saved American democracy, but it has also made it less egalitarian than other democracies. In large democracies with pronounced heterogeneity of territorial, ethnic, racial, social, economic, and ideological interests, it is extremely difficult to construct political coalitions to bring about change (e.g., the abolition of segregation, the promotion of redistributive policies, the introduction of universalistic social security). It is much easier to construct negative political coalitions for conservation of existing policies. In Dahl's view, American separation of powers has institutionalized a bias in favor of continuity. It is evident that this institutional system is an effective antidote against any hierarchical or paternalistic conception of the public good imposed from above (by the state). But it is less effective in counteracting conceptions that engender unequal relations among groups and individuals, even though they arise from below (from society). As a consequence, the United States has always faced the need to redress the balance among functional interests and stimulate the policy and political aggregation of fragmented interests. It was this endeavor that drove progressive liberalism during the twentieth century (see Brinkley 1995, 1998 for the most thorough treatment of this topic).

These considerations provide the basis for one of Dahl's most closely argued criticisms of the American political system. Having judged Madisonian democracy as decidedly antimajoritarian, he later tempers this interpretation with an acknowledgment that Madison did not greatly favor the "consensual model" of democracy (to use the contemporary expression); nevertheless, Dahl maintains that the historical development of Madisonian democracy led to the formation of a system of government that finds it difficult to aggregate fragmented interests and to counterbalance stronger organized and concentrated interests. [Elsewhere I have called this system "separated government" (Fabbrini 1999).]

In the United States, the growth of the modern presidency since the 1930s has been a response to the necessity of aggregating fragmented interests to produce a reasonably coherent political majority. But the presidency has constantly had to take account of the power of Congress, protected and fostered as it is by the separation of powers. This power is so substantial (especially in domestic politics) that it has no equivalent in any other Western legislature (Polsby 1997); Dahl has called America's a "presidential-congressional" government, as opposed to a presidential system in the conventional sense of the term.[1] Obviously, although this system needs parties to connect the various separate institutions so that it can function, it is not particularly hospitable to them, given that the institutional arenas in which the parties must act are so differentiated that their inner cohesion breaks down.

Thus, the United States, the democracy with the oldest political parties, is also the one with the weakest, as judged by their influence over the electorate and their ability to govern. According to Dahl (1994), this feature accounts for the "new political (dis)order" of American democracy, in that separated institutions—because they reciprocally reinforce and legitimate each other—hamper the aggregation of interests, and also of electors. In Dahl's view, when fragmented interests are unable to produce coherent majorities, then conditions are conducive to the interests of the stronger minorities. Once again, however, Dahl is careful not to throw the baby out with the bathwater. He also emphasizes the ability of those institutions to respond (though not uniformly) to the demands of citizens, and to guarantee their right to advance those demands. He does not propose a radical constitutional transformation of the American system, for instance in the direction of a parliamentary system. To be sure, he advances several institutional and constitutional proposals to strengthen the capacity of political parties to control the policy-making process; he even urges (Dahl 2001) the adoption of a sort of proportional representation electoral system. Nevertheless, Dahl's prescriptions remain within the American tradition of "separated institutions sharing power" (Neustadt 1990, p. 29).

Dahl's analysis is particularly useful for understanding EU political systems. Although not by constitutional design (as in the American case), the EU has gradually acquired the institutional features of a separation-of-powers governmental system. The main EU institutions (such as the European Council, the European Parliament, and the European Commission) are reciprocally independent. The Council represents the governmental leaders of the EU member states, the Parliament represents their electors, and the Commission is a sort of executive, chosen by the Council and approved by the Parliament but operationally independent from both. In fact, the Commission's president does not represent the political majority of the Parliament, nor that of the Council. Moreover, the decision-making power is so diffused in the EU governmental system that scholars have appropriately called it a "confusion of power system" (Schmidt 1997). Although the Commission has a monopoly on legislative initiative, the Council and the Parliament have to approve any law through differentiated and cumbersome procedures (the Council can adopt 25 different legislative procedures, which imply an equivalent number of different

---

[1]"[T]he American presidential system is unique. Incidentally, one might better call it the presidential-congressional system, because probably no other legislature in the world is as influential as the U.S. Congress" (Dahl 1997, p. 14).

institutional modalities of parliamentary involvement in law making). As Coultrap (1999, p. 127) remarks, "A comparison between the EU and the US highlights the essential similarities between the two systems."

Moreover, at the EU level, the political parties are significantly weak. They are confederations of state and regional organizations rather than political agencies identified by a program or an ideology. In Brussels, as in Washington, D.C., the diffusion of power complicates the life of the parties. Their capacity to aggregate interests and values is very low. Decisions arise from multiple negotiations between multiple actors in multiple arenas. As Scharpf (1988) explains, this system implies a "joint decision trap": Because a large consensus is needed to change the policy status quo, the outcome will be as close as possible to the policy status quo. Again, in this system, powerful national or subnational actors can exercise an effective veto power through their control of one of the many arenas in which the decision-making process has to take place. Institutionally nested veto powers prevent undesired decisions, but they also prevent the adoption of popular decisions that would challenge the power of powerful (national, economic, or social) actors.

The political disorder of the EU has been so evident that, in December 2001, the member states' leaders decided to convene a "constitutional convention for the future of Europe" to give some order to the Community institutional system. The convention will have to draft a "constitutional treaty" by 2003, which will then be discussed and approved by an Intergovernmental Conference (comprising the heads of state and government of the EU member states) before 2004—the year in which 10 new Central Eastern and Southern European states will join the EU and participate in the election of the European Parliament. It is too early to know whether the convention can solve the problems of the EU political disorder. But it is sure that Dahl's analysis could be useful to the EU constitution makers, because it could free them from the limitation of looking at the EU through the lens of European nation-states' experience. The EU is much more complicated than each of the EU member states, and this complexity may be managed only through institutional solutions more innovative than the traditional parliamentary ones.

CITIZENS' RIGHTS AND JUDICIAL POWER

Schattschneider, one of the greatest American political scientists of the postwar period, wrote that "democracy was created for the citizens, and not vice versa" (1975 [1960], p. 132). This is the point of view Dahl adopted to investigate democracy; after all, very little can be understood of democracy when it is viewed from the standpoint of those who have little interest in it because they already possess sufficient resources of power or influence, irrespective of democracy. It is the ordinary citizen, Thomas Paine's common man, who has the greatest need of democracy to advance his interests and aspirations (see Foot & Kramnick 1987 for a useful introduction to Paine's thought).

This emphasis on the ordinary citizen underlies Dahl's analysis of the relationship between democracy and citizenship. The analysis is, of course, conducted within the American political tradition, which has always considered rights as a natural prerogative of individuals and not as a concession of the state. For Dahl, the polyarchic democracies are marked by their respect for certain basic criteria of democracy. These criteria should guide the definition of the primary rights that turn an individual into a citizen. Moreover, these primary rights are not necessarily mutually compatible, and their exercise may have nondemocratic implications. For example, the consequence of the right to vote and its translation into majority decision making might be, in the absence of a specific constitutional protection, the denial of primary rights to the minority. Historically, whereas in Europe this possible contradiction between the rights of some and the rights of others has been resolved politically through parliamentary action, in the United States the solution to this possible contradiction has been removed from the political arena (i.e., Congress). This has been possible because, since the beginnings of the new republic, it has been the practice to recognize the existence of rights of a higher order than primary rights: those enshrined in the Constitution (or rather in its first 10 amendments of 1791, known as the Bill of Rights), which are unchallenged by contingent political majorities.

The point is that in the United States it was the judiciary that imposed itself as the last guarantor of those constitutionally enumerated rights of higher order. Since the historic decision by the Supreme Court (and in particular by its Chief Justice, John Marshall) in the *Marbury v. Madison* case of 1803,[2] a dualistic view of the Constitution has prevailed, dualistic in the sense explained by Ackerman (1991, p. 13): "the dualist believes that the Court furthers the cause of democracy when it preserves constitutional rights against erosion by politically ascendant elites who have yet to mobilize the People to support the repeal of previous higher lawmaking principles. Thus, unlike the monist, she will have no trouble supporting the idea that rights can properly trump the conclusions of normal democratic politics."

Of course, it is important not to confound (American) judicial review, celebrated by that early nineteenth-century Supreme Court ruling, with (European) constitutional review, introduced in most European constitutions in the second half of the twentieth century. In the American model of judicial review, Shapiro & Stone (1994, p. 400) remind us, "any judge of any court, in any case, at any time, at the behest of any litigant party, has the power to declare a law unconstitutional." Not so in Europe, where the "judiciaries do not possess jurisdiction over the constitution" (Stone Sweet 2000, p. 33). In Europe, this jurisdiction has been assigned to a special constitutional court, which operates in a legal space that is neither judicial nor political. The American separation-of-powers system, implying the formal equality of the executive, legislative, and judicial branches of government vis à vis the constitution, makes judicial review possible. "In contrast," writes Stone Sweet (2000, p. 32), "the subordination of the work of the judiciary to that of the legislature is a foundational principle of civil law systems, and therefore of Continental constitutional law."

---

[2]On the importance of this decision and its link with the previous colonial tradition, see Clinton (1989).

Moreover, whereas the American Constitution is at the apex of a hierarchy of legal norms the judges must protect, European constitutional laws are "formally detached from the hierarchy of laws which European judges are otherwise responsible for applying and defending" (Stone Sweet 2000, p. 33). Thus, postwar Europe adapted the principle of judicial review to its tradition of parliamentary sovereignty. In Europe, exclusive and final constitutional jurisdiction has been assigned to constitutional courts and not to the judiciary as in America. European constitutional courts are formally detached from both the judiciary and the legislature, whereas the American Supreme Court is the highest level of the judicial system. In Europe, "ordinary courts remain bound by the supremacy of the statute (legislation), while constitutional judges are charged with preserving the supremacy of the constitution" (Stone Sweet 2000, p. 34). In sum, in Europe, constitutional courts are restricted to the settlement of constitutional disputes, whereas in America the Supreme Court may settle all judicial disputes. The European model of constitutional review recognizes that, in post-authoritarian Europe, legislative supremacy has to conform to constitutional law, but this recognition does not extend the power of judicial review to ordinary judges.

Of course, historically, the U.S. Supreme Court or the judiciary has not always acted on behalf of rights of the higher order; indeed, in some cases it was Congress that upheld them. Nevertheless, with formalization of the principle of judicial review (that is, a judicial body's examination of the laws approved by Congress to ensure their conformity with the Constitution, or with the current interpretation of it), the conditions were created to distinguish between the contingent popular will (as represented in the various majorities in the various institutions of separated government) and the permanent public will (as expressed in the Constitution). In short, whereas in Europe the two have long tended to coincide, in the United States they never have, because of the role of judicial power in guaranteeing the pact between citizens and public institutions.

The decision to entrust the protection of superior rights to a nonelective institution is not without its incongruities if evaluated in the light of democratic principles. It implies, in fact, the acknowledgment that, in its ordinary functioning, the democratic process may not be sufficient to guarantee the primary rights of all citizens. This accounts for the use of guardians—the members of a judicial body relatively independent of the popular will—to supervise the popular will lest it threaten those rights. In a democracy, the democratic process may be subjected to nondemocratic (but not necessarily antidemocratic) constraints in the belief that it may not be able to guarantee its own democratic nature. Of course, insistence on the need for guardians is traditionally associated with conservative factions that have never entirely accepted the egalitarian implications of popular sovereignty. The socially and culturally elitist leanings of these factions have always made them suspicious of the common man's ascent to power. And there is no doubt that some of the proponents of guardianship during the debate at Philadelphia in 1787[3] saw the existence of judicial guardians as vital for the protection of the

---

[3]Still indispensable on this topic is Farrand (1966).

social and economic privileges of the dominant groups against possible attack by the representatives of the common man (that is, the members of the House of Representatives).[4]

Dahl, however, is not at ease with guardians, not only because he is a democrat but also because, as Shapiro (1988) has thoroughly established, no satisfactory answer has yet been given to the question "Who guards the guardians?" in a democracy. The question has become more urgent, one suspects, after the December 2000 decision of the Supreme Court regarding the unconstitutionality of the recounting of the presidential votes in some Florida electoral districts. In this regard, Dahl's sympathies lie with the European tradition, or with those democracies in which the exercise of the popular will is not limited by the existence of any nondemocratic institution. He prefers the vices of democracy to the virtues of nondemocracy. The absence of guardians, he argues, may encourage the representatives of the popular will to show greater self-control in the exercise of their powers. By contrast, the presence of such guardians may induce the popular representatives to evade their responsibilities. In a democracy, even mistakes serve a purpose: They heighten awareness, among both the representatives and the represented, of democracy's complexity. In short, it is Dahl's view that those who favor the existence of guardians in a democracy carry the burden of proof; they must demonstrate that guardians are necessary to guarantee democracy itself, particularly against unprecedented and threatening challenges for which it may be ill-prepared.

Yet the challenges to democracy may be multiple, and when they combine, they may distort the democratic process so that certain fundamental individual rights are not respected. It has already happened in Europe, and in Italy and Germany foremost, that the democratic process has ended up destroying itself; unfortunately, the Europeans have already assumed the burden of proof. Careful analysis is necessary, especially regarding the role of the judiciary, which only with great difficulty—and only recently—has managed to achieve autonomy from political power (that is, the representatives of the popular will). Consequently, one may ask, is it wiser to assign the defense of superior rights to the representatives of the popular will or to judicial guardians? Although Dahl prefers the former solution, the historical experience of Europe provides counterexamples. Moreover, the "constitutional" direction in which the EU has evolved seems to have given the European Court of Justice (ECJ) and domestic judiciaries a power of judicial review over national legislation unknown to the constitutional courts of the individual European countries. In fact, by imposing the supremacy of Community laws over domestic ones, the ECJ has created the legal conditions for favoring, within the scope of the Treaties, a process of judicial review in the EU member states. On the basis of art. 234 (previous art. 177) of the European Community Treaty, domestic courts (without exception) can refer to the ECJ whenever a domestic piece of legislation appears to be in conflict with Community laws, bypassing the domestic constitutional court. It is the domestic judiciaries that have to adopt and implement ECJ rulings. And

---

[4]The Senate was elitist in character and remained so at least until 1913, and arguably afterward.

they have, thus challenging de facto the principle of parliamentary supremacy. Of course, this practice concerns domestic legislation, not Community legislation.

Thus, it seems that Dahl looks to Europe precisely when Europe is growing closer to America. Both at the nation-state and Community levels, Europe is witnessing a process of judicialization of politics that has no precedent in its democratic experience. More and more, European leaders and representatives "govern with judges," as Stone Sweet (2000) aptly argued. This increasing role of the judiciary is obviously connected to the decreasing influence of political parties and representative institutions. Moreover, the power of the judiciary has been strengthened, at the EU level, by the separation of powers that was gradually institutionalized since its foundation in the 1950s. The EU undoubtedly would have constrained the policy-making role of the Court had it been informed by the principle of parliamentary sovereignty. This is a very new challenge for European leaders and publics. Dahl's analysis provides an interesting reference for thinking more thoroughly and critically on this matter.

INSTITUTIONS AND THE PUBLIC GOOD

Although in the United States large size and a plurality of interests have helped to neutralize the effects of factionalism, both features have made it difficult to define a common good that is recognized as such by the entire political entity. Of course, in extraordinary circumstances (war, for example), the common good (security or peace) is self-evident, but such circumstances are exceptional. This means that modern democracies require cooperation on a large scale, because the greater the number of people in a given community, the more diverse their interests become and the more problems there are to solve (a problem unknown to monistic Athenian society).

On what individual bases can this social cooperation be promoted or achieved? Dahl discusses two possible options. The first answer is provided by the economic theory of politics. By conceiving politics as the functional equivalent of the market, this theory assumes that the pursuit of selfish ends must necessarily produce a satisfactory collective outcome. The second answer is suggested by the communitarian theory of politics. By conceiving politics as the functional equivalent of the civic republic, this theory assumes that the pursuit of collective altruistic ends must inevitably produce a satisfactory individual outcome. For Dahl, neither answer is convincing; interindividual cooperation cannot be achieved on the basis of either selfishness or altruism.

The selfishness hypothesis is empirically unjustified. Although in contemporary democracies the public good is not clear or self-evident, there is no disputing the antisocial effects of interaction based solely on the pursuit of individual interests (as happens in all zero-sum and negative-sum games). Moreover, Dahl points out, as they accumulate, these effects may undermine the very legitimacy of the pluralist system. The altruism hypothesis is also empirically unjustified because, although in contemporary democracies there is a common good to pursue, physical and psychological distance and the plethora of interests involved do not foster reciprocal benevolence among individuals. In short, neither the hyperegoism posited by neoclassical economic theory nor the civic virtue proposed by communitarian political theory can help us to understand what social cooperation really is, why it occurs, and above all how we might expand and improve it.

From this impasse Dahl's normative question is derived: Is there an alternative to the politics of egoism and of altruism? His answer once again is realistic. When we talk about the public good, we can never answer the question, "*What* public?" Therefore, the solution to the problem of fostering social cooperation lies not in its substance but in the process that may give rise to it. To those who believe that they already have a normative answer to the question, Dahl's solution may appear unsatisfactory. In the past, radicals of various persuasions regarded Dahl as a mere defender of "procedural democracy," and an American one at that. But in reality, Dahl's position is anything but a simple celebration of procedures. For Dahl, procedures take concrete form in institutional arrangements that can be justified only on the basis of their compliance with the fundamental principles of democracy. This amounts to saying that institutions must be neutral with respect to the specific outcomes of political competition or conflict, but they cannot be neutral with respect to the value premises that justify their existence and their regulatory roles. (See Przeworski 1991 on these implicitly normative characteristics of institutional rules and procedures.)

While distinguishing him from the postwar pluralist approach (in whose development he nevertheless played a part), Dahl's later works have increasingly stressed the role of political institutions in shaping politics and in conditioning the outcomes of public policy. This role was analyzed by Polsby (1968) in an essay of seminal importance for the development of both institutionalist theory and the analysis of contemporary legislatures. Dahl maintains that it is the task of institutions to reduce the harmful effects of pluralism without threatening its existence. Consequently, his alternative to both the politics of hyperegoism and the politics of civic virtue—an alternative he calls the politics of robust civility—depends on neither the altruistic nor the selfish intentions of political actors or citizens but rather on an institutional (and constitutional) design that is adequate for the purpose because it is mindful of the structural and psychological constraints that act on individuals. Although it is true that in the 1960s and 1970s some pluralists conceived the public institutions as a "black box" or a "cash register" of pressures applied by a variety of interest groups, it is equally true that in the two decades that followed, the shrewdest of them came to realize that this interpretation of institutions was impracticable.[5] Dahl consequently came to specify that institutions are necessary not only to enable collective action but also to generate *good* collective action, or in other words, to sustain the politics of robust civility. As Ware (1999, p. 16) has pointed out, "Dahl's work has always been informed by a deep knowledge

---

[5]See Fabbrini (1988), my contribution (with Lowi and Nordlinger) to the debate that was stimulated by "The Return of the State" (Almond 1988).

of how political institutions actually work, and thus how they might work were reforms to provide for a more democratic society."

Perhaps it is no coincidence that, from Madison to Jefferson on up to Dewey and Dahl, the theory and practice of reform in the United States has focused on institutions and their improvement (see Young 1996 for one reconstruction of the matter). As a weighty legal and historical study has recently shown (Ackerman 1991, 1998), the political conflict that has marked the critical phases of the democratic regime in the United States has always been constitutional or institutional in character. Thus it was in the 1780s when the Constitution was drafted; thus it was in the 1830s when the fierce debate broke out over the role of financial power in democracy; thus it was in the 1860s when the Civil War exploded;[6] thus it was in the 1930s when the role of the federal government was redefined in the face of unprecedented economic crisis; and thus it was in the 1960s when the civil rights movement raised its radical challenge to the segregationist laws of the southern states. In all these cases of fierce or even bloody political conflict, the dispute has ultimately centered on the appropriate interpretation of the Constitution—and has therefore focused on the adequacy of the institutions derived from it with respect to the interpretation of the Constitution that prevailed. This, moreover, is the reason why constitutional language in the United States has regularly defined the order of legitimate political discourse. After all, if people are willing to die or go to prison to change the rules, then perhaps the rules are not so irrelevant to the pursuit of the public good.

These considerations may prove useful for discussion of the public good (or the "general interest," as the French, Italians, and Spaniards prefer to call it) in Europe. Especially in continental Europe, the legacy of the prolonged postwar ideological confrontation has been an entirely substantive view of the public good. Not only the general public but also a significant part of the political and cultural elite have adopted metapolitical views of democracy, views in which political principles are self-justifying and are never subjected to empirical verification. Moreover, those principles (however defined) were debated regardless of the specific institutional and public-policy arrangements that could better approximate them.

In the 1990s, Europe witnessed a resurgence of interest in institutional design. A debate on its normative and policy implications took place all over the continent. In Eastern Europe, the wave of democratization reopened the discussion on the various alternative forms of democratic constitution, with their implications for governmental organization and territorial distribution of power (Hesse & Johnson 1995). In Western Europe, the deepening of the process of integration, especially with the Maastrich Treaty of 1992, reopened the discussion about the congruence of European welfare states and the efficacy of centralized management of their policies in the context of a globalized economy (Ferrera & Rhodes 2000). For example, had it not been for the pressure from the EU and the fear of being excluded from the euro-zone, it is unlikely that Italy, Spain, and Greece would have reduced

---

[6]On the importance of the Civil War, in particular, in redefining constitutional liberalism, see the splendid book by Greenstone (1993).

their public debt after years of particularistic management by government and parliament had expanded it to staggering proportions.

Dahl maintains that it is not possible in contemporary democracies to establish a priori what the public good is (or better, what it should be), unless it is imposed from above by the state's elite (as occurred traditionally, for instance, in democratic France) (Chamorel 1994) or by fiat (as occurs in nondemocratic regimes). However, one can forgo the a priori idea of public good only if one is willing to reform institutions in a constant attempt to neutralize the fragmentation of the public good into an irrational welter of private goods, or to prevent the imposition of the most powerful group's good as the public good for everyone. Democratic politics takes place within institutions or at least is largely constrained by them. But, of course, to deal with institutions means to face the implications of constitutional design. Sunstein (2001, p. 224) argues, "Democracy is a distinct and limited ideal. It should not be confused with other social aspirations. But by ensuring reason-giving, by increasing exposure to diverse views, and by prohibiting second-class citizenship, a democratic constitution goes a long way toward promoting a wide range of social goals, emphatically including justice itself." Constitutions matter, as Dahl (2001) reminds us again in his recent book. It is a timely reminder in a historical period in which Europe, both Western and Eastern, faces the need to provide its new continental-integrated political system with democratic legitimacy and institutional efficacy.

CONCLUSION

Dahl's liberalism is the result of a personal journey distinguished by a constant passion for politics.[7] The dramatic events of the 1930s and 1940s affected Dahl deeply. His youthful experience profoundly influenced his work as a scholar. To a lesser extent, what happened to Dahl also happened to some European scholars, although they were involved in much more dramatic events in their youth, including those that preceded the crisis of the democratic Weimar Republic and the rise of Nazism. It seems that the events in which those young Europeans were either witnesses or protagonists endowed them with a particular intellectual charge when they became scholars. Today their writings still astonish us with the profundity of their insights, with their human empathy, and above all with their moral sensitivity.

"Cynicism is not attractive to me," says Dahl (1997, p. 30), "[nor] to people who may be searching for an alternative way of thinking about the world." It is true that Western democratic systems fall short of the criteria and values that constitute democracy, but it is equally true that they foster a moral responsibility and independence in individuals that have no equivalents in the regimes that stand as alternatives. Dahl makes no attempt to conceal his skepticism of those (postmodern)

---

[7]For discussion of Dahl's biography see "From Personal History to Democratic Theory" and "Interview with Nelson W. Polsby," Chapters 1 and 2, respectively, of the first volume of Dahl (1997).

theorists of cultural relativism who maintain that democracy is a Western product that is only feasible in the West. As he points out, people in nondemocratic regimes have no chance to say whether that presumption is true. In any case, he vows never to write anything "to give strength to the people controlling these regimes" (Dahl 1997, p. 30).

The task of the political scientist, Dahl says, is to examine problems with a certain empirical, as well as moral, importance, even if there is no methodology with which to do so. It is not the methodology that should furnish the criteria used to choose the problem to be investigated—quite the opposite: The problem should determine the methodology. Not surprisingly, therefore, Dahl's methodology is eclectic, in the sense that he has used different methodologies to examine different problems (or, indeed, a mix of methodologies to investigate the same problem). Whereas in the 1950s Dahl was a leader of the "behavioral revolution" in political science— that is, the use of a sociological approach in the empirical investigation of politics (most notably in *Who Governs?*)—he was never a total convert to that approach. Rather, he has shown a certain animosity toward the methodological dogmatism that has gradually spread through the American scientific community (a dogmatism strenuously defended today by the proponents of rational choice theory).

Dahl's methodological eclecticism jibes with his beliefs about the nature of democracy. The purpose of a political scientist's work should be to solve problems, to advance knowledge about the workings of institutions and policies, and to enlighten citizens and elites as to the features of democracy. There must be a connection between facts and theory. As a theory has to learn from facts, so a democratic regime needs to learn from its empirical experience. Democracy, Dahl argues, is not the perfect political regime, but it is the political regime of perfectibility. Dahl approves of the political changes necessary to make our polyarchies less unequal, but he is skeptical of calls for their large-scale structural transformation. Calls of this kind, in fact, underestimate the unwanted effects of change, as well as its costs (one need only remember, he adds, the enormous death toll of the American Civil War). After all, the history of democracies testifies that important structural changes can be achieved incrementally and pacifically. He declares, "If that is an 'American' perspective, so be it" (Dahl 1997, p. 10), but in fact it is the perspective of democratic reformism as a whole, not merely its American version.

It is true that incremental change has failed to eliminate many of the inequalities produced by the market. But the market capitalism analyzed by Marx has been pacifically transformed into a much more humane and decent economic order than he could have imagined. For Dahl (1997, p. 11), "the visible gap between what is and what ought to be, tempered by what could be" continues to drive the quest for alternative solutions. What is essential, he maintains, is that those who believe in democratic values should endeavor to sustain them as best they can, so that concrete polyarchies come to resemble ideal democracies as closely as possible. And they should do so by employing (principally) the instrument that is most legitimate in a democracy: argument, supported by raised voices if necessary. However, such argument should recognize the fact that every change occurs amid constraints and opportunities. "[A]ll life is given structure and meaning by its limits and opportunities, by the opportunities available within those limits, and the way those opportunities are seized and lost" (Dahl 1997, p. 12). Whereas conservatives see only the constraints and radicals see only the opportunities, the liberal Dahl reminds us that democracy, like collective life itself, is much more complex than either side would have us believe. But this complexity cannot release us from the obligation of seeking to improve both democracy and collective life, acknowledging their constraints while exploiting their opportunities.

In conclusion, Dahl has ended up emphasizing, in his long theoretical journey, the role played by institutions in promoting democratic citizens. If contemporary polyarchies are to function properly, they require citizens who are sufficiently competent and sufficiently interested in the deliberative process; but they do not necessarily require citizens who are virtuous "republicans." Dahl regards it as unrealistic, and perhaps ill-advised, to entrust the workings of democracy to citizens who set themselves up as champions of civic virtue. The institutions of democracy must be able to function adequately even in the absence of such citizens, although their presence may play a substantial part in improving the quality of democracy itself. What democracies need are fairly good citizens, that is, citizens who are neither altruists nor egoists. Such citizens should be induced to find reasonable solutions to collective problems by institutional rules that reward argument and penalize intimidation; in short, fairly good institutions make fairly good citizens.

Dahl, therefore, is not a communitarian, but neither is he a liberal individualist. He embraces a social liberalism that, in the tradition of Dewey (Ryan 1995), assigns institutions the task of fostering cooperation among individuals, as well their reciprocal empathetic understanding—which, moreover, is the indispensable premise for democratic self-government. In this sense, Dahl seems to reflect the progressive political tradition of Jefferson [well described and discussed by Shklar (1998)], with its search for an institutional design that provides not only the appropriate decisional framework for the problems that may arise but also the necessary variety of options for democratic self-government. In sum, Dahl's political tradition is both realistic and reformative, a tradition that is mindful of the beauty of virtue but does not view it as the salvation of politics. A dialogue with this tradition, I suspect, might be useful for those Europeans who are looking for practical alternatives to the ideologies of the past.

The *Annual Review of Political Science* is online at
http://polisci.annualreviews.org

LITERATURE CITED

Ackerman B. 1991. *We the People: Foundations.* Cambridge, MA: Harvard Univ. Press

Ackerman B. 1998. *We the People: Transformations.* Cambridge, MA: Harvard Univ. Press

Almond G. 1988. The return of the state. *Am. Polit. Sci. Rev.* 82(3):853–74

Beard CA, ed. 1964. *The Enduring Federalist.* New York: Frederick Ungar. 2nd ed.

Brinkley A. 1995. *The End of Reform. New Deal Liberalism in Recession and War.* New York: Vintage

Brinkley A. 1998. *Liberalism and Its Discontent.* Cambridge, MA: Harvard Univ. Press

Chamorel P. 1994. The integration of the U.S. political system in comparative perspective. See Dahl 1994, pp. 49–85

Clinton RL. 1989. *Marbury v. Madison and Judicial Review.* Lawrence: Univ. Press Kansas

Coultrap J. 1999. From parliamentarism to pluralism: models of democracy and the European Union's 'democratic deficit.' *J. Theor. Polit.* 11(1):107–35

Dahl RA. 1994. *The New American Political (Dis)order.* Berkeley, CA: Inst. Gov. Stud.

Dahl RA. 1997. *Toward Democracy—A Journey, Reflections: 1940–1997.* Berkeley, CA: Inst. Gov. Stud. 2 vols.

Dahl RA. 2001. *How Democratic Is the American Constitution?* New Haven, CT: Yale Univ. Press

Fabbrini S, with Lowi TJ, Nordlinger EA. 1988. The return of the state: critiques. *Am. Polit. Sci. Rev.* 82(3):891–901

Fabbrini S. 1999. The American system of separated government: an historical-institutional interpretation. *Int. Polit. Sci. Rev.* 20(1):95–116

Farrand M. 1966. *The Records of the Federal Convention of 1787.* New Haven, CT: Yale Univ. Press

Ferrera M, Rhodes M, eds. 2000. *Recasting the European Welfare State. West Eur. Polit.* 23(2) (spec. issue)

Foot M, Kramnick I, eds. 1987. *The Thomas Paine Reader.* Bungay, UK: Penguin Books

Greenstone JD. 1993. *The Lincoln Persuasion. Remaking American Liberalism.* Princeton, NJ: Princeton Univ. Press

Hesse JJ, Johnson N, eds. 1995. *Constitutional Policy and Change in Europe.* Oxford, UK: Oxford Univ. Press

Lipset SM. 1976. *The First New Nation. The United States in Historical and Comparative Perspective.* New York: Norton

Lipset SM. 1996. *American Exceptionalism: A Double-Edged Sword.* New York: Norton

Lowi T. 1969. *The End of Liberalism: Ideology, Politics, and the Crisis of Public Authority.* New York: Norton (2nd ed. 1979)

Neustadt RE. 1990. *Presidential Power and the Modern Presidents.* New York: Free

Polsby NW. 1968. The institutionalization of the U.S. House of Representatives. *Am. Polit. Sci. Rev.* 62(1):144–68

Polsby NW. 1997. On the distinctiveness of the American political system. In *New Federalist Papers. Essays in Defense of the Constitution,* ed. A Brinkley, NW Polsby, KM Sullivan, pp. 29–34. New York: Norton

Przeworski A. 1991. *Democracy and the Market: Political and Economic Reform in Eastern Europe and Latin America.* Cambridge, UK: Cambridge Univ. Press

Ryan A. 1995. *John Dewey and the High Tide of American Liberalism.* New York: Norton

Scharpf FW. 1988. The joint decision trap: lessons from German federalism and European integration. *Public Admin.* LXVI(9):239–78

Schattschneider EE. 1975 (1960). *The Semisovereign People. A Realist's View of Democracy in America.* Hinsdale, IL: Dryden

Schmidt S. 1997. European integration and democracy: the differences among the member states. *J. Eur. Public Policy* IV(1):128–45

Schmitter P. 2000. *How to Democratize the European Union and Why Bother?* Lanham, MD: Rowman & Littlefield

Shapiro M. 1988. *Who Guards the Guardians? Judicial Control of Administration.* Athens: Univ. Georgia Press

Shapiro M, Stone A. 1994. The new constitutional politics of Europe. *Comp. Polit. Stud.* 26(4):397–420

Shklar J. 1991. *American Citizenship. The Quest for Inclusion.* Cambridge, MA: Harvard Univ. Press

Shklar J. 1998. Democracy and the past: Jefferson and his heirs. In *Redeeming American Political Thought,* ed. S Hoffmann, DF Thompson, pp. 171–86. Chicago: Univ. Chicago Press

Skocpol T. 1992. State formation and social policy in the United States. *Am. Behav. Sci.* 35(4/5):559–84

Stone Sweet A. 2000. *Governing with Judges. Constitutional Politics in Europe.* Oxford, UK: Oxford Univ. Press

Sunstein CS. 2001. *Designing Democracy. What Constitutions Do.* Oxford, UK: Oxford Univ. Press

Tsebelis G. 2002. *Veto Players: How Political Institutions Work.* Princeton, NJ: Russell Sage Fdn.

Ware A. 1999. Dahl in perspective. Assessing a colossus of political science. *Public Aff. Rep.* 39(5):14–16

Young JP. 1996. *Reconsidering American Liberalism. The Troubled Odyssey of the Liberal Idea.* Boulder, CO: Westview

Annu. Rev. Polit. Sci. 2003. 6:139–60
doi: 10.1146/annurev.polisci.6.121901.085707
First published online as a Review in Advance on Jan. 8, 2003

THE MEDIA AND DEMOCRACY:
Beyond Myths and Stereotypes

Doris Graber

*Department of Political Science, University of Illinois, 1007 W. Harrison Street, Chicago,
Illinois 60607-7137; email: dgraber@uic.edu*

Key Words First Amendment assumptions, marketplace of ideas, participatory
citizenship, content analysis data, ownership patterns

■ **Abstract** This essay's point of departure is the hallowed belief that democracy
requires active citizens and news media that supply them with information they need
to participate effectively in politics. The main features of this model of a functioning democracy, including the underlying assumptions, are tested and found wanting.
Neither citizens nor media are capable of performing the roles expected of them. The
appropriateness of these roles for life in modern societies is also open to question, as are
the many myths and stereotypes that obscure the interface between media and democracy. The fact that democracy can persist despite citizens and media that fall short of
the expected performance suggests that political culture may be more important than
citizen wisdom and media excellence. Rallies in civic activism during crises may also
be a major factor in the durability of democratic governance in the United States.

Alexis de Tocqueville was among the first thinkers to recognize the importance
of the press as a powerful force for the promotion of democracy. In the 1830s,
in a chapter on the "Liberty of the Press in the United States" (Tocqueville 1984
[1835], pp. 94–95), he wrote that the press

> causes political life to circulate through all the parts of that vast territory. Its
> eye is constantly open to detect the secret springs of political designs and to
> summon the leaders of all parties in turn to the bar of public opinion. It rallies
> the interests of the community round certain principles and draws up the creed
> of every party; for it affords a means of intercourse between those who hear
> and address each other without ever coming into immediate contact.

DEFINING THE TARGET

Tocqueville's bold description hides the great difficulty of analyzing the interplay
between mass media and democratic governance. The subject is pervaded by many
long-standing myths, stereotypes, and controversies that obscure the relationship.
Like Tocqueville, politicians almost universally believe that the media substantially

139

influence politics. Therefore, they feel the need to control the media to ensure that the information that is supplied benefits their political fortunes. The media's great political significance is also acknowledged by those scholars (e.g., Cook 1998, Mazzoleni & Schulz 1999) who call the media a political institution that plays an important role in politics along with many other institutions.

Politicians' and pundits' belief that governments can control their citizens by manipulating the media is one of the myths surrounding the media. The totalitarian regimes that arose in the period prior to World War II were unable to translate their control and expert manipulation of the media into lasting support by their citizens. When readily observable events contradicted government-inspired media stories, these real-life experiences trumped the stories. Media power to create the political reality that surrounds the public is emasculated when media credibility plunges owing to stories that run counter to direct observations.

Why do myths and stereotypes about the media and their role in sustaining democracy persist? One reason is that they are essential parts of citizens' larger belief systems about how our social systems work. Changing essential parts would call the entire system into question, which is a frightening prospect. It is also difficult to dispel the myths because they are so entrenched and so often repeated. Findings that contradict established orthodoxies are rarely welcome.

The myths and stereotypes also persist because scholars have thus far failed to challenge them or to test most of them empirically to discover what is true, or partly or conditionally true, and what is false. Many broad and definitive judgments about the substantive content of mass media are still made without actual content analyses of these media. Similarly, most assertions about media effects still lack a solid empirical basis and totally ignore physiologic and psychological factors that determine how human beings process complex information about their world. It has been very tempting to oversimplify the role of the media and do so emphatically to defend questionable generalizations, because the interactions of media systems with other major human institutions is highly complex. Fortunately, the body of empirically tested knowledge has been growing rapidly.

"Media" as Myth

Every discussion about the role of the media immediately runs into the problem that this collective noun creates a mirage. It engenders visions of a fairly uniform body of institutions when, in reality, there is no such thing. If conveying information to large audiences about ongoing events, especially political happenings, is the salient characteristic of news "media," then newspapers, magazines, books, radio, over-the-air and cable television, and the Internet fall into this group. Do they all operate in the same way? Obviously not.

There are vast differences in content, framing, and mode of presentation among various types of news venues and within each venue. That makes it foolhardy to generalize about "the media" because any generalization leads to overly broad, deceptive summary judgments. Political news coverage by the *New York Times*, which is read carefully by political elites worldwide, cannot be equated with news coverage by the *Detroit News*, which takes a far more populist, tabloid approach. News broadcasts on C-SPAN, the cable network that presents live coverage of congressional debates and other government activities in the United States, offers far more serious, in-depth political coverage than most local television stations, which summarize the news at 10 PM.

If media vary so widely, can one generalize about their relation to democracy? Again, the answer is "no." The diversity of media is matched by the diversity of social, economic, and political conditions that shape the potential for democracy. The media's effects on politics spring from complex interactions of numerous causal factors that include basic political and media institutions, the sophistication of media technologies, and the characteristics of individual citizens. [These interactions are emphasized by Gunther & Mughan (2000), editors of a volume of comparative essays on the role of the media in democratic and nondemocratic countries.] The ideological orientation of the political elites and the governmental structures under which they operate are particularly potent factors. Because of the diversity of these elements, the interrelation between news media and the success or failure of democracy differs among cultures and subcultures and at various historical periods.

To skirt the myths and stereotypes that bedevil undue generalizations and to make my task more manageable, this essay focuses primarily on major U.S. print and television media that reach very large audiences—such as the *New York Times* or the *Chicago Tribune* and the ABC, CBS, NBC, and CNN networks—and on the Internet. I chose these news media because they are more influential for national politics in the United States than most of their less prominent prototypes.

Overview

My analysis begins with scrutiny of the assumptions and expectations that underlie the hallowed belief that the functions performed by the news media are essential for democracy in the United States. The list of assumptions and expectations is based on a comprehensive survey of pronouncements by First Amendment scholars, U.S. Supreme Court judges, and prominent political leaders throughout American history (Graber 1986). Following the initial analysis, I try to judge how the manner in which major U.S. media are performing these functions affects the quality of American democracy. That assessment encompasses the conflicting appraisals of scholars, including the projections by Internet scholars about the changes brought about by this newest technology. Finally, I attempt to answer the question of whether, on balance, the types of contemporary American media analyzed in this essay are an asset or a detriment to democratic governance in the United States.

PUBLIC VERSUS PRIVATE CONTROL

The relationship between media and government is unusual in the United States because the framers of the Constitution assumed that media in a democracy must be free from government control. Experience-based fears about tyrannical governments led the founders of the United States to create a government of limited powers. Checks and balances within the political systems would be strengthened by independent external safeguards provided by news media eager to preserve the people's control over their government.

Government Control as Myth

It is a myth that U.S. media, especially the electronic ones, are free from government controls. Many of the regulations regarding the size and reach of media business combinations, protection of national security, protection of the rights of individuals, and cultural safeguards strongly influence what may and may not be published. Violations are kept in check by the fear of regulatory legislation. In times of war or similar threats to national security, controls have often become quite severe, including laws that prohibited criticism of the government (Hemmer 2000, Tillinghast 2000). Finally, most of the information about government that the media present is supplied by government sources, giving government officials control over what to disclose or conceal and allowing them to present the information from the government's perspective. Whether government's role as the main supplier of news about its activities impairs democracy, and if so how much, remains an unsettled argument. So does the question of whether government control of the media is more likely to be a blessing or a curse.

Private Sector Control Myths

The alternative to government control through ownership of media or through substantial regulation of news content is control by the private sector. In the United States, where media ownership by private parties is the dominant pattern, it means control by self-selected business enterprises that are not beholden to the general public. Many media businesses try to serve the public's interests, but the extent of their public-service orientation varies greatly. Currently, most major media in the United States are owned by large business enterprises whose primary goal must be to produce revenue for the shareholders of their parent companies. That may mean that the public-service orientation yields to profit concerns occasionally or regularly. To serve huge, heterogeneous audiences, media enterprises feature sensationalized news of crime, sex, and violence and oversimplify serious news. Many media critics call that a disservice to democracy because "soft" news replaces "hard" political information; others hail it as praiseworthy populism (Franklin 1997, Brants 1998, Hermes 1997).

Critics are also unhappy that journalists, eager to retain the largest possible audiences, may avoid controversies that might offend sizeable audience segments. News enterprises may reduce the costs of news production by having fewer reporters pursue original stories. They may cut back on expensive foreign news bureaus in favor of parachute journalism, in which home-based commentators fly to the scene of breaking events without necessarily being familiar with the local political and cultural environment that has shaped these events.

One of the most damning accusations leveled against commercialized media in the United States is that they corrupt the election process by charging candidates money to broadcast their messages. That makes campaigning very expensive. Consequently, candidates largely limit themselves to 30-second advertisements that are apt to confuse voters rather than enlightening them. The ads are often nasty in tone and provoke anger that may then cloud judgments or keep voters away from the polls (Just et al. 1996, Fallows 1996).

Steep campaigning costs force candidates to spend inordinate amounts of time on fundraising rather than attending to politics. High costs prevent poor candidates from entering the race and allow rich candidates to "buy" elections. Wealthy contributors of large sums of money may have a better than average chance to influence politics. The turn to private commercial media has thus produced major hazards for democracy in the United States that were not expected when the restraints on major government controls of media were incorporated into the Constitution.

WHAT IS EXPECTED FROM THE MEDIA?

How can the media support American democracy so that their constitutionally protected privilege seems warranted? As First Amendment scholars and other prominent Americans see it, the press should do four things: (*a*) provide a forum for discussion of diverse, often conflicting ideas; (*b*) give voice to public opinion; (*c*) serve as citizens' eyes and ears to survey the political scene and the performance of politicians; and (*d*) act as a public watchdog that barks loudly when it encounters misbehavior, corruption, and abuses of power in the halls of government. A broad array of other requirements have also been mentioned occasionally, but they are subsumed in the four basic categories (Gurevitch & Blumler 1990, Curran 1996).

All of these expectations are based on the assumption that ideal democracy equates to participatory democracy, where politically well-informed citizens play an active role in government. This assumption, based on models dating back to ancient Greece, is questionable on multiple grounds. Is participatory democracy really feasible when modern mass publics are far too large to engage in policy debates where citizens have a reasonable chance to make themselves heard? Is it practical given the complexity of the public policy issues that face modern societies and often require insights based on high-level technical expertise? And is it realistic considering the disinclination of modern citizens to engage in such debates? Is it even the ideal form of democracy, or would other forms, such as direct democracy or communitarian democracy, provide better models (Becker & Slaton 2000, Dahlberg 2001)?

Mass Media and the Marketplace of Ideas

Among the contributions expected from American media is the provision of a forum for wide discussion of diverse, often conflicting ideas. Here again we encounter a number of questionable assumptions. Among them is the assumption that the public dialogue generated by media coverage will bring out the truth in political controversies so that the best policies can emerge. In the words of the U.S. Supreme Court, in "an uninhibited marketplace of ideas" the "truth will ultimately prevail" because many viewpoints will be heard (*Red Lion Broadcasting Co. v. FCC* 1969, p. 389). In reality, the cacophony of voices in today's marketplace of ideas often confuses nonexperts more than it enlightens them.

The problem is made worse by the "neutrality" norm that American journalists prize. That norm precludes telling their audiences where the "truth" might lie. Instead, the news is flooded with comments by "expert" sources with diametrically opposed opinions. That makes it difficult for lay people to judge the merits of complex policies (Neuman 1986, Zaller 1994). Of course, what is true and untrue in the policy realm, and the criteria by which policy alternatives should be judged, are matters of subjective choice. The marketplace of ideas, stocked with diverse news stories, gives little guidance.

A second assumption about the marketplace of ideas is that genuine news diversity requires that a large number of independent journalistic enterprises, representing many different perspectives on politics, must select and present the news. Many critics believe that increasing concentration of news enterprises precludes such diversity (Bagdikian 1996, Alger 1998, Picard 1998, Compaine & Gomery 2000, McChesney 2000). News media have multiplied steadily, but many are controlled by the same large business enterprises. In fact, the legal structure of the United States does not do well in promoting the establishment of large numbers of independent media and keeping them from combining. Media concentration, the critics claim, explains why so many of the largest media, like the major television networks, are rivals in conformity when they select and frame news stories (Picard 1998, Schudson 2002).

Research evidence does not substantiate the claim that the concentration of media enterprises in the United States since the 1980s has amounted to a dangerous shrinking of the interests represented by media voices. Although it has some facets of truth, the claim is largely a myth (Picard 1998). The number of media competing for audiences does not necessarily determine the diversity of viewpoints that are publicly aired. Media tycoons who control numerous media enterprises, such as Rupert Murdoch, often sponsor vastly different news outlets. Murdoch, for example, simultaneously controls a popular British tabloid, the *Sun*, and the venerable and elite London *Times* (Gunther & Mughan 2000). It is true that American media often are rivals in conformity, framing the news in line with political mainstream orientations. But that happens because they share notions about what is newsworthy and what appeals to their particular publics and because they tap the same sources of information.

What that mainstream orientation means for the quality of democracy is unclear. It is a typical "which came first, the chicken or the egg?" puzzle. Most Americans' political views are mainstream, and there is no evidence that they flock in large numbers to the extremist views available from alternative media and the Internet. So, is democracy served well or poorly when the media reflect the majority's approach to politics? The answer depends on one's political orientation. Many scholars and pundits whose ideology is far from the political mainstream cite the emphasis on mainstream orientations as a serious flaw in media content (Schiller 1989, McChesney 2000). They allege that, by favoring mainstream capitalist ideology, media help to perpetuate it. News stories are "messages in code about the nature of society, the nature of productive relations within the media themselves and institutional domains and social processes" (Altheide 1984, p. 478). In the eyes of critics, the media do not offer the electorate multiple, diverse frames of the many political issues that citizens should scrutinize. This is especially true in the foreign policy realm. Most discussions of U.S. foreign policies are presented from the perspective of the United States, which left-wing critics consider imperialist.

Mass Media as Voices for Public Opinions

Mass media in American democracy are expected to give voice to public opinion so that the government will know where majorities and minorities stand. The view that the media frame the news to reflect the opinion of various publics or the opinions of the majority is another myth that has little relation to political realities. Nonetheless, it has major consequences because political observers often equate the thrust of media coverage with a single, unanimous public opinion when such unanimity is a myth.

The press cannot function as a megaphone for public opinions because it does not keep in regular touch with various factions among the public. Journalists gather most of their information for news stories from media beats representing selected public and private institutions but not the mass public. The opinions of elites are featured while the views of the mainstream public are slighted; the views of ideological dissenters are largely ignored. Overall, the opinions of the mass public are treated as quaintly interesting but not necessarily consequential, except in connection with electoral politics and situations in which public support and compliance are essential. The closest that the mass media come to reporting details of public opinion are their reports of public opinion polls taken by their own or other organizations. Leaving aside the many questions that have been raised about how accurately public opinion polls reflect public views, the number of issues about which its opinions are reported is minuscule compared with the number of important public policy issues facing the nation at any particular time (Traugott & Lavrakas 2000, Asher 2001).

Journalists often claim to speak for the public but deny vehemently that this is an agency relationship in which publics have the right to insist that news stories report their opinions. On the whole, the news media have not been generous in granting access to the many viewpoints that people would like to air. To the contrary, political positions favored by a particular medium may be at odds with the views of its audience. Journalists tend to be more liberal about social policies and more conservative about economic policies than much of their audience (Weaver & Wilhoit 1996). Their stories reflect their orientation to varying degrees. Such discrepancies may explain why almost half of the public expresses only limited confidence in the accuracy of the media (Pew 1998a).

The notion that the media are a major catalyst of and contributor to public opinions is also at odds with the fact that average Americans do not form opinions on most political issues, whether or not the information to do so is available. If they do form opinions, these do not necessarily mirror the views presented in the media even when these views have been prominent (Zaller 2001). For these reasons, the accusation that the media hurt participatory democracy by destroying trust in government through cynical coverage rings hollow. Research does, indeed, show that trust in government dips when the public is plied with negative news that seems credible (Capella & Jamieson 1997, Rahn & Rudolph 2001). But, like other political phenomena, such attitudes are ephemeral and that should be reflected in the charges.

Public feelings of trust appear to be driven more by personal experiences and media reports about political events and the performance of politicians than by an excessively hostile tone of the media coverage of these events (Nye et al. 1997, Miller & Listhaug 1999). That fact was well illustrated by the soaring trust in government and the President's job approval ratings that followed the terrorist attack on the United States in 2001. The ratings dropped as soon as news stories about inattention to danger signals raised questions in people's minds about the effectiveness of the government in handling terrorism. Like most reported public opinions, trust in government depends heavily on the political situations that provide the context within which the public is forming the opinions that it relays to pollsters (Pew 1998b, Bishop 2001). Further exoneration of the media from the charge of promoting cynicism comes from research evidence that the segments of the public who pay most attention to news stories and are most receptive to new information display the highest sense of political efficacy and trust in government (Bennett et al. 1999, Norris 2000a,b).

Still, the press supplies the raw material from which public opinions are formed, so there is indeed a connection between the press and public opinions. If the press fails to alert people to information that they need to judge major aspects of the political scene, citizens' capacity to influence public officials suffers. Although the notion that people form their opinions based on what the media report is simplistic, news media can set the agenda for political thinking—the subject matter to which people will pay attention—without necessarily determining what they will think about these issues. Journalists' story choices may also influence the mental connections that people make between issues. For example, the issue of pay increases for police officers elicits different audience responses depending on whether the audience was primed by a story about police brutality or by a recollection of the events of September 11, 2001 (Iyengar 1991).

The Surveillance Function

The media are expected to serve as eyes and ears for citizens, who need to monitor the soundness of policies and the performance of politicians. The unstated assumption is that the media have the ability, resources, inclination, and mandate to perform oversight functions. In reality, their powers are very limited and no match for the power of politicians to hide what they are doing. The media lack subpoena powers to trace hidden information. They must depend on what is voluntarily supplied or what emerges when insiders leak information to the press. They also lack sufficient money and manpower for systematic oversight. Besides, they do not consider surveillance a compelling mandate. This is why the media usually wait for leaks and tips before delving into questionable political activities, rather than checking the activities of politicians routinely. Even then journalists rarely act unless the activities involved seem clear and easily investigated and unless the investigation seems likely to produce a newsworthy, appealing story. Impending institutional failures and the public's need to know about them have been insufficient to stimulate major investigations (Lang & Lang 1983, Jamieson & Waldman 2003).

The Watchdog Function

The situation is the same with regard to monitoring misbehavior, corruption, and abuses of power by government. Investigative journalism has enjoyed a few spectacular successes—unearthing the Watergate scandal in the Nixon administration, disclosing the My Lai massacre during the Vietnam War, reporting on excesses by CIA and FBI agents, and detailing the activities of corrupt individual politicians. But such investigations have been exceptional, not routine (Protess et al. 1991, Sabato et al. 2000). However, the monitoring function has a deterrent effect that may be more significant than the actual investigations of wrong-doing. Like all non-happenings, the extent of deterrence is hard to measure.

THE PERFORMANCE RECORD

Structural Obstacles

How well have major U.S. media performed the democracy-sustaining functions expected of them? It is clear that they have not done well, largely because they lack the power, resources, structure, and inclination to perform tasks that have become impossible to handle in a huge, heterogeneous country that must cope with extraordinarily complex political conditions. The news media, as Patterson (1993) has aptly described them, are a "miscast institution."

The media are not structured to perform the functions that America's founders expected of them. They do not operate as small, independent, diverse enterprises. Economies of scale have forced smaller units to merge with larger ones. Aside from the Internet, they are not common carriers open to all who desire to be heard. The media are not designed for systematic surveillance of the government and public opinion. There simply is too much news to cover and report on a daily basis. Journalists are often chided for providing too little context for news stories. Yet, because of time constraints, especially on television, they cannot repeat familiar contextual information at the expense of new elements of a perennial story. For example, the conflict between Israelis and Palestinians is decades old. There has been very little substantive change in the basic issues and the types of policies that have been proposed for dealing with them. Thus, journalists do not repeat this background information, hoping that audiences still remember the essence of past stories.

The media have no mandate to teach the public, nor has the public an obligation to learn from them. Most journalists therefore do not see themselves as teachers, and most audience members do not associate reading or watching or listening to political news with sitting in a classroom learning lessons that must be committed to memory. The capacity of audiences to absorb the contents of news stories is quite limited. So is their time and inclination to study the news. Attention to news is a leisure-time activity for most people, and leisure time is scarce.

Rather than being a venue for teaching civic knowledge, the media, as currently structured, are for-profit enterprises that must be concerned about their financial bottom line. Journalists know that average citizens are only mildly interested in the political life that surrounds them. People devour news about crime, disaster, and sexual exploits but slight the in-depth political analyses offered periodically by newspapers and television documentaries. Journalists therefore believe that they can serve their clients best by making the news entertaining. Consequently, news selection criteria relate more to audience appeal than to the political significance of stories or their relevance to civic goals. Under these circumstances, the surprise is not that media have failed to perform the functions that are deemed so essential for participatory democracy, but that they have retained a public-service orientation at all.

Surveillance Failures

Above all other criticisms, the media have been accused of major shortcomings in political surveillance, compounded by shallow presentations and a failure to feature diverse points of view. They do not assess the soundness of policies and the performance of politicians adequately to make a vigorous participatory democracy possible. As media critic Postman (1985, p. 141) has said about television, which is the most widely used information source, "it is a medium which presents information in a form that renders it simplistic, nonsubstantive, nonhistorical and noncontextual; that is to say information packaged as entertainment."

Patterson (1993) has highlighted numerous specific complaints about news quality. He accuses the media of failing to discuss the likely consequences of various types of political decisions. They may speculate about future events but they rarely tell their audiences what the political impact is likely to be. Talk about the horse-race aspects of elections is plentiful during campaigns, whereas analyses of the capabilities of various candidates are slighted. The media rarely point out patterns in political developments; they approach political happenings as if they were a series of discrete events. They emphasize novel twists that may be insignificant while ignoring long-term continuities. Lengthy analytical pieces are rare. The media favor stereotypes and perpetuate them because they are dramatic and easy to understand, rather than offering nuanced comments.

News Dosages for Political Health

The accusation that the current news supply is inadequate for the needs of citizens raises the highly controversial issue of what the public needs to know to be effective citizens (Popkin 1994, Rahn et al. 1994, Delli Carpini & Keeter 1996, Norris 2000a,b, Graber 2001). I have argued elsewhere (Graber 2001) that there is no uniform, widely accepted answer to that question. Neither scholars nor pundits nor average Americans agree what issues people need to be informed about to perform citizenship tasks adequately and how detailed their knowledge must be. Many theorists allege that the fully informed, participatory citizen is the ideal model and that the adequacy of media coverage should be assessed from that perspective. But this ideal citizen simply does not exist and cannot exist in most advanced industrialized societies, especially in large countries. This is why a major shift in the model of citizenship was needed to keep pace with political and social developments (Lupia & McCubbins 1998, Popkin & Dimock 1999, Neuman et al. 1992).

Schudson pointed that out in a 1999 keynote address on "The Transformation of Civic Life." Schudson describes successive stages of citizenship from the "deferential citizen" of the eighteenth century to the "partisan citizen" prior to World War I to the "informed citizen" who was in vogue until the 1960s to the "rights-bearing citizen" of the present day. The concept of the rights-bearing or "monitorial" citizen

> does not imply that citizens should know all the issues all of the time. It implies that they should be informed enough and alert enough to identify danger to their personal good and danger to the public good. When such danger appears on the horizon, they should have the resources—in trusted relationships, in political parties and elected officials, in relationships to interest groups and other trustees of their concerns, in knowledge of and access to the courts as well as the electoral system, and in relevant information sources to jump into the fray and make a lot of noise. (Schudson n.d., p. 23)

The modern press assists the monitorial citizen by surveying what government does and by critiquing its activities (Schudson 1998).

Do average Americans have sufficient political knowledge to cope with their duties as monitorial citizens? The answer is "yes." Research shows (e.g., Popkin 1994, Lupia & McCubbins 1998, Graber 2001) that the heuristics developed by most Americans to vote in elections and to participate in political discussions at home and in the workplace seem quite serviceable, although they are remote from the ideal of the fully informed citizen who enjoys in-depth knowledge about all aspects of politics. Even if that ideal were attainable, it would be impractical for most citizens in our complex age when citizens must attend to many other pursuits besides politics.

Citizens themselves feel that they are adequately informed by current media fare. In response to pollsters' questions, most citizens say that television news, which is the most widely used information source, provides them with sufficient information to carry out their civic functions. A majority of viewers (61%) claim to be very or fairly satisfied with television offerings in general, and viewers are overwhelmingly (85%) satisfied with news offerings. When asked "How good of a job does the evening news do in summing up the events of the day?" 18% of the respondents in a 1998 nationwide poll gave it an "excellent" rating and 50% called it "good," while 21% said it was "only fair" and 4% labeled it "poor." Seven percent gave no ratings (Pew 1998a).

Myths About News Quality

There are also many myths concerning the quality of media performance. It is far from stellar, as reflected in the critics' complaints. Still, if one judges adequacy by the availability of political news, the media are far better than their reputation (Graber 2001). Content analysis of the early evening national newscasts on ABC, CBS, CNN, and NBC for several months in 1997 and 1998 shows that over the course of a single week, viewers received roughly 43 min of foreign news, 32 min of general domestic stories, 30 min of news dealing with various social issues, 24 min of news about the environment, and 16 min of economic news. A viewer who watched the nightly 30-min network news six days per week and a 60-min CNN newscast once a week would get a political lesson lasting 2 h 24 min. That is almost equivalent to the weekly classroom time of a student enrolled in a political science college course, although it lacks tests and grades, which are a powerful incentive for learning.

To evaluate the overall quality of the news supply available to the American public requires looking at all the rivulets in the news stream, rather than examining single sources only, as is commonly done. A thorough examination (Norris 2001, Bimber 2003) shows that despite the decline of traditional political fare in many print and electronic news venues, the supply of political information, including hard political news, has never been more abundant when one considers the totality of offerings, including those available on the Internet. Gaps in one venue or one news format tend to be filled by programming in other venues or other formats. For example, although political documentaries on television have diminished, prime-time television news magazines now supply many in-depth and investigative stories that television news formerly provided. However, most people do not take full advantage of the rich feast.

At times, research problems intensify misconceptions about the quality and quantity of media coverage of particular topics. Even when content appraisals are based on systematic content analysis, these analyses usually have a very short focus. For example, most analyses of issue coverage during a U.S. presidential election focus on the last two months of the campaign and generally encompass a very small number of media. They ignore the information available earlier in the campaign as well as the fact that audiences have a large fund of prior information about many issues. Often, they count only one or two issues mentioned in a news story and ignore the rest, creating serious undercounts (Althaus et al. 2001).

Schudson (1998) does not mention that the modern citizen's focus of concern as a monitor of civic life is close to home rather than at the national or international level and that the modern rights-bearing citizen pays greater attention to economic and social issues than to traditional politics. But that, too, is part of the new package of citizenship concerns. Accordingly, the thrust of the information reported by the media has shifted, leaving media critics dismayed. There is greater emphasis on political issues that involve social and economic policies, including substantially more stories about business, health care, and crime, than on traditional reports about political maneuvers in the nation's capital and the activities of the President.

For example, a comparison of news offerings on ABC, CBS, NBC, the *Los Angeles Times*, the *New York Times*, and *Time* and *Newsweek* magazines over a 20-year span between 1977 and 1997 shows a 21% reduction in traditional political news and a 15% increase in economic and social news, although the pattern is uneven (Committee of Concerned Journalists 1999). The *New York Times*, for example, increased traditional political coverage, while *Time* magazine decreased it by more than 50%. The entertainment category, which includes sports and weather, grew only slightly—an average of only three percentage points—which runs counter to widespread stereotypes that entertainment features are mushrooming. Believers in the informed-citizen model regret changes in focus as a harmful deviation from supplying participatory citizens with traditional political news. But these changes are in tune with monitorial citizenship, which encourages citizens to monitor political issues selectively.

The continued willingness of the public to expose itself regularly to large amounts of national and international news nonetheless suggests that people, though frustrated with run-of-the-mill politics and political news, have not been alienated from the political process by the news media, as some critics allege. They are eager to learn information, especially when its salience is clear (Key 1965, Page & Shapiro 1991, Popkin 1994, Kuklinski et al. 2001). In fact, 87% of the public actually claims to enjoy keeping up with the news even though most of it does not interest them (Pew 1998a).

Despite these high rates of satisfaction among the public, academic critics and pundits excoriate television, complaining that it supplies inadequate political information to allow citizens to perform their civic duties. The wide divergence between the critics' harshly negative judgments and the much more positive appraisals of average citizens springs from their respective expectations. The critics base their expectations about what citizens ought to know about politics on the traditional model of the fully informed political actor. Rather than concentrating their analyses on knowledge that is essential to performing ordinary civic tasks, such as voting and political discussions, the critics focus on precisely remembered factual knowledge about past and current people and events. They judge civic intelligence by the ability to respond to questions with readily measurable facts and figures.

THE INTERNET AS PANACEA

Does Internet technology enhance the capability of the news media to perform the functions deemed essential for participatory democracy?

Major Contributions

It does so in part, although it cannot overcome the main physical and physiological barriers to participatory citizenship (Norris 2001, Bimber 2003). Compared with traditional media, it supplies information collected by a wider array of sources who represent more diverse viewpoints. Many of these sources are linked to traditional news media and public officials. They have been joined by thousands of political units, such as cities, counties, police departments, and school systems, that now have websites. These websites offer citizens more information than ever available before, making government more understandable, transparent, and accountable. Many of the sites permit and often invite two-way communication via the Web or email. Some of them enable citizens to observe and participate in legislative sessions and town meetings (Tsagarousianou et al. 1998, Bimber 1999). Opportunities for direct access to politicians at all levels, including the President and members of Congress, have mushroomed because nearly all have websites that set forth their political activities and invite comments and questions. However, meaningful responses from such officials still remain scarce (Davis & Owen 1998, Davis 1999).

Institutional websites are outnumbered by those of millions of people from all walks of life. Thousands of these websites provide political information. Some present information in regular news formats, enriched by links to websites that supply more in-depth information. Others specialize in detailed analyses of specific issues, such as global warming or prescription drugs for the elderly. Average citizens can reach and use this information faster and more easily and cheaply than ever before.

Many political issues have become the focus for usenet groups where interested citizens can engage in often spirited conversation with others who care about the same topics (Hill & Hughes 1998, Bucy & Gregson 2001). As Bucy & Gregson summarize it (2001, p. 369), "Quite possibly, the internet/world wide web presents more political information and opportunities for civic engagement than has [sic] ever existed." The Internet comes closer to being a "common carrier" open to the messages of all who desire to speak than any previous technology, and people from all walks of life have learned to use it. Since people's interests vary, the notion that one type of news coverage can serve all needs is naive. Diverse audiences are better served when the rich diet of news available on the Internet covers a broad array of topics, framed in multiple ways, and presented at various levels of sophistication.

Major Drawbacks

Still, the reality is not as rosy as some of the glowing appraisals suggest (Barber 1998, Hill & Hughes 1998, Keck & Sikkink 1998). Use of the Internet for political purposes has been disappointingly sparse compared with use for entertainment or business purposes. It is a political asset that is far from reaching its full potential and may never do so (Margolis & Resnick 2002, Bimber 2003, Graber et al. 2003). Access to audiences remains problematic. It is often difficult for news sources who are unfamiliar to the public to find audiences who will pay attention to their messages. Most of those who preach on the Internet preach primarily to those who are already converted.

The societal segments who already are immersed in valuable information—the well-educated and economically secure—dominate in Internet use. In that sense, the Internet contributes to inequality of opportunity rather than diminishing it. Nonetheless, the fact that subsets of politically engaged citizens are scrutinizing political activities and communicating their views to public officials decentralizes and democratizes political communication. Political and ideological dykes restricting information circulation have become porous.

When it comes to monitoring the activities of politicians, including performing the watchdog function, Internet news suppliers face the same problems as traditional media. Surveillance is better because more information is available from government and private websites and even from sources outside the United States. But the government's ability to hide what it does not wish to disclose remains formidable.

Along with the many other new media that have sprouted in recent decades, the Internet poses fragmentation problems for democracy. With audiences dividing their attention among more news venues, the bond of shared information that ties communities together may be vanishing. That loss puts democratic governance at risk because it depends on shared values and willingness to focus on a common agenda for public action. When shared social norms are diminished, norms of tolerance that are essential to democracy may weaken. Because of the diversity of information sources, Americans now have more variegated political agendas than ever before. There is a danger of fragmentation that may destroy the public sphere where people can discuss joint concerns, even though they may disagree about what solutions should be attempted (Dahlgren 2001, Sunstein 2001).

When people engage in more selective exposure to the media, their scope of interests tends to shrink. With more information and entertainment available, they may spend less time on political news. They may be lured away from the public sphere into their own communication ghettoes (Swanson 1997, Bennett 1998, Entman & Herbst 2001). Audience tallies show that this does indeed happen (Pew 2000). The upshot may be widening of cultural and knowledge gaps in society. Persuaders can then target their messages more effectively to the most receptive audiences. The threat of undue persuasion has become a major concern in an era when politicians hire public relations experts to craft their messages (Farrel 1996, Mayhew 1997, Kurtz 1998, Mancini 1999).

THE BALANCE SHEET

How could American democracy survive for more than 200 years when the news media, which are presumably essential for democratic governance, are badly flawed and the public shuns serious politics? This essay has recorded some of the public's and the media's serious shortcomings in surveillance of the political scene, in monitoring politicians and performing the watchdog role, and in mirroring America's vast array of public opinions (Schmitter & Karl 1991, Delli Carpini & Keeter 1996, Semetko 1996). The unavoidable verdict is that even the best U.S. media currently fall short of providing even the limited information needed by the monitorial citizen. For its part, the public fails to play the participatory citizenship role.

However, that verdict must be put into perspective. It is predicated on applying standards based on the prevailing myths about a politically well-informed participatory citizenry that requires ample hard news about all major political issues facing the nation. Stereotypes have exaggerated the media's failures to perform as handmaidens of democracy. The descriptions of the information diet offered by media critics are often mere caricatures that highlight its worst features. In fact, most print and electronic news media, except for tabloids, serve the four basic functions identified above reasonably well.

They serve as a forum of limited discussion of conflicting elite views about numerous political issues. The range of sources interviewed for news stories and the views that are publicized generally fluctuate only narrowly around the political center and many important issues are slighted. Still, news currently alerts the public to the range of political alternatives that have a chance to be selected because they are within the mainstream and propounded by influential individuals or groups.

When it comes to reflecting the opinions of their various publics, individual news venues often fall short. Still, they know that they cannot stray too far afield lest they lose their audiences. Hence they cling to the mainstream. For their part, the audience may not mirror the opinions expressed in the media but they use news stories as raw materials for shaping their own views. That assures that the gaps between media images and public opinions rarely become huge. Collectively, when public officials and private parties sample news offerings nationwide, they receive a reasonably good picture of the prevailing trends of opinions.

Measured against ideal standards, the surveillance and watchdog functions are also poorly performed by most news media. That harsh verdict softens substantially when one considers the practical obstacles to routine political surveillance and to investigative political journalism. Overall, surveillance of the political scene and monitoring of politicians have improved steadily in recent decades thanks to the many new media venues, including the Internet. Investigative journalism has had some spectacular successes and is a sword of Damocles that can scare corruptible politicians away from misdeeds.

A realistic standard of news evaluation based on actualities and feasible options also requires acknowledging that the quantity and quality of news vary widely among the thousands of news venues that are currently readily available in the United States. Many of these venues earn high ratings even from the severest critics of current media offerings. More would do so if they were judged by scientific content measurements rather than stereotypes and if content adequacy judgments were gauged by the needs of monitorial citizens.

Realistic standards also require foregoing criticism of conditions that are intrinsically unchangeable. News organizations cannot collect all available information and disseminate it rapidly. Much important information will never be collected or reported until it is too late to be useful. The promise of the *New York Times* that it offers "all the news that is fit to print" is a cruel joke. The capacity of citizens to pay attention to all they need to know is similarly limited because human capacity to absorb and process information is physiologically and psychologically bounded, and time available for dealing with citizenship concerns is short.

Nonetheless, focus-group evidence reveals that people from all walks of life are far more sophisticated about politics than currently used civic IQ tests indicate (Gamson 2001, Graber 2001). Current tests call for readily measurable recall of specific facts and figures that most people never store in their memories or forget rapidly. Like the drunkard who looks for his lost keys under the lamppost because the light is better, even though he dropped them elsewhere, most current tests miss their targets. Investigators fail to ask the productive, open-ended questions that allow citizens to frame their own responses in ways dictated by how they encoded information originally.

When people are allowed to tell what interests them and what they know, using their own words rather than responding to questions framed by investigators, the harvest of significant political information tends to be rich. Such open-ended tests reveal that most people know and use shortcuts for making sound political decisions, even when their detailed factual knowledge is sparse. For example, party labels in news stories allow them to infer which policies best serve their interests, and brief biographies furnish a basis for identifying trustworthy leaders whose opinions citizens then can adopt.

Granted that news media serve the public far better than their current reputation suggests and that monitorial citizens deserve upgraded ratings for political understanding and participation, is it enough? Can democracy still thrive? To answer that question requires going beyond the myth that the survival of democracy hinges predominantly on an excellent free press that supports effective, participatory citizenship. The focus must be expanded beyond the media/citizen dynamic to the interaction of the media with other parts of the political system. This essay has concentrated on those aspects of media performance by which media support of democratic governance has been traditionally judged; so I have not examined equally, if not more, important aspects of democratization in which the media have had a powerful influence. I refer to the impact of the media on the political system in general and on various political institutions.

To give a few examples: Scholars have chronicled how media coverage of the President affects his relationship with Congress, including his ability to have his legislative priorities enacted (Kernell 1997). Presidents who "go public" by asking citizens to support their policies may thereby use the news media to weaken Congress and strengthen the presidency. In fact, mobilization of the public via the media is a typical example of the two-step process in which elites first are aroused by news stories and then transmit their concerns to the public. Media coverage that mobilized elite opposition to the Vietnam War is another example. It ultimately generated public demands for major shifts in U.S. foreign policy (Braestrup 1983). Media coverage of obscure political parties and candidates occasionally has allowed them to emerge from the shadows, although it has rarely made them winners. These types of media impacts affect the quality of democracy even when mass publics are not involved initially.

Abroad, the media have been praised as crucial actors in promoting democracy in formerly authoritarian countries, either by showing images of thriving democratic societies or by depicting the weaknesses of dictatorships. These instances point to the vast influence modern media have had in promoting democratic governance at opportune moments in history. Media may not promote democracy very vigorously on a daily basis while still performing a key role in times of crisis. At such times, their power grows also because people who normally ignore the news flock to the media. For example, during the period following the presidential election of 2000, when control of that vital office was at stake, news audiences rose by as much as 250% on CNN and 440% on Fox news. Media coverage of the various complex aspects of that situation was far more detailed and helpful than during less critical times.

In a nutshell, democracy manages to function, albeit imperfectly, despite a media system that gives it too little support much of the time. As Gunther & Mughan (2000) concluded after studying the media/democracy interface in 10 politically diverse countries, what seems to matter most is the spirit in which political elites conduct the affairs of government. The historical evidence that they cite provides convincing proof that democracy is safe in political cultures pervaded by democratic principles, even when some practices stray from these principles. If that is true, then American democracy seems secure as long as American governments, American journalists, and the American public continue to be ideologically committed to democracy. In fact, governance is apt to become increasingly democratic. The history of the broadening of the suffrage in the United States and the civil rights movement are examples. American democracy does not work nearly as well as one would hope, and flaws in media offerings and citizen actions must share the blame. But, on balance, American democracy has managed to sustain its chief goals despite the imperfections of its tools.

The *Annual Review of Political Science* is online at
http://polisci.annualreviews.org

LITERATURE CITED

Alger D. 1998. *Megamedia: How Giant Corporations Dominate Mass Media, Distort Competition and Endanger Democracy.* Lanham, MD: Rowman & Littlefield

Althaus SL, Edy JA, Phalen PF. 2001 Using substitutes for full-text news stories in content analysis: Which text is best? *Am. J. Polit. Sci.* 45:707–23

Altheide DL. 1984. Media hegemony: a failure of perspective. *Public Opin. Q.* 48:476–90

Asher H. 2001. *Polling and the Public: What Every Citizen Should Know.* Washington, DC: CQ Press. 5th ed.

Bagdikian BH. 1996. *The Media Monopoly.* Boston: Beacon. 5th ed.

Barber BR. 1998. Three scenarios for the future of technology and strong democracy. *Polit. Sci. Q.* 113(4):573–89

Becker T, Slaton CD. 2000. *The Future of Teledemocracy.* Westport, CT: Praeger

Bennett SE, Rhine SL, Flickinger RS, Bennett LLM. 1999. Videomalaise revisited: reconsidering the relation between the public's view of the media and trust in government. *Harvard Int. J. Press/Polit.* 4(4):8–23

Bennett WL. 1998. The uncivic culture: communication, identity, and the rise of lifestyle politics. *P.S. Polit. Sci. Polit.* 31:741–62

Bennett WL, Entman RM. 2001. *Mediated Politics: Communication in the Future of Democracy.* Cambridge, UK: Cambridge Univ. Press

Bimber B. 1999. The internet and citizen communication with government: Does the medium matter? *Polit. Commun.* 16:409–28

Bimber B. 2003. *Information and American Democracy: Technology in the Evolution of Political Power.* Cambridge, UK: Cambridge Univ. Press. In press

Bishop G. 2001. Illusion of change. *Public Persp.* 13(3):38–41

Braestrup P. 1983. *Big Story.* New Haven, CT: Yale Univ. Press

Brants K. 1998. Who's afraid of infotainment? *Eur. J. Commun.* 13:315–35

Bucy EP, Gregson KS. 2001. Media participation: a legitimizing mechanism of mass democracy. *New Media Soc.* 3:357–80

Capella JN, Jamieson KH. 1997. *Spiral of Cynicism: the Press and the Public Good.* New York: Oxford Univ. Press

Committee of Concerned Journalists. 1999. *Changing Definition of News: Subject of News Stories by Medium.* http://www.journalism.org/lastudy2.htm

Compaine B, Gomery D. 2000. *Who Owns the Media? Competition and Concentration in the Media Industry.* Mahwah, NJ: Erlbaum. 3rd ed.

Cook TE. 1998. *Governing with the News: the News Media as Political Institutions.* Chicago: Univ. Chicago Press

Curran J. 1996. Mass media and democracy revisited. In *Mass Media and Society,* ed. J Curran, M Gurevitch, pp. 81–119. London: Arnold

Dahlberg L. 2001. Democracy via cyberspace. *New Media Soc.* 3:157–77

Dahlgren P. 2001. The public sphere and the net: structure, space and communication. See Bennett & Entman 2001, pp. 33–55

Davis R. 1999. *The Web of Politics: the Internet's Impact on the American Political System.* New York: Oxford Univ. Press

Davis R, Owen D. 1998. *New Media and American Politics.* New York: Oxford Univ. Press

de Tocqueville A. 1984 (1835). *Democracy in America (De la démocratie en Amérique),* ed. RD Heffner. New York: Penguin

Delli Carpini MX, Keeter S. 1996. *What Americans Know About Politics and Why it Matters.* New Haven, CT: Yale Univ. Press

Entman RM, Herbst S. 2001. Reframing public opinion as we have known it. See Bennett & Entman 2001, pp. 203–25

Fallows J. 1996. *Breaking the News: How the Media Undermine American Democracy.* New York: Pantheon Books

Farrel DM. 1996. Campaign strategies and tactics. In *Comparing Democracies: Elections and Voting in Comparative Perspective,* ed. L LeDuc, RG Niemi, P Norris, pp. 160–83. Thousand Oaks, CA: Sage

Franklin B. 1997. *Newszak and News Media.* London: Arnold

Gamson WA. 2001. Promoting political engagement. See Bennett & Entman 2001, pp. 56–74

Graber DA. 1986. Press freedom and the general welfare. *Polit. Sci. Q.* 101:257–75

Graber DA. 2001. *Processing Politics: Learning from Television in the Internet Age.* Chicago: Univ. Chicago Press

Graber DA, Bimber B, Bennett WL, Davis R, Norris P. 2003. The internet and politics:

emerging perspectives. In *The Internet and the Academy*, ed. M Price, H Nissenbaum. New York: Lang. In press

Gunther R, Mughan A. 2000. The media in democratic and nondemocratic regimes: a multilevel perspective. In *Democracy and the Media: a Comparative Perspective*, ed. R Gunther, A Mughan, pp. 1–27. Cambridge, UK: Cambridge Univ. Press

Gurevitch M, Blumler JG. 1990. Political communication systems and democratic values. In *Democracy and the Mass Media*, ed. J Lichtenberg, pp. 269–87. Cambridge, UK: Cambridge Univ. Press

Hemmer JJ. 2000. *Communication Law: The Supreme Court and the First Amendment.* Lanham, MD: Austin & Winfield

Hermes J. 1997. Cultural citizenship and popular fiction. In *The Media in Question: Popular Cultures and Public Interests*, ed. K Brants, J Hermes, L van Zoonen, pp. 157–67. London: Sage

Hill KA, Hughes JE. 1998. *Cyberpolitics: Citizen Activism in the Age of the Internet.* Lanham, MD: Rowman & Littlefield

Iyengar S. 1991. *Is Anyone Responsible? How Television Frames Political Issues.* Chicago: Univ. Chicago Press

Jamieson KH, Waldman P. 2003. *The Press Effect: Politicians, Journalists, and the Stories that Shape the Political World.* New York: Oxford Univ. Press

Just MR, Crigler AN, Alger DE, Cook TE, Kern M, West DM. 1996. *Crosstalk: Citizens, Candidates and the Media in a Presidential Campaign.* Chicago: Univ. Chicago Press

Keck ME, Sikkink K. 1998. *Activists Beyond Borders: Advocacy Networks in International Politics.* Ithaca, NY: Cornell Univ. Press

Kernell S. 1997. *Going Public: New Strategies of Presidential Leadership.* Washington, DC: CQ Press. 3rd ed.

Key VO Jr. with Cummings MC Jr. 1965. *The Responsible Electorate.* Cambridge, MA: Harvard Univ. Press

Kuklinski JH, Quirk PJ, Jerit J, Rich RF. 2001. The political environment and citizen deci-sion making: information, motivation, and policy tradeoffs. *Am. J. Polit. Sci.* 45(2):410–24

Kurtz H. 1998. *Spin Cycle: Inside the Clinton Propaganda Machine.* New York: Free

Lang G, Lang K. 1983. *The Battle for Public Opinion: The President, the Press and the Polls During Watergate.* New York: Columbia Univ. Press

Lupia A, McCubbins MD. 1998. *The Democratic Dilemma: Can Citizens Learn What They Need to Know?* New York: Cambridge Univ. Press

Mancini P. 1999. New frontiers in political professionalism. *Polit. Commun.* 16:231–45

Margolis M, Resnick D. 2000. *Politics as Usual: the Cyberspace Revolution.* Thousand Oaks, CA: Sage

Mayhew L. 1997. *The New Public: Professional Communication and the Means of Social Influence.* Cambridge, UK: Cambridge Univ. Press

Mazzoleni G, Schulz W. 1999. "Mediatization" of politics: a challenge for democracy? *Polit. Commun.* 16:247–61

McChesney RW. 2000. *Rich Media, Poor Democracy: Communication Politics in Dubious Times.* New York: New

Miller A, Listhaug O. 1999. Political performance and institutional trust. In *Critical Citizens: Global Support for Democratic Government*, ed. P Norris, pp. 204–16. New York: Oxford Univ. Press

Neuman WR. 1986. *The Paradox of Mass Politics: Knowledge and Opinion in the American Electorate.* Cambridge, MA: Harvard Univ. Press

Neuman WR, Just MP, Crigler AN. 1992. *Common Knowledge: News and the Construction of Political Meaning.* Chicago: Univ. Chicago Press

Norris P. 2000a. *A Virtuous Circle: Political Communications in Postindustrial Societies.* Cambridge, UK: Cambridge Univ. Press

Norris P. 2000b. The impact of television and civic malaise. In *Disaffected Democrats: What's Troubling the Trilateral Countries?*

ed. SJ Pharr, RD Putnam, pp. 231–51. Princeton, NJ: Princeton Univ. Press

Norris P. 2001. *Digital Divide: Civic Engagement, Information Poverty, and the Internet Worldwide*. Cambridge, UK: Cambridge Univ. Press

Nye JS Jr, Zelikow PD, King PD. 1997. *Why People Don't Trust Government*. Cambridge, MA: Harvard Univ. Press

Page BI, Shapiro RY. 1991. *The Rational Public: Fifty Years of Trends in American Policy Preferences*. Chicago: Univ. Chicago Press

Patterson TE. 1993. *Out of Order*. New York: Knopf

Pew Research Center for the People and the Press. 1998a. *1998 Media Consumption: Section 3: American News Habits*. http://www.people-press.org/med98rpt.htm

Pew Research Center for the People and the Press. 1998b. *How Americans View Government: Deconstructing Distrust: Questionnaire Part II*. http://www.people-press.org/reports

Pew Research Center for the People and the Press. 2000. *Media Report*. http://www.people-press.org/med00rpt.htm

Picard R. 1998. Media concentration, economics and regulation. In *The Politics of News, the News of Politics*, ed. D Graber, D McQuail, P Norris, pp. 193–217. Washington, DC: CQ Press

Popkin SL. 1994. *The Reasoning Voter: Communication and Persuasion in Presidential Campaigns*. Chicago: Univ. Chicago Press. 2nd ed.

Popkin S, Dimock MA. 1999. Political knowledge and citizen competence. In *Citizen Competence and Democratic Institutions*, ed. SL Elkin, KE Soltan, pp. 117–46. University Park: Penn. State Univ. Press

Postman N. 1985. *Amusing Ourselves to Death: Public Discourse in the Age of Show Business*. New York: Penguin

Protess DL, Cook FL, Doppelt JC, Ettema JS, Gordon MT, et al. 1991. *The Journalism of Outrage: Investigative Reporting and Agenda Building in America*. New York: Guilford

Rahn WM, Rudolph TJ. 2001. National identities and the future of democracy. See Bennett & Entman 2001, pp. 453–67

Rahn WM, Krosnick JA, Breuning M. 1994. Rationalization and derivation processes in survey studies of political candidate evaluation. *Am. J. Polit. Sci.* 38:582–600

Red Lion Broadcasting Co. v. FCC. 1969. 395 U.S. 367

Sabato LJ, Stencel M, Lichter SR. 2000. *Peepshow: Media and Politics in an Age of Scandal*. Lanham, MD: Rowman & Littlefield

Schiller HI. 1989. *Culture, Inc: the Corporate Takeover of Public Expression*. New York: Oxford Univ. Press

Schmitter PC, Karl TL. 1991. What democracy is . . . and is not. *J. Democr.* 2:75–88

Schudson M. n.d. *Good citizens and bad history: today's political ideals in historical perspective*. College of Mass Commun., Middle Tenn. State Univ.

Schudson M. 1998. *The Good Citizen: a History of American Civic Life*. New York: Free

Schudson M. 2002. The news media as political institutions. *Annu. Rev. Polit. Sci.* 5:249–69

Semetko H. 1996. The media. In *Comparing Democracies*, ed. L LeDuc, R Niemi, P Norris, pp. 254–79. Thousand Oaks, CA: Sage

Sunstein C. 2001. *Republic.com*. Princeton, NJ: Princeton Univ. Press

Swanson DL. 1997. The political-media complex at 50: putting the 1996 presidential election in context. *Am. Behav. Sci.* 40:1264–82

Tillinghast CH. 2000. *American Broadcast Regulation and the First Amendment*. Ames, IA: Iowa State Univ. Press

Traugott MW, Lavrakas PJ. 2000. *The Voter's Guide to Election Polls*. New York: Chatham House. 2nd ed.

Tsagarousianou R, Tambini D, Brian C, eds. 1998. *Cyberdemocracy: Technology, Cities and Civic Networks*. London: Routledge

Weaver DH, Wilhoit GC. 1996. *The American*

Journalist in the 1990's: U.S. News People at the End of an Era. Mahwah, NJ: Erlbaum

Zaller J. 1994. Elite leadership of mass opinion: new evidence from the Gulf War. In *Taken by Storm: the Media, Public Opinion, and U.S. Foreign Policy in the Gulf War*, ed. WL Bennett, DL Paletz, pp. 186–209. Chicago: Univ. Chicago Press

Zaller J. 2001. Monica Lewinsky and the mainsprings of American politics. See Bennett & Entman 2001, pp. 252–78

Annu. Rev. Polit. Sci. 2003. 6:161–80
doi: 10.1146/annurev.polisci.6.121901.085526

THE SUPREME COURT IN AMERICAN POLITICS

Lawrence Baum

*Department of Political Science, 154 North Oval Mall, Ohio State University, Columbus,
Ohio 43210; email: baum.4@osu.edu*

Key Words   judicial policy making, judicial review, strategic behavior,
implementation, policy impact

■ **Abstract**   The Supreme Court's role in American politics is a product of its interventions in public policy making and the impact of those interventions on government
and society. The Court's frequent and substantial interventions during the past half century are especially striking, and their extent and their beneficiaries cannot be explained
fully by major theories of the Court's behavior. The Court's rulings often receive negative responses from other policy makers, but even more noteworthy is the degree to
which judges and administrators carry out the Court's policies and legislators leave
those policies standing and the Court unscathed. Scholars who emphasize the Court's
limited ability to change society make a strong case, but it is not clear to what extent
the Court's limitations are unique to the judiciary and to what extent they reflect the
limited powers of government in general.

INTRODUCTION

The Supreme Court's ruling in *Bush v. Gore* (2000) attracted enormous attention
and a good deal of debate. In one sense this ruling and its aftermath were novel:
Never before had a court directly resolved a presidential election. But in another
sense *Bush v. Gore* was just one in a long series of significant judicial interventions
in public policy by courts in the United States.

For the most part, controversies over these interventions have focused on the
merits of court decisions in themselves. But the fact of intervention is often an
issue as well. The courts differ from the other branches of government in that their
involvement in the making of public policy is widely questioned.

Normative issues concerning the role of the courts in a democratic system
have interested both scholars and non-scholars. Political scientists participate in
the debates over these issues, but their more distinctive contribution is addressing
empirical questions about the courts' role as public policy makers. One set of
questions concerns the extent and content of judicial intervention in policy; another
concerns the impact of intervention when it does occur.

This review considers these questions, focusing on the Supreme Court. Its
interventions in policy are especially visible and consequential, so scholars have

given it the preponderance of their attention. An examination of the Court as intervenor can illuminate its behavior as a policy maker and its position in the political system.

JUDICIAL INTERVENTION IN POLICY

People who discuss judicial involvement in public policy making often characterize levels and forms of involvement in terms of "activism." That term is imprecise because it has taken on a wide range of meanings (Canon 1982). In the political arena, it is mostly an epithet; as Joel Grossman has said, "Basically, judicial activism is what the other guy does that you don't like" (Willing 1997). Thus I use the term intervention. That term has ambiguities of its own, but it can be given a straightforward definition: action by a court that substantially modifies or negates policies of the other branches of government.

The Extent of Intervention

How much does the Supreme Court intervene in policy, and what forces shape the pattern of interventions? One way to address these questions is from the perspective of the goals that motivate Supreme Court justices and the ways they act on those goals.

Among students of judicial behavior, there is a lively debate over the justices' hierarchies of goals (see Baum 1997). The most contentious issue is whether justices act almost exclusively on their interest in making good public policy or whether they balance that interest against the goal of interpreting the law well. Most students of judicial behavior explicitly or implicitly take the first position (Epstein & Knight 1998, Segal & Spaeth 2002; see Gillman 2001). The work of some political scientists challenges this position, explicitly or implicitly, in part by examining the legal frameworks in which decisions are made (Kahn 1994, Bussiere 1997, Richards & Kritzer 2002), and the issue remains open. But policy considerations certainly play a powerful part in shaping the justices' choices. Moreover, their impact is likely to be especially strong in cases involving possible interventions, cases that have high stakes for public policy. If justices balance legal and policy considerations, their policy goals can be expected to have the greatest impact when justices care most about the policy issues they face (see Kunda 1990). In any event, adopting the premise of policy-oriented behavior helps to illuminate the issues that I consider in this section.

If the justices' policy goals are the primary motivation affecting the Court's interventions, there remains the question of how justices act on those goals. Running through much of the scholarship on Supreme Court decision making is a conception of the justices as strategic actors (Murphy 1964, Rohde 1972, Maltzman et al. 2000). In this conception, justices depart from the policy positions that they most prefer under two conditions: when a departure helps to achieve the best feasible policy outcome in the Court and, ultimately, in government as a whole (e.g., modifying a policy position to avoid a congressional override of the Court's decision), or when a departure helps to preserve the Court's institutional standing and thus its capacity to make policy. This view of the Court, which emphasizes its interdependence with the other branches, has become increasingly popular in the past decade. That popularity reflects the growing use of formal theory and rational choice frameworks, with their assumption of strategic behavior, in the study of judicial behavior (Epstein & Knight 2000).

The extent to which justices think strategically is an open question. Some scholars treat strategic behavior as an inevitable concomitant of policy goals: If judges act on their policy preferences, they must choose between alternative positions on the basis of the prospective impact of each alternative on government policy as a whole. But judges might gain satisfaction chiefly from taking positions that reflect their policy preferences directly rather than from trying to influence the state of government policy (Posner 1995, p. 123; see Kuran 1995, pp. 30–35). Even if we assume that justices are strategic actors, it is uncertain how often they need to depart from their preferred positions for strategic purposes. The belief that justices seldom make such departures in voting on case outcomes is the basis for the "attitudinal model" of Supreme Court behavior.[1] In this model, the justices' positions in cases directly reflect their policy preferences (Rohde & Spaeth 1976, Segal & Spaeth 2002). The belief that such departures are frequent and substantial is the basis for analyses in which strategy plays a central role, analyses that follow a "strategic model" of Court behavior (Epstein & Knight 1998).

Different as the attitudinal and strategic models are, each provides reasons to predict limited judicial interventions in national policy. For the attitudinal model, these reasons were spelled out most clearly by Dahl (1957) in a classic article. As Dahl saw it, the Court's interventions are limited by the rules for selecting justices, which ensure that "the policy views dominant on the Court are never for long out of line with the policy views dominant among the lawmaking majorities of the United States" (Dahl 1957, p. 285). Thus, justices who act directly on their policy preferences generally support rather than attack policies established by the other branches. The Court, then, is "inevitably a part of the dominant national alliance" that "supports the major policies of the alliance" (Dahl 1957, p. 293).

Of course, the justices' life terms create a lag between the accession of a lawmaking majority and that majority's capture of the Supreme Court. As a result, there are "transitional periods" (Dahl 1957, p. 293) in which the Court's collective policy views are temporarily out of line, of which the early New Deal period was the most prominent example. But such periods are "short-lived" (p. 293) aberrations, terminated when presidents change the Court's membership sufficiently. Franklin

---

[1]As described by its leading proponents (Segal & Spaeth 2002), the attitudinal model allows for substantial strategic behavior in other stages of decision making, such as selection of cases to be decided on the merits. But these proponents argue that even justices who think in strategic terms depart very little from their preferred positions in response to their political environment (Segal 1997; Segal & Spaeth 2002, pp. 103–14).

Roosevelt had bad luck in that he could appoint no new justices in his first term. But once vacancies appeared during his second term, he was able to reshape the Court and its positions on federal regulatory power.

The strategic model seems to lead directly to a pattern of limited intervention. Justices who act strategically could be expected to focus much of their strategic behavior on the other branches of government, because they recognize the array of powers held by the legislature and executive. The other branches can limit the impact of the Court's decisions or even negate those decisions, thereby rendering interventions futile. More important, Congress and the president can attack the Court's institutional position when they are unhappy with its rulings, thereby reducing both its concrete powers and the authority or legitimacy on which its influence over policy presumably rests. Recognizing these potential consequences, strategic justices would avoid some interventions that might otherwise be attractive to them.

Scholars have given strategic interpretations to the Court's actions in some historical episodes. The Court under John Marshall (1801–1835) was assertive on behalf of national power and its own prerogatives, but accounts of the Marshall Court generally emphasize Marshall's efforts to avoid confrontations with the other branches in order to protect the Court and maximize its influence (Graber 1999; McCloskey & Levinson 2000, pp. 23–52). The end of the Court's opposition to New Deal policies in 1937 is usually interpreted as a consequence of the effort by one or two justices to head off a confrontation with the president and Congress that might do serious damage to the Court (but see Cushman 1998). The Court's conservative shift on civil liberties during the late 1950s is typically seen as a retreat under congressional attack (Pritchett 1961, Murphy 1962).

The implications of the strategic model for policy interventions depend in part on the form of strategic behavior in which the justices engage. One possibility is that justices continuously monitor their political environment and adjust their positions in response. Several scholars have argued that the Court engages in this "routine strategy" in interpreting federal statutes. As they see it, the justices depart from their most preferred positions when needed to avoid a likely congressional override of their decision (Eskridge 1991, Spiller & Gely 1992). A few scholars have argued that routine strategy occurs in constitutional cases as well (Epstein et al. 2001, Martin 2001). If this is the justices' mode of behavior, we might expect few significant interventions of the sort that could provoke confrontations with the other branches.

Another possibility is that the justices ordinarily give little attention to their political environment but take protective action when their decisions have aroused negative reactions from other policy makers. Justices might reason that it is a poor strategy to depart from their most preferred positions to avoid the possibility of an unfavorable response from the other branches. But when conflicts actually occur, the justices retreat as a means to limit the damage. What might be called crisis-driven strategy is analogous to the "fire alarm" form of congressional oversight over the executive branch (McCubbins & Schwartz 1984). Compared with routine strategy, it would lead to more interventions and more confrontations, but some periods of intervention would end abruptly as the justices responded to conflicts provoked by their decisions.

Thus, Dahl's version of the attitudinal model and these two versions of the strategic model all predict limited intervention by the Court, but they suggest somewhat different frequencies and patterns of intervention. The first issue to consider is whether their shared prediction is accurate. The second is their relative success in accounting for the Court's record of intervention.

The first issue is straightforward but very difficult to resolve. One difficulty lies simply in identifying significant interventions. Dahl (1957) restricted himself to rulings that strike down federal statutes on constitutional grounds, a reasonable limitation because this form of intervention seems to involve the most direct conflict with the other branches. Yet Dahl himself argued that many such rulings are not significant interventions, either because they come many years after enactment of the statute in question (and thus do not challenge a contemporary law-making majority) or because they involve minor issues. Of course, judgments about the significance of the issues involved in an invalidated statute may be contested. Dahl's limitation of analysis to decisions that strike down federal statutes itself could be contested. In the most important response to Dahl, Casper (1976) argued that invalidations of state statutes and even interpretations of federal statutes can constitute significant interventions.

Another difficulty lies in interpreting the frequency of interventions, a difficulty that has increased since the time Dahl wrote. Dahl counted only 86 provisions of federal law that had been struck down by 1957. It was reasonable to conclude that this type of intervention was infrequent. Further, Dahl was on firm ground in concluding that a good many of these invalidations were not very significant. Even so, another scholar might have read the record somewhat differently.

Shortly after Dahl wrote, the Court initiated a period of heightened intervention that has continued for nearly half a century. Since 1960, the Court has struck down more federal statutes and nearly as many state and local laws as it had in its entire history up to 1960 (Baum 2001, pp. 197, 199). Perhaps more important, the Court has invalidated legislative and administrative policy on a wide range of important issues. Among these issues are school segregation, school religious observances, legislative districting, criminal procedure, abortion, and (most recently) federal power to regulate state governments and the private sector. Casper (1976) pointed to this new wave of intervention in questioning Dahl's conclusions about the Court's role. A quarter century later, the questioning could be even more pointed.

Striking as it is, this record too can be interpreted in different ways. Of the many federal statutes that the Court has struck down since 1960, the great majority clearly were of minor importance. The Court's strongest attacks on existing policy were aimed at state laws and practices. Indeed, some scholars have suggested that the Warren Court actually was affirming values that had strong support in national government, as a part of the successful New Deal coalition (Shapiro 1978) or as "a functioning part of the Kennedy-Johnson liberalism" of the 1960s (Powe 2000,

p. 494). Still, the level of intervention over the past half century challenges both the strategic accounts and Dahl's account.

For Dahl, of course, the challenge stems partly from the sheer volume of intervention in the current era. Just as important, the Court's active participation in policy making has continued for a long period. Dahl suggested that significant interventions occur chiefly in transitional periods, similar to what other scholars have labeled realignments.[2] The several decades since 1960 are too long to be labeled a transitional period. On the other hand, this is an era in which partisan control of House, Senate, and presidency has been divided most of the time. In such an era, it is difficult even to identify a law-making majority, let alone characterize the Court's interventions in relation to that majority.

The attitudinal model in its more general form provides a ready explanation for the Court's record of interventions in the past half century. A series of appointments created and maintained a Court whose collective positions on civil liberties ran contrary to many national and state policies (see Schubert 1970, p. 180). More recently, another series of appointments produced a Court with five members who disagreed with the expansion of federal regulatory power in some areas. Following their preferences, the justices in the majority have struck down the statutes and other government practices with which they disagreed.

This attitudinal explanation cannot be fully tested until scholars develop fairly precise measures of the justices' preferences that are independent of their decisional behavior, an enormously difficult task (see Segal & Cover 1989). That matter aside, one feature of the Court's history over the past half century might be problematical for an attitudinal account: Why did Republican presidents from the 1950s to the 1990s appoint so many justices who supported and even spearheaded a wave of interventions with liberal content? The answer may rest heavily on chance, abetted by Democratic Senate majorities during much of that period. If so, the Court's sustained interventions might be regarded as an aberration (albeit a major one) from the process that Dahl described, and thus they create no difficulty for a generalized attitudinal explanation. But if there is something about the justices' social environments that has drawn some to the left, as conservative commentators complain (Bryden 1992, Sowell 1994), the attitudinal model is incomplete. Scholars have not probed this possibility.

The challenge of the Court's record to a conception of routine strategy lies partly in the frequency with which the Court has undertaken interventions that aroused strongly negative reactions, including attacks on the Court and its decisions by policy makers in the other branches. Justices should have been able to predict that

---

[2]Several scholars have analyzed the relationship between realignments and invalidations of federal statutes (Funston 1975, Canon & Ulmer 1976, Lasser 1985, Gates 1992). Taken as a whole, their studies indicate that the relationship is not strong. These inquiries do not fully test Dahl's argument: realignments need not coincide with the periods of strongest policy disagreements between the Court and the other branches, and the divisions involved in a realignment are more relevant to some judicial issues than to others (Gates 1992).

decisions mandating school desegregation, banning school religious observances, limiting police investigations, and overturning state abortion laws would arouse such reactions. Of course, strategic considerations may have prevented the Court from engaging in even more intervention. Indeed, an interest in avoiding conflict undoubtedly played into the Court's refusal to address the legality of American participation in the Vietnam War and the delay in its striking down state laws against interracial marriage, to take two examples. Still, the justices' willingness to get into so many conflicts indicates less caution on their part than we would expect if the justices engage in what I have called routine strategy.

Recent history also raises questions about a conception of crisis-driven strategy. Only in the late 1950s did the Court seem to undertake even a mild retreat under pressure. The justices' more common reaction has been to maintain the policies that had led to conflict with the other branches. In a typical episode, when the flag-burning decision of 1989 (*Texas v. Johnson*) was met with denunciations, a serious effort to amend the Constitution, and a federal statute designed to get around the decision, the five justices who formed the 1989 majority responded by reiterating their position (*United States v. Eichman* 1990) (see Goldstein 2000).

As noted above, one possible explanation for such behavior is that justices do not think strategically. But it might be that justices who do think strategically see little need to adjust their positions in the face of potential or actual threats to their institutional position. Congress sometimes acts to limit the impact of the Court's policy interventions or even to overturn them altogether, though it is unclear how frequently it does so (Dahl 1957, pp. 288–91; Casper 1976, pp. 53, 59; Meernik & Ignagni 1997, pp. 458, 461–62). But in the current era, it is striking how seldom Congress overturns even highly unpopular interventions. When Congress does act against the Court's policy, the Court ordinarily is no worse off than if it had not intervened. Thus, eschewing intervention to avoid possible reversal may constitute poor strategy, since it costs opportunities for justices to advance their preferred policies.

Congress can do more damage when it attacks the Court itself. But Congress seldom uses its institutional powers against the Court in significant ways. For example, the Court's size has not been changed since the 1860s. Over that period, its jurisdiction has never been cut back as a negative response to its policies despite a long list of bills with that purpose. Unpopular decisions may cost the Court a degree of public support in the short run (Hoekstra 2000), but in the long run the Court's standing tends to hold up well (Mondak & Smithey 1997). Thus, justices have reason to think that even under relatively difficult conditions, they can engage in policy interventions that they find appropriate without fear of serious consequences.

Bush v. Gore is a good example. Once it became clear that the Supreme Court would split along ideological lines in the case, the Court's conservative justices surely understood that a decision guaranteeing victory to Governor Bush would arouse vitriolic criticism. But they also had reason to think they could weather the storm. With a Republican president soon to take office and Republican majorities in both houses of Congress, the chance of legislative retaliation against the Court was nil. A good share of the elite and mass publics would question the integrity of the five justices, but a share of approximately equal size would applaud their judgment. And the breadth and depth of the attacks on these justices almost surely would die down month by month after the decision. Under the circumstances, even if the Court's conservatives were acting solely on policy considerations, the enormous satisfaction to be gained by ensuring the election of a Republican president and thereby advancing conservative policies would have outweighed the potential negatives of that decision. And that calculation would have been right; nothing concrete happened to the Court, and its public standing suffered no great harm (see Gibson et al. 2002).

Evidence about the Court's policy interventions is open to multiple interpretations. On the whole, however, the Court's record of policy interventions seems more consistent with an attitudinal account than with a strategic account (Segal & Spaeth 2002, pp. 112–14). As I have discussed, this record might reflect the calculations of justices who think strategically: At least since the Court secured general acceptance of its institutional position in the first half of the nineteenth century, it generally appears to be good strategy for policy-oriented justices simply to follow their preferences. Alternatively, some or all of the justices simply may not think in strategic terms; rather, they act directly on their preferences because they care more about the positions they take than about the ultimate impact of the Court's decisions. It is impossible to choose between these two explanations on the basis of the existing evidence. That choice is critical to our understanding of judicial behavior, but it is much less consequential for an understanding of the Court's role in policy making.

With their shared emphasis on the justices' policy preferences, the attitudinal and strategic models may not encompass fully the forces that shape Supreme Court intervention in public policy. Two other possibilities have been noted. Justices' interest in making what they see as good law might affect their choices of when and how to intervene. And elements of justices' social environment might exert a subtle impact on their policy orientations, as conservatives have claimed about some Republican appointees.

The justices' attitudes toward intervention in itself also might play into their judgments. Empirical research casts considerable doubt on the idea that "judicial restraint" deters justices from following their policy preferences (Spaeth 1964, Spaeth & Teger 1982, Spaeth & Altfeld 1986). Yet something broader and more subtle might affect the justices: They may feel more comfortable intervening in policy after intervention has become frequent and substantial. In particular, the active policy making of the Warren Court in the 1950s and 1960s may have altered expectations so that justices who served on the Court in the decades that followed found it easy to engage in their own interventions.

On a different level, judicial intervention in policy is affected by the litigation process. This consideration is especially relevant to determining the beneficiaries of intervention, so I consider it in that context.

Who Benefits from Interventions

The role of the courts in a democratic system depends not only on the extent of policy intervention but also on its content. Perhaps the most important aspect of its content is the allocation of gains and losses among segments of society. Judicial interventions on particular issues typically serve those who are unable to gain favorable policies on those issues elsewhere in government. To oversimplify, the primary beneficiaries of interventions in any period might fall into either of two broad classes. One is people and groups that are advantaged in the sense that they have high social and economic status, interests that seek redress from the courts at times when the other branches are relatively unfavorable to them. The other set of interests consists of disadvantaged people with little conventional political power, who seek to gain in the courts what they seldom could win in the other branches.

The attitudinal and strategic models do not predict the success of these two classes directly. However, the logic of each might lead us to expect the Court to tilt in favor of advantaged interests. Most justices have come from families of high socioeconomic status, most have achieved financial success in their careers, and in those careers most have associated chiefly with people of relatively high status. Thus their policy preferences might tend to reflect the interests of advantaged groups. Further, since those groups generally have the greatest political power, they would seem to be in the best position to affect the calculations of justices who take the Court's political environment into account.

In one of the most influential articles in the study of courts, law professor Marc Galanter (1974) argued that "the 'haves' come out ahead" in the courts because the various advantages of people with social and economic power translate into success in litigation. Galanter's analysis focused heavily on trial courts. Scholars responding to Galanter have taken a variety of positions, some of them emphasizing the difficulty of testing his argument (Kritzer & Silbey 1999). But the majority view appears to be that Galanter was more right than wrong, at least at the trial level.

In the early 1940s, two commentators reached a similar conclusion about the Supreme Court. Henry Steele Commager (1943, p. 428) and U.S. Attorney General Robert Jackson (1941, p. 187), shortly to join the Court, wrote in emphatic terms that the Court almost invariably favored socially advantaged interests. Commager focused on the Court's decisions striking down federal statutes. More than a decade later, Dahl (1957, pp. 291–93) took a similar position, though less emphatically (see also Galloway 1991). Commager and Jackson may have overstated their case, but they captured a basic truth.

The Court's civil liberties decisions from the 1950s on produced a fundamental change in perceptions of its beneficiaries. For the first time, the Court was widely viewed as an ally of people with little economic or conventional political power. This shift in perceptions was reflected in Casper's 1976 response to Dahl.

The Court's civil libertarian policies did not serve disadvantaged groups alone. More privileged sectors of society also benefitted, especially from the Court's expansions of privacy and freedom of expression. Moreover, the Court did little to protect the rights of the truly poor (see Lawrence 1990). Still, the Court built significant bodies of doctrine favoring racial minority groups, women, aliens, and criminal defendants, among others. This shift was reflected in the content of the Court's decisions striking down federal or state statutes (Baum 2001, p. 209). In the first four decades of the twentieth century, the preponderance of those decisions negated regulations of economic activity, usually in challenges brought by businesses. In the 1960s and 1970s, the preponderance negated restrictions on civil liberties, quite often in cases brought by litigants from lower-status groups.

Why was the Court now supporting disadvantaged groups? That stance was striking in contrast with both the Court's past history and the trial-court pattern that Galanter and others have depicted. As the Warren Court's interventions accumulated and the Burger Court maintained many of its predecessor's policies, it was tempting to link the Court's recent record with its basic position in the legal and political systems (see Epp 1998, pp. 11–14, 30–31). For one thing, the Court's role of protecting constitutional rights might make it uniquely receptive to the arguments of interests such as racial minority groups and political fringe groups. Further, conventional political power was less relevant to the Supreme Court than to other government bodies, because the Court's relative insulation from political forces allowed it to respond more even-handedly to the quality of legal arguments. But at most, these factors created the potential for the Court to support disadvantaged groups, a potential that the Court took a very long time to fulfill. The question was why the Court departed from its historical record, and scholars have offered two kinds of explanations.

The first, flowing directly from the attitudinal model, has already been discussed. In this explanation, a series of presidents appointed enough justices whose preferences favored the interests of disadvantaged groups to change the Court's stance. Whether the distribution of judicial preferences reflected the outcomes of presidential and senatorial elections or was largely a matter of chance, it led directly to the Court's civil libertarian policies. Consistent with this line of analysis, it has been shown that the relative success of high-status and low-status litigants in the Court varies with the Court's ideological composition (Sheehan et al. 1992).

This explanation requires some extension. Almost surely, broader changes in society facilitated the shift in the distribution of policy preferences on the Court. Those changes may have involved widened access to the legal profession and to the judiciary, and they surely involved evolution in the attitudes of American social elites. Students of the Court have not inquired extensively into the impact of these societal changes.

The second kind of explanation, best expressed by Epp (1998, pp. 44–70), relates to the litigation process. It is a truism that courts can decide only the cases that come before them, but the litigation process has broader and deeper effects as well. The quality of arguments made on behalf of a policy position affects its reception in court. A sustained litigation campaign can impress the seriousness of an issue on judges and condition their thinking about it.

Epp documented the development of strong litigation campaigns on behalf of relatively weak groups in American society during the twentieth century. Such campaigns were mounted by interest groups such as the NAACP Legal Defense Fund, and the federal government sometimes provided backing through participation as *amicus curiae*. At the least, these campaigns enabled Supreme Court justices who were favorably inclined toward the legal claims of disadvantaged groups to act on their inclinations. To some extent, they also may have shaped the justices' inclinations.

Since the 1970s, the Court's policies increasingly have favored the business community (Baum 2001, pp. 211–12). In the past decade, its most significant invalidations of federal laws have served primarily states through limitations of federal power to regulate state activity. Meanwhile, disadvantaged groups have not fared nearly as well as they did in the 1960s. This shift has resulted from change in the Court's membership, reinforced by increased litigation efforts of groups representing business and improved legal advocacy for the states.

Systematic comparison of the beneficiaries of legislative, executive, and judicial policy would be difficult but valuable for an understanding of American politics. With a dearth of research involving such comparison, any conclusions must be tentative. It may be that the Court's relative autonomy from its political environment gives it greater freedom to choose its beneficiaries. Over the full course of the Court's history, however, this freedom has not led the Court to consistently favor the interests of disadvantaged groups. In light of the paths of recruitment to the Court and the social and political forces around the Court, that result is not surprising.

THE EFFICACY OF INTERVENTIONS

Popular perceptions of the Supreme Court's role in the American political system are based primarily on observation of the Court's interventions in the policy process. The role that the Court actually plays is a function of both its interventions and their consequences. In turn, those consequences rest on responses to Court policies by people in and out of government.

Participants in politics and even students of politics sometimes take positive responses for granted, assuming that when the Supreme Court acts, other people follow its lead. In contrast, scholars who study the consequences of the Court's decisions frequently emphasize limits on the Court's power to change government and society. Those limits sometimes are depicted as the result of courts' attributes as policy makers, especially the weaknesses that Alexander Hamilton depicted in Federalist 78. The limitations on the Court's power are both substantial and consequential, but it is unclear to what extent these limitations distinguish the Court from other policy makers. Arguably, an emphasis on the Court's weaknesses obscures some important realities about its role.

Changing Government

The Supreme Court does not act directly on society. Rather, its decisions are directed at other public policy makers, usually lower-court judges and administrators, in the form of legal rules that they are asked to implement. In assessing the Court's efficacy, then, the first question is the extent to which the Court can get those policy makers to carry out its decisions.

Concerted research on compliance with Supreme Court decisions was spurred by the Warren Court. Some of that Court's major interventions met highly visible resistance from judges and administrators, resistance that dispelled any assumption of near-automatic compliance. Most dramatic were the responses to *Brown v. Board of Education* (1954). Research documented what news reports indicated: Across the Deep South, school boards seldom acted voluntarily to desegregate their systems. Perhaps more surprising, most of the federal district judges who were called upon to enforce *Brown* evaded the Supreme Court's intent and allowed school districts to continue their noncompliance (Bartley 1969, Peltason 1971).

Studies found widespread noncompliance with other Warren Court interventions. A high proportion of the public schools that included prayers and Bible reading in the school day maintained those practices after the Court prohibited them in 1962 and 1963 (Reich 1968, Way 1968). State courts often balked at applying the Court's expansions of rights for criminal defendants (Canon 1974), and police violations of the Court's procedural rules were widespread (Milner 1971). Altogether, the research inspired by the Warren Court (see Wasby 1970) left an impression that the Supreme Court enjoyed limited success in shaping the choices of lower court judges and administrators. Startling as this impression was for those who had assumed a high level of compliance with the Court's decisions, it seemed to confirm the depiction of judicial weakness in Federalist 78.

Yet both this impression and what it suggests about the Court are misleading in two respects. First, the early research overstated the Court's implementation failures. For one thing, scholars emphasized failures more than successes. Was it more remarkable that so many schools maintained religious exercises prohibited by the Court or that so many others eliminated exercises that had strong public support? The absence of desegregation in the Deep South in the decade after *Brown* was noteworthy, but so was the gradual elimination of school segregation in the border states. Moreover, this research reflected a strong selection bias in that scholars were attracted to the study of decisions that had run into visible implementation problems. Later research that avoided this bias indicates that, at least at the federal level, judges and administrators respond more favorably to Supreme Court decisions in general than the early research suggested (Johnson 1987, Songer et al. 1994, Stidham & Carp 1982, Songer 1987, Songer & Sheehan 1990, Spriggs 1997; see Canon & Johnson 1999).

Second, the early research typically treated implementation of Supreme Court decisions as a unique phenomenon. Scholarship on imperfect hierarchy elsewhere in government (e.g., Kaufman 1960, Pressman & Wildavsky 1973) and in work organizations (e.g., Mechanic 1962, Crozier 1964) had little impact on the judicial research. As a consequence, judicial scholars seldom considered whether noncompliance with Supreme Court decisions resulted chiefly from universal imperfections in implementation rather than special weaknesses of courts. The first possibility has become even more credible with the accumulation of research on policy implementation (e.g., Lipsky 1980, Wilson 1989, Brehm & Gates 1997).

In recent years, some scholars with a strategic perspective have analyzed relationships between the Supreme Court and lower courts in formal terms, terms that facilitate comparison between implementation processes in the judiciary and hierarchical relationships in other settings (Kornhauser 1995, Hammond et al. 2001; see Brehm & Gates 1997, pp. 13–20). Especially important is collaborative work by Segal, Songer, and Cameron (Songer et al. 1994, 1995; Cameron et al. 2000), who have employed principal-agent theory to guide empirical studies of the relationship between the Supreme Court and federal courts of appeals.

Even in this new wave of research, however, there has been little systematic comparison between courts and other policy enactors. The natural comparison is between the Supreme Court and Congress, each of which acts to shape administrative policy. It is reasonable to posit that Congress does better in getting what it wants from administrators, because its powers (especially fiscal) and its capacity to monitor the bureaucracy are appreciably stronger. The sequences of events that overcame school segregation and racial barriers to voting in the Deep South support that hypothesis. But it remains essentially untested, in part because good tests are difficult to design. Thus, we still know little about the relative success of implementation for legislative and judicial policies.

Once we know more about the implementation of the Court's decisions in absolute and relative terms, the most important question might well be why implementation is as successful as it is. The Court's limited concrete powers would seem to aggravate the difficulties faced by all organizational leaders, so why do judges and administrators follow the Court's lead so frequently? Within the judiciary, part of the answer undoubtedly lies in selection and socialization processes that enhance agreement about legal policy and acceptance of hierarchical authority. Even the Court's limited powers may be sufficient to rein in administrators, especially in the era of broad legal mobilization that Epp has described: Groups that undertake litigation campaigns to achieve favorable precedents can also litigate against organizations that refuse to accept those precedents. Both judges and administrators may reduce their decision costs by using the Court's legal rules as a guide. In any event, the relationship between the Court and policy makers who implement its policies may be an especially good subject for studies to probe the forces that reduce centrifugal tendencies in hierarchies.

It is also worth asking why the Court fares so well in Congress. As noted above, few of the Court's most controversial interventions in the past half century have been directly reversed. Nor has Congress enacted any of the numerous bills to remove the Court's jurisdiction over areas in which the Court has aroused congressional anger.

A large part of the explanation lies in the difficulty of enacting legislation in a process with so many veto points. That difficulty is especially great in an era like the current one, which lacks a strong or stable law-making majority. In such an era, interventions are likely to have significant support in government regardless of their ideological direction, and even decisions that strike down federal laws may enjoy majority support. The line of decisions since 1995 that has limited the regulatory power of the federal government (e.g., *Alden v. Maine* 1999, *United States v. Morrison* 2000) constitutes the most significant judicial attack on federal policy since the 1930s. But since 1995, Congress has had Republican majorities except for the bare Democratic Senate majority in 2001–2002. In that situation, any significant action to counter the Court's policies has been exceedingly unlikely.

Beyond the difficulty of enacting legislation, two other factors may come into play. First, Congress often adopts measures that limit the impact of a Court policy or that attack the policy symbolically, actions that suffice for members who want to vent their unhappiness with the Court or to claim credit with constituents who oppose the decision (see Keynes & Miller 1989). In response to *Roe v. Wade* (1973), for instance, Congress (often with presidential encouragement) has mandated various limits on federal funding of abortion. Two years after *Miranda v. Arizona* (1966), it enacted a statutory provision purportedly to supersede the *Miranda* rules in federal cases, a provision that federal prosecutors ignored and that the Court ultimately struck down in *Dickerson v. United States* (2000).

Second, the Court may enjoy a degree of institutional deference in Congress, similar to that found in other relationships among the three branches but buttressed by the symbolic status of the Constitution itself. This deference tinges certain courses of action, such as restrictions on court jurisdiction, with illegitimacy. The failure of proposals to overturn the flag-burning decisions with a constitutional amendment, despite broad and deep public opposition to those decisions, reflects the symbolic power of the First Amendment. Congressional deference to the Court is not limitless, but in combination with other factors it may help to explain why the Court's recent interventions and the Court itself have survived congressional scrutiny so well.

Changing Society

In practical terms, the most important issue concerning the Supreme Court's policy interventions is their impact on American society. But there is little basis for firm conclusions about that impact.

In the era that began with the Warren Court, the Court has been blamed for a range of social ills, most prominently crime (e.g., Cassell & Fowles 1998, p. 1132). Those who sympathize with the Court's policies are not so inclined to ascribe sweeping impact to the Court, but they sometimes depict the Court as a powerful force for good (e.g., Fiss 1991, p. 1118). The tendency to treat the Court as the hero or villain in the national debate over abortion policy illustrates the power that is often attributed to the Court.

In *The Courts and Social Policy*, Horowitz (1977) strongly challenged those who viewed judicial interventions as productive of good policy. Horowitz argued that interventions by both the Supreme Court and lower federal courts are problematical because of courts' poor capacities for effective policy analysis. Horowitz carefully discussed the characteristics of courts and of judicial decision making that he viewed as limiting their capacities. He then presented four detailed case studies to illustrate his generalizations. Two involved Supreme Court decisions that prohibited the use of illegally seized evidence in court (*Mapp v. Ohio* 1961) and that mandated greater procedural rights for juvenile suspects and defendants (*In re Gault* 1967). As related by Horowitz, the four studies suggested both that courts achieve less of their intended impact than they had sought and that their impact often takes unintended and undesirable forms. Horowitz's book attracted considerable attention and some strong disagreement (Cavanagh & Sarat 1980).

Rosenberg (1991) delivered an equally fundamental and more pointed challenge to the same audience in *The Hollow Hope*. As Rosenberg saw it, the Supreme Court could do little to bring about liberal social reform. Thus those who put their energies into litigation as a vehicle for social change were wasting their efforts. Rosenberg argued that courts suffer from serious constraints on their ability to achieve social reform: the "bounded nature of constitutional rights" (1991, p. 13), insufficient independence from the other branches of government, and lack of tools to make and implement policy effectively. Courts could be effective only when they received substantial help from other policy makers or from the market. Rosenberg then presented close analyses of several policy areas in which the Court had acted. In each, he concluded, the Court had made little difference.

The central case study concerned racial equality, and it was a wise choice. Scholars understood that the Court decisions mandating equality in education and voting had been implemented poorly and that Congress ultimately had rescued the Court in both areas. But many scholars and other observers thought that the Court had played a critical role as a catalyst, spurring action by the other branches of government and helping to stir the civil rights movement itself. Rosenberg analyzed a large body of evidence and concluded that the Court had exerted little impact on the political movement or on the legislative and executive-branch policies that improved the situations of African Americans.

Rosenberg was not the first to question the efficacy of litigation as a tool for social change (e.g., Scheingold 1974). But the breadth and depth of his questioning attracted new attention to this issue. The result was a debate that continues today. Most judicial scholars who address the issue have disagreed with Rosenberg at least in part. In particular, some have pointed to instances in which they argue that litigation has been an effective vehicle for social change (e.g., McCann 1994, 1999; Schultz 1998).

It is difficult to evaluate the competing arguments on this issue. In part, the difficulty lies in gathering and assessing relevant evidence. We have only limited information about the societal impact of Supreme Court decisions, and what we do have is open to differing interpretations. The chain of causality between Supreme Court decisions and broad social phenomena typically is complex, so that separating the Court's influence from that of other forces is problematic. Indeed, the task usually involves the analysis of counterfactuals: What would have happened if the Court had not acted? To ascertain the future course of state legislation in the absence of *Roe v. Wade* is difficult enough. To determine whether the civil rights movement would have achieved the same scope and impact without a series of Supreme Court decisions may be impossible. We simply lack the analytic tools to make good judgments about the societal impact of judicial interventions.

A second difficulty, one that also arises in gauging intervention itself, is the choice of standards. What kind of influence is reasonable to expect of the Supreme Court? Some enthusiasts of the Court's civil liberties decisions have made sweeping claims about their impact. Moreover, some interest groups have devoted substantial portions of their limited energy and resources to litigation on the assumption that this route is a key to achieving their goals. For these reasons, Rosenberg himself set a fairly high standard by which to assess the Court's contribution to social reform.

Such a standard may not be appropriate—not because it is unrealistic for the courts but because it is unrealistic for government in general. Horowitz cautiously suggested that the courts have more limited capabilities than other policy makers, and Rosenberg argued that groups seeking social change could gain more from favorable action by the other branches than from victories in court. As noted above, there is a basis for concluding that courts suffer from more weaknesses than other policy makers. Even so, the shared weaknesses of all three branches, the limitations on their capacity to change society, may be more significant than differences among them.

Although comparisons among policy makers usefully expand the focus of analysis, the impact of each branch should not be viewed in isolation from the others. Because policy makers do not act singly, the impact of government policy on society results from the intermixed actions of multiple actors. Government policies on civil rights or crime reflect so many choices by a disparate set of organizations that it is impossible to isolate the effects of any single organization. More important, it is very difficult for any single body of government, acting on its own, to achieve significant effects on society. Political scientists appropriately emphasize the interdependence of government bodies in making policy; their interdependence in shaping society is equally fundamental.

CONCLUSIONS

The Supreme Court occupies a complicated and ambiguous place in the political system. It is difficult to assess the extent and content of the Court's intervention in the policy process. The impact of the Court's interventions on government and society is even more uncertain.

In the past half century, the Court has taken on what can be considered a new role. This has been a period of sustained and substantial interventions that appears to have no parallel in earlier eras. Further, during much of this period, the Court has acted on behalf of disadvantaged groups whose interests it had given little support in earlier eras. In both respects, the Court looks very different from the Court portrayed by commentators and scholars in the 1940s and 1950s.

The Court has suffered relatively little damage from its interventions in the current period, and the interventions themselves have held up fairly well in the other branches of the federal government. These outcomes suggest that the justices have considerable freedom to intervene in national policy. The Court's record indicates that the justices make good use of that freedom: They appear to conform more closely to a model in which they act directly on their policy preferences than to one in which they frequently depart from those preferences to avoid negative reactions from their political environment. But neither model fully explains the growth in the Court's interventions and the change in their beneficiaries.

Implementation of the Court's policies is far from perfect; judges and administrators often balk at carrying out its rulings. The available evidence also indicates that the Court is quite constrained in its ability to secure social change. To a degree, the Court's limited impact on government and society may reflect unique weaknesses of the judiciary. But other policy makers also have difficulty in securing implementation of their policies and achieving change in society. For the most part, the Court's difficulties reflect universal imperfections in organizational hierarchy and inherent limitations in government capacity.

On this issue, as on others, our understanding of courts will be enhanced by comparing them with the other branches of government. Scholars increasingly probe the complex relationships between courts and the other branches, and by doing so they have given us a richer sense of how the courts fit into American politics. In the same way, comparison of the courts' role with that of legislatures and the executive branch can improve our comprehension of the forces that shape judicial policy and its impact.

The *Annual Review of Political Science* is online at
http://polisci.annualreviews.org

LITERATURE CITED

Alden v. Maine. 1999. 527 U.S. 706

Bartley NV. 1969. *The Rise of Massive Resistance: Race and Politics in the South during the 1950's.* Baton Rouge: Louisiana State Univ. Press

Baum L. 1997. *The Puzzle of Judicial Behavior.* Ann Arbor: Univ. Mich. Press

Baum L. 2001. *The Supreme Court.* Washington, DC: CQ Press. 7th ed.

Brehm J, Gates S. 1997. *Working, Shirking, and Sabotage: Bureaucratic Response to a Democratic Public.* Ann Arbor: Univ. Mich. Press

Brown v. Board of Education. 1954. 347 U.S. 483

Bryden DP. 1992. Is the Rehnquist Court conservative? *Public Interest* Fall:73–88

Bush v. Gore. 2000. 531 U.S. 98

Bussiere E. 1997. *(Dis)Entitling the Poor: The Warren Court, Welfare Rights, and the American Political Tradition.* University Park: Penn. State Press

Cameron CM, Segal JA, Songer D. 2000. Strategic auditing in a political hierarchy: an informational model of the Supreme Court's certiorari decisions. *Am. Polit. Sci. Rev.* 94:101–16

Canon BC. 1974. Organizational contumacy in the transmission of judicial policies: the

Mapp, Escobedo, Miranda, and Gault cases. *Villanova Law Rev.* 20:50–79

Canon BC. 1982. A framework for the analysis of judicial activism. In *Supreme Court Activism and Restraint*, ed. SC Halpern, CM Lamb, pp. 385–419. Lexington, MA: Lexington Books

Canon BC, Johnson CA. 1999. *Judicial Policies: Implementation and Impact.* Washington, DC: CQ Press. 2nd ed.

Canon BC, Ulmer SS. 1976. The Supreme Court and critical elections: a dissent. *Am. Polit. Sci. Rev.* 70:1215–18

Casper JD. 1976. The Supreme Court and national policy making. *Am. Polit. Sci. Rev.* 70:50–63

Cassell PG, Fowles R. 1998. Handcuffing the cops? A thirty-year perspective on Miranda's harmful effects on law enforcement. *Stanford Law Rev.* 50:1055–145

Cavanagh R, Sarat A. 1980. Thinking about courts: toward and beyond a jurisprudence of judicial competence. *Law Soc. Rev.* 14:371–420

Commager HS. 1943. Judicial review and democracy. *Virginia Q. Rev.* 19:417–28

Crozier M. 1964. *The Bureaucratic Phenomenon.* Chicago: Univ. Chicago Press

Cushman B. 1998. *Rethinking the New Deal Court: the Structure of a Constitutional Revolution.* New York: Oxford Univ. Press

Dahl R. 1957. Decision-making in a democracy: the Supreme Court as a national policy-maker. *J. Public Law* 6:279–95

Dickerson v. United States. 2000. 530 U.S. 428

Epp CR. 1998. *The Rights Revolution: Lawyers, Activists, and Supreme Courts in Comparative Perspective.* Chicago: Univ. Chicago Press

Epstein L, Knight J. 1998. *The Choices Justices Make.* Washington, DC: CQ Press

Epstein L, Knight J. 2000. Toward a strategic revolution in judicial politics: a look back, a look ahead. *Polit. Res. Q.* 53:625–61

Epstein L, Knight J, Martin AD. 2001. The Supreme Court as a strategic national policy-maker. *Emory Law J.* 50:583–610

Eskridge WN. 1991. Reneging on history?

Playing the Court/Congress/President civil rights game. *Calif. Law Rev.* 79:613–84

Fiss O. 1991. A life lived twice. *Yale Law J.* 100:1117–29

Funston R. 1975. The Supreme Court and critical elections. *Am. Polit. Sci. Rev.* 69:795–811

Galanter M. 1974. Why the "haves" come out ahead: speculations on the limits of legal change. *Law Soc. Rev.* 9:95–160

Galloway RW. 1991. *Justice for All? The Rich and Poor in Supreme Court History 1790–1990.* Durham, NC: Carolina Acad. Press

Gates JB. 1992. *The Supreme Court and Partisan Realignment: A Macro- and Microlevel Perspective.* Boulder, CO: Westview

Gibson JL, Caldeira GA, Spence LK. 2002. *The Supreme Court and the U.S. presidential election of 2000: wounds, self-inflicted or otherwise?* Work. Pap., Russell Sage Found.

Gillman H. 2001. What's law got to do with it? Judicial behavioralists test the "legal model" of judicial decision making. *Law Soc. Inq.* 26:465–504

Goldstein RJ. 2000. *Flag Burning and Free Speech: The Case of Texas v. Johnson.* Lawrence: Univ. Press Kansas

Graber MA. 1999. The problematic establishment of judicial review. In *The Supreme Court in American Politics: New Institutionalist Interpretations*, ed. H Gillman, C Clayton, pp. 28–42. Lawrence: Univ. Press Kansas

Hammond TH, Bonneau CW, Sheehan RS. 2001. *A court of appeals in a rational-choice model of Supreme Court decision-making.* Presented at Conf. Inst. Games and the U.S. Supreme Court, College Station, TX, Nov. 1–4

Hoekstra VJ. 2000. The Supreme Court and local public opinion. *Am. Polit. Sci. Rev.* 94:89–100

Horowitz DL. 1977. *The Courts and Social Policy.* Washington, DC: Brookings Inst.

In re Gault. 1967. 387 U.S. 1

Jackson RH. 1941. *The Struggle for Judicial Supremacy.* New York: Knopf

Johnson CA. 1987. Law, politics, and judicial decision making: lower federal court uses of Supreme Court decisions. *Law Soc. Rev.* 21:325–40

Kahn R. 1994. *The Supreme Court and Constitutional Theory, 1953–1993.* Lawrence: Univ. Press Kansas

Kaufman H. 1960. *The Forest Ranger: A Study in Administrative Behavior.* Baltimore, MD: Johns Hopkins Press

Keynes E, Miller RK. 1989. *The Court vs. Congress: Prayer, Busing, and Abortion.* Durham, NC: Duke Univ. Press

Kornhauser LA. 1995. Adjudication by a resource-constrained team: hierarchy and precedent in a judicial system. *South. Calif. Law Rev.* 68:1605–29

Kritzer HM, Silbey SS, eds. 1999. Do the "haves" still come out ahead? *Law Soc. Rev.* 33:795–1123 (spec. issue)

Kunda Z. 1990. The case for motivated reasoning. *Psychol. Bull.* 108:480–98

Kuran T. 1995. *Private Truths, Public Lies: The Social Consequences of Preference Falsification.* Cambridge, MA: Harvard Univ. Press

Lasser W. 1985. The Supreme Court in periods of critical realignment. *J. Polit.* 47:1174–87

Lawrence SE. 1990. *The Poor in Court: The Legal Services Program and Supreme Court Decision Making.* Princeton, NJ: Princeton Univ. Press

Lipsky M. 1980. *Street-Level Bureaucracy: Dilemmas of the Individual in Public Services.* New York: Russell Sage Found.

Maltzman F, Spriggs JF, Wahlbeck PJ. 2000. *Crafting Law on the Supreme Court: The Collegial Game.* New York: Cambridge Univ. Press

Mapp v. Ohio. 1961. 367 U.S. 643

Martin AD. 2001. *Statutory battles and constitutional wars: Congress and the Supreme Court.* Presented at Conf. Inst. Games and the U.S. Supreme Court, College Station, TX, Nov. 1–4

McCann MW. 1994. *Rights at Work: Pay Equity Reform and the Politics of Legal Mobilization.* Chicago: Univ. Chicago Press

McCann MW. 1999. How the Supreme Court matters in American politics: new institutionalist perspectives. In *The Supreme Court in American Politics: New Institutionalist Interpretations,* ed. H Gillman, C Clayton, pp. 63–97. Lawrence: Univ. Press Kansas

McCloskey RG, Levinson S. 2000. *The American Supreme Court.* Chicago: Univ. Chicago Press. 3rd ed.

McCubbins MD, Schwartz T. 1984. Congressional oversight overlooked: police patrols versus fire alarms. *Am. J. Polit. Sci.* 38:165–79

Mechanic D. 1962. Sources of power of lower participants in complex organizations. *Admin. Sci. Q.* 7:349–64

Meernik J, Ignagni J. 1997. Judicial review and coordinate construction of the Constitution. *Am. J. Polit. Sci.* 41:447–67

Milner N. 1971. *The Court and Local Law Enforcement: The Impact of Miranda.* Beverly Hills, CA: Sage

Miranda v. Arizona. 1966. 384 U.S. 436

Mondak JJ, Smithey SI. 1997. The dynamics of public support for the Supreme Court. *J. Polit.* 59:1114–42

Murphy WF. 1962. *Congress and the Court.* Chicago: Univ. Chicago Press

Murphy WF. 1964. *Elements of Judicial Strategy.* Chicago: Univ. Chicago Press

Peltason JW. 1971. *Fifty-Eight Lonely Men: Southern Federal Judges and School Desegregation.* Urbana: Univ. Ill. Press. Rev. ed.

Posner RA. 1995. *Overcoming Law.* Cambridge, MA: Harvard Univ. Press

Powe LA. 2000. *The Warren Court and American Politics.* Cambridge, MA: Harvard Univ. Press

Pressman JL, Wildavsky A. 1973. *Implementation.* Berkeley: Univ. Calif. Press

Pritchett CH. 1961. *Congress Versus the Supreme Court, 1957–1960.* Minneapolis: Univ. Minn. Press

Reich D. 1968. The impact of judicial decision-making: the school prayer cases. In *The Supreme Court as Policy-Maker: Three Studies on the Impact of Judicial Decisions,* ed. D Everson, pp. 44–81. Carbondale: Public Aff. Res. Bur., South. Ill. Univ.

Richards MJ, Kritzer HM. 2002. Jurisprudential

regimes in Supreme Court decision making. *Am. Polit. Sci. Rev.* 96:305–20

Roe v. Wade. 1973. 410 U.S. 113

Rohde DW. 1972. Policy goals, strategic choice and majority opinion assignments in the U.S. Supreme Court. *Midwest J. Polit. Sci.* 15:652–82

Rohde DW, Spaeth HJ. 1976. *Supreme Court Decision Making*. San Francisco: WH Freeman

Rosenberg GN. 1991. *The Hollow Hope: Can Courts Bring About Social Change?* Chicago: Univ. Chicago Press

Scheingold SA. 1974. *The Politics of Rights: Lawyers, Public Policy, and Political Change*. New Haven, CT: Yale Univ. Press

Schubert G. 1970. *The Constitutional Polity*. Boston: Boston Univ. Press

Schultz DA, ed. 1998. *Leveraging the Law: Using the Courts to Achieve Social Change*. New York: Peter Lang

Segal JA. 1997. Separation-of-powers games in the positive theory of Congress and courts. *Am. Polit. Sci. Rev.* 91:28–44

Segal JA, Cover A. 1989. Ideological values and the votes of Supreme Court justices. *Am. Polit. Sci. Rev.* 83:557–65

Segal JA, Spaeth HJ. 2002. *The Supreme Court and the Attitudinal Model Revisited*. New York: Cambridge Univ. Press

Shapiro M. 1978. The Supreme Court: from Warren to Burger. In *The New American Political System*, ed. A King, pp. 179–211. Washington, DC: Am. Enterprise Inst.

Sheehan RS, Mishler W, Songer DR. 1992. Ideology, status, and the differential success of direct parties before the Supreme Court. *Am. Polit. Sci. Rev.* 86:464–71

Songer DR. 1987. The impact of the Supreme Court on trends in economic policy making in the United States Courts of Appeals. *J. Polit.* 49:830–41

Songer DR, Cameron CM, Segal JA. 1995. An empirical test of the rational-actor theory of litigation. *J. Polit.* 57:1119–29

Songer DR, Segal JA, Cameron CM. 1994. The hierarchy of justice: testing a principal-agent

model of Supreme Court–circuit court interactions. *Am. J. Polit. Sci.* 38:673–96

Songer DR, Sheehan RS. 1990. Supreme Court impact on compliance and outcomes: Miranda and New York Times in the United States Courts of Appeals. *West. Polit. Q.* 43:297–316

Sowell T. 1994. Blackmun plays to the crowd. *St. Louis Post-Dispatch*, Mar. 4, p. 7B

Spaeth HJ. 1964. The judicial restraint of Mr. Justice Frankfurter: myth or reality? *Midwest J. Polit. Sci.* 8:22–38

Spaeth HJ, Altfeld MF. 1986. Felix Frankfurter, judicial activism, and voting conflict on the Warren Court. In *Judicial Conflict and Consensus*, ed. S Goldman, CM Lamb, pp. 87–114. Lexington: Univ. Kentucky Press

Spaeth HJ, Teger SH. 1982. Activism and restraint: a cloak for the justices' policy preferences. In *Supreme Court Activism and Restraint*, ed. SC Halpern, CM Lamb, pp. 277–301. Lexington, MA: Lexington Books

Spiller PT, Gely R. 1992. Congressional control or judicial independence: the determinants of U.S. Supreme Court labor-relations decisions, 1949–1988. *RAND J. Econ.* 23:469–92

Spriggs JF. 1997. Explaining federal bureaucratic compliance with Supreme Court opinions. *Polit. Res. Q.* 50:567–93

Stidham R, Carp RA. 1982. Trial courts' responses to Supreme Court policy changes: three case studies. *Law Policy Q.* 4:215–34

Texas v. Johnson. 1989. 491 U.S. 397

United States v. Eichman. 1990. 496 U.S. 310

United States v. Morrison. 2000. 529 U.S. 598

Wasby SL. 1970. *The Impact of the United States Supreme Court: Some Perspectives*. Homewood, IL: Dorsey

Way HF. 1968. Survey research on judicial decisions: the prayer and Bible reading cases. *West. Polit. Q.* 21:189–205

Willing R. 1997. "Activist" label actively applied. *USA Today*, Mar. 10, p. 3A

Wilson JQ. 1989. *Bureaucracy: What Government Agencies Do and Why They Do It*. New York: Basic Books

Annu. Rev. Polit. Sci. 2003. 6:181–204
doi: 10.1146/annurev.polisci.6.121901.085549
First published online as a Review in Advance on Jan. 8, 2003

WHY THE UNITED STATES FOUGHT IN VIETNAM

Larry Berman[1] and Stephen R. Routh[2]

[1]Department of Political Science, University of California, Davis, One Shields Avenue,
Davis, California 95616; email: lsberman@ucdavis.edu; [2]Department of Politics and
Public Administration, California State University, Stanislaus, 801 West Monte Vista
Avenue, Turlock, California 95382; email: srouth@csustan.edu

Key Words Vietnam conflict, presidential decision making, Ho Chi Minh, war
negotiations, Vietnam War scholarship

■ **Abstract** Scholarship on the Vietnam war has advanced understanding of why
the United States fought in Vietnam. An examination of this work leads us to consider several related topics, such as why North Vietnam won the war, why the United
States and its ally South Vietnam lost the war, and whether there were missed opportunities whereby the U.S. military intervention could have been avoided. The disciplines of history and political science have illuminated many important aspects of
the war ranging from such diverse subjects as presidential personality and leadership
to congressional-executive relations. Political science has also contributed significant
theoretical advances on the subject of why nations go to war and on the nature of
international conflict, belief systems, and conflict resolution processes. By and large,
however, we believe that most of the seminal discoveries on the subject of "why the
United States fought in Vietnam" have been made by historians. We review several
of these contributions with expectations that political science will build on this rich
empirical foundation in hypothesis testing and theory development.

INTRODUCTION

Scholarship on the Vietnam war has advanced our understanding of why the United
States fought in Vietnam. An examination of this work leads us to consider several
related topics, such as why North Vietnam won the war, why the United States and
its ally South Vietnam lost the war, and whether there were missed opportunities
whereby the U.S. military intervention could have been avoided (Logevall 1999,
McNamara et al. 1999, Gilbert 2002).

It has been three decades since America's war in Vietnam ended with the
Paris Agreement and Protocols on Ending the War and Restoring the Peace in
Vietnam (Porter 1975; Goodman 1978, 1986; Berman 2001; Asselin 2002; Loi
2002). Signed at the International Conference Center in Paris on January 27, 1973,
the agreement served as little more than a protocol for the return of American
prisoners of war and military disengagement. By the terms of the deal, over 150,000
North Vietnamese troops remained in the South, whereas the United States, over

the course of Nixon's presidency, had unilaterally withdrawn over 500,000 of its own troops. The final contingent of the U.S. commitment departed Vietnam 60 days after the signing, but the level of violence between Vietnamese adversaries did not significantly decline; no peace came to Vietnam (Le Gro 1981; Dillard 1982).

In the United States, Watergate was changing from amber to red, and as his presidency unraveled in 1973, President Richard Nixon's secret commitments to South Vietnam's President Nguyen Van Thieu were rendered meaningless (Hung & Schecter 1986). Less than two years later, faced with funding a $722 million budget supplement, the U.S. Congress showed little interest in providing military equipment or financial support to America's longtime ally, South Vietnam. On April 30, 1975, South Vietnam ceased to exist (Dung 1977, Hosmer et al. 1980, Engelmann 1990).

For most Americans, the last images of the war were of the dazed U.S. Ambassador Graham Martin carrying a folded American flag under his arm during the final evacuation from the U.S. Embassy; or perhaps the chaos surrounding the evacuation of U.S. personnel and Vietnamese families from the Embassy rooftop; or the looting and pillaging of the Embassy safe, furniture, and files once the Americans had departed.

These images of a bitter end to the war created a societal and academic amnesia. No one seemed interested in such critical questions as the nature of the war, why the United States chose to fight the way it did, how North Vietnam had prevailed, the relationship of political objectives to military strategy, or the lessons that could be derived from the public diplomacy and secret negotiations that had characterized so much of the conflict. In 1987, 12 years after the fall of Saigon, a feature article in *The Chronicle of Higher Education* bore the title "The Vietnam War Scores Well at the Box Office, but It Fails to Attract Many Researchers" (Winkler 1987).

That dire situation would change as scholars gained access to a series of significant declassifications of primary source documents located in archival depositories in the United States, Vietnam, China, and Russia, and as principal architects of policy—the so-called "best and brightest"—began to reflect and write on their roles during the period. In 1995, former Defense Secretary Robert S. McNamara broke his own long silence on the subject with the admission that "we were wrong, terribly wrong" (McNamara & Van De Mark 1995). Another principal architect of Vietnam policy, political scientist Henry Kissinger, has generated several books that address why the United States fought in Vietnam (Kissinger 1979, 1994, 1999).

We approach our topic chronologically by examining 30 years of war from 1945 to 1975–beginning with the historic Vietnamese proclamation of independence and ending with the fall of South Vietnam in April 1975. We have identified what we believe are important components of this unfolding saga, and we begin from the intellectual premise that truly understanding why the United States fought in Vietnam requires that we comprehend the roots of the conflict (before it became America's war in Vietnam) from the perspective of countries other than the United States—specifically, Vietnam, China, and the Soviet Union. After all, it was the United States that chose to fight in Vietnam's war (Young 1991, Werner & Huynh 1993).

The disciplines of history and political science have illuminated many important aspects of the war, including presidential personality and leadership, war powers, public opinion, the role of the media, advisory processes and interactions, political dissent, and congressional-executive relations. Political science has also contributed significant theoretical advances on the subject of why nations go to war and on the nature of international conflict, belief systems, and conflict resolution processes. By and large, however, we believe that most of the seminal discoveries on the subject of "why the United States fought in Vietnam" have been made by historians. We review several of these contributions so that political science can build on a rich empirical foundation in hypothesis testing and theory development (Nincic 1988, Fearon 1991, George 1993, Van Evera 1999, Elman & Elman 2003).

UNDERSTANDING VIETNAM WOULD HAVE HELPED

On September 2, 1945, before a crowd of 400,000 supporters, Ho Chi Minh issued the historic Vietnamese proclamation of independence with Jefferson's stirring words, "We hold the truth that all men are created equal, that they are endowed by their Creator certain unalienable rights, that among these are life, liberty and the pursuit of happiness." Ho told his followers that "this immortal statement was made in the Declaration of Independence of the United States of America in 1776. In a broader sense it means: All peoples on earth are equal from birth, all peoples have a right to live, be happy and be free." After Ho had completed his speech, Vo Nguyen Giap, the Minister of the Interior in the new government, told the throng that "America ... is a democratic country which has no territorial ambitions. Yet it bore the greatest burdens in defeating our enemy, fascist Japan. Therefore we consider America a good friend." Some in the crowd carried signs that read, "Vietnam Honors Truman" (Bradley 2000).

Ho had been preparing his entire life for the opportunity to rid Vietnam of colonial rule, both Japanese and French. Throughout Vietnam banners proclaimed, "Vietnam for the Vietnamese." Scholars have documented that the Vietnamese viewed the Americans and the Russians as historical models for overcoming imperialism (Marr 1995, Duiker 1996). Did this mean anything at the time to U.S. policy makers? In 1945, Vietnam was literally isolated from the international community and its leaders possessed only limited diplomatic experience. At the same time, the United States was emerging from World War II as a preeminent world power. Was this an opportunity for diplomatic maneuverability and fluidity on all sides?

It was nearly impossible in 1945 to envision the United States eventually sending over 550,000 troops to fight a land war in Asia in hopes of achieving what the United States always maintained was a limited political objective. Ho Chi Minh had received the translation of the American Declaration of Independence from Archimedes Patti of the Office of Strategic Services (OSS) (Patti 1980). Ho had also helped rescue American pilots and furnished intelligence reports on Japanese operations, earning the position OSS agent 19, code name Lucius. As well, Viet Minh militia had joined with the OSS Deer team for training and exercises near the Chinese border (Bradley 2000). So to some extent, Ho and the United States were cooperating against a common foe, and the evidence shows that Ho saw the United States as more likely to be friend than enemy of the Viet Minh, not only in defeating the Japanese but also in fostering fundamental rights in the Philippines.

In one of the most important archival revelations, Bradley shows that in late 1945 Ho made one final grasp for American support, writing President Truman and Secretary of State James Byrnes that Philippine independence offered a model for emulation: "It is with this firm conviction that we request of the United States as guardians and champions of World Justice to take a decisive step in support of our independence. What we ask has graciously been granted to the Philippines. Like the Philippines our goal is full independence and full cooperation with the United States" (Bradley 2000).

For many reasons, the United States and the Viet Minh did not bridge the chasm of the emerging Cold War forces that were already at work. In 1945 Ho Chi Minh was an enigma to policy makers in Washington, D.C. Born Nguyen Sinh Cuong in 1890, Ho left Vietnam in 1911 for a variety of jobs in Western Europe; he traveled to the United States, where he lived briefly in Brooklyn and Boston, and by 1917 had returned to France. He became one of the founders of the French Communist Party and agitated for Vietnamese rights. He was later sent to South China, where he organized and recruited Vietnamese students and dissidents. He became known as a pamphleteer, editor, and organizer. His writings attracted the attention of young Vietnamese such as Vo Nguyen Giap and Pham Van Dong, who would remain forever loyal to their leader and who themselves played important roles in Vietnam's diplomatic and military history. "One nation, one people, with four thousand years of history" was the foremost message of Ho Chi Minh's speeches and pamphlets (Tin 1995).

It was difficult for Truman and his advisors to discern whether Ho was a Vietnamese nationalist and patriot who calculatingly used Marxism as a means for achieving economic and social justice for his people or whether he was a Marxist-Leninist who was merely part of an expanding sphere for communism. The most sophisticated analysis of Ho's motives and thinking during the period comes in Duiker's (2000) extraordinary biography, which explores Ho's roots in the international communist movement and his staunch nationalistic principles. Ho came to Marxism-Leninism because it provided a belief system and a framework for organizing, training, and disseminating propaganda and analysis in pamphleteering. When Ho was asked directly why he did not choose the United States as his model framework, he answered that Moscow was the only place he received support for his ideas. The Soviet Union had been a friend in deed (Duiker 2000).

If policy makers did not understand Ho Chi Minh's roots, what did they know of the dynamics of this 1945 "revolution" in Vietnam—was it a war of national liberation or a war to help Moscow and Peking increase their influence in Southeast Asia (Pike 1966)? What did American policy makers know about the years

preceding the Vietnamese revolution, from 1941 to 1945? What filters and perceptions of historical analogies might they have applied to the moment? Or for that
matter, what was the level of understanding of the Vietnamese Communist Party
or of French colonial policy in Vietnam? Was there a capacity and a willingness
to historically and culturally contextualize the events unfolding there in terms of
actors' motivations?

In the months immediately preceding the August revolution of 1945, the Communist Party central committee convened over the question of how to deal with
the victorious Allied powers. Ho warned party members that the greatest threats
to Vietnam were the French and Chinese, and he was already calculating that a
relationship with the United States might help the Viet Minh fend off their new
occupiers. Marr's (1995) seminal work on the August revolution posits that the
communist movement and influence in the Vietnamese revolution was much less
organized and centrally structured than U.S. policy makers thought at the time. No
one party leader nor party central committee was directing Viet Minh activities from
the top. Indeed, the Viet Minh were a fragmented and loosely connected organization and not a collective with a tightly hierarchical command and control structure.
The effectiveness and success of communist efforts in 1945 resulted from the ability
of local party activists and Viet Minh to adapt to fluid situations and contingencies
and their capacity to adjust and accommodate to changing circumstances—without
direct guidance and supervision from a centralized party authority.

Brigham's exhaustive research in the archives of the National Liberation Front
(NLF) (Brigham 1999, Gilbert 2002) reveals that when the Front was created in
1960, the decision was not part of a carefully conceived plan by Hanoi's Politburo
for the North to eventually conquer the South. It in fact resulted from intense and
acrimonious debates within the Communist Party (created in 1929)—a party that
virtually no one in the United States really understood. The prevailing view of a
monochromatic and monolithic Communist Party demonstrated the policy makers'
blindness to the much more nuanced and contingent reality.

Scholars writing on this early period of the first Indochina war tend to focus
on Franklin Roosevelt's opposition to re-establishing the old European colonial
regimes in Vietnam. But what exactly did that mean? How plausible was it that
Roosevelt could keep de Gaulle and France, a World War II ally, from the spoils of
victory? Roosevelt saw the Vietnamese as children, a "small and passive people"
who were incapable of governing themselves. During World War II, Roosevelt
believed that if Vichy France lost the war, Indochina would belong to either Japan
or the United States. Japan's defeat presented a difficult dilemma for Roosevelt
because France now sought to recapture its colonial grandeur while the Vietnamese
wanted to rid their country of the French (Gardner 1988, Herring 1994).

Roosevelt's plan called for trusteeships of former European colonies whereby
disinterested nations would govern and help newly formed states mature into the
capacity for self-government. Winston Churchill opposed the idea. Roosevelt's
advisors, especially Harry Hopkins, recommended that the President abandon the
plan for trusteeship on grounds that the postwar world would require a strong

French-American partnership in any conflict with the Soviet Union (Gardner 1988). The State Department sided with Churchill, and concerns over Moscow's machinations pushed the United States away from an anticolonial orientation where international trusteeships would prevail (Bradley 2000).

Was there a missed opportunity at this early stage? Could the future war have been avoided during these first diplomatic gambits and games in 1945? Could both Vietnam and the United States have achieved their geopolitical goals? Could the early contacts by members of the OSS really have produced a situation in which the United States would have supported the Viet Minh in their struggle against French colonial occupiers? Certainly, at the end of the day, Ho Chi Minh would have sided with his communist/socialist brethren in any future confrontation with the exploitive forces of capitalism.

Ho used nationalist forces to advance communism, as evidenced by the land reform program in North Vietnam between 1952 and 1956. This campaign of terror in the name of class struggle triggered an exodus of Northerners to the South. Duiker (2000) convincingly argues that given the outcome of not supporting the Democratic Republic of Vietnam (DRV), the failure of policy makers in Washington to understand what Ho was offering had tragic consequences for the French, the Vietnamese, and the Americans. Of course, had the United States recognized the DRV in 1945, such news would not have been welcomed by the Indochinese Communist Party, whose primary allegiance was to Moscow. Moreover, both the Soviets and the Chinese were sponsors of "wars of national liberation," and it is reasonable to assume that promoting such revolutionary activity in neighboring Cambodia and Laos would have been rebuked by Washington (Duiker 2000).

It did not take Ho long to understand that, for the Truman administration, the fear of communism overrode all other concerns. In September 1945, the DRV controlled the region of Hanoi and the northern part of the country, but the French, determined to stop their declining world reputation, focused on reasserting control over Indochina. Following the shelling of Haiphong by French cruisers in November 1946, full-scale war broke out between the French and Viet Minh.

As the Cold War developed, Washington became more geopolitically sensitive to the colonial interests of its allies than to the "principled" decolonization of Indochina. Ho was categorized as a Leninist and pro-Moscow. The United States had no intention of questioning French sovereignty in Vietnam, but one of the most important new advances in our understanding of the period (and one ripe for future analysis) is the DRV's diplomatic initiative of the spring and summer of 1947, just prior to the Truman Doctrine and Marshall Plan, aimed at gaining support from the Truman administration for the Viet Minh cause. The reasons for the initiative's failure were rooted in the assumptions of racialized cultural hierarchies embedded in America's vision of postcolonial Vietnam (Bradley 2000).

Beginning in 1949 with the founding of the People's Republic of China, Beijing assisted Vietnam against both France and the United States. Mao considered the United States to be the primary threat to the security of China and saw helping Ho as a way to weaken U.S. influence in the region. Ho said he and Mao were not only comrades but also brothers (though by the 1960s and 1970s Mao would see the Soviet Union as the greater threat and seek to influence the Vietnamese to accept a negotiated settlement) (Zhai 2000).

In January 1950, the DRV recognized the People's Republic of China (PRC) and moved to establish diplomatic relations. Military advisors, economic support, and equipment soon followed—all to be used by the Vietnamese against the French colonialists. In turn, the PRC recognized the Vietnamese government. China set the terms of this deal by insisting first on diplomatic recognition in return for military support (Bradley 2000). Diplomatic recognition soon followed from the Soviet Union, Poland, Czechoslovakia, Hungary, Bulgaria, Albania, and Yugoslavia. In February, the Truman administration officially recognized the French-backed regime of Emperor Bao Dai and the Associated States of Vietnam and subsequently provided the French and Bao Dai with military assistance and financial backing to fight international communism in Vietnam.

Gaiduk's (1996) groundbreaking work in Soviet archives details the complex relationship between the Soviets and North Vietnamese. Without directly participating in the war, the Soviet Union provided economic and military aid to Hanoi in hopes of blunting China's influence in the area. One important finding in Gaiduk's study is that Soviet leadership feared being drawn into a confrontation between the United States and China that would result from American intervention. By arming, equipping, and advising the Vietnamese at these early stages, the Soviets sought to buy time for the Vietnamese and for themselves in the post World War II years (Pike 1969, Westad et al. 1998).

Dominoes and Containment

Writing in *Foreign Affairs* in July 1969, former Secretary of Defense Clark Clifford stated that "at the time of our original involvement in Viet Nam, I considered it to be based upon sound and unassailable premises, thoroughly consistent with our self-interest and our responsibilities. There has been no change in the exemplary character of our intentions in Viet Nam. We intervened to help a new and small nation resist subjugation by a neighboring country—a neighboring country, incidentally, which was being assisted by the resources of the world's two largest communist powers" (Clifford 1969, p. 602).

After the communist victory in China in 1949 and the outbreak of the Korean War in 1950, new pressures were added to the mix. The bitter recriminations in the United States over "who lost China?" produced a compelling domestic incentive for the Truman administration to prevent a communist victory in Vietnam or anywhere else in Indochina. The loss of Southeast Asia was defined as threatening the security of the United States and the collectivity of Free World nations. The sovereignties of Vietnam and other Southeast Asian countries were valued not on their own merit but rather as a test of U.S. global position and credibility—a perception that would have a profound impact on the nature on the decision to intervene. Vietnam became important for what its loss to the communists would portend.

Khong (1992) contributes important understanding on how policy makers use historical analogies in their foreign policy decision making and develops an insightful analogical model. Distilled, the United States fought in Vietnam because of the simplistic analogies invoked by decision makers—the "lessons" drawn from the Korean and Munich experiences predisposed decision makers to intervene and to escalate. In learning from history and developing analogies based on the Korean War, policy makers were predisposed not only toward intervention but also toward a specific option among the several pro-intervention options. The Korean analogy shaped the form as well as the fact of the U.S. intervention.

Neustadt & May (1986) hypothesize that decision makers used faulty historical conceptions about the nature of the conflict and failed to draw from more appropriate historical analogies when making the fundamental calculations on whether or not to intervene with military forces in Vietnam. The debacle of the French defeat at Dien Bien Phu in 1954 was seen by President Lyndon Johnson and his advisors as having little relevance in the period preceding the Americanization of the war.

Jervis (1976), George (1980), and Janis (1972) have also explored the role of cognitive biases, perceptions, and belief systems in strategic assessments and deterrence failures. Their important theory-driven explanations for common perceptual biases help us to understand what happened at the problem-definition stage of what became a war that cost the lives of over 58,000 Americans and millions of Vietnamese.

Based on the historical lessons of Munich, Korea, and China, not losing Vietnam became an increasingly important component in U.S. global objectives. In December 1950, the United States joined France, Vietnam, Cambodia, and Laos in signing a Mutual Defense Assistance Agreement. The United States agreed to provide military supplies and equipment through a U.S. military advisory group. This small contingent of U.S. advisors provided limited logistical services with all supplies and equipment being dispensed through the French Expeditionary Corps. Year by year, U.S. aid to the French military effort mounted: from $130 million in 1950 to $800 million in 1953, amounting to more than three fourths of the cost of the French war effort.

In May 1953, the French government appointed General Henri Navarre commander in Vietnam and charged him with mounting a major new offensive against the Viet Minh. One of Navarre's first moves, late in 1953, was to dispatch French troops to Dien Bien Phu, the juncture of a number of roads in northwestern Indochina about 100 miles from the Chinese border. In 1954, in Dien Bien Phu, the French and Viet Minh met in a major military confrontation. The French loss of this battle had important implications (Burke & Greenstein 1991).

The Viet Minh controlled most of Vietnam and sought a political settlement at Geneva that would lead to the withdrawal of French forces and to the establishment of an independent government led by Ho Chi Minh. But four of the men sitting around the map of Southeast Asia spread over the large horseshoe-shaped table at the old League of Nations building put their own interests ahead of those of the fifth person at the table, Pham Van Dong. The four—Foreign Secretary Anthony

Eden of the United Kingdom, Premier Pierre Mendes of France, Foreign Minister Vyacheslav Molotov of the Soviet Union, and Foreign Minister Chou Enlai of China—pressured the DRV to accept much less than the DRV had won in battle. The Vietnamese would never forget this "negotiation" (Devilliers & Lacouture 1969).

The Pentagon Papers make clear that the United States intended to disassociate itself from the results at Geneva, fearing a "sellout" of U.S. interests. The Chinese and Soviets, fearing American intervention under Secretary of State John Foster Dulles, forced Ho to accept two major concessions—a demarcation line drawn at the 17th parallel and free nationwide elections supervised by an international commission scheduled for 1956. The elections would settle the question of political control over Vietnam. In partitioning Vietnam at a nominally temporary "line of demarcation" between North and South at the 17th parallel, the Viet Minh took control of the Northern zone whereas France and an opposing Vietnamese government, ultimately led by Ngo Dinh Diem, controlled the South. Why did Ho Chi Minh accept these compromises? Ho recognized that without the support of the Chinese and Soviets, he could not have defeated the French. He acquiesced to the pressure, realizing that in two years Vietnam would be reunified (Zhai 2000).

Three months after Dien Bien Phu, Eisenhower convened the National Security Council (NSC) to review U.S. policy in Asia. The president was already on record as claiming that "strategically South Vietnam's capture by the Communists would bring their power several hundred miles into a hitherto free region. The remaining countries in Southeast Asia would be menaced by a great flanking movement. The freedom of 12 million people would be lost immediately and that of 150 million others in adjacent lands would be seriously endangered. The loss of the Republic of Vietnam, or South Vietnam, would have grave consequences for us and for freedom" (quoted in Berman 1982, p. 13). Eisenhower had also articulated the line of reasoning that came to be known as the domino theory, that the fall of one state to communism would lead to the next and the next being knocked over. Not losing Southeast Asia thus became the goal of the United States.

In an October 1954 letter to the president of South Vietnam, Ngo Dinh Diem, President Eisenhower was exceedingly clear: "I am, accordingly, instructing the American Ambassador to Vietnam to examine with you in your capacity as chief of Government, how an intelligent program of American aid given directly to your Government can serve to assist Vietnam in its present hour of trial, provided that your Government is prepared to give assurances as to the standards of performance it would be able to maintain in the event such aid were supplied. The purpose of this offer is to assist the government of Vietnam in developing and maintaining a strong, viable state, capable of resisting attempted subversion or aggression through military means" (quoted in Dommen 2001, p. 275).

Kaiser's (2000) study of the war's early years places responsibility with Eisenhower for establishing the underpinnings and "first principles" for American military intervention in Southeast Asia that guided subsequent presidents in their Vietnam policies. Strategic concerns stemming from the need to contain the threatening tentacles of communism drove Eisenhower's plans for defending this region. Even though he chose not to intervene militarily at Dien Bien Phu to help the French, he did provide the technical and financial support that allowed the Diem regime to gain power. The fear of falling dominoes and the accompanying threat to U.S. security led to the prominence of Vietnam's position in American national security policy. These fears and considerations, which apparently were never critically examined nor questioned by subsequent presidents, drove Johnson's foreign policy.

The 1954 division of Vietnam led the revolution to adopt two goals—socialism in the North and liberation in the South. By 1959, it had become evident to northerners and southerners that it was necessary to take up arms in the South in order to overthrow Diem and liberate South Vietnam. At the Fifteenth Plenum in January 1959, the Party leadership decided to make reunification the number one priority of the revolution. This began a political, diplomatic, and military struggle exemplified by the development of a multifaceted international strategy: a campaign of armed violence in the countryside paralleled by a new front for political warfare (Dommen 2001). The NLF would later be successful in promoting neutralism, establishing a relationship with China, engaging the United States in secret peace contacts, and driving a wedge between Washington and Saigon (Pike 1966, Brigham 1999, Prados 1999, Duiker 2000). The military arm of the NLF, then called the People's Liberation Army (PLA) and later known as the People's Liberation Armed Force (PLAF), bore the initial brunt of the battle in the South against Diem. Often overlooked is the fact that America's war of attrition succeeded in tipping the balance of power away from the PLAF, at which time the North dispatched PAVN (People's Army of Vietnam) filler units and then whole divisions to the South. At the time of the 1972 Easter Offensive, 90% of the day-to-day combat in the South was by the regular North Vietnamese PAVN units (Pike 1986, Andrade 1995).

Pike's (1966, 1969, 1986) lifetime of research on Hanoi's concept of general warfare shows that, when it came to understanding PAVN strategy, one of the great difficulties confronting policy makers in Washington was semantic. Pike categorizes five separate periods of war in which Hanoi's High Command altered strategy based on their perceptions of events and balance of forces: from early 1958 to late 1960—revolutionary war preparation; from 1961 to late 1964—revolutionary guerrilla war; from early 1965 to mid-1968—regular force strategy; from late 1968 to Easter 1972—neo-revolutionary guerrilla war; and from 1972 to the end of the war—high-technology regular force strategy. What we learn from Pike's work is that the these periods were delineated both by battlefield events and by serious disputes in Hanoi over doctrines of war. Pike's analysis distinguishes *dau tranh* (struggle), *dau tranh vu trang* (armed struggle), and *dau tranh chinh tri* (political struggle). *Dau tranh chinh tri*, which translates as "politics with guns," consists of three *van* (action) programs—*dich van* (action among the enemy), *dan van* (action among the people), and *binh van* (action among the military). Pike goes on to define *khoi nghia* (uprising, insurrection, to revolt), *tong koi nghia* (general uprising), and *chien tranh* (protracted conflict).

In English this translated to "regular force" battles versus "revolutionary" warfare; in official terminology, it was a debate over armed *dau tranh* versus political *dau tranh*. We now understand that when the United States considered fighting in Vietnam, policy makers were unaware that the conflict ahead was a new type of war—a struggle, *dau tranh*, more than a war—as the communists said it was (Pike 1986).

A complex relationship existed between Lao Dong's Political Bureau in Hanoi and the NLF's southern-based leadership. They had conflicts and disagreements over strategy, tactics, and diplomacy. For Brigham (1999), the difference between northerners and southerners is rooted not in any psychological-cultural explanation, but in their respective reaction to the American intervention. The realpolitik of southern revolutionaries often placed them at odds with Party leaders in Hanoi, and Brigham suggests that events after 1975 can be explained by the Political Bureau's lingering memories of these often bitter disputes (Brigham 1999, Gilbert 2002).

By 1961, Vietnam loomed as a test of President John F. Kennedy's inaugural commitment "to pay any price, to bear any burden, in defense of freedom." President Kennedy initiated a counterinsurgency campaign as a "limited" war that could be waged internally in South Vietnam (Hunt 1995, Lomperis 1996). Counterinsurgency was really unconventional counter-guerrilla warfare and a way of countering wars of national liberation (Taylor 1960). The idea of winning the hearts and minds of the civilian population was appealing to those who had doubts about the feasibility of defeating enemy forces on the battlefield. Counterinsurgency became the "other war" that the United States chose to fight in Vietnam. It consisted of population control, strategic hamlet programs, pacification, psychological warfare, and the Phoenix program that resulted in the execution of over 20,000 suspected Viet Cong guerrillas. All of these activities were coordinated by the Civil Operations and Revolutionary Development Support (CORDS). Counterinsurgency as a doctrine eventually contributed to failure because it diverted attention from the decisive enemy—the regular armed forces of the North.

Another result of the counterinsurgency campaign against the Viet Cong was a rise in revolutionary violence in the South against the Diem regime. The record shows that Ho Chi Minh persuaded Party leaders that the way to defeat the United States and Diem was not to place force against force, but to wage the battle politically through guerrilla warfare and by mobilizing the masses and worldwide opinion against Diem and the United States. Diem's government had evolved into a family oligarchy that ruled through force and repression. Opposition grew from a wide range of political, social, and religious groups. Protests raged, including the dramatic self-immolations by Buddhist monks (Catton 2003).

On November 1, 1963, Diem was removed from office and murdered in the back of a U.S.-built personnel carrier. The coup was planned and implemented by South Vietnamese military officers, but U.S. Ambassador Henry Cabot Lodge and the Central Intelligence Agency (CIA) had foreknowledge of the assassination. Kennedy, given the opportunity to instruct Lodge to stop the coup, issued no such order (Gardner & Gittinger 1997). The U.S. government's complicity in the coup heightened its sense of responsibility for finding a replacement. Diem's death was followed by political instability in Saigon—there would be five different governments and prime ministers over the next 12 months. The most significant event, however, occurred just three weeks after Diem's murder, when President Kennedy was assassinated (creating a vast "conspiracy" literature; see especially Newman 1992).

Americanizing the War

President Lyndon B. Johnson assumed office with the belief that the United States would be responsible for the stability and security of South Vietnam. He believed that his predecessor's complicity in the overthrow of Diem now gave the United States de facto responsibility for successive governments in South Vietnam. Many believe that it was the Diem assassination that set in motion a series of events that in July 1965 would force Johnson to choose between accepting defeat or Americanizing the war by introducing combat troops.

Was war inevitable? Logevall (1999) challenges this view by positing that a face-saving negotiated settlement was available in the 1964–1965 period, but that Lyndon Johnson chose war, seeing the challenge as a test of his own manliness. "The Long 1964," the period between August 29, 1963 and late February 1965, provided the window for a negotiated settlement. This period began with the approval to move ahead with the coup against Diem and ended with the decision to begin sustained bombing of North Vietnam and to land two marine combat battalions in South Vietnam.

Drawing on multi-archival sources, Logevall (1999) hypothesizes that Johnson had other options and few allies at the time but chose to listen to the hawks on his advisory team—McNamara, Bundy, and Rusk (Van De Mark 1991, Herring 1994, Gardner 1995). The window of opportunity for avoiding war was available because Hanoi was willing to compromise and accept a temporarily neutralized South Vietnam—fearing a massive U.S. escalation. Drawing on archival documents from international depositories, Logevall argues that China, Russia, and France were also predisposed toward this neutralist solution and that elite public opinion would have supported it. Moreover, Logevall makes extensive use of polling data from 1964 to show that the public was ill-informed and had not formed strong opinions on Vietnam. In the end, Logevall casts responsibility with Johnson and his close advisors for the critical decisions on America taking over the war. He correctly notes that this group, the so-called best and brightest, had been involved in policy making for several years and had a large personal stake in seeing that commitment succeed.

The Logevall thesis is part of a revisionist literature that rendered the "quagmire" thesis obsolete. First postulated by Schlesinger (1967), the quagmire thesis was that, with containment as the strategic backdrop, U.S. policy makers inadvertently stumbled into a war in Vietnam. Once an ill-conceived vital American interest was created, a series of decisions followed. There was no single deliberate calculation, but rather an incremental process whereby each prior decision was thought to have been the last best new decision, with hopes that no further action would be needed. The war became a quagmire, but there was no one to blame for the tragedy—decisions to escalate stemmed from ignorance, good-faith idealism, and unintentional bumbling rather than from strategic calculations.

The publication of *The Pentagon Papers* (Sheehan 1971) showed that the players were well aware of the odds of succeeding. Indeed, the decision to fight in Vietnam could not be explained merely as the inadvertent result of good intentions. The thrust of Kahin's (1986) seminal work is that a set of remarkably flawed decisions and advice given to Presidents Truman, Eisenhower, and Johnson resulted in the Vietnam tragedy. Rejecting the quagmire apologists, Kahin argues that the decisions were rendered not through error and ignorance but rather through strategic calculations based on the fear of communism. America's war in Vietnam was the result of the agenda of civilian advisers who were not fully cognizant of the importance and strength of Vietnamese nationalism and culture and who simply did not understand Vietnamese history, culture, language, and geography. As Daniel Ellsberg stated in 1972, "There has never been an official of Deputy Assistant Secretary rank or higher (including myself) who could have passed in office a midterm freshman exam in modern Vietnamese history, if such a course existed in this country" (Ellsberg 1972).

Political scientists are interested in understanding nationalist and indigenous sources of the war and windows of opportunity that existed before the Cold War mentality emerged. Once policies were implemented under Eisenhower that supported the Diem regime, it became increasingly difficult for subsequent presidents to roll back those obligations because the costs of losing increased with each presidential promise to maintain the government in the South. Many if not all advisors surrounding Truman and Eisenhower would have agreed with Clark Clifford's 1969 assertion that the original commitment was to a noble goal—ensuring that a separate, autonomous, sovereign, anticommunist, and pro-American (not just noncommunist and not neutralist) state would survive in Vietnam. Yet no one seemed interested in debating whether the nobler cause might have been in supporting the Viet Minh in their struggle for independence and self-determination.

No military strategy was ever matched with the limited political objective. In the *Art of War*, Tzu (1971) postulated that the most important aspect of war was to attack the enemy's strategy. North Vietnam's strategy was superior to that of the United States because it operated on several levels simultaneously in order to achieve both limited and total war objectives (Dommen 2001). For the United States, the result was not only disastrous policy but also bitter recriminations after the war between military and civilian policy makers, which fueled much misunderstanding about the appropriate use of force and military intervention (Krepinevich 1986, Levite et al. 1992). Only when Nixon changed the U.S. objective was it possible for bombing, as one example, to be effective as a tool of war (Clodfelter 1989).

Gelb & Betts (1979) also reject the quagmire thesis, maintaining that the bureaucracy of civilian policy makers knew the low odds of success but that politically no president wanted to be blamed for "losing" South Vietnam. This became known as the "Good Doctor" analogy—even if the patient (South Vietnam) died, the good doctor (the United States) would be seen as having done everything possible to prevent the expiration. In 1965, John McNaughton had already informed his boss, Secretary of Defense McNamara, of the poor probabilities for success with each increasing increment and year of American involvement. U.S. aims were identified as 70% to preserve national honor; 20% to keep South Vietnam free from communist control; and 10% to answer the call of a friend in order to help him enjoy a better life (Berman 1982, p. 140). This was no quagmire, but it was a sinkhole. The United States did not blunder into Vietnam; the bureaucratic system worked, in that McNamara knew the odds. But he and the President undertook a policy that was a compromise of competing beliefs—and decided to do what was minimally necessary to avoid losing Vietnam—which they pursued until they lost the "essential domino" of American public support.

Ellsberg (1972) compared this process to the card game "old maid." No one wanted to be the president who lost Vietnam, as China had been lost in 1949. It was Lyndon Johnson's misfortune to get caught with the old maid card, and he then felt compelled to dramatically escalate the war—in order not to be the president who lost Vietnam. Truman, Eisenhower, and Kennedy had avoided the old maid card by doing what was minimally necessary, with little hope for success.

Political scientists have made important contributions concerning Johnson and his advisors and the impact of advisory processes on policy outcomes. Burke & Greenstein (1991) compare 1954 and 1965, when two presidents with strikingly different leadership styles and advisory teams faced a similar challenge—committing American ground troops to Vietnam. In their Neustadt Award–winning book, Burke & Greenstein focus only on the quality of presidential reality testing. That is, how do presidents and their advisors assess their environment? How do they process information? How do they identify and explore possible courses of action? What is the independent impact of advisory processes on presidents? What is the impact of presidential personality and leadership style?

In posing these questions, Burke & Greenstein focus on the quality of the process and not the quality of the decision. This instrumental concern motivated an analysis of the structure, dynamics, and content of advisory systems. It also presented many opportunities for qualitative analysis of belief structures and of how instrumental rationality enhances the likelihood that a policy will attain its intended ends.

In *Planning A Tragedy*, Berman (1982) focuses on Johnson's decision in July 1965 to Americanize the war. Johnson believed that if South Vietnam went down the drain in 1965, so would his chances of passing most of his Great Society legislation. In order to avoid a divisive national debate on the American commitment to Vietnam, Johnson decided not to mobilize the military reserves, not to request a general tax increase for 1966, and not to publicize the anticipated manpower needs in order to accomplish the limited political objective. Johnson was not misled by his advisors. He used his great talents to forge a marginal political and military consensus that resulted in a guns-and-butter decision to fight a war at home and abroad with insufficient resources. In *Uncertain Warriors*, Barrett (1993) challenges Berman's thesis by positing that the Johnson advisory deliberations flowed from the actions of a rational leader and advisors pursuing a vision of an anticommunist world order.

In either case, Johnson's July 1965 decision was tantamount to slow political suicide and forced the administration to prove that there was a crossover point in the war of attrition. The administration became fixated on statistically demonstrating to the press and the American public that progress was being made—body counts, order of battle, kill ratios, pacification, bombing targets, and population control data were all measured, averaged, and manipulated to show that there indeed was a light at the end of the tunnel. Despite these efforts, the credibility gap and a failed policy soon forced Johnson from office.

Military revisionists have contributed to a fuller appreciation of how the war was fought and lost in Washington (D.R. Palmer 1978, Sharp 1978, Summers 1982, B. Palmer 1984, Record 1998, Sorley 1999). McMaster (1997) shows that Maxwell Taylor, Chairman of the Joint Chiefs of Staff from 1962 to 1964, consistently misled both Kennedy and Johnson on the views of the Chiefs and misled the Chiefs on the intentions of the commander-in-chief. Johnson certainly manipulated the Chiefs into accepting his guns-and-butter policy (Berman 1989, Van De Mark 1991), but the Chiefs played along and kept quiet, taking the path of least resistance. McMaster shows that this was as much the result of interservice rivalry as it was fear of challenging their commander-in-chief. Years later, many of these same senior military leaders lamented that they had not resigned in protest.

THE BOMBING

Why did bombing fail as a political tool for Johnson yet succeed for Nixon? This important and frequently misunderstood issue has also clouded discussion pertaining to the use of air power in subsequent interventions. Clodfelter (1989) evaluates bombing's efficacy by the standard of its contribution to a nation's war aims. Taking Clausewitz's definition of war as "a continuation of political activity by other means," Clodfelter analyzes the three separate air campaigns against the North—Rolling Thunder (March 2, 1965–October 31, 1968), Linebacker I (May 10, 1972–October 23, 1972), and Linebacker II (December 18–29, 1972). Rolling Thunder was the longest bombing campaign in the history of the U.S. Air Force, and it failed. Its objective was to destroy the North's means of production and distribution, but the communist forces in South Vietnam needed few external supplies. Rolling Thunder was strategically flawed because the war was stalemated in the South and conventional attacks against the North had little effect on the enemy's initiative. The enemy had no breaking point with respect to Rolling Thunder because the more Rolling Thunder attacked industry, rail, and roadways, the more successful the enemy was in developing the Ho Chi Minh Trail for transport (Prados 1999).

Linebacker II was more effective, since it was used against a large-scale conventional assault requiring massive logistical support. Linebacker II seriously disrupted and damaged North Vietnam's lines of communication. But most significantly, Nixon employed Linebacker II in support of very limited objectives. Whereas Johnson had explained the use of air power as the means of helping to establish an independent, stable, noncommunist South Vietnam, Nixon applied air power only to guarantee America's continued withdrawal and to assure that the South did not face imminent collapse after the U.S. departure. Opinion polls conducted immediately after the initiation of Linebacker II revealed that the American public approved of the bombing by wide margins. The "silent majority" spoke loudly. Nixon was also correct in his assessment that the Soviets would not risk détente over the bombings. There was a crucial irony to the Linebacker support: While Linebacker pushed Hanoi to make significant concessions, it also stiffened South Vietnam President Nguyen Van Thieu's opposition to any agreement. Viewing the concessions that Linebacker helped extract from Hanoi, the South Vietnamese president reasoned that continued strikes could bring him total victory (Berman 2001).

Just prior to the Easter 1972 bombing, President Nixon said, "the bastards have never been bombed like they're going to be bombed this time" (Andrade 1995, Berman 2001). The day before the Christmas 1972 bombing, Nixon told Admiral Moorer, "I don't want any more of this crap about the fact that we couldn't hit this target or that one. This is your chance to use military power effectively to win this war, and if you don't, I'll consider you responsible." Drawing a comparison between himself and his predecessor, Nixon frequently said that he had the "will" to punish Hanoi with B-52s.

Nixon intended Linebacker II to inflict maximum physical damage on the North Vietnamese. Whereas Linebacker I sought to wreck North Vietnam's war-making capacity, Linebacker II was intended to destroy the North's will to fight and to serve as a Western Union message to President Thieu that the United States intended to continually support South Vietnam. Hanoi was indeed rendered defenseless by the Linebacker assault, but the United States sustained serious losses as well. During the 12-day campaign (11 days, a pause on Christmas, and another day of bombing), the enemy downed 13 U.S. tactical aircraft and 15 B-52s. U.S. aircrew casualties during the expanded bombing of December amounted to 93 missing, with 31 reported captured.

One of the early studies of the bombing (Thies 1980) focused on Johnson's plan to utilize limited bombing as a means of encouraging North Vietnam to come to the negotiating table and settle on U.S. terms. The Rolling Thunder campaign was premised on three assumptions: (a) steadily intensifying military pressure would cause North Vietnam to cease supporting the Viet Cong, (b) military actions and diplomatic signaling would clearly convey the desired messages to Hanoi, and

(c) the White House would be able to control its use of force in congruence with alterations in policy aims.

In case after case, each of these three assumptions was proven to be in error because the war was not an ongoing bargaining process. The empirical reality in Hanoi and Washington did not comport with the base assumptions of a unitary rational actor. The bureaucratic conflict model captures reality much more accurately—the decision maker on both sides of the conflict is best seen as a collection of rival groups battling over policy rather than as a single individual who consistently engages in predictable cost-benefit analysis. Assuming such rationality on the part of one's enemy led to problematic and unsuccessful actions by the Johnson administration.

And what of the essential domino—American public opinion? Johnson found that he could not wage a war against poverty at home and against the Viet Cong in Asia without public backing, and his actions soon created a credibility gap. Nixon always insisted that his actions, especially bombing, were supported by the silent majority of Americans and that the American people believed he had secured a peace with honor.

Jacobs & Shapiro (1994) focus on the experiences of President Johnson and the challenges he faced during the Vietnam War. Their analysis of public opinion data suggests that Johnson was both unresponsive to public opinion toward American involvement in Vietnam and ineffective in trying to lead and direct that public opinion. The authors' assessment of archival material from the Johnson administration documents that Johnson and his aides had quite a bit of public opinion data available to them but opted not to use it. Perhaps Johnson was weighing voters' future reactions to his potential policies and these prospective assessments led him to his middle-way Vietnam policy—between the two poles of full-scale war and complete withdrawal.

Jacobs & Shapiro's analysis demonstrates the failure of Johnson's attempts to lead public opinion and change popular preferences about Vietnam. They find that the contours of public attitudes toward hawk and dove policies remained remarkably stable. Johnson independently formulated U.S. policy for Vietnam and then tried to get the public behind that policy. Problematically for Johnson, public opinion data showed that the strong hawk and strong dove positions drew the most public support; Johnson's centrist course led to discontentment on both sides with no profit for Johnson. Hawks and doves were united in their strong beliefs that Johnson was not doing enough to achieve their goals in Vietnam.

Mueller (1973) examined the dynamics of public opinion between the Korean and Vietnamese wars and identified strong connections between opinions and mounting casualties in both wars. Mueller's interpretation is that the populace is more sensitive to an increase in casualties at the beginning of a war and that they become somewhat desensitized to human loss as time passes. That is, the public's sensitivity is most pronounced at the beginning to small losses and then at later stages to large losses. Trajectories of popular reactions were markedly similar in the Korean and Vietnam conflicts, until Vietnam's casualty levels seriously surpassed Korea's.

Hallin (1986) also helps outline the causal paths between American public opinion and those changes within it that affected policy in Vietnam. By examining the conventional wisdom that print and television news media played a pivotal role in driving the public disenchantment with American involvement in Vietnam, Hallin finds that public dissent preceded reporters' more critical attitude toward the war (see Braestrup 1983, Hammond 1998).

The United States fought in Vietnam because of a Cold War consensus that Hallin shows was shared by journalists and policy makers alike. The critical crossover point in media criticism of policy came with the January 1968 Tet offensive, which challenged the administration's claims of progress. The oft-promised light at the end of the tunnel was that of an oncoming train. Tet revealed that despite over 525,000 troops, billions of dollars, and extensive bombing, the United States had not stopped the enemy from replacing his forces. The pace of the war and the capacity to sustain it were controlled not by America's superior technology but by the enemy. In effect, the United States faced stalemate in Vietnam (Oberdorfer 2001).

On March 31, 1968, Johnson announced a partial suspension of the bombing and asked that Hanoi's negotiators come to the table. The President then stunned the nation by announcing that he would not seek renomination for the presidency. The leader who committed forces abroad thereby removed himself from the disengagement process. The battle over disengagement and its meaning would now belong to his successor (Levite et al. 1992).

THE NEGOTIATIONS, DIPLOMACY, AND WAR TERMINATION

The war in Vietnam was negotiated over almost as long as it was fought (Goodman 1986, Asselin 2002, Loi 2002). The role of these negotiations in the political settlement remains one of the least understood aspects of the war. The negotiations became a contest of wills: the resolve of the United States to see the war through to an honorable end and the resolve of the North Vietnamese to reach an advantageous settlement that would allow them to continue their struggle toward unification of Vietnam under the flag of Hanoi.

The real negotiations were conducted in secret between Henry Kissinger and Le Duc Tho. This private channel meant that the United States and North Vietnam would negotiate the terms for South Vietnam's survival. President Thieu was kept in the dark, as were most bureaucratic entities in the United States. The veil of secrecy surrounding the talks meant that very few would be aware of the concessions being made. There was no precise negotiating position that had been agreed to within the U.S. government, nor even a general negotating position agreed on with the government of Vietnam. Nixon and Kissinger viewed secrecy as the key to a successful negotiating outcome.

The United States entered the negotiations during the Nixon presidency from the position of "mutual withdrawal" of troops as the essential component of any settlement. The United States would withdraw its troops from South Vietnam only if the North would do the same. The North Vietnamese position called for a unilateral withdrawal of all foreign troops and the removal of President Thieu from power.

North Vietnamese negotiator Le Duc Tho insisted that the only invading foreign army in South Vietnam was that of the United States. Kissinger soon capitulated (in secret). After the United States agreed to allow the Northern troops to remain, Hanoi waited until 1972, when the balance of forces in the South was decidedly in Hanoi's favor. The Politburo then instructed Tho to concede on the point of Thieu remaining in power because in Hanoi's eyes, Thieu would be irrelevant given the other concessions. In his memoirs, Kissinger describes Hanoi's concession as the one he had dreamed about for years—Tho had separated military from political issues. As John Negroponte quipped, "we bombed them into accepting our concessions."

President Thieu remained in power, buttressed with private assurances from Nixon, Kissinger, and Haig of massive, brutal retaliation for communist violations of the Paris Agreement—but only after the return of American prisoners of war in the 60 days following the signing of the Agreement in January 1973 (Dillard 1982). In private, Nixon promised Thieu that if he accepted the Agreement, it would be possible to rally the silent majority—"people with character of steel"—to support the renewal of bombing that Congress would not approve (Hung & Schecter 1986). Unity between allies was essential to the future conduct of the war, not the peace. Nixon expected communist violations and did almost nothing to prevent South Vietnamese violations. Aside from the return of American prisoners of war, Kissinger gave little attention to any of the post–60-day responsibilities for effective implementation of a ceasefire—status of opposing forces, territorial limits of control, policing and enforcing, and replacement of war materials. Kissinger displayed almost total indifference regarding treaty enforcement (Le Gro 1981, Dillard 1982).

The declassified record shows that President Thieu was encouraged (*a*) not to hold elections until the Northern troops went home, (*b*) to use political prisoners as hostages—even though Kissinger had promised Tho their release—to compel the North's withdrawal, and (*c*) to treat with contempt the National Council on Reconciliation. Thieu was being asked to accomplish something that Kissinger failed to achieve in three years of negotiations. Kissinger and Nixon repeatedly told their ally that there was no reason to risk a political solution until a North Vietnamese withdrawal from the South. The aged men in the Politburo had no intention of accommodating this daydream.

Thieu was informed and never consulted; Kissinger kept him in the dark while negotiating directly with Tho on the future of South Vietnam. The new documentation suggests a deceitful plan on the same level as Lyndon Johnson's manipulation of the Tonkin Gulf Resolution, which was used to justify expanded military engagement (Moise 1996). The Paris Agreement was intended to justify American reengagement, and as in the case of the Tonkin Gulf Resolution, the public and the Congress would not be told. The plan was for permanent war at acceptable political costs; only Watergate derailed it.

Nixon planned for an indefinite stalemate by using U.S. airpower to prop up the government of South Vietnam through 1976 and the end of his second term. He was prepared to take on Congress by appealing directly for the support of the silent majority. Nixon expected violations, but he had an enforcing mechanism—the return of the B-52s. The President would take whatever actions were necessary to guarantee that when he turned the keys of the White House over to the next occupant in 1976, there would be a South Vietnam.

At midnight Greenwich Mean Time on January 27, 1973, the war in Vietnam was declared officially over. Delegations representing the United States, South Vietnam, North Vietnam, and the Provisional Revolutionary Communist Government of South Vietnam signed the agreement known officially as the "Paris Agreement and Protocols on Ending the War and Restoring the Peace in Vietnam." The agreement provided for the end of the fighting and the withdrawal of American forces. The United States committed itself to ending all air and naval actions against North Vietnam and to dismantling or deactivating all mines in the waters of North Vietnam. Within two months after the signing of the agreement, all forces of the United States and of U.S. allies would depart Vietnam. The United States was barred from sending new war materials or supplies to South Vietnam and was required to dismantle all military bases there. The armed forces of the government of South Vietnam and the NLF were allowed to remain where they were, but the ceasefire barred the introduction of new troops, military advisers, military personnel (including technical military personnel), armaments, munitions, and war materials from North Vietnam or anywhere else. The disposition of Vietnamese armed forces in South Vietnam would be determined by the two South Vietnamese parties in a spirit of "national reconciliation and concord." In addition, the Agreement required the return of all captured military personnel and foreign civilians during the same two-month period. The two South Vietnamese parties would handle the return of Vietnamese civilians. The United States and North Vietnam promised to uphold the principles of self-determination for the South Vietnamese people, which included free and democratic elections under international supervision.

The treaty called for a Four-Party Joint Military Commission to be constituted by the four signatories to implement and monitor compliance with the provisions on withdrawal, ceasefire, dismantling of bases, return of war prisoners, and exchange of information on those missing in action. An International Commission of Control and Supervision, consisting of Canada, Hungary, Indonesia, and Poland, would oversee the agreement and report violations.

In the case of Vietnam, a set of limited political objectives in a region of political instability proved elusive, not only during the escalation stage, but during the protracted disengagement process as well. Here we see many promising avenues for research on how the processes of a negotiated settlement contributed to this outcome and what can be learned for future cases of protracted peace negotiations leading to a political settlement. What role did the Europeans play behind the scenes, and were there lost opportunities for peace? What lessons can be generated for future cases involving the cessation of hostilities and securing of a negotiated peace?

Was the deal negotiated in 1973 available in 1969? Why did the United States not try to secure more formal guarantees for President Thieu and sanctions against land grabbing and troop movement? Did President Nixon's advisors believe that continued American funding would guarantee a free and independent South Vietnam and that therefore no additional treaty provisions were necessary? Did Nixon or Kissinger envision conditions under which the United States would reenter the Vietnam conflict? Did either of these principals anticipate the return of U.S. air power as the instrument for maintaining the peace? If so, how did the President expect to sell politically a continuation of U.S. air power to the American people and to the Congress? Did President Nixon envision that the Paris Agreement would yield anything except an indefinite stalemate whereby South Vietnam would retain control over the major cities and key capitals, surrendering most of the countryside and part of the central highlands? As Watergate began to occupy more and more of Nixon's attention, just what did Kissinger tell him about the details of his negotiations? How well informed did the Secretary of State keep the President on the details of the treaty that was being negotiated to end the American involvement? Finally, did Kissinger and Nixon have differing visions of the so-called "decent interval" hypothesis on the fate of South Vietnam and the U.S. obligations to an ally (Snepp 2002)?

The *Annual Review of Political Science* is online at
http://polisci.annualreviews.org

LITERATURE CITED

Andrade D. 1995. *Trial by Fire: The 1972 Easter Offensive—America's Last Vietnam Battle.* New York: Hippocrene Books

Asselin P. 2002. *A Bitter Peace: Washington, Hanoi, and the Making of the Paris Agreement.* Chapel Hill: Univ. North Carolina Press

Barrett DM. 1993. *Uncertain Warriors: Lyndon Johnson and His Vietnam Advisors.* Lawrence: Univ. Press Kansas

Berman L. 1982. *Planning a Tragedy: The Americanization of the War in Vietnam.* New York/London: WW Norton

Berman L. 1989. *Lyndon Johnson's War.* New York/London: WW Norton

Berman L. 2001. *No Peace, No Honor: Nixon, Kissinger, and Betrayal in Vietnam.* New York: Free

Bradley MP. 2000. *Imagining Vietnam and America: The Making of Postcolonial Vietnam, 1919–1950.* Chapel Hill: Univ. North Carolina Press

Braestrup P. 1983. *Big Story: How the American Press and Television Reported and Interpreted the Crisis of Tet 1968 in Vietnam and Washington.* New Haven, CT: Yale Univ. Press

Brigham RK. 1999. *Guerilla Diplomacy: The NLF's Foreign Relations and the Vietnam War.* Ithaca, NY/London: Cornell Univ. Press

Burke JP, Greenstein FI, with L Berman and RH Immerman. 1991. *How Presidents Test Reality: Decisions on Vietnam, 1954 and 1965.* New York: Russell Sage Found.

Catton P. 2003. *Diem's Final Failure:*

Prelude to America's War in Vietnam. Lawrence: Univ. Press Kansas

Clifford CM. 1969. A Vietnam reappraisal. *For. Aff.* 47:601–22

Clodfelter M. 1989. *The Limits of Air Power: The American Bombing of North Vietnam.* New York: Macmillan

Devilliers P, Lacouture J. 1969. *End of a War: Indochina, 1954.* New York/London: Frederick A. Praeger

Dillard WS. 1982. *Sixty Days to Peace: Implementing the Paris Peace Accords.* Washington, DC: Natl. Defense Univ.

Dommen AJ. 2001. *The Indochinese Experience of the French and the Americans: Nationalism and Communism in Cambodia, Laos and Vietnam.* Bloomington: Indiana Univ. Press

Duiker WJ. 1996. *The Communist Road to Power in Vietnam.* Boulder, CO: Westview. 2nd ed.

Duiker WJ. 2000. *Ho Chi Minh.* New York: Hyperion

Dung VT. 1977. *Our Great Spring Victory: an Account of the Liberation of South Vietnam.* New York: Monthly Rev.

Ellsberg P. 1972. *Papers on the War.* New York: Simon & Schuster

Elman C, Elman MF, eds. 2003. *Progress in International Relations Theory: Appraising the Field.* Cambridge, MA: MIT Press

Englemann L. 1990. *Tears Before the Rain.* New York: Oxford Univ. Press

Fearon JD. 1991. Counterfactuals and hypothesis testing in political science. *World Polit.* 43:169–95

Gaddis JL. 1982. *Strategies of Containment.* New York: Oxford Univ. Press

Gaiduk IV. 1996. *The Soviet Union and the Vietnam War.* Chicago: Ivan R. Dee

Gardner LC. 1988. *Approaching Vietnam: From World War II Through Dienbienphu.* New York/London: WW Norton

Gardner LC. 1995. *Pay Any Price: Lyndon Johnson and the Wars for Vietnam.* Chicago: Ivan R. Dee

Gardner LV, Gittinger T, eds. 1997. *Vietnam:*

The Early Decisions. Austin, TX: Univ. Texas Press

Gelb LH, Betts RK. 1979. *The Irony of Vietnam: The System Worked.* Washington, DC: Brookings Inst.

George AL. 1980. *Presidential Decisionmaking in Foreign Policy: The Effective Use of Information and Advice.* Boulder, CO: Westview

George AL. 1993. *Bridging the Gap: Theory and Practice in Foreign Policy.* Washington, DC: U.S. Inst. Peace

Gilbert MJ, ed. 2002. *Why the North Won the Vietnam War.* New York: PALGRAVE

Goodman AE. 1978. *The Lost Peace: America's Search for a Negotiated Settlement of the Vietnam War.* Stanford, CA: Hoover Inst. Press

Goodman AE. 1986. *The Search for a Negotiated Settlement of the Vietnam War.* Berkeley, CA: Inst. East Asian Stud.

Hallin DC. 1986. *The Uncensored War: The Media and Vietnam.* New York/Oxford: Oxford Univ. Press

Hammond WM. 1998. *Reporting Vietnam: Media and Military at War.* Lawrence: Univ. Press Kansas

Herring GC. 1994. *LBJ and Vietnam: A Different Kind of War.* Austin: Univ. Texas Press

Hosmer ST, Kellen K, Jenkins BM. 1980. *The Fall of South Vietnam.* New York: Crane, Russak

Hung NT, Schecter JL. 1986. *The Palace File.* New York: Harper & Row

Hunt RA. 1995. *Pacification: The American Struggle for Vietnam's Hearts and Minds.* Boulder, CO: Westview

Jacobs LR, Shapiro RY. 1994. *Lyndon Johnson, Vietnam, and public opinion: rethinking realists' theory of leadership.* Presented at Annu. Meet. Midwest Polit. Sci. Assoc., Chicago

Janis IL. 1972. *Victims of Groupthink: a Psychological Study of Foreign-policy Decisions and Fiascoes.* Boston: Houghton Mifflin

Jervis R. 1976. *Perception and Misperception in International Politics.* Princeton, NJ: Princeton Univ. Press

Kahin GM. 1986. *Intervention: How America Became Involved in Vietnam.* New York: Alfred A. Knopf

Kaiser D. 2000. *American Tragedy: Kennedy, Johnson, and the Origins of the Vietnam War.* Cambridge, MA: Harvard Univ. Press

Khong YF. 1992. *Analogies at War: Korea, Munich, Dien Bien Phu, and the Vietnam Decisions of 1965.* Princeton, NJ: Princeton Univ. Press

Kissinger H. 1979. *White House Years.* Boston/Toronto: Little, Brown

Kissinger H. 1994. *Diplomacy.* New York: Simon & Schuster

Kissinger H. 1999. *Years of Renewal: The Concluding Volume of His Memoirs.* New York: Simon & Schuster

Krepinevich AF. 1986. *The Army and Vietnam.* Baltimore/London: Johns Hopkins Univ. Press

Le Gro WE. 1981. *Vietnam from Cease-fire to Capitulation.* Washington, DC: U.S. Army Cent. Mil. Hist.

Levite AE, Jentleson BW, Berman L, eds. 1992. *Foreign Military Intervention: the Dynamics of Protracted Conflict.* New York: Columbia Univ. Press

Logevall F. 1999. *Choosing War: the Lost Chance for Peace and the Escalation of War in Vietnam.* Berkeley/Los Angeles: Univ. Calif. Press

Loi LV. 2002. *Fifty Years of Vietnamese Diplomacy, 1945–1995.* Hanoi: Thê Gioi

Lomperis TJ. 1996. *From People's War to People's Rule: Insurgency, Intervention, and the Lessons of Vietnam.* Chapel Hill: Univ. North Carolina Press

Marr DG. 1995. *Vietnam 1945: The Quest for Power.* Berkeley: Univ. Calif.

McMaster HR. 1997. *Dereliction of Duty: Lyndon Johnson, Robert McNamara, the Joint Chiefs of Staff, and the Lies That Led to Vietnam.* New York: HarperCollins

McNamara RS, Blight JG, Brigham RK, Biersteker TJ, Schandler HY. 1999. *Argument Without End: In Search of Answers to the Vietnam Tragedy.* New York: Public Aff.

McNamara RS, Van De Mark B. 1995. *In Retrospect: The Tragedy and Lessons of Vietnam.* New York: Times Books

Moise EE. 1996. *Tonkin Gulf and the Escalation of the Vietnam War.* Chapel Hill: Univ. North Carolina Press

Mueller JE. 1973. *War, Presidents, and Public Opinion.* New York: Wiley

Neustadt RE, May ER. 1986. *Thinking in Time: The Uses of History for Decision Makers.* New York: Free

Newman JM. 1992. *JFK and Vietnam: Deception, Intrigue, and the Struggle For Power.* New York: Warner Books

Nincic M. 1988. *United States Foreign Policy: Choices and Tradeoffs.* Washington, DC: CQ Press

Oberdorfer D. 2001. *Tet!* Baltimore: Johns Hopkins Univ. Press

Palmer B. 1984. *The 25-Year War: America's Military Role in Vietnam.* New York: Simon & Schuster by arrangement with Univ. Press Kentucky

Palmer DR. 1978. *Summons of the Trumpet: U.S.–Vietnam in Perspective.* Novato, CA: Presidio

Patti AL. 1980. *Why Viet Nam? Prelude to America's Albatross.* Berkeley: Univ. Calif. Press

Pike DE. 1966. *Viet Cong: The Organization and Techniques of the National Liberation Front of South Vietnam.* Cambridge, MA: MIT Press

Pike DE. 1969. *War, Peace, and the Viet Cong.* Cambridge, MA: MIT Press

Pike DE. 1986. *PAVN : People's Army of Vietnam.* Novato, CA: Presidio

Porter G. 1975. *A Peace Denied: The United States, Vietnam, and the Paris Agreement.* Bloomington: Indiana Univ. Press

Prados J. 1999. *The Blood Road: The Ho Chi Minh Trail and the Vietnam War.* New York: Wiley

Record J. 1998. *The Wrong War: Why We Lost in Vietnam.* Annapolis, MD: Naval Inst. Press

Schlesinger AM. 1967. *The Bitter Heritage: Vietnam and American Democracy 1941–1966.* Boston: Houghton Mifflin

Sharp USG. 1978. *Strategy for Defeat : Vietnam in Retrospect.* Novato: Presidio

Sheehan N. 1971. *The Pentagon Papers: as Published by the New York Times.* Toronto/New York: Bantam Books

Snepp F. 2002. *Decent Interval: an Insider's Account of Saigon's Indecent End Told by the CIA's Chief Strategy Analyst in Vietnam.* Lawrence: Univ. Press Kansas

Sorley L. 1999. *A Better War: The Unexamined Victories and Final Tragedy of America's Last Years in Vietnam.* New York: Harcourt, Brace

Summers HG. 1982. *On Strategy: A Critical Analysis of the Vietnam War.* Novato, CA: Presidio

Taylor MD. 1960. *The Uncertain Trumpet.* New York: Harper

Thies WJ. 1980. *When Governments Collide: Coercion and Diplomacy in the Vietnam Conflict: 1964–1968.* Berkeley: Univ. Calif. Press

Tin B. 1995. *Following Ho Chi Minh: Memoirs of a North Vietnamese Colonel.* Honolulu: Univ. Hawaii Press

Tzu S. 1971. *The Art Of War.* Oxford, UK: Oxford Univ. Press

Van Evera S. 1999. *Causes of War: Power and the Roots of Conflict.* Ithaca, NY: Cornell Univ. Press

Van De Mark B. 1991. *Into the Quagmire: Lyndon Johnson and the Escalation of the Vietnam War.* New York: Oxford Univ. Press

Werner JS, Huynh LD, eds. 1993. *The Vietnam War: Vietnamese and American Perspectives.* Armonk, NY: Sharpe

Westad OA, Jian C, Tonesson S, Nguyen VT, Hershberg JG, eds. 1998. *77 Conversations Between Chinese and Foreign Leaders on the Wars in Indochina, 1964–1977.* Washington, DC: Woodrow Wilson Cent.

Winkler KJ. 1987. The Vietnam war scores well at the box office, but it fails to attract many researchers. *Chron. Higher Ed.* Sept. 30, p. 1

Young MB. 1991. *The Vietnam Wars, 1945–1990.* New York: HarperPerennial

Zhai Q. 2000. *China and the Vietnam Wars: 1950, 1975.* Chapel Hill: Univ. North Carolina Press

Annu. Rev. Polit. Sci. 2003. 6:205–32
doi: 10.1146/annurev.polisci.6.121901.085731
First published online as a Review in Advance on Jan. 24, 2003

WHAT IS THIRD WORLD SECURITY?

Raju G.C. Thomas
*Department of Political Science, Marquette University, Milwaukee,
Wisconsin 53201-1881; email: raju.thomas@marquette.edu*

Key Words   postcolonial states, less developed countries, civil wars and
revolutions, weapons of mass destruction, transnational terrorism

■ **Abstract**   This paper examines three images of the Third World (postcolonial,
nonaligned, and less developed states) and four types of security (international, transnational, regional, and internal) on three continents (Asia, Africa, and Latin America).
In the first image, the Third World is defined by a postcolonial racial divide between
the former European colonial powers and their decolonized empires. The second image of the Third World is the lingering legacy of the Non-Aligned Movement, which
comprised the states outside of the American and Soviet blocs. The third image is that
of the less developed world and the continuing struggle between rich and poor, both
among and within states. The four forms of security—international, transnational, regional, and internal—encompass interstate conflicts; civil wars, revolutions, and their
spillover effects; nationalism and interethnic conflict and the prospect of failed states;
the spread of nuclear, biological, and chemical weapons; transnational terrorism; the
illicit narcotics trade; and perceived negative consequences of globalization.

INTRODUCTION

"Third World" and "security" are ambiguous terms, subject at times to new meanings, expansion, contraction, and obsolescence. What is customarily called the
Third World at the beginning of the twenty-first century is a conceptual mixture
of decolonized nations and their relations with their former European colonial
rulers across a largely racial divide; former nonaligned states in the now defunct
East-West Cold War ideological divide; and the poorer, less developed countries in
the North-South economic divide. In the Western public image, "the Third World"
conjures up the poor and problematic regions of Asia, Africa, and Latin America.

   Likewise, the term security carries varying connotations. It now pertains to
any conflict issue or intense political differences among states and peoples. It
continues to be used in the traditional interstate context to denote the defense
capabilities and policies of states against threats from other states and nonstate
actors. This is familiarly the subject of international security and, where such
problems are geographically circumscribed, the subject of regional security. The
term transnational security covers the protection of peoples from a variety of destructive forces that transcend state boundaries. Broadly, these problems include

1094-2939/03/0615-0205$14.00

TABLE 1   The three continents and Third World security

	Postcolonial image	Nonaligned image	Less developed image
International Security	Asia, Africa, Latin America	Asia	Asia, Africa, Latin America
Transnational Security	Asia, Africa	Insufficient relevance	Africa, Latin America
Regional Security	Asia, Africa	Asia	Africa, Latin America
Internal Security	Asia, Africa	Insufficient relevance	Asia, Africa, Latin America

environmental degradation, famines and epidemics, and human rights violations (Paris 2001, Homer-Dixon 1994, Singer 2002, Forsythe 2000, Donnelly 2002). More narrowly, the main concern of transnational security involves violence conducted by nonstate actors across national boundaries. Finally, internal security is concerned with violence that threatens the survival of the state or regime from within, especially through insurgencies and civil wars. Again, all such problems are believed to be more critical in the poorer regions of Asia, Africa, and Latin America than in the advanced industrialized countries of the West (Ayoob 1995, Acharya 1997). Table 1 depicts the three Third Worlds and four securities and their relevance to the three continents.[1]

An alternative perspective of three worlds that displaced the old Cold War system of the First World (Western capitalist), Second World (Eastern communist), and Third World (nonaligned states) was provided by retired British diplomat Robert Cooper (2002a,b), who postulated newer patterns of postmodern, modern, and premodern worlds. The postmodern world is best exemplified by the European Union, where balance-of-power politics and *realpolitik* have become irrelevant. Here borders no longer matter and state sovereignty is defunct. In the modern world, the traditional interstate system continues as before, revolving around security dilemmas, arms races, balance-of-power politics, and the territorial integrity and sovereignty of states. States that remain part of this world include China, India, Pakistan, the United States (because of its global military commitments), and Japan (because of its East Asian strategic neighborhood). The premodern world consists of those countries and regions where elements of the Hobbesian world of anarchy are still evident. Examples include Afghanistan and many parts of Africa, such as Sudan, Somalia, Congo, Liberia, and Sierra Leone.

The study of Third World security suggests considerable conceptual discontinuities and disparities as well as geographical and cultural distances. There are no comprehensive or integrated theories and literature on "Third World security" except those based on widely different and narrow interpretations of the subject.

---

[1]In this paper, Latin America is referred to as a continent in a political context, not a geological context.

For example, studies of development, environmental degradation, famines and epidemics, human rights violations, regional interstate wars, revolutions and civil wars, and terrorism are discrete security issue-areas, usually unrelated to each other. Other non-security-related issues of the Third World outside the field of politics are spread through the disciplines of economics, sociology, and anthropology.

The varied security issue-areas are usually linked by their common concentration mainly in decolonized nations with less developed economies, which were members of the nonaligned group of states during the Cold War. Two related questions are pertinent. First, are race and/or poverty the underlying causes of their security problems? Second, would economic advances to the levels of prosperity found in the industrialized Western nations dissipate the security problems associated with the Third World? The answers to these questions would be largely "no" and "yes." South Korea, Taiwan, Malaysia, Singapore, and Thailand are nonwhite states that have moved rapidly into the economic ranks of the advanced industrialized states of the West, albeit mainly through their links with the Western economies. Also note that South Korea, Taiwan, and Thailand do not fit the decolonized or nonaligned concepts of the Third World. They were not part of European empires and were members of the American alliance network during the Cold War. This would suggest that their American alliance enabled these states to move out of Third World confinement, but the failure of American allies Pakistan and the Philippines to accomplish the same feat discounts this hypothesis.

Beyond problems associated with dire poverty among the masses, the common denominator of security issues in many of these Third World regions is endemic violence or the threat of violence, both external interstate wars and internal insurgencies and civil wars (Harkavy & Neuman 2001, C. Thomas 2003). The multilayered and interactive dynamics of the "three Third Worlds" and the "four securities" on the three continents, and the fit of these pieces in the larger puzzle of global security, are explored further below. The analysis is accompanied by references to the discrete and varied literatures that fall within the scope of this conceptual framework.

THE THREE THIRD WORLDS

Perceptions of three Third Worlds as subjects of interest have been chronological and cumulative. Although most security concerns are common to all three continents, the primary natures of problems that spring from the three Third Worlds are different, namely, interethnic and quasi-racial in the postcolonial, ideological and strategic in the nonaligned, and economic and social in the less developed. There is, however, considerable overlap and interplay among the three Third Worlds.

The Postcolonial World

In the postcolonial conception, the Third World comprises the states that emerged after the decolonization of the mainly nonwhite populations of Latin America, Asia, and Africa. The process of new state formation began with the colonies of the Spanish, Portuguese, British, French, and Dutch empires in the Americas in the eighteenth and nineteenth centuries. (The withdrawal of the British from North America was an exceptional case because the dominant populations of these colonies and their rulers were of the same racial stock.) Colonial withdrawal from the Americas was succeeded by the independence of the non-European states of the Middle East and North Africa (as well as parts of Southeastern Europe) following the collapse of the Ottoman Empire after the First World War. Finally, a steady stream of new states emerged in Asia and Africa with the end of all empires after the Second World War, beginning with the withdrawal of the British from India in 1947 and ending with the withdrawal of the Portuguese from Angola, Mozambique, East Timor, and Macao in 1974.

It should be kept in mind that "world politics" before the end of these empires was simply an extension of European great power politics. Herein lay one linkage among the disparate states that emerged in Asia, Africa, and Latin America. The legacy of European political institutions and practices, as well as memories of racial and economic subjugation of nonwhite regions by white colonial powers, is reflected in the postcolonial age through occasional expressions of resentment in these states toward Western intrusions into their domestic politics. Such intrusions include condemnations of human rights violations, demands for democratic regimes, and the right of multinational corporations to operate freely under unprotected global market conditions. The postcolonial relationship also finds expression indirectly in issues of migration, immigration (e.g., the status in European countries of nonwhite immigrants from their former colonies), and the rights of black, "Hispanic," and/or Asian residents in the New World states of the United States, Canada, and Australia.

The postcolonial conception of the Third World, based on the relationship between the former rulers and the formerly ruled, has an unusual twist in the case of Latin America. Here the uneven distribution of wealth and power between the indigenous and mixed Indian populations relative to the white settler populations is internal to the states and not external. The struggle between the First and Third Worlds, between North and South, exists concurrently within the countries of Latin America. It is sometimes expressed through revolutions, insurgencies, and terrorism by mainly indigenous Indian populations against the elite ruling establishments, which are often dominated by the descendants of the European colonial settlers. This adversarial white-Indian relationship was highlighted amid the Latin American economic crisis of 2000–2003 as states from Argentina and Brazil to Uruguay and Venezuela faced economic bankruptcy. For instance, "White, middle-class, urban, sophisticated Venezuela has convinced itself that all the problems will be solved once [Hugo] Chavez is gone. Darker, poorer Venezuela . . . suspects . . . that Chavez's enemies are its enemies as well" (Falcoff 2002). In 2002, Peru elected Alejandro Toledo, the first president of Indian ancestry since a military dictator in the 1920s, ridding the country of Alberto Fujimoro, a president of Japanese ancestry who had been supported by an allegedly corrupt group of mainly white ethnic Peruvians. The Peruvian electorate believed that control by a leader of

Indian stock in the predominantly Indian nation would end exploitation and resolve their economic woes. Indigenous Indian revolts against the more white ruling elites have been a recurring phenomenon in Mexico.

However, the Indian-white racial divide in Latin America is neither clear-cut nor predominantly radicalized because of large populations of mixed racial heritage. Whites, Indians, mulattos, and Mestizos have been represented on both sides of the revolutions and civil wars of the past two centuries. Often guerrilla movements have lacked widespread indigenous Indian support, especially in Guatemala, Bolivia, Colombia, Venezuela, and Peru (Loveman & Davies 1997).

An example of the postcolonial consciousness was India's rejection of proposed Western observers of the October 2002 elections in the violence-racked Indian state of Kashmir. India's Chief Election Commissioner (CEC), J.M. Lyngdoh, declared that the idea of Western election monitors was absurd: "The days of the white man telling natives what to do and how is long past. . . . We have crossed the Stone Age [sic]. . . . They are not superior to us" (Rana 2002). The Indian news report claimed that "the CEC was effectively voicing the nation's collective psyche over the issue." Such sensitivity and sentiment about Western intrusions and meddling are even more intense in the postcolonial African states (Davidson 1992, pp. 197–242; Stiglitz 2002, pp. 23–52).

In countries such as the Philippines, India, Iraq, Zimbabwe, Mexico, and Argentina, and throughout much of the postcolonial world, condemnation of NATO's bombing of Serbia in 1999 was severe because it brought back historical memories of colonial conquests and great power military interventions. *Washington Post* correspondent Anthony Faiola (1999) observed,

> Here in Argentina, one of Washington's closest Latin American allies, a poll last week showed that 64 percent of the public opposed the NATO air campaign against Yugoslavia. More respondents had a negative opinion of NATO than of Yugoslav President Slobodan Milosevic. In Latin America, Asia, Africa, the Middle East and other regions with little direct interest in the conflict, opposition is surfacing in statements by elected officials, newspaper editorials, opinion polls, public protests, Internet banter and street graffiti. Increasingly, there is little subtlety in NATO-bashing.

The main destabilizing legacy of European colonial rule in this Third World was that the boundaries of the state and those of the ethnic nation did not coincide. This was true in Asia and especially sub-Saharan Africa but was much less relevant in Latin America, although even here boundaries were artificially carved out through European conquests and settlements. Conflicts over East Timor, Tamil Ealam, Kashmir, Palestine, Iraq's claim to Kuwait, and especially the endemic and bloody intertribal wars in Africa are mainly the outcome of artificial boundaries in states where the ruling elites now speak English, French, Dutch, or Portuguese.

In the case of Africa, Rotberg (2000, p. 98) observed that "many of the postcolonial independent states inevitably included a mishmash of peoples, some not even of similar linguistic and ethnic origins. The larger the new state, the more numerous its component parts and frequently, the more those components differed in culture, outlook, education and political attitudes." The African problem was first highlighted in the demand by the Catholic Ibos of Biafra for independence from dominant Muslim Hausa, Yoruba, and Fulani tribes. The Ibos argued that the colonial territorial boundaries were illegitimate and that Biafra had a right to secede from Nigeria, setting off a bloody civil war with the Muslim-dominated government between 1967 and 1970. Subsequently, more anarchic and implosive civil wars and spillover interstate wars have erupted in Angola, Mozambique, Tanzania, Uganda, Congo, Liberia, Sierra Leone, Rwanda, Ethiopia, Somalia, and Sudan (Davidson 1992; Schraeder 1992, 2002; Clapham 1998; Reno 1998; Ayittey 1999; Cliffe & Luckham 1999; Herbst 2000; Kieh & Mukenge 2002; Zartman 1995; Ahmed & Green 1999; USIP 2001).

The Nonaligned World

During the Cold War, "the Third World" referred to states that were not part of the First World of capitalist states led by the United States nor the Second World of communist states led by the Soviet Union. Many of these states practiced varying degrees of socialism, and most, with some exceptions such as India and Sri Lanka, were under authoritarian regimes. Security in this Third World concerned primarily the impact of East-West superpower politics on the security of the nonaligned world, or, conversely, the spillover effects of security problems in the nonaligned world on East-West politics. Ideologically, and to a certain extent geographically, the nonaligned states lay somewhere between East and West. There were problems with this conception of the Third World because the nonaligned group of countries included Marshal Tito's Yugoslavia, a European communist state that had broken off from the Soviet bloc, and Fidel Castro's Cuba, a communist but less developed state of Latin America (Deutschmann & Shnookal 1990). The "West" included Japan, an Asian capitalist state with military ties to the United States. South Korea, Taiwan, and the Philippines were allied with the West but not considered part of it.

Indian Prime Minister Jawaharlal Nehru first expressed the doctrine of non-alignment. In a speech to the Indian Constituent Assembly on December 4, 1947, Nehru declared, "We have proclaimed this past year that we will not attach ourselves to any particular group. That has nothing to do with neutrality or passivity or anything else. . . . We are not going to join a war if we can help it; and we are going to join the side which is to our interest when the time comes to make the choices. There the matter ends" (quoted in R.G.C. Thomas 1978, pp. 29–65 and 1986, pp. 14–19).

The spirit of the nonaligned movement was given shape at the 1955 conference in Bandung, Indonesia, where 29 countries from Asia (including the Middle East) and a few from Africa were represented (http://www.encyclopedia.com/html/T/ThirdW1or.asp). Nonalignment began mainly as an Asian movement of countries that had emerged from colonialism in the immediate aftermath of the Second World War beginning with India in 1947. Later, the Non-Aligned Movement (NAM) was set up as a formal global institution in 1961. The decolonization of Africa, beginning with the independence of Ghana in 1957, turned the NAM into an Afro-Asian movement in the 1960s, with some Latin American countries, notably Mexico and Cuba, joining as well. Therefore, the NAM also carried an anti-imperialism agenda. This explains why it was more sympathetic to the East, since the West comprised the former European colonialists of Asia, Africa, and Latin America.

With the collapse of communism in the Soviet Union and Eastern Europe and the embracement of capitalism in China, the NAM would appear to be irrelevant. However, diehard proponents of the movement claim that the main underlying goal of nonalignment was to resist domination and control by great powers, and therefore the concept and purpose remain relevant (Rajan 1994, Damodaran 1997). The rationale of the new nonalignment after the Cold War would be to resist Western political control, economic exploitation, and military intervention. The preservation of the territorial integrity and sovereignty of states remains paramount. Post–Cold War nonalignment is also expressed through resistance to globalization, perceived as a new form of Western domination and exploitation of the former colonized states (Scholte 2000).

The Less Developed World

A third impression of the Third World focuses on the less developed countries of the so-called South conceived along a North-South axis. This is now the most pervasive and popular image of the Third World. The North consists of the more developed countries, encompassing both capitalist Western and erstwhile communist Eastern European states. North-South relations involve an economic struggle between rich and poor countries, but the line between them remains ill-defined. The East Asian economies of South Korea and Taiwan were once part of the South and became part of the North as their economies advanced under capitalism. Since the Islamic oil-producing countries of the Middle East raised the price of oil fourfold after the Arab-Israeli war of 1973, many of these countries, especially oil-rich kingdoms such as Saudi Arabia, Kuwait, the United Arab Emirates, Oman, and the Shah's Iran, achieved per capita incomes that rivaled those of North America and Western Europe. The Third World defined by economic criteria must then be perceived as a changing group of countries.

Like the East-West struggle, the North-South axis has a geographical dimension. The richer countries are mostly in the northern hemisphere or away from the equatorial and tropical zones. Climatic factors based on latitude appear to be the underlying cause of this rich-poor distribution, although cultural factors also play a part. Indeed, until recently, even within the more developed countries, the richer areas were in the colder or more comfortable climatic regions. For example, until the 1970s, the East, the Midwest, and the West in the United States were more developed than the hotter and more humid South. Likewise, the colder climatic regions of northern and northwestern Europe were more developed than the hotter southern regions. Such economic disparities may be seen even between northern and southern Italy. However, the growing differentials in labor costs among regions and technological advances that make working conditions in hot climates more comfortable have broken down these North-South generalizations. Factories and jobs have moved south in search of cheaper labor. This is true not only in the Americas and Europe but also in Asia, where Thailand, Singapore, Malaysia, and Indonesia have joined the rapidly growing "tigers" of the colder Asian north.

The economic disparities may be explained also by cultural and religious factors (Harrison 1993, Harrison & Huntington 2001). The Protestant Reformation in early sixteenth-century Europe and the Meiji Restoration in late nineteenth-century Japan played important roles in raising economic standards of living. In both cases, work ethics and general value systems were radically overhauled so that the "blessed" of Christ were no longer the "poor" and the "meek" in the West, and Buddha's exhortation to renounce worldly goods and seek nirvana was no longer the guiding light in the East. Hard work and the generation of wealth and prosperity became measures of a person's worth. The earlier preeminence of spiritual and learned pursuits and respect for those who renounce worldly goods, and the high status granted to the mainly nonproductive occupations of the landed and military classes, are exemplified by the hierarchy of the Indian caste system, in which Brahmins (priests and teachers) and Kshatriyas (kings and warriors) superseded Vaishyas (merchants and traders) and Sudras (workers).

As these value systems were abandoned in the Catholic regions of Europe (more recently in Ireland and Poland), and now in countries such as Brazil, China, India, and Indonesia (all with different but once traditional religious-cultural value systems), rapid economic growth and prosperity also became evident. Economic policies of privatization and marketization, instead of socialism or communism, would appear then to be the main determinant of standards of living, rather than exploitation by the West. This image of the Third World, therefore, suggests a constantly changing world. However, Huntington (1993) insists that economic disparities are caused by higher and lesser civilizations—the highest being Western civilization—with fundamentally different values, which lead eventually to conflicts among them. This view was challenged by Ajami (1993), among others, who argued that growing global communications and cross-fertilizations made such differences irrelevant, although Mahbubani (1991) earlier projected an emerging cultural and political confrontation between the "West and the Rest."

The struggle in this Third World involves a search for economic security through consolidation of strategies to provide better bargaining capabilities in dealing with the advanced industrialized states. The larger Group of 77 (G-77) and the smaller Group of 19 major developing countries (formerly Group of 15) were forged to negotiate favorable economic terms for the South in the several "Rounds" of the General Agreement on Tarriffs and Trade (GATT). GATT was set up in 1948 and was succeeded by the World Trade Organization (WTO) in 1994. The G-19 countries of Asia, Latin America, and Africa (Algeria, Argentina, Brazil, Chile, Colombia, Egypt, India, Indonesia, Iran, Jamaica, Kenya, Malaysia, Mexico, Nigeria, Peru, Senegal, Sri Lanka, Venezuela, and Zimbabwe) comprise 35% of the world's population but carry only 10% of world trade (*New York Times* 2000).

Thus, the economic bargaining relationship between the rich and poor countries is one of dependency rather than interdependency. For smaller less developed countries that survive on the export of one cash crop or mineral, the dependency is much more precarious.

The situation is different, however, between the oil-producing states and the West, where an unusual interlocking relationship has been forged. Western imports of oil from the Middle East and the large quantity of petrodollars accumulated by the oil-exporting Muslim countries are balanced by large-scale Western exports of civilian and military goods and services and large-scale construction projects in the region.

At the beginning of the twenty-first century, the threat to the Third World's economic security and political stability is perceived by critics to come from globalization, the result of open world markets among states and of free markets within less developed states (Hurrell & Woods 1997; Chomsky & Heinz 1999; Kiely 2000; Mittelman 2000a,b; Scholte 2000; Shari 2000; Main 2001; Berger & Huntington 2002; Hertz 2002; Palast 2002; Stiglitz 2002). After the formalization of the WTO in 1994 with membership requiring open and unprotected markets, the major Latin American economies were reduced to shambles by mid-2002, requiring multibillion dollar bailouts by the United States. Rosenberg (2002b) observed that the WTO "has become an unbalanced institution largely controlled by the United States and the nations of Europe, and especially the agribusiness, pharmaceutical and financial-services industries in these countries." Important decisions at WTO meetings are negotiated by the trade ministers of a handful of rich industrialized countries of the West, while the poor countries can only accept what is imposed. Likewise, Rosenberg claimed that the International Monetary Fund (IMF) "has become a long-term manager of the economies of developing countries, blindly committed to the bitter medicine of contraction no matter what the illness. It . . . has become a champion of market supremacy in all situations, echoing the voice of Wall Street and the United States Treasury Department, more interested in getting wealthy creditors repaid than in serving the poor."

The globalization of the less developed countries also aggravates political instability, especially in multiethnic states. The London-based Control Risks Group pointed out that the pursuit of foreign investment and IMF loans compels Asian and African countries to adopt Western economic ideas such as smaller governments and reduced public spending. Such changes intensify violent separatist movements and civil wars among disgruntled ethnic groups whose loyalties to the state had been bought earlier by government subsidies (Reuters 1999).

The growing gap between the few rich and the many poor within and among states is seen often as one of the main underlying sources of international, transnational, regional, and internal conflicts. Underdevelopment theories of conflict postulate that widespread poverty amid relative wealth and prosperity leads to despair, and despair leads to violence (Holsti 1975). If the rich-poor gap is between different ethnic groups within a state or among states, this leads to conflict between the two. Or the gap causes radical and violent ideologies to rise. But this is not a problem of concern to the Third World alone. Revolutions and civil wars within states, and regional conflicts among poor states, could suck in the advanced industrialized states on opposing sides, especially where resources essential to rich states are at risk.

THE FOUR SECURITIES

The "four securities" may be viewed in a vertical and descending order from international to transnational, regional, and internal. But they are also concurrent and interactive; much of the separation provided here is for analytical convenience.

International Security

International security issues primarily involve the defense capabilities and deterrence postures adopted by states against threats from each other under conditions of strategic interdependence. "Strategic interdependence" denotes the relative power distributions among states, although the constitution and measurement of power remain subject to debate. Traditionally, "power" referred to existing military capabilities and mobilization potential based on a state's economic and technological capacities. However, military capability and potential as a measurement of power was complicated by the advent of nuclear weapons, when absolute capabilities became irrelevant and the psychology and motivation to deter an attack became the more important, though intangible, factors in the calculus of power.

Given the economic and technological gap between the advanced Western states (including Japan) and the less developed states, and the absence of a conventional military balance of power between rich and poor, Third World states with sufficient economic and technological capacity have sought weapons of mass destruction as a way of leveling the playing field (Mozley 1998). States such as Iran, Iraq, North Korea, China, and India perceive some utility in acquiring or preserving a nuclear deterrent capability in case of American military intervention that contravenes their internal or regional security interests, whether such a policy posture is meaningful or not (Jervis 1988, Sagan & Waltz 1995, Sagan 1996–1997, Perkovich 1999, Synnott 1999, Tellis 2001, Subrahmanyam 2002, R.G.C. Thomas 2002c).

From the perspective of weak states, one of the lessons learned from NATO's use of massive conventional force against Russia's ally Serbia in 1999 is that although Moscow can deter such military intervention by the United States over human rights violations in Chechnya with the threat of a nuclear retaliatory strike, it cannot deter an attack against third parties (R.G.C. Thomas 2000). A weak state with nuclear weapons and delivery systems may deter an attack on itself (basic deterrence), but nuclear guarantees provided by major powers to their weaker allies and client states (extended deterrence) carry no credibility. Thus, for instance, had Iraq first acquired nuclear weapons and delivery systems capable of retaliating against U.S. allies in the region, then it would seem unlikely that the United States and its allies would have used force to reverse the Iraqi invasion and annexation of

Kuwait in 1990. The search for basic deterrence against the United States by North Korea, China, India, and Iraq generates regional security dilemmas and actual or potential nuclear counter-responses in South Korea, Taiwan, Pakistan, and Israel. Many aspects of this problem of international security arising from the absence of a global conventional military balance pertain to the Asian Third World.

An alternative theory to the balance-of-power system claims that global peace and prosperity are more likely in a world dominated by a single state or alliance. In a study of the European balance-of-power system over several centuries, Organski (1958) concluded that balance-of-power politics was likely to generate instability and wars, whereas a preponderance of power was likely to produce peace and stability. According to Organski, under conditions of military preponderance, the weaker state dares not attack, while the stronger state needs not attack, and therefore peace is sustained. Especially when the dominant state or group of states is considered to be benevolent, just, and without territorial ambitions, a noncompetitive military preponderance of power may be the most desirable condition for world peace. For example, now that the Cold War is over, the United States believes that an expanding, unthreatened, American-led NATO alliance system is good for the world. Peace, security, and justice for all will prevail under the new Pax Americana.

This view is emphasized by Cooper (2002b), who points out that stability before the twentieth century was either sought through military balances, which often broke down and led to wars, or achieved through the spread of European empires, within which order and stability were enforced. There was, for instance, relative order within the far-flung British Empire. Therefore, Cooper argues that a post–Cold War world order would be best achieved through the restoration of a liberal global empire under the West but without territorial conquest and permanent occupation. Such a Western policy outlook was apparent in the U.S. use of military force and subsequent nation building in Bosnia, Kosovo, and Afghanistan. Western military occupations are deemed temporary until stability and human rights standards are established. This Western outlook reflects an ominous return to nineteenth-century acceptance of what Rudyard Kipling called the "white man's burden" and in America's "manifest destiny," now extended outside the American hemisphere (R.G.C. Thomas 2000, 2002c).

Such Western theories and visions are not acceptable to much of the rest of the world. For example, following the unrestrained use of conventional military force by an unrivaled NATO alliance against Yugoslavia in 1999, Chinese military strategists proposed new rules of unrestricted war, which would include the resort to terrorism, ecological destruction, cyber-warfare through the spread of computer viruses, and trafficking in drugs to undermine the enemy population from within, thereby bringing destruction into the heart of the Western countries, especially the United States (Pomfret 1999). According to Colonels Qiao Liang and Wang Xiangsui, the authors of *Unrestricted War*, this strategy was the only viable method of balancing unequal military states. "Unrestricted War is a war that surpasses all boundaries and restrictions. . . . It takes nonmilitary forms and military forms and creates a war on many fronts. It is the war of the future." In an interview (quoted in Pomfret 1999), Colonel Wang declared, "We are a weak country. So do we need to fight according to your rules? No. War has rules, but those rules are set by the West. But if you use those rules, then weak countries have no chance. But if you use nontraditional means to fight, like those employed by financiers to bring down financial systems, then you have a chance. . . . If today you impose your value systems on a European country, tomorrow you can do the same to Taiwan or Tibet."

Likewise, an Indian editorial (*Times of India* 1999) during NATO's 1999 war argued that weak actors who feel threatened have two ways to counter the unrivaled power of NATO: nuclear weapons and terrorism. Whereas nuclear weapons may be the likely option of Third World states to deter unrivaled U.S. military power, terrorism may be the option of disgruntled nonstate actors who resent American policies abroad. One of the basic problems with Organski's (1958) preponderance theory is that under conditions of preponderance, the stronger state is not supposed to initiate a war against a weaker state. However, it is also apparent that under conditions of benevolent preponderance, weaker states would prefer not to challenge the United States for military and especially economic reasons. In the extended Iraq and Afghanistan crises, the phenomena of "bandwagoning" with the dominant power (Walt 2000)—instead of "balancing"—has become commonplace. States no longer dare or care to challenge the sole superpower.

Except for India, Pakistan, and Israel, virtually all states with the capability or potential of producing nuclear weapons have signed the Nuclear Non-Proliferation Treaty, which went into effect in 1970 and was renewed indefinitely without change in 1995. But the treaty has not stopped clandestine nuclear weapons programs (R.G.C. Thomas 1998, 2000, 2002a; Cirincione 2000; Utgoff & Welch 2000; Sokolski 2001). And the Comprehensive Test Ban Treaty, which went into effect in 1996, does not preclude nuclear testing under laboratory conditions. Several key countries, including the United States, have yet to ratify this treaty. Similar but more serious dangers prevail in the spread of biological and chemical weapons, sometimes referred to as "the poor man's bomb." The entry into force of the Biological Weapons Convention in 1975 and the Chemical Weapons Convention in 1996 have not alleviated the threat from these weapons from both states and nonstate actors (Falkenrath et al. 1998, Tucker 2000, Lavoy et al. 2001, Miller et al. 2001). The simple dual-use nature of these technologies and the ease with which they may be produced without detection further levels the military playing field between the technologically advanced industrialized countries and the poorer regions of the Third World.

Transnational Security

Transnational security issues are those that transcend national boundaries and are believed to be the common concerns of mankind, not confined to interstate relations. They include the global consequences of environmental destruction and the spread of diseases; human rights violations; violations of women's rights (often referred to as gender security); the illegal production of and international trade in narcotics, along with actions by states to combat this menace; internet security and cyberwarfare; and large-scale migrations, which raise concerns about illegal immigrants threatening the stability of advanced industrialized states (Paris 2001, Singer 2002). Human rights and women's rights are also issues of internal security, but they have taken on a transnational dimension as the inherent rights of all peoples (Tickner 1992, Hurrell & Woods 1997, Forsythe 2000, Steiner & Alston 2000, Agosin 2001, Paris 2001, C. Thomas 2001, Donnelly 2002). The demand for such rights is often expanded into demands for democracies everywhere.

The illegal narcotics trade, especially in cocaine and heroin, constitutes a security problem at both the international and internal security levels but is primarily transnational because it affects the social and physical well-being of the societies affected, in both the poor and rich states (McCoy 1991, Scott & Marshall 1998, Farer 1999, Haq 2000, Davids 2002). This may be seen in one sense as a market supply-and-demand problem. Without the demand for narcotics in the rich states where domestic production is prevented by law, there would be no covert production and supply from the poor states. The security aspect arises from the extreme violence that accompanies the illegal narcotics trade, both in the less developed producer states and in the advanced industrialized consumer states (Williams 1994, Friman 1996, Dupont 1999, Friman & Andreas 1999, Flynn 2000, Lintner 2000).

The illicit drug trade now extends beyond drug cartels seeking commercial profit. Illegal drugs have become a lucrative source of income for dissident ethnic groups who use the proceeds to purchase arms and equipment for conducting violent campaigns for secession, or for other domestic or international political causes. The Kosovo Liberation Army in Yugoslavia, the Liberation Tigers of Tamil Ealam in Sri Lanka, and the Kachin separatist guerrilla forces in Burma have used profits from their drug trade to buy arms and other supplies for their wars of independence (Davids 2002). In Afghanistan, the Taliban and al Qaeda grew poppy and sold its heroin derivative to advance their domestic and international wars (Bergquist et al. 2001, Davids 2002). In Africa, however, narcotics have not been the source of income for conducting internal and external wars. Here the international trade in diamonds and other mineral resources have provided the means of obtaining weapons of war (Reno 1998, Malaquias 2001, Rosenberg 2002a).

Increasingly, the form of violence being adopted to achieve a balance between the strong and the weak, especially between states and nonstate actors, is terrorism (Hoffman 1998, Cameron 1999, Tanter 1999, Whittaker 2001, Talbot & Chanda 2001, Cooley 2002). The problem took on greater urgency after al Qaeda's attack on the World Trade Center in New York on September 11, 2001. Just as nuclear weapons were once perceived as the great equalizer among unequal states, terrorism has the potential to become the great equalizer between powerful states and weak nonstate actors who are disgruntled about the global state of affairs (R.G.C. Thomas 2000). It has become the supplementary tactic of choice in the Third World in interstate wars and domestic insurgencies. Likewise, indiscriminate violence, to terrorize civilians who may become informants, has become a means of conducting the illicit drug trade that weakens the predominantly Western consumer countries.

In addressing the problem of terrorism, it is useful to distinguish between terrorism that may be classified as irredentist and that which may be called millenarian, both religious and ideological or secular. The goals of irredentist terrorists are no different from those of insurgents. They seek to change the territorial status quo or distribution of land among existing states, either through the carving out of new states by violent secessionist movements or through one state's violent annexation of another's land. In the First World, for example, the Irish Republican Army, the Basques of Spain, and the Kurdish Workers Party of Turkey are irredentist groups. A millenarian terrorist's objectives are more vague and even grandiose, derived from feelings of global socioeconomic injustice. The actions of the Symbionese Liberation Army in the Berkeley area, the Red Brigade of Italy, the Baader-Meinhoff gang in Germany, and Timothy McVeigh in Oklahoma City are examples of millenarian terrorism. Whereas such problems may be intermittent and lack direction in the First World, they are perennial and destabilizing in the Third World.

Religious-millenarian terrorist objectives may overlap or merge with the strategy of insurgency. For example, the goals of Palestinian Liberation Organization factions that attack Israeli security forces do not differ from those of Palestinian terrorist groups such as the Palestine Liberation Front, Hamas, and Islamic Jihad, which attack Israeli civilians. All seek to end Jewish settlements in the occupied territories, to claim East Jerusalem, and to establish an independent Palestinian state. However, the Al Fatah faction's terrorism is of the territorial-irredentist type, whereas that of Hamas and Islamic Jihad is of the religious-millenarian type. The Palestine Liberation Front has the specific territorial goal of creating an independent Palestine, and its terrorist activities may be expected to dissipate once its territorial objectives are achieved. The goals of Hamas and Islamic Jihad tend to revolve around broader and more long-term Muslim antagonism toward Jews.

A similar distinction may be drawn between groups in Kashmir, such as the Jammu and Kashmir Liberation Front and Hizbul Mujahideen on the one hand and the Lashkar-e-Tayeba and Jaish-e-Mohammed on the other. The first two are insurgency groups that also indulged in irredentist terrorism; the latter two are millenarian-type terrorist groups with broader and more long-term antagonism toward Hindus and Hindu India. They seek to mobilize Muslims against Hindus. Likewise, in the Philippines, the Muslim separatist Moro National Liberation Front has been eclipsed by the radical Islamic terrorist organization, the Abu Sayyaf Group, which is motivated by the desire to create an independent state on the island of Mindanao and to separate and expel Filipino Christians. Muslim extremist groups with links to al Qaeda, such as the Kumpulan Mujahideen of Malaysia and the Jemaah Islamiah of Indonesia, operate across the complex waterways of Indonesia and Malaysia, which makes them elusive (*Strategic Survey* 2001, pp. 297–302). Their goal is to carve out a pan-regional Daulah Islamiah Nusantara (Sovereign Islamic Archipelago) that would include Malaysia and all Muslim areas of Indonesia and southern Philippines. As the strategy of terrorism by nonstate actors operating across national boundaries is perceived as cheap and effective, it increasingly becomes the weapon of choice for wars against the state.

Regional Security

The term regional security is used here to refer to problems that are indigenous to a particular subregion, such as Southeast and South Asia; the Middle East; the Horn of Africa; Central, West, and Southern Africa; Central, Andean, or more broadly South America; and the Caribbean. Various transnational issues, such as narcoterrorism and illegal migrations, are also part of the regional security problematique. The somewhat subjective demarcations of these regions are based on common political perceptions and popular usage. Such hypothetical boundaries of regions are elastic; for example, Pakistan straddles South Asia, the Middle East, and Central Asia. Security problems of South Asia and the Middle East are often interrelated and treated together as part of a broader region, Southwest Asia. The conflict in Kashmir has attracted Afghan, Chechen, and Arab mujahideen (Ataov 2001). The Arab world in general, stretching from Morocco to Iraq, has been physically or emotionally involved in varying degrees with the Palestinian question since the creation of Israel in 1948. African mercenaries have moved across regions in sub-Saharan Africa (Folz & Bienen 1987, Clapham 1998). Likewise, security issues in East and Southeast Asia, Central America, and the Caribbean do not have clear regional boundaries.

Regional security issues involve the threat of wars among states of a particular region and the various regional and global measures adopted to prevent or mitigate such conflicts. The notion of security here does not differ from that enunciated above in the section on international security. Differences lie in its sources and orientation (that is, whether the problems are rooted in local security conditions) and often in the nature of regional interethnic dynamics or in great power politics. Arms races and military capabilities at the regional level are inextricably linked to international security issues (Buzan & Herring 1998). The ability of Third World countries to obtain an abundance of arms is often facilitated by great power struggles, especially during the Cold War, with rival powers willing to arm regional antagonists, e.g., India and Pakistan, Iran and Iraq, Israel and Syria, Ethiopia and Somalia. Increasingly, producers of arms are selling them to the Third World for commercial profit, especially after the Cold War. Interstate regional security issues primarily concern the Asian Third World, the Horn of Africa, and Arab North Africa (Cliffe 1999, Diehl & Lepgold 2003). No doubt, there are more ongoing wars in Central and West Africa than anywhere else in the world. However, these interstate tensions and conflicts arise from spillovers of interethnic conflict and civil wars in Congo, Sierra Leone, Liberia, Nigeria, and Rwanda (Rotberg & Mills 1998, Rotberg et al. 2000, Kieh & Mukenge 2002). They do not resemble traditional wars among states.

Internal Security

Internal security issues involve domestic strife and instability that may result from revolutionary threats to existing regimes and violent secessionist movements that threaten to destroy the state from within (Kim 1997, Halliday 1999). They may arise from competing ideologies, a struggle for ethnic minority or majority democratic rights, or power struggles between civil and military authorities or among rival individuals or groups. Such internal threats to regimes and states invariably involve violent street demonstrations, insurgency and terrorism, and coups and counter-coups. Internal security problems are pervasive in the Asian, Latin American, and especially African Third Worlds, where interethnic conflicts, insurgencies, and civil wars have been endemic and prolonged (Loveman & Davies 1989, 1997; Loveman 1993, 1999; Selbin 1993; Migdal et al. 1994; Evans 1997; Clapham 1998; M.J. Smith 1999; R.G.C. Thomas 2001; Cooley 2002; Shaw 2003; Zartman 2003). The term civil war, as used here, includes all forms of armed internal war between insurgents and/or terrorists, on the one hand, and government security forces on the other, or between two opposing groups of armed forces with the state. The conflict in Sri Lanka between Tamil secessionists (who resort to insurgency and terrorism) and government forces is an example of the first. The civil war in Yemen in the 1960s is an example of the second.

Many civil wars in the Third World arise not only from interethnic rivalry and demands for independent states but also from economic grievances and a struggle for the control of resources within the state, such as cocaine in Colombia and diamonds in Sierra Leone (Berdal & Malone 2000, Safford & Palacios 2002).

Among insurgency groups worldwide, as among terrorists, we could distinguish territorial-irredentist and secular/ideological-millenarian types. Insurgency is primarily an internal security problem, but to the extent that insurgents operate from sanctuaries across national boundaries and are aided by neighboring states, it may be viewed also as transnational. Territorial-irredentist insurgents seek decolonization, territorial changes through secession from an existing sovereign state, or annexation of territory from another state. Examples include the Viet Cong who expelled the French from Indochina, the Mukhti Bahini of East Pakistan who fought for an independent Bangladesh, and the Kurdish Workers Party, which attempts to carve out an independent Kurdistan from parts of Turkey. In India, territorial-irrendentist insurgents include the Jammu and Kashmir Liberation Front, fighting for Kashmiri independence, and the earlier Mizo National Front and Naga Federal Army, which sought an independent Mizoram and Nagaland. Ideological-millenarian insurgents seek changes in the regime or ideological makeup of the state. Examples are Mao Zedung's communist guerrillas, who overthrew the Nationalist regime in China, the Viet Cong who defeated the American-backed South Vietnamese regime, the Marxist Shining Path in Peru, and the Maoists operating in Nepal and in the West Bengal Andhra Pradesh provinces of India.

Insurgencies have been more prolonged and successful near the borders or coastlines of states, across which guerrillas and weapons may be moved more readily. Moro insurgents in Mindanao in the Philippines, Kachins in the Kachin Hills of Burma, Tamils in the Jaffna peninsula of Sri Lanka, Muslims of Kashmir in India bordering Pakistan, Kurds of the areas adjacent to Iraq and Turkey, Eritreans in the region bordering the Red Sea in Ethiopia, have all benefited from proximity to borders or coasts; and economic or ideological insurgents in many parts of Latin America are able to move freely across states, especially in the central and Andean regions (Byman et al. 2001, Rabasa & Chalk 2001b).

The principle of the sovereignty and equality of states has generally prescribed that outside powers have no right to intervene on any side. However, since the end of the Cold War, arguments have been made for intervention in civil wars on humanitarian grounds. The problem is that most civil wars and many insurgencies invariably involve humanitarian nightmares, as in the cases of Bosnia, Abkhazia-Georgia, Chechnya-Russia, Sudan, Ethiopia, Rwanda, Congo, Angola, and Mozambique (Wickham-Crowley 1992, Zack-Williams 1999, Harkavy & Neuman 2001, Diehl & Lepgold 2003). But the level of international attention has varied—higher where whites are killed, as in Bosnia, and lower when black lives are lost, as in Rwanda. The loss of lives in Congo civil war may be as high three million.

If we accept the notion of the sovereignty and territorial integrity of existing states, internal security issues and how governments deal with them should be beyond the purview of other states. Intervention in the internal affairs of sovereign states that were claimed to affect the security of other states was considered legitimate. Thus, direct or indirect American interventions in Vietnam and Nicaragua were considered part of the U.S. global security policy of the containment of communism. Direct U.S. military intervention in Iraq was deemed essential to protect vital American economic and strategic interests and to reverse the illegal Iraqi invasion and annexation of Kuwait. The Soviet military intervention in Afghanistan was supposedly to preserve the Marxist government that had seized power there in 1978. In the post–Cold War era, NATO's military intervention against rump Yugoslavia (Serbia and Montenegro), once a member of the nonaligned world, was declared to be for humanitarian reasons, although much of the rest of the world (including Russia, China, India, Indonesia, and Mexico) considered the action illegal and unwarranted (Faiola 1999).

THE THREE CONTINENTS

The "three Third Worlds" and the "four securities" are concurrent, overlapping, and interactive. Although security issues in Asia, Africa, and Latin America appear geographically separate and unrelated, linkages occur through the involvement of the great powers in these regions, or from the common security concerns that they raise coupled with the need for unified global agendas in resolving those concerns. For the purpose of this analysis, environmental issues such as the destruction of the rain forests in Latin America, health issues such as the AIDS epidemic in Africa, and social issues such as the denial of women's rights and the exploitation of child labor will be excluded (Tickner 1992, LeBlanc 1995, Agosin 2001, Singer 2002). Discussions of security in the Third World are confined to actual or potential violence stemming from the issues named in Table 2.

TABLE 2 Security issues on the three continents

Security issue	Asia	Africa	Latin America
Regional security and great power linkages	India-Pakistan, China-Taiwan, North Korea–South Korea, Arab-Israel, Iraq-Iran	Ethiopia-Eritrea, Ethiopia-Somalia, Congo-Rwanda, Tanzania-Uganda, Angola-Mozambique	Colombia, Cuba, Peru, Argentina (Falklands)*
Interstate conventional wars	India-Pakistan, Arab-Israel, Iraq-Iran	Ethiopia-Eritrea, Ethiopia-Somalia, Congo-Rwanda, Tanzania-Uganda	Not applicable
Weapons of mass destruction (nuclear, biological, chemical)	North Korea, India, Pakistan, Israel, Iran, Iraq, Libya	South Africa*	Argentina,* Brazil,* Cuba*
Cross-border terrorism (recipient victims)	Philippines, Malaysia, India, Sri Lanka, Israel	Insufficient relevance	Peru, Venezuela, Colombia
Insurgency, civil wars, regime instability	Philippines, Indonesia, Burma, India, Bangladesh,* Sri Lanka, Iraq, Algeria	Sudan, Somalia, Rwanda, Burundi, Congo, Sierra Leone, Guinea, Liberia, Angola, Mozambique	Colombia, Peru, Mexico, Nicaragua,* Honduras,* Guatemala,* El Salvador*
Illicit narcotics or diamond trade for profit or political objectives	Afghanistan, Pakistan, Burma, Thailand	Sierra Leone, Congo	Colombia, Ecuador, Bolivia, Mexico
Criminalization of government activity	Occasional relevance	Congo, Liberia, Sierra Leone	Occasional relevance

*May not be a security issue at the present time.

Asia

The key international and regional security issues of East Asia are inseparable (Alagappa 1998). The ideological confrontation between the United States and the Soviet Union aggravated the divisions and security tensions between North and South Korea, China and Taiwan, and North and South Vietnam. The unification of Vietnam in 1974 following 10 years of U.S. military intervention greatly reduced security tensions here. However, the problems of the two Koreas and the two Chinas remain unresolved legacies of the Cold War. Claims by Vietnam and the Philippines to the Spratly Islands in the South China Sea now appear futile. China's occupation of the islands has been a long-standing fait accompli, and unless it willingly relinquishes them, the situation is unlikely to change (Valencia 1995). North Korea's nuclear and missile program, which threatened to provoke nuclear countermeasures by South Korea and Japan, was contained hitherto by U.S. policy measures in East Asia. The significant internal threat to the territorial integrity of an East Asian state is found in the Chinese region of Xinjiang. The Tibetan question has not been raised in recent years, while the movement of large numbers of Han Chinese into sparsely populated Tibet is steadily reducing Tibetans into a minority in the province.

Since the end of the Vietnam War in 1974, security problems in Southeast Asia have arisen primarily from internal sources—demands for territorial secession and the potential of state disintegration through both insurgency and terrorism. The separation of the former Portuguese Catholic colony of East Timor from pre-dominantly Muslim Indonesia under Western diplomatic pressure has threatened to unravel the rest of Indonesia. Christian-Muslim clashes and violent insurgencies for independence have broken out in Aceh, Ambon, Irian Jaya, and the Maluku Islands, with similar conditions developing in Riau and East Java (Acharya 2001, Rabasa & Chalk 2001a, Sulistiyanto 2001, Huxley 2002). In the Philippines, the Muslim insurgents of the Moro National Liberation Front agreed to a ceasefire with the government in 1996, but a faction called the Moro Islamic Liberation Front continued the struggle. The latter was then superseded by the Abu Sayyaf Group, which resorts to terrorism to pursue the goal of independence for the Moro Muslims of the island Mindanao. Separatist movements among the Kachins and the Shans of Burma have not yet been subdued. Meanwhile, in Burma, the illicit heroin industry continues to thrive within the continuing stranglehold of an op-pressive military regime. The independence of East Timor has offered justification for past secessionist movements and a precedent for future secessions in Southeast Asia.

In South Asia and the Middle East, security issues between India and Pakistan, Israel and the Arab countries, and Iran and Iraq were rooted primarily in subregional ethnoreligious differences but got caught up in Cold War politics as the two rival superpowers supported and supplied arms to the regional antagonists (C.D. Smith 2000, Hiro 2001, Ganguly 2002). Since the roots of these conflict situations are regional, the end of the Cold War made little difference to the conflict relationships here—except that the United States and the new Russia are involved now in a more cooperative relationship in attempting to bring about peace in these regions (although they continue to arm various sides for commercial profit). Regional, internal, and transnational security problems are linked, especially in India and Israel, where insurgency and terrorism by resident Muslim and Arab extremists are aided often by other Islamic nonstate actors from across national borders.

Meanwhile, the basic structure of conflict relations in the Middle East and South Asia remains the same. The political direction of the regime in Iran looks uncer-tain, although the prospect of another Iran-Iraq war seems remote (Chubin 2002). However, the alleged clandestine stockpiling of weapons of mass destruction by Saddam Hussein's Iraq continues to provoke an American military intervention with potentially destabilizing repercussions (or stabilizing effects, according to those who advocate war) in the rest of the Middle East. Iran has opposed an American military strike against Iraq. The continuity of the Saud royal family's regime and the stability of Saudi Arabia remain in question (Peterson 2002). Revolution and the collapse of the Saud regime may produce a domino effect among the other oil-rich Arab kingdoms. Overall, American ability to manage conflict in the Middle East has been tenuous (Lewis 2001). Apart from domestic-based acts of terrorism by ideological left-wing or right-wing groups, almost all terrorism directed at the United States has emerged from the Muslim world (Hoge & Rose 2001).

The India-Pakistan conflict is complicated by the possession of nuclear weapons on both sides, generating what Snyder (1976) conceptualized as the "stability-instability paradox." Snyder's paradox postulates that when mutual nuclear deterrence prevails between two nuclear powers, they are forced down to lower levels of conventional or unconventional warfare. For example, the United States and the Soviet Union were compelled to fight each other's armed proxies in Vietnam and Afghanistan and suffer defeat (Herring 1986, Moss 1990, Karnow 1991, Goodson 2001, Rashid 2001). Without the support of the other noncombatant superpower, Vietnam and Afghanistan could not have emerged victorious in their wars of attrition. A similar pattern has prevailed in Kashmir following the covert and then overt acquisition of nuclear weapons by India and Pakistan (R.G.C. Thomas 2002b). India has been compelled to fight Pakistan's armed proxies since 1989. Meanwhile, violent secessionist movements continue among the disaffected Tamils in Sri Lanka; Assamese, Tripurans, and Manipuris in northeast India; and among the Kurds of Iraq and Turkey.

Africa

The security problems of sub-Saharan Africa are characterized by widespread ethnotribal conflicts, economic mismanagement, tendency toward anarchy, famines caused by both droughts and civil wars, and the criminalization of state activity (Davidson 1992, Clapham 1998, Rotberg & Mills 1998, Bayart et al. 1999, Cliffe 1999, Herbst 2000). What is most startling is the scale of death and destruction that has occurred in Africa compared to Asia and Latin America with little worldwide attention (Schraeder 2002).

At the heart of the African security problem are states constantly on the brink of collapse, a legacy of the sudden carving up of Africa between 1870 and 1900 (Schraeder 1999, Rotberg et al. 2000, Kieh & Mukenge 2002). In 1870, only about 10% of Africa was colonized. By 1900, only about 10% of Africa was not colonized, with only Ethiopia and Liberia escaping the colonial drive. The negative legacy of colonialism is acutely represented in many parts of sub-Saharan Africa. Zartman (2003) points out that it is not the prolonged and ongoing conflicts that cause African states to collapse but rather the perennial tendency toward state collapse that causes conflicts in the African states. "State collapse is a process rather than a single well-defined event, and so even when the state does not fully disintegrate, the near-occurrence of collapse has similar effects" (Zartman 2003). The constantly collapsing state in Africa weakens political society, making it difficult for new groups to restore the state. Where the process generates a brutal regime, the state lacks a social base and the ability to control its territory. And where the state is simply weak rather than brutal, it is unable to care for its population, which results in the privatization of security by individuals and groups. Zartman identifies Somalia, Liberia, Sierra Leone, and the two Congos (Kinshasa and Brazaville) as collapsed states at the beginning of the twenty-first century. Meanwhile, the effects of previous collapses from the 1990s are still felt in Rwanda, Burundi, and Angola, with similar conditions likely in Guinea, Cameroon, Togo, and other states in Central and West Africa.

The phenomena of wars of secession within the state and interstate wars that characterize Asia are comparatively rare in Africa despite the irrationality of its colonial borders. Two major secessionist movements have taken place in Africa, one of which succeeded. The struggle for independence between 1967 and 1970 by the Ibos of the Biafran province was crushed by Nigerian federal forces. The Italian colony of Eritrea was captured by the British in 1941 and administered as a U.N. trusteeship until it was federated with Ethiopia and then made a formal province in 1962. The Eritrean secessionist movement began almost immediately thereafter, first against the emperor Haile Selassie and then against the Marxist regime of Mengistu Haile Mariam. Eritrea became formally independent in 1993.

There have been occasional and brief border wars among African states. Zartman (2003) observed, "Border wars occur when one side considers the other internally weak enough to succumb to the challenge, and they are natural aftermaths—immediate or delayed—of situations unresolved at the time of independence." A good example of this is the Eritrean initiation of a war against Ethiopia over border demarcations that it disputed. After a two-year war with a high human cost, a ceasefire and peace treaty finally came in 2000. Other marginal interstate wars occurred between Dahomey and Benin in 1963, Ethiopia and Somalia in 1964 and 1978, Mali and Upper Volta in 1965 and 1976, Uganda and Tanzania in 1979, Chad and Libya in 1980, Nigeria and Cameroon in 1981 and 1993, and Senegal and Mauritania in 1989. However, surpassing the loss of lives from these wars are the millions of deaths from the AIDS epidemic that has ravaged much of Africa (Singer 2002).

Assessing the overall African conflict situation, Rotberg (2000) came to two general conclusions: that the violent civil wars of Africa are "largely a modern phenomenon, with multiple causes and complicated remedies," and that such intrastate conflict is not apt to disappear soon. If Africa's conflicts are of modern making and not entirely the legacies of its colonial past, then solutions to the pervasive conflicts throughout the continent have to come from Africans themselves. In mid-2002, two quick agreements raised hope for peace and stability in Africa. First, at the meeting of the Organization of African Unity in South Africa, the 53 member nations agreed to replace it with the African Union, whose goal would be the eventual uniting of Africa along the lines of the European Union. Meanwhile, a series of ongoing and newly initiated peace negotiations had succeeded or were nearing resolution (Lacey 2002). Wars in Burundi, Somalia, Sudan, and Congo were being advanced at negotiating tables rather than on the battlefield. The wars in Angola and Sierra Leone and the Eritrean-Ethiopian war have been settled. However, if the past is prologue, the prospects of sustaining these positive conditions and trends remain uncertain.

Latin America

Following the end of the Cold War, Latin American security issues have become primarily internal and transnational, and secondarily regional. The international dimension of security, involving great power rivalry and intrusions, ended with the disintegration of the Soviet Union; some Marxist-oriented insurgencies continue as before but without encouragement or support from outside the hemisphere. Like North Korea, Fidel Castro's Cuba remains stuck within the political culture of the old Cold War, although Castro's mindset is perpetuated by the continuation of an uncompromising U.S. policy toward Cuba.

As discussed above, the globalization of Latin American economies is perceived by its critics as the cause of the economic meltdowns in major Latin American countries. The economic crisis exacerbates many of the continuing security issues in the region. A 1995 U.S. Department of Defense report identified three major threats to Latin America (Loveman 2002): internal conflicts, such as guerrilla movements in Colombia, Peru, Guatemala, and Mexico; border disputes, such as the brief Ecuador-Peru war in 1995; and transnational threats, such as drug trafficking, terrorism, and international criminal organizations. Concerns about nuclear weapons proliferation in Latin America dissipated after Brazil and Argentina signed the Nuclear Non-Proliferation Treaty in 1995 and 1998, respectively. The major volatile security issues concern narcoterrorism and organized international crime; arms smuggling; insurgencies, usually involving indigenous movements of varying intensities that demand "relative autonomy" for Indian groups (Mexico, Bolivia, Ecuador, Peru, Guatemala); and problems of large-scale migrations and illegal immigration (Mexico-Guatemala, Peru-Chile, the entire Amazon basin, United States–Mexico). Some of these security issues were mere "problems" in the past but have now reached higher levels of concern.

An important concern in Latin America remains the frequent coups and military interventions into the civilian sphere (Loveman 1993, 1999). According to Shaw (2003), civilian representative government and keeping the military out of politics were principles embodied in the Charter of the 1948 Organization of American States. They became a top regional priority following the passage of the Santiago Commitment and Resolution 1080 in 1991 (Shaw 2003, Loveman 1999).

Organized crime associated with drug cartels and the drug-related domestic insurgency in Colombia have regional and hemispheric repercussions (Davids 2002, Safford & Palacios 2002). Drug trafficking in Latin America undermines civil society through pervasive corruption or intimidation of politicians and officials and through the breakdown of law and order (Bergquist et al. 2001, Davids 2002, Shaw 2003). Frequent references to "narcoterrorism" began in the 1980s with the Reagan administration's focus on the Marxist-oriented Revolutionary Armed Forces of Colombia (FARC), as well as the Shindero Luminoso (Shining Path) of Peru, the Sandinistas in Nicaragua, and Castro's regime in Cuba (Friman 1996, Friman & Andreas 1999). The use of the term narcoterrrorism was intended to be politically explosive; the Reagan administration claimed a linkage between leftist groups and drug trafficking in Nicaragua, Colombia, and Peru. To critics of the United States, this claim was a means to generate greater support for the U.S. war against drugs and an excuse for the United States to engage in various military interventions in Latin America. With the collapse of the Medellin and Cali cartels and the rise of the FARC in Colombia, the link between drug trafficking and Marxist terrorist actions may have become more credible, though even right-wing paramilitary groups engage in the trade.

CONCLUSION

The "three Third Worlds," "four securities," and "three continents" are not always apparent or linked. Despite similarities and parallels, security issues on the three continents are discrete and autonomous with marginal overlaps or spillover effects. There is no cause for or probability of a war between the three Third World continents, in contrast to the frequent political and economic struggles between Asia, Europe, and North America. However, common concerns and strategies among these states continue to be manifest at world political forums and global economic negotiations. The search for solutions to the Third World's economic, political, and social problems calls for a united front and pooling of resources. The mutual security ties of the Third World are evident in the tricontinental membership of the Group of 19, the "ganging up" against the advanced Western industrialized nations at world forums, the resistance to Western political or military interventions, and the determination to maintain existing national boundaries despite their colonial heritage. The First and Third Worlds have substantially different perceptions of the shape and direction of the future world order.

The *Annual Review of Political Science* is online at
http://polisci.annualreviews.org

LITERATURE CITED

Acharya A. 1997. The periphery as the core: the third world and security studies. In *Critical Security Studies: Concepts and Cases*, ed. K Krause, MC Williams, pp. 299–328. Minneapolis: Univ. Minn. Press

Acharya A. 2001. *Constructing a Security Community in Southeast Asia: ASEAN and the Problem of Regional Order*. London: Routledge

Agosin M, ed. 2001. *Women, Gender, and Human Rights: a Global Perspective*. Piscataway, NJ: Rutgers Univ. Press

Ahmed II, Green RH. 1999. The heritage of war and state collapse in Somalia and Somaliland: local-level effects, external interventions and reconstruction. *Third World Q.* 20(1):113–27

Ajami F. 1993. The summoning. *For. Aff.* 72(4):2–9

Alagappa M, ed. 1998. *Asian Security Practice: Material and Ideational Influences.* Stanford, CA: Stanford Univ. Press

Ataov T. 2001. *Kashmir and Neighbours: Tale, Terror, Truce.* Hants, UK: Ashgate

Ayittey GBN. 1999. *Africa in Chaos.* New York: St. Martin's

Ayoob M. 1995. *The Third World Security Predicament: State Making, Regional Conflict and the International System.* Boulder, CO: Lynne Rienner

Bayart JF, Ellis S, Hibon B. 1999. *The Criminalization of the State in Africa.* Indianapolis, IN: Indiana Univ. Press

Berdal M, Malone DM, eds. 2000. *Greed and Grievance: Economic Agendas in Civil Wars.* Boulder, CO: Lynne Rienner

Berger PL, Huntington SP, eds. 2002. *Many Globalizations: Cultural Diversity in the Contemporary World.* New York: Oxford Univ. Press

Bergquist C, Penaranda R, Sanchez GG. 2001. *Violence in Colombia: Waging War and Negotiating Peace.* Wilmington, DE: Scholarly Resources

Buzan B, Herring E. 1998. *The Arms Dynamic in World Politics.* Boulder, CO: Lynne Rienner

Byman D, Chalk P, Hoffman B, Rosenau W, Brannan D. 2001. *Trends in Outside Support for Insurgent Movements.* Santa Monica, CA: RAND

Cameron G. 1999. *Nuclear Terrorism: a Threat Assessment for the 21st Century.* New York: Palgrave-Macmillan

Chomsky N, Heinz D. 1999. *Latin America: From Colonization to Globalization.* Melbourne, Austr.: Ocean

Chubin S. 2002. *Whither Iran: Reform, Domestic Politics and National Security.* Int. Inst. Strategic Stud. Adelphi Pap. 342. Oxford, UK: Oxford Univ. Press

Cirincione J. 2000. *Repairing the Regime: Preventing the Spread of Weapons of Mass Destruction.* Cambridge, MA: MIT Press

Clapham C, ed. 1998. *African Guerrillas.* Bloomington, IN: Indiana Univ. Press

Cliffe L. 1999. Regional dimensions of conflict in the Horn of Africa. *Third World Q.* 20(1):89–111

Cliffe L, Luckham R. 1999. Complex political emergencies and the state: failure and the fate of the state. *Third World Q.* 20(1):27–50

Cooley JKK. 2002. *Unholy Wars: Afghanistan, America, and International Terrorism.* London: Pluto

Cooper R. 2002a. Why we still need empires. *The Observer* (London), Apr. 7

Cooper R. 2002b. The new liberal imperialism. *The Observer Worldview Extra* (London), Apr. 7

Damodaran AK. 1997. NAM: the road ahead. In *Indian Foreign Policy: Agenda for the 21st Century,* pp. 261–78. New Delhi: Konark Pub. For. Serv. Inst. (India)

Davids DJ. 2002. *Narco-Terrorism: a Unified Strategy to Fight a Growing Terrorist Menace.* Ardsley, NY: Transnational

Davidson B. 1992. *The Black Man's Burden: Africa and the Curse of the Nation-State.* New York: Three Rivers

Deutschmann D, Shnookal D. 1990. *The Right to Dignity: Fidel Castro and the Nonaligned Movement.* Melbourne, Austr.: Ocean

Diehl P, Lepgold J, eds. 2003. *Regional Conflict Management.* Boulder, CO: Rowman & Littlefield

Donnelly J. 2002. *Universal Human Rights in Theory and Practice.* Ithaca, NY: Cornell Univ. Press

Dupont A. 1999. Transnational crime, drugs and security in East Asia. *Asian Surv.* 39(3):433–55

Evans G. 1997. *Responding to Crises in the African Great Lakes.* Int. Inst. Strat. Stud. Adelphi Pap. 311. Oxford, UK: Oxford Univ. Press

Faiola A. 1999. Air campaign ignites anti-U.S. sentiment. *Wash. Post For. Serv.*, May 18

Falcoff M. 2002. South America on the edge of disaster? *Latin Am. Outlook*, July, http://www.aei.org/lao/lao14190.htm

Falkenrath RA, Newman RD, Thayer BA. 1998. *America's Achilles Heel: Nuclear, Biological and Chemical Terrorism and Covert Attack.* Cambridge, MA: MIT Press

Farer T. 1999. *Transnational Crime in the Americas.* London: Routledge

Flynn SE. 2000. The global drug trade versus the nation state: why the thugs are winning. In *Beyond Sovereignty: Issues for a Global Agenda*, ed. MK Cusimano, pp. 44–66. New York: Bedford/St. Martin's

Folz WJ, Bienen HS, eds. 1987. *Arms and the African: Military Influences on Africa's International Relations.* New Haven, CT: Yale Univ. Press

Forsythe DP. 2000. *Human Rights in International Relations.* Cambridge, UK: Cambridge Univ. Press

Friman R. 1996. *Narco-Diplomacy: the United States and the Export of Drugs.* Ithaca, NY: Cornell Univ. Press

Friman R, Andreas P, eds. 1999. *The Illicit Global Economy and State Power.* Boulder, CO: Rowman & Littlefield

Ganguly S. 2002. *Conflict Unending.* New York: Columbia Univ. Press

Goodson LP. 2001. *Afghanistan's Endless War: State Failure, Regional Politics and the Rise of the Taliban.* Seattle, WA: Univ. Wash. Press

Halliday F. 1999. *Revolution and World Politics.* London: Macmillan

Haq EM. 2000. *Drugs in South Asia: From the Opium Trade to the Present Day.* Houndmills, UK: Macmillan; New York: St. Martin's

Harkavy RE, Neuman SG. 2001. *Warfare in the Third World.* New York: Palgrave Macmillan

Harrison LE. 1993. *Who Prospers?: How Cultural Values Shape Economic and Political Success.* New York: Basic Books

Harrison LE, Huntington SP, eds. 2001. *Culture Matters: How Values Shape Human Progress.* New York: Basic Books

Herbst J. 2000. *States and Power in Africa: Comparative Lessons in Authority and Control.* Princeton, NJ: Princeton Univ. Press

Herring GC. 1986. *America's Longest War: the United States and Vietnam, 1950–1975.* New York: McGraw-Hill

Hertz N. 2002. *The Silent Takeover: Global Capitalism and the Death of Democracy.* New York: Free

Hiro D. 2001. *Neighbors, Not Friends: Iraq and Iran after the Gulf Wars.* London: Routledge

Hoffman B. 1998. *Inside Terrorism.* New York: Columbia Univ. Press

Hoge JF, Rose G, eds. 2001. *How Did This Happen? Terrorism and the New War.* New York: Public Aff.

Holsti KJ. 1975. Underdevelopment and the "gap" theory of international conflict. *Am. Polit. Sci. Rev.* 69(3):827–39

Homer-Dixon T. 1994. Environmental scarcities and violent conflict. *Int. Sec.* 19(1):5–40

Huntington S. 1993. The clash of civilizations? *For. Aff.* 72(3):22–49

Hurrell A, Woods N. 1997. *Inequality, Globalization and World Politics.* New York: Oxford Univ. Press

Huxley T. 2002. *Disintegrating Indonesia? Implications for Regional Security.* Int. Inst. Strat. Stud. Adelphi Pap. 349. Oxford, UK: Oxford Univ. Press

Jervis R. 1988. Political effects of nuclear weapons: a comment. *Int. Sec.* 13(2):80–90

Karnow S. 1991. *Vietnam: a History.* New York: Penguin Books

Kieh GK Jr, Mukenge IR. 2002. *Zones of Conflict in Africa: Theories and Cases.* Westport, CT: Praeger

Kiely R. 2000. Globalization: from domination to resistance. *Third World Q.* 21(6):1059–70

Kim QY, ed. 1997. *Revolutions in the Third World.* Leiden, Netherlands: Brill Acad.

Lacey M. 2002. Combatants in African nations may soon give peace a chance. *New York Times*, Aug. 20

Lavoy P, Sagan SD, Wirtz J. 2001. *Planning the Unthinkable: How New Powers Will Use*

Nuclear, Biological and Chemical Weapons. Ithaca, NY: Cornell Univ. Press

LeBlanc LJ. 1995. *The Convention on the Rights of the Child: United Nations Lawmaking on Human Rights.* Lincoln, NE: Univ. Nebraska Press

Lewis B. 2001. *What Went Wrong: Western Impact and Middle Eastern Response.* New York: Oxford Univ. Press

Lintner B. 2000. *Burma in Revolt: Opium and Insurgency Since 1948.* Chiang Mai, Thailand: Silkworm Books

Loveman B. 1993. *The Constitution of Tyranny: Regimes of Exception in Spanish America.* Pittsburgh, PA: Univ. Pittsburgh Press

Loveman B. 1999. *For La Patria: Politics and the Armed Forces in Latin America.* Wilmington, DE: Scholarly Resources

Loveman B. 2002. *The U.S. regional security agenda and civil-military relations in Latin America since 1990.* Work. Pap. Dept. Polit. Sci., San Diego State Univ.

Loveman B, Davies TM, eds. 1989. *The Politics of Antipolitics: the Military in Latin America.* Lincoln, NE: Univ. Nebraska Press. 2nd ed.

Loveman B, Davies TM, eds. 1997. *Che Guevara: Guerrilla Warfare.* Wilmington, DE: Scholarly Resources. 3rd ed.

Mahbubani K. 1991. The West and the rest. *Natl. Interest* Summer:3–13

Main L. 2001. The global information structure: empowerment or imperialism? *Third World Q.* 22(1):83–97

Malaquias A. 2001. Diamonds are a guerrilla's best friend: the impact of illicit wealth on insurgency. *Third World Q.* 22(3):311–25

McCoy AW. 1991. *The Politics of Heroin: CIA Complicity in the Global Drug Trade.* Brooklyn, NY: Lawrence Hill Books

Migdal JS, Kohli A, Shue V. 1994. *State Power and Social Forces: Domination and Transformation in the Third World.* New York: Cambridge Univ. Press

Miller J, Engelberg S, Broad WJ. 2001. *Germs: Biological Weapons and America's Secret War.* New York: Simon & Schuster

Mittelman JH. 2000a. *The Globalization Syndrome: Transformation and Resistance.* Princeton, NJ: Princeton Univ. Press

Mittelman JH. 2000b. Globalization: captors and captive. *Third World Q.* 21(6):917–29

Moss GD. 1990. *Vietnam: an American Ordeal.* Englewood Cliffs, NJ: Prentice-Hall

Mozley RF. 1998. *The Politics and Technology of Nuclear Proliferation.* Seattle, WA: Univ. Wash. Press

New York Times. 2000. Developing countries hold summit. June 19

Organski AFK. 1958. *World Politics.* New York: Knopf

Palast G. 2002. *The Best Democracy Money Can Buy: an Investigative Reporter Exposes the Truth about Globalization, Corporate Cons, and High Finance Fraudsters.* London: Pluto

Paris R. 2001. Human security: paradigm shift or hot air? *Int. Sec.* 26(2):87–102

Perkovich G. 1999. *India's Nuclear Bomb: the Impact on Global Proliferation.* Berkeley/Los Angeles, CA: Univ. Calif. Press

Peterson JE. 2002. *Saudi Arabia and the Illusion of Security.* Int. Inst. Strat. Stud. Adelphi Pap. 348. Oxford, UK: Oxford Univ. Press

Pomfret J. 1999. China ponders new rules of "Unrestricted War." *Wash. Post For. Serv.*, Aug. 8

Rabasa A, Chalk P. 2001a. *Indonesia's Transformation and the Stability of Southeast Asia.* Santa Monica, CA: RAND

Rabasa A, Chalk P. 2001b. *Colombian Labyrinth: the Synergy of Drugs and Insurgency and Its Implications for Regional Stability.* Santa Monica, CA: RAND

Rajan MS. 1994. *Nonalignment and the Nonaligned Movement in the Present World Order.* Columbia, MO: South Asia Books

Rana A. 2002. On white man's burden. *Pioneer* (New Delhi), Aug. 3

Rashid A. 2001. *Taliban: Militant Islam, Oil and Fundamentalism in Central Asia.* New Haven, CT: Yale Univ. Press

Reno W. 1998. *Warlord Politics and African States.* Boulder, CO: Lynne Rienner

Reuters. 1999. Western economic forces threaten bloody new century. *Reuters*, Nov. 11

Rosenberg T. 2002a. To prevent conflicts, look to commodities like diamonds. *New York Times*, July 15

Rosenberg T. 2002b. The free trade fix. *New York Times Magazine*, Aug. 18

Rotberg RI. 2000. African responses to African crises: creating a military response. See Rotberg et al. 2000, pp. 98–110

Rotberg RI, Albaugh EA, Bonyongwe H, Clapham C, Herbst J, Metz S. 2000. *Peacekeeping and Peace Enforcement in Africa: Method of Conflict Prevention*. Washington, DC: Brookings Inst.

Rotberg RI, Mills G. 1998. *War and Peace in Southern Africa*. Washington, DC: Brookings Inst.

Safford F, Palacios M. 2002. *Colombia: Fragmented Land, Divided Society*. New York: Oxford Univ. Press

Sagan SD. 1996–1997. Why do states build nuclear weapons? Three models in search of a bomb. *Int. Sec.* 21(3):54–86

Sagan SD, Waltz KN. 1995. *The Spread of Nuclear Weapons: a Debate*. New York: Norton

Scholte JA. 2000. *Globalization: a Critical Introduction*. New York: Palgrave-Macmillan

Schraeder PJ. 1992. *Intervention into the 1990s: U.S. Foreign Policy in the Third World*. Boulder, CO: Lynne Rienner

Schraeder PJ. 1999. *African Politics and Society: a Continental Mosaic in Transformation*. Belmont, CA: Wadsworth

Schraeder PJ. 2002. *United States Foreign Policy Towards Africa: Incrementalism, Crisis and Change*. Cambridge, UK: Cambridge Univ. Press

Scott PD, Marshall J. 1998. *Cocaine Politics: Drugs, Armies, and the CIA in Central America*. Berkeley, CA: Univ. Calif. Press

Selbin E. 1993. *Modern Latin American Revolutions*. Boulder, CO: Westview

Shari I. 2000. Globalization and economic disparities in East and Southeast Asia: new dilemmas. *Third World Q.* 21(6):963–75

Shaw CM. 2003. Conflict management in Latin America. In *Regional Conflict Management*, ed. P Diehl, J Lepgold. Boulder, CO: Rowman & Littlefield. In press

Singer PW. 2002. AIDS and international security. *Survival* 44(1):145–58

Smith CD. 2000. *Palestine and the Arab-Israeli Conflict*. New York: Bedford–St. Martin's

Smith MJ. 1999. *Burma: Insurgency and the Politics of Ethnicity*. London: Zed Books

Snyder GH. 1976. Conflict and crisis in the international system. In *World Politics: an Introduction*, ed. JN Rosenau, KW Thompson, G Boyd, pp. 682–720. New York: Free

Sokolski HD. 2001. *Best of Intentions: America's Campaign Against Strategic Weapons Proliferation*. Westport, CT: Praeger

Steiner HJ, Alston P. 2000. *International Human Rights in Context: Law, Politics, Morals*. New York: Oxford Univ. Press

Stiglitz JE. 2002. *Globalization and Its Discontents*. New York: Oxford Univ. Press

Strategic Survey 2001–2002. 2001. London: Int. Inst. Strategic Stud.

Subrahmanyam K. 2002. India and the international nuclear order. In *Nuclear India in the 21st Century*, ed. S Damodar, RGC Thomas, pp. 63–84. New York: Palgrave-Macmillan

Sulistiyanto P. 2001. Whither Aceh? *Third World Q.* 22(3):437–52

Synnott H. 1999. *The Causes and Consequences of South Asia's Nuclear Tests*. Int. Inst. Strat. Stud. Adelphi Pap. 332. Oxford, UK: Oxford Univ. Press

Talbot S, Chanda N, eds. 2001. *The Age of Terror: America and the World After September 11*. New York: Basic Books

Tanter R. 1999. *Rogue Regimes: Terrorism and Proliferation*. New York: St. Martin's

Tellis AJ. 2001. *India's Emerging Nuclear Posture: Between Recessed Deterrent and Ready Arsenal*. Santa Monica, CA: RAND

Thomas C. 2001. Global governance, development and human security: exploring the links. *Third World Q.* 22(2):159–62

Thomas C. 2003. Third World security. In *International Politics: Enduring Concepts and Contemporary Issues*, ed. RJ Art, R Jervis, pp. 263–273. New York: Longman

Thomas RGC. 1978. *The Defence of India: a Budgetary Perspective of Strategy and Politics*. Delhi: Macmillan

Thomas RGC. 1986. *Indian Security Policy.* Princeton, NJ: Princeton Univ. Press

Thomas RGC, ed. 1998. *The Nuclear Non-Proliferation Regime: Prospects for the 21st Century.* Basingstoke, UK: Macmillan; New York: St. Martin's

Thomas RGC. 2000. India's nuclear and missile programs: strategy, intentions, capabilities. In *India's Nuclear Security,* ed. RGC Thomas, A Gupta, pp. 87–122. Boulder, CO: Lynne Rienner

Thomas RGC. 2001. The nationalities question in South Asia. In *The Post Colonial States of South Asia,* ed. A Shastri, AJ Wilson, pp. 196–214. London: Curzon

Thomas RGC. 2002a. The shifting landscape of India's foreign policy. In *Comparative Foreign Policy: Adaptation Strategies of the Great and Emerging Powers,* ed. S Hook, pp. 170–93. Upper Saddle River, NJ: Prentice-Hall

Thomas RGC. 2002b. Whither nuclear India? In *Nuclear India in the 21st Century,* ed. D SarDesai, RGC Thomas, pp. 3–24. New York: Palgrave-Macmillan

Thomas RGC. 2002c. *The South Asian security balance in a western dominant world.* Presented at conf. "The Balance of Power Revisited," McGill Univ., Montreal, Quebec, Can., May 17–18

Tickner AJ. 1992. *Gender in International Relations: Feminist Perspectives on Achieving Global Security.* New York: Columbia Univ. Press

Times of India. 1999. Apr. 3

Tucker JB. 2000. *Toxic Terror: Assessing Terrorist Use of Chemical and Biological Weapons.* Cambridge, MA: MIT Press

United States Institute of Peace (USIP). 2001. *Responding to War and State Collapse in West Africa.* Spec. Rep., Washington, DC

Utgoff V, Welch LD. 2000. *The Coming Crisis: Nuclear Proliferation, U.S. Interests, and World Order.* Cambridge, MA: MIT Press

Valencia MJ. 1995. *China and the South China Sea Disputes.* Int. Inst. Strat. Stud. Adelphi Pap. 298. Oxford, UK: Oxford Univ. Press

Walt S. 2000. Alliances: balancing and bandwagoning. In *International Politics,* ed. R Art, R Jervis, pp. 110–17. New York: Addison Wesley Longman

Whittaker DJ, ed. 2001. *The Terrorism Reader.* London: Routledge

Wickham-Crowley T. 1992. *Guerrillas and Revolution in Latin America.* Princeton, NJ: Princeton Univ. Press

Williams P. 1994. Transnational criminal organisations and international security. *Survival* 36(1)

Zack-Williams AB. 1999. Sierra Leone: the political economy of civil war, 1991–98. *Third World Q.* 20(1):143–62

Zartman WI, ed. 1995. *Collapsed States: the Disintegration and Restoration of Legitimate Authority.* Boulder, CO: Lynne Rienner

Zartman WI. 2003. Regional conflict management in Africa. In *Regional Conflict Management,* ed. P Diehl, J Lepgold. Boulder, CO: Rowman & Littlefield. In press

Annu. Rev. Polit. Sci. 2003. 6:233–56
doi: 10.1146/annurev.polisci.6.121901.085655
Copyright © 2003 by Annual Reviews. All rights reserved
First published online as a Review in Advance on Feb. 6, 2003

ELECTORAL FRAUD: Causes, Types, and Consequences

Fabrice Lehoucq

*Division of Political Studies, Centro de Investigaciones y Docencia Económica (CIDE),
Carret. México-Toluca 3655, Lomas de Santa Fe, Mexico City, DF, Mexico 01210;
email: Fabrice.Lehoucq@cide.edu*

Key Words   electoral corruption, ballot rigging, vote buying, electoral laws

■ **Abstract**   This article reviews research on electoral fraud—clandestine and illegal efforts to shape election results. Only a handful of works classify reports on electoral fraud to identify its nature, magnitude, and causes. This review therefore looks at the larger number of historical works (as well as some ethnographies and surveys) that discuss ballot rigging. Its conclusions are threefold. First, fraud takes on a panoply of forms; it ranges from procedural violations of electoral law (that may or may not intend to distort results) to the outright use of violence against voters. Second, even when ballot rigging is an integral part of electoral competition, it is infrequently decisive. Fraud, nevertheless, undermines political stability because, in close races, it can be crucial. Third, political competition shapes the rhythm and nature of electoral fraud. Efforts to steal elections increase with inequality, but competitiveness—which institutions help to shape—determines the ballot-rigging strategies parties adopt.

INTRODUCTION

"The illusion of transparency" (Gueniffey 1993) is responsible for the scarcity of scholarship on the operation—and corruption—of balloting procedures. For decades, researchers assumed that electoral laws straightforwardly converted preferences into outcomes, a notion that encouraged many social scientists and historians to use election results to identify the social bases of political parties. Yet, as social choice research demonstrates (Riker 1982), the procedures for converting votes into political power can distort the meaning of the general will and, worse still, produce a collective choice that violates the preferences of many citizens. Indeed, the opportunities generated by voter registration, polling station operation, and tallying procedures often lead parties to stuff the ballot box, an outcome that can wreak havoc with more sociologically minded views of politics.

If, as a first approximation, we define electoral fraud as clandestine efforts to shape election results, it becomes clearer why scholarship on electoral fraud is so uncommon. No one who stuffs the ballot box wants to leave a trail of incriminating evidence. Fraud is also difficult for social scientists to study because the most abundant sources for studying fraud—from first-hand accounts to partisan denunciations of electoral shenanigans—are not "objective." These obstacles, however, are not insurmountable. Indeed, once we recognize that important areas of human activity are typically beyond the gaze of the social scientist, yet nevertheless are studied (e.g., crime and human sexuality), there is no reason to suppose that fraud is empirically intractable.

In this review, I critically assess the handful of studies that discuss the types, magnitude, and determinants of electoral fraud. Like entomologists, historians and some social scientists concentrate on cataloguing and describing fraudulent activities. Historians, in fact, have been among the few analysts to move beyond the anecdotal or prurient interests of so many chronicles of the electorally illicit—accounts that titillate and amuse us. Several historians and social scientists have also explored what I call the ethnography of electoral fraud. The ethnographers of fraud help us understand what separated right from wrong to the people who participated in fraud-tainted elections. Understanding justifications for activities that the contemporary observer condemns (perhaps too easily), the anthropologists of fraud try to make sense of the dilemmas that fraud posed to its perpetrators, its audience, and its observers.

I also survey efforts to assess the consequences or the magnitude and causes of electoral fraud. Efforts to assess the role of electoral fraud in politics range from claims that fraud is an isolated, random event to claims that ballot rigging was rampant in, for example, the United States until the 1960s. Understanding the extent of fraud is indispensable for deciding whether it merits systematic attention. I then examine the handful of accounts that conjecture why and how it happens. Finally, I classify hypotheses about the causes of fraud.

Selecting work for review was difficult for two reasons. In the first place, social scientists and historians have not written much about electoral fraud. I found fewer than two dozen articles with titles that contained such terms as electoral fraud, electoral corruption, vote buying, or ballot box stuffing. I found a slightly larger number of legal texts on fraud and vote buying, which are typically normative discussions of what should be considered illegal electoral behavior. In the second place, a great number of articles and books refer to electoral fraud in very general terms. Indeed, it is hard to study any democratic or quasidemocratic system of the past 200 years without acknowledging that governments or their rivals resorted to less than transparent methods to alter the results of the ballot box.

I therefore base my review on articles and books that analyze ballot rigging from an empirical perspective. By "empirical," I mean any effort to document and theorize about the types, magnitude, and spatial distribution of ballot rigging. Though electoral fraud plagues political systems around the world, I only found research about the countries of the Americas, Asia, and Europe and available in English, French, and Spanish. I also discuss books and articles that have important things to say about electoral fraud, even if their subject matter revolves around clientelism, political parties, elections, or the operation of the formal political arena.

WHAT IS ELECTORAL FRAUD? HOW DO WE STUDY IT?

Common sense initially suggests that an activity is fraudulent if its perpetrator wants it hidden from the public gaze. Manifestly fraudulent behaviors—such as coercing voters at the polling station to cast ballots for party X or filling the ballot box with votes for party X—are things that only its victims want publicized. Even procedural violations, such as a polling station opening late and closing early or failing to advertise its location before election day, sound like fraud because the accused would prefer that no one learn of these facts. Both blatantly coercive acts and voting irregularities are also fraudulent because they can throw election results.

There is a fine line between fraud and political pressure. To take a particularly glaring example, landlords are not guilty of electoral fraud when all their retainers vote for their party. Regardless of whether peasants have been duped into voting in favor of the landlord's party or wish to avoid the reprisals associated with voting against their employer, these activities are not really fraudulent, even if they are morally reprehensible. Even if we can demonstrate that retainers voted against their own interests, we cannot call this fraudulent unless a law has been broken.

So, in addition to being concealed and potentially affecting election results, an act is fraudulent if it breaks the law. Indeed, parties go out of their way to do things in the dark precisely because they are doing something wrong before or on election day. They are taking advantage of the legal machinery of the electoral process to steal an election they believe they cannot win fairly. A key advantage of a legalistic conception of fraud is that it permits assessing the location of the boundaries between acceptable and unacceptable political activity. Indeed, ethnographers of electoral fraud need to juxtapose what citizens and parties believe is morally reprehensible with what is legally possible to understand why, at particular places and times, many activities are no longer deemed appropriate to win an election.

There are six sources for the study of electoral fraud. The first two are "objective"—that is, not partisan in inspiration, even if they are, like any source, imperfect reflections of reality. One largely unexploited source of information is scientific surveys. Cornelius (2002) identifies the social and partisan correlates of vote buying from surveys of the 2000 Mexican election, the one in which the Institutional Revolutionary Party (PRI) was defeated after 70 years in power. To my knowledge, only a research team at the Latin American Social Sciences Faculty (Aparicio 2002) in Mexico City has also used surveys to make sense of electoral fraud. A second and similarly underused method is ethnographic. Like pollsters, ethnographers use interviews to make sense of electoral law violations. Schaffer (1998, 2001) is one of the few political scientists to sit with villagers in developing countries to plumb their views of democratic practices; he has done this in Senegal and the Philippines. Schedler (2002b) also uses in-depth interviews to gauge the attitudes of Mexicans toward what is known as "electoral alchemy."

The next three information sources are partisan. One consists of the memoirs left by the participants or the victims of electoral chicanery. Like ethnographic accounts, memoirs often sacrifice statistical representativeness for detailed coverage of fraud of particular places and times. Former U.S. President Jimmy Carter's (1992) tale of how he personally witnessed his rivals in the Georgia Democratic Party stuff the ballot box against him is a marvelous example of this genre. A second partisan source consists of the denunciations of fraud that parties file with political authorities. Historically, parties sought legal redress of violations of electoral law with legislatures. According to eighteenth- and nineteenth-century constitutional doctrine (Lehoucq 2002a), executives ran elections and legislatures certified their results—an institutional framework that often placed losers in the paradoxical position of seeking justice from their aggressors. Bensel,[1] Anderson (2000), Charnay (1964), and Lehoucq & Molina (2002) study complaints filed with the U.S. Congress, Imperial German Reichstag, French National Assembly, and Costa Rican Congress, respectively. A third partisan source consists of newspaper accounts, a body of information that Cox & Kousser (1981) use to understand electoral corruption in late-nineteenth-century rural New York.

A final source of information consists of the reports of organized civil society. As international electoral observation took off in the last decades of the twentieth century (Middlebrook 1998, Pastor 1999), nongovernmental organizations (NGOs), with domestic and international funding, have often displaced parties as poll watchers. Although NGOs may be more impartial than parties (then again, no one really knows) in monitoring activities on election day, their increasing visibility deprives parties of a principal—and unrecognized—function, as I explain later in this review. The Mexican Civic Alliance organized more than 18,000 observers to monitor more than 10,000 polling stations in 1994, an effort that has generated a voluminous record (Calderón Altzati & Cazés 1996, Cazés 1996).

TYPES OF BALLOT RIGGING

It is hard to find a book on unreformed political systems that does not refer to electoral fraud. Pre-reform systems are polities that do not meet minimal democratic standards, that is, they restrict franchise rights to something less than all adults of age 18 or older and civil liberties are unenforced. More important, elections are imperfectly administered in unreformed systems—which leads to outcomes whose credibility ranges from nonexistent to partial. Notable accounts of unreformed systems that, to some extent, analyze electoral fraud include books by Botana (1979) and Sabato (2001) on Argentina, Anderson on Germany (2000), Basadre on Peru (1980), Graham on Brazil (1990), Hanham (1959) and Seymour (1915) on England, Hoppen (1984) on Ireland, Kousser (1974) and Perman (2001) on the U.S. South, and Varela-Ortega on Spain (2001a,b). Much of this work suggests that fraud was commonplace, even if relatively few authors try to classify and count acts of ballot rigging. I begin by discussing the works that refer to electoral fraud in the most general terms before moving on to more systematic efforts.

---

[1]Bensel RL. 2002. *The American Ballot Box: Law, Identity, and Voting, 1850–1900.* Unpublished manuscript.

Both Kousser (1974) and Perman (2001) rely on legislative records, newspapers, and census records to relate how the Democratic Party in the 11 states of the former Confederacy deprived African Americans and poor whites of their suffrage rights through the end of the nineteenth century. Even though the Republican Party added the thirteenth (1865), fourteenth (1868), and fifteenth (1870) amendments to the Constitution to ensure the suffrage rights of recently emancipated slaves, the planter-dominated Democratic Party gained control of southern governorships and legislatures to enact poll taxes and other restrictive procedures to eradicate the electoral base of their Populist and Republican opponents. Kousser (1974) tells this story particularly well, with abundant examples of the Democratic Party's use of fraud and violence to regain control of southern politics.

Students of U.S. politics, nevertheless, have not written systematic accounts of ballot rigging, even though irregularities continue to plague U.S. elections (National Commission on Federal Election Reform 2002). Bensel's (2002) study is an exception. Based on the appeals losers filed with the U.S. House of Representatives during the heyday of the public ballot (1850–1900), Bensel shows that the most common allegations of fraud involved either intimidating or using violence against undecided or opposition voters and/or questioning whether voters met suffrage requirements. In urban areas, citizens cast party-supplied ballots in precincts that their party and/or ethnic group controlled. Population densities necessitated multiple polling stations in the nineteenth-century urban United States, an administrative fact that allowed rival parties and factions to capture precincts that parties made safe for their followers and dangerous for their adversaries. In a rural community, peer pressure could replace blunter forms of intimidation to ensure results at its sole polling station.

A rare and pioneering study of rural New York examines why parties went from paying citizens to vote to paying them to stay at home on election day (Cox & Kousser 1981) after this state adopted the Australian Ballot—the use of a single, government-supplied ballot—in 1890. Another paper documents how a Court of Common Appeals judge disenfranchised some 1700 voters or 26% of the electorate in Adams County, Ohio in 1910 for having sold their votes for prices ranging from a drink of whiskey to $25 (Gist 1961, p. 77), some 20 years after Ohio residents got Australian Ballots. The overall absence of scholarship nevertheless is notable because Congressional and Judicial archives contain a wealth of evidence about these activities (Argersinger 1992). Unlike in many other democracies, legislative bodies still certify election results in the United States, a process that has produced a record of contested House elections and recounts (Garber & Frank 1990).

Historians have produced studies that shed light on pre-reform political systems in several Latin American countries (Annino 1995, Malamud 2000, Posada-Carbó 1996, Sabato 1999). In his review of electoral corruption in Latin America between 1830 and 1930, Posada-Carbó (2000) lists the research that examines how governments and parties stuffed the ballot box. The author draws attention to how commonplace fraud was and how little we understand it. In an all-too-general analysis of Guatemalan elections, Sloan (1970, p. 78; see also McDonald 1967) also points out that "electoral fraud has never been studied carefully," even though "the case for choosing the revolutionary path of development is partly dependent upon proof that the electoral system is corrupt."

In his own work on Colombia, Posada-Carbó (1994, 1997, 2000) uses newspapers, party pamphlets, and period publications to show how Colombian conservatives and liberals were organized into political machines and that fabricating votes was an integral part of electoral strategy. Graham (1990) shows that the constitutional monarchy of nineteenth-century Brazil had a political life remarkably similar to that of nineteenth-century England. An electorate consisting of "50.6 percent of all free males, 20 years or older, regardless of race or literacy" voted for parliaments that governed alongside Brazilian emperors (Graham 1990, p. 108). Graham shows that cabinets took elections very seriously because they needed to maintain the parliamentary majorities necessary to enact the federation's laws. As a result, elections were contests among regional power brokers, where fraud and violence determined who occupied legislative and other elected posts.

In a study of the 1872 election in Peru, Mücke (2001) shows that parties struggled to gain control of town squares, where winners held elections. Losers, in turn, would organize their own polling stations in squares of lesser importance. Rival polling stations often squared off against each other, and did little to collect the votes from all voters. Indeed, the idea of an impartial polling station receiving the votes of all citizens seemed to be the farthest thing from parties' minds. Both then forwarded their results to parallel provincial boards, which would each then send them to Congress, in which partisan majorities certified the results they found most acceptable. Basadre (1980), the great Peruvian historian, describes how electoral fraud prompted legislators to reform laws to make it harder to steal elections.

Ballot rigging is an integral part of Argentine political history. Argentine historians typically argue that electoral fraud has been pervasive (Ferrero 1983). Tjarks (1963) relates how, in the 1876 elections in the Province of Salta, government forces and their opponents surrounded polling stations with militias to prevent their rivals from voting, purchased votes and polling station officials, and purged the electoral rolls of rival voters. Using legislative records, newspapers, and private correspondence, Sambruccetti (1980) mentions that parties packed the electoral rolls, set up parallel polling stations, bought votes, and destroyed opposition ballots in the 1886 elections. Both also discuss government parties' use of their legislative majorities to dismiss allegations of fraud to certify the vote. The accounts of Tjarks (1963) and Sambruccetti (1980) also suggest that, in Argentina, packing the electoral registry with the names of ineligible males was a key source of fraud. In a society receiving massive numbers of immigrants from the Old World, parties faced powerful incentives to register any male aged 18 years or older (all of whom possessed suffrage rights), regardless of whether he had become a naturalized Argentinian. According to Botana's (1979) classic study of the Argentine conservative order between 1886 and 1916, fraud permitted provincial governors to deliver the requisite votes so that their party could maintain control of the presidency, the Chamber of Deputies, and the provincial legislatures (which appointed the members of the federal Senate).

Vote buying was the key source of fraud in nineteenth-century England (Hanham 1959, O'Gorman 1989, O'Leary 1962, Seymour 1915) and Ireland (Hoppen 1984). Even after the 1832 Reform Bill, which outlawed many of the districts with less than a handful of registered voters, English grandees used their parliamentary influence to maintain what were known as the rotten boroughs. The continuation of public voting allowed landlords to control the behavior of their retainers in the counties, the largely rural constituencies, without overt fraud. In the urban boroughs, the enfranchisement of an increasing number of voters fueled a market of votes, an outcome that did not begin to decline until after the establishment of the secret franchise in 1872 in England and Ireland. Along with small district size and the casual enforcement of anticorruption laws (until 1868, the English House of Commons reviewed petitions to nullify electoral results, few of which it ever endorsed), rampant electoral corruption began to dissipate after the dismantling of the public franchise and the enactment of anticorruption Acts.

Vote buying is a major issue in several Asian political systems as well, even if specialists complain about scarcity of evidence for the market of votes. Rigger (2002) cites a survey that found more than two thirds of voters and politicians in Taiwan believed candidates offered favors and/or cash to vote on election day. The consensus among specialists on the island, Rigger notes, is that vote buying declined in the 1990s, which she attributes to growing electoral competition and the urbanization of Taiwanese society. Callahan (2000, Callahan & McCargo 1996) and Hicken (2002) discuss the centrality of vote buying in Thailand. Before the 1997 constitutional reform, Thai voters cast as many ballots as there were seats in their plurality districts. Hicken argues that a "surplus" of votes encouraged citizens to sell votes to the highest bidder. Both Callahan and Hicken contend that vote buying has declined since 1997, when Thailand adopted a mixed-member electoral system (400 single-member, plurality seats plus 100 seats selected in a nationwide district through proportional representation) and an independent electoral commission that aggressively prosecuted vote buyers and vote sellers.

Several historians use complaints filed with the Reichstag to make sense of nineteenth-century German elections (Anderson 2000; Fairbairn 1990, 1997). In her study on Imperial Germany, Anderson (2000) uses the election "scrutinies" or audits (*Wahlprüfungen*) that parties filed with the Reichstag between 1867, when the German Empire established suffrage rights for men 25 years or older, and 1912, the last elections held before the Kaiser's abdication. She seeks to understand how "the Germans experienced their new franchise" (p. 18). This is an important point: Anderson's book does not classify acts of fraud to understand how and why votes were fabricated. Her key finding is that Germans did not complain about bribery, physical force, or the falsification of results on election day. Without providing any hard numbers, she claims that electoral complaints condemned the Catholic hierarchy, landlords, and factory owners for using "influence" on voters. And "influence" ranged from the pressure of the congregation on each of its members to the threat of eviction that landlords used against retainers and the possible dismissal that capitalists used against their employees. Much of the controversy surrounding electoral misconduct, Anderson's book suggests, revolved around ways of using procedural violations of electoral law to overturn election results, especially since the Reichstag considered employer pressure to be a "private matter" until 1912 (Anderson 2000, p. 233)—11 years after the Reichstag replaced party-supplied ballots with the Australian Ballot to safeguard the privacy rights of voters. Fairbairn's work is consistent with Anderson's portrait; his research on the 1898 and 1903 Imperial elections indicates that "many election protests involved purely technical errors by officials untrained for their tasks, quirks of human behaviour, and opportunistic allegations by candidates who had narrowly lost elections" (Fairbairn 1990, p. 817).

Spanish historians have produced the largest national historiography that discusses ballot rigging as part of the post-Francoist effort to come to terms with the failure of earlier republican experiments in Spanish history (for reviews, see Dardé 1996, Tusell 1991, Varela Ortega 2001a,b). Varela Ortega's (2001a,b) study, in particular, of restoration Spain between 1875 and 1900 describes how the central government and locally based strongmen (caciques) manipulated voting returns. Varela Ortega's book is particularly noteworthy because it combines a narrative of the election cycle with a listing of violations of electoral laws. He shows that the government and the caciques, which often opposed each other, tried to gain the upper hand before election day by purging the electoral rolls of the names of opposition citizens, a process that the establishment of universal suffrage for men 25 years or older in 1890 did not thwart. According to Varela Ortega, there was little fraud in most (largely rural) districts, because collusion between the government and caciques cooked results in favor of mutually agreed-upon candidates. In more competitive districts, fraud included stuffing ballot boxes with false votes; ballot substitution; preventing opposition voters from casting ballots; locating polling stations in disagreeable places, such as a hospital's infectious wards; having citizens vote repeatedly or on behalf of deceased, nonexistent, or opposition voters (this practice when done collectively became known as *escuadrillas volantes* or "flying squads"); and, during the tally of the vote, falsely claiming that rival candidates had withdrawn from races (Varela Ortega 2001a, pp. 478–79).

Civic Alliance of Mexico uses reports of more than 1870 observer teams of a stratified sample of rural polling stations to produce a comprehensive portrait of election-day irregularities and legal violations in 1994, the first time in Mexico that an independent court and administrative system ran an election (Calderón Alzati & Cazés 1996, pp. 169–89). These observers note that more than two thirds of the polling stations witnessed the arrival of citizens whose names were not on the electoral rolls (and who possessed electoral identification). They also find that more than a third of the voting precincts could not maintain the secrecy of the ballot and that parties or electoral authorities pressured voters in a quarter of the polling stations. The observers report numerous procedural violations, including that more than a third of the polling stations opened after 9:00 a.m. and that results were not posted outside the polling station after officials and party observers tallied the vote in 6% of these stations. Civic Alliance also finds that 7.5% of the voting precincts had voters whose thumbs were not dipped in indelible ink; staining thumbs is a common way of distinguishing voters from nonvoters and thus preventing voters from casting more than one ballot per election. What distinguishes Civic Alliance's work from previous efforts is that it presents a classification of acts of fraud and quantitatively measures them, objectives necessary to a more systematic understanding of electoral fraud.

Lehoucq & Molina (2002) use the petitions to nullify electoral results parties presented to Costa Rica's unicameral Congress between 1901 and 1948 to provide a comprehensive listing of electoral fraud. Table 1 catalogs the charges parties made in more than 123 petitions, from which we extract 1131 complaints (and to whose total the authors add 235 accusations made during the tally of the vote). Accusations range from the procedural (e.g., opening or closing polling stations out of schedule) to the hardcore (e.g., stealing ballot boxes) to expelling voters or poll watchers from the voting precinct. Table 2 lists the charges parties lodged against polling stations, which rise from 30% of all complaints filed between 1901 and 1913 to 68% of all accusations during the 1940s. I include these tables to summarize the types of fraud that incumbents, parties, and machines seem to perpetrate everywhere, not just in prereform Costa Rica.

These tables reveal that the petitions denounce increasingly blatant acts of fraud through time. Table 2 indicates that the absence of formal requisites and questions about whether voters met suffrage requirements fell from 74% to roughly 36% of all accusations lodged against polling stations between the 1910s and the 1940s. Table 1 reveals that acts of coercion against voters and polling stations went from ~10% to 15% between these periods. These trends suggest that parties increasingly began to condemn more blatant types of electoral fraud, a process fueled by electoral reform and, in particular, the shift from a public voting system where parties supplied voters with ballots to one where voters cast Australian ballots in secret.

Under the heading of the nature of fraud, I also want to mention several examples of ethnographic research, efforts that depict the nature and meaning of ballot rigging. To date, one of the best works in this genre is Aziz-Nassif's (1987) fine study of the 1986 Governor's race in the northern Mexican state of Chihuahua. Trained as an anthropologist, Aziz-Nassif describes a highly controversial election, one that the opposition claimed the PRI stole from them. Aziz-Nassif pays careful attention to pro- and antigovernment understandings of their behavior, apparently interviewing many of the participants before and after election day. His account reflects the moral outrage that both left and right felt about the PRI's control over yet another election. Aziz-Nassif describes how a broad antireform coalition formed to contest the PRI's hegemony. He relates that PRI manipulation of the electoral arena included a biased voter registry, the pre-election reform of state electoral law to deprive opposition parties of poll

TABLE 1   Accusations of electoral fraud by type and time period in Costa Rica, 1901–1946 (in percentages and numbers)[a]

Accusation	Time periods				
	1901–1912	1913–1923	1925–1938	1940–1946	Total
2nd-stage elector excluded	2.8% (4)				0.3% (4)
2nd-stage elector not qualified to vote	7.8% (11)				11.9% (11)
Formal requirements for 2nd-stage election were violated	5.6% (8)				0.6% (8)
2nd-stage elections held outside of official time period	0.7% (1)				0.1% (1)
Authorities did not take an electoral census	0.7% (1)	0.2% (1)			0.2% (2)
Official coercion against 2nd-stage electors	0.7% (1)				0.1% (1)
Official coercion against voters	0.7% (1)	10.9% (48)	5.5% (20)	11.3% (33)	8.2% (102)
Official coercion against polling station	3.5% (5)	0.9% (4)	0.8% (3)	4.8% (14)	2.1% (26)
Nonofficial coercion against voters		0.2% (1)	0.8% (3)		0.3% (4)
Official intimidation against voters		0.3% (3)	1.4% (5)	2.8% (8)	1.3% (16)
Nonofficial intimidation against voters			0.3% (1)	3.4% (10)	0.9% (11)
Officials show favoritism toward a party	45.1% (64)	3.9% (17)	5% (18)	3.1% (9)	8.7% (108)
Elected official not qualified for post	2.1% (3)	1.4% (6)	1.6% (6)		1.2% (15)
Purchase of votes		2.3% (10)	13.7% (50)		4.8% (60)
Liquor distributed on election day		1.1% (5)	2.5% (9)	2.4% (7)	1.7% (21)
Accusations against polling stations	30.3% (43)	73.5% (325)	65.1% (237)	68.7% (200)	65% (805)
Unknown		2.9% (13)			1.1% (13)
Other		2% (9)	3.3% (12)	3.5% (10)	2.5% (31)
Total	100% (142)	100% (442)	100% (364)	100% (291)	100% (1239)

[a]Source: Molina & Lehoucq (1999).

TABLE 2   Accusations of fraud against polling stations by type and time period, 1901–1946 (in percentages and numbers)[a]

Accusation	Time periods				
	1901–1912	1913–1923	1925–1938	1940–1946	Total
Inappropriate exclusion of voters	11.6% (5)	3.7% (12)			2.1% (17)
Party observer expelled or threatened	4.7% (2)	8.9% (29)	10.6% (25)	12.5% (25)	10.1% (81)
Absence of formal requisites	48.8% (21)	56.9% (185)	35% (83)	10.5% (21)	38.5% (310)
Voter cast more than one ballot	2.3% (1)	3.1% (10)	5.9% (14)	3% (6)	3.9% (31)
Voting booth in an inappropriate place	2.3% (1)	3.1% (10)	3.4% (8)	1 (2)	2.6% (21)
Elections held outside of official time period	4.7% (2)	2.8% (9)	2.1% (5)	9.5% (19)	4.3% (35)
Voters did not meet requirements (too young, not citizens, etc.)	26% (11)	12.3% (40)	0.8% (2)		6.6% (53)
Voters prevented from casting ballots		1.2% (4)			0.5% (4)
Number of votes inflated		2.5% (8)	7.2% (17)	10% (20)	5.6% (45)
Number of votes exceeds number of voters		0.6% (2)			0.2% (2)
Elections were not held		0.9% (3)	0.8% (2)	1% (2)	0.9% (7)
Votes not received		0.6% (2)	0.4% (1)		0.4% (3)
Substitution of votes was permitted		3.1% (10)	9.3% (22)	18.5% (37)	8.6% (69)
Location of polling stations changed on election day		0.3% (1)			0.1% (1)
Voters were intimidated			0.4% (1)		0.1% (1)
Ballots were altered			3.4% (8)		1% (8)

(*Continued*)

TABLE 2   *(Continued)*

Accusation	Time periods				
	1901–1912	1913–1923	1925–1938	1940–1946	Total
Votes were annulled			1.7% *(4)*	4.5% *(9)*	1.6% *(13)*
Number of ballots exceeds number of voters			3.8% *(9)*	7% *(14)*	2.9% *(23)*
Electoral identification was rejected			3.4% *(8)*		1% *(8)*
Electoral identification not demanded of a citizen			0.4% *(1)*		0.1% *(1)*
Number of ballots does not equal number of identification cards			0.8% *(2)*		0.2% *(2)*
Ballots substituted			0.4% *(1)*	2% *(4)*	0.6% *(5)*
Electoral identification removed			2.1% *(5)*	3.5% *(7)*	1.5% *(12)*
Ballots removed			0.4% *(1)*	1% *(2)*	0.4% *(3)*
Ballot box altered			1.3% *(3)*	5% *(10)*	1.6% *(13)*
Voting was public			6.4% *(15)*	6% *(12)*	3.4% *(27)*
Vote tally conducted by unauthorized individuals				2% *(4)*	0.5% *(4)*
Electoral documentation not surrendered for legislative elections				1.5% *(3)*	0.4% *(3)*
Electoral documentation opened before election day				0.5% *(1)*	0.1% *(1)*
Electoral documentation collected by unauthorized individuals				0.5% *(1)*	0.1% *(1)*
Wrongfully counted absentee ballots from other provinces				0.5% *(1)*	0.1% *(1)*
Total	100% *(43)*	100% *(325)*	100% *(237)*	100% *(200)*	100% *(805)*

[a]Source: Molina & Lehoucq (1999).

watchers at all voting tables, and the certification of the results by the state legislature (where only the PRI had Representatives) instead of by an impartial electoral tribunal.

In his exploration of 81 open-ended interviews with poor Mexicans before the 2000 elections, Schedler (2002b) shows that respondents had much more ambiguous views regarding vote trading than images of pliant clients portray. Many of them expressed misgivings regarding public authorities and parties that exchange individual benefits for political support. Although they find it acceptable that parties promise to improve social conditions—universalistic goods, according to Schedler—many disapproved of candidates who trade votes for money or benefits. In Senagal, although community leaders and government officials spoke of the "traditional African" virtues of public voting, Schaffer (1998) finds that voters preferred the secret ballot because it allowed them to vote their conscience and to remain on good terms with members of their family, fellow villagers, and, of course, local notables and public officials. Most Senagalese, therefore, welcomed the 1988 reform that reintroduced the mandatory use of (secret) ballot boxes. The colonial French had established this practice in 1914 in urban areas, and it cost them the election of the colony's representative in the mainland's National Assembly.

Through in-depth interviews with 139 registered voters randomly selected from four areas of Barangay Commonwealth, Quezon City, Philippines, Schaffer (2001) also shows that many respondents also disapproved of vote trades—explicit promises to vote for X in exchange for Y—or undeniable acts of corruption (Rose-Ackerman 1999). They, however, expressed empathy for individuals who made such deals. They also find nothing controversial about politicians promising to make people's lot better as long as there is no explicit quid pro quo for their support. Distinguishing between what Rose-Ackerman calls bribes (payments to voters with a quid pro quo) and tips (payments with no formal payback) is, in fact, the objective of a handful of lawyers (Karlan 1994, Hasen 2000) and two social scientists (Kochin & Kochin 1998), who concede that, if politics is about the exchange of support for goods, then it is not easy to argue that vote trades are morally wrong. According to Schaffer, the failure of middle- and upper-class reformers to understand these distinctions dooms their efforts to create a political consensus to uproot corruption from Filipino political life.

This overview suggests that electoral fraud is commonplace in many political systems. Furthermore, there are many clandestine ways to increase vote totals, ranging from procedural violations to outright coercion on election day. The study of Costa Rica indicates that parties used some combination of at least 47 different types of fraud (Lehoucq & Molina 2002). Though there may not be an infinite number of ways to rig electoral results, the techniques for manipulating the vote are varied and artful. This review also points out that blatant types of fraud—including the use of intimidation or the stealing of ballot boxes—do not comprise a majority of fraudulent acts. Most efforts to fabricate votes are mundane; they involve surreptitious efforts to increase vote totals. Finally, this survey suggests that electoral fraud incenses parties and citizens. There is a normative dimension to electoral fraud that makes it more than simple violations of electoral law; in many places, the accusation of fraud has become part of the discourse of democratic movements, an accusation that refers to the desecration of civil liberties and liberal democratic principles.

THE MAGNITUDE AND CONSEQUENCES OF ELECTORAL FRAUD

How common is electoral fraud? How important is it? Although much of the research on unreformed electoral systems paints a rough portrait of ballot rigging, only a few of these studies try to assess its weight in electoral competition. This is an important issue because certifiers of electoral returns often dismiss allegations of fraud by claiming that legal violations do not affect results.

Both Schedler (2002b) and Schaffer (2001) cite surveys that ask citizens whether they were offered benefits for their votes. Schedler draws on work by Cornelius (2002), whose post-election survey of a panel of Mexicans finds that 26.1% of respondents received gifts from parties or candidates in the 2000 elections. Cornelius uses several statistical models to show that PRI operatives were much less successful than either of the main opposition parties in nailing down vote trades, perhaps because electoral safeguards allowed voters to take advantage of the PRI's largesse and vote their consciences. According to an unpublished report (cited in Schaffer 2001), 10% of Filipinos say a party offered them a gift before the May 2001 election day. As in contemporary Mexico, vote buying showed that it was not often effective: Only 38% of the Filipino poor mentioned voting for the candidate that offered them money.

As all these authors recognize, however, these surveys do not permit inferring whether vote buying occurs. Vote buying involves an explicit quid pro quo for votes, an exchange that only seems to proliferate when parties can ensure that voters or their agents cast ballots in prearranged ways (Lehoucq 2002b). Depending on how the question is phrased and how voters are approached (via telephones, face-to-face on the street, in their homes, etc.), surveys can generate contradictory findings. Three surveys of Mexican voters in 2000 found that some respondents—estimates ranged from 4.7% to 26.1%—felt pressure or got something of value for their votes (cited in Cornelius 2002, p. 17). Fine-tuning questions and improving sampling techniques will go a long way toward making surveys a highly useful means of understanding the nature and dynamics of electoral fraud.

Domínguez and McCann's study of Mexican public opinion is perhaps the most ambitious attempt to use surveys to determine the decisiveness of electoral fraud (Domínguez & McCann 1996, McCann & Domínguez 1998). They demonstrate that, contrary to conventional wisdom, the opposition probably did not win the

1988 general election, one that resulted in Carlos Salinas's controversial election to the presidency. By taking into account the preferences of nonvoters—who disproportionately favored opposition candidates—they suggest that Salinas would have won anyway, but perhaps by less than an absolute majority of the popular vote (Domínguez & McCann 1996, pp. 162–64). The PRI's nervousness on election night, when the central computer system mysteriously shut down—its concern that it would simply outpoll its rivals and perhaps lose the Federal District (where 1 out of 5 voters resides)—led to shenanigans that robbed the election result of legitimacy and ushered in a decade of electoral reforms. In a review of public opinion polls, Schedler (1999) shows that the share of respondents believing that fraud would mar elections went from over 50% in the 1988 elections to less than 30% in the 1997 midterm elections.

Another way to gauge the magnitude of fraud is to correct for the impact of ballot rigging on vote totals. The most creative and sensitive effort to assess the impact of fraud is Powell's (1989) statistical analysis of the 1868 Mississippi ratification election. In June 1868, 53.4% of the voters rejected the Republican-inspired constitution, a charter that threatened to bar former white (and Democratic) officials from ever holding office again. Powell uses regression analysis of the 61 counties to identify outliers—places with large shares of black registered voters who rejected the proposed constitution. By correcting results in these counties based on vote totals and approval rates in normal counties, Powell plausibly argues that the vote should have been 52.5% in favor and 47.5% against the constitution. Because the outlier counties tend to be the places with allegations of fraud, Powell (1989, p. 651) suggests that the "swing vote was the stolen vote." King (2001) also uses ecological analysis of 32 counties to argue that South Carolinian Democrats stole the gubernatorial election from the Republican candidate, Daniel Chamberlain, in the 1876 elections.

Other statistical analyses of voting returns include Baum's (1991) analysis of the 1861 Texas secession referendum and Oberst & Weilage's (1990) study of the 1982 Sri Lankan referendum. Baum suggests that "apathy, intimidation, or possible 'counting out'" may have caused underrepresentation of voters wishing to remain part of the United States in three counties of Texas. His paper implies, however, that fraud was not responsible for the 3 to 1 vote in favor of joining the U.S. Confederacy. Oberst & Weilage use simple tests of significance to demonstrate that the difference between the yes and no votes was far greater in the 16 (of 133) districts where there were allegations of fraud than in the districts with no such allegations. Although they do not claim that the government stole the referendum to ensure that parliamentarians could remain in office until 1989 (and thus inaugurate a semipresidential system), they show how t-tests can identify areas ripe for more intensive study.

These academic studies have their political counterparts. Hotly contested elections in Africa, the Americas, Asia, and Eastern Europe often involve NGOs that organize a parallel count of the vote to generate an independent basis for evaluating the performance of authoritarian systems forced to hold elections. In

1994, Civic Alliance of Mexico fielded more than 10,000 observers, covering 1 out of 10 polling stations with their sample. Though their parallel vote count was within 1% of official returns, Civic Alliance documented numerous infractions of electoral law. According to their observers (Calderón-Alzati & Cazés 1996, p. 179), for example, 39% of Mexican polling stations violated the secrecy of the ballot, whether because some voters showed their ballots (18.58 of these polling stations) or someone saw for whom they voted (16.53 of the total). What is unclear from these reports is whether these and other irregularities constitute grounds to invalidate the results of the 1994 Mexican presidential or legislative elections.

Using the legal challenges parties file regarding election outcomes is another way to assess the impact of fraud on election outcomes. Gómez-Tagle (1988, pp. 21–24) reveals that the share of impugned votes in Mexico's single-member legislative districts went from 46% in the 1979 elections to 62% in the 1985 elections. Renzato (1991, p. 126) points out that parties, on average, complained about results in five times more districts in Spain than in Italy between 1904 and 1914. On average, parties complained about results in more than a third of Spain's mostly single-member districts; in 1914, they filed complaints in nearly half of them. Similarly, Tusell (1970, p. 618) notes that this ratio remained steady until 1923 in Spain, even with the establishment of an Electoral Tribunal in 1907 to judge complaints about election outcomes (even as the Cortes remained the body that ultimately certified election results). Lehoucq & Molina (2002, p. 242) show that parties presented an average of nearly 6 petitions to nullify electoral results in each of the 20 elections held in Costa Rica between 1901 and 1948. In a different vein, Eisenstadt (2002) shows that the rule-of-law ratio—the ratio of street protests, or what he calls postelectoral conflicts, to electoral court cases filed by opposition parties—began to approach zero by the second half of the 1990s among Mexican states, suggesting that opposition parties began to trust autonomous electoral courts to resolve their disputes about the results from the ballot box.

Identifying the number of impugned races must be complemented with an analysis of the charges raised in the petitions to gauge the effects of this electoral litigation on the magnitude of fraud. On the basis of such an analysis, Lehoucq & Molina (2002, p. 22) conclude that three Costa Rican presidents—out of the 12 elected at four-year intervals between 1901 and 1948—owed their election to fraudulent practices. Even with very permissive assumptions about the extent of fraud, the proportion of impugned votes does not typically exceed the percentage of votes separating winners from losers. Yet, 20% of 12 presidential elections is not an insignificant share over a 50-year period. Though the constant accusations of fraud that accompany elections in unreformed systems exaggerate the impact of fraud, the fact that ballot rigging could be decisive suggests that its denunciation is justified.

Knowledge about the magnitude of fraud suggests that it is not always efficacious. The handful of surveys suggests that parties offer an array of promises, gifts, and even cash for votes, but that does not mean that vote buying always works.

Analysis of election results raises the possibility that outcomes can be fixed—that, given past performance or the behavior of voters, recorded outcomes do not always express the unfettered will of the people. Legal petitions indicate that parties will denounce an array of practices in the hopes of overturning unfair (or even fair) election returns. All three types of evidence suggest that complaints are not infrequently exaggerated; the 1988 Mexican survey and the legal data on Costa Rica suggest that fraud is usually not the cause of an electoral defeat. Nevertheless, ballot rigging can reduce turnout, contribute to cynicism, and therefore fabricate enough votes to tip the scales in one party's favor. Because electoral fraud can be decisive in close races, its ultimate cost may be that it undermines democratic stability. Regardless of whether fraud is decisive, it encourages incumbents and opponents to discredit elections and their outcomes. Precisely because it is so hard to determine the efficacy of ballot rigging, electoral fraud and its denunciation corrode the democratic body politic.

THE CAUSES OF BALLOT RIGGING

If stuffing the ballot box can be decisive and acts of electoral fraud can be classified and counted, how can fraud be explained? Why do parties and machines rig ballot results? Though few studies explicitly analyze motives, the underlying argument seems to be that incumbents, parties, and machines will try to get away with anything to retain or obtain control of the state. Less consensus exists about the interests these agents protect. Some analysts underscore the importance of economic interests—landlords and industrialists come to mind—while others emphasize the role of partisan interests. In this section, I review the evidence about why parties fabricate fraud, which is even scarcer than the research on its magnitude and consequences.

Of the historical studies about fraud, Anderson's (2000) is the best exponent of the argument that economic interests perpetrate electoral fraud. She uses the German Imperial electoral audits to show how eastern *Junkers*, coal mine owners, and factory owners policed their peasants and employees to ensure that conservative parties won elections. Graham (1990), Hoppen (1984), Kousser (1974), and O'Gorman (1989) imply that landlords use fraud to ensure that the representatives elected from their districts maintain their class power.

Dardé (1996), Botana (1979), Tusell (1991), and Varela Ortega (2001a) suggest that partisanship explains the incidence of fraud. Botana argues that incumbent manipulation of the electoral system in Argentina preserved the conservative order's control of a political system until 1916, when the opposition Radical Civic Union won the general elections. The 1916 defeat of the conservative candidate was the result of the 1912 Sáenz Peña electoral law, which, among other reforms, had cleaned up the voter registry. Dardé surveys much of the Spanish historiography to identify economic and partisan motives of the cacique. Tusell (1991) and Varela Ortega (2001a) adopt a political angle, that of the local machine operator; the cacique served his own interests as well as those of the local grandees and of the central government. Indeed, the cacique cut deals with landlords and government officials to obtain particularistic benefits ("pork"), such as roads, bridges, and related construction projects, useful for holding "his" voters together and therefore maintaining his power. Like other Spanish historians, they usefully distinguish between rural areas, where, because of some collusion between central government officials, landlords, and caciques, there was no effective political competition—and therefore no election-day fraud—and competitive urban areas, where all manner of electoral atrocities occurred (Varela Ortega 2001b).

Several studies of electoral fraud shed light on the relative importance of sociological and political factors. Using survey data, Domínguez & McCann (1996, pp. 164–70) argue that accusations were more common in competitive, typically urban, districts. Exit polls recorded fewer denunciations of voting irregularities as the share of the vote that incumbent PRI gubernatorial candidates obtained in districts increased (Domínguez & McCann 1996). Eisenstadt (1998) demonstrates that infractions of electoral law picked up in the 1980s and 1990s, precisely when the PRI's decades-long domination of politics began to crumble (also, see Gómez-Tagle 1988, Molinar-Horcasitas 1991).

Three studies explicitly vary social structural and institutional factors to identify the determinants of electoral fraud. First, Eisenstadt's (1999) analysis of more than 3000 municipal elections between 1989 and 1998 in Mexico reveals that post-election conflicts increased where political competition was more intense and where citizens had a tradition of engaging in collective action. He measures competitiveness as the ratio of the votes the two principal opposition parties receive to those of the PRI. Eisenstadt claims this variable performs better than the conventional indicator for competitiveness, the difference in votes between the first- and second-place winners (Cox 1988). Eisenstadt also uses an invaluable database from the federal Attorney General for Agrarian Issues. The relationship between collective agrarian conflicts per capita and post-election conflicts is positive.

Second, Trejo & Aguilar-Rivera (2002) show that election conflict in 803 municipalities (or approximately a third of all municipalities—those whose population is at least 30% indigenous) in Mexico during the 1997 federal elections is largely a function of sociological factors. They use ordinal probit models to show that procedural violations of electoral law and reports of intimidation in the organization of elections are negatively related to geographic dispersion. The models also demonstrate that voting irregularities are positively related to the monolingual share of the population, the effective number of ethnic groups, gender discrimination, and the effective number of religions. Their study, which also includes 10 focus groups, finds that an institutional factor also leads to election conflict. The use of customary law in local elections, a common practice in the State of Oaxaca, augments difficulties for voters using different procedures and rules in federal elections.

Third, in a study of 1300 accusations of ballot rigging between 1901 and 1946 in Costa Rica, Lehoucq & Molina (2002) discover that institutional as well as sociological factors explain the rhythm and spatial distribution of accusations of fraud. Slightly less than half of the accusations of fraud took place in the three poorest and least populated provinces, which never contained more than 25% of the electorate. Social differentiation was much more pronounced in the periphery, where laborers were often completely landless and worked on large cattle or banana estates. In contrast, citizens of the four central provinces—where most voters resided—tended to live in tightly knit, highly literate communities capable of organizing themselves to protect their civil liberties. Nevertheless, Lehoucq & Molina (2002) argue that the structure of electoral competition was equally—if not more—responsible for regional distributions of electoral fraud. Unlike most races in the center, most elections in the periphery were single- or double-member districts whose seats went to the parties that only needed to obtain one more vote than their rivals. In the center, in contrast, proportional representation typically allocated seats among parties because most races involved parties competing for three or more legislative seats at a time. Unless the quotient—the number of seats divided by the number of valid votes—was small and/or the number of impugned votes was large, parties stood little chance of ever electing one of their members to Congress. Parties, in other words, faced incentives to commit and, most importantly, to denounce acts of fraud precisely where voters were disproportionately poorer, less literate, and more ethnically discriminated against.

The paucity of findings makes it harder to generalize about the causes of fraud than about its nature or magnitude. Though the study of Spain and one study of Mexico (i.e., Domínguez & McCann 1996) suggest that fraud is more common in urban than in rural areas, this conclusion has to be qualified. Ballot rigging may be less common in rural areas because political or economic domination makes it pointless to complain about fixed results. The urban bias in reports, in other words, seems to be a product of an incumbent monopoly. Civic Alliance's finding (Calderón Altzati & Cazés 1996, Cazés 1996) that violations of the secret ballot are more common in rural polling stations suggests that local machines use subtle techniques to control voters, tactics that electoral observation picks up in an increasingly competitive electoral environment. Existing studies also indicate that properties of electoral laws—district size and electoral formula—can increase the uncertainty of political competition, the factor through which social and political variables shape the nature and frequency of ballot rigging.

CONCLUSION: DIRECTIONS FOR FUTURE RESEARCH

The research on electoral fraud tells a consistent story. First, fraud takes on a panoply of forms. It ranges from procedural violations of electoral law (that may or may not intend to distort results) to the outright use of violence to intimidate voters and poll watchers. Moreover, only a minority of the accusations involves blatant types of fraud. Second, ballot rigging does not appear to be decisive most of the time. The colorful history of vote fabrication probably exaggerates its role in determining election outcomes. Fraud, nevertheless, undermines political stability because, in close races, it can be decisive. Even when elections are not competitive, ballot rigging robs elections of credibility and therefore prevents the consolidation of democratic institutions. Third, political competition shapes the rhythm and nature of electoral fraud. Efforts to steal elections increase with social inequality, but political competitiveness—which institutions help to shape—determines the ballot rigging strategies parties adopt.

Studying electoral fraud is not easy because it is supposed to remain clandestine. Yet, analyzing ballot rigging is far from impossible. There is a wealth of legal material about the nature and incidence of ballot rigging. In virtually all places, parties filed complaints about election returns with legislatures until the late nineteenth century. By the beginning of the twentieth century, electoral tribunals or commissions began to run elections and to judge the complaints parties filed about them (Lehoucq 2002a). Whatever the system a country uses (or used), candidates and parties therefore generate the detailed legal trail that researchers, to date, rarely exploit. Indeed, most of the historical work on elections refers to such materials but almost never tries to classify, count, and analyze them. True, these petitions cut both ways: They exaggerate as well as denounce acts of fraud. Carefully used, though, accusations of fraud provide a wealth of information about ballot rigging—how it worked, how extensive it was—and help shed light on what it means to its targets and its plaintiffs.

Surveys can also uncover the facts and the causes of electoral fraud. To date, only a handful of surveys cover ballot rigging. Questions need to focus on activities deemed fraudulent and to encourage respondents to report how they are cajoled, pressured, or bought. Focus groups or even more ethnographic research techniques can also reveal how citizens react to clandestine efforts to shape election outcomes and even participate in them.

Future studies of electoral fraud need to be theoretically focused. Researchers tend to select countries and time periods for idiographic reasons or on the dependent variable. The study of country X for country X's sake, however, can lead researchers to neglect issues that are causally important. For example, Dardé's (1996) effort to come to grips with a history of controlled rural elections or fraudulent urban ones in Spain pushes him to focus on cultural limitations. That the existing research emphasizes the impact of sociological and institutional factors—and that, to date, there is no systematic study of ballot rigging for Spain—suggests that students of this case may not be choosing the best approach to make sense of electoral fraud in Spain. Similarly, picking cases on the dependent variable can prejudice efforts to distinguish actual from spurious causes. A study limited to places with charges of fraud runs the risk of producing conclusions that do not hold true for districts with no such reports. Comparison between countries or of districts within a country is a research strategy useful to overcome the selection bias problem (King et al. 1994).

I end this review with several hypotheses worth investigating. The first is whether majoritarian electoral laws encourage higher levels of ballot rigging and election litigation than more proportional systems. If seats are allocated on a first-past-the-post basis, parties may commit—and denounce—ballot rigging because a relatively small number of votes may determine an election outcome. To the extent that majoritarian systems encourage personal as opposed to party-centered campaigns, first-past-the-post systems may generate additional incentives for candidates, for example, to buy votes and for voters to sell them (Hicken 2002). The cases for which we know the most—England, Germany, Ireland, Spain, and the United States—uphold this claim; all of these cases used plurality to allocate seats among candidates. The study of Costa Rica adds further support to this hypothesis: Plurality districts generate more accusations of fraud than proportional-representation ones. Majoritarian formulas such as the Thai multiple-seat, multiple-vote plurality system or the Taiwanese single-nontransferable vote (Grofman et al. 1999) also appear to be linked with high levels of vote buying in both countries.

Electoral systems that dampen turnout may simultaneously encourage fraud. Many electoral authoritarian regimes (Schedler 2002a)—systems where incumbents hold elections but manipulate laws for partisan advantage—hinder voter registration or prevent opposition parties from observing the electoral process or the tally of the vote in order to reduce turnout. If rates of voter participation fall, then fabricating a handful of votes may be sufficient to retain power, a fact that opposition or regional parties may exploit as elections become more competitive. This claim, I should add, dovetails with the previous hypothesis. As Cox (1999) points out, proportional systems increase turnout more than majoritarian laws because the expected utility of a vote cast for a third party is greater in the former than in the latter systems. Thus, plurality electoral laws may decrease turnout so that the impact of stealing votes becomes greater. Finally, both hypotheses are part of the broader theory that political competition fuels ballot rigging. Indeed, only the existence of anticorruption legislation and nonpartisan electoral commissions can thwart competition from propagating all manner of strategies for winning elections.

The *Annual Review of Political Science* is online at
http://polisci.annualreviews.org

LITERATURE CITED

Anderson ML. 2000. *Practicing Democracy: Elections and Political Culture in Imperial Germany.* Princeton, NJ: Princeton Univ. Press. 483 pp.

Annino A, ed. 1995. *Historia de las elecciones en Iberoamérica, Siglo XIX.* Buenos Aires: FCE. 481pp.

Aparicio R. 2002. La magnitud de la manipulación del voto en las elecciones federales del año 2000. *Perfiles Latinoam.* 20:79–100

Argersinger P. 1992. *Structure, Process and Party: Essays in American Political History.* Armonk, NY: Sharpe. 219 pp.

Aziz-Nassif A. 1987. Chihuahua y los límites de la democracia electoral. *Revista Mexicana de Sociología* 49:159–226

Basadre J. 1980. *Elecciones y centralismo en el Perú: Apuntes para un esquema histórico.* Lima: Univ. del Pacifico. 173 pp.

Baum D. 1991. Pinpointing apparent fraud in the 1861 Texas secession referendum. *J. Int. Hist.* 22:201–21

Botana N. 1979. *El orden conservador: la*

política Argentina entre 1880–1916. Buenos Aires: Ed. Sudamericana. 345 pp.

Calderón-Alzati E, Cazés D. 1996. *Las elecciones presidenciales de 1994*. México, DF: La Jornada/CIICH, UNAM. 257 pp.

Callahan W. 2000. *Pollwatching, Elections and Civil Society in Southeast Asia*. Burlington, VT: Ashgate. 218 pp.

Callahan W, McCargo D. 1996. Vote-buying in Thailand's northeast. *Asian Surv.* 26:376–92

Carter J. 1992. *Turning Point: a Candidate, a State, and a Nation Come of Age*. New York: Times Books. 273 pp.

Cazés D, and 843 coauthors. 1996. *Memorial de las elecciones de 1994: testimonios de observadores*. México, DF: La Jornada/CIICH, UNAM. 422 pp.

Charnay JP. 1964. *Les scrutins politiques en France de 1815 à 1962: contestations et invalidations*. Paris: Cah. De la Fond. Nat. Des Sci. Polit. 281 pp.

Cornelius W. 2002. La eficacia de la compra y coacción del voto en las elecciones mexicanas de 2000. *Perfiles Latinoam.* 20:11–32

Cox GW. 1988. Closeness and turnout: a methodological note. *J. Polit.* 50:768–75

Cox GW. 1999. Electoral rules and the calculus of mobilization. *Leg. Stud. Q.* 24:387–419

Cox GW, Kousser JM. 1981. Turnout and rural corruption: New York as a test case. *Am. J. Polit. Sci.* 25:646–63

Dardé C. 1996. Fraud and passivity of the electorate in Spain, 1875–1923. In *Elections Before Democracy*, ed. E Posada-Carbó, pp. 201–23. New York: St. Martin's

Domínguez JI, McCann JA. 1996. *Democratizing Mexico: Public Opinion and Electoral Choices*. Baltimore, MD: Johns Hopkins Univ. Press. 269 pp.

Eisenstadt TA. 1998. *Courting democracy in Mexico: party strategies, electoral institution-building, and political opening*. PhD thesis. Univ. Calif., San Diego. 379 pp.

Eisenstadt TA. 1999. *Weak electoral institutions or legacies of social conflict? Modeling causes of Mexico's local post-electoral mobilizations, 1989–1998*. Presented at Annu. Meet. Am. Polit. Sci. Assoc., 95th, Atlanta, GA

Eisenstadt TA. 2002. Measuring electoral court failure in Mexico. *Int. Polit. Sci. Rev.* 23:47–68

Fairbairn B. 1990. Authority vs. democracy: Prussian officials in the German elections of 1898 and 1903. *Hist. J.* 33:811–38

Fairbairn B. 1997. *Democracy in the Undemocratic State: the German Reichstag Elections of 1898 and 1903*. Toronto: Univ. Toronto Press. 328 pp.

Ferrero RA. 1983. Los fraudes electorales. *Todo es Hist.* 197:48–64

Garber M, Frank A. 1990. *Contested Elections and Recounts*. 2 vols. Washington, DC: Gov. Print. Off.

Gist G. 1961. Progressive reform in a rural community: the Adams County vote-fraud case. *Miss. Valley Hist. Rev.* 48:60–78

Gómez-Tagle S. 1988. Conflictos y contradicciones en el sistema electoral mexicano. *Estud. Sociol.* 6:3–38

Graham R. 1990. *Politics and Patronage in Nineteenth Century Brazil*. Stanford, CA: Stanford Univ. Press 382 pp.

Grofman B, Lee SC, Winckler EA, Woodall B, eds. 1999. *Elections in Japan, Korea, and Taiwan under the Single Non-Transferable Vote: the Comparative Study of an Embedded Institution*. Ann Arbor: Univ. Mich. Press. 390 pp.

Gueniffey P. 1993. *Le nombre et la raison: la Révolution française et les élections*. Paris: École des Hautes Études en Ciencias Sociales. 559 pp.

Hanham HJ. 1959. *Elections and Party Management: Politics in the Time of Disraeli and Gladstone*. London: Longmanns. 468 pp.

Hasen RL. 2000. Vote buying. *Calif. Law Rev.* 88:1323–71

Hicken AD. 2002. *Parties, pork and policy: policymaking in developing democracies*. PhD thesis. Univ. Calif., San Diego

Hoppen KT. 1984. *Elections, Politics and Society in Ireland, 1832–1885*. Oxford, UK: Clarendon. 569 pp.

Karlan P. 1994. Not by money but by virtue

won? Vote trafficking and the voting rights system. *Va. Law Rev.* 80:1455–75

King RF. 2001. Counting the votes: South Carolina's stolen election of 1876. *J. Interdiscip. Hist.* 32:169–91

King G, Keohane RO, Verba S. 1994. *Designing Social Inquiry: Scientific Inference in Qualitative Research.* Princeton, NJ: Princeton Univ. Press

Kochin MS, Kochin LA. 1998. When is buying votes wrong? *Public Choice* 97:645–62

Kousser JM. 1974. *The Shaping of Southern Politics: Suffrage Restriction and the Establishment of the One-Party South, 1880–1910.* New Haven, CT: Yale Univ. Press. 319 pp.

Lehoucq FE. 2002a. Can parties police themselves? Electoral governance and democratization. *Int. Polit. Sci. Rev.* 23:29–46

Lehoucq FE. 2002b. *When do parties buy votes? Theoretical and empirical perspectives on electoral corruption.* Presented at Annu. Meet. Am. Polit. Sci. Assoc., 98th, Boston, MA, Aug. 28–Sep. 1

Lehoucq FE, Molina I. 2002. *Stuffing the Ballot Box: Fraud, Electoral Reform, and Democratization in Costa Rica.* New York: Cambridge Univ. Press. 277 pp.

Malamud C, ed. 2000. *Legitimidad, representación y alternancia en España y América Latina: las reformas electorales (1880–1930).* México, DF: FCE. 318 pp.

McCann JA, Domínguez JI. 1998. Mexicans react to electoral fraud and political corruption: an assessment of public opinion voting behavior. *Elec. Stud.* 17:483–503

McDonald RH. 1967. Electoral fraud and regime controls in Latin America. *West. Polit. Q.* 20:694–708

Middlebrook KJ, ed. 1998. *Electoral Observation and Democratic Transitions in Latin America.* La Jolla, CA: Cent. US-Mexican Stud., Univ. Calif., San Diego

Molina I, Lehoucq FE. 1999. Political competition and electoral fraud: a Latin American case study. *J. Interdiscip. Hist.* 30:199–234

Molinar-Horcasitas J. 1991. *El tiempo de la legitimidad: elecciones, autoritarismo y democracia en México.* México, DF: Cal y Arena. 265 pp.

Mücke U. 2001. Elections and political participation in nineteenth century Peru: the 1871/1872 presidential campaign. *J. Latin Am. Stud.* 33:311–46

National Commission on Federal Electoral Reform. 2002. *To Assure Pride and Confidence in the Electoral Process.* Washington, DC: Brookings Inst. 385 pp.

Oberst RC, Weilage A. 1990. Quantitative tests of electoral fraud: the 1982 Sri Lankan referendum. *Corrupt. Ref.* 5:49–62

O'Gorman F. 1989. *Voters, Patrons and Parties: The Unreformed Electoral System of Hanaverian England, 1734–1832.* Oxford, UK: Oxford Univ. Press. 445 pp.

O'Leary C. 1962. *The Elimination of Corrupt Practices in British Elections, 1868–1911.* Oxford, UK: Clarendon. 253 pp.

Pastor R. 1999. The role of electoral administration in democratic transitions: implications for policy and research. *Democratization* 6:1–27

Perman M. 2001. *Struggle for Mastery: Disfranchisement of the South, 1888–1908.* Chapel Hill: Univ. North Carol. Press. 416 pp.

Posada-Carbó E. 1994. Elections and civil wars in nineteenth-century Colombia: the 1875 presidential campaign. *J. Latin Am. Stud.* 26:621–49

Posada-Carbó E, ed. 1996. *Elections Before Democracy.* New York: St. Martin's

Posada-Carbó E. 1997. Limits to power: elections under the conservative hegemony in Colombia, 1886–1930. *Hispan. Am. Hist. Rev.* 77:245–79

Posada-Carbó E. 2000. Electoral juggling: a comparative history of the corruption of the suffrage in Latin America, 1830–1930. *J. Latin Am. Stud.* 32:611–44

Powell LN. 1989. Correcting for fraud: a quantitative reassessment of the Mississippi ratification election of 1868. *J. South. Hist.* 5:633–58

Renzato G. 1991. La forja de la soberanía nacional: las elecciones en los sistemas liberales italiano y español. *Ayer* 3:115–38

Rigger S. 2002. *Weighing a shadow: toward a technique for estimating the effects of vote-buying in Taiwan.* Presented at "Trading Political Rights: The Comparative Politics of Vote-Buying," Mass. Inst. Technol., Cambridge, MA

Riker WH. 1982. *Liberalism Against Populism: The Theory of Social Choice Confronts the Theory of Populism.* San Francisco: Freeman. 311 pp.

Rose-Ackerman S. 1999. *Corruption and Government: Causes, Consequences, and Reform.* New York: Cambridge Univ. Press. 266 pp.

Sabato H, ed. 1999. *Ciudadanía política y formación de las naciones: perspectivas históricas de América Latina.* México, DF: FCE. 449 pp.

Sabato H. 2001. *The Many and the Few: Political Participation in Republican Buenos Aires.* Stanford, CA: Stanford Univ. Press

Sambruccetti SIR. 1980. El fraude electoral en 1886. *Bol. Inst. Hist. Argent. y Am. "Dr. Emilio Ravgnon"* 16:415–82

Schedler A. 1999. Percepciones públicas de fraude electoral en México. *Perfiles Latinoam.* 14:103–27

Schedler A. 2002a. The menu of manipulation. *J. Democracy* 13:36–50

Schedler A. 2002b. *Citizens resent clientelism: on the moral economy of vote trading in México.* Presented at Annu. Meet. Am. Polit. Sci. Assoc., 98th, Boston, MA

Schaffer F. 1998. *Democracy in Translation: Understanding Politics in an Unfamiliar Culture.* Ithaca, NY: Cornell Univ. Press. 168 pp.

Schaffer F. 2001. *Clean elections and the "great unwashed": electoral reform and the class divide in the Philippines.* Presented at Annu. Meet. Am. Pol. Sci. Assoc., 97th, San Francisco, CA

Seymour C. 1915. *Electoral Reform in England and Wales: The Development and Operation of the Parliamentary Franchise, 1832–1885.* New Haven, CT: Yale Univ. Press. 564 pp.

Sloan JW. 1970. Electoral fraud and social change: the Guatemalan example. *Sci. Soc.* 34:78–91

Tjarks GOE. 1963. Las elecciones salteñas de 1876 (un estudio de fraude electoral). *Anuario de Historia* 1:417–75

Trejo G, Aguilar-Rivera JA. 2002. Etnicidad y consolidación democrática: la organización de las elecciones en las regiones indígenas de México. In *Los Dilemas de la democracia en México*, ed. A Hémond, D Recondo, pp. 195–224. México, DF: CEMCA and IFE

Tusell J. 1970. Para la sociología política de la España contemporánea: el impacto de la ley de 1907 en el comportamiento electoral. *Hispania* 30:571–631

Tusell J. 1991. El sufragio universal en España (1891–1936): un balance historiográfico. *Ayer* 3:13–62

Varela Ortega J. 2001a. *Los amigos políticos: partidos, elecciones y caciquismo en la restauración, 1875–1900.* Madrid: Marcial Pons/Junta de Castilla y León, Consejería de Educación y Cultura. 568 pp.

Varela-Ortega J, ed. 2001b. *El poder de la influencia: geografía del caciquismo en España (1875–1923).* Madrid: Marcial Pons/CEPC. 776 pp.

Annu. Rev. Polit. Sci. 2003. 6:257–74
doi: 10.1146/annurev.polisci.6.121901.085715
First published online as a Review in Advance on Mar. 6, 2003

RAWLS AND HABERMAS ON PUBLIC REASON:
Human Rights and Global Justice

J. Donald Moon

*Department of Government, Wesleyan University, 238 Church Street, Middletown,
Connecticut 06459; email: dmoon@wesleyan.edu*

Key Words political liberalism, international justice, rights, common-good
conceptions of justice, agency

■ **Abstract** Many have argued that Rawls's and Habermas's accounts of public
reason have converged in their latest writings, as both support the basic structure of
the modern, constitutional, democratic state. But an analysis of their views of global
justice reveals deep differences in their views of public reason. For Rawls, public
reason is a substantive set of principles to be used to answer fundamental questions,
whose content varies with the context in which these questions arise. Habermas, on the
other hand, endorses the public use of reason, which provides criteria determining the
universal validity of moral norms, though it does not itself ground substantive norms.
Ironically, at the global level Rawls's substantive principles of public reason are more
inclusive than Habermas's formalist account, which rules out moral and legal systems
that Rawls's theory would accommodate.

1. INTRODUCTION

Despite their indebtedness to Kant, Rawls and Habermas are in many ways heirs
to contrasting theoretical traditions. Rawls's work grows out of liberalism, and he
self-consciously presented his *Theory of Justice* as a development of the social
contract tradition of political theory (1999c, p. xviii). Habermas's work, on the
other hand, grows out of the Frankfurt School of critical theory, and he sought,
in the words of a sympathetic observer, "to provide conceptual and normative
foundations for a reconstructed Marxist social theory that provides a critical analysis of modernity" (Seidman 1989, p. 1). In recent years, however, their work
has converged in many respects, motivating a number of efforts to examine both
their similarities and the remaining differences. Most notable, perhaps, is the exchange between Rawls (1995) and Habermas (1995) themselves, though the issues
they addressed have been examined by many others. McCarthy (1994) has placed
"Rawls and Habermas in Dialogue," and Baynes (2001, p. 1) has suggested that
their accounts of "public reason," when carefully examined, do "not differ significantly." In one of the strongest statements of this view, McMahon (2002, p. 111), in
an article entitled "Why There Is No Issue between Habermas and Rawls," argues

that their "procedures of moral thinking are not in competition with each other," as "Rawls can make use of Habermas's procedure, and Habermas could employ a theoretical device that plays the role of Rawls's original position."

Most of these discussions focus on Rawls's political liberalism, which seeks to identify "the correct principles of justice for a modern pluralistic democracy" (McMahon 2002, p. 111). If we restrict our attention in that way, the positions of Rawls and Habermas appear similar in many important respects. But a shift to the political context of international affairs reveals deep differences between them, involving such fundamental matters as the basic human rights that should be universally respected and realized, and their ideals of world order. Although both advance a universalist account of human rights, Rawls's account affirms only a restricted class of rights that does not include claims rooted in distributive justice (such as equality of opportunity and the difference principle) nor even rights of civic and political equality and freedom of conscience and thought. And Rawls's vision of international society is that of a society of "peoples," whereas Habermas calls for a global political order, though not a world government. Some of the differences between Rawls and Habermas regarding global justice reflect different beliefs about the political and economic forces shaping the world today, but at a deeper level their views reflect their different accounts of public reason.

In this paper I do not try to resolve the differences but to locate their sources. Section 2 presents Rawls's account of international justice. Section 3 sets out elements of Habermas's account, and in the final section I show that their differences are ultimately rooted in contrasting conceptions of public reason.

2. RAWLS ON INTERNATIONAL JUSTICE

Although Rawls is most often associated with a neo-Kantian turn in political theory and philosophy, a turn that explains some of the convergence between him and Habermas, there are important non-Kantian roots to his theory, roots that I will call "Humean" (or neo-Humean, since I do not wish to make strong claims about their connection to Hume's own work). As is well known, Rawls signals the Humean side of his theory in discussing the "circumstances of justice." Following Hume, he argues that the question of distributive justice arises in part because we exist under conditions of moderate scarcity and have conflicting interests rooted in "different ends and purposes," which lead us to "take no interest in one another's interests" (Rawls 1999c, p. 127). The need for justice is a response to the twin problems of organizing social cooperation and resolving social conflict. Living in a society in which our actions are coordinated with others', we produce far more resources than we could otherwise produce. But because we have different plans of life or "conceptions of the good," we come into conflict over the distribution of the advantages of social coordination.

But this Humean moment goes deeper than Rawls's own account suggests, or at least deeper than most critics realize. For Rawls's general account of justice is thoroughly conventional and tied to a particular society or "people." Thus, his theory is based on the assumption of a "society conceived for the time being as a closed system isolated from other societies" (Rawls 1999c, p. 7), and his account of political liberalism is intended for societies, including the United States, Canada, and many European countries, that share traditions of democratic rule and commitments to ideals of freedom and equality. Rawls's political liberalism may best be thought of as a species of a general account of "justice as social cooperation." The principles of justice are seen as regulating (or serving as critical principles for) those who actually share a set of social and political institutions that have pervasive effects on the life chances of individuals. These institutions produce the set of social advantages whose distribution is contested.

2.1 Common-Good Conceptions of Justice

The idea of justice as social cooperation contrasts with a more common view, in which a specific conception of justice is rooted in some overarching moral and political theory. What Rawls calls "common good conceptions of justice" are radically different from the political liberal conception he champions. He does not explain fully what he means by a common-good conception of justice, so it is necessary to interpret his schematic comments in light of his other writings. We should begin by noting that both the conception of justice as social cooperation and common-good conceptions of justice see society as a system of social cooperation, and not merely the site of "socially coordinated activity—for example, activity coordinated by orders issued by an absolute central authority" (Rawls 2001, p. 6). Social life is impossible without coordination; "cooperation" is coordination realized through rules or procedures that participants accept as "appropriate to regulate their conduct," in part because these rules enable them to realize their own good in ways they regard as fair. As Rawls puts it (2001, p. 6),

> Fair terms of cooperation specify an idea of reciprocity, or mutuality: all who do their part as the recognized rules require are to benefit as specified by a public and agreed-upon standard.

Reciprocity or mutuality does not necessarily mean that people benefit equally; whether equality is required depends on publicly accepted standards. A well-ordered society "is a fair system of social cooperation over time from one generation to the next" (Rawls 2001, p. 5), in which the "role of the principles of justice . . . is to specify the fair terms of social cooperation" (p. 7).

But where do those standards or principles of justice come from? One source is Rawls's own account of justice as social cooperation, but he also acknowledges another source, which he calls common-good conceptions of justice. Such accounts appear to view social justice as applied moral philosophy, that is, as an application of a general (or, as Rawls puts it, comprehensive) moral, religious, or philosophical doctrine to the issue of how the advantages of socially coordinated activity should be distributed, and in general what principles should govern the political and other key institutions of society. Comprehensive doctrines offer a vision of human life and well-being from which flows an account of how society should be structured in order to allow its members to flourish and to cultivate human excellence. As in Plato's *Republic*, justice requires each person to play his or her proper role in realizing this vision, and these roles define the claims people can make on each other. Desert often figures prominently in this kind of account, for one's contribution to realizing the shared vision of human life and well-being, and one's instantiation of the virtues that vision requires, provide the necessary grounds for judging that one deserves some honor or recognition, some privilege or advantage. The warrior hero in MacIntyre's (1984, ch. 10) heroic society deserves recognition and honor. On the other hand, the monk who exemplifies humility and piety may be deserving, but his desert would not take the form of dominion over others.

In common-good conceptions of justice, the rights and obligations of individuals are typically derived from the role they play in a society unified around a particular view of the common good, or at least around an account of socially shared priorities (which appear to be a rather loosely articulated comprehensive doctrine) (Rawls 1999b, p. 77). Because individuals occupying different social positions may play very different roles in the realization of the common good, their basic rights may well be unequal. Because the society is organized around a specific comprehensive doctrine or "special priorities," there is often not even a presumption of equal standing in public life for other doctrines. There may even be some restrictions on religious liberty or liberty of thought, though—for reasons I address below—these restrictions must not be so onerous as to constitute persecution or repression of minority religions (Rawls 1999b, p. 74). Needless to say, rights of political participation may also be unequal. Whether or not a society based on a common-good conception of justice accepts such structured inequalities depends on its specific conception of the common good; even if most actually existing societies that approximate this idea have been hierarchical, some theoretical visions based on civic humanist, socialist, or communitarian ideals have been strongly egalitarian.

2.2 Political Liberal Conceptions of Justice

Common-good conceptions of justice are obviously problematic in democratic societies characterized by moral pluralism, that is, by a diversity of comprehensive moral, philosophical, and religious doctrines, each supported by a significant number of adherents. In democratic societies, different visions of human life lead to conflicting moral claims. Those who subscribe to natural-law-inspired ideals have rather different views about just deserts from those who accept a socialist conception of human solidarity and positive freedom, though they no doubt share a certain repugnance for what utilitarians have to say.

Rawls's political liberalism offers an account of social justice that is a response to moral pluralism, and the resulting disagreements about questions of justice. As long as the requirements of justice are rooted in comprehensive moral doctrines, this conflict will continue, and the likely outcome will be either (*a*) a structure of domination, in which the adherents of some particular account (or a coalition of groups) gain enough power to impose their views on the rest, or (*b*) some uneasy compromise reflecting a balance of power among factions. Such a society cannot be well ordered; it is not based on a common understanding and acceptance of the principles of justice, which are effectively realized in its practices and institutions, and which guide the settlement of major disputes about the division of social advantages that arise within it. And when people have good reasons to persist in their own particular beliefs, but they suffer the imposition of other values, there is an obvious sense in which their society is unjust, for it is based on domination and held together by force.

If there were some way to find the truth, we could resolve these disagreements, but Rawls views that as unlikely because of what he calls the "burdens of judgment." Reasonable disagreement about our fundamental commitments, he writes, "is disagreement among reasonable persons," who "share a common human reason, similar powers of thought and judgment: they can draw inferences, weigh evidence, and balance competing considerations" (Rawls 1996, p. 55). Disagreement among reasonable persons is possible, he argues, because the grounds on which we make judgments (both theoretical and practical) are often inadequate. The evidence may be conflicting and thus hard to assess, or people may disagree about the weight to be assigned to different considerations, or different normative considerations may be found on each side of an issue. Although it is possible to resolve many issues, others cannot be settled, and reasonable people may continue to hold different views even after sincere consideration of the arguments and evidence that others have offered.

Thus, a different approach is required. The essence of the problem and the form of the solution were stated long ago by Rousseau (1997 [1762], p. 66):

> All justice comes from God, he alone is its source; but if we were capable of receiving it from so high, we would need neither government nor laws. No doubt there is a universal justice emanating from reason alone; but this justice, to be admitted among us, must be reciprocal.

Rawls's political liberalism can be thought of as spelling out this requirement of reciprocity in the presence of moral plurality. Reciprocity is expressed in the commitment to living cooperatively with others, which requires that one be "ready to propose principles and standards as fair terms of cooperation and to abide by them willingly, given the assurance that others will likewise do so" (Rawls 1996, p. 49). One must be prepared, as Scanlon (1982, p. 116) puts it, "to justify one's actions to others on grounds they could not reasonably reject." By being prepared to justify one's actions to others, one expresses the commitment to live cooperatively with them, rather than seeking to dominate them.

Because people differ in their comprehensive moral, religious, and philosophical commitments, justification cannot take the form of reaching full agreement on the truth or correctness of these principles. If one acknowledges that those who do not share one's beliefs are "reasonable" in the sense that they have defensible (though not persuasive) grounds for holding their views, then one cannot simply dismiss others' views as irrational or dogmatic. In response to this situation, political liberalism conceives of the principles of justice as the object of reasonable agreement among citizens who seek to live cooperatively while acknowledging reasonable disagreement on comprehensive moral, religious, and philosophical doctrines. Political liberalism therefore seeks principles that all citizens have reason to accept as a basis for governing the basic institutions of their society and for adjudicating their claims regarding the distribution of the advantages of social cooperation. There is no attempt to ground these principles in some overarching account that vindicates them as, in some sense, true. It is not that political liberalism denies the truth of its principles, but it seeks to avoid the question of truth and to substitute for it the idea of reasonable agreement. It offers principles that can be accepted despite moral, philosophical, and religious differences. Rawls's own theory of "justice as fairness" is one of a family of such conceptions (see 2001, pp. 39–42, and passim).

These reasonable political conceptions of justice specify the content of what Rawls calls the "idea of public reason" for a democratic society (1999a, pp. 132–33). In his account, "public reason specifies at the deepest level the basic moral and political values that are to determine a constitutional democratic government's relation to its citizens and their relation to one another" (Rawls 1999a, p. 132). Public reason, then, is substantive, comprising the principles and values that citizens and public officials should employ in determining the basic principles of justice and the constitutional essentials of a particular society.

In passing, Rawls remarks that a liberal society also has a common-good conception of justice in that its members share "the common good of achieving political justice for all its citizens over time and preserving the free culture that justice allows" (1999b, p. 71, fn. 10). Although his comment appears to be somewhat ironic, the point is important. The common good of political liberalism is, above all, the commitment to living cooperatively in the special sense defined above. This means that the principles on which society is organized are based on a subset of one's fundamental commitments, and thus may on occasion come into conflict with other values or norms one holds, but that one is in general willing to let the more narrow, political or shared values prevail in the face of such conflicts. This means our social lives are necessarily alienated inasmuch as the structure of our society does not reflect, and may sometimes conflict with, some of our deepest beliefs and aspirations. To value this particular conception of social cooperation to this extent is no trivial thing.

2.3 Basic Human Rights and the Idea of a Well-Ordered Society

Common-good and political liberal conceptions of justice both represent ways in which a society may be well ordered, that is, constitute a system of social cooperation rather than one of mere social coordination. For a society to be a system of social cooperation, its members must accept rules that they view as "appropriate to regulate their conduct" and that specify the claims of its members according to "a public and agreed-upon standard" (Rawls 2001, p. 6). Although Rawls does not spell out the connection between social cooperation and human rights, it would appear that any society that can be characterized as cooperative will, by definition, respect certain basic rights, because they are necessary to protect the minimal capacities of agency that one must have if one's actions are to be described as following from one's own will or reflecting one's own choices or affirmations. Without the protections these rights provide, conformity to the basic rules of a society would not in any sense reflect the willing cooperation of its members. Although protecting such vital interests as subsistence need not take the form or employ the language of "rights," without the protection of basic interests, the social practices of the society would not be mutually beneficial, and the social order would involve "command by force, a slave system, and no cooperation of any kind" (Rawls 1999b, p. 68).

That is not to say that force is always present in noncooperative social orders, and not only because the dominated know that resistance is futile. As Berlin suggests, "the victim may prefer to have no responsibility; the slave may be happier in his slavery" (2002, p. 28). But only when one's basic agency is protected does the notion of "willing acceptance" make any sense. Even if the victim prefers not to have any responsibility, the point is that the victim's preferences are beside the point. Victims have no say. And slaves, as Rawls points out (2001, p. 24, following Patterson 1984), suffer social death.

Because social cooperation is possible only if people are able to exercise some basic capacities of agency, even a society founded on a common-good conception of justice must have what Rawls calls a "consultation hierarchy" in which its members have some degree of representation in the process of political decision making, albeit perhaps less than the rights of full democratic participation (1999b, p. 71–75). Rawls does not explain precisely why a consultation hierarchy is necessary, but it seems to be based on the idea of a society organized in accordance with a common-good account of justice. Although the view of justice accepted in such a society may limit the terms within which political discussion may proceed, there will always be the possibility of disagreement about the implications of that framework (and other relevant considerations) for particular issues of policy. Because such differences are inevitable, rulers can demonstrate their adherence to a particular conception of justice only by being prepared both to acknowledge such disagreements and to explain their decisions in terms of that conception. Without an institutional process through which dissent is encountered and decisions explained, it would be impossible for authorities to show that their actions are based on their understanding of the requirements of justice, and so to give their subjects reason to acknowledge an obligation to conform to their decisions. Thus, a well-ordered society must acknowledge the principle that rulership is rule over people with the capacity of agency, who have voices, and is legitimate only when those voices have opportunities to be heard.

As Beitz (2000, p. 686) has argued, Rawls does not specify with any care the basic rights that all societies must respect, nor does he explain their basis. Rawls lists the right to life (including "the means of subsistence and security"), the right to liberty (including "freedom from slavery, serfdom, and forced occupation, and to a sufficient measure of liberty of conscience to ensure freedom of religion and thought"), the right to "personal property," and the right to "formal equality" (in the sense that "similar cases be treated similarly") (1999b, p. 65). We can add to this list a right to emigrate (Rawls 1999b, p. 74) and a right to participate in a political process in which those who exercise power must justify their use of power in terms of the society's public conception of justice. I would suggest that what unifies this list is the idea of agency. These rights in some form are necessary to protect the minimal capacities of agency that are presupposed by the idea of social cooperation, or willing participation in the social order. So long as most members accept a particular substantive idea of the common good, or a specific comprehensive doctrine, these rights do not have to be equal, nor do they have to be extensive, so long as they provide space and resources sufficient for individuals to dissent if they are unable to identify with socially enforced expectations and objectives. Rawls refers to societies that are based on a common-good conception of justice and that meet this standard as "decent" peoples, and he allows that they may be full members of an international society of peoples.

Critics fault Rawls for distinguishing between liberal and decent peoples on the one hand and all other societies on the other, holding that the distinction is arbitrary, or at least its basis unclear. I have argued that the distinction is not arbitrary but reflects an ideal of society as a system of social cooperation, which is therefore based on some conception of justice. I have argued that any form of social cooperation must protect basic capacities for agency and so must provide the protections and resources necessary to effectively realize certain basic rights. The standard of protecting agency is not as demanding a standard as the liberal ideal of autonomy, for it does not require that individuals have the capacities (and dispositions) to engage in critical reflection on their choices and the social expectations to which they are subject, but it does provide a minimal set of human rights that limits the range of societies that can be full members of an international society of peoples. Because these rights are necessary to any system of social cooperation, they are universal rights.

2.4 The Boundaries of a People

Beyond the universal but quite limited set of basic rights, different societies may construct different systems of rights and obligations binding their members. The boundaries of these societies in Rawls's theory are defined both in "objective" terms and in terms of the identifications and orientations of their members, giving rise to a certain ambiguity in Rawls's theory. On the one hand, he sometimes writes as if a "people" presupposes a "cultural nation," a group sharing a set of particularistic identities or "common sympathies," so that they see themselves as a people. But he acknowledges that (at least in the case of a democratic society) a people may not be "united by a common language and shared historical memories" (1999b, p. 25). What is crucial is not that they share a pre-existing identity but that they share a "basic structure" that has a pervasive impact on the life chances of all. Thus, the limits to social justice are not particularistic.

In Rawls's account, contrary to various nationalists and communitarians, my claims against my fellow citizens are not based on our valuing our common membership for noninstrumental reasons, thus giving rise to special rights and obligations (though I may have such reasons as well). Rather, they are based on the fact that we share a "basic structure," which is (or should be) regulated by principles of justice. This basic structure consists of institutions constituted by rules and procedures that give rise to rights and obligations and that bring about a distribution of benefits. Because the basic structure defines rights and obligations, and because of its pervasive impact on individuals' life chances, it necessarily gives rise to questions about the justice of the rights it defines and the distribution of benefits and burdens it imposes. Thus, the limits of the claims of social justice reflect the limits of social cooperation organized through a basic structure.

This conclusion is similar to one advanced by Miller (1998), who distinguishes between "comparative" and "noncomparative" principles of justice. "Comparative principles . . . assess the justice of a mode of treatment or of a resulting distribution by comparing how each member of the relevant group fares when compared with everyone else," whereas noncomparative principles "assert that certain forms of treatment are inherently just regardless of what is happening to others" (Miller 1998, p. 169). Rawls's basic rights are noncomparative: They assert that individuals should be protected in certain ways, have access to certain goods and services, and enjoy certain liberties; determining whether these conditions are met does not require comparing one person's condition to another's. Most principles of distributive or social justice, such as equality or Rawls's difference principle, by contrast, are comparative. Miller argues that principles of international justice must be noncomparative because "comparative judgments . . . have force" only if they "apply to persons who are connected together in some way, for instance by belonging to the same community or association" (1998, p. 171). But Miller does not explain why the "relevant group" within which comparative judgments are to be made should be a "community or association." If the relevant group is the whole of humanity, there is no reason why comparative principles would not be applicable. For Rawls, what determines the relevant group is that its members share a basic structure, and what makes it relevant is the fact that the basic structure largely determines the production and distribution of the social advantages whose distribution is to be regulated by principles of justice. Thus, the reason that one set of strangers (fellow citizens) have different claims on each other than another set (foreigners) is that they, unlike foreigners, share a basic structure. Sharing a basic structure, they are subject to claims of reciprocity with one another that do not extend to outsiders. Thus, Rawls's argument does not rest on the idea that there is some moral priority to be given to compatriots, simply by virtue of their being compatriots (cf. Beitz 1999, p. 215). There may be a variety of reasons why people who see themselves as joined in a certain way are more likely to be able to create a (just) basic structure, but—again contrary to the claims of various nationalists and communitarians—the causal relationship may go in the opposite direction: Being linked in a basic structure (sometimes even an unjust one) creates the sense of being joined with others.

2.5 International Society and the Law of Peoples

Rawls assumes that the world is made up of different peoples, each of whom shares a basic structure of social and political institutions, which has a pervasive impact on the life chances of its members. In his view, "transnational" social and economic forces have only a limited impact on a society's well-being, since the primary determinants of economic prosperity are "internal" to the society (a matter I take up in Section 4). Thus, the problem of justice at the global level becomes a problem of defining norms that can be accepted by these peoples to regulate their relationships. Rawls's solution to this problem involves an extension of his idea of the "original position," in which those who deliberate on the principles of justice for the international society of peoples are conceived as representatives of separate "peoples" rather than of "individuals." This argument (which I do not detail here) involves a two-stage procedure. First, representatives of liberal peoples—those sharing liberal principles of justice—articulate a set of norms governing their relationships and agree to such basic principles as the freedom and independence of peoples, nonintervention, the prohibition of the use of force as an instrument of foreign policy, and the requirement to honor human rights. At a second stage, the representatives of "decent peoples" deliberate on the norms governing their relationships, and they come to accept the same set of principles. These principles, then, constitute the "public reason" in terms of which fundamental issues arising within the society of peoples should be decided. Thus, the principles of global justice govern the relationships of both "liberal" and "decent" societies, as both have similar basic interests and—being well ordered—have reason to observe similar constraints in the conduct of foreign policy. Needless to say, these principles are radically different from the principles governing democratic societies, they apply to different questions, and they govern people acting in different roles and capacities.

3. HABERMAS ON GLOBAL JUSTICE AND UNIVERSAL HUMAN RIGHTS

My account of Rawls has focused on two views of justice, namely his own political liberalism and common-good conceptions that rest on more or less comprehensive moral visions, but Habermas's view of justice fits neither of these models. Habermas distinguishes "morality" from "ethics," arguing that "[m]oral commands are categorical or unconditional imperatives that express valid norms" (Habermas

1993, p. 8) whereas ethical statements tell us "that it is 'good' for you to act in this way in the long run, all things considered" and are based on some account of "the highest good of a self-sufficient form of life that has its value in itself" (Habermas 1993, pp. 5). Unlike common-good conceptions of justice, Habermas views justice as part of morality, not ethics, for the requirements of justice are not rooted in a particular understanding of a good life nor in some comprehensive religious, cultural, or philosophical worldview. But unlike Rawls's political liberalism, Habermas seeks principles of justice that are "valid" or in some sense "true," not merely something that people can "reasonably" accept.

In Habermas's theory, moral norms are invoked in what he calls communicative action, in which people coordinate their actions "on the basis of mutual understanding" (Baynes 1992, p. 84). That is to say, in acting communicatively, I try to achieve my goals not by manipulating or coercing others but by (perhaps implicitly) invoking a norm that I expect others will accept as valid, leading them to respond accordingly. To take a trivial example, when I stop a stranger to ask for directions, I implicitly invoke a social norm to the effect that one ought to give truthful answers when asked for directions. In this case, I expect to get the correct directions not because I am able to coerce, bribe, or manipulate a passer-by, but because she will accept an obligation to give me truthful directions if she can, and my action implicitly invokes our common understanding of that norm. Of course, I may be mistaken when I invoke a norm. Expecting my interlocuter to accept its validity, I may find that she contests it. When that happens, I must be prepared to offer reasons why I think the norm is valid. As Habermas puts it, the possibility of a common understanding of valid norms invoked in communicative action must be based on "the speaker's guarantee that he will, if necessary, make efforts to redeem the claim" that a norm is valid "by adducing reasons" and, more generally, engaging in "practical discourses" (1990, pp. 58–59). But, according to Habermas, "what it means to discuss hypothetically whether norms of action ought to be adopted" (1990, p. 92) amounts to "implicitly acknowledging" the principle of universalization, (1990, p. 63) which holds that a valid norm must fulfill the following condition:

> *All* affected can accept the consequences and the side effects its *general* observance can be anticipated to have for the satisfaction of *everyone's* interests (and these consequences are preferred to those of known alternative possibilities for regulation). (Habermas 1990, p. 65).

According to Habermas, the principle of universalization is implicit in the idea of moral argumentation itself. Thus, principles of justice cannot be based on a conception of the common good, since any such conception is necessarily rooted in a particular way of life and set of cultural self-understandings and therefore will fail the test of universalization. On the other hand, the principles that meet this test are not merely "reasonable" but are genuinely valid or true. They are not restricted to particular contexts; their scope is universal, applying not only to specific societies, but globally. Thus, Habermas rejects fundamental aspects of

Rawls's account of global justice—the idea that the objects of a global account of justice are peoples rather than individuals and the idea that some societies may reject the claims of human freedom and equality.

Not surprisingly, then, Habermas's account of human rights is deeply at variance with Rawls's. Habermas contrasts liberal and republican understandings of rights. The liberal understanding assigns priority to the rights of private individuals, rights that protect their interests as natural persons, including the right to own property, freedom from harm and arbitrary treatment by political authorities, freedom of conscience and belief, and privacy. The republican account assigns priority to the rights of political participation, the right to engage in the processes through which rights are themselves defined. Habermas considers both positions mistaken, for these rights are cofoundational: "private and public autonomy reciprocally presuppose one another" (2001, p. 118). As Habermas explains,

> on the one hand, citizens can make appropriate use of their public autonomy only if, on the basis of their equally protected private autonomy, they are sufficiently independent; on the other hand, they can realize equality in the enjoyment of their private autonomy only if they make appropriate use of their political autonomy as citizens. Consequently, liberal and political basic rights are inseparable. (Habermas 2001, p. 118)

To be sure, any specific polity will be "rooted in particular collective identities," but the universality of rights rests on "the solidarity of *world* citizens," which "generates a kind of cosmopolitan cohesion in the first instance through feelings of indignation over the violations of rights, i.e., over repression and injuries to human rights committed by states" (Habermas 2001, p. 108).

In Habermas's view, world citizenship will not be realized through a world state, but the key point is that it presupposes a world of democratic states, and a political process that realizes "the democratic legitimation of decisions beyond the schema of the nation-state" (Habermas 2001, p. 110). In contrast to Rawls, then, Habermas rejects both the idea of a pluralist world containing domestic regimes based on nondemocratic conceptions of justice, and the idea of international society as consisting essentially of a society of "peoples," governed by norms that are not democratically legitimated but rather are the objects of agreement among representatives of peoples. Rather, policy making at the international level should conform to the requirements of democracy, though not through the standard mechanisms of elections and political representation but through devices that ensure "the general accessibility of a deliberative process whose structure grounds an expectation of rationally acceptable results" (Habermas 2001, p. 110). Habermas does not explicitly spell out the characteristics of such a deliberative process. He does, however, call for a "functioning public sphere" that allows for serious discussion of global issues and that is widely accessible. To be sure, "discursive structures of opinion- and will-formation . . . could never entirely replace conventional procedures for decision-making and political representation," but he insists that "they do tip the balance" (Habermas 2001, pp. 110–11). Concretely, these democratized processes of global governance could take a variety of forms, perhaps including "the institutionalized participation of non-governmental organizations in the deliberations of international negotiating systems" and empowering international organizations "to demand that member states carry out referendums on important issues" (2001, p. 111). Although falling short of the procedures of domestic democratic systems, such innovations could extend "the democratic legitimation of decisions beyond the schema of the nation-state" (2001, p. 110).

Both Habermas and Rawls draw inspiration from Kant's vision of perpetual peace, but the different ways in which they appropriate Kant's ideas reveal the deep differences between them. Habermas argues that an examination of Kant's ideal in light of the two centuries that have passed since he first articulated it shows the need for revisions in three fundamental areas. In the first place, he rejects Kant's notion of a "federation of nations" that respects the sovereignty of each country, insisting that the "community of peoples must be able to ensure that its members act at least in conformity with the law through the threat of sanctions," thereby transforming the "external character of international relations between states" into "a domestic relationship between the members of a common organization based on a legal code or a constitution" (Habermas 1998, p. 179). Second, he views Kant as inconsistent in imagining "the cosmopolitan community as a federation of states, not of world citizens," since "every legal order" derives "from the original right that attaches to every person 'qua human being'" (Habermas 1998, p. 180). Because every "individual has a right to equal liberties under universal law," it follows that "the autonomy of citizens" may not "be preempted even by the sovereignty of their states" (Habermas 1998, pp. 180–81). Finally, Habermas finds that Kant's notion of world peace as the absence of war must be altered in light of the growing interdependence of all parts of the world owing to globalization and increasing ecological imbalances. Instead, peace must be understood "as a process which unfolds in a nonviolent manner" aiming "to satisfy the real preconditions for a peaceful coexistence of groups and peoples," and which requires "strategies of nonviolent intervention designed to promote processes of democratization," including appropriate economic and environmental policies (Habermas 1998, p. 185).

In Habermas's vision, what is required is a transformation of the institutions of international society (notably the United Nations) from a "congress of states" to incorporate features of a cosmopolitan democracy, and the institutionalization of democracy within each of the individual units (states) of the world system. In some ways, his appropriation of Kant is closer to Kant's vision than is Rawls's ideal—in particular, in insisting that the subunits of international society consist of democratic states, a natural extension of Kant's view that each of the peoples of world society would have a republican constitution. In other ways, Habermas goes beyond Kant in calling for structures of international governance in which individuals and not just states have a central role, structures whose jurisdiction extends to social, economic, and environmental issues. By contrast, Rawls allows for a plurality of political forms in international society and envisions much more restricted forms of international organization.

4. THE TASKS AND POSSIBILITIES OF THEORY

The differences between Rawls and Habermas regarding international justice are rooted partly in their different views of the tasks of philosophy—in particular in their conceptions of public reason—and partly in disagreements about important empirical issues. Their empirical differences are obvious. Key to Rawls's argument is the idea that there is no global structure. Addressing the terrible inequalities and deprivation that we see in the world, Rawls argues that there is a duty of assistance: Rich countries must aid burdened societies. But, as I have indicated, he insists that the primary causes of a country's poverty are "internal" to that country, specifically, "its political culture—its members' political and civic virtues" (Rawls 1999b, p. 117). Although he does not spell his argument out fully, he appears to claim that, with the right "political and cultural traditions," these societies will be able to acquire the "human capital and know-how" and "the material and technological resources needed to be well-ordered" (Rawls 1999b, p. 106). What these societies need, then, is not material aid so much as help in rectifying "basic political and social injustices" through "an emphasis on human rights," particularly the rights of women (Rawls 1999b, pp. 108–10).

By contrast, for Habermas, the forces of globalization clearly undermine the relative independence of national economies. Globalization destroys the capacity even of wealthy countries to fulfill the requirements of social justice for their own citizens, and it creates the need for a new global order and "global domestic policy."

> If current trends continue, the progressive undermining of national sovereignty will necessitate the founding and expansion of political institutions on the supranational level, a process whose beginnings can already be observed. (Habermas 1998, pp. 106–7)

The great danger we face, in Habermas's view, is the "abdication of politics," the abandonment of the effort to control and direct economic forces to realize the requirements of justice. Unfortunately, with the decline of "national economies," governments have less and less power to control economic forces at the national level, including in particular the power to levy taxes for redistributive purposes. We thus see growing levels of unemployment and the dismantling of the welfare state, problems that can only be tackled in new political venues.

Without trying to resolve the disagreement between Rawls and Habermas here, I would suggest that both positions are exaggerated. Contrary to Habermas's claims, states apparently still have considerable freedom from international constraints in the design of social policies. Among OECD countries, there is "a wide variation in both the content of policies and the associated institutional frameworks" (Quiggin 2001, p. 71) in the areas of education, health, and taxes and transfers. The countries most exposed to international economic forces—small, relatively open economies—have the largest and most redistributive social welfare programs, which could hardly be the case if international constraints were so powerful. Significantly, levels of taxation in OECD nations rose (from 42% to 44% of gross domestic product) during the 1990s, and the growth was greater in the smaller economies (presumably more subject to global economic forces) than in the larger, G7 countries (Crook 2001, p. 14). In short, frequently repeated claims that nation-states are losing the capacity to manage their economies and maintain social programs appear to be exaggerated.

Similarly, Rawls's claim that the principal causes of a country's poverty are internal to that country, in particular its political culture, is one-sided. It neglects the structure of the international political-economic regime and fails to develop principles of justice that apply in this area. For example, the World Trade Organization requires that countries respect intellectual property rights (by adopting and enforcing laws that define intellectual property according to international standards). Under this policy, countries such as India and South Africa have been blocked from producing pharmaceuticals covered by foreign patents, which has increased morbidity and mortality as well as health care costs in those countries. The best-known example, no doubt, is the (ultimately unsuccessful) effort on the part of drug companies to block the production and use of patented AIDS medications in Africa and other third-world countries. Similarly, other cases raise serious issues of justice, e.g., the Multifiber Agreement, which blocks access to rich-country markets for the textile and clothing exports of poor countries, or U.S. opposition to special treatment for poor countries under the Kyoto Accord.

As important (and problematic) as these empirical claims might be in illuminating the differences between Habermas and Rawls on international morality, the deeper differences are conceptual and philosophical, and reflect their views about the tasks of philosophy and political theory. For Habermas, philosophy aims to show that our moral judgments can be rationally grounded, or "to provide a characterization of the moral point of view suitable for all moral reasoning" (McMahon 2002, p. 111). Although in his political writings he advances substantive positions, he insists that "it is incumbent on moral theory to explain and ground the moral point of view. What moral *theory* can do and should be trusted to do is to clarify the universal core of our moral intuitions and thereby to refute value skepticism," but "what [moral theory] cannot do is make any kind of substantive contribution" (Habermas 1990, p. 211). Nonetheless, as I pointed out above, the moral point of view itself rules out common-good conceptions of justice and supports a strong and universal set of human rights, even if it does not specify their content. Just as there is a certain irony in Rawls's observation that political liberalism is committed to a "common good" (of social cooperation), so it is ironic that, despite Habermas's insistence on the purely formal character of his account, his theory delegitimates more types of social and political arrangements than does Rawls's more "substantive" account.

In contrast to Habermas, Rawls (2001, pp. 1–5) sees philosophy as having four tasks: the practical task of clarifying and resolving conflicts, the task of orienting and reconciling us to our political life, and the task of projecting a realistic utopia. Each of these tasks shows his central preoccupation with the "reasonable" as opposed to the "true," that is, with finding principles that participants in political discourse and conflict have reason to accept, while side-stepping the question of whether they are true or valid. The practical concern of political philosophy "is to see whether, despite appearances, some underlying basis of philosophical and moral agreement can be uncovered" so as to resolve or at least narrow the "divisive political differences" that divide people in a particular society (Rawls 2001, p. 2) or that divide societies from each other. The orienting task of political philosophy, closely related to the reconciling task, involves providing a unified account of how we may think about our political and social institutions as a whole and how we collectively share "basic aims and purposes as a society with a history," so that we may see how our various "ends can cohere within a well-articulated conception of a just and reasonable society" (Rawls 2001, pp. 2–3). In this way political philosophy helps reconcile us to our way of life by enabling us to see "the way in which [our] institutions, when properly understood from a philosophical point of view, are rational, and developed over time as they did to attain their present, rational form" (Rawls 2001, p. 3). But philosophy apparently cannot perform the work of reconciliation by itself. For we can be reconciled to our world only if, by acting on the "belief that the social world allows at least a decent [in the ordinary sense of this word, not the special sense used above] political order," we can probe "the limits of practicable possibility" to project an image of a just order that can be attained "under reasonably favorable but still possible historical conditions, conditions allowed by the laws and tendencies of the social world" (Rawls 2001, p. 4). Thus, for Rawls the task of philosophy is substantive, rooted in the exigencies and conflicts of a particular setting.

These different views of the tasks of theory are nowhere more evident than in Rawls's willingness to accept nonliberal, hierarchical regimes as full members of the society of nations, in contrast to Habermas's (implicit) rejection of such regimes as violating fundamental and well-grounded moral norms. Both Rawls and Habermas agree that international morality is subject to the test of public reason, but they have different conceptions of public reason and its powers. Habermas revealingly speaks not of "public reason" but of the public use of reason, a form of practical reason accessible to all, giving rise to the criteria determining the validity of moral norms. But Rawls insists that, in explicating the idea of public reason, "at no point are we deducing the principles of right and justice, or decency, or the principles of rationality, from a conception of practical reason" (1999b, p. 86). Rather, public reason is substantive, consisting of the normative ideas, the principles and values, that may properly be invoked in answering fundamental questions. And its content varies with the context in which it is employed—whether it applies to the constitutional essentials and basic principles of justice of a democratic society, or to the principles governing international relations or what Rawls calls the society of peoples. An account of public reason (such as the one Rawls offers) is not deductively unified but worked out for each particular case, and though there can be no guarantee, the hope is that when "laid out properly, the resulting principles and standards of right and justice will hang together and will be affirmed by us on due reflection" (Rawls 1999b, p. 87). Indeed, Rawls criticizes Habermas in part on the grounds that his position is "a comprehensive doctrine" offering "a general account of meaning, reference, and truth or validity both for theoretical reason and for the several forms of practical reason" (Rawls 1995, p. 135), and is "metaphysical" in the sense that "it presents an account of what there is" (p. 137).

Rawls does not, of course, reject Habermas's view as incorrect in any way. Rather, he argues that some citizens have reasonable grounds to reject it, and so it is necessary to develop a different account of public reason if society is to be organized as "a fair system of cooperation." The centrality of the value of "fair cooperation" to Rawls's thinking may reflect the origins of his theory in the social contract tradition, the idea of society as based on an agreement of free and equal people on the terms of their ongoing social life. On the other hand, Habermas's rejection of the "reasonable" in favor of the "true" may reflect the roots of his thinking in the tradition of critical theory, and the aspiration for a fully rational society in which the "free development of each is the condition for the free development of all."

ACKNOWLEDGMENTS

I would like to thank Arash Abizadeh and Stephen White for their helpful comments on an earlier version of this article.

The *Annual Review of Political Science* is online at
http://polisci.annualreviews.org

LITERATURE CITED

Baynes K. 1992. *Normative Grounds of Social Criticism.* Albany, NY: SUNY Press

Baynes K. 2001. *Public reason and liberal values.* Presented at Annu. Meet. Am. Polit. Sci. Assoc., San Francisco, Aug. 30

Beitz C. 1999. *Political Theory and International Relations.* Princeton, NJ: Princeton Univ. Press. 2nd ed.

Beitz C. 2000. Rawls's law of peoples. *Ethics* 110:669–96

Berlin I. 2002. On human dignity: a letter to George Kennan. *New Republic* 4(541):23–30

Crook C. 2001. Globalisation and its critics. *Economist* 360(8241) (Suppl.)

Habermas J. 1990. *Moral Consciousness and Communicative Action.* Transl. C Lenhardt, S Weber Nicholsen. Cambridge, MA: MIT Press

Habermas J. 1993. *Justification and Applica-*

tion. Transl. C Cronin. Cambridge, MA: MIT Press

Habermas J. 1995. Reconciliation through the public use of reason: remarks on John Rawls's political liberalism. *J. Philos.* 92:109–31. Reprinted in Habermas 1998

Habermas J. 1998. *The Inclusion of the Other.* Cambridge, MA: MIT Press

Habermas J. 2001. *The Postnational Constellation.* Cambridge, MA: MIT Press

MacIntyre A. 1984. *After Virtue.* Notre Dame, IN: Univ. Notre Dame Press

McCarthy T. 1994. Kantian constructivism and reconstructivism. *Ethics* 105:44–63

McMahon C. 2002. Why there is no issue between Habermas and Rawls. *J. Philos.* 99(3):111–29

Miller D. 1998. The limits of cosmopolitan justice. In *International Society*, ed. D Mapel,

T Nardin, pp. 164–81. Princeton, NJ: Princeton Univ. Press

Patterson O. 1984. *Slavery and Social Death.* Cambridge, MA: Harvard Univ. Press

Quiggen J. 2001. Globalization and economic sovereignty. *J. Polit. Philos.* 9:56–80

Rawls J. 1995. Reply to Habermas. *J. Philos.* 92:132–80. Reprinted in Rawls 1996

Rawls J. 1996. *Political Liberalism.* New York: Columbia Univ. Press. 2nd ed.

Rawls J. 1999a. The idea of public reason revisited. See Rawls 1999b, pp. 129–80

Rawls J. 1999b. *The Law of Peoples.* Cambridge, MA: Harvard Univ. Press

Rawls J. 1999c. *A Theory of Justice.* Cambridge, MA: Harvard Univ. Press. Rev. ed.

Rawls J. 2001. *Justice as Fairness: a Restatement.* Cambridge, MA: Harvard Univ. Press

Rousseau JJ. 1997 (1762). *Of the Social Contract.* Transl./ed. V Gourevitch. New York: Cambridge Univ. Press

Scanlon T. 1982. Contractualism and utilitarianism. In *Utilitarianism and Beyond*, ed. A Sen, B Williams, pp. 103–28. Cambridge, UK: Cambridge Univ. Press

Seidman S. 1989. *Jürgen Habermas on Society and Politics: a Reader.* Boston: Beacon

Annu. Rev. Polit. Sci. 2003. 6:275–305
doi: 10.1146/annurev.polisci.6.121901.085719

DEMOCRATIC INDIVIDUALISM AND ITS CRITICS

George Kateb

*Department of Politics, Princeton University, Princeton, New Jersey 08544;
email: kateb@princeton.edu*

Key Words   democracy, Plato, Tocqueville, communitarianism

■ **Abstract**   Where democracy exists, there will be individualism. The historical record shows that democracy inevitably engenders individualism. This proposition will be challenged by those who think either that individualism can obtain in nondemocratic cultures or that democracy can exist without engendering individualism. The paper rejects both contentions. The defining characteristic of democracy is freedom, and the oldest democratic concept of freedom is the Greek one: To be free is to live as one likes. Versions of that definition are found wherever people are or aspire to be democratic. To live as one likes means that one is allowed to try out various roles in life. Each person is more than any single role, function, or place in society. Individualism consists in that idea. Only democracy inspires it. It is also true that democracy, in reaction, produces antidemocratic individualism. The greatest students of democratic individualism are Plato and Tocqueville, and they are also its profoundest critics. But contemporary critics are certainly worth scholarly attention.

WHAT INDIVIDUALISM IS

Individualism is both a normative doctrine and a set of practices that people engage in whether or not they explicitly adhere to the normative doctrine. They may engage in these practices because of the pervasive influence of the habits, traditions, and common spirit of their society. As a normative doctrine, individualism may receive elaboration in various degrees of theoretical sophistication, and it may also encourage or deepen existing social tendencies. Advocates of the doctrine defend what they see or merely catch hints of, but they usually want more. Their espousal of individualism may be tinged by disappointment; or they may harbor a hope that by refining the individualism that they observe, they may induce people to approach more closely the ideal that is practiced imperfectly. The critique of individualism, on the other hand, can also contribute to second thoughts in both theory and practice. There may also be fairly neutral theoretical analysis of individualism that helps to fill out our understanding. What is most instructive is theoretical elaboration based on the individualist practices that are noticed: individualism as it is embodied and lived in society. Without some evidence that individualism actually is pursued, individualism may be a suggestive theoretical construction but lacks a certain solidity or warrant.

It turns out that some of the greatest writing on individualism is the work of its critics, especially those who are not completely hostile and who combine theoretical discussion, moments of analytic neutrality, moments of appreciation, and keen sensitivity to the evidence of individualism that they observe. The two most important critics of individualism are Plato and Tocqueville, and they are, as well, its most subtle and most comprehensive general observers. Hence, they are among the principal benefactors of individualism.

The normative doctrine, as an espousal of individualism, is put forth as a guide to how people should think of themselves, what treatment they should expect from society, how to treat others, and—most grandly—how to live. As a doctrine, it is not meant as a rationalization for the self-assertion of the person who propounds it. It is meant for all people or, in its antidemocratic variant, for only certain sorts of people who may be few in number.

When thinkers speak of democratic individualism, they often refer to the kind or, more usually, kinds of individualism that best suit people in democracy or that people actually practice in the spirit of democracy. The implication is that individualism, in theory or practice, may exist outside of and be completely untouched by democracy. But on one reading of the historical record, individualism (in several kinds), in theory and practice, is exclusively democratic in the first instance and may later provoke a deliberately antidemocratic individualism (also in several kinds). The emergence of individualism is thus bound up with democracy, whether democracy is established or insurgent or only an aspiration or influence, and later when democracy is disliked. There is probably no espousal of individualism that is not democratic to begin with; and, by definition, no assertion of antidemocratic individualism until democracy exists and dominates, or fails but cannot be smothered completely. There has not been, it seems, any individualism outside a democratic context. Individualism is entwined with democracy and is a borrowed and forever alien element in any other political theory or society. Needless to say, the critique of individualism, whether democratic or antidemocratic, is also tied to democratic experience. What is not acknowledged, however, is that any critique of individualism is necessarily a critique of democracy. Democracy and individualism are inseparable phenomena.

If such is the case, how to account for it? Before speculating on that question I must try to say what individualism is. Individualism, as theorized or regularly lived, maintains the view or exemplifies the sentiment that people—whether all or only some—count or matter apart from their roles, functions, or place in society. Of course, there is no society without roles, functions, and locations, without a division of labor, without differences that are often obvious and sometimes crucial. But to say or feel that people matter apart from their work and their involvements and relationships—and even that they matter more—is to say that no finite value can be put on them. Their value is not finite because they—their identities—are not exhaustively definable; they are capable of unpredictability and creativity, for good (and bad). No single act provides the key to anyone. You cannot say for certain who a person is, much less who he may become. Unlike other species members, each person initiates (more than ecological) change in the world just by living in it and remakes it indefinitely in a tangled web of cause and effect. Each is distinctive to an extent or in a way that a member of some other species is not (or appears to us, at least, not to be). In the words of the late English poet and essayist, Stephen Spender, the truth is that "the world is experienced by each individual uniquely—that there are as many inner worlds as there are people" (1975, p. 208). Whatever the performance or behavior of a person, or the outward expression in work or everyday life, the person's uniqueness (or individuation) remains; it is the distinctness of a whole world. It is invisible and often barely articulate, and it awaits its occasions, which may be infrequent, to come out of hiding, to the person's surprise and the surprise of others. There are no ordinary persons, except to the unimaginative observer. If each person is a world, then society must approach him or her with due respect. This is not a logical entailment, but it may be the most appropriate response.

Individual uniqueness, as it figures in individualist doctrines or everyday sentiment, is not the same as a religious assertion of the immortal soul, although the idea of the uniqueness of each soul has of course lent substantial though indirect support to individualism. Indeed, the very notion of soul is a rich resource when it blends with the notion of self, and self is seen as vast and unfathomable, as Augustine sees it when he discusses memory in the *Confessions*. Nevertheless, individualism is for the most part a secular doctrine or common disposition, not tied to views of religious origin and destiny, and able to flower only in more secular circumstances.

WHAT DEMOCRATIC INDIVIDUALISM IS

Let us for the time being concentrate on democratic individualism and turn later to the antidemocratic kinds. The supposition of every person's individual uniqueness may be thought vaporous and even doubtful. But I think that without such a thought or subconscious feeling, the whole energy and pathos of reforming the world, or keeping it as it is, so that it may properly house democratic individualism cannot be understood. The case for counting each person as priceless and therefore inviolate cannot rest solely, as it is sometimes made to, on undeniable traits putatively shared by all people. These traits include the capacity to suffer such moral injuries as insults, indignities, and humiliations, not just physical injuries and losses; the capacity to make choices; and the capacity to reciprocate right or fair treatment, not just to inflict retribution or revenge. The commitment to basic individual rights, to which every person is entitled, is certainly shored up by emphasis on these universal traits, but the underlying conception of what it means to be a human being must sooner or later be exposed. It must be exposed because democratic individualism is a full code of life, the life that should grow and flower when rights are genuinely recognized. If the practice—better, set of practices—of democratic individualism does not develop in a society of rights, then something has gone wrong. Individual rights ultimately acquire, and must acquire, an existential premise, which is found in the idea of individual uniqueness and which makes the rights all the more precious. This is not to say that rights are mere instruments of democratic individualism or individual uniqueness; rights are rather the irreplaceable medium or atmosphere. If individualism did not develop, that would not mean that people would no longer deserve rights. The universal traits mentioned above would still have to be honored and accommodated by the recognition of rights. But no discussion of reasons for rights is complete without substantial reference to democratic individualism and its premise of individual uniqueness.

The concept of individual uniqueness may be slow to emerge. Awareness of the premise may come later than the establishment of democracy and the codification (or more informal conventions) of basic individual liberties or rights. The final cause is apprehended last. What is more, it may come even after democratic individualism, an outgrowth of a society of rights, manifests itself. But once it comes, it can intensify both the devotion to rights and the will to democratic individualism.

I must admit that although democratic individualism existed in ancient Athens, I suspect that the surviving Greek literature contains no formal articulation of the modern concept of individual uniqueness: the idea that every person is, in important respects, a distinct world. Intimations can certainly be found in the Stoic doctrine of inner freedom, according to which the self can rise above slavish passivity by correct interpretation or mental rearrangement of experience. But by the time of Stoicism, Athenian democracy was overridden by Macedonian and then Roman domination. Yet it is possible that in the myth of Er, which closes Plato's *Republic*, the doctrine of the passage of the soul from one kind of life to another (after intervals in the afterlife), and indeed from one species to another, all on the basis of constrained choice made by the soul's undying but unnameable temperament, may suggest that every human being is, as a unique creature, indefinable. To fantasize that one lives many times and many different kinds of life is to say mythically that one contains everything and is always on the verge of leaving behind what one has been. But I would not press the point. On the other hand, the idea of the distinctiveness of the human race is strongly present in Greek thought. I refer not only to Aristotle's assertion that a human being is not "a beast or a god" (I:2, p. 55), but also to the chorus in *Antigone*, which announces the ambiguous dignity of man by delineating his distinctiveness—"Many the wonders but nothing walks stranger than man" (Sophocles, line 332)—and then amplifies the thought by reference to human creativity in the face of needs and perils but also in the name of adventure. Still, human species distinctiveness does not entail individual distinctiveness.

DEMOCRATIC INDIVIDUALISM IN ATHENIAN THOUGHT AND PRACTICE

Even if the idea of individual uniqueness in an existentialist sense may not appear in Greek thought, democratic individualism was practiced in Athens, anachronistic though it may sound to say so, especially because formal individual rights were not as established as they were later to be. I wish to mention a few moments that illustrate aspects of the normative doctrine that all people—at least all citizens—count or matter apart from their roles, functions, or place in society. Such manifestations of individualism usually incurred the dismay of philosophical observers but the applause of politicians. This essay devotes what may seem a disproportionate amount of space to Greek democracy, more in practice than in doctrine, in order to reinforce the thesis that individualism is entwined with democracy and only with it. When I come to individualism in the United States and its greatest student, Tocqueville, I can be briefer; much of the modern story is already told by a few ancient Greek thinkers, especially Plato. From our own experience, we are intimately familiar with individualism, democratic and antidemocratic, but Tocqueville helps us see it more roundedly. Then, when I take up a few of the contemporary critics of individualism, we can see that by being critics of individualism, they are perforce critics of democracy, whether they mean to be or not.

The essential nature of democratic individualism is nicely summarized by Aristotle in the *Politics*. He says that there are two basic principles of democracy. The first (though not in importance) is political equality: All citizens should rule and be ruled in turn, and the majority should prevail. The second is that "a man should live as he likes." [All Aristotle quotations come from *Politics* VI (2):1317a–b, p. 260.] Aristotle indicates that the second principle is embedded in popular sentiment; the people say that living as one likes is "the privilege of a freeman, since, on the other hand, not to live as a man likes is the mark of a slave." From the ideal of living as one likes is derived "the claim of men to be ruled by none, if possible, or if this is impossible, to rule and be ruled in turns." Individual freedom is a stronger passion than even political equality. Freedom is loved for its own sake, whereas political equality is accepted as necessary to the preservation of freedom. There is no doubt, however, that the standing that political equality gives every citizen permeates his feeling and thinking to such an extent that all the relations in life, especially his dealings with noncitizens, tend to undergo a democratic transformation. Any citizen can say, "I want to be free to try everything, so let me move out of my present role, function, or place." The restless movement of democratic individuals is driven by this sentiment. Freedom pushes all sorts of equality, and equality guides all sorts of freedom.

Compressed in Aristotle's few sentences is the democratic insistence that unless one lives as one likes, one is reduced to one's assigned function and thus frozen in it. One's place should not define oneself exhaustively. Furthermore, although living by rules is imperative, even the arrangement by which each democratic citizen shares in making and enforcing those rules does not completely efface the odium of external constraint. Democracy is second-best freedom; benign anarchy is best. A loose-textured democracy, a political and legal style of tolerance and leniency, is the most commendable compromise. And living as one likes includes letting live, acknowledging that others, one's equals, must be allowed to live as they like, free of imposition or oppression.

I begin with Aristotle's apparently neutral summary of democratic sentiment, rather than Pericles' renowned Funeral Oration in Thucydides' *The Peloponnesian*

War, because Pericles' project of imperial greatness frames his characterization of democratic culture in such a way as to make that culture instrumental to the project. Near the beginning of his speech, he says that his questions are "under what form of government our greatness grew, out of what national habits it sprang" (Thucydides, II:36, p. 108). Whatever people may have thought and felt, Pericles subordinates them to the purposes of society and thus displaces individuals from the center of democratic concern. The project of imperial greatness obviously requires large sacrifices in life and wealth beyond those involved in defending individuals and their society. There seems little doubt that imperialism enriched the Athenian demos and made democracy more democratic by subsidizing the citizenship of the poor. Pericles sees nothing exploitative of the demos in the imperialism that makes it less poor. Yet a well-treated instrument is still an instrument. In a later speech given after "their land had now been twice laid waste; and war and pestilence at once pressed heavy upon them" (II:59, p. 120), he mitigates the instrumentalism. He says that "national greatness is more for the advantage of private citizens, than any individual well-being coupled with public humiliation. A man may be personally ever so well off, and yet if his country be ruined he must be ruined with it; whereas a flourishing commonwealth always affords chances of salvation to unfortunate individuals" (II:60, p. 121). It is noteworthy that a leader in a democracy must make the effort to yoke the interest of society (howsoever defined) to the interest of individuals. This rhetorical gesture pays obeisance to democratic individualism. Nonetheless, Pericles must appeal to non- and anti-individualist considerations to carry the real burden of his plea: a sense of group honor and an almost mystically erotic attachment to the city. He thought the demos could be more strongly persuaded by such undemocratic considerations. The purest political democracy that ever existed was, in spite of all, grossly impure in its democratic spirit. (That is always true of a democracy.)

Undeniably, a number of formulations in Pericles' speech show pride in the freedom of everyday life in Athens and the opportunity that the democracy afforded for individual enhancement and aspirations, and pride as well in the equal protection of the law extended to all citizens regardless of wealth and social standing. Despite the instrumentalization that permeates Pericles' words, he does voice many of the feelings and attitudes inherent in the everyday practice of democratic individualism, not only in Athens but also in modern democratic circumstances. But the story of democratic individualism in the first and purest political democracy that ever existed does not end there. For thought about democratic individualism in ancient Greece, we owe the most to Plato, who is both the greatest observer and the most perceptive, if not the harshest, critic of democracy. When I say that he is the greatest observer, I do not mean to imply that his perspective is solely external. He seems to have caught the mentality of democratic citizens from the inside, despite his privilege and his distaste. (The same goes more or less for Thucydides.)

In Book 8 of the *Republic*, Plato (through the character Socrates) writes comparatively about various types of soul and types of city. The tone is not neutral, but it is not merely polemical, either. It does not matter for our purposes that the structural analogy between soul and city, on which his analysis rests, perhaps raises more problems than it settles, or that it is so fluid that Plato's observations about individual souls are sometimes about the cultural tendencies of whole cities and vice versa. What emerges is a striking depiction of what it means to be a democratic individual in some main aspects, what feelings and attitudes inhere in the effort to be and live like one. As later with Aristotle, the key to democracy is everyone's love of freedom, where freedom is defined as a condition in which "a man may say and do what he likes" (Plato, *Republic*, VIII:557b, p. 311). It is to the philosopher's advantage to study democracy because there alone will the observer (who may happen to be, like Plato, an antidemocratic reformist designer of polities) find a "complete assortment of [individual] constitutions" (VIII:557d, p. 311). The widest spectrum of human beings is found in democracy because people take advantage of the opportunity to live as they like. This means their lives unfold in accordance with their diverse inclinations and wishes—perhaps we could say in accordance, if only indirectly, with their uniqueness or at least distinctiveness. Plato claims not to be as charmed by the spectacle of diversity as he says that people of questionable taste (especially democratic citizens) are likely to be. But he does not deny the power of democracy to instruct the observer in a way that other types of polity—all of them built on strictness, suppression, stratification, exclusion, and unyielding habituation—can never do. The implication, of course, is that even those who choose to live against the spirit of democracy need take almost no trouble to disguise that fact. Democracy accommodates even those who despise it—within limits that are very broad. It is not an accident that Athens was the capital city of philosophers, who are often most in need of tolerance and who are more likely than many others to be appalled aesthetically by democracy.

When we read the *Republic*, we see that Plato's reflections on democracy are bifurcated. He analyzes the causes of the emergence of democracy from the oligarchic rule of the rich and the causes of the degeneration of democracy into tyranny. The key to both causal patterns is class struggle: first, the successful effort of the many poor, the demos, to throw off the cruel oppression of oligarchic rule, and then, when democracy is entrenched and prone to disturb the rich in their privilege, the successful effort to enlist a strong-man, a tyrant, to put the rich down, with a consequent loss of freedom for all, the demos included. When Plato writes about the struggle between rich and poor, he posits the poor as the great majority and as a single-minded political force intent only on unjust economic gain. There is no democratic individualism involved. But when Plato writes about established democracy in its regular suspension of coercive class struggle, in periods during which the people remain unswayed by self-interested agitators, he provides an unsurpassed glimpse of democratic individualism. The subject is not the demos as an undifferentiated mass, but as an aggregation of souls, each trying to be itself. Here I deal with this part of Plato's analysis.

For Plato in the *Republic*, democracy is the scene of human diversity because the love of freedom is a rejection of inhibition. Freedom is often license or at least is always on the verge of turning into license, but this does not mean, at its best, wickedness toward others. Living as one likes tends to mean living for the gratification of one's numerous uncultivated and ill-disciplined appetites and desires. There is a pervasive wish, however, that life be a spectacle, full of color, motion, speed, noise, violence, and novelty, and that one's own life partake of these qualities. (In Plato's eyes, democracy is childish or perhaps childlike.) Underneath the surface diversity, common urges rule. But these common urges are nevertheless shaped differently by each person. Indeed, each person is an "epitome of the lives of many" (VIII:561e, p. 317). Plato discerns the restlessness in each person that is indistinguishable from perpetual experimentation. Democratic citizens play at life; all the major social roles are assumed and then dropped as if they were theatrical roles. The person is now self-indulgent, now ascetic; now athletic, now idle; even a philosopher now and then; occasionally he plays the role of active citizen or warrior or businessman. Plato does not say that the reason for such restlessness or experimentation is the sense that no role seems to fill out the yearnings of the soul or is felt as finally adequate to the soul's largeness; nor, alternatively, that people believe that only when they break out of themselves and do or say something out of character and unpredictable are they on the road to becoming new to themselves. It may be that only the attainment of the metaphysical vision of the Good (the cause and measure of the "beautiful and right" in all things, VII:517b–c, p. 257) measures up to anyone's soul, but Plato leaves no doubt that only a rare soul can attain such a vision. The remedy he prescribes for restlessness or perpetual experimentation is a simplicity of life for most people that is marked by an underdeveloped sense of self and hence a trained inability to look at oneself as from the outside.

Plato is certainly not amused by another aspect of democratic individualism. The spirit of democratic freedom encourages each person not only to play many roles in the course of his life because no role is as large as the soul, but also to reverse roles. When roles that usually define people exhaustively and in a starkly contrastive manner are exchanged, such reversal shows that the individual behind the role matters more than the role, and that anyone is capable of doing just about anything. Versatility is the sign of individualism. Democracy "would have subjects who are like rulers, and rulers who are like subjects" (VIII:562d, p. 319). Notice this is not quite the same as ruling and being ruled in turn, which means that each takes his turn in office and when not in office obeys magistrates with a perfect sense that they are to be obeyed just because of their offices. Rather, subjects are always citizens whose obedience is never forgetful of their rulership, and rulers are not really rulers but merely temporary and dependent office holders. Ruling is assimilated to obeying and obeying to ruling. There is no chasm between holding and not holding office. Human authority has no mystique; the individual is all. Plato's bemused satire goes so far as to claim that democratic citizens see no necessity in ruling or being ruled at all, if they do not feel like it; and even no necessity to "go to war when the rest go to war, or to be at peace," unless they are so disposed (VIII:557e, p 312).

The reversal of roles, which is the same as the permeability of all roles, extends to some of the principal relationships in everyday life. When certain roles are reversed, "anarchy" (what I have called benign anarchy) appears to take hold: "young and old are all alike" (VIII:563a, p. 319). When young and old are alike, children instruct their fathers and students their teachers. Youth is assimilated to age and age to youth.

From Plato's critical perspective, there is worse yet. Usually inferior people claim equality with their superiors. The superiors accede, but they do not in turn lower themselves. Democracy dispenses "a sort of equality to equals and unequals alike" (VIII:558c, p. 312). (Unequals means superiors.) Of course, the most blatant example of this leveling upward is granting all free-born males of the right lineage equal political power as citizens, even though it is obvious that some people are wiser or more energetic or more virtuous than others. Such canceling of hierarchy is, after all, what democracy is and what allows, to begin with, individualism to develop and become infused with a tendency to regard all roles as impermanent, exchangeable, or improvable. Democracy democratizes everything; and that process includes encouraging the lowly to rise out of place, and not necessarily or even mainly to subordinate those who once lorded it over them. Where individualism is powerful, democracy cannot mean leveling or egalitarian sameness. The lowly, too, just want to be free enough to live as they like and not be told that their self is their place and that they must stay there. The last extremes are reached when women claim equal liberty with men to act as they please and become what they want; when resident aliens and even strangers regard themselves and are regarded as equal to citizens; when freed slaves act with impunity like full citizens; and when "many persons, although they have been sentenced to death or exile, just stay where they are and walk about the world—the gentleman parades like a hero, and nobody sees or cares" (VIII:558a, p. 312). The guilty are not defined by one bad act and the innocent are sometimes strongly tempted to do wrong.

All the roles of subordination, whether ascribed roles, inherited roles, or even roles that seem to have their basis in nature or moral necessity, are blurred and therefore played or abandoned at will. Or, at least, there is a readiness to play or abandon a role at will. In general, the person is always struggling against the confinement of definition for the sake of becoming an individual. Because of democracy's remarkable leniency toward different natures, even the animals are much freer in a democracy than elsewhere. The line between human privilege and animal servitude is blurred. The "horses and asses have a way of marching along with all the rights and dignities of freemen; and they will run at anybody who comes in their way if he does not leave the road clear for them; and all things are just ready to burst with liberty" (VIII:563c–d, p. 320).

Perhaps the most interesting manifestation of democratic individualism that Plato mentions is the tendency of untutored people to philosophize. In the *Republic*, Plato painfully admits that many lower-class people in various trades crave philosophy or at least are strongly attracted to its prestige. They are like "prisoners running out of prison into a sanctuary" when "they take a leap out of their trades into philosophy" (VI:495d–e, p. 230). Alas, only a rare individual can escape from the prison (or cave) of an un-philosophical life. The mismatch between philosophy and the lowly must engender only "sophisms captivating to the ear, having nothing in them . . . akin to true wisdom" (VI:496a, p. 231). But even in Plato's rebuke there is some mild though unspoken praise. After all, the restlessness of individualism need not ever turn in philosophy's direction—unless there is some intrinsic bond between them. The wish to take hold of oneself and be thoughtful about one's metaphysical (not sociopolitical and not necessarily religious) place in existence is not smothered in a democracy as it is likely to be in other types of city. In Plato's *Apology*, Socrates engages with artisans, not only with politicians and poets, as he goes about seeking wisdom and endeavoring to decipher the oracle's answer that no one is wiser than he is (21a, p. 25). Of course, the artisans, too, disappoint him, but not worse than the two other categories, who tend to be socially more respected and honored. "I found that the men whose reputation for wisdom stood highest were nearly the most lacking in it, while others who were looked down on as common people were much more intelligent" (22a, pp. 26–27).

The sketch of democratic individualism in ancient Athens and specifically of the relation between philosophizing and democratic individualism cannot end without taking Socrates a little more fully into account. He enriches the democratic battle against imposed definitions of the self by emphasizing self-examination. Even though thinking about one's existence from a philosophical perspective is not the same thing as self-examination, the two inner processes may cooperate with each other. The Delphic injunction "know yourself" was not addressed solely to Athens, but it seems that Socrates of Athens is the first to expect all people to adhere to it and thus to want to know, if only minimally, who they are. Such knowledge cannot mean to know one's role or function or place in society, but rather to have the beginnings of an idea of what a human life is about. The highest wisdom is knowing what it means to excel in doing what human beings are "naturally capable of," doing what is most appropriately human (Plato, *Apology*, 20a–b, p. 24). Socrates searches for this wisdom and claims never to find it. At least, however, he is aware of his ignorance, unlike all those who let their practical expertise in a line of work inflate the estimate they make of their own wisdom about human things. Still, it is noteworthy that practically everyone in Athens gives thought to the subject matter of wisdom, however faultily.

It is not clear that Socrates expects everyone to undertake the practice of self-examination. It may be that he is alone or almost alone in subjecting himself to his own perpetual self-interrogation, to live by a silent internal dialogue about life. But he does suggest that if one can put up with being examined by someone else, especially a self-examining one like Socrates or some other (if there are others), then one can be disabused of pretended self-knowledge. When ignorance about the most important issue is mistaken for wisdom, self-hurt and harm to others must follow.

Socratic individualism consists in taking oneself seriously as an object of existential and moral inquiry. His general tendency is to believe that greater self-knowledge must increase one's ignorance about the highest development of individuality but, in compensation, will increase one's moderation. Moderation is increased when susceptibility to the thralldom of conformity is reduced. More moderate people here and there can set examples of restraint. Socrates is famous (at least to us) for his dissent on legal procedure as a member of the council of the Assembly and for his refusal to obey a command from the Thirty to assist in the capture of a putatively innocent man. Socratic individualism therefore includes a willingness, though tinged by a pained reluctance, to elevate one's own moral judgment above the state's, even when the state is deemed acceptable in form. Socrates starts the practice of individualist resistance to injustice perpetrated by the state and permitted or encouraged by an intimidated or a conformist and self-inconsistent people. His notion of what it means to be an individual, to be oneself, therefore transcends the democratic individualism that Plato describes as the democratic wish not to be defined exhaustively by role or function or place and the consequent wishes to play many roles, to allow roles to be reversed, and to see people raised above their due. Socratic individualism, then, is not expressive. It is in fact anti-expressive. It consists of a struggle with oneself to avoid delusion, no matter what others think. One courts both dislike and the appearance of deviance. One is oneself mainly in the sense that one does not spend one's life in an energetic but conformist imitation of life. Thoughtfulness produces inhibition; by not acting reflexively one may, oddly enough, be taken nearer to oneself.

It may very well be that democratic individualism in its normal condition of role fluidity, as Plato describes it, would be for most people an indispensable preliminary to Socratic individualism. It probably will not get there, but it may be closer than any other way of being. After all, what is more likely to make people tired of roles than a steady disposition to see social activity as role-playing and seeing no role as adequate to oneself? By loosening every definition of identity, and therefore making one's selfhood elude one's own grasp, everyday democratic individualism may help to induce greater appetite for self-knowledge, a greater detachment or at least a greater distance from all roles, and thus a greater tentativeness and thereby a greater moderation. With greater moderation, one's capacity to inflict harms is somewhat reduced in comparison to the harmful efficacy of unexamined lives. An individual stops being a puppet (at least occasionally) and stops being transfixed by the puppet show. And although Socratic self-examination is not clearly expected of everyone, even though willingness to examine and be examined by others is urged as within everyone's reach, later on secularized Protestantism sets up self-examination as a democratic expectation for everyone. Examination and self-examination are not the same as Catholic confession, in which one recites one's sins to a figure of unquestioned authority, but no doubt Catholic Christianity got people used to talking in earnest about themselves. In any case, the Socratic suggestion is that thoughtfulness about oneself as a soul or self, rather than as a social role or function or place-keeper, helps to complete one's experience and perhaps rescues one from the inevitable frustrations that all experience throws up. Frustrations are felt more acutely when expectations are high—made higher by democracy itself. Democratic individuals need a philosophical element in their lives more than other people do. It is entirely fitting that, as Plato observes, the lower classes have a craving for philosophizing.

ANTIDEMOCRATIC INDIVIDUALISM IN ATHENS

There was in Athens not only democratic individualism but also, in reaction, antidemocratic individualism, in doctrine and practice. By antidemocratic individualism in the Greek setting, I do not mean the self-assertion of the well-born when such self-assertion suits the rules of one's position, one's inherited aristocratic role. Of course every social role requires individual interpretation; living an aristocratic life, for example, is not like following a recipe routinely. Still, for aristocrats, one's role is one's world; and the rules of their station constitute a barrier between the aristocratic class and all other classes, as well as a project that may tax their talents and fulfill their self-conception. Aristocrats may cross every line but that does not mean that they abandon their role. In contrast, antidemocratic individualism is shown by those who are loyal only to themselves as individual selves, who assert themselves defiantly, and who, when they cross lines, do so without a sense that they are taking their whole caste or class with them. They are not likely to come from the lower classes; they must have unusual ambitions and define themselves as individual resisters to democratic equality. Their passion to be superior is stimulated by the prevailing commitment to equality, while the sight of many people straining to resist definition in order to be themselves sanctions their will to succeed in a similar effort but on a much grander scale. They are guided by an inflamed imagination.

Greek history gives at least one case of an antidemocratic individual in action and one sustained doctrinal exposition of antidemocratic individualism. Furthermore, certain formulations by political speakers about the conduct of intercity relations are powerfully suggestive about the nature of antidemocratic individualism. The supreme antidemocratic individual in action is Alcibiades; the quasi-theorist is the character Callicles in Plato's *Gorgias*; and the speakers include Alcibiades and those anonymous others who defend or condemn Athenian imperialism.

I begin with Callicles, who is known to us as a character in Plato's dialogue. Socrates is his adversary, but a Socrates somewhat more somber and self-confident than the Socrates of Plato's *Apology*. In the course of exploring the nature of rhetoric and its power in life, especially public life, Callicles justifies individual self-assertion. Really to be an individual is to be restlessly acquisitive, especially of power, for the sake of oneself. Callicles does seem to endorse the restless acquisitiveness of Athens as a whole, as if to imply an analogy between individuals and cities and also to imply a desirable consonance between the nature of a city and the nature of the citizens who live in it. But these implications are not worked out. What is interesting is that certain individuals have no regard for the success or failure of their city, except to the degree that these individuals need the city as a base for their own self-aggrandizement. If Pericles instrumentalizes people for the sake of the city, Callicles does the reverse—but not on behalf of every individual as an equal of all others, as with democratic individualism. Cities exist for the sake of a few individuals, but those individuals are not a class or faction. Self-assertive individuals in their competition may even be at cross purposes. Who are they? Those who are the most intelligent, courageous, and energetic (Plato, *Gorgias*, 491b, p. 60). How should they behave? They should take more than their share. "A man who is going to live a full life must allow his desires to become as mighty as may be and never repress them. When his passions have come to full maturity, he must be able to serve them through his courage and intelligence and gratify every fleeting desire as it comes into his heart" (491e–492a, p. 61). How does Callicles vindicate his doctrine? He maintains that it is a matter of right that these few should rule and exploit the rest. The right is by nature. Equal morality is moral only by convention—the morality of the numerous weak-willed, timid, and comparatively unintelligent. Their morality is merely self-protection against a few superiors (483b–c, p. 51). But an honest perception of nature everywhere shows that life is a struggle in which not all survive and only a few prevail. "But my opinion is that nature herself reveals it to be only just and proper that the better man should lord it over his inferior: it will be the stronger over the weaker. Nature, further, makes it quite clear in a great many instances that this is the true state of affairs, not only in the other animals, but also in whole states and communities" (483d, pp. 51–52). Nature is the standard, not convention or man-made rules. By that standard, superior talent should not be impeded by artificial obstacles. That would be unnatural, and society—certainly democratic society—is unnatural.

The oddities are two: first, Callicles' doctrine as a code for individuals would never have come into being except in a democracy, and second, Callicles is repeatedly called by Socrates a lover of democracy. For the study of democratic individualism, the first point is more relevant: Democracy engenders individualism, not only democratic but also antidemocratic. Does it matter more in human history that antidemocratic individualism, whether of one kind or several, is individualist than that it is antidemocratic? Perhaps. By reaction to itself, democracy elevates the human mind by leading it to see through and outside society, but not religiously. The trouble is that Callicles applauds tyrants and imperialists. He is willing to see democracy destroyed in his own city or by one city that conquers others.

This trouble becomes glaring when we encounter in Thucydides' *The Peloponnesian War* the speeches and deeds of Alcibiades and the speeches of those who defend or condemn Athenian imperialism. Alcibiades, whose native talents made him capable of the greatest contribution to the well-being of his city, acts as if he were above the city, not merely as a tyrant stands above it, but as an individual for whom nothing matters but his own—what? It is easy to say pleasure or pride, arrogance or hubris. All these designations would be correct. But there is something more. When he speaks in 416 B.C. in support of the Athenian invasion of Sicily, some of his strangeness comes through doctrinally. He strikes a new note. To be sure, he is advocating a policy for the city, not for particular individuals in it (as Callicles does). But he turns the city into one person. I do not think that he is confused; he knows better than anyone that a city is not a person. Yet he wants the city to guide itself as an individual of inflamed imagination, like himself, would do. He finally wins the debate (with disastrous results for Athens in Sicily), although not for the reasons he gives to sustain his position. As Thucydides makes clear, those who voted for his plan to conquer Sicily had a mixture of reasons. Some reasons were ostensibly public, but most were private, such as a taste for adventure, or self-interested, such as a desire for wages at the moment and the capture of "a never-ending fund of pay for the future" (Thucydides VI:24, p. 373). Democratic individuals learn from antidemocratic individuals to use their city as if indeed it were one person, but an antidemocratic one, a tyrant to other cities. In using their democratic city, they reverse the longstanding custom whereby other cities, including domestic tyrannies, use their citizens.

Alcibiades, however, has special reasons, and their essence is that the very idea of limitation is ruinous. He turns Greek thought inside out. It is hard to resist the feeling that he is projecting onto the city an outlook on life that suits him best as an antidemocratic individual in a democratic city. He is asking the city to imitate him—not merely reward him—in his sovereign disregard of limitation, just as, to begin with, his egotism was transmuted into individualism by the democratic culture of his city. There is always something deranged in imperialism, whether undertaken by a democracy or some other type of polity. In any case, imperialism is in its very nature antidemocratic because it treats outsiders as if they were lesser human beings who had no valid moral claims or only minor ones. But there is something peculiarly individualist or singular in Athenian imperialism as Alcibiades conceives it. Athens should be, in relation to other cities, individualist, not merely one city among many, and all with the same motives. Athenian imperialism is different from other imperialisms because Athens is different from all other polities. It is not only strongly individuated, it is individualist, but antidemocratically so. Alcibiades says that "we cannot fix the exact point at which our empire shall stop" (Thucydides VI:18, p. 370). Any imperialism will be disposed to think and act in that spirit, whatever it may say. It will have, up to a far point, the dynamism of insatiability. But Alcibiades is willing to go beyond insatiability and be candid about it. In his candor, he reaches for an idea that exceeds the extremism of the usual imperialism. He says that "by sinking into inaction, the city, like everything else, will wear itself out, and its skill in everything decay; while each fresh struggle will give it fresh experience" (VI:18, p. 371). This view may remind us of that of Callicles, but it is enhanced to the point of a perverse sublimity. Perpetual movement is for purposes that surpass even inordinate self-regard and that display an intoxication that can disappear only after disaster. Alcibiades is teaching an ultra-imperialism and using himself as the model. His life shows an extreme form of antidemocratic individualism and he wants it to be a model for a democratic imperialism that is not only antidemocratic in itself but is also eventually self-destructive. The glory of Alcibiades and Athens ends in premature violent death or in defeat—but lives in memory forever after.

Those who earlier in Thucydides' text explain or denounce Athenian imperialism also speak like Callicles, as if they, too, see Athens as unique in the coloration of its imperialism, even if not quite as in love with action for the sake of the experience of action as Alcibiades wants it to be. In the first congress of Sparta's allies, held at Sparta in 432 B.C. on the eve of Sparta's commencement of

hostilities against Athens, the Athenian delegation there on other business volun-
teers to speak, not to pretend that their imperialism is not imperialism but to justify
it. Their Corinthian adversaries have just accused them of being limitless: "they
were born into the world to take no rest themselves and to give none to others"
(Thucydides I:70, p. 41). In rebuttal, the Athenians use the language of individual
motivation to encompass the behavior of cities: fear, interest, and honor are their
principal motives, as they are allegedly everyone else's. (In these descriptions,
which rest on an ontological analogy rather than a Platonist structural one, there
is a two-way traffic between the individual as the model for the city and the city
for the individual.) What stands out in the speech is their invocation of a certain
law. They do not say whether the law is natural or conventional, but they claim
that "it has always been the law that the weaker should be subject to the stronger"
(I:76, p. 44). This is much like the formulation that Callicles uses in expounding
what I have been calling antidemocratic individualism. Later on, in 416 B.C., the
Athenians justify their conquest of the neutral island-city of Melos by claiming
that "Of the gods we believe, and of men we know, that by a necessary law of
their nature they rule wherever they can ... [this law will] exist for ever after us"
(V:105, p. 353). Thus, the law of limitless self-assertion (whether the self of individuals or groups) is built into the nature not only of humanity but also and
most importantly of what is immortal and above humanity. No higher justification
can be envisaged. But I think that it is fair to say that individualism has coached
the Athenians in this manner of thinking. What resembles candor may be only a
convenient rationalization.

PLATO'S CRITIQUE OF INDIVIDUALISM

To repeat: Individualism will emerge only in association with democracy and will
remain entwined with it. In theory and practice, individualism is committed to the
idea that individuals matter apart from role, function, or place in society. Society
exists for individuals, not the other way around. With these notions, individualism
becomes either democratic (egalitarian) or antidemocratic (restricted). Democratic
individualism rests on the further idea that all, not just a few, people matter as
individuals because no one is exhaustively definable by role, function, or place.
All people exceed definition, and each is a world, and a distinctive one at that. This
sense of indefinability shows itself in a readiness to live many lives in one lifetime,
to play many roles, to see roles reversed, and to see the lowly raised to equality with
the rest. In contrast, antidemocratic individualism rests on the notion that only a
select few deserve the opportunities of individualism, and society ideally exists for
the purpose of allowing them to develop themselves to the fullest and then to assert
themselves with impunity, typically but not exclusively at the expense of others. It
is no surprise that all these premises and the results that ensue when they are acted
on (in varying degrees of deliberateness) should arouse opposition from a wide
range of critics. In the Greek world, Plato, as I have said, is the greatest critic, as
he is one of the main sources of our knowledge, of Athenian individualism in both

its democratic and antidemocratic varieties. Insofar as he has a doctrine—and if he does not, he surely has a fairly persistent tendency of sentiment—he may be called the theoretical founder of anti-individualism, just as he is, for most of his readers, the most powerful of antidemocrats. This is not to say that he is favorably disposed to any actual polity (no matter its kind), even though in the *Republic* he ranks the main kinds. Every actual polity refuses to allow philosophical wisdom any share of power; much less does it give such wisdom its due, which is absolute power.

Democracy is ranked below philosophical monarchy, warrior aristocracy, and plutocracy, and above only tyranny. Plato provides numerous and complex reasons for his ranking. Every actual city, whatever its form, is equally remote from philosophy, but the superiority of one form to another lies in its proximity to the character structure that is the precondition of the sort of philosophy (and only that sort) whose methods and teachings do not tend toward the destruction of the city (Plato, *Republic*, VI:497d, p. 233). Plato says his standard is the greatest general (mutually compatible) happiness of all groups in society (IV:420b, p. 129; V:466a, p. 192). He gives many indications of believing that most people everywhere are unhappy, whatever their status or wealth. The *Republic* is an effort to delineate a society where people are less unhappy and indeed positively happy. Plato's strategy is to make people in society less developed and less experienced, less covetous and less materialist, less self-conscious and less mindful of themselves as selves, less aware of differences and varieties that exist elsewhere. Even those who are allowed to pursue philosophy are steered away from argument for the sake of argument and probably would never be allowed to visit a democracy to learn about the variety of human nature.

The just society is simple, static, orderly, harmonious. It contains no restlessness or vague longings. It disallows works of the literary imagination because they nurture passions and desires. It strives to shrink everyone's ego. It assigns everyone a role, place, and function, and not only induces contentment in such boundedness but sustains it by means of the feeling that one is exhaustively defined by role, function, and place. Only the philosopher exceeds social identity. Everyone is given work, and the work fulfills them, partly because they are left comparatively undeveloped and hence more easily fulfilled and partly because they are given an opportunity to do something that is socially valuable and exercises whatever talents they have been allowed to develop. The mind is fed only wholesome food. Everyone exists for the city, not the other way around. Although the just city stands in contrast with all actual cities, the sharpest contrast is obviously with democracy.

This is the case because the just city is systematically against what we are calling individualism, whether democratic or antidemocratic. In a democracy, the greater number move out of place and presume to equality when they are unsuited to that status, while some few presume to superiority when they have no legitimate warrant for their self-estimation. Everyone is restless; everyone is ill-defined; people try to fill themselves up but never feel satisfied. No one's mind is focused where it should be: on the best contribution each can make to the well-being of all. When excited by itself, or seduced or corrupted by unscrupulous orators and false philosophers, the multitude becomes a "beast" (Plato, *Republic*, VI:493a–c, p. 227), capable of monstrous deeds of injustice. No individuals remain when a multitude is aroused and becomes a single-minded force for wickedness. Their leaders are themselves relentless monsters who cynically manipulate the people and thus ultimately instrumentalize them for purposes that go against even the most practical interests of the people. Empire turns into weakness and class struggle into a wretched tyranny.

Above all, the *Republic* teaches that it is delusion to believe that anyone but a genuine philosopher can be an individual. The soul of everyone but a philosopher is so torn by inner conflict waged against one's reason by the desires and appetites, in collusion with the sheer disposition to assert oneself in ambition and anger, that the unphilosophical person becomes the helpless, passive victim of his own energies, no more than the scene of a conflict over which he has no control. Not being a unity under the governance of reason, one ceases being a unit, a whole and single-minded agent. Only a genuine philosopher can escape this fate; only he or she is both a unity and a unit—a person who is capable of being a self, a harmonious soul. At such an elevation, individual distinctiveness counts for nothing. A philosophical soul has no merely personal identity, only an impersonal and self-obliterating communion with a higher reality, and all social roles and functions and places become to the mind's eye mere shadows of the highest reality. As Aristotle in the *Nicomachean Ethics* later put the Platonist point: "[trained and philosophically directed] intelligence far surpasses everything else in power and value. One might even regard it as each man's true self, since it is the controlling and better part. It would, therefore, be strange if a man chose not to live his own life but someone else's" (X:1178a, p. 291).

Many of the main elements of democratic individualism, antidemocratic individualism, and the critique of individualism as such are found in the writings of Plato, with valuable hints from Thucydides and Aristotle among other Greek writers. We learn from Plato especially that democracy and individualism are inseparable and that to think poorly of individualism is necessarily to think poorly of democracy. The picture of course changes appreciably when the next democracy after Athens—namely, the United States—comes into view. But to spend some time with Athens is part of the preparation for thinking about individualism (whether democratic or antidemocratic) and its critics in the modern age. It is a tremendous leap from ancient Athens to the United States. But the resemblances—at least to the susceptible mind—are not insignificant.

It was Nietzsche who yoked Athens and the United States together in order to present a serious indictment of the latter. [1] Nietzsche loved the Greeks. His philosophy is unimaginable without a Greek inspiration. He said little about the United States, but because it was the only democracy in his world, he had to

---

[1]I grant willingly that Nietzsche is rarely of one mind about any human phenomenon.

dislike and fear it. In Book V of *The Gay Science*, added five years later to the first edition of 1882, he produces a striking section on the individualizing effects of democracy. (All Nietzsche quotations below are from Section 356, pp. 302–3.) Under the ironic title "How things will become ever more 'artistic' in Europe," he suggests that in democratic cultures, established or on the way, people give up the faith that the work they do is what they were predestined to do. "A certain cocky faith" becomes ever more prominent: "the Athenian faith that first becomes noticeable in the Periclean age, the faith of Americans today" and that is spreading to Europe. What is that faith? "The individual becomes convinced that he can do just about everything and *can manage almost any role*." The result of that conviction is that "everybody experiments with himself, improvises, makes new experiments, enjoys his experiments." And the further and most important result is that "all nature ceases and becomes art." After accepting this "*role faith*—an artist's faith, if you will," the Greeks "really became actors." Every job or vocation turned into a role that could be played; but that also meant the roles could be dropped and replaced by other roles. If everything is a role, no fixed identity remains, no sense remains that each person is exhaustively defined by the work he does and that he was born to do it and can do nothing else. Nietzsche's obvious implication is that Americans are that way, too.

Nietzsche is enraptured by the spectacle he deplores. "It is thus that the maddest and most interesting ages of history always emerge, when the 'actors,' *all* kinds of actors, become the real masters." But the costs, in Nietzsche's estimate, are immense. Great projects for the future are aborted because they must rest on "the faith that man has value and meaning only insofar as he is *a stone in a great edifice*; and to that end he must be *solid* first of all, a 'stone' and above all not an actor." A democrat must say, however, that to accept being as solid as a stone is to accept being a merely useful means to ends beyond one's own, and thus a slave. The ignominy of slavery comes not from abuse alone but also from the mere fact of coerced submission as an owned being. A self-consistent democracy—not that there has ever been one—will never inflict such total extinction of individualism on anyone.

And yet the highest Nietzschean imperative, to become what one is, captures a good part of the meaning of individualism. As Nietzsche says later in *Ecce Homo*, becoming what one is paradoxically requires that one does not have "the faintest notion *what* one is" (1969 [1908], p. 254). One must forget and misunderstand oneself in order to reach one's highest potentiality. To lead a life is to lead many lives in succession, each life a new start and an unstable achievement. Isn't such an attitude, in some way, already incipiently present in all the role-playing intrinsic to democratic individualism? Some restlessness that is urgent but will probably never be satisfied—a yearning to find and become oneself? Doesn't the imperative in democracy of becoming what one is override everything else? In any case, let us notice that a thinker who loves Athens and hates and pities democracy shows that the way to understand democratic individualism in the modern age is to study first its ancient version in Athens.

TOCQUEVILLE AND DEMOCRATIC INDIVIDUALISM

I do not mean to say that the Greeks do all the work of thinking about individualism. Rather, they offer us the substantial beginnings. It is obvious that Athens and the United States are profoundly different. The most determined effort to assimilate one to the other must confront numerous obstacles, among them the impact of Christianity and capitalism on modern democracy. The fact remains, however, that Athens and the United States are the two purest democracies, for good and bad. And their examples show that where there is democracy, there will be individualism, both democratic and antidemocratic. To gain a broad vision of American democracy, the best guide is still Tocqueville. He has never been equaled as an observer of the culture of American democracy and, by extension, of modern democracy wherever it is established or strongly desired and struggled for. One of his concepts is individualism, a term he did not invent but helped to circulate widely. The heart of the matter for Tocqueville is what it was for Plato: democracy as the culture in which people think of themselves as individuals, not as members of society defined exhaustively by their role, function, or place.

Most of the generalizations about democracy and its bond with individualism that Plato formulates are present in Tocqueville's *Democracy in America*, which was published in two volumes in 1835 and 1840. Whereas Plato takes roughly 20 pages to tell his story, Tocqueville takes hundreds. The longer analysis has the advantage of much greater detail, but Tocqueville is so discursive that his book sustains some loss of conceptual power. He is also free of the rhetorical need to posit the city as the soul enlarged; and he is much more sober than Plato, though no less determined to generalize. One inestimable value of Tocqueville's analysis is the systematic comparison between Old World hereditary aristocracy and modern democracy, with the result that an alternative title of his book could almost be *Aristocracy in Europe*. He keeps his sights steadily fixed on aristocracies that exist or have recently existed, rather than interesting himself in hypothetical rule by politically disciplined philosophers.

Perhaps the main theoretical difference is that Plato believes the basic passion of democracy is (equal) freedom to live as one likes. Equality becomes an issue only after being free—not being a slave—is held dear. Living as one likes must mean, until antidemocratic individualism arises in reaction, that everyone is entitled to do so. But the craving is not to have everyone the same but to allow people to become themselves diversely. In democracy according to Plato's (and Aristotle's) conceptualization of Athenian democracy, freedom is prior to equality. Equality means all citizens vote equally in the Assembly and are equally eligible for offices; thus, the real force of equality, as I have said, is to protect everyone's freedom to live an unconstrained life to the fullest extent that is compatible with a like freedom for everyone else.

In contrast, Tocqueville holds, with some qualification, that in the United States equality (especially in the form of legal equality of social condition and equality of opportunity) is prior to freedom. Furthermore, Americans often appear to value freedom simply as instrumental to higher productivity and more wealth (Tocqueville 1954 [1840], II:2, ch. 14, p. 148). To be sure, they cherish freedom; they were politically free from the start; but Tocqueville's fear is that in the modern age, even if less fatalistically in the United States than in Europe, people will tend to accept equality under despotism rather than freedom under hierarchy, if the choice is forced on them or if they act in such a way as to force the choice on themselves (II:2, ch. 1, p. 103). He says chidingly that though democracies have "a natural taste for freedom," their passion for equality is " ardent, insatiable, incessant, invincible" (II:2, ch. 1, p. 102). Tocqueville calls his worst fear "democratic despotism": a condition in which state bureaucracies regulate every sphere and aspect of life, while retaining the forms of representative democracy. Their mission is to give security in possessions but above all to reassure people that powerful private individuals or small groups of them are not public usurpers or aggrandizers in violation of the spirit of equality.

Tocqueville may be right about the ranking of freedom and equality in modern democracy, although I think that the ranking is an open question that is not likely to find a conclusive answer. But if he is right, the explanation would lie in the impact of advanced capitalism on modern democracy. Athens was a market society and had gross disparities of wealth; but even with a vigorous, predatory imperialism, Athens' economy was not nearly as expansionist as modern capitalist economies are. If the love of social equality in modern times turns out to be indissociable from the love of wealth, as Tocqueville's analysis suggests (II:3, p. 240), then capitalism would be responsible. But of course there would be no dynamic capitalism unless the people wanted what it incessantly and innovatively gives. On the other hand, if only for the time being, and long after Tocqueville, advanced capitalism has suspended class warfare (domestically if not globally) of the sort that was always in the Athenian background and that surfaced on occasion to upset democratic political arrangements. It is a structural feature, though not always a cultural and psychological force, in Plato's account.

In any case, the threat of democratic despotism is by now only partly realized, though time seems to be on its side, at least as much in the United States as elsewhere. The bureaucratic supervision and regulation of human beings and the lives they lead is close and increases constantly. What is clear is that whatever the direct influence of Plato on Tocqueville, his analysis of democracy in the United States shows numerous similarities to the treatment of democracy in the *Republic*. Tocqueville confirms Plato; they both confirm our own observation, even though they may often regard what they observe with distaste and disdain, or at least with detachment. What does Tocqueville see? He sees the restless effort that everyone makes to change one's life now and then in order to find a way of living that comes closer to one's understanding of oneself as being more than any role; he also sees that roles are often reversed and that immemorial subordinates are raised to a level nearly equal. There is much less inequality between the sexes in the United States than in Europe, and the ease in relations between fathers and sons is so marked that one could say that democracy radically revises fatherhood and thus masculinity. Servants identify with their masters because their masters are not harsh and unbending like masters elsewhere. Servants can plausibly imagine themselves masters.

We have seen such fluidity of self and such role-playing and role-switching in Plato's characterization of Greek democracy. I have attributed this condition of life to a commitment to individualism, which I have defined as the belief that people are more than their roles, functions, and place in society. I know no other way of describing the essence of individualism. If I am right, then the fact that the concept of individualism does not seem to exist among the Greeks, or exists just barely, does not matter. Greek democracy manifested the basic everyday phenomena of individualism. Individualism follows when the equal claim of all to live as they like is honored without making everyone the same in all respects or leveling downward. The curious thing is that although Tocqueville speaks directly of individualism, his individualism does not include the phenomena of successive roles or lives within a life, role reversal, and leveling the condition of the role-player upward.

What is individualism, democratic individualism, as Tocqueville conceives it? He says that it is "a mature and calm feeling, which disposes each member of the community to sever himself from the mass of his fellows and to draw apart with his family and friends, so that after he has thus formed a little circle of his own, he willingly leaves society at large to itself" (Tocqueville 1954 [1840], II:2, ch. 2, p. 104). Individualism, Tocqueville makes clear, is not the same as egotism or selfishness, which is as old as humanity. No, individualism is of "democratic origin" (p. 104). Thus, individualism is a disposition to build a life for oneself that is one's own; it is a deliberate privatism. Negatively, such a life is a shelter from the enormous mass of one's equals who must not be allowed to press on each person in a society that lacks the barriers set up by the several classes in the old order. Positively, such a life is one's own creation, an expression of who one is, outwardly changeable and inwardly distinctive. By Tocqueville's conception, individualism comes down to the freedom of living as one likes, which means living for oneself and one's intimates. (It is not the literal isolation of a hermit's life.)

The deficiency in Tocqueville's conception is that he does not connect the various phenomena of personal fluidity and role permeability with individualism. That deficiency may not signify much; after all, Tocqueville presents these phenomena in a manner that is both general and vivid. Nonetheless, a conception of individualism that is too narrow denies it some features that many (not all) critics admire; confining it to privatism distorts it. One must grant, however, that a tendency to privatism is intrinsic to individualism, ancient and modern, which shows that it is inseparable from a self-conception formed independently of role, function, and place—a self-conception that defines individualism. Indeed, it is hard to see how such a self-conception could not result in the effort to build one's life on one's own terms. Only a few will ever make public life constitutive of themselves, except in occasional episodes. Privatism sponsors self-exploration, which is another term for personal fluidity and role permeability. The long and short of it is that to allow Tocqueville to assist us in understanding the bond between democracy and individualism we must study the whole picture he presents, and not just those few chapters that have the word individualism in the title (II:2, chs. 2–4, pp. 104–113).

There are other continuities between Plato and Tocqueville and hence between Athens and modern democracy. Resemblances include the widespread will to philosophize among the people, which Tocqueville sketches as the natural Cartesianism of Americans—a wish to think things through for oneself rather than accepting tradition and authority (Tocqueville 1954 [1840], II:I, ch.1, p. 4). Religion is revered, but rather than a religion of transmitted revelation, it is a "commonly received opinion" (II:1, ch. 2, p. 12). This natural Cartesianism, however, does not prevent that process of intimidation by which everyone is awed by the cumulative power of mass public sentiment, of the anonymous "they," even though one is able to stand up to one's face-to-face equals. Pride (or at least a lack of shame) in the physical presence of others gives way to a feeling of "insignificance and weakness" at the thought of the huge body of one's equals in society at large (II:1, ch. 2, p. 11). In Tocqueville's analysis, borne out by our experience, independence and intimidation are in continuous and sometimes invisible struggle within the souls of democratic individuals. I suppose what is remarkable is the intermittent and unexpected independence of mind that grapples speculatively with issues that go far beyond one's practical needs.

Has there been and is there antidemocratic individualism in the United States? Recurrent in Tocqueville's book is the idea that hereditary aristocracies sponsor the individualism of members of the nobility, though he does not apply the word individualism to them. Rather he praises their largeness of character, their initiatory and defensive power vis-à-vis central authority, and their self-reliance in the face of various cultural pressures. From the individualist perspective that I develop in this paper, what Tocqueville admires in aristocracy is not a self-conception that holds that a person is more than his or her role, function, and place in society. Rather, he admires the way in which aristocrats live up to their role and play it as if they were born to play it and could play no other. They may, they must, interpret their role, function, and place; they will perhaps practice eccentricity; a few may even abandon their position. But what they characteristically display is better not seen by us as individualism, even as antidemocratic individualism. Aristocrats do not say that society exists for individuals, even a few special individuals like themselves. They say instead, at the extreme, that society exists for their class or caste; they keep the traditional arrangements going; they matter above all as temporary occupants of positions in an order that is supposed to last indefinitely. Those beneath them must stay in their positions, too. Some aristocrats may avoid extreme class-centrism and rise to a view that sees empirical or religious worth in the hierarchical system. But they have no doubt that role and function and place transcend individuals in importance.

The democratic analogy to hereditary aristocracy is racial supremacy, at least in the United States. White people could rarely imagine themselves as nonwhite or even imagine themselves in a position comparable to that of nonwhites, because they could not recognize nonwhites as equal to themselves or even equally human.

Racism is perhaps the greatest democratic inconsistency of popular (as distinct from elitist) origin, the most complete failure of mutual recognition; there is no understanding modern slavery and other modern democratic atrocities without it. Toward the end of the first volume of *Democracy in America* (1954 [1835]), Tocqueville writes powerfully about the white race's tyranny. These pages (I, ch. 18, pp. 343–412) are full of sadness and foreboding: "although the law may abolish slavery, God alone can obliterate the traces of its existence" (p. 372). Racism is not an individualist but a group phenomenon; it is an extreme example of antidemocratic anti-individualism.

From our perspective, a clear case of antidemocratic individualism found in Tocqueville's analysis and more starkly present in American life from the 1870s on is the entrepreneur. Tocqueville devotes a whole chapter to the problem of "How an Aristocracy May Be Created by Manufactures" (II:2, ch. 20, pp. 168–71), well before the technological intensification of capitalism had begun. The division of labor in a manufacturing system, even when Tocqueville was writing, stultifies the worker by limiting him or her to a repetitive performance of a minor task, while the costs of production decrease when the scale of the enterprise is enlarged. As a result, "in proportion as the workman improves, the man is degraded" (p. 168). Selfhood is diminished; the worker "no longer belongs to himself, but to the calling that he has chosen" (p. 169). In our terms, his capacity to believe that he is more than his role or function or place vanishes. At the same time, the magnitude of enterprise attracts ambitious and energetic individuals. They are given an apparently legitimate way of using others undemocratically by commanding them and relegating them to inferiority. The entrepreneur "resembles more and more the administrator of a vast empire," while the worker looks like a "brute" (p. 169). Each takes on the appearance of being born to his position, one to rule, the other to submit. "What is this but aristocracy?" (p. 169). Yet the new aristocracy is not really an aristocracy: "the class of rich man does not exist" (p. 170). The entrepreneurs, the unconcerted aggregation of "rich individuals have no feelings or purposes, no traditions or hopes, in common; there are individuals, therefore, but no definite class" (p. 170).

Did entrepreneurs in Tocqueville's time justify themselves in the manner of Callicles? Was there a doctrine of antidemocratic individualism in the midst of the only democracy? Not yet, but it was coming. Social Darwinism arose in the second half of the nineteenth century, formulated by Herbert Spencer in England and by his American followers, including William Graham Sumner. The doctrine is more accurately called Social Spencerism because Spencer produced the basic arguments before Darwin published *The Origin of Species*. In his valuable study, *Social Darwinism in American Thought* (1955, p. 201), Hofstadter says, "There was nothing in Darwinism that inevitably made it an apology for competition or force." The trouble is that Darwin's immense reputation added prestige to existing social evolutionary ideas that were applied to human life independently of Darwin's efforts.

In its pure form, Social Darwinism (to stick with this familiar term) is not a justification of exploitation, as Callicles' view was. Although competition between entrepreneurs is posited as desirable, the real competition is between each person and himself. If one is self-disciplined and applies oneself to the task at hand, one will rise above others, but not at their expense. There is opportunity for everyone, but most are lazy and many are ruinously self-indulgent. Winners triumph over themselves, while losers lose to themselves. However, Social Darwinism is like Callicles' doctrine in one respect. Both doctrines claim that inequality of the right sort is in accordance with nature. Nature, in the Social Darwinian scheme, dictates that society can make progress only if society does not interfere with the struggle between each man and himself. It should allow the lazy and self-indulgent to perish and their stock to die out. Social Darwinism is thus an individualist doctrine but an antidemocratic one. It is individualist because it sees life as an opportunity for everyone, but it is antidemocratic not only because it welcomes the furtherance of inequality—unequal individualism—through freedom, but also because it denies the moral claims of individuals not to perish in misery. The economic division of humanity into winners and losers is seen to be definitive of the human condition. Even worse, Social Darwinism in its extended versions justifies the idea that life is a struggle between groups, rather than between each individual and himself. It lends a naturalistic cover to an unending process whereby groups always struggle to a conclusion: victory and its spoils for some groups, defeat and humiliating exploitation for others. But a democracy cannot self-consistently embrace such a view. Imperialism is more odious when democratic because of the additional vice of hypocrisy. It appears nonetheless that democratic individualism is hospitable to the individualist idea that life is a struggle of each with himself.

Tocqueville's harsh words about the "aristocracy" that the newly industrializing economic system may create indicate that he would have been appalled by the uninhibited capitalism that began its reign in the second half of the nineteenth century. He admired the old order, the hereditary aristocracy that modern democracy was overthrowing, for its luster, its refinement, its dedication to rare and difficult achievements, its decorum and sense of honor, its ability, in sum, to elevate the human stature—but also for the structural barriers it maintained, though with ever greater difficulty, against an indefatigable central power that threatened to swallow up all life and make it subject to authoritarian command.

But for Tocqueville, a capitalist subordination of masses of people in industrial enterprises would be only a part, and not the worst part, of a larger process that he conceptualized as democratic despotism (to which I referred above). In his analysis, individualism makes democratic despotism a strong possibility in modern democracies. Specifically, democratic individualism reduced to privatism is the culprit. Tocqueville does not assign the blame to democratic individualism in the largest sense (as I have worked with it). But if privatism is intrinsic to, even if it is not the totality of, democratic individualism—if, that is, in modern circumstances privatism will inevitably exist wherever democracy exists and engenders (as it must) democratic individualism—then Tocqueville's most important criticism of democratic individualism is that it may very well prepare society for a new kind of despotism, formally democratic but actually elitist and bureaucratic. Capitalism's contribution is to make the core of individualism the love of getting ahead and then using the wealth obtained to lead one's whole life as one sees fit. Everyone is economically obsessed, so that one may gain the resources to live to oneself and as one pleases. The public sphere is left to those few who aspire to rule and thus find their individualism realized undemocratically.

Tocqueville projects a soft despotism, but soft or not, it represents the degradation of the human being to a mere subject. In his view, only active citizens can resist the tendency to despotism. Only democracy in the mode of freely and actively associated civil and political groups can restrain privatist individualism from becoming the accomplice of despotism. The trouble is that once the career of imperialism in the modern age is begun, the secret and discretionary power of executive agencies (even when elected) dominates government and society and thereby establishes a kind of garrison state that makes welfarist democratic despotism seem minor in moral importance. Imperialism can happily coexist with a vibrant citizenship of the associational type that Tocqueville celebrates, but such citizenship is powerless in the face of the imperialist project; it becomes a sideshow that misleads people into thinking that their citizenship reaches to the most significant issues of public policy. Imperialism is the slow death of democracy. To be sure, democratic individualism can go on for a while despite democratic self-betrayal; but it should become guilty and worry about its future.

PLATO AND TOCQUEVILLE COMBINED

Most of the fundamental elements of democratic and antidemocratic individualism are contained in Greek literature, especially Plato. The description of democratic practices and their explanation by reference to democratic sentiments and attitudes are memorably presented. Tocqueville's contribution is an invaluable analysis of modern democratic practices and their underlying sentiments and attitudes, which reveals to what extent modern democratic individualism differs from that of Athens. The impact of capitalism is especially significant in accounting for the difference, though between Athens and the United States lie Stoic and then Christian intimations of human equality that also must be noticed. But capitalism, at least in the United States, means that the people are not a demos, a great majority condemned to a life of poverty, even a mitigated poverty. Modern democracy as a system is essentially middle class and working class, not proletarian (in the Marxist sense). The majority are not poor. Although the Athenian demos cherished the ideal of living as one likes and reflexively preferred no-rule, individual self-government, and private pursuits, it was much harder to attain the comparative luxury of privatism, a whole life organized around the will to make up one's own world in such a way that family, friends, and everyday life and business pleasurably dominated one's preoccupations. Modern democratic individuals are fully aware of their political and moral status as free individuals and prepared for episodic citizenship. But the enticements of private life, on the one hand, and the scale of society, on the other, prevent active citizenship from forming a central component of the self-definition of most people. As for antidemocratic individualism, it may be odd to say so, but it is possible that Plato is a better guide even to modern antidemocratic individualism than Tocqueville. Greek literature is a splendid preparation for the mentality of Social Darwinism, in its pure as well as its extended forms.

Is there anything theoretical in modern democratic individualism and its critique not already found in Plato and Tocqueville? I think that Emerson initiated a philosophical renovation of democratic individualism; hence neither Plato nor Tocqueville saw all its existential possibilities. (I doubt that all its existential possibilities could be even so much as glimpsed until its story is finished.) There are actual phenomena that meet Emersonian theoretical expectations. I briefly turn to the Emersonian strand at the end of this essay, but first I must say a word about a few contemporary critics of democratic individualism.

CONTEMPORARY CRITICS OF INDIVIDUALISM

What do contemporary critics add to the critique of individualism enunciated by Plato and Tocqueville? Let us remember that neither of the two is a principled democrat. Their deepest loyalties are with philosophical and hereditary aristocracies, respectively. The greatest students of individualism and democracy are skeptics of genius. What of contemporary critics? If they only elaborate criticisms that are already found in Plato and Tocqueville, does that have to mean that they, too, are not principled democrats? If they add new points, are those points internal to democracy? I think that contemporary critics add a little to Plato's and Tocqueville's criticisms and also serve the purpose of redirecting our attention to aspects of these earlier criticisms. Of course in their details our contemporary critics enrich our understanding of the life around us. But though all the critics either endorse democracy or offer no alternative to it despite their reservations, they make their criticisms on the supposition that democracy could exist without individualism. More accurately, they suppose that individualism could disappear or be drastically purged and democracy still remain and grow ever stronger. They do not tend to advocate democracy as a weapon in the class struggle between the many and the few. Their interest in democracy is not demotic, for the most part. They are especially concerned with the culture of democracy but do not see or want to concede that democracy as a culture is necessarily individualist, for good and bad. The point is that even in city-state form, in ancient Athens, individualism characterized the culture of democracy. How could it not define the culture of modern democracy in its large-scale nation-state form with a capitalist economy?

Diverse contemporary critics have made distinguished contributions to political theory. I cannot attend to the subtleties of their work and their disagreements with one another. Instead, I offer a composite of contemporary criticism of democratic individualism. Its tenets are as follows. Society is prior to individuals, not only temporally but in existential and moral significance. Hence, individuals exist for society, not the reverse. The individual is less than the role or function or place that he or she occupies. The self flourishes or is really a self only as a part or member of a larger entity. Indeed, every individual is greater as a part than as a pretended whole. One can be whole, can be completed and fulfilled, only projectively through identifying with a group or several groups, whether the fellow citizens of one's society or some lesser cultural groups within it. One's identity is simply the sum of groups one identifies with, affiliations that one has inherited or chosen. One is too small in oneself. The higher authenticity consists in merging one's identity with a larger identity. Consequently, for a society or a lesser group to go on, as it supremely deserves to, individuals must wholeheartedly accept tradition and authority. The autonomy that matters is the group's. Individual autonomy is largely fictional, given the multiple determinisms to which every human being is subject. The moral upshot is that duties come before rights and that rights must give way for the sake of the preservation or excellence of the society or lesser group. The highest morality shows itself in a readiness for self-denial and self-sacrifice, when called for. Self-denial and self-sacrifice are marks of a genuine private life as well, not only of social or public life. Society or group life is active cooperation and dedicated performance; private life should consist of putting others ahead of oneself. The world is good when there are plural societies in it, but also when each society is fairly unitary.

If we turn to such thinkers as Robert Bellah, Christopher Lasch, Alasdair MacIntyre, Michael Sandel, Charles Taylor, and Michael Walzer, we find in each case many, though not necessarily all, of the above tenets developed with skill and passion. (Numerous thinkers have engaged in the critique of individualism, but the ones listed have been influential and are representative.) Naturally, the emphases and elaborations vary, as does the urgency of the intellectual temper. But the name "communitarian" is a more or less accurate designation for the position of these thinkers, each of whom exemplifies, it must be said, a richness that exceeds any ideological category.

Bellah believes that, divorced from Protestantism and from civic republicanism, individualism in the form of "self-contained individuals" cannot sustain "either a public or a private life." Privatism deserts the public sphere and thus erodes it, while turning into a self-absorbed and unsatisfiable "therapeutic ethos" (Bellah et al. 1985, p. 143). Lasch, in a somewhat different idiom, likens individualism to narcissism and therefore to mental disturbance. The symptoms are "dependence on the vicarious warmth provided by others combined with a fear of dependence, a sense of inner emptiness, boundless repressed rage, and unsatisfied oral cravings" (Lasch 1978, p. 33). Only a restored vigor of public life can loosen the hold of narcissistic individualism. MacIntyre challenges the idea that one human life can consist of many unconnected and heterogeneous lives by praising the narrative unity, the coherent shapeliness, that a well-led life can have. A life in segments is ill composed. A person should inhabit a role and perfect the virtues that sustain it. We all "approach our own circumstances as bearers of a particular social identity. I am someone's son or daughter . . . I am a citizen of this or that city, a member of this or that guild or profession; I belong to this clan, that tribe, this nation. Hence what is good for me has to be the good for one who inhabits these roles. As such, I inherit from the past of my family, my city, my tribe, my nation, a variety of debts, inheritances, rightful expectations and obligations'' (MacIntyre 1981, pp. 204–5). Sandel (1982, p. 62) protests that individualism espouses the erroneous view that "No commitment could grip me so deeply that I could not understand myself without it." Proper self-understanding will show that "fraternal sentiments and fellow-feeling" are "partly constitutive of the agent's identity" and that people's identities are "defined to some extent by the community of which they are a part. For them, community describes not just what they *have* as fellow citizens but also what they *are*, not a relationship they choose (as in voluntary association) but an attachment they discover, not merely an attribute but a constituent of their identity." What individualism wars against is a "strong view" of community (Sandel 1982, p. 150). Taylor likens individualism to "atomism," a doctrine that encourages human isolation and self-enclosure. The "primacy of rights," which is promoted as the source and expression of individualism, denies "the same status to a principle of belonging or obligation, that is a principle which states our obligation as men to belong to or sustain society, or a society of a certain type, or to obey authority or an authority of a certain type" (Taylor 1985, p. 188). To accord primacy to rights is to posit the impossible ideal of "the self-sufficiency of man alone or, if you would prefer, of the individual" (p. 189). Walzer, in a barely qualified defense of what he calls "tribalism," praises group identity when it reflects a strong commitment to a distinctive way of life. "Tribalism names the commitment of individuals and groups to their own history, culture, and identity . . . . The parochialism, the moral thickness, that it breeds is similarly permanent. It can't be overcome; it has to be accommodated . . . it must [i.e., should] always be accommodated" (Walzer 1994, pp. 81–82). The tribe, not the individual, is the unit of overriding significance.

Like individualism, anti-individualism is a normative doctrine or set of doctrines. It combines analysis and aspiration, along with some metaphysics. Undeniably, it accurately perceives serious shortcomings in a society in which democratic individualism is or appears to be dominant. Equally important, it catches the longings that many, perhaps most, people have for a lightening of the burden of being or becoming an individual. Most anti-individualists are also troubled by antidemocratic individualism, the self-assertion of a few who rise high above the rest, whether or not at their expense, even though this theme is not always salient. Yet for all their impressive effort, I believe that individualism is still essentially a democratic phenomenon. We cannot have democracy without it; it owes its existence to democracy. If the human and social situation is as bad as the critics say—and it sometimes seems to be so, or worse—the indictment must be directed at democracy itself. Capitalism and imperialism may make certain manifestations of democratic individualism (and antidemocratic individualism, too) pathological. Plato may be right: A society without individualism may make everybody happier and even outwardly more sane. The proclivity of individualism toward confusion and outbursts may make it seem on average less admirable than a more orderly society. But the basic situation is inherent in democracy. What alternative is there?

When a much stronger group feeling exists, when one's identity is unthinkable without one's particular social attachment, when it is urged that we treat the given as the chosen, when one thinks that one owes society infinitely more than it owes oneself, when deference to tradition and authority is praised seemingly without reservation, and when we are discouraged from allowing a thoughtful disposition to maintain some distance between oneself and one's surroundings, the result in modern times is much more appropriate for, say, a Hegelian society than for a democratic one.

It could be asked, isn't Rousseau a democrat without being an individualist? My answer is that by the time Rousseau gets done outlining the good society, he effaces its individualist origins by an unrelenting sociality, and abandons democracy—that is, popular self-government in a loose sense—for an executive despotism. No, Rousseau does not provide an example of a democrat who is anti-individualist. He may be a populist, but he is not a democrat, and as an antidemocrat, he is an anti-individualist.

In any case, the tendency of the contemporary critique of individualism is antidemocratic, even though the thinkers I have mentioned would deny the imputation. In her excellent discussion of communitarian thinkers—many of them mentioned here—Gutmann says (1985, p. 320), "The critics' failure to undermine liberalism suggests not that there are no communitarian values but that they are properly viewed as supplementing rather than supplanting basic liberal values." Gutmann's liberalism is not identical to what I have been calling democratic individualism, but there is sufficient overlap to permit me to disagree slightly and say that the value of the communitarian critics is not to offer supplementary values but rather to provoke disquiet with individualist values and to further the attempt to refine them. Communitarian values cannot be absorbed into democracy without compromising democracy, but they can help to diminish complacency. The work of refining democratic individualism is not the business of communitarians.

REFINING DEMOCRATIC INDIVIDUALISM

The work of refining democratic individualism was the business of Emerson, Thoreau, and Whitman. They did it with unsurpassed power, and the study of individualism has not caught up with them a century and a half later. Among the contemporary critics I have mentioned, only Lasch takes up Emerson (and favorably). Now at the end of this paper I can only assert that if what is wanted is an internal critique, a democratic and philosophical critique of democratic individualism as it is rationalized and practiced, the best attempt so far is the writing of Emerson and his two great colleagues. What makes reading Emerson, Thoreau, and Whitman so unsettling is the sense that unless democratic individualism reformed itself, it could turn hideous in its predatory and boundless egomania. But if reformed in the spirit of its best possibilities, democratic individualism would be a brighter page in human history, all the brighter for being rare and perhaps precarious.

I know that the Emersonian tradition is friendly to privatism; it does not think that in modern conditions, privatism is avoidable and replaceable by an active life of republican citizenship in which all or many people take part. The scale of causes and effects, their remoteness, their abstraction, their frequent unintelligibility, and their irrationality all must induce alienation. Politics is necessary, but it cannot define an individualist life for most people; its realism is indistinguishable from fantasy, especially group fantasy. The associative life, though needed in emergencies (such as standing up to the expansionary policies of the slave states), is not an end in itself. Its discipline smothers more virtues than it fosters. The permanent aim is to reform privatism. In what direction does this reform go?

It heads away from those kinds of self-concern and self-expression that indicate entrapment in the coils of conformity: too much anxiety about competing successfully, too much insistence on finding oneself through the accumulation of goods, too much belief that care of the self means reliance on professional healers. The Emersonian teaching, articulated in strikingly various ways by Emerson first and then by Thoreau and Whitman, tries to move its audience toward an unegotistical individualism, an ideal that, adapting Whitman, I have called democratic individuality (Kateb 1992). The gist is to regard with skepticism such proposed solutions to the problem or puzzle of the self as tradition, authority, belonging, identity submerged in a group, docile loyalty, and fixed notions of oneself. Each person is unique, but this is a realization that eventually comes, not a purpose deliberately to be pursued. One must remain somewhat strange to oneself and respect the strangeness of other individuals. Only then is there honesty in the face of human complexity. One must welcome the dialectic in one's soul of resistance and acceptance. Emerson (especially in "Self-Reliance" and "Circles," 1983 [1841]) voices the central individualist idea that a self is more than role or function or place and that therefore one may take on many roles experimentally and delight in seeing roles reversed and the lowly elevated. But there is a self beyond even these engagements, a self that at last carves out an area for its distinctive work and busies itself above all in the receptive and appreciative apprehension of experience. Only thus can the normal condition of sleep be thrown off and life be entered into. Everyone can have philosophical moods of the sort that Plato defines and Emerson encourages (and Emerson is a Platonist in a manner of speaking): to become, even if fleetingly, "the spectator of all time and all existence" (*Republic* VI:486a, p. 217).

Are there rewards to democratic individuality? Perhaps a cleaner conscience because of resistance and a sharper wonder that grows out of acceptance. Is there evidence of democratic individuality in democratic life? Not enough, but there is some, if only now and then.

The *Annual Review of Political Science* is online at
http://polisci.annualreviews.org

LITERATURE CITED

Aristotle. 1943. *Politics*. Transl. B Jowett. New York: Modern Library

Bellah RN, Madsen R, Sullivan WM, Swidler A, Tipton SM. 1985. *Habits of the Heart*. Berkeley: Univ. Calif. Press

de Tocqueville A. 1954 (1835/1840). *Democracy in America*. 2 vols. Transl. H Reeve, F Bowen, P Bradley. New York: Vintage

Emerson RW. 1983 (1841). *Essays and*

Lectures, pp. 257–282, 401–414. New York: Library of America

Gutmann A. 1985. Communitarian critics of liberalism. *Philos. Public Aff.* 14(Summer): 308–22

Hofstadter R. 1955. *Social Darwinism in American Thought*. Boston: Beacon. Revised ed.

Kateb G. 1992. *The Inner Ocean: Individualism and Democratic Culture*. Ithaca: Cornell Univ. Press

Lasch C. 1978. *The Culture of Narcissism*. New York: Norton

MacIntyre A. 1981. *After Virtue*. Notre Dame: Univ. Notre Dame Press

Nietzsche F. 1974 (1882). *The Gay Science*. Transl. W Kaufmann. New York: Vintage

Nietzsche F. 1969 (1908). *Ecce Homo*. Transl. W Kaufmann. New York: Vintage

Plato. 1952. *Gorgias*. Transl. WC Helmbold. New York: Liberal Arts Press

Plato. 1956. *Apology*. Transl. FJ Church. New York: Bobbs-Merrill. 2nd ed.

Plato. n.d. *Republic*. Transl. B Jowett. New York: Modern Library

Sandel M. 1982. *Liberalism and the Limits of Justice*. Cambridge: Cambridge Univ. Press

Sophocles. 1959. *Antigone*. In *The Complete Greek Tragedies*, Vol. 2, ed. D Grene and R Lattimore. Transl. E Wyckoff. Chicago: Univ. Chicago Press

Spender S. 1975. *Love-Hate Relations: English and American Sensibilities*. New York: Vintage

Taylor C. 1985. Atomism. In *Philosophical Papers*, 2:187–210. Cambridge: Cambridge Univ. Press

Thucydides. 1982. *The Peloponnesian War*. Transl. R Crawley, T Wick. New York: Modern Library

Walzer M. 1994. Justice and tribalism: minimal morality in international politics. In *Thick and Thin*, pp. 63–83. Notre Dame, IN: Univ. Notre Dame Press

Annu. Rev. Polit. Sci. 2003. 6:307–26
doi: 10.1146/annurev.polisci.6.121901.085538
First published online as a Review in Advance on Feb. 5, 2003

DELIBERATIVE DEMOCRATIC THEORY

Simone Chambers

*Department of Political Science, University of Toronto, 100 St. George Street, Toronto,
Ontario M5S 3G3, Canada; email: schamber@chass.utoronto.ca*

Key Words   democracy, law, pluralism, accountability, public sphere

■ **Abstract**   Deliberative democratic theory has moved beyond the "theoretical
statement" stage and into the "working theory" stage. Although this essay revisits
some of the main theoretical debates, this is done via a survey and evaluation of the
state of deliberative democratic theory as it is being *applied* in a number of research
areas and as it intersects with related normative debates. Five research areas are covered: public law, international relations, policy studies, empirical research, and identity
politics.

INTRODUCTION

It is now commonplace to talk about the deliberative turn in democratic theory
(Dryzek 2000). Indeed, this turn is so striking that it has spawned a small industry
of review articles and edited volumes attempting to sum up its meaning and content
(Bohman & Rehg 1997, Bohman 1998a, Elster1998a, Macedo 1999, Freeman
2000). For the most part, these articles and books focus on the central theoretical
principles underlying deliberative democratic theory and compare and contrast
the major theoretical statements defining this view. This article will take a slightly
different approach. Rather than go over already well-covered ground, I look beyond
the question of what deliberative democratic theory is, to the question of what
deliberative democratic theory is doing these days. Deliberative democratic theory
has moved beyond the "theoretical statement" stage and into the "working theory"
stage. Although I revisit some of the main theoretical debates, this is done via a
survey and evaluation of the state of deliberative democratic theory as it is being
applied in a number of research areas and as it intersects with related normative
debates. I have chosen five research areas: public law, international relations, policy
studies, empirical research, and identity politics.

This list is not exhaustive, nor are the categories mutually exclusive. Furthermore, I want to stress that the number of scholars working with a model of deliberative democracy or writing about this model is enormous. Any one of these
subfields could furnish enough material for a survey article on its own. I cannot
mention, let alone discuss, all the work being done in these fields and I am sure to
leave out some potentially significant contributions.

1094-2939/03/0615-0307$14.00   **307**

WHO IS A DELIBERATIVE DEMOCRATIC THEORIST?

In 1999, Rawls joined the deliberative turn and explained that he was "concerned with a well-ordered constitutional democracy ... understood also as a deliberative democracy" (1999, p. 139). A recent review article about deliberative democracy devoted a good half of its analysis to Rawls (Freeman 2000). Although Rawls endorses a deliberative democracy and his conception of public reason is central to that understanding of democracy, for the purposes of this review he is not considered a theorist of deliberative democracy. A great many other theorists who also endorse deliberation are not considered deliberative democracy theorists in this review. Let me explain. The problem is that nearly everybody these days endorses deliberation in some form or other (it would be hard not to). And more and more people understand constitutional democracy as entailing deliberation in some fundamental way (Tully 2002). The language and concepts of deliberative democratic theory have filtered into many discourses and debates. But not all appeals to or endorsements of deliberation can be considered deliberative democratic theory. For the purposes of this review, democratic theory is a more restrictive domain than appeals to deliberation. Rawls does not qualify because, although he discusses some aspects of democracy, his is not a democratic theory per se (for an alternative view see Laden 2000). This is a somewhat arbitrary distinction to be sure, but appeal to deliberation is now so widespread that without drawing some distinction I would have to survey liberal theory rather than just deliberative theory.

Although I think most political scientists have a fair idea of what is meant by deliberative democratic theory, I include a quick list of its key components as a starting point. Deliberative democratic theory is a normative theory that suggests ways in which we can enhance democracy and criticize institutions that do not live up to the normative standard. In particular, it claims to be a more just and indeed democratic way of dealing with pluralism than aggregative or realist models of democracy. Thus, it begins with a turning away from liberal individualist or economic understandings of democracy and toward a view anchored in conceptions of accountability and discussion. Talk-centric democratic theory replaces voting-centric democratic theory. Voting-centric views see democracy as the arena in which fixed preferences and interests compete via fair mechanisms of aggregation. In contrast, deliberative democracy focuses on the communicative processes of opinion and will-formation that precede voting. Accountability replaces consent as the conceptual core of legitimacy. A legitimate political order is one that could be *justified* to all those living under its laws. Thus, accountability is primarily understood in terms of "giving an account" of something, that is, publicly articulating, explaining, and most importantly justifying public policy. Consent (and, of course, voting) does not disappear. Rather, it is given a more complex and richer interpretation in the deliberative model than in the aggregative model. Although theorists of deliberative democracy vary as to how critical they are of existing representative institutions, deliberative democracy is not usually thought of as an alternative to representative democracy. It is rather an expansion of representative democracy.

Definitions of deliberation and how to distinguish it from other forms of talk—for example, bargaining or rhetoric—vary a great deal among theorists (compare Elster 1997 and Bohman 1996 on bargaining; see Remer 1999, 2000 on rhetoric). Furthermore, even when a strong distinction is made between, say, bargaining and deliberation, this rarely means that bargaining is illegitimate or undemocratic. It means that citizens need to deliberate about and decide when and where bargaining is a fair and appropriate method of dispute resolution (Habermas 1996). Generally speaking, we can say that deliberation is debate and discussion aimed at producing reasonable, well-informed opinions in which participants are willing to revise preferences in light of discussion, new information, and claims made by fellow participants. Although consensus need not be the ultimate aim of deliberation, and participants are expected to pursue their interests, an overarching interest in the legitimacy of outcomes (understood as justification to all affected) ideally characterizes deliberation.

Theorists of deliberative democracy are interested in such questions as: How does or might deliberation shape preferences, moderate self-interest, empower the marginalized, mediate difference, further integration and solidarity, enhance recognition, produce reasonable opinion and policy, and possibly lead to consensus? Deliberative democratic theory critically investigates the quality, substance, and rationality of the arguments and reasons brought to defend policy and law. It studies and evaluates the institutions, forums, venues, and public spaces available for deliberative justification and accountability. It looks at the social, economic, political, and historic conditions necessary for healthy deliberation as well as the attitudes, behaviors, and beliefs required of participants. Finally, deliberative democratic theory contains a deep reading (some would say rereading) of foundational issues regarding rights, popular sovereignty, and constitutionalism. This last is most visible when deliberative democratic theory meets law and constitutionalism.

PUBLIC LAW

With the publication of *Between Facts and Norms*, subtitled *Contributions to a Discourse Theory of Law and Democracy*, Habermas announced that what began in language philosophy had ended in legal theory (1996). Even before this, of course, legal scholarship had taken note of the deliberative turn or perhaps taken its own deliberative turn especially in the area of constitutional theory (Michelman 1988; Ackerman 1991, 1998; Sunstein 1993; Preuss 1995; Tully 1995; Nino 1996). Is there a common theme to deliberative legal theory? At the most abstract level, there is a shared theme of reconciling democracy and rights. Deliberative democratic theorists for the most part steer a middle course between rights foundationalism—which sees the will of the People, usually understood as majority will, in direct opposition to individual rights and so in need of clear and inviolable limits (Dworkin 1996)—and strong democracy and/or communitarian theory, which sees individual rights, or at least a culture obsessed with individual rights, as a pernicious impediment to the common good (Sandel 1996). Deliberative democratic theory can be described as a rights-friendly theory of robust democracy, with some theorists leaning toward the rights side (Gutmann & Thompson 1996, 2002) while others lean more toward the democracy side (Dryzek 2000, Tully 2002).[1]

Habermas has developed this middle ground into a deep theory of legitimacy. In answer to the liberal objection that deliberative democracy privileges the People's will over rights, and to the democrat's objection that it privileges rights over the People's will, Habermas defends the "co-originality" (*Gleichursprünglichkeit*) of rights and popular sovereignty (1996, 2001b). There is no People's will to speak of without rights and there are no rights without some theory of popular sovereignty to create an original justification. The relationship between constitutional rights and popular sovereignty mirrors the relationship between law and democracy. The rule of law is inherent in democracy and democracy cannot function without the rule of law (Habermas 2001b). We are legal persons protected by rights only to the extent that we are authors of those laws. We are authors only to the extent that we are persons under the law.

Habermas's legal theory has generated much debate and criticism (Rosenfeld & Arato 1998, Chambers 2002, Honnig 2002). A common question running through the criticisms (Michelman 1996, Scheuerman 1999) has been: Where exactly is robust democracy in all this? One problem is that Habermas wants to do two things that are not always compatible. He wants to offer a grand legal theory that redescribes and reinterprets the modern legal tradition in deliberative terms. But at the same time he wants to offer a normative theory that has some critical bite—that can tell us what is wrong with the modern legal tradition or at least what is wrong with the way it is working today. The prescriptive project is often overshadowed by the descriptive one. Thus, the picture that emerges sometimes looks not much different from what we appear to have right now, and Habermas is very vague about the best or most efficacious institutional arrangements for deliberative empowerment.

Another problem is that Habermas is dealing with law at the highest level of abstraction. In contrast, questions of institutional design are best addressed within a particular legal and constitutional tradition. Habermas is much better when he talks about particular constitutions, the German or American for example, or when he engages in debate with legal scholars writing within a given tradition. The work of Ackerman (1991, 1998) demonstrates the effectiveness of this focus. He too is involved in a grand redescription that is supposed to lead to a significant set of prescriptions, but he begins deep within the American constitutional tradition. The redescription of American constitutional history is informed by a theory of constitutional dualism. Constitutional politics has two gears. Most of the time,

---

[1]Rather than a continuum, both Dryzek (2000) and Tully (2002) see a clear divide in deliberative theory along these lines. Dryzek distinguishes between liberal constitutionalist and discursive conceptions of deliberative democracy, whereas Tully contrasts a constitutional theory approach to an activist approach. I discuss this divide below.

the Constitution is a relatively stable set of principles that judges apply but do not radically alter. These principles form the backdrop to "normal politics." In this gear, citizens have little to do with the Constitution and court decisions stay within a given interpretive paradigm. But every once in a while, constitutional politics changes gears. During these "constitutional moments," citizens engage in higher law making. These are often times of crisis or great change when nations are galvanized by issues and debate spreads and intensifies. In these moments, elites call on and listen to the People. A collective reassessment of values and principles results in a constitutional paradigm shift. These moments represent a popular constitutional amendment process outside the formal institutional channels of amendment. Ackerman identifies three such moments (1998, p. 11): "The Founding, Reconstruction, and the New Deal were all acts of constituent authority."

An interesting aspect of Ackerman's reading of American history, from the point of view of deliberative democracy, is the situating of constituent authority and power of the People in informal but widespread deliberation. Although throughout all these periods there were national elections, the epicenter of popular sovereignty cannot be identified with one vote. Indeed there is no epicenter. This complements and furthers a Habermasian theme that runs through much deliberative democratic theory. As I noted at the outset, deliberative democratic theory moves the heart of democracy away from the vote and into the public sphere and practices of accountability and justification. Of course democratic polities still vote, and deliberative democracy is not an alternative to representative democracy. This results in a two-tiered view of democratic politics: One tier contains formal institutions of representation (sometimes called strong publics), and the second tier contains informal citizen deliberation (weak publics) (Fraser 1993, Habermas 1998). Habermas has been much criticized for being vague about how these two relate to each other. In particular, how can the informal opinion and will formation that goes on in civil society and the public sphere have the power to influence the formal institutions other than by simply mobilizing voting majorities? Historically focused studies like Ackerman's can show us how the People exercise constituent power that is not completely captured in the power of the vote.

This theme can also be seen in Michelman's (1999) recent study of Supreme Court Justice William Brennan. Here again we see a discussion of the intersection between rights and democracy being understood in terms other than the clash between majority will and individual rights. Brennan is depicted as a "responsive" judge who listened and was accountable to the People without being swayed by the majority. Habermas, Ackerman, and Michelman, along with others, are trying to work out a relationship between law and democracy that goes beyond majoritarianism. Another way to put this is that deliberative legal theory is trying to articulate a relationship between the public and legislative authority that goes beyond the voting booth to investigate how law might be an expression of popular will via communicative power. This translates into a constitutional theory concerned with the general conditions of communicative power. Deliberative legal theory investigates what ought to be in a constitution if we are to promote a deliberative order

(Nino 1996), how we ought to interpret a constitution to maintain and enhance deliberation (Sunstein 2001), and finally how we ought to be making constitutions if we are to establish a deliberative legitimacy (Elster 1998b, Chambers 1998).

A related trend in legal theory is worth mentioning. Recently, theorists have begun exploring a reflexive-law model of regulation (Arato 1998; J.L. Cohen 1999, 2002; Scheuerman 2001). Borrowing from systems theory (Teubner 1993), such scholars as Cohen develop "a new understanding of legal regulation and of state/society relations, allowing one to see how state regulation can foster autonomy and recognize plurality while still satisfying the demands of justice" (J.L. Cohen 2002, p. 4). Whereas the foundational theory we reviewed above steers a middle course between rights and democracy, regulatory law raises a slightly different set of antinomies. Here the middle course sought is between freedom and equality, often translated into decentered versus state-centered regulation. Reflexive law is an alternative to, on the one hand, liberal models of regulation and, on the other, welfare models. Liberal models are concerned with maintaining freedom and minimalizing interference. The result is that justice sometimes suffers. The welfare model, in a drive to establish justice and equality, is often intrusive and can lead to unwanted juridification, hence a loss of autonomy. Reflexive law seeks "regulated autonomy" (J.L. Cohen 2002). With the two mainstream paradigms at work, we see "the tendency to over- or underregulate, and to turn equality (secured by regulation) and liberty (secured by nonregulation?) into a zero sum-game" (J.L. Cohen 2002, p. 16). Reflexive law involves the public regulation of self-regulation to promote local problem solving. Rather than the state directly fixing a problem, the state sets up and guarantees fair procedures through which citizens fix a problem. Some collective bargaining procedures are forms of reflexive law. Not as decentered as the systems theory version, the deliberative democratic version of reflexive law stresses the *public*-regulation aspect of local self-regulation as much as the local aspect of it. Universal principles of reciprocity as well as substantive ends of justice should inform the design of self-regulation. In general, we need to promote procedures that empower citizens while safeguarding their autonomy.

Cohen applies this model to questions of intimacy and sexual harassment, where privacy versus justice is already a central concern. In a very different domain, Scheuerman (2001) applies it to questions of transnational economic legal coordination. He suggests that a reflexive-law paradigm can help us think about a global legal order that stands between freedom and equality. "This basic approach arguably combines precisely the right mix of realism and radicalism called for by globalization: a normatively acceptable model of global economic regulation must aggressively confront the glaring inequalities of the emerging global economy, but it will need to do so while recognizing the irrepressibility of some institutional restraints on the quest to achieve greater equality" (Scheuerman 2001, pp. 87–88). Although one might quibble with the articulation of the freedom side of the equation, Scheuerman nevertheless seeks procedures for regulation that would maintain the autonomy of economic regulatory agencies while subjecting them to procedural guidelines for their internal decisions. This leads directly to our next topic.

INTERNATIONAL RELATIONS

Paralleling the deliberative turn in democratic theory has been an explosion in debate and literature on postnational sovereignty, multilevel governance, cosmopolitanism, and the new global order. A common theme within the transnational discourse has been the question of democratic deficit. As economic globalization intensifies and market zones such as the European Union (EU) expand, we are reminded of nineteenth-century enthusiasm for free market forces and the early twentieth-century attempt to control them via the welfare state. Does globalization represent the escape of market forces from the political controls of the welfare state? Do we need to re-embed those forces within a coherent social and political vision of the good society? Does the national political arena have enough reach to accomplish a re-embedding? Just as deliberative democratic theory steers a middle course between rights foundationalism and communitarian democracy, it also steers a middle course between free markets and statism. While acknowledging the benefits of healthy markets, deliberative democratic theorists want to embed them in politics, and particularly in democratic politics. Political units such as the EU and institutions such as the World Trade Organization raise the question of political and democratic accountability. These are just some of the concerns that have sent deliberative democratic theorists beyond the nation-state to investigate postnational politics.

The two focal points of the debate regarding democratic accountability are international governance and the EU.[2] On the question of cosmopolitanism, the range of views within deliberative democratic theory is quite broad,[3] running from those who argue that global issues and cosmopolitan perspectives must inform national politics but sovereignty needs to stay within the nation-state (Thompson 1999) to those who argue for a full-fledged new order in which we develop democratically accountable international governmental organizations (Held 1995). Between these two views are theorists who envision governance without government and accountability without formal representation via such mechanism as nongovernmental organizations (Dryzek 2000) and what could be called the global public sphere (Bohman 1998b, 1999).

This debate is still in its early stages and its impact on the wider field of international relations is not yet clear, although there does appear to be a growing discussion of transnational governance in general, even if it is not informed by deliberative democratic theory in particular. More interesting is the way in which this debate is reflecting back onto deliberative democratic theory by asking theorists to identify clearly the ties that bind citizens into a democratic enterprise. For

---

[2]The literature on transnational democracy, especially as it relates to the EU and EU constitutionalism, is vast. In this section, I highlight only debates within deliberative democratic theory and make no attempt to address the wider discussion.

[3]Stock A. *Deliberative democracy and international governance*. PhD manuscript. Dep. Polit. Sci., Univ. Colorado, Boulder, CO.

example, Habermas (2001a, p. 107) has had to admit that "any political community that wants to understand itself as a democracy must at least distinguish between members and non-members . . . . Even if such a community is grounded in the universalist principles of a democratic constitutional state, it still forms a collective identity, in the sense that it interprets and realizes these principles in light of its own history and in the context of its own particular form of life. This ethical-political self-understanding of citizens of a particular democratic life is missing in the inclusive community of world citizens." The issues that Habermas raises here are the focal point of the most interesting debate. One also sees innovative suggestions regarding institutional design of international organizations (Held 1995, Archibugi 2000). But the more difficult questions have to do with how much and what sort of commonality is necessary for democracy. The answers have implications not only for how far beyond the nation-state we can imagine democracy moving, but also for how far pluralism can expand within the nation-state before we see cracks in our democratic walls (Benhabib 2002). Obviously, Habermas does not mean collective identity on an ethnic model, but he does mean it on some model of "civic solidarity," and this might be problematic as our populations become more diverse and are in continual flux.

The relationship between collective identity and workable deliberative democracy is also raised in the EU debate, especially as the EU is on the brink of a major enlargement that will bring in countries with different civic traditions. The focus has been on the question of a constitution for the EU (Weiler 1999, Eriksen & Fossum 2000, Habermas 2001c). Although there is a considerable amount of talk about European integration through deliberation, it is sometimes vague and occasionally suffers from an institutional deficit. There are very few concrete suggestions for citizen venues that could, for example, counterbalance the technocratic bent of the EU. The constitutional debate, although it too vaguely nods toward institutionalized deliberation, is really directed at a deeper level.

Deliberative democratic theory, for the most part, weighs in on the side of a European constitution. The reasons for this include the maintenance and recognition of universal principles of reciprocity as well as the placement of an overarching political framework above the economic framework. But one reason that certainly seems implicit in Habermas's endorsement of the constitution is that constitutions can bind citizens into a common enterprise. Thus, deliberative democracy is seen by some as needing a relatively coherent and bounded *demos* that shares a collective identity in order to function. The questions, then, as I have said, are: How much commonality? And what kind? Habermas (2001a) and Benhabib (2002) endorse a form of constitutional patriotism that requires commonality mediated through constitutional principles. But even this might be too demanding if it can only be generated through a common history.

Some deliberative democracy theorists take issue with this constitution-centered understanding of deliberative democracy. The constitutional model highlights the possibility of a People collectively shaping and steering society according to democratically worked-out principles or values—indeed, for Habermas, a shared life form. From this point of view, we need to make Europe more like a nation-state in order for democracy to work, and conversely [for Habermas (2001a) and Thompson (1999)], democracy is not really appropriate for the international sphere because there can be no People with shared aspirations. In contrast, such theorists as Dryzek (2000) and Bohman (1997, 1998b) (see also Shaw 1999, Tully 2001) are developing more genuinely postnational models of democracy that do not rely on traditional "ties that bind," a *demos*, or a collective identity. Democracy is centered not in a collective will but rather in making institutions, elites, and governments accountable to a plurality of voices often joined together by issues, interests, or causes. "The politics of transnational civil society is largely about questioning, criticizing and publicizing" (Dryzek 2000, p. 131). We might add that it is not about pursuing a "shared life form." This model eschews traditional notions of sovereignty that need a clear and constituted authority to stop the buck and offers a decentered democracy in which a plurality of grass-roots forces engage in global campaigns of discursive harrying. Decentered democracy locates democratic voice in a largely uncoordinated civil society and public sphere (Warren 2002). To be sure, constitutionally oriented theorists also place much stock in civil society, but in the constitutional model, the opinions formed in the crisscrossing debates of civil society and the public sphere are ultimately funneled into representative institution that coordinate our shared life. A fully decentered view of democracy focuses on the way representative institutions answer to the multiple and uncoordinated voices of civil society. National-level civil societies are the most developed and so are the richest ground for decentered democracy, but the international arena is an ideal context to illustrate the fundamental components of decentered democracy precisely because there is no center in the form of a state.

PUBLIC POLICY

Public policy research was one of the first subfields in political science to embrace a deliberative model. The late 1980s and early 1990s saw a pronounced shift away from an expert-centered policy science and toward the inclusion of citizens in policy debates (Fischer & Forester 1993, Majone 1990). Generally speaking, deliberative policy studies can be divided into two not entirely distinct areas. The first involves a procedural approach and concentrates on the design of venues for choosing and developing policy. The second area involves using a deliberative model to generate substantive public policy outcomes. We could, of course, divide up public policy by subject matter. An attempt to cover public policy by subject would lead us into a huge literature as it would have to include environmental policy, bio- and medical ethics, educational policy, energy and space policy, and media studies, to name only a few of the areas most noticeably influenced by deliberative models.

Procedurally focused public policy runs the gamut from discussions of small neighborhood initiatives to grand nation-encompassing conversations. Sometimes proposals are very specific, for example, instituting a "National Deliberation Day"

(Ackerman & Fishkin 2002) or suggesting that the funding and establishment of citizen panels be a top priority in electoral reform (Gastil 2000 is particularly helpful in giving an overview of deliberative initiatives around the country). Other times, the approach is more general, investigating general models of policy analysis and dispute resolution (Gutmann 1999, Fischer 1993). It is in the realm of policy initiative and analysis that deliberative democratic theory is at its most concrete. One often hears the complaint that deliberative democratic theory is very abstract, lacking a clear institutional core or agenda. But even the briefest foray into policy initiative literature indicates that deliberative initiatives are springing up all over the country, in all sorts of policy areas. Citizen consultation, for example, in the form of open meetings has always been around. But in conjunction with a growing theoretical literature on deliberation and deliberative democracy, these sorts of initiatives are getting more sophisticated, innovative, and sensitive to such issues as including marginalized groups or canvassing silent sectors (Kahane 2003). Citizen conferences, citizen panels, and citizen juries are proliferating, sponsored by local, state, and national governments as well as a growing number of private foundations (e.g., Kettering and Carnegie Mellon) dedicated to citizen deliberation (Gastil 2000, Gastil & Gina 1995). These initiatives are furnishing good empirical data on how deliberation might work in various settings as well as, of course, bringing citizens into the process in a meaningful way. Such phenomena as the Oregon initiative on publicly funded health care (Daniels 1991, Gutmann 1999), the Kettering Foundation's National Issues Forums on education (Button & Mattson 1999, O'Connell & McKenzie 1995), and Fishkin's experiments in Deliberative Opinion Polls (Fishkin 1995, Gastil 1996) are often cited as flagship examples of deliberation in action. But these three are just the tip of the iceberg.

Although I have been talking about a procedural approach to public policy, it is important to remember that procedures are designed to enhance and facilitate *deliberation* rather than a fair decision rule.[4] Decisions need to be taken and fair decision rules need to be in place, but a deliberative approach focuses on qualitative aspects of the conversation that precedes decisions rather than on a mathematical decision rule. In designing and proposing deliberative forums, scholars generally have four goals in mind: to augment legitimacy through accountability and participation; to encourage a public-spirited perspective on policy issues through cooperation; to promote mutual respect between parties through inclusion and civility; and to enhance the quality of decisions (and opinions) through informed and substantive debate (Gutmann & Thompson 1997).

Deliberative democracy should not be confused with direct democracy. For example, it might be suggested that citizen participation in local policy issues should not be encouraged because it will be dominated by parochial attitudes exemplified by NIMBY ("not in my back yard"). Deliberative policy analysts respond

---

[4]Gutmann & Thompson (1997) associate the term procedural with a decision-rule emphasis and so reject it as a way of describing deliberation. I do not disagree; I simply use "procedural" in a somewhat broader way.

that this criticism of participation assumes citizens take part only at the end point (Fischer 1993). A deliberative model involves citizens at every stage of policy formation, including research and discovery stages. Thus, a deliberative model offers a way to overcome NIMBY by getting citizens to cooperatively solve policy dilemmas rather than simply vote on policy options. Furthermore, within the public process of deliberation, many NIMBY-type arguments are difficult to justify.

Although the actual public policy recommendations that come out of deliberative democratic theory are predominantly procedural ones, procedure blurs into substance at a certain point. But we need to be careful about the status of substantive proposals vis-à-vis deliberative theory. For example, Habermas recently contributed to bioethics by coming out against human cloning on the grounds that it would undermine individual autonomy (Habermas 2001a). He argues that in replacing blind chance by human intention as the determining factor in an individual's genetic makeup, we necessarily shift the basis of moral self-understanding. It becomes more difficult to see oneself as free and equal. This is especially true when we think of ourselves in relation to the "original" who furnished the genetic material. Without evaluating the merits of Habermas's argument, I want to consider its connections with deliberative democracy. First, Habermas could be endorsing a no-human-cloning policy because the arguments he outlines are the ones that are the most likely to be agreed to in a deliberation of all those affected. Second, he could be saying that autonomy is a condition of healthy citizenship and so the no-human-cloning principle is a precondition of democracy in the same way that the recognition of certain human rights is a precondition of democracy. Or finally, he could simply be making a contribution as a citizen to an ongoing debate that we, as democratic citizens, must work out over the course of the next years.

If he thinks his position on cloning is reasonable, then he thinks that he could (ideally) persuade others of its cogency, that is, it could be the object of general agreement. But he does not think, nor do most theorists of deliberative democracy think, that a theory of deliberation is a tool for arriving at determinate solutions to substantive policy disputes. In this respect, deliberative democratic theory is not like game theory. Models of deliberative democracy are rather blunt instruments for "determining" what people would agree to. One reason for this is that the very question often changes as it is subject to public and democratic debate. The deeper normative issue is that, in principle, substantive outcomes should be the result of actual and not virtual deliberation. But sometimes what appear to be substantive issues are, deep down, procedural issues. On this reading, Habermas might be endorsing a no-human-cloning policy because it is a necessary condition of a democratic society—in other words, it is a procedural requirement of deliberation. But these requirements are themselves subject to democratic debate and deliberation. So, ultimately, Habermas's policy stand on cloning should be seen as a citizen's contribution to an ongoing ethical debate. His reasoning, however, is based on the moral self-understanding most conducive to the practice of public and private autonomy. The general point is that the more substantive, as opposed to procedural, the policy recommendations to flow from a deliberative perspective are, the more one risks bypassing democracy itself (Chambers 2002; for a criticism of this procedural approach see Gutmann & Thompson 2002).

EMPIRICAL RESEARCH

Theories of deliberative democracy contain many empirical claims and assumptions, particularly about preference and opinion formation. For example, a central tenet of all deliberative theory is that deliberation can change minds and transform opinions. What if that is not the case or rarely the case? In addition to the assumption that minds are changed through deliberation, one also finds arguments concerning the direction in which minds are changed. Although few adhere to the view that deliberation inevitably leads to consensus, many believe that deliberation under the right conditions will have a tendency to broaden perspectives, promote toleration and understanding between groups, and generally encourage a public-spirited attitude (Benhabib 1992, Chambers 1996, Gutmann & Thompson 1996, J. Cohen 1997, Dryzek 2000). There is a widespread belief that deliberation and publicity associated with deliberation will have a salutary effect on people's opinions. But again we can ask, is this true? Perhaps deliberation sharpens our disagreements, intensifies social competition, and polarizes opinion (Mansbridge 1996, Sunstein 2002). Or perhaps empirical realities make it impossible to even approximate deliberative conditions, especially the equality condition (Hooghe 1999, Sanders 1997). These and other empirical questions raised by deliberative theory have spawned a growing literature concerned with testing its claims.

Empirical research falls into three categories. The first involves deep forays into fields such as social psychology, jury research, and public opinion research (Mackie 2002). The second involves designing and running experiments especially geared to test claims of deliberative democratic theory (Neblo 1998, Weber 1998, Sulkin & Simon 2001). The third category looks at "real world" cases as test cases for theoretical claims. This third area is very rich and involves many different techniques, including participant-observer methods (Quell 1998, Mendelberg & Oleske 2000), surveys and questionnaires of participants in various deliberative initiatives (Price & Neijens 1998, Pelletier et al. 1999), qualitative analysis of deliberative initiatives (Button & Mattson 1999, Smith & Wales 2000, Mutz 2002), and quantified content analysis of public statements using, for example, a Discourse Quality Index to measure whether statements live up to ideals of deliberation (Steenbergen et al. 2003, Steiner et al. 2004).

What does empirical research tell us about normative theory? The literature is quite mixed. Although "empiricists" agree that normative theory has generally been somewhat cavalier with its empirical claims, there is no consensus about whether such research generally supports the normative claims or undermines them. Some of the experimental material is particularly ambiguous because it is impossible to recreate all the crosscutting conditions that shape deliberation in an ongoing political community. The cumulative effect of this research, however, has given us a better idea about the nuts and bolts of deliberation and especially insight into questions of institutional design. Let's look quickly at one such case.

Sunstein (2002) has noted that deliberative democratic theorists would do well to look at group polarization research, which appears to challenge many central claims of deliberative democracy. Group polarization research indicates that "members of a deliberating group predictably move toward a more extreme point in the direction indicated by members' predeliberation tendencies" (Sunstein 2002, p. 176). Research seems to suggest the group polarization can be associated with two factors. The first has to do with social dynamics: Members of groups seek approval of and recognition from other group members. This tends to lead members to present themselves as champions of the most prevalent opinion of the group. The second factor is a limited argument pool that is skewed in a particular direction. Thus, the more like-minded and similar the members of a group are to start with, the more intense the group polarization effect will be.

These findings do not challenge very general claims of deliberative theory. Ideally, a well-ordered deliberation is based on full information and the representation of all points of view. Thus, the claim that under these (ideal) conditions participants are likely to become accommodating of others and more broad-minded is not directly undermined. The real question is whether the conditions of group polarization experiments offer a more plausible representation of real deliberative conditions than does normative theory. The answer is not as obvious as one might think. Experimental data record empirically observable phenomena whereas normative theory often relies on inference and conjecture about how opinions will shift in deliberation. But our political reality is no more like a controlled experiment than it is like the ideal speech situation. It is a good idea to read experimental research in a comparative framework that highlights alternative conditions. The significance and limitation of the group polarization research comes to light if we read it alongside other experimental data. For example, Sunstein (2002) notes that Fishkin's (1995) Deliberative Opinion Polling (DOP) experiments found no polarization effect.

In struggling with the feasibility of nationwide face-to-face deliberation, Fishkin proposed, developed, and implemented a series of national issues conventions intended to simulate a national deliberation (Fishkin 1995, Gastil 1996, Merkle 1996, Fishkin & Luskin 1999). These conventions are designed to gather valuable data about the dynamics of deliberation, and if they succeed, the findings could make their way into national debates. Thus, rather than appeal to "raw" public opinion, elites might be encouraged to appeal to deliberated public opinion (Ackerman & Fishkin 2002). The public would also be encouraged to think about and engage the deliberated opinion on any given policy question. The idea that small-group deliberation can at least put deliberated opinions on the agenda is also behind such proposals as citizens panels and citizen juries. One objection to these proposals is that citizens need to experience the face-to-face deliberation to find deliberated opinions persuasive in the first place. A number of objections to DOP (Mitofsky 1996, Flaven & Dougherty 1996), not the least of which is that it is undertaken under highly controlled experimental conditions, make it a questionable place holder for national debate. But as an experiment, and in comparison with polarization studies, it has produced interesting results.

Conference participants were drawn from a random sample of the population and brought to an all-expense-paid three-day issues conference (conferences have taken place in Britain, Australia, and the United States). There they participated in small-group discussions as well as larger plenary sessions on major policy questions facing the nation. A predeliberation and postdeliberation opinion survey were administered. Polarization research predicts that opinions will tend to shift toward the median predeliberation opinion. No such strong tendency emerged in DOP surveys. What explains the difference? Sunstein (2002) notes five relevant differences between Fishkin's experiment and group polarization experiments: (*a*) No votes were taken during DOP conferences; (*b*) DOP conferences were random-sample forums whereas groups polarization research usually studies groups; (*c*) moderators oversaw the discussions and insured that all points of view were heard (such moderators were usually absent in group polarization studies); (*d*) DOP conferences provided expert panelists to answer questions; and (*e*) extensive informational material was distributed to conference participants.

Sunstein concludes correctly that these differences have implications for institutional design. Moderators, random sampling (or at least bringing together people with very different viewpoints), and no voting will reduce group polarization and to that extent enhance deliberation. I would add that deliberation and deliberative democracy are appealed to in a wide range of contexts, from small one-on-one dispute resolution models proliferating at the margins of the judicial system to global "debates" about human rights and the environment. The variety of institutions, contexts, venues, and conditions in which these deliberations take place is almost inexhaustible. A comparison of group polarization studies and DOP studies provides a glimpse of some of the dynamics we must attend to in some sorts of deliberation and in designing certain sorts of institutions. But it is unclear what we should conclude from these studies with regard to the informal, free-wheeling deliberation of civic society, for example. Empirical research can be invaluable in keeping normative theorists on their toes and in zeroing in on some specific institutional design questions. Empirical research cannot be either the last or the leading word in deliberative democratic theory, however.

IDENTITY, DIVERSITY, AND RECOGNITION

Deliberative democratic theory's confrontation with the claims of identity, diversity, and recognition has pushed deliberative theory in promising new directions. This debate has led deliberative theorists to reformulate and specify aspects of the theory to make it both more concrete and better able to deal with pluralism. The criticisms voiced by diversity theory begin with a general misgiving with regard to the emphasis on agreement. As Gould notes (1996, p. 172), "the telos of discourse, what characterizes its aim and method, is agreement. Difference is something to be gotten past. And the reciprocal recognition is for the sake of common agreement rather than also for the sake of enhancing and articulating diversity." This general theme is taken up in two related but distinct tracts of political theory: postmodern difference theory and critical diversity theory. Difference is the more abstract concept; diversity almost always refers to social groups.

The exchange between postmodernism and deliberative theory has been lively and at times heated (Villa 1992, Kelly 1998, Connolly 1999, Mouffe 2000, Dean 2001). I do not discuss it in detail because, first, it has not been as productive as the exchange with diversity theory. The intersection with diversity theory has moved deliberative democratic theory in significant new directions. The debate with postmodernism has contributed to our self-understanding as moderns and highlighted the ways modernity limits rather than expands freedom, but it has not led deliberative democratic theory to major reformulations. Deliberative theory has moved away from a consensus-centered teleology—contestation and indeed the agonistic side of democracy now have their place—and it is more sensitive to pluralism. All this has more to do with a confrontation with other peoples, cultures, and identities, however, than a confrontation with postmodernism. To be sure, much of postmodernism is concerned with other peoples, cultures, and identities. The divisions between deliberative theory, diversity theory, and postmodern difference theory are very blurry at the edges, with some very good work being done at the intersection of all three (Markell 1997, 2000; White 2000; Honig 2001; Tully 2002). But for the most part, postmodernism has not compelled deliberative theory to take a closer look at how groups and specific identities fare within the model. This leads to my second reason for concentrating on identity theory. I have chosen to look at some applications of deliberative theory rather than debates about its epistemological foundations. Again we see that the exchange between diversity theory and deliberative theory has helped to make the latter more concrete. The debate with postmodernism is often very abstract.

Williams (2000) argues that diversity theory has two major concerns about deliberative theory. The first involves the notion of reasonableness and reason-giving and the second the conditions of equality. With regard to the first, Williams argues (2000, p. 125), "Whether or not citizens will recognize others' reasons *as* reasons may be a socioculturally contingent matter. Moreover, it seems likely that the contingency of this recognition may tend to be resolved in a manner that systematically disadvantages the reasons of marginalized groups in a discursive exchange" (see also Young 1996, Deveaux 2000). This sort of concern pushes deliberative theory to interrogate the process of reason-giving. Gone, with only a few exceptions (Elster 1998b), is the narrow, highly rationalistic view of reason-giving that stresses a model of impartiality rising above all difference. First as a response to feminist criticism that the impartial perspective excludes many issues and points of view that are context bound (Benhabib 1992, Phillips 1995), and second in response to multicultural criticisms that impartiality is in fact not impartial when it comes to other cultures (Williams 1998), most deliberative democratic theory has adopted a flexible and pluralistic idea of reason-giving (Bohman 1995, Benhabib 2002).

Here we see a definite expansion of the sorts of things that could be considered arguments and reasons. This expansion is sometimes the result of deep theorizing about reason but is also the result of confrontations with real-world practices.

Deliberative democracy has benefited from the "what about . . . " line of argument. What about aboriginal peoples and their use of story telling and greeting, what about African Americans and their repertoire of meanings, what about women and their appeal to the personal (which is after all political), what about the religious and their appeal to the faith, what about the oppressed and their appeal to anger and passion, what about . . . ? This does not lead to ad hocism. It leads to a richer and more useful idea of public reason that addresses real-world challenges. It concretizes the debate in positive ways and forces deliberative democratic theory to grapple with real-world cases. The intersection between deliberative theory and diversity theory is becoming less an intersection and more a merger (De Greiff 2000, Valadez 2001, Benhabib 2002). Proponents of identity politics will continue to criticize Habermas because he is too Kantian and challenge Gutmann & Thompson because they are not radical enough. But I predict that the next generation of deliberative theory will also be diversity theory.

The second concern that comes out of diversity theory is about conditions of discourse, in particular the equality condition. All deliberative democratic theory contains, either implicitly or explicitly, an idea of a well-ordered public sphere. The organizing principles of a well-ordered public sphere are drawn loosely from an ideal notion of deliberation. For the process of deliberation and accountability to work as it should, participants need to be on equal footing. But what does this mean? Theorists concerned with diversity have argued that deliberative theory has been blind to the inability of marginalized groups to even minimally meet the conditions of discourse (Fraser 1997, Williams 2000). They argue that at best deliberative theory has been too vague and abstract about the real-world barriers to authentic deliberation, and at worst it understands the problem in such minimal and negative terms (e.g., the debate about free speech and campaign finance regulation) as to fail miserably to confront it (Sanders 1997).

What sort of equality is necessary for deliberative democracy? What conditions are required to give marginalized groups voice and empowerment? These are not really questions that diversity theory brings to deliberative theory but questions that diversity theory and deliberative theory together need to answer. Where have distribution questions gone in all this talk of recognition and the public sphere? Some authors are indeed reengaging the question of distribution and poverty (Phillips 1997, Fraser 2000, Tully 2000, Fraser & Honneth 2003). Deliberative democratic theory needs to pursue questions of its own material conditions (in both the national and global context) more vigorously. This, too, I predict, will be a central concern of the next generation of deliberative theorists.

ACKNOWLEDGMENTS

I would like to thank Jeff Kopstein, Grace Skogstad, Melissa Williams, Andy Stock, Lori Weber, and David Kahane for helpful discussions and suggestions.

The *Annual Review of Political Science* is online at
http://polisci.annualreviews.org

LITERATURE CITED

Ackerman B. 1991. *We the People: Founda-tions.* Cambridge, MA: Harvard Univ. Press

Ackerman B. 1998. *We the People: Transforma-tions.* Cambridge, MA: Harvard Univ. Press

Ackerman B, Fishkin J. 2002. Deliberation day. *J. Polit. Philos.* 10(2):129–52

Arato A. 1998. Procedural law and civil society: interpreting the radical democratic paradigm. In *Habermas on Law and Democracy*, ed. M Rosenfeld, A Arato, pp. 26–36. Berkeley: Univ. Calif. Press

Archibugi D. 2000. Cosmopolitical democracy. *New Left Rev.* 4:137–50

Benhabib S. 1992. *Situating the Self: Gender, Community and Postmodernism in Contem-porary Ethics.* New York: Routledge

Benhabib S, ed. 1996. *Democracy and Differ-ence: Contesting the Boundaries of the Po-litical.* Princeton, NJ: Princeton Univ. Press

Benhabib S. 2002. *The Claims of Culture: Equality and Diversity in the Global Era.* Princeton, NJ: Princeton Univ. Press

Bohman J. 1995. Public reason and cultural plu-ralism: political liberalism and the problem of moral conflict. *Polit. Theory* 23:253–79

Bohman J. 1996. *Public Deliberation: Plu-ralism, Complexity, and Democracy.* Cam-bridge, MA: MIT Press

Bohman J. 1997. The public spheres of the world citizen. In *Perpetual Peace: Essays in Kant's Cosmopolitanism*, ed. J Bohman, M Lutz-Bachman, pp. 179–200. Cambridge, MA: MIT Press

Bohman J. 1998a. Survey article: the coming of age of deliberative democracy. *J. Polit. Phi-los.* 6(4):400–25

Bohman J. 1998b. The globalization of the pub-lic sphere: cosmopolitan publicity and the problem of cultural pluralism. *Phil. Soc.Crit.* 24:199–216

Bohman J. 1999. International regimes and democratic governance: political equality and influence in global institutions. *Int. Aff.* 75(3):499–513

Bohman J, Rehg W, eds. 1997. *Deliberative Democracy: Essays on Reason and Politics.* Cambridge, MA: MIT Press

Button M, Mattson K. 1999. Deliberative democracy in practice: challenges and pros-pects for civic deliberation. *Polity* 31:609–37

Chambers S. 1996. *Reasonable Democracy: Jürgen Habermas and the Politics of Dis-course.* Ithaca, NY: Cornell Univ. Press

Chambers S. 1998. Contract or conversation: theoretical lessons from the Canadian con-stitutional crisis. *Polit. Soc.* 26(1):143–72

Chambers S. 2002. Can procedural democracy be radical? In *Studies in Contemporary Con-tinental Political Philosophy*, ed. D Ingram, pp. 168–88. Oxford, UK: Blackwell

Cohen J. 1997. Deliberation and democratic le-gitimacy. See Bohman & Rehg 1997, pp. 67–91

Cohen JL. 1999. Personal autonomy and the law: sexual harassment and the dilemma of regulating "intimacy." *Constellations* 6(4):443–72

Cohen JL. 2002. *Regulating Intimacy: a New Legal Paradigm.* Princeton, NJ: Princeton Univ. Press

Connolly W. 1999. *Why I Am Not a Secularist.* Minneapolis: Univ. Minn. Press

Daniels N. 1991. Is the Oregon rationing plan fair? *JAMA* 265(17):2332–35

Dean J. 2001. Publicity and deliberation: demo-cratic ideals in dispute: publicity's secret. *Polit. Theory* 29(5):624–51

De Greiff P. 2000. Deliberative democracy and group representation. *Soc. Theory Pract.* 26(3):397–415

Deveaux M. 2000. *Cultural Pluralism and the Dilemmas of Justice.* Ithaca, NY: Cornell Univ. Press

Dryzek JK. 2000. *Deliberative Democracy and*

Beyond: Liberals, Critics, Contestation. Oxford, UK: Oxford Univ. Press

Dworkin R. 1996. *Freedom's Law: the Moral Reading of the American Constitution*. Cambridge, MA: Harvard Press

Elster J. 1997. The market and the forum: three varieties of political theory. See Bohman & Rehg 1997, pp. 3–33

Elster J, ed. 1998a. *Deliberative Democracy*. Cambridge, UK: Cambridge Univ. Press

Elster J. 1998b. Deliberation and constitution making. See Elster 1998a, pp. 97–122

Eriksen E, Fossum J, eds. 2000. *Democracy in the European Union: Integration through Deliberation*. London: Routledge

Fischer F. 1993. Citizen participation and the democratization of policy expertise: from theoretical inquiry to practical cases. *Policy Sci.* 26:165–87

Fischer F, Forester J. 1993. *The Argumentative Turn in Policy Analysis and Planning*. Durham, NC: Duke Univ. Press

Fishkin J. 1995. *The Voice of the People: Public Opinion and Democracy*. New Haven, CT: Yale Univ. Press

Fishkin J, Luskin R. 1999. Bringing deliberation to the democratic dialogue: the NIC and beyond. In *A Poll with a Human Face: the National Issues Convention Experiment in Political Communication*, ed. M McCombs, A Reynolds, pp. 30–38. New York: Erlbaum

Flaven C, Dougherty R. 1996. Science and citizenship at the NIC. *Public Persp.* 7(3):46–49

Fraser N. 1993. Rethinking the public sphere: a contribution to the critique of actual existing democracy. In *Habermas and the Public Sphere*, ed. C Calhoun, pp. 109–42. Cambridge, UK: Cambridge Univ. Press

Fraser N. 1997. *Justice Interruptus: Critical Reflections on the "Postsocialist" Condition*. New York: Routledge

Fraser N, Honneth A. 2003. *Redistribution or Recognition? A Philosophical Exchange*. New York: Verso

Freeman S. 2000. Deliberative democracy: a sympathetic comment. *Philos. Public Aff.* 29(4):370–418

Gastil J. 1996. *Deliberation at the National Issues Convention*. Albuquerque, NM: Inst. Public Policy

Gastil J. 2000. *By Popular Demand: Revitalizing Representative Democracy through Deliberative Elections*. Berkeley: Univ. Calif. Press

Gastil J, Gina A. 1995. *Understanding Public Deliberation*. Albuquerque, NM: Inst. Public Policy

Gould C. 1996. Diversity and democracy: representing difference. See Benhabib 1996, pp. 171–86

Gutmann A. 1999. How not to resolve moral conflicts in politics. *J. Dispute Resolut.* 15(1):1–18

Gutmann A, Thompson D. 1996. *Democracy and Disagreement: Why Moral Conflict Cannot Be Avoided in Politics, and What Should Be Done about It*. Cambridge, MA: Harvard Univ. Press

Gutmann A, Thompson D. 1997. Deliberating about bioethics. *Hastings Cent. Rep.* 27(3):38–48

Gutmann A, Thompson D. 2002. Deliberative democracy beyond process. *J. Polit. Philos.* 10(2):153–74

Habermas J. 1996. *Between Facts and Norms: Contributions to a Discourse Theory of Law and Democracy*. Transl. W Rehg. Cambridge, MA: MIT Press

Habermas J. 1998. *The Inclusion of the Other: Studies in Political Theory*. Cambridge, MA: MIT Press

Habermas J. 2001a. *The Postnational Constellation: Political Essay*. Transl. M Pensky. Cambridge, MA: MIT Press

Habermas J. 2001b. Constitutional democracy: a paradoxical union of contradictory principles? *Polit. Theory* 29(6):766–81

Habermas J. 2001c. Why Europe needs a constitution. *New Left Rev.* 11:5–26

Held D. 1995. *Democracy and the Global Order: From the Modern State to Cosmopolitan Governance*. Stanford, CA: Stanford Univ. Press

Honig B. 2001. *Democracy and the Foreigner*. Princeton, NJ: Princeton Univ. Press

Honig B. 2002. Dead rights, live futures: a reply to Habermas's "Constitutional Democray." *Polit. Theory* 29(6):792–806

Hooghe M. 1999. The rebuke of Thersites: deliberative democracy under conditions of inequality. *Acta Polit.* 4:287–301

Kahane D. 2003. Dispute resolution and the politics of cultural generalization. *Negot. J.* In press

Kelly M. 1998. *Critique and Power: Recasting the Foucault/Habermas Debate.* Cambridge, MA: MIT Press

Laden A. 2000. *Reasonably Radical: Deliberative Liberalism and the Politics of Identity.* Ithaca, NY: Cornell Univ. Press

Macedo S. 1999. *Deliberative Politics: Essays on Democracy and Disagreement.* Princeton, NJ: Princeton Univ. Press

Mackie G. 2002. *Does deliberation change minds?* Presented at Am. Polit. Sci. Assoc. Annu. Meet., Boston, Aug. 29–Sep. 1

Majone G. 1990. Policy analysis and public deliberation. In *The Power of Public Idea*, ed. R Reich, pp. 157–78. Cambridge, MA: Harvard Univ. Press

Mansbridge J. 1996. Using power/fighting power: the polity. See Benhabib 1996, pp. 44–66

Markell P. 1997. Contesting consensus: rereading *Habermas and the Public Sphere*. *Constellations* 3(3):377–400

Markell P. 2000. Making affect safe for democracy? On "constitutional patriotism." *Polit. Theory* 28(1):38–63

Mendelberg T, Oleske J. 2000. Race and public deliberation. *Polit. Commun.* 17:169–91

Merkle D. 1996. The National Issues Convention deliberative poll. *Public Opin. Q.* 60:588–619

Michelman F. 1988. Law's republic. *Yale Law J.* 97:1493–537

Michelman F. 1996. Constitutional authorship. In *Constitutionalism: Philosophical Foundations*, ed. L Alexander, pp. 64–98. Cambridge, UK: Cambridge Univ. Press

Michelman F. 1999. *Brennan and Democracy.* Princeton, NJ: Princeton Univ. Press

Mitofsky W. 1996. The emperor has no clothes. *Public Persp.* 7(3):17–19

Mouffe C. 2000. *The Democratic Paradox.* London: Verso

Mutz D. 2002. Cross-cutting social networks: testing democratic theory in practice. *Am. Polit. Sci. Rev.* 96:111–26

Neblo M. 1998. *Deliberative Actions: Identifying Communicative Rationality Empirically.* http://www.src.uchicago.edu/politicaltheory/ptarch.htm

Nino CS. 1996. *The Constitution of Deliberative Democracy.* New Haven, CT: Yale Univ. Press

O'Connell D, McKenzie R. 1995. Teaching the art of public deliberation—national issues forums in the classroom. *Polit. Sci. Politics* 28(2):230–33

Pelletier D, Kraak V, McCullum C, Uusitalo U, Rich R. 1999. The shaping of collective values through deliberative democracy: an empirical study from New York's north country. *Policy Sci.* 32:103–31

Phillips A. 1995. *The Politics of Presence: Issues in Democracy and Group Representation.* Oxford, UK: Oxford Univ. Press

Preuss U. 1995. *Constitutional Revolution: the Link Between Constitutionalism and Progress.* Transl. DL Schneider. Atlantic Highlands, NJ: Humanities

Price V, Neijens P. 1998. Deliberative polls: toward improved measures of "informed" public opinion? *Int. J. Public Opin. Res.* 10:145–76

Quell C. 1998. Citizenship concepts among Francophone immigrants in Ontario. *Can. Ethn. Stud.* 30(3):173–89

Rawls J. 1999. *The Law of Peoples.* Cambridge, MA: Harvard Univ. Press

Remer G. 1999. Political oratory and conversation: Cicero versus deliberative democracy. *Polit. Theory* 27(1):39–64

Remer G. 2000. Two models of deliberation: oratory and conversation in ratifying the Constitution. *J Polit. Philos.* 8(1):35–54

Rosenfeld M, Arato A, eds. 1998. *Habermas on Law and Democracy.* Berkeley: Univ. Calif. Press

Sandel M. 1996. *Democracy's Discontent: America in Search of a Public Philosophy.* Cambridge, MA: Harvard Univ. Press

Sanders L. 1997. Against deliberation. *Polit. Theory* 25(3):347–76

Scheuerman W. 1999. Between radicalism and resignation: democratic theory in Habermas's *Between Facts and Norms.* In *Habermas: a Critical Reader,* ed. P Dews, pp. 153–77. Oxford, UK: Blackwell

Scheuerman W. 2001. Reflexive law and the challenges of globalization. *J. Polit. Philos.* 9(1):81–102

Shaw J. 1999. Postnational constitutionalism in the European Union. *J. Eur. Public Policy* 6(4):579–97

Smith G, Wales C. 2000. Citizens' juries and deliberative democracy. *Polit. Stud.* 48:51–65

Steenbergen M, Bächtiger A, Spörndli M, Steiner J. 2003. Measuring political deliberation: a discourse quality index. *Comp. Eur. Polit.* 1:1–28

Steiner J, Bächtiger A, Spörndli M, Steenbergen M. 2004. *Deliberative Politics in Action: Crossnational Study of Parliamentary Debates.* Cambridge, UK: Cambridge Univ. Press

Sulkin T, Simon A. 2001. Habermas in the lab: a study of deliberation in an experimental setting. *Polit. Psychol.* 22(4):809–26

Sunstein C. 1993. *The Partial Constitution.* Cambridge, MA: Harvard Univ. Press

Sunstein C. 2001. *Designing Democracy: What Constitutions Do.* Oxford, UK: Oxford Univ. Press

Sunstein C. 2002. The law of group polarization. *J. Polit. Philos.* 10(2):175–95

Teubner G. 1993. Substantive and reflexive element in modern law. *Law Soc. Rev.* 17(2):239–85

Thompson D. 1999. Democratic theory and global society. *J. Polit. Philos.* 7(2):111–25

Tully J. 1995. *Strange Multiplicity: Constitu-tionalism in an Age of Diversity.* Cambridge, UK: Cambridge Univ. Press

Tully J. 2000. Struggles over recognition and distribution. *Constellations* 7(4):469–82

Tully J. 2001. Introduction. In *Multinational Democracies,* ed. A-G Gagnon, J Tully, pp. 1–34. Cambridge, UK: Cambridge Univ. Press

Tully J. 2002. The unfreedom of the moderns in comparison to their ideals of constitutional democracy. *Mod. Law Rev.* 65(2):204–28

Valadez JM. 2001. *Deliberative Democracy: Political Legitimacy and Self-Determination in Multicultural Societies.* Boulder, CO: Westview

Villa D. 1992. Postmodernism and the public sphere. *Am. Polit. Sci. Rev.* 86:712–21

Warren M. 2002. What can democratic participation mean today? *Polit. Theory* 30(5):677–702

Weber L. 1998. *The effect of democratic deliberation on political tolerance.* Presented at Annu. Meet. Midwest Polit. Sci. Assoc., Chicago, IL

Weiler J. 1995. Does Europe need a constitution? Reflections on demos, telos, and the German Maastricht decision. *Eur. Law J.* 1(3):219–58

White SK. 2000. *Sustaining Affirmation: the Strengths of Weak Ontology in Political Theory.* Princeton, NJ: Princeton Univ. Press

Williams M. 1998. *Voice, Trust, and Memory: Marginalized Groups and the Failings of Liberal Representation.* Princeton, NJ: Princeton Univ. Press

Williams M. 2000. The uneasy alliance of group representation and deliberative democracy. In *Citizenship in Diverse Societies,* ed. W Kymlicka, W Norman, pp. 124–54. Oxford, UK: Oxford Univ. Press

Young I. 1996. Communication and the other: beyond deliberative democracy. See Benhabib 1996, pp. 120–36

Annu. Rev. Polit. Sci. 2003. 6:327–43
doi: 10.1146/annurev.polisci.6.121901.085546
First published online as a Review in Advance on Jan. 24, 2003

THE POLITICAL ECONOMY OF HEALTH IN THE UNITED STATES

John D. Wilkerson
Department of Political Science, University of Washington, Seattle, Washington 98195;
email: jwilker@u.washington.edu

Key Words health politics, health markets, health care reform, politics of health

■ **Abstract** The United States pays a high price for its health system, and governments pay about half the costs. At the same time, the United States distinguishes itself by failing to provide health insurance for 15% of its population. In this article, I review research on the politics and economics of health to investigate three questions. Does this spending represent good value? Why does the United States spend so much on health? Finally, what technical and political challenges do policy makers face as they turn away from government solutions and toward market-based solutions to the challenge of balancing costs, access, and quality?

INTRODUCTION

Tax-financed health expenditures constituted nearly 60% of all health-related spending in the United States in 1999 (Woolhandler & Himmelstein 2002, p. 91). Government-sponsored public health and safety programs have led to some of the most important accomplishments of the twentieth century (Centers for Disease Control 1999), while government subsidies and policies have played a central role in the development of the U.S. health care system. Because of these investments, Americans are living longer and they are living better.

On the other hand, the health system that government has promoted is inefficient and unfair. The United States spends 50% more of its gross domestic product on health care than other OECD nations and seems to get less in return (Anderson et al. 2000). In 1960, Canada was spending 5.4% of its GDP on health and the United States was spending 5.1%. By 2000, the United States was spending >13% of its GDP on health (about $1.2 trillion) compared to Canada's 9%. Life expectancy in the United States was 2–3 years shorter, infant mortality was one third higher, and Canada had improved more quickly in both areas since 1960.

A recent report projects that private health insurance premiums will increase by >15% in 2003 (*New York Times* 2002). The Congressional Budget Office projects that federal health program spending will increase from 4% today to nearly 15% of the GDP by 2030 and will surpass Social Security as the most expensive federal entitlement (Congressional Budget Office 2002). Despite recent reforms making health insurance more portable and expanding public program eligibility for children, the number of uninsured Americans is above 40 million (15% of the population) and rising.

Is the U.S. health care system in crisis? Health care spending in the public and private sectors continues to spiral upward with no end in sight, and with questionable benefits for the nation's overall health. Certainly, health care costs constitute something of a crisis for the governments, businesses, and consumers who pick up the tab. More spending on health means less spending on other programs, higher taxes, less profit, and less disposable income. But a focus on costs alone does not answer the central question—do we get good value for the dollars we spend? Research offers three answers to this question.

First, it is easy to demonstrate that this spending has yielded beneficial health effects (Cutler et al. 1999, Hadley 2002). For example, an additional $4000 investment in treating a heart attack extends a Medicare patient's life by an average of eight months. Five hundred dollars seems a small price to pay for an additional month of life. Cutler et al. conclude (1999, p. 69) that "although we pay more for medical care than we used to, we also get more in return." Murphy & Topel (1999) estimate the economic value of reductions in death rates since 1970 at $57 trillion, well below the cumulative health care costs of the period.

Second, these benefits have come at a high cost. The McKinney Group compared medical services in the United States and Germany and found that the U.S. system was 26.5% more productive but 65% more expensive. The Dartmouth Health Atlas Project documented variations in Medicare costs across the nation and found that the cost of treating a typical Medicare patient is three times higher in some regions (Wennberg & Gittelson 1973, Wennberg & Cooper 1999). Moreover, these higher costs usually do not translate into better outcomes for patients (Reinhardt 2000, Newhouse 2002, Wennberg et al. 2002).

Finally, the most significant benefits of medical care do not come from the most sophisticated and expensive interventions. Many health economists would question whether advances in medical care are responsible for the mortality reductions that are at the center of Murphy & Topel's economic analysis. Figure 1 graphs the percentage of the population that could be expected to survive to a particular age at four points during the last century (Anderson 2001). Clearly, the most dramatic gains occurred between 1900 and 1950, when modern medicine was still in its infancy. Public health innovations were primarily responsible for these gains. Between 1900 and 1960, the death rate from pneumonia, tuberculosis, diarrhea, enteritis, and diphtheria declined by 90% owing to improvements in sanitation and immunizations. Deaths among children <5 years of age declined from 20% of all deaths in 1900 to <2% today. In 1900, heart disease, stroke, and cancer accounted for 18% of all deaths. These diseases account for 65% of all deaths today, in part because so many more people are living longer (Centers for Disease Control 1999).

Perhaps the best evidence that spending on medical care services is not the primary driver of health differences comes from the fact that other nations have

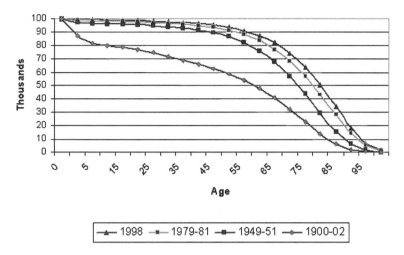

Figure 1   Survivorship rates 1900–1998.

managed to achieve similar mortality reductions with substantially smaller per capita investments. The key drivers seem to be differences in basic living conditions across societies and increased access to basic medical care, such as preventive services and antibiotics, rather than access to the latest technologies (see also Wilkinson 1986, House 2001).

Taken as a whole, these findings suggest that the United States pays a high cost for its health system. It is more productive, but these productivity gains are offset by higher prices. It is more expensive, but these higher costs do not translate into better health outcomes or even similar levels of access.

DEVELOPMENTS AND POLITICS

Most health policy scholars place the initial blame for this situation squarely on the shoulders of private providers and the unwillingness or inability of governments to rein them in. The United States committed itself to this path early in the twentieth century (Skocpol 1997, Hacker 1998, Tuohy 1999). Starr (1984) argues that physicians drew on their claims of expertise and on public suspicion of government to define illness and to turn back repeated government efforts to "socialize" medicine. When the federal government finally did become involved, it did so in ways that explicitly avoided interfering in the practice of medicine. As a result, early developments in the U.S. health care system were oriented toward the priorities and perspectives of medical providers.

The power of the medical lobby and its allies in the insurance and hospital industries during this period is difficult to exaggerate (Morone 1990). Advances in modern medicine made access to health care increasingly important and increasingly expensive after World War II. Presidents from Truman to Kennedy tried unsuccessfully to address these problems by tiptoeing around the medical lobby. Truman's single-payer proposal was soundly defeated. When Eisenhower proposed his version of Medicare, the American Medical Association vowed to fight it "with every resource" (*Congressional Quarterly Almanac* 1960, p. 163). When Kennedy proposed a different version, he went out of his way to argue that it was not "a program of socialized medicine" (*Congressional Quarterly Almanac* 1961, p. 870). Johnson's first attempt to pass a Medicare program failed just as Kennedy's had. Johnson ultimately succeeded, but only after he asked voters to make the 1964 election a referendum on the issue and won by a landslide (*Congressional Quarterly Almanac* 1964, p. 239).

Medicare represented a radical departure from past federal policies because it made the federal government a purchaser of health care services. Like earlier policies subsidizing the construction of hospitals and medical education, Medicare's reimbursement policies were designed to be as innocuous as possible. Providers were to be reimbursed for each service provided based on "reasonable and customary" costs. (Prepayment, in which providers receive a single payment to provide all required care, existed at the time but was never seriously considered because the independent practitioners represented by the American Medical Association staunchly opposed it.) Medicare Part A offered limited hospital benefits similar to those of private plans. Medicare Part B placed no limits on reimbursement for physician services, although both parts of the program included substantial deductibles and copayments.

The cost implications of these generous policies were probably appreciated at the time. Conservative Ways and Means Chairman Wilbur Mills (D-AR) opposed Medicare for many years, partly because he believed that program costs would rise rapidly without proper controls (Patashnik & Zelizer 2001). For the dominant political coalition, getting the federal government's foot into the door of government-sponsored health insurance was the priority (Marmor 1973, Ball 1995). Fewer than half of the elderly possessed health insurance of any kind. Partly because of the devastating costs of an illness, the poverty rate among the elderly (24%) was twice that of the nonelderly population.

By the 1970s, health care costs were rising about twice as quickly as general inflation. The increased availability of private and public insurance made health care services affordable for an increasingly large segment of the population, and the increased demand created pressure on short-term prices. What was not expected was that prices failed to moderate with increased supply. The primary culprit was soon identified. Rapid medical developments expanded the range of services available to patients, while comprehensive fee-for-service insurance gave both providers and patients little reason to ration access to those services. Newhouse (1996) and Peden & Freeland (1995, p. 235) estimate that 70% of this growth has been the result of "cost-increasing advances in medical services induced by insurance coverage." The standard variables of population increases, changing demographics, and general prices account for less than half of this growth.

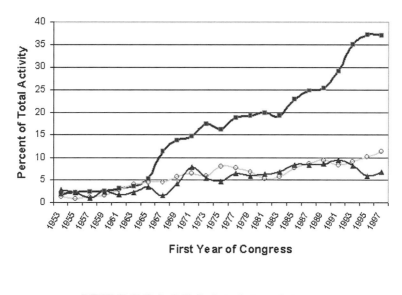

Figure 2   Federal health activity 1953–1998.

Between 1953 and 1998, the percentage of the federal budget devoted to health programs rose from <2% to >36% (Figure 2). Health also consumed an increasingly large share of Congress's legislative agenda, rising from <2% of all bills to nearly 12% in 1998. During the 1970s, federal policy tried to limit utilization of services through health system planning and reforms designed to realign provider incentives (Brown 1982, Ruggie 1992, Patel & Rushevsky 1995, Weissert & Weissert 1996). The Health Planning Act of 1974 required hospitals to demonstrate need for additional services in a community before they could build or expand. The HMO Act of 1973 offered subsidies to stimulate prepaid health systems in which providers profit by limiting unnecessary care rather than by providing it.

During the 1980s, the focus of attention shifted to more direct control over prices. The Prospective Payment System of the Medicare program replaced the "reasonable costs" approach with government rate setting. Diagnosis-related groups (DRGs) reimbursed Medicare providers by diagnosis, instead of for each specific service provided. The 1980s also saw employers becoming more actively involved in efforts to identify private as well as public solutions to the cost problem (Martin 1993, 2000).

Cost concerns did not completely displace concerns about access. National health insurance was on the agenda, to varying degrees, under Presidents Nixon, Ford, Carter, and Clinton. During the 1980s and 1990s, Congress passed laws expanding access and coverage. In 1988, President Reagan signed the Medicare

Catastrophic Coverage Act, only to see it repealed after objections from seniors (Himelfarb 1995, Wilkerson et al. 2002). Medicaid was strengthened. The private long-term care insurance market received a boost. New laws made it somewhat easier for people to change jobs without losing their health insurance coverage and created incentives for states to provide health insurance for all children through age 18 (Patel & Ruschevsky 1995).

These incremental efforts have been beneficial, but they have not come close to solving the access problems they were promoted as addressing. Other nations have placed much less faith in markets and have been willing to negotiate wages, ration care, and limit spending. This is a path the United States is unlikely to take for broader ideological and structural reasons. Comprehensive government reform went out the window with the decisive rejection and political repercussions of the Health Security Act in 1994.

Private and public payers have turned to market competition as the solution to rising health care costs, if for no reason other than an absence of alternatives. Such an approach conforms to a broader ideological shift away from government (Skocpol 1997). However, the assumption that competition will shake out the inefficiencies of the health care market is unproven and theoretically problematic. Left alone, markets cannot be expected to allocate health efficiently, and they will certainly not allocate it equitably. The future of the U.S. health care system will depend on the public and private sectors' abilities to restructure health markets to promote collective goals. To better appreciate the challenges these efforts will face, we need to better understand why health markets fail.

ECONOMIC MARKETS AND HEALTH

Health economists tend to focus on the limits of markets as a means for promoting the efficient allocation of health care services. According to Aaron (2002, p. 33), health markets operate on "faulty price signals" (p. 34) that lead to inefficient transactions. According to Newhouse (2002, p. 16), the "Darwinian process found in most markets does not operate as ruthlessly in medical care."

The normative appeal of competitive markets is that if an equilibrium exists, it is Pareto efficient: Any other distribution cannot make some people better off without making others worse off. The "if" of the theory is that the equilibrium prediction holds only if the market is "competitive." Producers and consumers are assumed to have good information about the prices, values, and choices available in the market. No participant is able to manipulate prices. Producers and consumers consider the total benefits and costs of a commodity in evaluating how much it is worth to them.

Arrow (1963, p. 951) brought health into the mainstream economics literature by arguing that "uncertainty as to the quality of the product is perhaps more intense here than in any other commodity."

Arrow saw professional norms in medicine as responses to consumer uncertainty about the value of medical care. The physician's knowledge "is necessarily very much greater than that of the patient, or at least so it is believed" and "their relation is colored by this knowledge" (Arrow 1963, p. 946). Through advertising prohibitions, free care, and nonprofit hospitals, providers try to signal that the patient's health, rather than their bottom line, comes first. Through exclusive licensing practices and adherence to socially accepted "best" treatments, providers try to reassure doubtful consumers that they are receiving quality care.

Arrow's explanation stands in sharp contrast to the portrayals of other scholars, who argue that practices such as restrictive licensing were designed not to reassure patients but to limit entry in order to extract rents (Starr 1984). This debate over the motives behind private as well as public policies relating to the medical profession continues today (Arrow 2001, Robinson 2001). Both perspectives are consistent with the facts, and institutions created with one purpose in mind can serve other purposes as well.

In addition to the centrality of uncertainty, Arrow made several other important observations about medical care markets that remain relevant today. First, the normative goal of Pareto efficiency limits the range of possible outcomes to those in which no party ends up worse off than he began. Societies may have good reasons to object to this standard.

Second, some commodities are not marketable because the benefits or costs extend beyond the market participants or into the future. Immunizations, for example, serve a public as well as a private purpose in preventing the spread of illness. For an individual, the cost of an immunization may seem too high relative to its direct benefits. As a result, fewer immunizations will be purchased than is socially optimal. Genetic research benefits the firm that is developing a product, but the same research would also be expected to yield knowledge that benefits other companies and society as a whole. Once again, market incentives alone may lead to investment levels that are below what is socially optimal.

Finally, Arrow notes that Pareto efficiency is a theoretical prediction under an assumed set of conditions. If a health care market fails to meet the conditions for a competitive market, then a decision to rely on market principles to allocate health care may no longer be defendable in terms of economic theory (Arrow 1963, p. 943; Reinhardt 2001). This point is often ignored in public debates about the virtues of markets, which seem to proceed on the assumption that fairly competitive markets yield fairly efficient outcomes. How much efficiency are we willing to trade to promote equity? In fact, economic theory offers no such general reassurance that a market that meets more of these conditions will be more efficient than a market that meets fewer of them.

ROLES OF GOVERNMENT

Many in government and the private sector believe that we are spending too much on health, period. Politically, such perceptions are important because policy makers and their publics may be less supportive of additional health-related spending if they believe that the current system is wasteful or corrupt. Reinhardt (2000,

p. 162) argues that "by its very nature the typical health care transaction lacks legitimacy . . . because health care transactions are not based on the personal cost-benefit analysis that the purchasers of ordinary commodities routinely make in the marketplace."

Much of the literature on the politics of health focuses on why governments of the past have failed to produce health policies that serve the public interest and why governments have failed to act when action was needed. These explanations run the gamut of political science perspectives. Elected officials tend to be most responsive to attentive special interests, and those who bear the direct costs of a policy change tend to be the most attentive (Feldstein 1977, Skocpol 1997, Balbach & Glantz 2000). Minority interests use institutional veto points to thwart the will of the majority (Brady & Buckley 1995, Evans 1995, Steinmo & Watts 1995). Regulatory agencies are captured and end up serving the interests of those they are supposed to regulate (Balla 1998, Huber & Shipan 2002). On the other hand, special interests often have competing agendas that limit their influence (Walker 1991, Peterson 1993, Baumgartner & Talbert 1995). Public enthusiasm is not a necessary condition for policy reform (Jacobs & Shapiro 1995). And nonincremental reforms do sometimes pass despite institutional veto points (Baumgartner & Jones 1993).

In my view, however, the complexity of the underlying issue tends to be under-emphasized in this research (Peterson 1995). Governments can intervene for the right reasons and still produce the wrong policies. Reviewing a journal volume on the managed-care backlash, Peterson (1999) noted the authors' consensus that it was real and demanded a political response. But he found "relatively little agreement [among the authors] about which government initiatives are most sensible and how aggressive either state or federal policy makers ought to be in their efforts to soften managed care's hard edge" (Peterson 1999, p. 875). On one hand, there was a legitimate concern that managed care organizations would deny necessary care. On the other hand, there was a legitimate concern that policies limiting abuse would prevent managed care organizations from limiting unnecessary care.

It was not a coincidence that the Health Security Act was developed with the assistance of more than 500 experts and was over 1300 pages long. Nearly everywhere in the health care arena, efforts to reform the system in one area bump up against efforts to advance other goals. Commoner's law in reference to the environment also applies to health: "Everything is connected to everything else" (Commoner 1971, p. 163). Politics aside, creating the proper incentives has been a stumbling block of past efforts by governments and private sector payers to control costs, increase access, and improve quality simultaneously, and it remains the central challenge today.

REDUCING UNCERTAINTY

Costs (not value) have been a central motivating factor for both public and private reform efforts (Oberlander 1995). Both public and private sector payers have been frustrated by their longstanding inability to rein in health care costs. However, it is also important to recognize the challenges facing reformers on the quality side of the equation. The value of a product is a function of both its price and its quality. An effective health care system rewards providers for the health they produce, not for the services they provide. An efficient health care system maximizes the health produced for a given level of resources.

Critics contend that government reimbursement policies have been ill designed to promote efficiency (De Parle 2002). They note that government policies have a strong status quo bias (Newhouse 2002, p. 17). Medicare payments to health maintenance organizations (HMOs) begin with average costs for the local service area. This practice, which is still in place today, assumes that there are good reasons for costs to be higher in some areas than in others despite a growing body of evidence to the contrary. Regions that have innovated to hold down costs are penalized—exactly the opposite of the policy's intended effect. Across-the-board cuts perpetuate a preexisting bias in favor of expensive, specialized treatment and reward regions with historically high rates of utilization or historically high reimbursement rates.

The same holds true for reimbursements for specific services and diagnoses.

Ambulatory procedure codes (APC) schedules provide higher reimbursements for complicated and intensive procedures, even if no evidence indicates that they are more effective. Diagnosis-related group (DRG) schedules pay a fixed rate to provide all necessary care for a given diagnosis. They too are criticized as not creating incentives that promote efficiency (Wynia et al. 2000). For example, a physician might diagnose and admit a heart attack patient to the hospital and later decide that the patient can be treated on an outpatient basis. The decision to admit places the patient in a DRG that assumes more intensive services and therefore pays more. The physician's subsequent decision to treat the patient on an outpatient basis saves the system money. However, the Department of Health and Human Services interprets such actions as fraud. The assumption is that the provider knows how best to treat the patient, and such erratic behavior indicates an effort to game the system. In this case, the provider could file an amendment to her original diagnosis, but it is probably easier to keep the patient in the hospital.

What is needed is an incentive system that rewards the benefits of the provided service by comparing inputs to outputs. Unfortunately, information about the comparative effectiveness of different treatments or the performance of different providers is the exception more than the rule. Such information is difficult to obtain because it requires an accurate diagnosis of the patient and an understanding of the effect of the intervention. How sick was the patient? If the patient was treated and died, is that evidence of poor care? If the provider did little and the patient died, is that evidence of poor care?

When Medicare first began to contract with private HMOs, the government assumed that managed-care firms would be able to operate more efficiently than traditional fee-for-service Medicare. The reimbursement rate for HMOs was set at 95% of risk-adjusted costs for an enrollee in the service area. It turned out that areas with higher reimbursement rates attracted more HMOs than did areas with lower reimbursement rates. Moreover, in areas with higher rates, HMOs were adding remarkable benefits, such as coverage for prescription drugs, at no additional cost.

Was this evidence of increased efficiency? Or was it evidence of something else? The evidence indicated that HMOs profited not by being more efficient but by attracting healthier Medicare enrollees (De Parle 2002). Medicare HMOs appeared successful in holding down costs because their enrollees used fewer services. Medicare has subsequently altered adjustments for enrollment mix and has reduced payments to HMOs—so much so that HMOs are scaling back benefits or raising premiums, and even fleeing from the Medicare program altogether.

Medical savings accounts (MSAs) have also been promoted as a means for making health care markets operate more efficiently by making consumers more price sensitive (Pauly & Goodman 1995). This argument for MSAs assumes that consumers are able to compare the value of alternative health care services, an assumption that seems to be contradicted by both Arrow's observation that information is what providers sell in a health care system, and by research at RAND (Newhouse 2002, p. 17). The results of the RAND Health Insurance experiment indicate that increased cost sharing led consumers to reduce their number of visits to physicians but had little impact on their use of the most expensive services (Newhouse 1996). Lower costs do not imply increased efficiency if, for example, additional cost sharing deters consumers from seeking out cost-effective preventive services (Hsaio 2001).

Society as a whole benefits from knowing whether a particular approach to health is beneficial or cost-effective, or whether a particular hospital provides quality care. Unfortunately, markets cannot always be counted on to provide the necessary data. Information is often costly to obtain, and the benefits are distributed. Consumers may have good reasons to resist sharing their medical information for the greater good. Providers may resist collecting data, especially high-quality data, because it is time consuming or because it is threatening (Newhouse 2002, p. 20). Recent research suggests that medical mistakes are a leading cause of death in the United States (Kohn et al. 2000). Better information may serve to reduce such mistakes, but it is also damaging to the providers responsible. "Better transparency and speedier communication in U.S. health care actually [have] more powerful enemies than friends" (Reinhardt 2001, p. 987). More generally, information about the effectiveness of treatments is proprietary.

And information, if it is available, may not be used. Consumers (and providers) may not be well equipped to balance the tradeoffs that are often inherent in medical care choices. Providers may believe that proper medical care cannot be guided by statistical patterns, or they may operate according to norms and financial incentives that provide little reason to deny access to treatments that have only marginal benefits. Fully insured consumers may have little incentive to question the decisions of providers, unless they perceive that the interests of the provider are at odds with their own. The moral hazard predicts that consumers who appreciate that generic drugs are largely equivalent to brand-name drugs and are considerably cheaper will nonetheless choose the brand-name drug. Legislators from Florida who complain about rising health care costs will resist reductions in Medicare reimbursements to their state, even if the evidence demonstrates that average costs in Florida are twice as high as another state's with no improvement in health. Corporations may oppose reforms that would promote greater information sharing because they fear that the end result would be increased state or federal regulation of their health plans.

VALUES BESIDES EFFICIENCY

Information is valued for its ability to reduce waste and harm. But information cannot tell us what our goals are, or how we should trade off among competing objectives. Information can tell us whether angioplasty is more economical than bypass surgery, but it cannot tell us whether we are spending too much on treating heart disease. Information cannot answer the "who counts?" and "what's fair?" questions that are central to health policy debates.

Even in a competitive market, a society may legitimately choose to intervene to promote fairness or to address problems of undersupply and oversupply of public goods. The public may want to control how their medical records are shared. The public may want to subsidize immunizations or weight-loss programs when private insurers are unwilling to provide them. The public may want to tax tobacco products because the market price of cigarettes does not include the future costs of smoking for the individual and society. And of course markets will not allocate health care and health equitably.

Equity concerns have been most visible in reform efforts promoting health insurance coverage for the uninsured. The case can be made that income security, rather than health security, has been the central motivation behind such efforts. Medicare was promoted primarily as a program to protect seniors and their families from financial ruin. In 1994, President Clinton's Health Security Act was a response to public concerns about the tenuous state of the economy. People were worried about losing their jobs and their employment-based health insurance.

Health equity probably requires that policy move in a different direction. Fuchs (1994, p. 109) finds "little evidence either in this country or abroad to suggest that providing universal coverage or changing the delivery system will have significant favorable effects on health, either in the aggregate or for particular socioeconomic groups." Access to health insurance coverage does appear to be related to better health outcomes (Hadley 2002), but other factors are more important in explaining health differences across populations. Income disparities, not health care spending differences, are the best predictors of differences in health status across developed nations. As House puts it (2001, p. 530), conditions of poverty (discrimination and poor housing, sanitation, education, and recreation) are not "promotive of health."

Public health initiatives that extend beyond health care services are controversial, not because they are less effective but because they would primarily benefit the "undeserving" poor (Ingram & Schneider 1993). Medicaid has received much less political support over the years than Medicare, even though two thirds of Medicaid spending supports the elderly and disabled. Improved public housing is good public policy for improving the health of children, but it will be much more controversial than providing those same children with access to health insurance. Needle-exchange programs may be a very effective and inexpensive method for preventing the spread of HIV/AIDS to children, but they are opposed as supporting the chosen habits of "deviants" (Donovan 1998).

HEALTH AND THE POLITICS OF INDIVIDUAL RESPONSIBILITY

Stone (1989) argues that whether a problem such as the uninsured deserves a government response depends on which causal story ends up dominating the debate. The original logic for health insurance was that illness occurred rarely and was beyond the control of the individual. In this story, the uninsured are victims of circumstances beyond their control. President Clinton reflected on Kerry Kennedy, a small businessman who had "poured his heart and soul, his sweat and blood" into his business but could no longer afford health insurance for his workers because his mother and father, who had started the business, "had become high risks because of their advanced age" (Clinton 1993, p. 1558). Tobacco reform efforts claim to be protecting the health of children, who are victims of unwanted advances by Joe Camel.

On the other side is the argument that health is largely a matter of individual responsibility and choice. Shortly after Clinton gave his speech, Senate minority leader Robert Dole (R-KS) questioned Administration claims of a health crisis by suggesting that many of the uninsured could purchase health insurance but elected not to. [A Kaiser Family Foundation (2000, p. 12) survey of the uninsured found that 19% of uninsured adults felt that they did not need insurance, and 3% cited this as their primary reason for not purchasing it.] Similar arguments about individual responsibility are presented in objection to policy initiatives designed to mitigate the consequences of risky behaviors, such as sexually transmitted diseases, lung cancer, and the growing problem of obesity (Shiltz 1987, Rosin 1998, Kessler 2001).

THE MYTH OF RATIONING

The complaint that government-based reforms will lead to rationing has been a powerful weapon in the arsenal of opponents of health care reform. This claim is undoubtedly true, if only because *any* system for allocating health care services rations. The Health Security Act proposed an alternative rationing scheme to the one that was already in place. The current system places the burden on the 15% of the population that is uninsured. The Health Security Act would have redistributed that burden over the 85% of the population who already had coverage.

The assumption that government-funded health care is less efficient is also far from evident. There are reasons to expect that consumers collectively would get more out of a government-based health care system. Private health insurance has substantially higher administrative costs than the Medicare program, largely because of marketing costs. And, as discussed, much of the health care spending in the United States is wasteful in the sense that more service use does not always translate to better health outcomes. A government-based system might better control utilization and prices and, as a result, costs. Canada regulates utilization, salaries, and how much the nation spends on health. Although these actions would clearly constitute rationing for those who can currently afford the best in care under the U.S. system, the end result might be increased access and improved population health.

A universal health care system would cost more, but it would not necessarily be less efficient. A government reform that expanded coverage for poorer individuals would be expected to increase utilization and perhaps even raise average costs if wealthier individuals tend to be healthier. But judging whether these higher costs indicate inefficiency requires a comparison of the added costs to the added benefits. Those benefits would include improved health, improved economic productivity, and increased protection from financial hardship.

CONCLUSIONS

The holy grail of health care reform is a proposal that promotes quality and increases access while controlling costs (Reinhardt 2000). Public perceptions that such a reform must exist have been a central stumbling block of health care reform efforts. These three objectives are dynamically related. Most people who lack health insurance cannot afford it. Health insurance costs are high because consumers and providers have weak incentives to limit access to services when those costs are broadly distributed. The existence of dramatic geographic variations in utilization rates without evidence of improved health outcomes suggests that costs could be dramatically lowered, given sufficient political will. This, in turn, would lower overall costs and make health insurance more affordable. More people would purchase insurance. Costs would be distributed even more broadly, reducing premiums once again.

Most Americans believe that we are spending too much on health, but they are also reluctant to embrace the solutions that have been proposed. Polls suggest that Americans (collectively speaking) want it all. They would like to see everyone covered. At the same time, the vast majority of Americans express satisfaction with their own care and have resisted reforms that would limit their own health care choices in order to control costs or provide coverage for others (Brodie & Blendon 1995). The fictional Harry and Louise captured the sentiments of a nation when they rejected the Health Security Act as flawed, while failing to provide any hint of the "better way" they preferred (West et al. 1996).

Policy makers have followed the public's lead. They have tried to address the problem of rising costs while avoiding accusations of rationing (at least for the most politically active constituencies). When policy makers have addressed rationing, they have attempted to make it more difficult for providers to limit access to services, instead of easier. When policy makers have enacted reforms designed to promote greater attention to quality, they have worried too much about short-term political consequences and not enough about long-term benefits. And for the most part, these efforts have had little impact on the problems they were designed to address.

Some suggest that many of these challenges will be resolved as technological advances lower the costs of promoting and preserving health, and warn against reforms that might suppress the innovation that will cause this to happen. Physician Lewis Thomas (1983) argued that the current medical care system emphasizes what he calls expensive "halfway" technologies, such as organ transplants and dialysis, whose purpose is to treat diseases that cannot be cured or managed. The future of medicine, according to Thomas, rests with "decisive technologies" that attack the fundamental underlying causes of illnesses at the molecular level. For example, HIV interventions have become more effective over time, but they remain prohibitively expensive and do little to reduce the spread of the disease. The vaccine that will prevent HIV/AIDS, saving millions of lives and billions of dollars in the process, remains elusive because researchers do not fully understand the biological processes underlying the disease. There are reasons to think that technical evolution may address many of the concerns that seem so problematic today (Gelijns et al. 2001). The past century, indeed the past decade, has witnessed dramatic advances in health and our scientific understanding of the human body. Perhaps technology will soon solve the cost and equity problems that resist simple solutions today.

Belkin (1997) calls such thinking the "technocratic wish," because it appeals to science and objectivity to resolve contentious political issues. As discussed, we also need to consider whether the innovations that we would like to see are the things that markets of the future are likely to produce. The answer to this question is far from obvious, even if our understanding of disease and interventions expands much more rapidly than past patterns would lead us to expect. There will be tremendous advances in our understanding of disease and how to treat it, but the benefits of those advances will be tempered by the same factors that shape health care decisions today. Market actors will always have limited incentives to share information, to promote quality, and to supply public goods. Governments will always have an important role in reshaping market incentives to promote the public interest or in supplying what markets cannot supply. Despite the best wishes of the technocrats, politics cannot be avoided. The challenge of politics, on the other hand, is to persuade governments to focus on the right question: How can health, as opposed to health care services, be allocated efficiently and equitably?

The *Annual Review of Political Science* is online at
http://polisci.annualreviews.org

LITERATURE CITED

Aaron HJ. 2002. A funny thing happened on the way to managed competition. *J. Health Polit. Policy Law* 27:31–36

Anderson RN. 2001. United States life tables. *Natl. Vital Stat. Rep.* 48(18):1–39

Anderson GF, Hurst J, Hussey PS, Jee-Hughes M. 2000. Health spending and outcomes: trends in OECD countries, 1960–1998. *Health Aff.* 19:150–57

Arrow KJ. 1963. Uncertainty and the welfare

economics of medical care. *Am. Econ. Rev.* 53:941–73

Arrow KJ. 2001. Reflections on the reflections. *J. Health Polit. Policy Law* 26:1197–1203

Balbach E, Glantz S. 2000. The implementation of California's tobacco tax initiative: the critical role of outsider strategies in protecting Proposition 99. *J. Health Polit. Policy Law* 25:689–715

Ball RM. 1995. What Medicare's architects had in mind. *Health Aff.* 14:62–72

Balla SJ. 1998. Administrative procedures and the policy process. *Am. Polit. Sci. Rev.* 92: 663–73

Baumgartner FR, Jones BD. 1993. *Agendas and Instability in American Politics.* Chicago: Univ. Chicago Press

Baumgartner FR, Talbert JC. 1995. From setting a national agenda on health care to making decisions in Congress. *J. Health Polit. Policy Law* 20:437–45

Belkin GS. 1997. The technocratic wish: making sense and finding power in the "managed" medical marketplace. *J. Health Polit. Policy Law* 22:509–32

Brady DW, Buckley KM. 1995. Health care reform in the 103rd Congress: a predictable failure. *J. Health Polit. Policy Law* 2:447–57

Brodie M, Blendon R. 1995. The public's contribution to congressional gridlock on health care reform. *J. Health Polit. Policy Law* 20: 403–10

Brown L. 1982. *The Political Structure of the Federal Health Planning Program.* Washington, DC: Brookings Inst.

Centers for Disease Control. 1999. Achievements in public health 1900–1999: infectious diseases. *Morbid. Mortal. Wkly. Rep.* 48:621–29

Clinton WJ. 1993. Address to a joint session of the Congress on health care reform. *Public Papers of the President*, 2:1556–65. Washington, DC: Gov. Print. Off.

Commoner B. 1971. The closing circle: nature, man and technology. In *Thinking About the Environment*, ed. MA Cahn, R O'Brien, pp. 161–66. New York: Sharpe

Congressional Budget Office. 2002. *The Budget and Economic Outlook* (ch. 6). http://www.cbo.gov/showdoc.cfm?index=3735&sequence=0

Congressional Quarterly Almanac. 1960, 1961, 1964. Washington, DC: Congr. Q. Press

Cutler D, McClellan M, Newhouse J. 1999. The costs and benefits of intensive treatment for cardiovascular disease. In *Measuring the Prices of Medical Treatments*, ed. JE Triplett, pp. 34–71. Washington, DC: Brookings Inst. Press

De Parle NA. 2002. As good as it gets? The future of Medicare+Choice. *J. Health Polit. Policy Law* 27:495–512

Donovan MC. 1998. *Taking Aim: Target Populations and the War on Drugs and AIDS.* Washington, DC: Georgetown Univ. Press

Evans LM. 1995. Committees and health jurisdictions in Congress. In *Intensive Care: How Congress Shapes Health Policy*, ed. TE Mann, NJ Ornstein, pp. 25–52. Washington, DC: AEI/Brookings

Feldstein PJ. 1977. *Health Associations and the Demand for Legislation.* Cambridge, MA: Ballinger

Fuchs VR. 1994. The Clinton plan: a researcher examines reform. *Health Aff.* 13:102–14

Gelijns AC, Zivin JG, Nelson RR. 2001. Uncertainty and technological change in medicine. *J. Health Polit. Policy Law* 26:913–24

Hacker JS. 1998. The historical logic of national health insurance: structure and sequence in the development of British, Canadian and US medical policy. *Stud. Am. Polit. Dev.* 12:57–130

Hadley J. 2002. *Sicker and Poorer: Health Insurance, Health, and the Consequences for Work, Income, and Education of a Large Uninsured Population.* Washington, DC: Kaiser Comm. Medicaid and the Uninsured

Himelfarb R. 1995. *Catastrophic Politics: the Rise and Fall of the Medicare Catastrophic Coverage Act of 1988.* Philadelphia: Penn. State Univ. Press

House JS. 2001. Relating social inequalities in health and income. *J. Health Polit. Policy Law* 26:523–32

Hsaio WC. 2001. Behind the ideology and theory: What is the evidence for medical savings accounts? *J. Health Polit. Policy Law* 26:733–37

Huber JD, Shipan CR. 2002. *Deliberate Discretion: the Institutional Foundations of Bureaucratic Autonomy.* Cambridge, UK: Cambridge Univ. Press

Ingram H, Schneider A. 1993. The social construction of target populations: implications for politics and policy. *Am. Polit. Sci. Rev.* 87:334–47

Jacobs LM, Shapiro RS. 1995. Don't blame the public for failed health care reform. *J. Health Polit. Policy Law* 20:411–23

Kaiser Family Foundation. 2000. *National Survey of the Uninsured.* San Francisco: Kaiser Family Fdn.

Kessler DA. 2001. *Question of Intent: a Great American Battle with a Deadly Industry.* New York: Public Aff.

Kohn LT, Corrigan JM, Donaldson MS, ed. 2000. *To Err is Human: Building a Safer Health System.* Washington, DC: Natl. Acad.

Marmor TR. 1973. *The Politics of Medicare.* Chicago: Aldine

Martin CJ. 1993. Together again: business, government and the quest for cost control. *J. Health Polit. Policy Law* 18:359–93

Martin CJ. 2000. *Stuck in Neutral: Business and the Politics of Human Capital Investment Policy.* Princeton, NJ: Princeton Univ. Press

Morone JA. 1990. *The Democratic Wish: Popular Participation and the Limits of American Government.* New York: Basic Books

Murphy KM, Topel R. 1999. *The Economic Value of Medical Research.* Chicago: Univ. Chicago Press

New York Times. 2002. Cost of health benefits are seen rising by 15%. *New York Times* Oct. 15, 2002, p. C6

Newhouse JP. 1996. *Free For All? Lessons from the Rand Health Insurance Experiment.* Cambridge, MA: Harvard Univ. Press

Newhouse JP. 2002. Why is there a quality chasm? *Health Aff.* 21:13–25

Oberlander J. 1995. *Medicare and the American state: the politics of federal health insurance.* PhD thesis, Dep. Polit. Sci., Yale Univ.

Patashnik EM, Zelizer J. 2001. Paying for Medicare: benefits, budgets, and Wilbur Mills' policy legacy. *J. Health Polit. Policy Law* 26:7–36

Patel K, Rushevsky ME. 1995. *Health Care Policy and Politics in America.* New York: Sharpe

Pauly MV, Goodman JC. 1995. Tax credits for health insurance and medical savings accounts. *Health Aff.* 14:125–39

Peden EA, Freeland MS. 1995. A historical analysis of medical spending growth, 1960–93. *Health Aff.* 14:235–47

Peterson MA. 1993. From iron triangles to policy networks. *J. Health Polit. Policy Law* 18:395–438

Peterson MA. 1995. How health policy information is used in Congress. In *Intensive Care: How Congress Shapes Health Policy,* ed. TE Mann, NJ Ornstein, pp. 79–126

Peterson MA. 1999. Introduction: politics, misperception, or apropos? *J. Health Polit. Policy Law* 24:873–86

Reinhardt UE. 2000. International perspectives on health care reform. In *Social Security and Medicare: Individual Versus Collective Risk and Responsibility,* ed. S Burke, E Kingson, UE Reinhardt, pp. 161–82. Washington, DC: Brookings Inst.

Reinhardt UE. 2001. Can efficiency in health care be left to the market? *J. Health Polit. Policy Law* 26:967–92

Robinson JC. 2001. The end of asymmetric information. *J. Health Polit. Policy Law* 26:1045–53

Rosin H. 1998. The fat tax. *New Republic* May 18, pp. 18–19

Ruggie M. 1992. The paradox of liberal intervention: health policy and the American welfare state. *Am. J. Sociol.* 97:919–44

Shiltz R. 1987. *And the Band Played On: Politics, People, and the AIDS Epidemic.* New York: St Martin's

Skocpol T. 1997. *Boomerang: Health Care Reform and the Turn Against Government.* New York: Norton

Starr P. 1984. *The Social Transformation of American Medicine*. New York: Basic Books

Steinmo S, Watts J. 1995. It's the institutions stupid. Why comprehensive national health insurance always fails in America. *J. Health Polit. Policy Law* 20:329–72

Stone DA. 1989. Causal stories and the formation of policy agendas. *Polit. Sci. Q.* 104:281–300

Thomas L. 1983. *The Youngest Science: Notes of a Medicine-Watcher.* New York: Viking

Tuohy CH. 1999. *Accidental Logics*. Oxford, UK: Oxford Univ. Press

Walker J. 1991. *Mobilizing Interest Groups in America*. Ann Arbor: Univ. Mich. Press

Weissert CA, Weissert WG. 1996. *Governing Health: the Politics of Health Policy*. Baltimore, MD: Johns Hopkins Univ. Press

Wennberg JE, Cooper MM. 1999. Practice variation and the quality of surgical care for common conditions. In *The Dartmouth Atlas of Health Care for 1999*, ed. Cent. Eval. Clin. Sci. Staff. Am. Hosp. Assoc.

Wennberg JE, Fisher ES, Skinner JS. 2002. Geography and the debate over Medicare reform. *Health Aff.* 21:96–114

Wennberg JE, Gittelson A. 1973. Small area variation in health care delivery. *Science* 182:1102–8

West DM, Heith D, Goodwin C. 1996. Harry and Louise go to Washington: political advertising and health care reform. *J. Health Polit. Policy Law* 21:35–68

Wilkerson JD, Feeley TJ, Scheiereck NS, Sue C. 2002. Using bills and hearings to trace attention in Congress: policy windows in health care legislating. In *Policy Dynamics*, ed. BF Baumgartner, BD Jones. Chicago: Univ. Chicago Press

Wilkinson RG. 1986. Socioeconomic differences in mortality: interpreting the data on their size and trends. In *Class and Health: Research and Longitudinal Data*, pp. 1–20. London: Tavistock

Woolhandler S, Himmelstein DU. 2002. Paying for national health insurance—and not getting it. *Health Aff.* 21:88–98

Wynia MK, Cummins DS, VanGeest JB, Wilson IB. 2000. Physician manipulation of reimbursement rules for patients: between a rock and a hard place. *JAMA* 283:1858–65

Annu. Rev. Polit. Sci. 2003. 6:345–76
doi: 10.1146/annurev.polisci.6.121901.085827

ANCIENT EMPIRES, MODERN STATES, AND THE STUDY OF GOVERNMENT

George E. Von der Muhll

*Politics Department, Merrill College, University of California, Santa Cruz,
1156 High Street, Santa Cruz, California 95064; email: mozart@ucsc.edu*

Key Words   ancient history, comparative government, civilizations, political modernization, states and society

■ **Abstract**   Samuel Finer's *The History of Government from the Earliest Times* is not only a major contribution to the history of governance in the ancient world; it is, in certain crucial respects, the only one. This essay surveys the uses of history within the discipline of political science to establish that surprising conclusion. In certain other social sciences—most notably in economics and above all in sociology— numerous leading scholars have applied the theories of their disciplines to illuminate the study of past civilizations while using data from those periods as a check on contemporary theories. Political scientists have, however, rarely ventured into world history before the eighteenth century. This essay considers some possible explanations for that discrepancy, then delineates and assesses Finer's massive and penetrating exploration of some 5000 years of institutional governmental history.

INTRODUCTION

Can modern political scientists profit from studies of the ancient world? Many reviewers of Samuel Finer's *The History of Government from the Earliest Times* (1999) insist they could. "If there were a Nobel Prize for political science," one reviewer has declared (*Economist* 1997), "Sammy Finer would deserve to win one." Luttwak (1997) judges Finer's work to be "'Political science' at its best"; Crick (1998) contends that it may rank as "the masterpiece of postwar British political studies." Power (1999) finds Finer's "remarkable" work "so rich as to defy comprehensive ordering through any single comparative theoretical framework." Three years before the turn of the millennium, the *Economist*'s reviewer concluded (acknowledging the near inevitability of the pun), "No finer work of political science . . . has been published in this century" (*Economist* 1997).

"No finer work of political science" in a century containing some 90% of such works? "The masterpiece" of modern British political studies? Even presidents of the most competitive political science associations seldom elicit such assessments of their work. Yet these judgments seem restrained compared with the timeless metaphors and references Finer's *History* suggests to some readers.

"To read [Finer's study] is like seeing the pyramids and the Taj Mahal for the first time," the *Economist* asserts. *"The History of Government from the Earliest Times* is likely to be read as long as Aristotle" (*Economist* 1997). Readers of this remarkable prediction are unlikely to be able to check its veracity. Zeno's Paradox may further complicate the test. Yet its possible hyperbolism faithfully reflects the impact a first encounter with Finer's magnum opus can have.

Not all reviewers have been dazzled. Brisbin (1999) invokes numerous criteria of modern social science to support his contention that Finer "fails to provide either a social scientific explanation of historical variations in government or a historical interpretation of the construction of political institutions." Deficient, he writes, both as history and in terms of the explanatory objectives of contemporary social science, *The History of Government* fails to convert its categories into true variables to test key hypotheses. Moreover, it employs only a limited range of secondary sources to construct an unwarrantedly selective study of governmental history. At best, it provides "a primer for students interested in a brief, literate introduction to governance in historical regimes," and therefore "large university research libraries" may want "to include it in their collections."

These charges (and perhaps even more the damnation through the faintest of praise) must necessarily ring unpleasantly in the ears of both political scientists and professional historians. They serve as a warning that the attempt to use historians' methods to cast light on the concerns of analytically disposed political scientists may end up displeasing both groups. Such charges therefore demand the consideration they will receive below. For the present, however, the point to be noted is that Brisbin's (1999) reference to "variables" to "test hypotheses," and his evident distaste for a work "deliberately hostile to structural functionalism and empiricism and ignorant of both the new institutionalism and rational choice approaches to state formation and analysis," are articulated in the authentic accent of postwar American political science. Similar reservations apparently led the Social Science Research Council to turn down Finer's request for research grant funds in the mid-1980s (Finer 1999:v–vi).

It is, of course, perfectly consistent to pass adverse judgment on a particular work of social science while denying that, in so doing, one has simultaneously judged the approach it purports to embody. In the instant case, however, this dissociation is not so easily effected. In the review cited above, Crick (1998) claims that Finer's *History* "fills a huge gap in political studies." But Crick's metaphor raises the question: What is the structure within which he discerns a "gap"? Which are the comprehensive comparative studies of political history that political scientists have undertaken for purposes of advancing political science amid which Finer's work can be said to take its place? Huge though his study is, its 1701 pages do not suffice to fill a "huge gap" because there is no "gap," large or small, for it to fill. Like Central Australia's Ayers Rock, it stands massively alone on a deserted plain, with only a few analogous formations of far smaller compass on the horizons. To assess Finer's *History* is accordingly to assess the state of the subfield it metonymically monopolizes.

HISTORY AND POLITICAL THEORY

Scholarship is conventionally deemed a collective enterprise. Ascribing to Finer's work the isolated grandeur of Ayers Rock accordingly incites two questions: Was the terrain of political studies of the ancient world truly so barren before his book appeared; and, if so, what might account for this improbable condition? This essay obliges its writer to address these questions. It is predicated on the synecdochic proposition that, as asserted above, the achievements and shortcomings of Finer's monumental volumes constitute most of the achievements and shortcomings of a cell with few members. Finer's *History* cannot be compared with other similar enterprises because they do not exist. Since the titles of other seemingly parallel undertakings may already have sprung to readers' minds, this declaration demands some clarification.

The first step requires confronting a paradox. Historical consciousness as such is certainly not lacking in political science. On the contrary, in some domains and in certain respects it is more highly developed than in any of the other social sciences. The use of all but the most recent centuries of human history as a data base for political science may be rare. Yet no other discipline in the social sciences has assigned so central a role to the intellectual history of theories about its subject as has the academic study of politics. "Political theory" commonly constitutes one of three or four basic subdivisions of the discipline. Critical exposition of the history of such theory comprises a vocation in itself. In the other social sciences, theory provides an instrumental guide to research and is absorbed into its substantive findings. In political studies, theory holds a proudly autonomous place.

This unusual status of political theory as a disciplinary subdivision may be partly due to its long history. The other social sciences typically trace the first clearly recognizable formulations of their theoretical foundations no farther back than to the early nineteenth century. With respectful bows to Adam Smith, and before him perhaps the Cameralists, economists usually adopt David Ricardo's elegant post-Napoleonic analyses of the phenomena of rent and of comparative advantage in foreign trade as the founding models of their discipline. The inauguration of sociology as a distinctive field of study is commonly ascribed by sociologists to Saint-Simon, Karl Marx, and Emile Durkheim in the second half of that century. Psychology as a science began to separate from shrewd insights into human personality in the later nineteenth century, and anthropology diverged from perceptive travelers' narratives at about the same time.

Although the intellectual historians of these disciplines may disagree on the exact dates, particular contributors, and publications that constitute the starting points for their tale, the tale itself rarely spans more than two centuries. Here the contrast with political theory is dramatic. No history of what is commonly called political theory could purport to completeness without the inclusion of Plato, Aristotle, Bodin, Machiavelli, and Hobbes, all of whose works had appeared over the two millennia preceding the earliest plausible dating of a distinctive founding contribution to the other social sciences. Contemplation of this long tradition, moreover, has induced among its contemporary students a historical piety not found in those disciplines. Political theorists do not treat classical Athenian and Renaissance political treatises as interesting early statements of theories subsequently subject to more incisive, more adequately differentiated and conclusively substantiated formulations. On the contrary, a common practice of modern writers on ancient political theory is to provide an interpretive reaffirmation of the enduring insights first developed in certain "classics" of political thought.

To be sure, the paradox referred to above is in some respects superficial. Its validity depends on an ambiguity in the concept of theory itself. In the other social sciences, as in the natural sciences, a theory is understood to be a logical elaboration of a small set of explicit axioms into a model containing indications of the conditions under which certain empirical observations can be taken to confirm or disconfirm its utility as an economical representation of a specified domain of the phenomenal world. Not so within the tradition of political theory. Here, "theories" are seldom judged by the extent to which they generate validated empirical predictions. Instead they are evaluated by such criteria as the degree to which their formulations, internal consistency, compelling clarification of moral dilemmas, and apparent relevance to the larger concerns of reflective political observers merit sustained attention by those observers. Attempted analogies between such "theories" of politics and the theories of the other social sciences (let alone the natural sciences) seem much less apt than the English philosopher Michael Oakeshott's (1962) description of political theory as "a conversation through the ages" among philosophers concerned with political matters. In so describing political theory, Oakeshott thus incorporated into its very definition a dimension of historical time.

Oakeshott's characterization of the distinctive tradition of political theory does not apply to all theorizing about politics, nor did he claim that it did. Practitioners of contemporary political science include many political scientists with aspirations directly paralleling those of other social scientists. Since the postwar "behavioral revolution," they have committed themselves to developing a body of explanatory, empirically predictive "positive" theories of politics. Such theorizing does not of itself carry any greater historical baggage than similar undertakings in other disciplines. A "science of politics" can as well be a science of contemporary politics as of any other era. Indeed, contemporary politics is by far the most common empirical domain of positive theory. So it is not from such positive theorists, but rather from the continuing participants in the "conversation through the ages," that we might expect to encounter a distinctive commitment to viewing the history of those ages as a valuable resource for students of politics; and it is within that domain that the paradox arises.

Insofar as historical consciousness has been manifested in these circles on such terms, it is more prominent in political science than in the other social sciences. Such consciousness is shaped, however, by a tradition—peculiar to political scientists—of conceiving of theoretical studies as the study of the modes of discourse employed by philosophers regarding their subject. Political theorists have traditionally been primarily interested in what other political philosophers have said and how they said it. They are struck by Locke's failure to confront the challenge in Hobbes's *Leviathan*, interested in what Kant learned or could have learned from Rousseau, concerned with John Stuart Mill's unwittingly parricidal abandonment of Utilitarianism in favor of a rediscovered Aristotelian developmentalism. Wolin (1960) broke new ground in locating a discursive convention within the works of such contemporary positive social scientists as Philip Selznick and Herbert Simon. Even so, his critique centered on the implicit political perspectives reflected in their formulations, not on the structural properties and changing capabilities of the organizational entities they purported to analyze.

Such delineations and debates are drawn from a study of texts. They do not seek to identify the working rules of historical actors. As Beer (1965) noted in his study of doctrinal evolution in the unarticulated political theories of British parliamentary politics, political theorists have shown little interest in charting changes in the philosophical premises entailed in the strategic justifications and critical exchanges of practicing politicians. Still less have they seen the philosophical underpinnings of institutional rules of ancient governance as their proper domain (their interest in available indications of the practices of ancient Athenian democracy may form a partial exception). To be sure, students of political theory commonly find associations between philosophical discourses about politics and their authors' encounters with their world. Many have emphasized that the unbridgeable distance between Machiavelli's contingently instrumentalist morality and Thomas Aquinas' universalistically deductive absolutism reflects the experiential separation between the flux of Florentine politics and the peace of a medieval cloister. Nonetheless, such contrasts of historical context are assigned significance for the study of political theory because of their perceived doctrinal consequences. They do not command or receive attention for their intrinsic structural properties. The points of interest are the philosophers themselves and their writings, not the degree to which their philosophies demonstrate a superior capacity to illuminate the workings of the political institutions of their time.

The distinctively preeminent status of the history of political philosophy within the academic study of politics, then, does not betoken any markedly greater disposition of political scientists than of other social scientists to search through the records of the past for insights to incorporate into their quest for a lawful social science. If anything, it derives from the autonomy accorded the "conversations" of classical political theorists—the exceptional degree to which discussions of their works have remained disconnected from any instrumental construction and revision of empirically contingent postulates regarding the contemporary politics of their eras. The mission of political theorists—in the traditional sense of that term—remains the mission of political philosophers: to examine past and present philosophical discourse about politics for its internal integration and meta-theoretical resonances and entailments. Much illumination has come through this ancient and honorable method. But for a disposition to use historical studies of the ancient world to enrich a scientific understanding of contemporary social institutions, we must look elsewhere.

HISTORY, POLITICAL SCIENCE, AND THE SOCIAL SCIENCES

What has traditionally been known as political theory, as we have just seen, has not inexorably led its students and critics to the study of ancient political institutions and the actors whose powers and disabilities derived from their rules. But are not such arenas the natural preserve of historians? Are not political scientists adhering to a firmly established tradition in the social sciences when they leave such investigations to historians? Are not the ends of political science better served when they apply their disciplinarily distinctive theories and techniques to uncovering and analyzing human relationships in the contemporary settings in which the collection and processing of pertinent data can most readily and reliably proceed?

Such questions rest on a misperception. To answer them properly is to emphasize the paradoxical relation of history to political science. For what we find is that many social scientists have made outstanding contributions to locating recurrent or evolving patterns within human history. But very few of these contributions have been made by those who professionally classify themselves as political scientists.

The record is plain. Comparative historical sociology has emerged in the past three decades as one of the major subfields of that discipline, one that has attracted a high fraction of the leading names in the profession (Skocpol 1984). A severely shortened list would include such profoundly influential, agenda-setting works as (sociological historian) Anderson's *Passages from Antiquity to Feudalism* (1974a) and *Lineages of the Absolute State* (1974b), Bendix's *Nation-Building and Citizenship: Studies of Our Changing Social Order* (1964) and *Kings or People* (1978), Eisenstadt's *The Political System of Empires* (1963), Homans's *English Villagers of the Thirteenth Century* (1941), Lipset's *The First New Nation* (1963), Mann's *The Sources of Social Power* (1986), and Moore's *Social Origins of Dictatorship and Democracy* (1966). Such a list would continue with Parsons' *Societies in Evolutionary and Comparative Perspective* (1966) and *The Evolution of Societies* (1977), Polanyi's *The Great Transformation* (1944), Sjoberg's *The Pre-Industrial City: Past and Present* (1965), Skocpol's *States and Revolutions* (1979), Thompson's *The Making of the English Working Class* (1963), Tilly's *Coercion, Capital, and the European States, AD 990–1992* (1992), and Wallerstein's *The Capitalist World-Economy* (1979). And despite differences in selection and range of cases for analysis, despite differences in duration of chosen era, despite major differences in preferred interpretive approach, kinds of data examined, and even political emphasis, these works have much in common. All are guided by overarching sociological theories prevalent in the discipline, yet all are continuously conditioned by the necessities of providing convincingly fine-grained contextual explanation. All employ an explicitly comparative framework to define and justify their focus. All show control over an awesome bibliography of historical studies that visibly set the agenda for research, generate puzzles requiring explanation, provide data that confirm hypotheses or compel their revision, and give rise to reflections on the interplay between human intention, social institutions, and ecological constraints. In all cases, the authors must struggle with novel methodological issues as they confront the irregular, imperfect, culturally remote, and unrecoverable elements in the available record of the past. As they engage in this struggle, they find themselves obliged to devise concepts [e.g., Eisenstadt's "free-floating" (freely deployable) politico-administrative resources] that not only supply a thematic *basso ostinato* to their historical studies but subsequently become incorporated into their contemporary analyses. In every case, finally, these scholars find reason to draw attention to the unacknowledged and probably unperceived exceptionalism of cases presumed to be paradigmatic by colleagues in their discipline who restrict their studies to contemporary social systems. In short, they use the resources of history as a continuous check on the state of the discipline.

Anthropology and psychology contain no comparable subfields. Because these disciplines are defined as much by their methods as by their substantive focus of inquiry, their lack of a large corpus of disciplinarily defined historical investigation is readily explicable. The disciplinary techniques of physical anthropology have developed out of drawing inferences from surviving physical data to reconstruct the preliterate past; anthropological field observations of the cultural practices of other eras might well be thought a contradiction in terms. The three branches of psychology might find one another's theories nearly unintelligible, but one element these subdivisions have in common is the lack of any compelling reason to view research into the past as either feasible or rewarding. In the case of psychobiological laboratory work, the irrelevance of history is self-evident; likewise in the case of the experimental and survey-research techniques refined by social psychologists. Some interesting efforts have been made to apply the insights of clinical psychology to explain the behavior of prominent historical figures. But such exercises have necessarily been applications of contemporary theory to past events (George 1956), not—as in the case of historical sociology—a two-way circuit of findings, explanation, and revision of general theory.

Economics is, of course, the most proudly theoretical and positivist of the social sciences. And for some time, most economists perceived economic history as something of a backwater within the discipline. Much that was labeled economic history was, in essence, a sociological inquiry into the history of economic institutions (Polanyi et al. 1957). This characterization held whether economic history was investigated for its own sake, as in the classic works by Pirenne (1956) and Rostovzeff (1963–1966) and in the many influential later works of Cipolla (1975) and Braudel (1975), or—as in the case of Schumpeter (1950) and most famously, of course, Marx (1962)—to support a general thesis concerning the dynamics of economic institutions. For a time, Schmoller and his German historicist associates further contributed to giving economic history a bad name among analytically disposed economists by advocating an institutionalist approach as a paradigmatically superior empiricist alternative to the Austro-British positivist tradition. But the past few decades have been marked by an efflorescence of state-of-the-art work in economic history by economists who have no quarrel with their discipline's axiomatic precepts. Such leading economists of impeccable disciplinary credentials as Milton Friedman, John Kenneth Galbraith, and Charles Kindleberger have sought to show how economic reasoning could be used to resolve—or at least, to structure—the historical debate over the causes of the Great Depression (Friedman 1965, Galbraith 1988, Kindleberger 1973). Similar work is now being done on the economic rationale for the British Empire (Offer 1993). Jones (1981, 1988), Elvin (1973), Perkins (1969), and Landes (1969, 1998) have employed insights explicitly derived from economic theory to develop macrohistorical theses about China's economic stagnation over many centuries and the rise of the West. Indeed, Landes does this so provocatively, with such clear implications for so many historical debates, that his latest book has become something of a popular best seller. In the opening chapter of a more general study of the political economy of security policy, Gilpin (1987) has traced the long-term impact on China's economy of the defense burden imposed by its inner-Asian frontiers. And economist Mancur Olson similarly attracted large cross-disciplinary readerships with his rational choice explanation for social rigidities and the rise and fall of national economies (Olson 1982).

Yet before Samuel Finer took up the challenge, it would be hard to name a single political scientist whose contributions to historical interpretation, or whose sustained and searching use of historical data to frame and substantiate a major treatise on political science, invited comparison with any of the long list of leading economists and sociologists cited above. Put differently, it would be hard to name a single president of the American Political Science Association who owed his or her election primarily to such a work. And it is an equally remarkable fact that this contrast among the social sciences regarding the continuing significance of historical data to the field has excited little comment within political science.

To be sure, many of the scholars on the above lists—sociologists Barrington Moore, Seymour Lipset, and Charles Tilly come immediately to mind, along with the historian Paul Kennedy (Kennedy 1988)—have written in terms that have aroused intense interest and generated intense controversies among political scientists. To that extent, one might argue that the whole issue of the different status of historical investigations among the disciplines can only be raised in terms of a kind of factitious essentialism. Yet that response, however appealing, ignores or denies the promptings of intradisciplinary theoretical agendas. Moore, Lipset, and Tilly may present findings and speak a language with which political scientists can readily identify. But each, on other occasions, has written books concerning reigning theoretical conventions within their discipline that are explicitly addressed to its other members [e.g., Moore's polemical attacks on other sociologists in *Political Power and Social Theory* (1962)]. Although Lipset, Moore, and Tilly are thought of as political sociologists, they remain sociologists. The shades of Max Weber and Karl Marx provide controlling binary points of reference for their work to an extent few political scientists would acknowledge for themselves (Bendix 1977).

Certainly the differences among the disciplines in their engagement with the history of the ancient world has nothing to do with the distinctive methods of political science. If anything, the interpenetration of works of contemporary history (understood, in this context, as the period since World War I) with works of political science is nearly complete. In the case of political biography, the point is particularly self-evident. Can Bullock's (1960, 1992) magnificent biographies of Hitler and Stalin be said to be contributions to the disciplined study of politics? What of Burns's (1956) study of Franklin Roosevelt, Goodwin's (1976) of Lyndon Johnson, Brown's (1989) of Gandhi, and the nearly innumerable penetrating biographies of Mao Zedong's rise to and exercise of power? For purposes of understanding how political power can be accumulated and maintained, does it matter that Bullock has never been anything but a conventional Oxford historian whereas Burns wrote his first book, on the shortcomings of Congress, as a political scientist (Burns 1949)? Such questions answer themselves. But they are replicated in every public arena of politics, whether of policies (Williams 1962, Conquest 1968, Gaddis 1997), movements (Schuman 1936, Schurmann 1966), eras (Schlesinger 1957–1960, Matusow 1984), or the history of regimes (Malia 1994). To seek differentiation between historians and political scientists in such domains, to claim that the questions asked and answered and the methods used to facilitate their resolution are a significant function of the authors' academic vocations, is truly to traffic in disciplinary essentialism.

Political scientists retain a sufficient interest in the founding of the American Republic, the emergence of parliamentary government and mass parties, the rise of European nationalism, the rigidities of Imperial Russia, the expansion of European colonialism overseas, and the disintegration of the Qing Empire under such pressures to assure that historians who serve such interests will be cited in their footnotes. They may even try their hand at historical works on such subjects (Anderson 1983, Huntington 1981). But as we step back through World War I into the nineteenth century, the distinction between political scientists and political historians becomes much sharper, the balance of contributions to the total enterprise tilts notably toward the historians, and the analyses by political scientists themselves become more and more clearly first chapters to the main body of work. And then, once we have passed back through the French and American Revolutions, we swiftly approach something resembling absolute zero in the disposition of political scientists to engage in institutional analysis. Kautsky's *The Politics of Aristocratic Empires* (1982) is an impressive exception that in its isolation and lack of wider disciplinary influence confirms the general rule. This remarkable fact— it is a slight overstatement of a central core of truth, qualified mainly (as noted already) by an interest in Athenian democracy—is of the highest significance for measuring Samuel Finer's contribution to the study of government.

What might account for this striking pattern? Why should leading sociologists so freely deploy their theoretical resources and methods to the study of historical eras no reputable political scientist has ventured into? Why should the most positivist of economists sometimes show a greater disposition than any political scientist to formulate analytic issues in the historical context of the ancient world? One answer might be that political scientists since the behavioral revolution have professionally focused on "politics," understood to mean the processes by which societal demands and support are transformed into public policy outcomes that feed back into such processes; and that before the French and American Revolutions the "public" was only tangentially, sporadically, and unpredictably enmeshed in any readily observable way with the policy flows of governance. Another possible answer is that the quality of data regarding such societal dispositions thins out dramatically as we move back in time beyond the last two centuries. There is some evident truth in both these suggestions. However, they hardly explain political scientists' durable fascination with the inner workings of international policy-making bureaucracies, or with the conflict over authority and resources between leadership staffs and semipermanent civil servants—let alone their interest in attempting to chart the infighting within secretive, tightly controlled totalitarian regimes. Studies of African politics have shown a marked progression over the past decade from explication of how divisive ethnic patterns in African society are mirrored within governmental structures to questions of "governability" and "governance" itself. Such concerns, as one might expect, have redirected the attention of many political scientists to internal governmental channels and choices indicating a more complex understanding of the relationship of governmental policy making to assimilative societal cleavages. Furthermore, the lowered quantity of reliable data has not deterred sociologists and economic historians from probing the taxation policies of the Roman Empire or the class structures and recruitment of leadership in Han China, Tokugawa Japan, and Imperial Russia.

A more convincing explanation may lie in the history of political science as a discipline. That still most universally admired of sociologists, Max Weber, set an agenda for his discipline at the beginning of the twentieth century with his confident demonstration that trained sociologists could ask fruitful new questions concerning ancient history (Weber 1963). Political science had no such figure at its founding. Indeed, a primary quest of the new discipline was to establish a "new science of politics" (the phrase is Catlin's) that could be recognized as something more than contemporary history (Catlin 1964 [1927], Easton 1953). The post–World War II behavioral revolution in American political science attained this objective in considerable measure. But historically trained postwar European political scientists were initially disposed to dismiss the "behavioral persuasion" (Eulau 1963) as pretentiously obscurantist scientism; and precisely because of these critics' continuing preference for traditional historical approaches to the study of politics, many American political scientists have felt pressure to demonstrate the value-added component of their discipline in generating and structuring data in paradigmatic terms exceeding the informed insight of historians and journalists. Their research agendas have been shaped by the acclaim accorded those whose analytic imagination and methodological skills helped differentiate political science from topically limited current history. In such an academic climate, there was little incentive to bring these hard-won techniques to bear on remote eras with unpromising theoretical payoffs.

It would be preposterous to suggest that political scientists, in their effort to establish themselves as true social scientists, have shown no willingness to explore such resources as noncontemporary history might afford. A significant number have clearly done so. Leaving aside straightforward histories of such institutions as the American presidency, political parties, and public administration (Rossiter 1960, Binkley 1962, White 1965), their uses of history can be grouped in four categories. From these we can learn much that bears on Finer's study.

Some eminent political scientists have enriched their contemporary studies through historical points of reference. Despite his behavioralist statistical proclivities, Key (1949) frequently chose the mid–nineteenth century as the starting point for the narrative element in his classic *Southern Politics*. Huntington (1968) drew on concise accounts and subsequent analyses of episodes from the past—e.g., Joseph II's unsuccessful attempts to modernize the late-eighteenth-century Habsburg Empire, the unhappy outcome to the Guangxu Emperor's "Hundred Days Reform" in 1898, and Kemal Ataturk's combination of Fabian and "blitzkrieg" strategies to circumvent Islamic resistance to his policies—to clinch general theses concerning the requisites for engineering political change in traditional societies. As these have been familiar expository techniques since the days of Machiavelli, they require no further comment here beyond noting their relative rarity in contemporary treatises on political science.

Second, some political scientists have identified cultural continuities in a nation's history that, they argue, have led to increasingly institutionalized political expectations. Hoffman's opening essay in *France: Continuity and Change* (Hoffman et al. 1963) and Huntington's *American Politics: the Promise of Disharmony* (1981) provide prominent examples. Nearly two decades earlier, Burns (1963) sought to show that the American political system of separated and "balanced" powers had rendered Congress incapable since its earliest years of undertaking large-scale collective tasks in the public interest because of a persistent fourfold division within both major political parties. All three scholars argued that disappointments arising from the apparent effects of specific electoral outcomes could be regarded as wholly predictable when viewed from a larger historical perspective.

A third possible analytic connection between politics and history derives from applying a concept or theoretical approach of recognized power within political science to a particular historical case. Polsby (1968) demonstrated how a sociological theory of institutionalization could be used to retell the early history of the U.S. House of Representatives in terms strikingly linking its study to the literature on political development. Similarly, Levi's *Of Rule and Revenue* (1988) elegantly applies "the theory of predatory rule"—a variant of rational choice theory—to several historical case studies widely separated in time and space to reach generic conclusions about public finance. The opening chapter of Doyle's (1986) study of nineteenth-century colonialism provides a novel perspective on that familiar subject by drawing attention to parallels between the European metropolitan powers' export of their political institutions overseas and the common practice in Caesar Augustus's Roman Empire of transferring templates of governance from Rome to its colonies. Because the purpose of this literature is to spotlight the fruitfulness of a particular form of analysis, it tends to establish the stimulatingly organizational power of the theory itself more than the returns to political science from the study of history.

A final group of political scientists have brought their trained sensibilities and techniques to bear on particular episodes of the past in order to illuminate a larger conceptual perspective within the discipline. The strategies underlying the founding of the American Republic have exercised the imagination of political scientists for some time (Roche 1968, Smith 1987). Certain accounts of the early days of the American political parties have moved beyond routine narrative by presenting their emergent organization in sociological terms as an experimental response to the novel exigencies of mass politics (Cunningham 1957, Chambers 1963). Burnham's (1970) statistical analysis of "critical elections" has passed into the vocabulary of the discipline. The ninth volume in the Princeton University Press series on "political development" offered a stimulating comparison of several European nations over the past millennium in response to a set of specified "political crises" (of identity, legitimacy, etc.), although—tellingly—the individual chapters were nearly all written by professional historians (Grew 1978). Skowronek's (1982) study of the expansion of the administrative capabilities of the American state between the end of the Reconstruction and World War I is part of a promising sequence of studies of "nation building" inaugurated by the volumes edited by Tilly (1975) and Eisenstadt & Rokkan (1973). In the 1990s, four works by political scientists on the expanding military and fiscal capabilities of the European states and Japan since the early Middle Ages suggest that conceptually driven political history is at last beginning to acquire independent academic momentum (Downing 1992, Silberman 1993, Porter 1994, Ertman 1997).

Yet four limitations are common to all or nearly all of the above studies. In most, a single institution or theme—political parties, the House of Representatives, techniques for raising revenue, alternating periods of tranquility and utopian demands for change—predominate. In many, explication of historical systems and processes is secondary to, and shaped by, the author's theoretical interests; what falls outside the range of these interests is not accounted for. Third, virtually all the studies are limited to the United States and Western Europe, and many are comparative only by implication. Finally (partly because of this geographical limitation), with the exception of Doyle's opening chapter, Levi's study, and a few of the books in the final category, none press back beyond the time boundary of the American and French Revolutions noted above. It is in this light that Finer's *The History of Government from the Earliest Times*—a work that encompasses the entire Eurasian continent, along with North and Spanish South America and North Africa; that devotes its first third to an analysis of governments that preceded the Roman Empire; that enters into the intricate details of the daily work of government in such matters as personnel procedures, military organization, revenues raised and spent, criminal laws enforced, and administrative bureaus maintained in outlying provinces while seeking to relate these to overall governmental capabilities; and that, having done so, seeks to maintain continuous and cumulative comparative tension among the individual cases considered—stands alone.

SAMUEL E. FINER: MAN AND VISION

Finer's *History of Government* must astonish any reader by its scope, its erudition, the density of its tellingly assembled details, and the precision of its arguments. But equally astonishing is that a project of such monumental dimensions was taken on by one of the most tightly focused, most thoroughly professional of political scientists.

Nothing in Finer's active career inside the British academy hinted that he would one day be offering fine-grained comparisons of the Assyrian Empire with ancient Persia, the Byzantine Empire with Ming China. After some early work on public administration and a biography of the Utilitarian public health reformer Sir Edwin Chadwick, he first made his distinctive mark as a political scientist with a book on pressure-group politics in Great Britain (Finer 1958). Crisply written, with a political insider's insight into the behind-the-scenes manipulative techniques of Britain's organized interests, it established his identity as one of the alert, young, American-influenced political scientists around W.J.M. MacKenzie who had learned much from Truman's *The Governmental Process* (1951) and for whom the traditional moralistic deprecation of such pressures on properly parthenogenic policy making now became an unsatisfactory analytic pose (Finer 1980). But the work remained firmly empirical, more notable for its findings than for its formulations; and a similarly low level of abstraction remained evident in Finer's other projects from this period, ranging from studies of local government in England and Wales to Early Day motions and "back-bench" opinion in the House of Commons. Indeed, as Finer entered the 1960s, he became increasingly vocal in his criticisms of the universalistic conceptualism of Talcott Parsons, Gabriel Almond, and David Easton, whose writings, as he saw them, had reduced government to an empty and theoretically inconsequential black box surrounded by an all-determining environment.

Yet all this time Finer saw himself as moving purposefully beyond the point he had reached in 1950 as a recent Oxford graduate who was "as much an historian as a political scientist" (Finer 1980). His studies of history had not only given him respect for the techniques of meticulous documentary research; they had given him "an historical breadth and perspective without which the study of politics is either a barren *a priorism* or an empty set of mechanical computations" (Finer 1980). But they had not given him an analytic approach that could cut through masses of surface detail to elementally functional nonconstitutional causal forces. These he found—for a time, at least—in the writings of Vilfredo Pareto, whose work he eventually edited. And although he came to reject much that he encountered in a Social Science Research Council report that formed the basis for a Round Table in Florence in 1954, he found "enormously appealing" its call for a "systematic politics" that would include a search for "patterns of uniformity and difference" in non-Western as well as Western systems (Finer 1980).

His first answer to this call came with *The Man on Horseback: the Role of the Military in Politics* (Finer 1962), the work for which he is best known. This study traversed the contemporary Third World while connecting its instabilities to those found earlier in Europe. It was followed by a 600-page, single-authored textbook on comparative government (Finer 1970) that inevitably evoked comparisons with an earlier comparative text by his admired older brother Herman but self-consciously broke with its conventional restriction to the governments of Western Europe (Kavanagh & Peele 1984). Already Finer had become involved in the Social Science Research Council's extension of its comparative series on political development to include a volume on nation building in Europe (Tilly 1975)—a volume to which he contributed an article on the military and the formation of the modern West European state (Finer 1975). By this point, Finer's scholarly horizons had clearly broadened well beyond the days of *Local Government in England and Wales*; yet this trajectory was not uncommon in the political science of that era and hardly signaled his next step.

That move occurred—just why, the editors of his "most ambitious and encompassing" work do not say in their otherwise illuminatingly candid Preface—at the point of his formal retirement from Oxford in 1982. Almost in a flash, it seems, he resolved to use his new freedom to write the first academically serious history of human government from the Sumerians to the present. Since his previous studies had not prepared him to write about many of the countries and millennia he planned to cover, his first act was to consult colleagues (mainly historians, it would seem) for bibliographical recommendations. Once accumulated, these provided the base for what must rank as one of the most relentlessly focused pursuits of a vision of its scope in academic history. He was not deterred by the Social Science Research Council's decision not to fund a project that represented a "combination of historical and analytic typologies," with insufficiently clear criteria for selection of the regimes to be discussed (Finer 1999). He was only briefly checked in 1987 by a near-fatal heart attack that left him with the deteriorating heart condition from which he died six years later. He was still two chapters away from completing his treatise at that point. But he had completed 34, bringing his analysis up to the eve of the twentieth century; and knowing for those last six years that every day he was writing against the clock, he constantly updated on his computer a conceptual prolegomenon intended as a guide to whoever might have to edit his unfinished work, and to his prospective readers as well. What they now encounter, then, in the three volumes of his last and greatest work, constitutes a remarkably complete and faithful enactment of the vision with which he was seized 11 years before his death.

THE HISTORY OF GOVERNMENT
FROM THE EARLIEST TIMES

Scope and Methods

In surveying five millennia of governmental history, Finer establishes at the outset an implicit agenda for his analysis. After the "Conceptual Prologue" it does not significantly vary throughout his three volumes. In each chapter, he first briefly considers the distinctive significance of the state he is about to examine and the rationale for its study. With a few bold strokes, he then depicts the societal context of the government, emphasizing how this context both defines the tasks of governance in that society and constrains their execution. Finer is now ready to undertake what always forms the core of his chapters. He opens with inventories of what might be called the constitutional rules—some of them formally proclaimed, more of them implied in daily transactions—that prescribe the capital division of decision-making authority within the central government and the roles that emerge within these rules. Next he considers the degree to which these prescriptions become offset through ambiguities and outright contradiction among the rules themselves or as outcomes of mismatched allocations of political resources. This discussion typically obliges him to examine how the government he is analyzing copes with five basic challenges of governance: how to maintain territorial boundaries against hostile outside pressure; how to recruit and keep responsive a competent palace staff; how to maintain civilian control over the coercive resources of the military; how to balance sovereign will with the judiciary's responsibilities for adjudication of conflicting claims; and how to manipulate or absorb the potentially competing legitimacy of religious figures. After examining the nominal areal division of governmental responsibility between the central government and the provinces— always a source of tension in imperial regimes in an epoch of weak transport and weaker communication links—he looks, in conclusion, for evidence of the degree to which governmental figures actually succeed in imprinting their societies in accordance with their intentions.

Finer focuses on two underlying dimensions of these challenges. He asks close questions about how resources are extracted from society at large to support the governmental agenda. He identifies typical impediments to their movement up through governmental pipelines with a relatively modest rate of attrition, and he views the probability of their diversion to private pockets as a near-fatal flaw of most ancient governments. He also identifies those governmental role incumbents who have most commonly exercised strategic leverage over the terms on which governmental interests become integrated to form authoritative policy declarations, and he probes the lines and degree of their accountability. These concerns lead to assessments of the performance of the government both on its own terms and in comparison with other governments he has previously examined. Of particular interest to Finer is whether a government's record in these respects can be related to intrinsic structural flaws in its design and to happy or dysfunctional institutional innovations it has adopted.

A comparativist to the core, Finer seeks the rewards of comparative analysis in his *History* in several ways. While expositing a particular feature of a government, he often seeks to illuminate its significance by referring to seemingly analogous practices in a government he has already taken up, always asking what can be learned from the juxtaposition and whether the implied similarity is misleading. At a higher level of generality, he looks for parallel faultlines in similar structures of government and weighs explanations for superior performance in coping with similar challenges. Finally, Finer does not hesitate to offer judgments regarding a state's concern for the welfare of its subjects, its overall fairness in distributing public resources, the lawful integrity of its procedures, and the degree to which it exercises starkly brutal, uncontrolled, indiscriminate collective violence beyond the evident necessities of the day. Here again he makes use of comparative perspectives to keep these assessments appropriately scaled to their time and place.

As described, this analytic agenda is one of classic simplicity. Aristotle would recognize its leading injunctions readily enough. Finer makes no effort to elaborate a functional conceptual scheme at one remove from the governmental institutions and actors he examines. He thereby departs not only from a strong trend in the past several decades of comparative political analysis (Almond & Powell 1966, Easton 1979) but even from his own earlier practice [when, as we shall see (Finer 1970), he grouped the governments of the world into four categories on the basis of their favored mode for gaining civic compliance]. We return to the possible costs of this departure in the concluding pages of this essay. For the present, what bears stressing is Finer's determination to depict the institutions and processes of governance in the past much as they would probably have been understood by the participants themselves and at the same time not to sacrifice comparative perspectives to that objective.

There can be no doubt as to the unprecedented range of his project. The full title of Finer's massive treatise makes no claim Finer does not substantiate. Following the conceptual prologue, it begins with a weighty chapter on the Sumerians, reserves two for the Old and New Kingdoms of Egypt, then provides an extended tour of the polities in Mesopotamia and its borders, to arrive, after nearly 300 pages, at the Persian Empire, which most readers are likely to know best from its role as the nemesis of Sparta and democratic Athens. An account of the formation of the Chinese state lies ahead, as do long chapters on the Roman Republic and Empire, Byzantium, the Arab Caliphate, and the Tang Empire. By this point, persevering readers are nearly halfway through the *History's* 1651 pages of text. No previous comparative treatise on government has had a chronological center of gravity so far back in the human past.

Moreover, *The History of Government* maintains a disciplined focus on its purported subject to the exclusion of all historical data and civilizational commentary that cannot be related to it. That subject is government—not politics, but government. Finer is very insistent on that point. It is not conceivable that the man who wrote *Anonymous Empire* would minimize the influence of nongovernmental actors on the agenda of government. But Finer, on several previous occasions, lamented in print that in making the properties of societies the determinative variables of political life, the currently fashionable models of political systems—whether neo-Marxist, pluralist, or structural-functionalist—had essentially eclipsed the significance of states as semiautonomous and potentially potent actors. He contended, to the contrary, that the internal structure of governments might prove in many cases as crucial to their efficacy within their jurisdictional domains as the constraining effects of low agrarian productivity, class divisions, congruent societal subcultures, ethnic balances, geopolitical positioning, and other favored environmental variables commonly used to account for their performance (Finer 1969).

In this *History*, Finer does not further argue the point; he demonstrates it. He scrutinizes the circuitry within the "black boxes" of government. He believes that the design of governments—their arrangements for selecting and maintaining leaders, their information-gathering capabilities, their mechanisms for mediating internal conflicts among key administrators, their methods for raising revenue and controlling its use, their devices for controlling military actors while filtering the demands of temple priests, their degree of institutionalized accountability to societal constituencies—is sufficiently consequential to justify an extended history of institutional innovation and institutional failure within government. That, at any rate, is the premise from which his treatise proceeds.

Yet despite the disheartening bulk of Finer's three volumes, rendered all the greater by a tightly intercalated prose saturated with comprehensive lists and specific enumerations, the omissions and allocations of space within them are surprising. Venice "La Serenissima" receives 35 pages of discussion. The Aztec and Inca Empires are noted in one eighth of a sentence on p. 204, and the Mayans not at all. Government on the Indian subcontinent before the coming of the Mughals is said to be unworthy of attention. Sub-Saharan Africa is totally ignored without comment, as is the institution of the *deva raja* in the empire of the Cambodian Khmers; and the account of the history of government in Japan begins for most purposes with the Tokugawa drive to power in the seventeenth century. Finer is surely the first political scientist ever to write about the ancient Middle Eastern kingdoms of Elam, Ebla, and Mari (Finer 1999, pp. 170–75), which makes his passing over of the much better known and more colorful Minoan and Mycenaean kingdoms of the Aegean all the more surprising. It is probably too much to have expected Finer to discuss the sacred kingships of Bali and Java, the nomadic Turkic kingdoms of Central Asia, and the distinctive fusion of religion and kingship into nationalist sentiment in Ethiopia and Safavid Persia—on so vast a canvas, one can always spot corners that need touching up—but the earlier omissions seem to demand more justification than Finer offers. Similarly, we are told that his two unfinished chapters would have dealt with twentieth-century totalitarianism and the export of the paradigmatic Western state; but could the Ayatollah Khomeini's spectacular installation of a clerical regime have been properly fitted in either category?

Such seemingly unprincipled inclusions and omissions appear to have troubled the Social Science Research Council's reviewers of Finer's project proposal. One might have expected Finer to meet their understandable concern head-on in subsequent drafts of his manuscript. In fact, he did not. The nearly 100-page "Conceptual Prologue" covers many points, but not why his three volumes discuss some governments and exclude others. A first indication of his criteria is reserved for his opening traverse of the historic world before 1700 BC. Self-evidently, as he notes at that point, we must have some "fathomable" record of the social and political life of a society if we are to analyze the structure and functions of its government

(p. 99). Archaeological artifacts alone will not do; we need decipherable written accounts of religious covenants with kings, of payments made, of treaties signed, of imperial directives to subordinates, if we are to understand how a country was governed. It is not enough, Finer's criterion implies, to speculate on the organizational capacities required to build a pyramid or to derive a monarch's status from his depiction on a frieze of a triumphal march. Such signs may tell us much about the symbolic archetypes of the great civilizations of the past; they do not yield the more intimate information we require to comprehend the working rules of a social institution.

"Fathomability" as a criterion goes some way toward accounting for Finer's omission of several well-known, much-studied civilizations and their governments from his *History*. Its invocation points to a distinctive difficulty in studying the politics of the past. Government is quintessentially relational, a matter both of allocations of authority and of gaps between rules and their enforcement. The very nature of Finer's project commits him to penetrating and untangling evanescent patterns that leave few physical traces. Differences in the nature and decipherability of the archives uncovered by archaeologists explain why he discusses in depth the governing of the Sumerian and Egyptian kingdoms while passing over Minoan Crete (p. 99). The inability of archaeologists (at least in his lifetime) to decode the writing employed in the early kingdoms of the Indus Valley and the Maya helps explain his omission of them (though not so clearly his silence concerning the Aztecs and the Inca, about which we have at least the observations of the Spanish *conquistadores* and their accompanying priests to go by). Conversely, Finer devotes many pages to the Assyrian Empire. Though best remembered for the well-founded horror with which it was regarded by all its unfortunate neighbors, it is of singular importance for his purposes because we have an impressively rich and intimate transcript, without parallel in the ancient world, of the hopes and fears of the Assyrian rulers' minds in the form of well-preserved archives of clay tablets recording questions the kings posed to their oracles (pp. 223–24).

Beyond their "unfathomability," such states as Minoan Crete were "'one-off' states, dead-end states. As they arose suddenly and in mystery, so they perished suddenly, in mysterious circumstances; and dead, left no progeny" (p. 99). Once again, the terms of Finer's enterprise explain his decision to ignore them despite their intrinsic historic fascination. He is interested, he tells us, in inventions in the art of governance and in their diffusion (a further reason for the space he give to the Assyrian Empire, the first state to work out the institutions of imperial rule). States without imitators require other qualities to attract his analytic attention.

These qualities are revealed contextually over the next several chapters. Even if fathomable written records did not inform us so fully about government in Ancient Egypt, it demands scrutiny for its unique durability—*three thousand years* (the italics are Finer's) of "a set of variations on a few perennial themes" (p. 133). Sheer territorial immensity provides sufficient warrant for including the Persian and Chinese Empires and the enormous and radically heterogeneous Arab Caliphate in Finer's study (pp. 286, 442, 665). As for both the Roman Republic and the subsequent Empire, "it must seem redundant, perhaps impertinent even, to seek to justify a place for Rome in a general history of government" (p. 385), but he risks impertinence to recapitulate the many familiar dimensions of their "inventive" governmental legacies to the extraordinarily diverse societies that emerged on the European peninsula a millennium later.

Three quarters of the way through his three-volume work, Finer at last produces a systematic list of the criteria for inclusion by which he has been governed throughout (p. 1210). Falsely claiming that he is repeating himself, and dropping "fathomability" in the process, he cites the following as determinative: (*a*) durability, populousness, or contemporary power; (*b*) archetypicality; (*c*) innovative or inventive contributions to governance; and (*d*) the quality of being "vivid variants" on a generally autocratic theme. Given such elastic categories for inclusion and exclusion ("vivid variants" must rank as a stand-out!), it is entirely clear why Finer's enterprise could never hope to meet the minimum statistically representative standards for "a social scientific explanation of historical variations in government" (Brisbin 1999). Whether serious distortions are thereby introduced into the conclusions Finer draws from his comparative survey of government since the Sumerians is less clear.

The issue of inclusion and exclusion arises again as one inspects the sources on which Finer relies for his study. Unsurprisingly, they are for the most part secondary, at least as regards language: common mastery of Akkadian, Arabic, Persian, Sanskrit, Chinese, Japanese, Russian, and Ancient Greek is not to be expected of historians of the ancient world, let alone of a political scientist who studies the processes of government conducted in those languages. But Finer shows his early training as a historian in his passion for getting as close as he can to raw or lightly processed, empirically ascertainable data. Legal manuals, translations of scribal chronicles, tables of rank, tabulations of palace expenditures fascinate him. Despite his warnings to the contrary, he makes use of these monographs to develop such data-saturated portraits of the regimes he studies that readers may imagine we know almost as much about the governments of Assyria, Diocletian's Rome, and Tang China as we do about the France of Louis XIV.

So far as his radically uneven and incomplete sources permit, Finer inserts specific numbers into his sentences. One learns that under the Wu Ti Emperor's reign in Han China, fiscal levies were standardized through setting the poll tax "at 120 coins (cash) per adult and twenty-three for each child over the age of 7" (p. 514). In the medieval Arab Caliphate, "in 923–4 [fines] are believed to have formed no less than 48 per cent of the total revenue" (p. 723). Under the Guelphs, an oligarchical commission controlled membership in the key governing bodies of Florence by screening the lists of names submitted by the guilds to the point that "750 (out of 5000 names)" survived in 1382 (p. 969). Japanese shogunal inspection records for 1764 show, we are told, 1568 enfeoffed vassals and 4725 stipended vassals (p. 1106). When no one else has performed pertinent calculations, Finer does so himself. During the Ming Dynasty, he notes, governmental control by a fixed staff over a swelling population was becoming a matter of form. But not content (as most historians of China have been) with that important but abstract generalization, he estimates that each inspector from the Imperial Censorate, "on a rough calculation, assuming a figure of 1,100 *hsien c*. 1600, . . . had fifty-two *yamens* to visit whose population (out of a national total of 160 million) would have been some 145,500 apiece" (p. 833). When others' figures seem implausible, Finer engages in similar recalculations as a reality check (p. 827).

Finer's determination to freight every generalization with specific numbers, to spell out every category of punishment in a legal code and every institutionalized responsibility of a Roman Emperor, to inform us of the frequency and locations of satrapal revolts in the Persian Empire and compare them in depth with provincial rebellions in China, can make his three volumes seem many times their already awesome length. His chapters emphatically do not lend themselves to skimming. Yet this unrelenting empiricism is not idle show or an indication of inability to step back from thickets of contextual detail. His ten-page "overviews" of successive stages of human history are marvels of panoramic concision. His cumulative comparisons among regimes repeatedly remind readers of his larger objectives. But Finer appears to have set himself the challenge of mapping as never before, to the fullest extent permitted by the available data, a comprehensive set of determinate power relationships within each government he studies and the resources used to maintain or alter them. To this end, he feels obligated to locate and assess whatever data can cast light on the terms of recruitment to central positions of leadership within the government. He wants to leave readers in no doubt as to the identity of the specific cadres of personnel intervening between rulers and lower-echelon administrative officials. In his eyes, identifying the recurrence of general patterns does not suffice to justify exempting himself from examining in differentiated detail the always-troublesome relations between a capital city and its provincial agents, the degree of independence enjoyed within superficially similar regimes by the judiciary and the military in the exercise of their authority, the relative efficacy with which resources were extracted to maintain this structure. Cumulatively, these carefully and critically amassed details give special weight to his concluding comparative judgments concerning the regimes he examines.

Finer's nominalist conception of how to compare governments is curiously conventional—indeed, outmoded—in its objectives and the inventories to which they lead. Even so, for most of the countries covered in Finer's first two volumes (i.e., preceding 1500 AD), its execution is virtually without precedent. To appreciate the validity of this claim, one has only to look at the standard works on almost any of the civilizations of the ancient world other than China, Rome, and the city-states of Ancient Greece. What will strike any political scientist in such cases is how swiftly the chapters on government thin out as the writer descends below an analysis of sacral kingship. One simple reason is the paucity of relevant data on the subject. This is, perhaps, to be expected when one considers how little is known about several crucial years in the life of even so prominent a figure as the Emperor Hadrian, greatest of the Antonine emperors, despite the comparatively high literacy rate of the Roman upper classes and despite their intense interest in politics (Perowne 1961, Birley 1997). Furthermore, as noted above, since manipulations of the operative relational networks within the corridors of palatial power leave no physical traces, their reconstruction depends heavily on the availability of written testimony by strategically placed observers, many of whom must be presumed to have had a keen interest in concealment or distortion of such matters. But another causative factor is the sheer tedium of such reconstruction. Lacking satisfactory data in most cases, students of the governments of many of these societies must construct a coherent picture of palace administration out of shards of evidence—a surviving letter of complaint, a receipt for grain delivered, the chance recording on a durable material of a law relating to enforcement of a regulatory statute. One measure of Finer's achievement in his *History* is his success in weaving these incomplete, often distorted fragments of texts, and the often narrowly focused monographs that report them, into his smoothly flowing, comprehensive, and comparative narrative.

Finer's conception of his task, and his clear need for primary sources to support it, may likewise account for his striking indifference to a large fraction of the theory-oriented historical studies noted above. Weber is mentioned occasionally and briefly, but Wittfogel's (1957) provocative "hydraulic" thesis not at all. Anderson's *Lineages of the Absolutist State* (1974b) appears in Finer's bibliography but not as an active presence in the text. Bendix, Eisenstadt, Kautsky, Mann, Moore, and Parsons are simply passed over despite theses directly applicable to his work. Toynbee is acknowledged only for an appended volume on topics ancillary to his monumental study of ancient civilizations (Toynbee 1956–1962). It is not with such theorists, but rather with specialists' data, interpretations, and calculations that Finer picks his scholarly quarrels.

Theoretical Substructure

Finer's *History of Government* does not, in the end, purport to be about *all* government. His self-defined task is not to develop a general structural theory of governance within the social order; rather, he scrutinizes a broad panoply of historical governments as closely as surviving data permit, hoping both to identify their individual operative codes and capabilities and to pinpoint the chronological moment at which their structure significantly altered. In undertaking his detailed and nearly exhaustive survey, however, Finer does not exhibit the ideological hostility to conceptual abstractions shown by deconstructionist historians. In an earlier critical review of Almond's contributions to comparative theory, he challenges not Almond's reduction of political systems to four transactional categories but rather his elimination of the state in the process (Finer 1969). His own earlier treatise on comparative government consistently employs a quadrifold scheme (coercion, manipulation, regimentation, persuasion/bargaining) for differentiating governments by their core techniques (Finer 1970).

When needed, as in his efficient millennial surveys of the historical contexts for the governments he examines in each section, he restates with admirable clarity and concision the boldest of sociological characterizations of historical phenomena. For example, in relating religion to politics, he embraces, with some qualifications, Bellah's (1969) five-fold classification of the religions of humanity and Rokkan's (1973) tabulation of "secular-religious differentiation" (Finer 1999, pp. 23–28). Confronting the task of charting the history of government in medieval Europe, he pens a preface designed to assure his permanent exclusion from the fraternity of contemporary historians (p. 864):

> Certain medievalists will not use the concept "feudalism" or "feudal system". They find the Middle Ages too protean, too full of exceptions and local idiosyncrasies to be captured in a formula . . . . This approach is not open to me. I am not, like them, trying to write a history of an epoch nor even a history of the form of government in a particular epoch, but trying to present a history of successive and repetitive forms of government throughout the world, and this cannot proceed without constant comparison and contrast, and these in turn require formulae, constructs, and models to make similarities and differences plain.

Rejection of ontological nominalism could not be put more plainly.

Indeed, Finer structures the exposition of his entire *History* around an introductory schematic classification of governments so disarmingly simple as to risk discrediting his enterprise in sophisticated readers' eyes. Nearly all historically recorded governments, he contends, can be grouped into just two types of regime—those in which the critical processes of governance occur within "the Palace" and those in which the constituency of "the Forum" must be included in the analysis. These two types are hardly of equivalent empirical weight. Until the mid-eighteenth century, at least, virtually all the regimes in Finer's comprehensive history are "Palace polities," so that until well into third volume the dichotomy chiefly serves to accentuate the stunning exceptionalism of Athenian democracy. In combination, however, "Palace-Forum" polities have a pedigree traceable back to the Greek tyrants and Julius Caesar and extending through the despotisms of certain medieval Italian city-states to modern totalitarian regimes in which "the ruler governs in true Palace fashion" but claims legitimation from below.

For the sake of completeness, Finer acknowledges two further classificatory entities—"the Church" and "the Nobility." As "pure types," such polities have established at most an exceedingly marginal niche in world history. Finer cites the Vatican and Tibet 1642–1949 as the only examples of a pure Church polity, eighteenth-century Poland as one of the few examples of a Nobility polity. Even their combinatorial variants cover few cases. Seeking examples of a Church-Nobility polity in history, he comes up with nothing beyond the thirteenth-century Teutonic Order in the eastern Baltic region. But far more important than a further inventorying of such possibilities is the implicit thesis underlying them. Finer's sweepingly comprehensive survey of some five millennia points to the conclusion that human inventiveness is startlingly limited in its design of basic governmental structure. Throughout all but the last two centuries, human beings have relied on forms of government that lie almost exclusively under the rubric of "Palace polities." Immense variations in scale, in topography, in ecological resources, in location, in exposure to invaders, in social stratification, in religious creeds and cultural values extending back over some 5000 years have not precluded a near-universal disposition to locate collectively binding, purportedly sovereign decisional authority in a single individual and (nearly always) his court, leaving at issue within that restricted format such further questions as how these individuals are selected, how their reign is legitimized, what resources they command, how extensively their effective power is dispersed among their courtiers, how liable they are to deposition, and what consequences typically ensue. Monocratic, autocratic rule has been the common lot of humanity throughout nearly all of its written history. It is a rule with startlingly few exceptions.

How is one to account for such strikingly limited variations on a single theme? Finer's argument, more evident in the uniform subdivisions of his chapters than in any explicit declaration, is that everywhere and always throughout the preindustrial world the expected functions of government have been similar. They include—but are typically limited to—the attempt to achieve and maintain centralized control over coercive resources, the internal integration of governmental decision making, the protection or expansion of jurisdictional borders, the authoritative resolution of societal conflicts, the provision of a limited number of public works enhancing the productivity of an agrarian society, the creation of artifacts and rites designed to add luster to monarchical rule, and the mobilization of the financial, informational, and personnel resources required to sustain these tasks. Individual polities have given greater emphasis to some of these functions. They have also varied in their degree of reliance on any one (for instance, Chinese imperial governments through the centuries have remained at one extreme in their efforts to obtain the compliance of the governed through intensive doctrinal socialization). From time to time, though rather rarely, the monarch and his courtiers have come up with an invention in the art of governance. Nevertheless, the commonality and restricted agenda of governments across continents and centuries appears to justify the presentational uniformity of Finer's case studies.

The special strength of Finer's study lies within these confines. Finer is relentless—at times, one feels, merciless—in articulating the internal patterns and tensions of his governments. He carefully notes the cross-currents and ambiguities in these patterns, the typical sources of challenge to governments' implicit constitutions, and the resources employed to maintain these "contested concepts" (p. 822) against such challenges. He looks closely for evidence as to the actual imprint of governments' policy decisions on their societies. Not content with listing every function performed by the early Roman emperors, he examines the precise terms of legitimation for each role, the constraints within which each could be effectively exercised, and the subtly calibrated degree to which these patterns deviated from those of a Han Chinese emperor, an Egyptian pharoah, a Babylonian monarch (pp. 542–50). He patiently inventories the tier of provincial and court officials in the Byzantine and Moghul courts, giving each his indigenous name along with estimates of who was likely to prevail in the event of conflict (pp. 639–45, 1233–47). He is unfailingly attentive to the mechanisms of control over the military and the specific kinds of taxes that support it. Despite its relative brevity, his outline of Islamic justice under the Caliphate in precept and practice leaves little of leading importance to be said (pp. 712–21).

At some points, Finer's determination to tie down every loose end, to pinpoint each structural inconsistency in a government, seems a grievous strain on the nonspecialist's attention. It requires a special kind of commitment to stay with him as he meticulously unravels the almost unbelievably complex system of checks and counter-checks institutionalized in the Roman Republic to head off absolutism (pp. 397–417)—a design so effective in paralyzing the potential exercise of executive energy on behalf of collective goals as to make virtually inevitable the coming of a Caesar. When Finer offers a similarly dedicated tour of the labyrinthine constitution of the medieval Florentine republic (pp. 966–70), one's disposition to step off the bus cannot help but quicken. Both exercises are virtuoso performances in tracing pathways through a seemingly impenetrable forest. One is awed as much by the author's ability to maintain his bearings as by the gloriously inventive complexity of the human mind such governments reveal, yet it is hard to fight down the wish that Finer had eschewed these challenges. But this same determination to back up broad structural generalizations by precisely drafted blueprints works splendidly when Finer provides a definitive account of "paperwork and paralysis" in China's sixteenth-century Ming Dynasty (pp. 832–37). Minutely quantitative yet sweepingly comparative, highly specific as to what Chinese imperial officials could learn about their society in illuminating contrast to the informational resources generated by modern democracy, cogently linking the intricacies of governmental structure to the challenges of monitoring huge populations, he accomplishes in five pages what numerous more celebrated scholarly specialists on China have conveyed imperfectly in whole volumes—a conclusive portrait of the seizing up of an ancient and glorious empire's collective capacities at a critical turning point in its history.

As Finer moves into the era of the post-Renaissance European nation-state—the era and geographical locale in which, on previous evidence (Finer 1975), one might expect to find him most at home—such moments become rarer. Here Finer is, of course, traversing much-mapped territory; yet one could have hoped that by this point the unique perspective derived from his long and densely contextual exploration of the internal intricacies of ancient governments would yield more startling comparative insights than it does. Few readers will be struck by his differentiation of British constitutional government from Continental absolutism. He identifies six important inventions contributed by the 1787 Philadelphia Convention to the art of governance, and he concisely and convincingly depicts the rise of Brandenburg-Prussia as a triumph of governmental engineering in an unpromising environment; but these tales have been well told many times before (Rosenberg 1958, Smith 1987). He sees what others have seen in the French Revolution, using an extended account of its month-to-month trajectory to establish that the mass mobilization of "citizens" to protect and enlarge *la patrie* was something new under the sun in the history of government. In perhaps the least refreshing chapter of his study—a narration of the advance toward the constitutionalization of the European monarchies between 1815 and 1871—he inserts a six-page calendar of reasonably familiar events of which, for once, he makes no subsequent use in his analysis (pp. 1583–88). In a three-volume work remarkable, despite its bulk, for the weightiness and elegantly latinate compression of nearly every sentence, this ballast marks an unwelcome innovation of its own. It would be easy to conclude from this chapter that Finer had long since said what he had most compellingly to say; and yet the final surviving chapter on industrialization and the radical expansion of governmental capacity is a magnificent summation that could only have been written by a scholar as richly versed in the exiguous and nominal character of government throughout most of its history as Finer could now claim to be. Although not intended as a coda to his monumental study, it is a coda worthy of Beethoven.

Assessment

In a 1651-page treatise as factually saturated as Finer's, one that spans the Eurasian continent and the Americas across five millennia, it would be remarkable if specialists failed to spot errors of fact and empirically unsustainable interpretations. Despite Finer's critical discussion of his sources and data, the elementary laws of probability suggest no less. What is equally remarkable is the sheer range of specialists whose expertise Finer's three volumes implicitly (and sometimes explicitly) challenge. This reviewer will not be so foolhardy as to add himself to their numbers. Suffice it to say that Finer's scrupulous attentiveness to the trustworthiness of his sources, as well as his marked disposition to cross-check and run independent calculations to correct their claims, inspire confidence that, had he lived longer, those critics would have faced tenacious rebuttals. In any case, in arenas where so few have ventured before him, many convictions concerning errors of fact would only marginally diminish the magnitude of his contribution.

Less easily dismissed are misgivings concerning his manifest indifference to the potential applicability of macrosociological theories to his subject. Comparative history, as Skocpol (1984) concisely reminds her readers, offers opportunities to depict the course of human events as an economically lawful ordering through repeated application of theoretical argument, through systematic construction of an ideal type, or through comparing cases to test a proposition. Finer does none of the above. His approach precludes doing so. At the start of each chapter, he sometimes rhetorically, sometimes implicitly, asks his readers, "What can we learn from studying the regime I am about to examine?" It is a good question, and Finer generally answers it very well; but the lessons learned are diverse and do not fall into place as successive confirmations or disconfirmations of an identifiable, explicit set of interrelated propositions. They are, instead, a function of structural faultlines uncovered in the course of surveying particular terrains. As a consequence, the conclusions of one chapter, however intrinsically fascinating, do not provide the starting point for the next.

What Finer and his readers learn from his study of any particular government results from a confrontation of a penetrating, sensitive, sophisticated political observer's mind with the distinctive nodules, networks, and hierarchies of governmental power that the available data make salient for a particular regime. His chapters' subdivisions (the territorial framework, the central government, administrative services, the judiciary, the provinces) are, with little variation, topical; they derive not from the functions governments must perform but from those they have performed. In a general way, Finer seeks to chart how an inward flow of resources extracted from society is allocated among those whose locations within the prevailing structures of a government give them strategic advantages or systematically strategic handicaps as they seek to capture, convert, and deploy the positive externalities of governmental organization into collective outcomes in accordance with their intentions. Finer is strongly committed to the proposition that the institutionalized rules of governmental design have a powerful influence on that process. However, he resolutely rejects a priori theoretical guidance in his undertaking, preferring instead to identify the sign and potency of the attractive or repelling charges of the individual governmental roles he depicts and then matching their revealed properties accordingly until patterns emerge within his mosaic. Something like Mendelyeev's table of the chemical elements would seem to constitute his theoretical ideal.

These patterns are necessarily empirical patterns. They are identified and elaborated in the particular form Finer ascribes to them because he believes that their delineation in these terms provides an economical and illuminating ordering to the recurrent contests for dominance he observes. They do not derive from any one explicitly postulated set of axioms concerning theoretically conceptualized actors, nor do his actors act within an environment of systemically specified constraints and requisites. Finer, as noted, is not at all opposed in principle to constructing theories of society. An ardent advocate of comparative methods, he freely uses nonstatistical comparisons to confirm and extend propositions. His internal charting of regime structures is laced with comparative references that attain a level of explicit generality in the concluding sections of his chapters. He only insists that it is in the conclusions—not at the outset of his inquiries—that such propositions belong.

The costs of this empiricist approach have often been inventoried (e.g., Deutsch 1963). It does not tell the reader where and how the author will start his or her inquiry. It does not provide advance indication of the direction in which the chosen starting point will logically lead. It does not make clear what propositions are being tested, what commitments the investigator has made to any particular outcome, or what constitute decisive refutations of these commitments. It neither invites nor permits an orderly articulation of the processes selected for exposition and analysis (processes of governance in the instant case) with other environing variables theoretically identified as requisite or antithetical to these processes (e.g., the economy, the physical ecology, pattern maintenance through religious creeds). It therefore does not tell the reader how the terms of their interaction can be used to define critical ranges within which the variables of (in this case) government must remain if it is not to collapse (Easton 1979). The limited level of theoretical explicitness and abstraction afforded by this approach precludes both the ready transfer of its implicit explanatory paradigm to new settings and the use of parallel models from elsewhere to strengthen confidence in its conclusions.

To some degree, Finer's approach stands justly indicted under all these headings. It is true, for example, that he can offer no general explanation for the collapse of governments, nor can he systematically relate their properties and performance to the fate of the civilizations in which they are embedded. Beyond incisive description of the lineaments of governmental power, his explorations are so multiform and so embedded in their specific historical contexts that it is hard to state in general terms what questions concerning government he sought to answer and to what extent he succeeded in answering them. Whether these limitations reduce his work to an encyclopedia of information about ancient governments for the use of more scientifically sophisticated researchers is quite another matter. Finer's objectives are at a lower order of abstraction than these criteria demand. He is fascinated by the early manifestations of a governmental order among the Sumerians, and he invites and expects the reader to share that fascination. Although he notes that the command economy of the Egyptians showed symptoms of the same problems as Brezhnev's Soviet Union over a period of nearly 3000 years, he also notes that its rigidities did not preclude the survival of an unchanging pattern of governance for the same period. Constitutional rigidity also characterized the Venetian government, which preserved that small city-state's independence with remarkable serenity and efficiency for 1300 years (the last 500 under an unchanging constitution) despite turbulent and greedy neighbors. The inadequacies of the Marxist proposition that government can best be understood as the executive committee of the interests of some social class, rather than as a semiautonomous entity with a consequential internal design, is documented in virtually every chapter of Finer's work. Finer concludes that the secret of durable governments lies in the details of their political arrangements and that political scientists have something to learn from those details.

If Finer has any general ideological bias, it might be his conviction that 5000 years of governmental history support the argument that the welfare of citizens is more secure under the rule of law than under the unconstrained will of the ruler. The medieval Arab Caliphate was much larger, much wealthier, and much less subject to invasion than the Byzantine Empire. It sustained a far more glittering scientific and literary community. The Byzantine Empire was sunk in religious superstition and so unstable at the top that all but 34 of its 107 emperors over 1068 years died of "poison, smothering, strangulation, stabbing, or mutilation." Nevertheless, the Byzantine Empire maintained throughout these years such an authentic legal regime below the top level that it retained the loyalties of its citizens under endless states of siege for a millennium. The Caliphate, in contrast, disintegrated in less than three centuries (pp. 636, 727). Civilizational brilliance proved less consequential than pervasive lawfulness in sustaining a government under continuous siege. Like the other middle-range propositions noted above, this is no trifling conclusion to draw from a historically oriented study of government.

CONCLUSION

At the beginning of this essay, a metaphorical comparison was drawn between Finer's *History of Government* and Ayers Rock. Many of its remaining pages were devoted to establishing the validity of this trope. But the analogy is misleading in one crucial respect. Ayers Rock has remained in isolation in the central Australian desert through a combination of inexorable natural forces. Finer's book, in contrast, stands in isolated grandeur because it occupies a terrain few political scientists have chosen to explore in their work.

There are, at present, few signs that such exploration is now under way. The postwar interest in expanding the comparative study of politics from its former North Atlantic domain to such global outposts as contemporary Mongolia and New Guinea has not yet prompted a parallel quest to extend that enterprise through time. Despite the rhapsodic terms in which Finer's *History of Government* was first reviewed, it is already heading for the publisher's remainders shelves. Had the Arab Caliphate not preserved Aristotle's *Politics*, its fate might have been worse; yet at the moment, it seems improbable that these two works will maintain a coterminous existence through the ages. Present indications suggest that Finer's magnum opus is destined to remain a largely unread curiosity in the eyes of most political scientists. But those who have worked their way through its three volumes will know how gravely the discipline stands to be impoverished if none of its members are stirred by the challenge this study presents.

The *Annual Review of Political Science* is online at
http://polisci.annualreviews.org

LITERATURE CITED

Almond GA, Powell GB. 1966. *Comparative Politics: A Developmental Approach.* Boston: Little, Brown. 348 pp.

Anderson B. 1983. *Imagined Communities: Reflections on the Origin and Spread of Nationalism.* London: Verso. 160 pp.

Anderson P. 1974a. *Passages from Antiquity to Feudalism.* London: New Left Books. 304 pp.

Anderson P. 1974b. *Lineages of the Absolutist State.* London: New Left Books. 573 pp.

Beer SH. 1965. *British Politics in the Collectivist Age.* New York: Knopf. 390 pp.

Bellah RN. 1969. Religious evolution. In *Sociology of Religion*, ed. R Robertson, pp. 262–94. Hammondsworth, UK: Penguin

Bendix R. 1964. *Nation-Building and Citizenship.* New York: Wiley. 314 pp.

Bendix R. 1977. *Max Weber: An Intellectual Portrait.* Berkeley: Univ. Calif. Press. 522 pp.

Bendix R. 1978. *Kings or People: Power and the Mandate.* Berkeley: Univ. Calif. Press. 692 pp.

Binkley WE. 1962. *American Political Parties: Their Natural History.* New York: Knopf. 486 pp.

Birley AR. 1997. *Hadrian: The Restless Emperor.* London: Routledge. 399 pp.

Braudel F. 1975. *Capitalism and Material Life: 1400–1800.* New York: Harper Colophon Books. 462 pp.

Brisbin RA. 1999. *The History of Government from the Earliest Times* (review). *Persp. Polit. Sci.* 28:170

Brown J. 1989. *Gandhi: Prisoner of Hope.* New Haven, CT: Yale Univ. Press. 440 pp.

Bullock A. 1960. *Hitler: A Study in Tyranny.* New York: Harper. 776 pp.

Bullock A. 1992. *Hitler and Stalin: Parallel Lives.* New York: Knopf. 1081 pp.

Burnham WD. 1970. *Critical Elections and the Mainsprings of American Politics.* New York: Norton. 210 pp.

Burns JM. 1949. *Congress on Trial: The Legislative Process and the Administrative State.* New York: Harper. 224 pp.

Burns JM. 1956. *Roosevelt: The Lion and the Fox.* New York: Harcourt Brace. 553 pp.

Burns JM. 1963. *The Deadlock of Democracy: Four-Party Politics in America.* Englewood Cliffs, NJ: Prentice Hall. 338 pp.

Catlin GEG. 1964 (1927). *The Science and Method of Politics.* Hamden: Archon. 360 pp.

Chambers WN. 1963. *Political Parties in a New Nation: the American Experience, 1776–1809.* New York: Oxford Univ. Press. 231 pp.

Cipolla CM. 1975. *Before the Industrial Revolution: European Society and Economy 1000–1700.* New York: Norton. 326 pp.

Conquest R. 1968. *The Great Terror: Stalin's Purge of the Thirties.* New York: Macmillan. 633 pp.

Crick B. 1998. *The History of Government*, 3 vols. (review). *Polit. Q.* 69:102–4

Cunningham NE. 1957. *The Jeffersonian Republicans: the Formation of Party Organi-*

zation 1789–1801. Chapel Hill: Univ. North Carolina Press. 279 pp.

Deutsch KW. 1963. *The Nerves of Government: Models of Political Communication and Contrast.* London: Free. 316 pp.

Downing BM. 1992. *The Military Revolution and Political Change: Origins of Democracy and Autocracy in Early Modern Europe.* Princeton, NJ: Princeton Univ. Press. 308 pp.

Doyle MW. 1986. *Empires.* Ithaca, NY: Cornell Univ. Press. 407 pp.

Easton D. 1953. *The Political System: An Inquiry into the State of Political Science.* New York: Knopf. 320 pp.

Easton D. 1979. *A Framework for Political Analysis.* Chicago: Univ. Chicago Press. 142 pp.

Economist (U.S.). 1997. *The History of Government from the Earliest Times* (review). 345(Oct. 18):S4–5 (Suppl.)

Eisenstadt SN. 1963. *The Political System of Empires.* London: Free/Glencoe. 524 pp.

Eisenstadt SN, Rokkan S, eds. 1973. *Building States and Nations.* 2 vols. Beverly Hills, CA: Sage. 903 pp.

Elvin M. 1973. *The Pattern of the Chinese Past.* Stanford, CA: Stanford Univ. Press. 346 pp.

Ertman T. 1997. *Birth of the Leviathan.* New York: Cambridge Univ. Press. 363 pp.

Eulau H. 1963. *The Behavioral Persuasion in Politics.* New York: Random House. 141 pp.

Finer SE. 1958. *Anonymous Empire: A Study of the Lobby in Great Britain.* London: Pall Mall. 150 pp.

Finer SE. 1962. *The Man on Horseback: the Role of the Military in Politics.* London: Pall Mall. 342 pp.

Finer SE. 1969. Almond's concept of "the political system": a textual critique. *Gov. Oppos.* 5:3–21

Finer SE. 1970. *Comparative Government.* London: Penguin. 615 pp.

Finer SE. 1975. State and nation-building in Europe: the role of the military. In *The Formation of National States in Europe*, ed. C Tilly, pp. 84–163. Princeton, NJ: Princeton Univ. Press

Finer SE. 1980. *Political Science: An Idiosyncratic Retrospect of a Putative Discipline.* Gov. Oppos. 15:346–63

Finer SE. 1999. *The History of Government from the Earliest Times.* 3 vols. Oxford: Oxford Univ. Press. 1701 pp.

Friedman M. 1965. *The Great Contraction: 1929–1933.* Princeton, NJ: Princeton Univ. Press. 150 pp.

Gaddis JL. 1997. *We Know Now: Rethinking Cold War History.* Oxford, UK: Clarendon. 425 pp.

Galbraith JK. 1988. *The Great Crash: 1929.* Boston: Houghton Mifflin. 206 pp.

George AL. 1956. *Woodrow Wilson and Colonel House: A Personality Study.* New York: J. Day. 362 pp.

Gilpin R, with assistance from Gilpin J. 1987. *The Political Economy of International Relations.* Princeton, NJ: Princeton Univ. Press. 449 pp.

Goodwin DK. 1976. *Lyndon Johnson and the American Dream.* New York: Harper & Row. 432 pp.

Grew R, ed. 1978. *Crises of Political Development in Europe and the United States.* Princeton, NJ: Princeton Univ. Press. 434 pp.

Hoffman S, ed. 1963. *France: Change and Tradition.* London: Victor Gollancz. 443 pp.

Homans GC. 1941. *English Villagers of the Thirteenth Century.* Cambridge, MA: Harvard Univ. Press. 478 pp.

Huntington SP. 1968. *Political Order in Changing Societies.* New Haven, CT: Yale Univ. Press. 488 pp.

Huntington SP. 1981. *American Politics: The Promise of Disharmony.* Cambridge, MA: Belknap. 303 pp.

Jones EL. 1981. *The European Miracle: Environment, Economics, and Geopolitics in the History of Europe and Asia.* New York: Cambridge Univ. Press. 279 pp.

Jones EL. 1988. *Growth Recurring: Economic Change in World History.* New York: Oxford Univ. Press. 246 pp.

Kautsky JH. 1982. *The Politics of Aristocratic Empires.* Chapel Hill: Univ. North Carolina Press. 416 pp.

Kavanagh D, Peele G, eds. 1984. *Comparative Government and Politics: Essays in Honour of S.E. Finer.* London: Heinemann. 242 pp.

Kennedy PM. 1988. *The Rise and Fall of the Great Powers.* New York: Random House. 677 pp.

Key VO. 1949. *Southern Politics in State and Nation.* New York: Knopf. 675 pp.

Kindleberger CP. 1973. *The World in Depression: 1929–1939.* London: Allen Lane. 336 pp.

Landes DS. 1969. *The Unbound Prometheus: Technological Change and Industrial Development in Western Europe from 1750 to the Present.* London: Cambridge Univ. Press. 566 pp.

Landes DS. 1998. *The Wealth and Poverty of Nations: Why Some Are So Rich and Some So Poor.* New York: Norton. 655 pp.

Levi M. 1988. *Of Rule and Revenue.* Berkeley: Univ. Calif. Press. 253 pp.

Lipset SM. 1963. *The First New Nation: the United States in Historical and Comparative Perspective.* New York: Basic Books. 366 pp.

Luttwak E. 1997. *The History of Government from the Earliest Times* (review). *Times Lit. Suppl.* Aug 29:5–6

Malia ME. 1994. *The Soviet Tragedy: A History of Socialism in Russia, 1917–1991.* New York: Free. 575 pp.

Mann M. 1986. *The Sources of Social Power. Vol. I: A History of Power from the Beginning to 170.* Cambridge, UK: Cambridge Univ. Press

Marx K. 1962. *Capital.* 2 vols. Transl. E Paul, C Paul. London: Dent. 929 pp.

Matusow AJ. 1984. *The Unravelling of America: A History of Liberalism in the 1960s.* New York: Harper & Row. 542 pp.

Moore B. 1962. *Political Power and Social Theory: Seven Studies.* New York: Harper & Row. 243 pp.

Moore B. 1966. *Social Origins of Dictatorship and Democracy: Lord and Peasant in the Making of the Modern World.* Boston: Beacon. 559 pp.

Oakeshott MJ. 1962. *Rationalism in Politics and Other Essays.* New York: Basic Books. 335 pp.

Offer A. 1993. The British Empire, 1870–1914: a waste of money? *Econ. Hist. Rev.* 46:215–38

Olson MS. 1982. *The Rise and Decline of Nations: Economic Growth, Stagflation, and Social Rigidities.* New Haven, CT: Yale Univ. Press. 273 pp.

Parsons T. 1966. *Societies: Evolutionary and Comparative Perspectives.* Englewood Cliffs, NJ: Prentice Hall. 120 pp.

Parsons T. 1977. *The Evolution of Societies.* Englewood Cliffs, NJ: Prentice Hall. 269 pp.

Perkins DH. 1969. *Agricultural Development in China: 1368–1968.* Chicago: Aldine. 395 pp.

Perowne S. 1961. *Hadrian.* New York: Norton. 192 pp.

Pirenne H. 1956. *Economic and Social History of Medieval Europe.* Transl. IE Clegg. New York: Harcourt Brace. 239 pp.

Polanyi K. 1944. *The Great Transformation.* Boston: Beacon. 315 pp.

Polanyi K, Arensberg CM, Pearson HW. 1957. *Trade and Market in the Early Empires: Economics in History and Theory.* Glencoe, IL: Free. 382 pp.

Polsby NW. 1968. The institutionalization of the U.S. House of Representatives. *Am. Polit. Sci. Rev.* LXII(1):144–68

Porter BD. 1994. *War and the Rise of the State: The Military Foundations of Modern Politics.* New York: Free. 380 pp.

Power J. 1999. *The History of Government from the Earliest Times* (review). *Austr. J. Polit. Sci.* 34:95–99

Roche JR. 1968. The Founding Fathers: a reform caucus in action. In *The Reinterpretation of the American Revolution, 1763–1789,* ed. JP Greene, pp. 437–69. New York: Harper & Row

Rokkan S. 1973. Cities, states, and nations. In *Building States and Nations,* ed. SN Eisenstadt, S Rokkan, pp. 73–97. London: Sage

Rosenberg H. 1958. *Bureaucracy, Aristocracy,*

and Autocracy: the Prussian Experience, 1660–1815.* Boston: Beacon. 237 pp.

Rossiter CL. 1960. *The American Presidency.* New York: Harcourt Brace. 281 pp.

Rostovzeff MI. 1963–1966. *Social and Economic History of the Roman Empire.* 2 vols. Oxford, UK: Clarendon. 847 pp.

Schlesinger AM. 1957–1960. *The Age of Roosevelt.* 3 vols. Boston: Houghton Mifflin. 1975 pp.

Schumpeter JA. 1950. *Capitalism, Socialism, and Democracy.* New York: Harper. 431 pp.

Schuman FL. 1936. *The Nazi Dictatorship: A Study in Social Pathology and the Politics of Fascism.* New York: Knopf. 516 pp.

Schurmann F. 1966. *Ideology and Organization in Communist China.* Berkeley: Univ. Calif. Press. 540 pp.

Silberman BS. 1993. *Cages of Reason: the Rise of the Rational State in France, Japan, the United States, and Great Britain.* Chicago: Univ. Chicago Press. 487 pp.

Sjoberg G. 1965. *The Pre-Industrial City: Past and Present.* New York: Free. 353 pp.

Skocpol T. 1979. *States and Revolution: A Comparative Analysis of France, Russia, and China.* New York: Cambridge Univ. Press. 407 pp.

Skocpol T, ed. 1984. *Vision and Method in Historical Sociology.* New York: Cambridge Univ. Press. 410 pp.

Skowronek S. 1982. *Building a New American State: the Expansion of National Administrative Capacities, 1877–1920.* New York: Cambridge Univ. Press. 389 pp.

Smith DG. 1987. *The Convention and the Constitution: the Political Ideas of the Founding Fathers.* Lanham, MD: Univ. Press Am. 120 pp.

Thompson EP. 1963. *The Making of the English Working Class.* New York: Vintage Books. 848 pp.

Tilly C, ed. 1975. *The Formation of National States in Western Europe.* Princeton, NJ: Princeton Univ. Press. 711 pp.

Tilly C. 1992. *Coercion, Capital, and the European State: AD 990–1992.* Cambridge, MA: Blackwell. 271 pp.

Toynbee AJ. 1956–1962. *A Study of History.* 10 vols. London: Oxford Univ. Press

Truman D. 1951. *The Governmental Process: Political Interests and Public Opinion.* New York: Knopf. 544 pp.

Wallerstein IM. 1979. *The Capitalist World-Economy.* New York: Cambridge Univ. Press. 305 pp.

Weber M. 1963. *The Sociology of Religion.* Boston: Beacon. 304 pp.

White L. 1965. *The Federalists: A Study in Administrative History.* New York: Free. 538 pp.

Williams WA. 1962. *The Tragedy of American Diplomacy.* New York: Dell. 309 pp.

Wittfogel KA. 1957. *Oriental Despotism: A Comparative Study of Total Power.* New Haven, CT: Yale Univ. Press. 556 pp.

Wolin SS. 1960. *Politics and Vision: Continuity and Innovation in Western Political Thought.* Boston: Little, Brown. 529 pp.

Annu. Rev. Polit. Sci. 2003. 6:377–98
doi: 10.1146/annurev.polisci.6.121901.085631
First published online as a Review in Advance on Mar. 6, 2003

TRADE, FOREIGN INVESTMENT, AND SECURITY

Richard Rosecrance and Peter Thompson

*Department of Political Science, University of California at Los Angeles, 4250 Bunche
Hall, Los Angeles, California 90095-1472; email: rosecran@polisci.ucla.edu;
pthomp@ucla.edu*

Key Words   factor flows, symmetry/asymmetry of investment, portfolio
investment, conflict

■ **Abstract**   Trade interdependence does not always reduce hostility between states.
It depends on whether the trade represents vulnerability or sensitivity interdependence.
Portfolio investment also does not represent a tie that binds politically. Even more
important, foreign direct investment (FDI) represents a link that is costly (and time-
consuming) to break. Thus, FDI links between countries are more likely to reduce
conflict than trading links. Evidence shows that symmetrical FDI is the most stable
guarantor of low conflict between countries. One factor generating conflict may be
that scarce factors of production are in political command. Abundant factors, now
more generally in power among developed states, may be partly responsible for the
diminishment of conflict among these states in recent years.

INTRODUCTION

The relationship between international economic ties and security has been much
mooted and remains controversial. Economic relationships between countries affect their security links, but how important they are is uncertain. Among developed
nations, trade may forge a closer security relationship, reducing the likelihood of
military conflict; yet, there are notable exceptions. Developed states linked by trading ties have sometimes gone to war with one another. Less developed countries
dependent on more developed nations have been taken over (Hirschman 1945) or
they have sought to cut ties with advanced countries. In the nineteenth century, advanced nations undertook imperialist expansion to conquer dependent colleagues.
In the 1960s and 1970s there was a *dependencia* reaction that led some southern countries to think that they might be better off decoupling themselves from
the North (Cardoso 1979, Galtung 1971, Gunder Frank 1966). The opponents of
northern domination assumed, however, that if the relationship could be made more
equal, it would facilitate cooperation and economic exchange beneficial to both
sides (Russett & Oneal 2001). The critics of globalization today call for greater
equality, contending that the increased international flow of factors of production
has benefited the rich more than the poor (Stiglitz 2002, Soros 2002). Yet, there are
few prospects of a dissociation of southern countries from trade with the North.

The argument for trade as an enhancement of international security contends that if countries can dependably acquire needed assets or goods from other nations through trade, they do not need to seek them through military expansion.[1] Under conditions of international openness, trade benefits both parties. The traditional economic argument for free trade presumes that international specialization and trade produce welfare benefits to both even where those benefits are based only on comparative, not absolute, advantage (Ricardo 1817, Caves & Jones 1999). Commerce under these conditions leads to a beneficial interdependence of trading partners. Developing this argument further, Mundell (1957) showed that factor flows of investment could also compensate for trade, benefiting both parties and overcoming the prior effects of a tariff. Factor flows are movements of capital or labor between countries.

Yet, despite the correlation between trade as a proportion of gross domestic product (GDP) and peace (Russett & Oneal 2001), it seems clear that trade is only one of many factors that may help to produce peace and that sometimes it may actually favor war (Barbieri & Schneider 1999). Democratic states generally do not fight with each other, although the process of democratization is often fraught with violence (Mansfield & Snyder 1995). Ideological community or the absence of ideological conflicts may also produce a more homogeneous and peaceful international system (Aron 1962). And as discussed below, the development of ties forged by mutual foreign direct investment (FDI) between a pair of states can create an even stronger and more peaceful bond than trade. Cultural and communication factors are also relevant. In the 1950s, Deutsch and his associates argued that pervasive and intense international communication between two peoples could in time increase the similarity of norms and ultimately cultures, helping to dissolve contrary nationalisms (Deutsch 1954, Deutsch et al. 1957). Cultural differences today have been claimed to be a major factor producing violence along national frontiers (Huntington 1993). Some assert that differences in national power and in the rate of growth of national power also lead to security tensions between countries (Gilpin 1981). The outcome of the relations between China and the United States will be important to unraveling this conundrum because in power terms the economic rise of China might be expected to produce conflicts with the United States, the heretofore dominant power. If these are assuaged or moderated through reciprocal trade and investment links, however, the result could still be cooperative. At any rate, economic connections are only one of a set of factors that could lead to security or cause conflict among nations.

In what follows, we argue that trade ties, though capable of mitigating conflict, have not always produced peaceful relationships. This is because trade ties frequently involve sensitivity interdependence, not vulnerability interdependence

---

[1]Under conditions of high tariffs and trade restrictions, commerce may actually be a way of carrying on mercantilist conflict, as was true for much of the seventeenth and eighteenth centuries (see particularly Levy & Ali 1998).

(Russett & Oneal 2001). Sensitivity interdependence refers to trading relations in which prices of goods are altered as a result of increases or decreases in trade. Vulnerability interdependence refers to ties that are costly to break (Cooper 1968). Sensitivity interdependence may not be sufficient to prevent conflict. Portfolio investment links have not ensured peace either (Gartzke et al. 2001), but reciprocal FDI between two countries tends to reduce the threat of conflict.[2]

It would be premature, however, to conclude that economic ties between producing nations have become too strong to break. In many past eras, international trade and investment collapsed, leaving nations in limbo. In some cases, military conquest followed as great powers sought to gain access to the raw materials or markets that they had previously been able to tap through trade or factor flows. In the past, world depressions and economic contractions generated tariffs and exchange controls that cut international trade by large amounts. Under certain conditions, these could occur again. Yet during the Far Eastern financial crisis of 1997–1998, although portfolio investments were withdrawn from East Asia, FDI ties remained strong. (China, the beneficiary of great amounts of FDI, was much less affected than other nations.) Even higher tariffs might not deter continuing factor flows, since productive investment in another country is one means of obviating the effect of customs restrictions. Thus, while security does not depend solely on economic linkages, FDI has been directly correlated with peaceful ties in recent years.

FOREIGN TRADE AND PEACE

Although aggregate data demonstrate a modest correlation between peace and trade among politically relevant dyads (Russett & Oneal 2001), there are too many obvious exceptions to rely on this systemic finding in individual cases. Two types of situations must be considered: (*a*) economic relations among major states and (*b*) relations between developed and less developed countries.

Among major states, trade interdependencies have too frequently merely reflected "sensitivity" interdependence, that is, relations in which one trading partner

---

[2]Economists have recently testified to the rapid distribution of production blocks overseas joined by service links to the originating firm in the home country. (Production blocks are manufacturing capabilities now generally located abroad. Service links are the means by which the output of these production blocks can be coordinated by the home industry.) Jones (2000, p. 130) writes, "This process has been aided by recent drastic falls in the cost of the service links that are required to connect various production blocks that are located in various disparate regions or countries. Costs have fallen both because of some remarkable technological improvements in communication and because of a greater degree of deregulation of service activities, both nationally and internationally . . . ." The fall in such costs is also directly related to the establishment of peaceful economic relations between the countries that divest the production unit and those that do the producing.

could easily find a substitute for its existing trade with another major power.[3] Such was clearly the case in 1913. Although France, Great Britain, and Germany had important trading relationships (so important that factor price equalization had begun to take place among their markets) (Rosecrance et al. 1977), the goods that they bought from one another could easily have been provided by other countries. Neither in agricultural nor in industrial trade, for example, was commerce between Britain and Germany essential. Britain desperately needed food but Germany did not generally provide it. Germany needed iron ore but did not get it from Britain.

In contrast, today the United States depends on oil from the Middle East and may or may not be able to find substitutes elsewhere (from Russia, the Caspian, Latin America, or the North Sea). In this case, interdependence raises questions of "vulnerability," not merely "sensitivity" (Keohane & Nye 1989). U.S. interdependence with Middle Eastern countries reflects a tie that is costly to break, although it may not involve any particular country.

Among major powers, however, industrial trade seems less essential because such countries all produce high-technology goods,[4] and in any event, industrial components can be found in many places around the globe. American imports of European manufactured goods could be replaced by products from Japan, East Asia, Mexico, and Brazil, all abundant suppliers of industrial equipment. In addition to the United States, military products can be purchased from Israel, India, Russia, and European nations; aircraft components can also be bought from China, Europe, and Russia. Software comes from India, Israel, Europe, the Ukraine, and Russia, as well as America. The range of foreign production of manufactured goods, moreover, is increasing with time, as we discuss below.

There is one sense, however, in which trade creates strong interdependencies that were not present in 1913. Before World War I, democratic publics did not expect or require government to manage the economy, and recessions were considered (like earthquakes) to be acts of God. In the then prevailing climate of "laissez-faire," governments were not implicated in economic downturns and were not asked to work with other countries to avoid them. That has all changed since 1914. As a result, the political significance of trading ties and their ensuing interdependence has become much greater. Particular relationships may not be costly to break, but the general maintenance of a high level of trade with other industrial countries has become an important method of maintaining employment and growth in the GDP. Today, more than before, the United States, Japan, and Europe are well-nigh irrevocably tied in a network of economic relations in which they broadly prosper

---

[3]On the other hand, some studies assert that interdependencies of trade bind developed states much more closely than they bind developing nations. Hegre (2000) concluded that interdependence has little bearing on conflict involving less developed states but that it reduces conflict among developed states.

[4]The early work of Deutsch & Eckstein (1961) suggested that economic ties among countries could decline in importance as they industrialized.

or decline together.[5] Chinese economic development is also affected by foreign purchases and FDI by the major powers. India is increasingly influenced in the same way. Such ties are, after all, the rationale for international organizations such as the International Monetary Fund and World Trade Organization, to say nothing of G-8 and OECD. Increasingly, all developed countries seek to maintain stable exchange rates, low inflation, high employment, and economic growth through policies of reciprocity and adjustment. No democratic government would now subject itself to the "beggar thy neighbor" policies of the 1930s.

Relations between developed and less developed nations, however, do not evince the same reciprocity. Globalization has brought many countries within its ambit without equalizing the profound economic differences among them. Less developed nations, certainly one- or two-product nations, have had great difficulty selling to northern and developed states. There is a one-way dependence. Sometimes their product is in oversupply, and the price falls drastically. Sometimes governments of developing countries distort the price mechanism and cheapen agriculture, leading to a flight of population from the countryside to the cities, where there is no secondary industry to sop up unemployment. Foreign investment does not enter under these uncertain conditions. In some instances, capital-surplus nations have not seized the opportunities available in labor-surplus countries (Olson 1996). As a result, many have argued that if capital is not invested in labor-surplus locations, labor should be freer to migrate to areas of capital surplus (see Bhagwati 1998, O'Rourke & Williamson 1999). Despite Central American migration to the United States, however, this has not generally happened. Neither Europe nor, especially, Japan has offered sanctuary to large numbers of migrants from the Third World. Thus, the inequality between North and South increases.

Few less developed countries today, however, believe that dissociation from the world economy provides an answer to this problem. First, many such countries offer similar primary products and could not benefit greatly from trading solely among themselves. Second, most Third World states are indebted to First World nations or private banks. They must export to the North to pay back their loans. But developed country tariffs on primary products, textiles, steel, and other imports make this difficult. Accordingly, developing nations seek entrance to the World Trade Organization and favor further cuts in industrial and agricultural

---

[5]Important changes have taken place both in the international economy and in national policies toward it since the late 1970s. At that time, there appeared to be two different approaches to the oil crisis. The first involved currency depreciation and inflation; the second involved stable currencies and relatively higher interest rates. As a result, one could hazard that there were two disparate responses to interdependence, leading to wholly different national and international outcomes. Since then, the world's experience with inflation (particularly in the 1970s and 1980s) has led to common and agreed-on policies internationally, favoring stable currencies, low inflation, and ultimately low interest rates among many countries. There are, thus, no longer two different responses to international economic interdependence (see Rosecrance et al. 1977).

tariffs in the next negotiating round, facilitating greater openness in northern markets.

At all events, the tensions between North and South are not likely to involve military solutions. The long-term trend has been for developing nations to seek entrance to the North and northern economies and ultimately to the OECD, as South Korea has just done. New members of the European Union (EU)—largely in the developing category—will also seek even closer relations with key developed economies. President Vladimir Putin is clearly moving to associate Russia with the EU and other industrial nations. The North American Free Trade Agreement (NAFTA) also stimulates linkages between developed and less developed nations in the western hemisphere. With the proposed creation of the Free Trade Area of the Americas (FTAA), ties will become closer and decoupling will become an anachronistic response. In more general terms, what might have been a new source of tension with security implications is being resolved by the gradual spread of a network of regional economic clubs, each offering new benefits to Third World adherents. As new members join and stabilize politically and economically, European, American, and Japanese capital will increasingly proceed to erstwhile developing locations. New capital will go into Argentina and Brazil; investment in Mexico will increase. There will be new capital flows to India and China. Ultimately, the economic quandary in which the Third World remains labor-abundant and capital-short while the First World is capital-abundant and labor-short will be resolved. As Olson (1996) has shown, northern capital will increasingly pick up the "missed opportunities" that exist elsewhere.

In the nineteenth century, however, southern dependence on the North frequently led to colonization. The flag followed trade. Africa, Oceania, and much of Asia fell under the sway of European nations as Europe sought raw materials and markets overseas. This was not true across the board, however. Whereas British dominions and French colonies provided key raw materials as well as markets to their metropoles—thereby cementing the imperialist tie—the United States, Argentina, and some Scandinavian primary producers remained outside the colonial bond (O'Rourke & Williamson 1999). Britain increasingly needed American grain and cotton and sought grain supplies from Odessa and Buenos Aires as well, but she did not try to annex those primary-producing areas. And even parts of the empire had autonomous policies. Such dominions as Australia, New Zealand, South Africa, and Canada retained a degree of commercial latitude. Thus only part of the then-developing world was subject to imperialist control. Today, trade dependence would be even less likely to lead to military expansion because potential colonies now contain nationalist and mobilized populations ready to resist foreign intrusion. Cost-benefit calculations favor "access" to such economies rather than any attempt to assert "control" (Huntington 1973, Rosecrance 1986, Nye 1990).

In more general terms, trade facilitates but does not guarantee peaceful security relationships. In the past, some countries sought to take over political entities on which they had become dependent as a result of trade. This response is much more unlikely today.

PORTFOLIO INVESTMENT AND PEACE

Portfolio investment is a powerful instrument in the modern international economy, and it might also be regarded as a harbinger of peace between creditors and debtors. Countries generally do not invest where political uncertainty exists. The world has become sufficiently peaceful that now huge foreign exchange transactions occur, sometimes equaling $2 trillion per day. During the 1997–1998 financial crisis, perhaps as much as $1 trillion was pulled out of East Asian and Russian banks and stocks, crippling the local economies as they one-by-one had to devalue their currencies and increase interest rates. The money that left Russia and the Far East was by and large reinvested in the U.S. stock market, with a large increase in the Dow index of industrial stocks between 1998 and 2000. Nonetheless, these shifts did not reflect or present fundamental security problems. They had to do with too much Asian borrowing, "crony capitalism," and imbalance in the exchange rate between the dollar and the yen.[6]

Portfolio shifts, however, can entirely destabilize an economy, as Austria and Germany found out in 1931–1932 (De Long 1997). England was also forced to devalue the pound when gold and foreign currency left London in those years. Sixty years later, in 1992, the British pound sterling collapsed under speculative attack, and England had to withdraw from the European "snake" in which its currency values had been linked to the mark and the franc. Ten years after that, in the first half of 2002, the dollar depreciated vis à vis the euro as funds left the United States in the aftermath of the fall in American stocks during that period.

It seems unlikely, however, that foreigners will completely desert the U.S. dollar. The dollar provides the key reserve currency besides gold. It finances trade with a huge profusion of countries, from China and Japan to Europe, East Asia, and Latin America. Most world debts are denominated in dollars, requiring borrowers to acquire that currency to pay back their loans. Thus, in the U.S. case, international holdings of dollars or American stocks are in part an index of foreigners' need to continue to trade with the United States to gain dollar assets to finance their trade with each other. Because the return on American stocks has (at least until recently) been substantially higher than the growth in the prices of Japanese or European equities, the dollar is likely to be in continuing demand as the U.S. stock market revives. In this one particular instance, foreign support for the dollar indicates long-term support for the U.S. economy and is a factor for greater interdependence between America and other countries that is not likely to change.

On the other hand, one should not draw general conclusions from this apparently stable relationship. The British pound, along with gold, had been the major medium of exchange in the late nineteenth century, but after World War I there was

---

[6]Before 1997, Asian countries assumed that dollar-yen values would remain stable and were prepared to borrow money in yen and spend it in dollars. When the dollar fell, however, they could no longer repay in yen values. Their currencies had to depreciate to regain export balances (see also Stiglitz 2002, ch. 4).

a huge diversification out of British pounds and into the U.S. dollar and the French franc, undermining sterling values. The dollar was the pillar of the Bretton Woods monetary system, but after 1971, the Japanese yen rose quickly against it. The exchange rate went from $360Y = \$1.00$ to $110Y = \$1.00$ in the 1990s, an appreciation of nearly 120%. Currencies, moreover, have a tendency to overshoot their purchasing power–parity values, causing an even greater disruption in financial markets. Huge waves of currencies now slosh in and out of particular economies, causing turbulence. Without some attempt to regulate currency values or at least limit their fluctuation, dependable economic relationships among countries cannot be assured. Periodic financial crises will affect stock and bond markets (Kindleberger 1989). Given the instability of the U.S. dollar in the 1970s and 1980s, European leaders did not want to import dollar inflation, and between 2000 and 2002 they moved to create a single currency, the euro. In response, the United States may also seek to limit fluctuations among the euro, the yen, and the dollar.[7]

One has to admit, however, that the actual record of short-term and portfolio financial flows does not indicate a general pattern of stable interdependence among economies. Close financial relationships among great powers in the 1890s and early 1900s did not prevent World War I. The British sold their enemy assets on open markets in early August, 1914. The financial tie to Germany was relatively easy to break; it did not forge a stable link between London and Berlin, nor did it prevent conflict between the two countries. In contrast to FDI, in which one country takes a significant productive stake in another, portfolio relationships can be easily terminated.

FOREIGN DIRECT INVESTMENT AND PEACE

The rise of FDI has been greater than trade or growth in GDP since 1970 (Figure 1). This is because of the transformation in the industrial structure of modern economies, including the newly industrialized countries. Whereas most developed nations initially produced most of their industrial goods at home, they have increasingly diverted production abroad, gaining cost advantages through employment of lower-priced foreign labor. In so doing, they have moved much of their production plant elsewhere. Ten percent of Japanese production and >20% of U.S. manufacturing now occurs overseas. Some states have de facto become "virtual" in that home production is <10% of GDP while services total>80%.[8] Hong Kong, Singapore, and Taiwan have increasingly become virtual states as they move their manufacturing to China, Malaysia, and Indonesia. While producing abroad,

---

[7]See the proposals by Volcker (1999), which favored establishing bans of permissible fluctuation among major currencies—the dollar, the euro, and the yen—in order to achieve greater stability in trading relationships.

[8]"Virtual states" are analogues of the "virtual corporations" in Silicon Valley that design new products but have them produced by other companies. Such companies have been very productive and cost-efficient (see Houlder 1995).

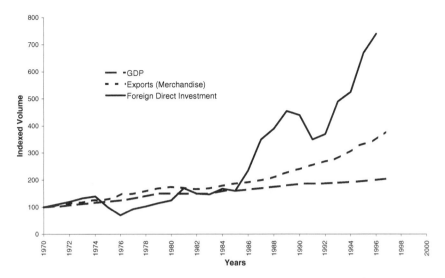

Figure 1   Relative growth of worldwide gross domestic product, manufacturing exports, and foreign direct investment since 1970. Sources: WTO, UNCTAD, and *The Economist* June 20, 1998, p. 5.

they still retain research, development, product design, financing, marketing, and transport functions at home. In recent years, Taiwan in particular has found its labor costs too high and has moved much of its manufacturing plant to Fujian Province in China.[9] This change also reflects the movement from manufacturing to services in the domestic economy. More and more, services have become high-value components of the GDP, and their increase in value has exceeded that of manufacturing since 1970 (Ripoll 1996). Intangibles have increasingly outpaced tangible items in the GDP.

With this shift has come a "thinning" of the state analogous to the "thinning" of the corporation. According to Coase (1937) and Williamson & Bercovitz (1996), corporations only existed because they could bundle certain services and components into a product more efficiently than could the more dispersed process of individual contracting in a wider market.[10] The corporation's "vertical" blending

---

[9]This investment brings the mainland and Taiwan closer together and makes war less likely between them.

[10]Coase (1937, p. 388) points out that within a firm "market transactions are eliminated and in place of the complicated market structure with exchange transactions is substituted the entrepreneur-coordinator, who directs production." Essentially, Coase argued that the size of the firm depends on the cost of bringing in services from outside the firm as compared with the overhead cost of providing them inside the firm. Williamson makes an essential distinction between the corporation's decision to "make or buy" a product or component (Williamson & Bercovitz 1996, p. 334).

of raw materials and components into finished products occurred more cheaply than the "horizontal" contracts of buyer and seller, partly because of information costs. If a homeowner could act as her own prime contractor, she could horizontally arrange separate deals with electricians, bricklayers, carpenters, plumbers, and providers of building materials to build a house without outside assistance. In most cases, however, one would require the services of a corporate prime contractor to bring all the separate services together in a single construction process—building the new house.

In both state and corporation, however, the greater information base provided by the Internet and other types of communication has made individual contracting more efficient (Mueller 1999). Corporations outsource back-office functions as well as production. They hire network specialists to design their internal communications systems. They locate production facilities overseas. So does the state. Like virtual corporations, virtual states slim their domestic functions and rely on production abroad to provide much of their consumption (Rosecrance 1999). Virtual states are dependent on labor that exists in other places, but all states increasingly need capital as well as labor from other countries. Their success as economic entities increasingly comes to depend on their access to technology and markets located elsewhere. To succeed, states must cut interest rates as well as inflation, provide stable currencies, and keep government spending under control. Having decentralized their past functions, national governments compete with one another for spare capital and educated labor. They provide incentives to capital and technology to enter their economies. With full capital mobility (which did not exist in the 1930s), policy makers are forced to choose between setting interest rates or currency values (these are the well-known Mundell-Fleming conditions). If they depreciate their currencies, capital may leave, causing interest rates to rise. If they wish to hold interest rates constant or to lower them, they cannot depreciate their currency. The armory of national policy instruments has been reduced.[11] Similarly, governments cannot induce foreign capital to enter their economies and still engage in unlimited deficit spending. This will only bid up interest rates and limit the returns on industrial investment.

In the past, Heckscher-Ohlin and other typical factor endowment models presumed that goods were mobile but that capital and other factors of production were fixed. This assumption is no longer true. As Mundell showed, factors can move to compensate for the failure of goods to move. No country can rest assured that it will always have at its beck and call all the goods and factors it needs to provide a modern economic existence for its population. In the 1997 financial crisis, Malaysia put on capital controls, limiting short-term speculation, but it may also

---

[11]In Europe today, the existence of the common currency, the euro, means that countries can no longer independently depreciate their currencies. Germany is presently in recession but it cannot control rates or currency values. It can increase government (fiscal) spending, but then it may violate the Stability Pact set up with the creation of euro. Under it, government deficits cannot exceed 3% of GDP.

have reduced the inflow of foreign capital over the longer term by changing the climate of acceptability (Stiglitz 2002, Kaplan & Rodrik 2001). In the 1960s, the U.S. attempt to prevent capital outflow with the interest equalization tax did not succeed and led instead to the creation of the Eurodollar market and to financing abroad. American dollars and FDI still proceeded to Europe. Unlike in the 1930s, when tariffs and exchange controls prevented capital flows and guaranteed the independence of the national market, countries today cannot manipulate their economies at will. They are dependent on selling abroad and to some degree on receiving capital and labor from abroad.

The greatest measure of this dependence has been the need for FDI. FDI has gone in different directions in the years since 1960. The first decade showed large amounts of U.S. productive investment going to Europe, prompting Servan-Schreiber's (1968) call to respond to "le defi americain"—the American challenge. After 1970, however, cooler heads prevailed, and European and Japanese investment rapidly entered the U.S. economy to compensate for the lower-valued dollar that had made foreign exports less competitive. In the 1980s, the incentives changed again; American investment went rapidly to Europe and abroad to outweigh the effects of the extremely high-valued dollar, which had diminished U.S. exports. In the 1990s, however, a lower-valued dollar attracted huge amounts of foreign investment to the United States. Portfolio investment increased as well in response to the rise of American stocks. As the Japanese currency rose and fell, U.S. investment went in and out of Japan.

Not surprisingly, countries that relied on foreign direct (that is, productive) investment were less impeded by the crisis of 1997–1998. When currency values collapsed elsewhere, capital left in a rush whereas productive investment stayed. But China was scarcely affected, and most of the FDI in Guangdong and elsewhere remained. There was no downward pressure on the *renminbi*. The very existence of FDI (as opposed to speculative flows of currency or portfolio investment) suggests a long-term commitment on the part of foreign investors who know that they cannot remove their capital in the short term.[12] In the same manner, FDI indicates favorable security relations between investor and recipient countries. Otherwise, long-term capital would not enter and stay in the host country.

In fact, for economic as well as security reasons, a division of labor is developing internationally between what might be called "head" and "body" nations. Head nations fundamentally decide what will be produced and do the designing, marketing, and financing. Body nations, like China, India, Mexico, and Brazil, do the producing. Superficially, this distinction might appear to suggest imperial and colonial relationships like those in the nineteenth century. Nothing, however, could be further from the truth. Producing nations such as China and Brazil have enormous leeway and have been able to play head nations such as Germany, Japan,

---

[12]This does not mean that corporations will not sometimes have a "fire sale" to get rid of unneeded productive investment overseas. But such transactions are extremely costly, as Chrysler found out in the 1970s and early 1980s.

and the United States off against each other—they are not tied to any one head. Equally, head nations can select other producing outlets. Besides, body nations can rapidly become heads, as South Korea and Taiwan have done. Initial ganglia develop quickly into cerebral cortexes, and new body nations are born further afield.

And sometimes the very distinction between head and body begins to blur. Reciprocal FDI demonstrates this shift.[13] Canada produces some things and the United States others. Europe produces particular goods and Japan different ones; both have heavy FDI in the United States, and the United States has reciprocated. Chinese investment in the United States is growing rapidly, although most of it is still portfolio in character. Korean direct investment, however, is making inroads on a worldwide basis. Previous producers have become designers and developers. In many cases, ties are being established that would be costly to break—the criterion of vulnerability interdependence.

If this is true, security relations among countries tied together by FDI should be more favorable than those based on portfolio investment. It should also be the case that nonreciprocal (or one-way) foreign investment should constrain conflict less than fully reciprocal FDI relationships. A variety of studies point in this direction. Modelski (1972) examined the impact of transnational corporations on conflict between countries during 1945–1970. Fundamentally, he concluded that high corporate presence and activity correlate with low levels of conflict. The higher the ratio of subsidiaries to countries, the lower the level of conflict in those countries. Western and developed countries with a large number of subsidiaries had no major conflict locations during that period. On the other hand, 87 developing countries with fewer subsidiaries had 22 conflict locations (Modelski 1972). More recently, Gartzke et al. (2001) studied conflict as it might be related to both FDI and portfolio investment. They concluded that FDI is negatively correlated with conflict, whereas there is no relationship between portfolio investment and conflict. Gartzke et al. (2001) looked at openness to FDI (inward and outward flows) and its effect on conflict. They did not consider whether the conflicts stemmed (or explicitly did not stem) from those making the investments. Their measure was entirely systemic. Brooks (1999, p. 665), in a conceptual analysis of trade, FDI, and the benefits of conquest, found that "the increased ease of FDI reduces the willingness to engage in conquest." This was in part because FDI was no longer concentrated in a few locations on whose production the home country depended, but rather was spread throughout the world. Brooks writes (1999, p. 666), "So long as holdings or overseas supply operations were centered in a particular country or

---

[13]Some may believe that reciprocal foreign investment is a contradiction in terms. If labor costs favor investing abroad, how can the host country invest back in the United States or Europe? Yet, for a variety of reasons, including exchange rates, market participation, and niche markets, FDI has frequently gone both ways. If a head nation invests in a body nation because of its lower labor costs, the body nation may reciprocate in order to get access to research and development and product design functions.

geographic region, instability in that country or region posed a substantial threat, and states consequently had a strong incentive to forcibly intervene." No longer. Important FDI is widely dispersed, facilitating reliance on other producers or suppliers and reducing the incentive to use force.

All previous studies have looked at systemic factors, not particular FDI relationships and their effect on conflict between the countries doing and receiving the investing. We have constructed a database that tests for the direction of FDI flows and conflict (see Appendix for details). Do the countries that invest the most in each other have the least conflict with each other? Unfortunately, few nations except the United States collect data on FDI flows with particular countries. Thus, to test for such relationships, we had to limit ourselves to looking at data on U.S. FDI and conflict with other countries over the period 1950–1992. Broadly, we found that two-way FDI relationships limit conflict more than one-way relationships do. Both reduce conflict, however. In addition, we tested for internal political and power variables that might be positively or negatively correlated with conflict relationships. Democracy has a very slight negative correlation with conflict whereas power has a more substantial positive relationship. Powerful countries such as members of the Big Five are more likely to be involved in conflict. We also looked at the direction of flows. Flows into the United States were more likely to produce conflict than flows from the United States, which suggests that the United States had less conflict with countries in which it was investing. Contiguity was also modestly related to conflict (since countries at greater remove from one another can almost by definition have less conflict). The simple model tested was as follows:

$$\text{CONFLICT} = \beta_0 + \beta_1 {}^*\text{RECIP} + \beta_2 {}^*\text{ONESIDED}$$

Table 1 lists the basic relationships.

In addition, we examined the exposure-to-FDI level of the United States and the other country and sought to assess their effects on conflict. If exposure does not affect conflict, then reciprocal and unilateral flows should be taken less seriously. Exposure was measured by FDI inflows plus outflows divided by GDP. Exposure was significantly (negatively) related to conflict in the U.S. case and negatively related to conflict in the partner case (though the relationship was not significant).

Finally, we compared the effect of trade exposure (exports + imports toward a particular country over GDP) with two-way and one-way FDI flows. Trade exposure here was measured with regard to a specific trading partner, not systemically. Although our findings only cover the period 1950–1992, we find a positive, though not fully significant, relationship between bilateral trade and bilateral conflict.[14] For this period, it appears that X's trade with another particular

---

[14]Russett & Oneal (2001, pp. 145–48) also do not correlate bilateral trade and conflict directly. Instead, they measure the probability or risk of conflict by increasing, one by one, the standard deviations of their variables. At these higher levels, bilateral trade is correlated with less conflict. Russett also includes the entire period of 1886–1992.

TABLE 1   Conflict and investment relations: the United States and other countries, 1950–1992[a]

Independent variables	Model 1	Model 2
RECIP	-0.3268^{b} (0.1736)	-0.4075^{c} (0.1783)
ONESIDED	-0.1697^{b} (0.0943)	-0.1625^{b} (0.0949)
MAJ_POWER	1.073^{d} (0.1529)	1.1641^{d} (0.1642)
DEM	-0.0508^{d} (0.85)	-0.0398^{d} (0.0149)
CONTIG		0.1990 (0.1745)
DIR		-0.2738 (0.2946)
Constant	-1.8045^{d} (0.0893)	-1.7473^{d} (0.1160)
N	2300	2300

[a]Source: Maoz 1999 (DYMID 1.1 data). Numbers in parentheses are robust standard errors.
[b]$p < 0.1$
[c]$p < 0.05$
[d]$p < 0.01$

country, Y, does not necessarily reduce conflict with Y, however much it may reduce conflict in general.[15] Again, it appears that studies of particular country relationships (in both economic and conflict terms) are preferable to measures of general openness or trade toward the outside world as a whole. Table 2 charts these relationships.

In addition, we examined the scatterplots linking levels of conflict with amounts of FDI (Figure 2). The general direction of relationships showed that higher levels of FDI produced lower levels of conflict, but there were outliers. At various times, the United States was in conflict (though not war) with countries in which it had substantial productive investments. The three cases are Canada, Switzerland, and Panama at various times during the 1950s to the 1980s. Except for "Operation Just Cause" (designed to capture General Noriega), they involved no casualties and lasted no more than two days.

The greater the FDI exposure of the United States (inflows plus outflows of FDI toward the particular country divided by GDP), the less the conflict with that country (see Table 3). The same results were found for the partner country, although the relationship was less strong (Table 4). Again, as the conflict level goes up, the FDI exposure of the partner state goes down, although FDI exposure is not negligible.

---

[15]It may be that the United States is an outlier in this process. Polachek (unpublished manuscript) found that aggregating all dyads produced a negative relation between commerce and conflict, but the U.S. dyads were more likely to have a positive relationship (see also Mansfield & Pollins 2001).

TABLE 2 Conflict and trade relationships, the United States and other countries, 1950–1992[a]

Independent variables	Model 1	Model 2
RECIP	-0.4206^c (0.1976)	-0.2987 (0.2187)
ONESIDED	-0.2148^b (0.1179)	-0.1856 (0.1192)
TRADEXUSA	0.0533^b (0.0279)	0.0421 (0.0283)
TRADEEXB	-0.0047^b (0.0026)	-0.0037 (0.0025)
MAJ_POWER		0.7790^d (0.1663)
DEM		-0.0343^d (0.0096)
CONTIG		0.0223 (0.3038)
Constant	-1.3189^d (0.0572)	-1.690^d (1.024)
N	1795	1735

[a]Source: Maoz, 1999 (DYMID 1.1 data). Numbers in parentheses are robust standard errors.
[b]$p < 0.1$
[c]$p < 0.05$
[d]$p < 0.01$

CONCLUSIONS AND QUESTIONS

For analytical as well as empirical reasons, we have found that FDI provides a stronger and more peaceful link between countries than trade and portfolio investment. This is not surprising under modern economic and technological conditions. Costs press for productive investments overseas, which can only take place and be maintained if security relations are mutual and benign. This finding is quite robust, but it is uncertain whether security paves the way for investment or investment generates peace, or, more likely, whether the two are mutually reinforcing. In the early days of the Cold War, the U.S. government encouraged American FDI in areas such as Berlin that might be thought insecure in order to stabilize the economic and political situation there. FDI in France and Italy immediately after World War II had a similar function and result. The present-day investment in China both rests upon and helps stabilize China's security relationship with the United States. FDI is now proceeding in large amounts from Taiwan to China with dual motivations: to improve the political relationship and to create a situation in which neither political unit can think realistically of getting along without the other.

Domestic politics and economics can of course impinge on these ties. According to the Stolper-Samuelson model, free trade benefits the abundant factor of production and hurts the scarce factor. Hence, scarce factors favor tariffs, and if the dominant coalition in competing major powers consists of scarce factors, tariff conflicts between them will result. In France at the end of the nineteenth century, capital and land were both scarce, and labor was abundant. The same was true in

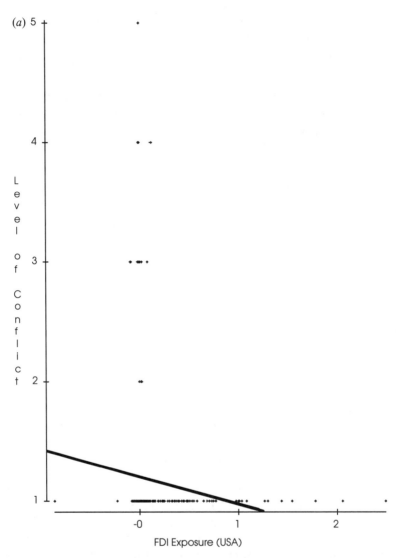

Figure 2 (*a*) This scatterplot shows the relationship between the highest level of conflict reached by the United States in each dyad and the level of foreign direct investment (FDI) exposure. The outlier cases of Canada—as mentioned in the text—have been removed and the new regression line is shown. (*b*) This scatterplot shows the relationship between the highest level of conflict reached by the partner country in each dyad and the level of FDI exposure for that country. The outlier cases of Panama—as mentioned in the text—have been removed and the new regression line is shown.

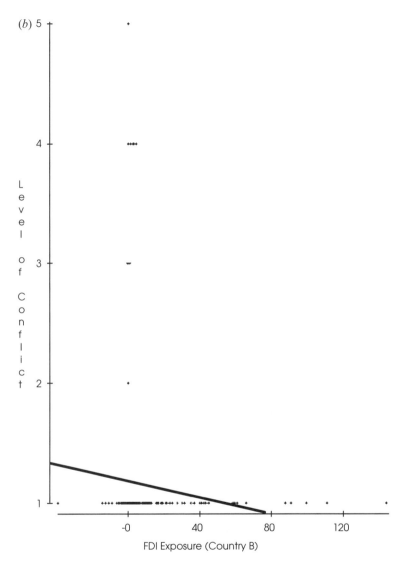

Figure 2   (*Continued*)

Germany (Rogowski 1989), but labor was not dominant in either country politically. Economic conflicts between them were foredestined. If, however, Germany had possessed abundant capital and labor and if (as in Britain) they had formed a dominant political coalition, the differences leading to World War I would have been greatly mitigated.

Today, in contrast, most major powers are led by coalitions that represent abundant factors. In China the abundant factor is clearly labor, and in Europe it is clearly

TABLE 3 FDI exposure of the United States (country A) and conflict

Conflict level	Mean	Std. Dev.	Frequency
0 level	.038765	.1841006	2195
1 level	.008895	.0539886	197

capital. Like the abundant capital and land of the United States, those abundant factors favor openness. In this sense, the pattern of factor abundance today makes for a more peaceful environment than the pattern in place at the end of the nineteenth century. This is why the political balance attained by factors of production internally can be of enormous importance in economic relationships. If, on the other hand, agriculture in Europe and Japan and labor in the United States attained political dominance, economic conflicts would rise. The globalization protestors, though still in a political minority, make this apparent. In the past, some great powers have been dominated by factors that sought economic closure while others favored openness. In the 1890s and the 1930s, this led to higher economic and ultimately political conflict.

We have sought to show that FDI is a very important part of the process involved in forging new economic relationships. It is important because factor mobility can compensate for trade immobility. Through direct investment, former exporters can produce and therefore sell abroad even in the presence of high tariffs. This relationship is strong but not monotonic. Even countries with high direct investment in each other's economies can have occasional conflict, though generally not of the military sort. We hope that this essay will encourage much more investigation of this important but neglected topic in both economics and security.

APPENDIX

Data

The data for conflictual dyads are taken from the Dyadic Militarized Interstate Dispute (DYMID) dataset compiled by Maoz (1999). The dataset consists of conflict between countries in a dyad during the period 1812–1992. We began with 1950 because we were interested in the post–World War II period, when FDI began to

TABLE 4 FDI exposure of the other country (country B) and conflict

Conflict level	Mean	Std. Dev.	Frequency
0 level	1.9926935	0.1841006	2115
1 level	1.4495825	12.151615	183

accelerate for many countries. Only U.S. FDI data differentiate FDI by target and recipient beginning in 1950. The dataset we constructed thus covers the period 1950–1992 and includes all dyads in which the United States was a member.

We took out all multiple entries. Some cases involved multiple entries per dyad in a given year. The multiple entries were of two kinds: first, several dyads had exact multiple listings in one year if there was conflict; second, some multiple entries for a given dyad in one year had different levels of conflict. These were condensed by taking the highest level of conflict for each country in the year as the overall hostility measure for that country in that dyad. We also removed the cases in which the level of hostility exhibited by the United States and the other country was missing.

We then modified the dataset to conform to the availability of data on FDI. First, as mentioned above, this meant using the United States as one dyad member. Second, this limited the years in the study to 1950–1992. We used U.S. data from the Department of Commerce on inflows and outflows of direct investment.[16]

One advantage of using the United States as a member of a dyad is that some theories might predict a smaller effect for such a large country. First, the United States, because of its major power status in the post–World War II period, had relations, peaceful and otherwise, with many different countries around the world. This meant that the United States as a great power had less freedom to interact with whomever it chose and was potentially active in many more conflicts. Second, because the U.S. FDI exposure level is lower than that of many smaller states, one might expect FDI to have a smaller effect on U.S. policy decision making. Because the results demonstrate a significant statistical result, this is stronger confirmation of a deterrent effect from FDI.

Trade data come from various years of the *Direction of Trade Statistics*, which is published jointly by the International Monetary Fund and the United Nations Office of Statistics. These data are available for both inflow and outflow of trade in dyadic relationships for all of the years in the study.

The Maoz (1999) data listed cases in which various levels of militarized dispute occurred between the United States and another country. We added in all other years in which the United States had peaceful relations with the various countries in the dyads. For example, if the United States and Peru were in two conflictual dyads, in 1960 and 1980, we added the United States–Peru dyads of peaceful years for 1950–1959, 1961–1979, and 1981–1992. These were then coded as having no conflict. This was done to insure that there was variance on the dependent variable.

---

[16]Two entries in the investment data in the official statistics were disregarded. First, an asterisk in U.S. data represents cases that are between –$500,000 and $500,000, thus extremely small but unrecorded flows. Second, a "D" value in the data indicates a high likelihood that only one firm has invested in a country or been the recipient of investment flows from that country and that to divulge the amount of the flow would indirectly divulge confidential information about a firm's financial transactions. Cases in which either of these conditions was present were removed.

After starting with the DYMID dataset, extracting all of the U.S. cases from 1950–1992, removing multiple entries, removing missing data on the level of military action, adding cases for years of peaceful relations, and removing cases where FDI data were absent, we were left with 2418 total dyad years consisting of 1209 dyads. We examined the actions of each side of the dyad, doubling the number of cases. However, the lack of additional data in some cases reduced the number of observations. The number of observations in a given model is listed in each regression table.

Because the DYMID dataset contains responses for the highest level of hostility reached by each side in the dyad, we examined the specific FDI exposure level for a country on its highest level of hostility. This gives a more precise measure of the effect of FDI on hostility than a systemic analysis.

Variables

In order to test our approach, we collected the data into two separate variable sets. The first set consisted of dummy variables of whether a given dyad had reciprocal flows (RECIP), one-sided flows (ONESIDED), or no flows of FDI in the dyad. These variables were then used to predict whether there would be conflict (CONFLICT) in a given dyad. "Conflict," in this case, is a measure of whether there was any level of force exhibited or used by one country against the other. These were all cases above a hostility level of one in the DYMID dataset. This simple model is as follows:

$$\text{CONFLICT} = \beta_0 + \beta_1{}^*\text{RECIP} + \beta_2{}^*\text{ONESIDED} \ldots$$

The levels of FDI outflow and inflow used were specifically the levels of FDI flow from each country to the other in the dyad. This gives a rough estimate as to whether there was financial openness in a given dyad. By constructing the variable in this way, we get a more accurate impression of how FDI flows between two countries affect their relations with each other at a given point in time.

In addition to the FDI variables, we added several political and military control variables. The first is a measure of whether the country was a major power (MAJ_POWER), in effect one of the five permanent members of the United Nations Security Council. The second variable was a measure of the level of democracy, or autocracy, in a country based on the POLITY III dataset (available at ftp://isere.colorado.edu/pub/datasets/polity3/politymay96.data). Here, we subtracted the autocracy score from the democracy score to obtain an overall level of democracy (DEM). We also devised a variable to measure whether the states were physically contiguous (CONTIG) and a dummy variable to show the direction of the investment flow (DIR). A CONTIG value of 1 indicates the countries are contiguous; a DIR value of 1 indicates that the capital is flowing from the United States to the other country. These control variables were added to the RECIP and ONESIDED variables to gain a better understanding of the post–World War II environment.

In several dyads, it was not clear whether both investment and divestment had occurred, or only divestment. Accordingly, we made a second review of the data using variables that measured the exposure level of a country to FDI flows. We constructed two variables that measure this level of exposure—EXPOSUREUSA for the level of U.S. exposure to flows of FDI and EXPOSUREB for the level of exposure of the other dyad member. The variable construction is as follows:

$$\text{EXPOSURE}_{\text{USA}} = \frac{\text{Inflows}_{\text{B}} + \text{Outflows}_{\text{USA}}}{\text{GDP}_{\text{USA}}}$$

$$\text{EXPOSURE}_{\text{B}} = \frac{\text{Inflows}_{\text{USA}} + \text{Outflows}_{\text{B}}}{\text{GDP}_{\text{B}}}$$

This is a more exact method of determining how specific FDI flows between countries affect the level of conflict in the dyad year.

The *Annual Review of Political Science* is online at
http://polisci.annualreviews.org

LITERATURE CITED

Aron R. 1962. *Paix et Guerre Entre les Nations.* Paris: Calmann-Levy

Barbieri K, Schneider G. 1999. Globalization and peace: assessing new directions in the study of trade and conflict. *J. Peace Res.* 36:387–404

Bhagwati JN. 1998. *A Stream of Windows: Unsettling Reflections on Trade, Immigration, and Democracy.* Cambridge, MA: MIT Press

Brooks SG. 1999. The globalization of production and the changing benefits of conquest. *J. Confl. Resolut.* 43:646–70

Cardoso FH. 1979. *Dependency and Development in Latin America.* Berkeley, CA: Univ. Calif. Press

Caves R, Jones R. 1999. *World Trade and Payments.* Reading, MA: Addison-Wesley

Coase R. 1937. The nature of the firm. *Economica* n.s. 4:386–405

De Long B. 1997. *The role of international economic institutions.* Presented at UCLA Colloq. War and Peace, Los Angeles, CA, Nov. 7–8

Deutsch KW. 1954. *Nationalism and Social Communication.* Cambridge, MA: MIT Press

Deutsch KW, Burrell SA, Kann RA, Lee M Jr, Lichterman M, et al. 1957. *Political Community and the North Atlantic Area.* Princeton, NJ: Princeton Univ. Press

Deutsch KW, Eckstein A. 1961. National industrialization and the declining share of the international economic sector: 1850–1959. *World Polit.* 13:267–99

Galtung J. 1971. The structural theory of imperialism. *J. Peace Res.* 8:81–117

Gartzke E, Li Q, Boehmer C. 2001. Investing in the peace: economic interdependence and international conflict. *Int. Organ.* 55:391–438

Gilpin R. 1981. *War and Change in World Politics.* Cambridge, UK: Cambridge Univ. Press

Gunder Frank A. 1966. *The Development of Underdevelopment.* Boston: New Engl. Free

Hegre H. 2000. Development and the liberal peace: What does it take to be a trading state? *J. Peace Res.* 37:5–30

Hirschman AO. 1945. *National Power and the Structure of Foreign Trade.* Berkeley, CA: Univ. Calif. Press

Houlder V. 1995. Today's friend, tomorrow's foe. *Financial Times* Oct. 2, p. 14

Huntington S. 1973. Transnational organizations in world politics. *World Polit.* 25:333–68

Huntington S. 1993. The clash of civilizations? *For. Aff.* 73:22–49

Jones RW. 2000. *Globalization and the Theory of Input Trade.* Cambridge, MA: MIT Press

Kaplan E, Rodrik D. 2001. *Did the Malaysian capital controls work?* Work. Pap. W8142. Natl. Bur. Econ. Res.

Keohane RO, Nye JS Jr. 1989. *Power and Interdependence: World Politics in Transition.* Glenview, IL: Scott, Foresman

Kindleberger C. 1989. *Manias, Panics, and Crashes: a History of Financial Crises.* New York: Basic Books

Levy J, Ali S. 1998. From commercial competition to strategic rivalry to war: the evolution of the Anglo-Dutch rivalry, 1609–1652. In *The Dynamics of Enduring Rivalries,* ed. PF Diehl, pp. 29–63. Urbana-Champaign: Univ. Ill. Press

Mansfield E, Pollins B. 2001. The study of interdependence and conflict. *J. Confl. Resolut.* 45:834–59

Mansfield ED, Snyder J. 1995. Democratization and the danger of war. *Int. Sec.* 20:5–38

Maoz Z. 1999. Dyadic Militarized Interstate Disputes (DYMID 1.1) dataset. ftp://spirit.tau.ac.il/zeevmaoz/dyadmid60.xls (dataset); ftp://spirit.tau.ac.il/zeevmaoz/dyadmid.doc (codebook)

Modelski G. 1972. *Multinational Corporations and World Order.* Beverly Hills, CA: Sage

Mueller J, ed. 1999. *Politics, Prosperity and Peace.* Colorado Springs, CO: Westview

Mundell R. 1957. International trade and factor mobility. *Am. Econ. Rev.* 47:321–35

Nye JS, Jr. 1990. *Bound to Lead.* New York: Basic Books

O'Rourke K, Williamson J. 1999. *Globalization and History.* Cambridge, MA: MIT Press

Olson M. 1996. Big bills left on the sidewalk: why some countries are rich and others poor. *J. Econ. Persp.* 10:3–24

Ricardo D. 1817. *On the Principles of Political Economy and Taxation.* London: Murray

Ripoll J. 1996. *The future of trade in international services.* UCLA Burkle Cent. Work. Pap.

Rogowski R. 1989. *Commerce and Coalitions: How Trade Affects Domestic Political Alignments.* Princeton, NJ: Princeton Univ. Press

Rosecrance R. 1986. *The Rise of the Trading State: Commerce and Conquest in the Modern World.* New York: Basic Books

Rosecrance R. 1999. *The Rise of the Virtual State: Wealth and Power in the Coming Century.* New York City: Basic Books

Rosecrance R, Alexandroff A, Koehler W, Kroll J, Laqueur S, Stocker J. 1977. Whither interdependence? *Int. Organ.* 31:425–71

Russett B, Oneal J. 2001. *Triangulating Peace: Democracy, Interdependence, and International Organization.* New York: Norton

Servan-Schreiber J. 1968. *The American Challenge.* New York: Atheneum

Soros G. 2002. *George Soros on Globalization.* New York: Public Aff.

Stiglitz J. 2002. *Globalization and Its Discontents.* New York: Norton

Volcker P. 1999. *Arnold Harbenger Lecture: The art of central banking: how it can solve financial crisis.* UCLA Burkle Cent. Int. Relat., Feb. 19

Williamson O, Bercovitz J. 1996. The modern corporation as an efficiency instrument: the comparative contracting perspective. In *The American Corporation Today,* ed. C Kaysen, pp. 327–59. New York: Oxford Univ. Press

Annu. Rev. Polit. Sci. 2003. 6:399–431
doi: 10.1146/annurev.polisci.6.121901.085635
Copyright © 2003 by Annual Reviews. All rights reserved

CURRENT CONTROVERSIES IN FEMINIST THEORY

Mary G. Dietz

*Department of Political Science, University of Minnesota, 267 19th Avenue S.,
Minneapolis, Minnesota 55455; email: dietz@polisci.umn.edu*

Key Words   gender, sex, subjectivity, identity, difference feminism, diversity
feminism, deconstruction feminism

■ **Abstract**   Over the past two decades, academic feminism has differentiated and
fragmented substantially in light of a wide range of new approaches in theory. This
overview and assessment of the wide, diverse, and changing field of feminist theory
gives particular attention to contestations surrounding the political theorizing of gender,
identity, and subjectivity. Three divergent and oppositional perspectives—difference
feminism, diversity feminism, and deconstruction feminism—frame current discussions regarding the "construction" of the female subject; the nature of sexual difference;
the relation between sex and gender; the intersection of gender, race, class, sexuality,
etc.; and the significance of "women" as a political category in feminism. The problem of epistemic identification (locating or dislocating the female subject, analyzing
gender difference, politicizing identity) is also a central element in the theorizing of
feminist politics, multicultural citizenship, justice, power, and the democratic public
sphere. Within this domain, we find equally intense debates among feminist theorists
concerning the meaning of feminist citizenship and the politics of recognition, as well
as the relations between gender equality and cultural rights, feminism and multiculturalism, democracy and difference. Although the field is far from convergence even on
the meaning of feminism itself, we might take its current state as a sign of its vitality
and significance within the discourses of contemporary social and political theory.

INTRODUCTION

Before assessing current controversies in the domain of academic feminist theorizing, it is important to recognize that feminism is a historically constituted,
local and global, social and political movement with an emancipatory purpose and
a normative content. It posits a subject (women), identifies a problem (the subjection and objectification of women through gendered relations), and expresses
various aims (e.g., overturning relations of domination; ending sex discrimination; securing female sexual liberation; fighting for women's rights and interests,
raising "consciousness," transforming institutional and legal structures; engendering democracy) in the name of specific principles (e.g., equality, rights, liberty,
autonomy, dignity, self-realization, recognition, respect, justice, freedom). As a
historical movement, feminism is geared toward action-coordination and social

1094-2939/03/0615-0399$14.00

399

transformation, interrogating existing conditions and relations of power with a view toward not only interpreting but also changing the world. Consequently, the philosophical and analytical debates that arise from feminist theorizing are unavoidably political (not purely philosophical), insofar as every emancipation project that aims toward freedom must undertake the historical and theoretical analysis of power, and every theoretical project that arises out of real, material contexts of action must speak to the political and ethical dimensions of transformation and change. In the face of the world diversification of the feminist movement over the past 20 years, Western feminist theory (a problematic category in itself) has been forced or encouraged to think through the limitations of previous North Atlantic, Anglo-American, second-wave formulations that were largely untouched by the histories of women not of the West, and the work of African, South Asian, and Middle Eastern scholars. Consequently, and in its most salutary manifestations, contemporary feminist theory is becoming less unthinkingly Western and more thoughtfully Western, more global, more comparative, and more democratic in its efforts to grasp the complexities of human cultures, social orders, and practices as it addresses women in the world. Yet, at the same time, the conflict of interpretations that appears to be a permanent feature of current feminist theory has not produced anything like a smooth alignment with the social and political movement called feminism, wherever it is practiced in the world.

Over the past two decades within the academy, feminist theory has transformed substantially in light of a wide range of intellectual and philosophical discourses and new approaches in theory. Feminist theoretical contestations have moved well beyond the ideological terms "liberal," "socialist," and "radical" that used to frame them (Jaggar 1983, Tong 1989). Of course, feminist theory and gender studies are themselves part of this range of new theoretical approaches; but one notable trait of feminist theory has been its tactical capacity to appropriate and deploy various, often irreconcilable, methods and theories in the course of engaging with its own subject matter. These theories emanate from numerous forms of contemporary critique and include critical theory, discourse ethics, political liberalism, analytic philosophy, hermeneutics, structuralism, existentialism, phenomenology, deconstruction, genealogy, poststructuralism, postcolonial theory, psychoanalysis, semiotics, cultural studies, language analysis, pragmatism, neo-Marxism, and post-Marxism. Many feminist theorists deploy inventive combinations of these discourses and methods, creating their own hybridized critical-interpretive positions; but it would be a mistake to assume (and inadvisable to wish) that their various positions ultimately or coherently conjoin under "feminist" as a unitary category. There is today, for example, no agreement in feminist theory about the meaning and status of the concept "women" or "gender identity," nor even consensus about how to appropriate gender as a useful category of analysis (Scott 1988a, Nicholson 1994, Carver 1996). Thus, what really exists under the standard rubric of feminist theory is a multifaceted, discursively contentious field of inquiry that does not promise to resolve itself into any programmatic consensus or converge onto any shared conceptual ground. Whether or not this is a welcome situation in the long term, it is certainly a sign of the dynamism and vitality that mark feminist theory today.

CONSTRUCTING THE STATUS OF "GENDER"

Despite the multifarious divergences within academic feminism, one general conceptual strategy seems to have informed its theorizing since the mid-1970s: the articulation of gender as a phenomenon separate from but related to biological claims of natural sex difference between men and women. The latter view is itself a by-product of the eighteenth- and nineteenth-century science of reproductive physiology, which located sex difference in the male and female anatomies (Schiebinger 1989, Laquer 1990). The disentanglement of the concept of gender from the dichotomous variable of biological sex, with which it had previously been considered synonymous, was an emergent property of second-wave feminist philosophy and social science research ever since Beauvoir's (1949) celebrated formulation, "one is not born a woman, but, rather, becomes one." Within social science research, the first systematic articulation of gender as a formal category of critical feminist analysis appeared in Rubin's (1975) structuralist anthropological account of a "sex/gender system." Drawing on Freud, Lévi-Strauss, and Lacan, Rubin specified certain cultural and institutional mechanisms that transform biological males and females into a gender hierarchy (and a corollary heterosexual disposition) that subordinates women. What is important here is the operating premise behind this particular moment in the development of analytic feminism. As Lovenduski distills it (1998, p. 337), "sex and gender are analytically distinct, gender is relational, and the concept of sex is meaningless except when understood in the context of gender relations."

The political significance of the conceptual innovation regarding gender can hardly be overestimated. Under this argument the supposedly natural relation of "male and female" could be theorized as the product of specific social, cultural, historical, and discursive processes, a move that throws into question the very concept of naturalness as well as the meaning of social construction (Butler 1987, 1990; Nicholson 1990). Furthermore, the sex/gender system that this hitherto "natural" relation represented could now be theorized as a social condition constituted through relations of power, thus open to critique and the possibility of change. Although not all modes of feminist theorizing abandoned biological foundational or essentialist arguments, the "social constructivist" framework for understanding gender became integral to contemporary feminist discourses and research programs across the social sciences (e.g., Chodorow 1978, Gilligan 1982, Ferguson 1984, Keller 1984, Fausto-Sterling 1985, Klein 1986, Scott 1988a, MacKinnon 1989), and in the interpretation of Western political theory and philosophy (e.g., Okin 1978, Elshtain 1981, Pitkin 1984, Brown 1988, Di Stefano 1991, Coole 1993, Lloyd 1993). However, despite refinements in the notion of gender as a social construction constituted by and constituting a culture, a system, or a specific structure of relations, in feminist theory the concept remains, as Butler writes (1990, p. 16), "a complexity whose totality is permanently deferred, never fully what it is at any given juncture in time." Indeed, notwithstanding the constructivist turn and the proliferation of "gender studies," feminist theorists today regularly, and often radically, disagree over the practical-normative significance of maintaining a conception of gender as, on the one hand, a binary configuration of masculine/feminine or male/female rooted in the idea of gender or sexual difference or, on the other hand, as a process or an effect of discourse that is constantly in production and therefore changeable and fluid. As various formulations of gender and sex and their relation to difference began to emerge in the 1980s, they moved feminist theory toward what was widely understood as a "crisis of identity" within the field (Alcoff 1988).

From Gender to Subjectivity: the Controversy over "Women"

Within a philosophically diversified and politically volatile context, perhaps the most pressing issue in feminist theory during the 1980s and 1990s was how (and whether) to construct a subject of feminism under the category of woman or women. Indeed, of all the concerns that have accompanied the conceptualization of gender over the past two decades, none have produced more theoretical divisiveness than the effort to rethink the meaning of gender difference, or the idea of the feminine within sexual difference, as a social, cultural historical, and psychosymbolic phenomenon. The controversy can be framed in the form of two questions: Is there a coherent concept of woman that stands prior to the elaboration of women's interests or point of view, or a concept of the feminine that functions as a symbolic unconscious? If so, what epistemic identity or meaning adheres to such concepts of subjectivity?

To put matters schematically, we might cast the current controversy over woman (or "the subject") in terms of three dominant perspectives that have developed over the past two decades of feminist theorizing: difference feminism, which is itself divided into "social" and "symbolic"; diversity feminism; and deconstruction feminism. Difference feminism, whether social or symbolic, is preoccupied with revaluing "women" or the feminine in order to affirm a positive account of the female side of the gender binary or the female aspect of sexual difference. Both forms of difference feminism theorize the tenacity of gender identity as male/female difference and locate women's subordination or the repression of women's agency within a social or symbolic system of gender bifurcation rooted in psychological relations or psychic structures. Both also appeal, though with different emphases, to the female body, the maternal, or women's universal oppression as unique means of access to ways of knowing in the world or speaking/being within the patriarchal system.

Primarily in opposition to social difference feminism, diversity feminism challenges, both philosophically and politically, the notion of a female subject and the very coherence of the concept of "woman." Diversity feminism complicates and multiplies the concept by considering race, class, ethnicity, sexuality, and other ascriptive identity categories. In effect, diversity feminism questions the primacy of sexual or gender difference and its elision of other collective forms of difference and identity.

Deconstruction feminism argues for dismantling gender's inhibiting polarities of male and female altogether. This perspective rejects any notion of an a priori female subject grounded in a presexed body, any concept of "woman" as the foundation of a feminist politics, or any conception of sexual difference that instantiates the feminine or a presumptive heterosexuality as the privileged locus of ethics or existence. From the deconstructive perspective, neither sex nor the body are brute, passive, or given; they constitute systems of meaning, signification, performance, reiteration, and representation. Thus, instead of inscribing sex as an essential, biological, or psychically foundational category and gender as a social construction, deconstructive feminism rejects the opposition between sex and gender, essentialism and constructivism, altogether.

Of course, given the academic multiplicity of feminist theory, there are important theoretical variations not only within difference feminism but also within diversity and deconstruction feminisms. Indeed, the effort simply to name, categorize, and review the alternatives has become a small industry in the literature (e.g., Echols 1983; Harding 1987a; Moi 1987; Alcoff 1988; Hawkesworth 1989; Snitow 1989; Braidotti 1991, 1994; Ferguson 1991; Grant 1993; Grosz 1994; Coole 1994; Nicholson 1994; Fraser 1997; Arneil 1999; Kruks 2001). (Feminist theory is extremely self-conscious.) The stakes in these debates are, however, every bit as practical and political as they are categorical, analytical, and philosophical. As Butler puts it (1990, p. 5), "In the course of this effort to question 'women' as the subject of feminism, the unproblematic invocation of that category may prove to *preclude* the possibility of feminism as a representational politics." Or, as Nicholson asks rhetorically (1994, p. 100), "Does not feminist politics require that the category *woman* have some determinate meaning?" Hence, the controversies over sexual difference, gender identity, and the concept of woman in feminist theory, as well as the politics of the difference, diversity, and deconstruction perspectives, require closer examination.

THE SUBJECTIVITY PROBLEM IN FEMINISM: THEORIES OF DIFFERENCE

Not the least of the controversies within feminist theory involves the confusion that attends the theorization of gender or sexual "difference." Any effort to make sense of this term must begin with recognition of two separate, though distantly related, approaches within the field. The first approach is the social difference feminism of primarily Anglo-American theorists who understand gender in terms of its social or psychological construction and often rely on empirical descriptions regarding gender development and the internalization of norms. The second approach is the symbolic difference feminism of primarily French theorists whose projects begin psychoanalytically, exploring the effects of sexual difference within the unconscious, the symbolic, and the imaginary domains. As Zakin points out (2000, p. 22), these two logics of difference feminism need not be incommensurable, but they do tend to operate in different fields of reality (historical-material and symbolic-psychical) that rarely overlap at the level of critical commentary within feminist theory (but see Eisenstein & Jardine 1980, Meyers 1992, Butler 1994, Zakin 2000). Thus, it is not surprising that the controversy over "difference" bifurcates into two separate literatures, with diversity feminists responding primarily to social difference feminism and deconstruction feminists responding primarily to symbolic difference feminism.

Difference Feminism I: Gender as Social Reality and Feminist Standpoint

The dominant discursive context of Anglo-American feminist theorizing in the late 1970s through the early 1980s was forged out of second-wave feminism, including the existential feminism of Beauvoir (1949), the liberal feminism of Friedan (1963), the radical feminism of Millet (1970), the socialist-Marxist feminism of Rowbotham (1972), the psychoanalytic feminism of Mitchell (1973), and other "women's liberation" writers of the 1960s and early 1970s. In response to the dominant concepts and categories of these diverse literatures (e.g., patriarchy, androgyny, misogyny, consciousness raising, sisterhood), socialist-feminist critiques of capitalist patriarchy and "dual-systems" theory (Young 1981), and radical Beauvoiresque proclamations about child bearing, family life, and the role of wife and mother as the site of woman's oppression, a new perspective on "the woman question" emerged. We now have a series of terms to identify it: feminist standpoint theory, standpoint epistemology, cultural feminism, social feminism, gynocentric feminism, woman-centered theory, and difference theory. Social difference feminism advances insights variously drawn from (or combining) dialectical and Marxist historical materialism (O'Brien 1981, Hartsock 1983, MacKinnon 1983); the object-relations school of psychoanalytic theory (Chodorow 1978, Flax 1980, Hartsock 1983); cognitive development analysis and moral psychology (Gilligan 1982); social psychology and situational sociology (Miller 1976, Smith 1987); interpretive social science (Rose 1983, Harding 1986); and the literatures on female spirituality and bodily essence (Rich 1976, Daly 1978). The collective aim of these theorists is to thematize a feminism rooted in the realities of women's lives and in ways of knowing or being that flow from women's experiences (Harding 1987b) or from the female body (Rich 1976).

The most systematic account of social difference feminism's epistemology is that of Hartsock (1983, 1987), with whom the term feminist standpoint is most closely associated. The idea of a feminist standpoint (or standpoint feminism) became something of a flagship or, to paraphrase MacKinnon (1987, p. 151), an epistemic term of art for a sector of academic feminist theory. In developing the feminist standpoint, Hartsock (1983, 1987) posits (*a*) a historical-materialist thesis indebted to Marx but attuned to gender rather than class analysis; and (*b*) an object-relations psychology influenced by Chodorow (1978) and Flax (1980) that asserts a distinctively female self attuned to connection rather than separation, continuity rather than dissociation, and relational knowledge rather than abstract reason. Accordingly, Hartsock notes a profound structural difference between the "lived realities" of women and of men in a society structured by compulsory heterosexuality and masculine domination. Within this materialist framework, Hartsock (1987, p. 164) finds an epistemological consequence: The "double aspect" of women's lives is the basis for a particular "understanding of social relations" and a "privileged vantage point on male supremacy," which can ground a powerful critique of the phallocratic institutions and ideology that constitute the capitalist form of patriarchy. The task of feminism is to revalue female experience, search "for common threads which connect the diverse experiences of women," and articulate a standpoint that offers "the possibility of a fully human community" grounded in an analysis of women's claims to knowledge (Hartsock 1987, pp. 174–75; also Harding 1987b, 1991).

Despite the divergences between biological accounts on the one hand and psychological, social, or cultural explanations of women's commonalities on the other, social difference feminists do share three theoretical strategies worth noting. First, at the level of social theory, difference perspectives all bring to the feminist project an implicit epistemology substantively geared toward accessing the true (if nonbiological) nature and social reality of women. Second, at the level of conceptual analysis, social difference theorists all assume the coherence of an account of gender identity rooted in the difference between two sexes. Regardless of how they get there, in other words, persons are preeminently male or female in social difference feminism. The point is not to challenge the reality of this dyadic formulation or deny its logic as an analytical framework but rather to explore its social, moral, and political meanings and how it structures power. Within this theoretical perspective, to paraphrase Adams & Minson (1990), male/female simply "mark[s] the always already given gender in the category of humanity." Third, social difference feminism does not merely register women's difference from men; it mobilizes gender difference in order to shed a "distinct light" (MacKinnon 1987, p. 57) on epistemological issues, to espouse the superiority of women's ways of knowing, or to reclaim their moral voice.

Difference Feminism II: Sexual Difference and Psychosymbolic Structure

The dominant discursive context of Continental feminist theorizing of the 1980s was constituted by structuralist (Lévi-Strauss), psychoanalytic (Lacan), poststructuralist (Foucault, Deleuze), and deconstructive (Lyotard, Derrida) influences within the academy, and radical forms of practice in the European political sphere (Fraser & Bartky 1992). Together, these forces produced within feminist theory a unique complex of positions called French feminism, associated primarily with the philosophical and literary writings of Cixous (1976), Irigaray (1985a,b, 1993), Le

Doeuff (1989), and Kristeva (1980, 1982, 1984), although other significant feminist thinkers influenced by post-Marxist approaches emerged as well (e.g., Wittig 1976, 1980; Plaza 1978; Delphy 1984). Over the past two decades, French feminism has received wide attention within Anglophone feminist philosophy and literary, cultural, and film studies; numerous volumes are devoted to critical commentaries on and interpretive applications of French feminist psychoanalytic writings (e.g., Marks & de Courtivron 1980; Gallop 1982; de Lauretis 1987; Moi 1987; Spivak 1988; Brennan 1989; Butler 1990; Whitford 1991; Braidotti 1991, 1994; Cornell 1991, 1995; Fraser & Bartky 1992; Grosz 1989, 1994; Burke et al. 1994; Zerilli 1994; Deutscher 1997). French feminism has much in common with deconstruction feminism (particularly in its view of sexual identity as a linguistically or discursively mediated phenomenon); but its commitment to the concept of irreducible sexual difference warrants its inclusion under the category of difference feminism, its various strategies of displacement notwithstanding.

A distinctive aspect of French feminism, especially in the writings of Kristeva and, even more influentially, Irigaray, is the tenacity with which it holds to sexual difference as a primary critical-analytical concept and a fundamental ontology of human existence. Simultaneously appropriating and subverting Lacan's categories of "symbolic order" (or the "Law of the Father"), the "imaginary," and *jouissance*, Kristeva (1980) locates sexual difference in the semiotic (feminine) zone of the preverbal, pre-Oedipal maternal body, the time of mother/child bonding and maternal rhythms that precedes the (masculine) zone of the symbolic order, in which the child's desire of the mother is fully repressed. Kristeva (1984, 1986) deploys the symbolic and the semiotic to mark sexually differentiated forms of language; the latter retains logical connections and linearity, but the former "marks a point of resistance to paternally coded cultural authority," unbounded by linguistic rules and keyed to the expression of libidinal drives (Fraser 1992, p. 187). Thus, within the unconscious psychic roots of patriarchal power, Kristeva (1986, p. 294) identifies a transgressive "dissident" embodied in Woman as the sign of the feminine, if not in real, historically situated women as social beings. In this respect, Kristeva's conception of female subjectivity remains "firmly on the interface between the psychic and the political" (Braidotti 1991, p. 231), engaged in a perpetual poetic subversion of the logicosymbolic, phallogocentric code.

If Kristeva's thought exhibits the power of the French feminist psychoanalytic account of the tenacity of gender, then Irigaray's writing exemplifies French feminism's continuing insistence on "the fundamental nature and, indeed, the infrastructural status of sexual difference to human existence as a whole" (Cheah & Grosz 1998, pp. 3–4). It is within this position that Irigaray (1985b, p. 136) explores the specificity of woman symbolically as a "being-two" ("not One"). She invokes the metonymic figure of the half-open sex whose two lips displace the phallic signifier to become the basis for imagining "speaking (as) woman should" (*parler femme*), against the symbolic order. At the crux of this psycholinguistic maneuver lies the sexual difference between woman and man, or what Irigaray calls the different modes of articulation "between masculine and feminine desire and language" (1985b, p. 136). Like Kristeva, Irigaray (1985b, pp. 110, 134) wants to model a new kind of linguistic exchange, a "feminine syntax" that would no longer privilege "oneness" or "any distinction of identities" but rather articulate itself within the unconscious as the play of metonymy. Irigaray's earlier work was, therefore, directed toward theorizing the feminine and speaking the female body not as already given "essences" but as utopian categories that point toward or inaugurate a future within language and intelligibility. Her more recent work (Irigaray 1993, 1996) has shifted from the feminine within sexual difference to sexual difference itself, or the "figure of being-two," in an effort to rethink rights and ethics. For Irigaray (1993, pp. 13–14; 1994, 1996), "the fecund couple" of sexual difference, as a "generative interval," is an analytical category that serves to critique gender oppression and neocolonial globalization (e.g., Berger 1998, Fermon 1998), and to provide for the dissemination of new values and the transfiguration of cultural and sociopolitical life (e.g., Schwab 1998).

"The Issue Which Simply Refuses to Die": Essentialism and Difference

No philosophical matter is more tenacious within feminist theory's subjectivity problem than essentialism, "the issue which simply refuses to die," partly because its status within feminism cannot be readily resolved (Fuss 1992, p. 95, 1989; Heyes 2000). Both social and symbolic difference feminisms have had to face the problem of essentialism in the form of questions about whether it is possible or desirable to forward a collective concept of "women," valorize a symbolic appeal to "the feminine," or posit irreducible "sexual difference" without asserting some invidiously exclusive or normalizing metaphysical substance, natural life form, or deep structure with regard to these entities. This matter is particularly complicated because, with few exceptions (e.g., Rich 1976, Daly 1978), neither social nor symbolic difference feminists have sought recourse to a foundational concept of the essential female, or declared a natural or innate difference between women and men. Social difference feminism, whatever one makes of its efforts to articulate an identity for women, remains committed to a concept of gender as a social and psychological construction and condition (Alcoff 1988); and symbolic difference feminism, whatever one makes of its efforts to secure a place for the feminine, remains committed to the deployment of irony, tropes, literary devices, and a "strategic" essentialism that refuses to submit to the dualisms of Western "phallomorphism," including the binary category of essence/accident (Fuss 1992, p. 108). Nevertheless, these commitments have not secured social difference feminism from diversity theorists' charges of (latent) essentialism and universalism (see below). Nor have they rescued French feminism from attacks concerning its alleged metaphysical idealism (Burke 1981, Moi 1985); its psychologistic reductionism (Plaza 1978); its reliance on an inadequate political psychology and an inhibiting (Freudian) gender bifurcation (Leland 1992, Meyers 1992); its structuralist ahistoricism (Spivak 1988, Fraser 1992); and, on the matter of irreducible sexual difference, its presumptive heterosexuality (Butler in Cheah & Grosz 1998). Thus, intense debates about "risking essence" proliferate within feminist theory, especially at the intersection of symbolic difference and deconstruction feminisms.

MULTIPLYING THE SUBJECT: DIVERSITY FEMINISM

Social difference feminism's tendency to appropriate the concept of "women" as an unproblematic universal invites charges of essentialism, raises the question of exclusion, and ignites the identity crisis within feminist theory (Lugones & Spelman 1983, Alcoff 1988, Fraser & Nicholson 1990, Grant 1993). Surveying the contemporary classics of feminist theory, Spelman (1989) argues that, beginning with Beauvoir, feminism was insufficiently attentive to ethnicity, class, and race and was captured by unexamined heterosexist assumptions. By presupposing the lives of white, middle-class, heterosexual women as paradigmatic for the situation of all women, Spelman contends, the dominant strains of feminist theorizing fail to appreciate how the social constructions of race, class, and sexuality profoundly alter the status of gender, complicate identity, and fundamentally pluralize and particularize the meaning of "women." Difference feminism, it seems, could not adequately theorize differences among women (Hekman 1999) or incorporate cultural and historical diversity into the notion of standpoint that relies philosophically on a "speaking subject who is an autonomous, self-conscious individual woman" (Alarcón 1990, p. 363). Thus, at the level of practical politics and strategic organization, social difference feminism's articulation of women's experience and the quasi-prescriptive character of its generalizations appear limited and reductive, not only privileging whiteness and "consciousness" but also excluding axes of domination and oppression other than gender (Alarcón 1990, Fraser & Nicholson 1990). Cott (1986, p. 49) effectively summarizes the conceptual dilemmas of social difference feminism: "It acknowledges diversity among women while positing that women recognize their unity. It requires gender consciousness for its basis, yet calls for the elimination of prescribed gender roles."

In response to these Anglo-American inadequacies, redefinitions of female subjectivity begin to take form in what Rich (1976) terms a "politics of location" and Kruks (2001, p. 86) later calls "a politics of identity affirmation." (The generic term is "identity politics.") On both counts, feminist thinkers begin to press demands against the existing women's movement and the "class biased ethnocentrism" (Alarcón 1990, p. 364) of mainstream feminist theory, calling for recognition, power, respect, and voice for women of color (Moraga & Anzaldúa 1983, Lorde 1984, Trinh 1989, Anzaldúa & Keating 2002). Collins' (1991) articulation of an "Afrocentric feminist epistemology" or a "Black women's standpoint" is a systematic attempt to counter the whiteness of feminist theory in the name of a "politics of empowerment" rooted in a recognition of the marginality and outsider status of black women (see also Hull et al. 1982; Smith 1983; hooks 1981, 1984, 1989, 1990; Carby 1987; Christian 1988). Critiques of "compulsory heterosexuality" (Rich 1983) and, later, the "heterosexual matrix" (Butler 1990) further challenge the hegemonic status of mainstream (difference) feminism's concepts of gender and sexuality (see also Wittig 1976, 1980; Fuss 1989; Phelan 1989; Card 1995). The whiteness and ethnocentrism of Western feminist theories of gender, sexual difference, and subjectivity are also scrutinized by postcolonial and Third World critiques that engage the "subaltern" (Spivak 1988), interrogate colonizing practices (Alexander & Mohanty 1997), and analyze the production of women as socioeconomic political groups within particular local and historical contexts, with a view toward asserting the material and discursive processes of identity formation (Lazreg 1988, Mohanty et al. 1991). Finally, Haraway (1990, p. 201; 1991) subjects feminist standpoint theories to epistemological and technological interrogation, rejecting the notion of a single feminist standpoint and criticizing the "unintended erasure of polyvocal, unassimilable, radical difference[s]" within the approach first formulated in Hartsock's work.

Given the array of views within the diversity feminisms (which are themselves as theoretically and methodologically varied as the diversity they champion), it is difficult to identify a set of philosophical or political features that allow them to coalesce into a unified whole. Collins' (1991) approach, for example, has far more in common with Hartsock's (1983) standpoint theory than with Haraway's construct of social identity as fragmentary, contradictory, and ungrounded in color, which is closer to deconstruction feminism. Anzaldúa's (1987) cultural/group identity politics is considerably distant from Mohanty's (1991, p. 51) historical-materialist critique, which vehemently eschews the production of "a singular monolithic subject" out of putatively shared experiences of subordination, dependence, oppression, or victimization, or a preconstituted group identity.

Nevertheless, the diversity perspective, at least as I construe it here, exhibits four key features: First, it brings to the feminist project an emphasis on differences, pluralities, heterogeneity, and multiplicity in the theorizing of women, thereby rejecting the notion of a unitary group or singular gendered category (much less an experientially or morally superior gendered category). Second, it emphasizes the situated, specific, historically embodied condition of the female subject primarily with attention to so-called sociocultural identities based on ethnicity, religion, sexuality, class, color, and so on. Third, as part of a political project of empowerment, diversity feminism repeatedly invokes those subjugated and silenced "others" who are displaced, marginalized, exploited, or oppressed under structures of domination that privilege the white, male, heterosexual, Eurocentric, or Western subject. Fourth, in the diversity perspective, the articulation, negotiation, and recognition of previously submerged, negated, or dismissed identities or subjectivities (along a range of politicized differences not simply focused on women) are a central task of a feminist politics of resistance.

Theorizing Subjectivities from an Epistemological Point of View

In the wake of these diversity feminisms, an "ensemble of epistemological and political conundrums" (Brown 1995, p. 43) enters onto the stage of academic feminist theory in the form of encounters between social difference and diversity feminists. To paraphrase Haraway (1988) and Hartsock (1997, 1998), the problem is how simultaneously to hold to a radical and contingent account of knowledge claims and knowing subjects, thereby dissolving the false "we" of the feminist standpoint, while maintaining solidarity, across differences, among women in the name of a long-term or wide-ranging feminist movement. Is it possible to incorporate a concept of differences and diversity without ceding the privileged (truth) ground of a "women's standpoint," or the concept of sexual difference? As hooks contends (1989, pp. 22–23), "recognition of the inter-connectedness of sex, race, and class highlights the diversity of experience, compelling redefinition of the terms for unity"; but the challenge remains to determine exactly what the redefinition requires.

Confronted with this problem, feminist theory took a philosophical turn toward questions about the meaning of the self, the subject, and gendered subjectivity, as well as the content of a feminist epistemology (e.g., Jaggar & Bordo 1989, Code 1991, Gunew 1991, Harding 1991, Alcoff & Potter 1993, Scheman 1993, Campbell 1998). In response to Hekman's (1997, 1999) challenge that standpoint theory address the question of differences, for example, Hartsock (1997; 1998, pp. 240–41) begins to reformulate her initial views in terms of the "real multiplicity and variety" in the epistemologies contained in the experience of dominated groups; and Collins (1997) appeals to "group-based experiences." Haraway's (1988) effort to achieve a rapprochement with standpoint theory replaces a unitary and privileged epistemological position with a concept of diverse and publicly communicable (but not necessarily privileged) "situated knowledges" and "partial perspectives." Benhabib (1992, pp. 10–11) envisions an ethical continuum that moves from the "standpoint" of the generalized to the "concrete," particularized, and distinct other(s); Weeks (1998, pp. 8,10) appeals to the feminist standpoint as an "inspiring example" for a collective feminist subjectivity, constructing "antagonistic subjects" and rooted in a sense of commonality with other women. Hirschmann (1992, pp. 338–39) develops a feminist theory of the variety and multiplicity of standpoints that recognizes "the interdependence of different kinds of oppression" and underscores the articulation of identity as a "collaborative enterprise" involving conversation and mutual recognition. Kruks (2001, p. 176), invoking Beauvoir, recommends an intersubjectivity "that can acknowledge and accept otherness" and respect difference as part of "the project of feminist world-travelling."

These multiplications take place not only at the level of interaction among subject positions and subjectivities but also within the individual, theorized as self and subject. Alcoff (1988, pp. 432–33) forwards "a conception of the subject as positionality," where identity is a matter of "choices" made "relative to a constantly shifting context" that is mutable, fluid, and persistently enacted. Anzaldúa (1987, p. 98; Anzaldúa & Keating 2002) introduces the concept of *mestiza* consciousness to capture identity not as a set of compartmentalized components (race, sexuality, class, etc.) but as a complex of border crossings and admixtures; similarly, Clough (1994, pp. 115–16) and Sandoval (1991) valorize identity as a hybrid "rather than the unified subject-identity." Alarcón (1990, p. 366) cites a "plurality of self" and "multiple antagonisms" in grasping the subjectivity of women of color; Haraway (1991) pursues the concept of feminist subjectivity and hybridity through the dislocated image of the "cyborg"; de Lauretis (1990) theorizes the subject as a process of embodied, material, interconnected relations, a multiplicity of positionalities and entanglements. Despite considerable differences in substance, all of these projects seek to describe the constituents of the subject(s) for whom feminism speaks and to assign a normative value to these descriptions, even as they acknowledge that privileging the subject, albeit a "multiple-voiced" subject, is not enough (Alarcón 1990).

The rapprochement between at least some social difference and diversity feminists means that gender is absorbed into a mixture of identifications and that feminist subjectivity is now a pluralized phenomenon woven of many different strands. Yet, despite its view of "women" as an identity complex of color, class, ethnicity, culture, sexual identity, sexuality, etc., this sector of feminist theory by no means abandons the "subject"; it merely complicates and situates it, so that the prevailing political question is how these variously situated knowledges, partial perspectives, or complex subjects connect or translate across "multiple intersecting differences" (Fraser 1997, p. 180) that are by no means limited to gender. As we shall see, "diversity theory" or "pluralist multiculturalism" (Fraser 1997, p. 185) and the attendant epistemological problem of "recognition" generate a great deal of controversy about the meaning, processes, and procedures of a (feminist) politics of identity.

Before turning there, however, we need to examine deconstruction feminism, the third perspective in contemporary feminist theory, wherein the feminist politics of identity theorizes its own negation by designating "women" as a field of differences that cannot be summarized through any descriptive identity content or category. Deconstruction feminism disrupts and dismantles all the multivocal, preconstituted categories (race, color, class, gender) and the "et cetera" (Butler 1990, p. 143) that diversity theories promote as culturally and politically paramount.

DISMANTLING THE SUBJECT: DECONSTRUCTION FEMINISM

The challenge to theorizing the "subject" in the category of women is perhaps most famously and controversially exemplified in the early writings of Butler (1986, 1987, 1990, 1991, 1993), especially *Gender Trouble: Feminism and the Subversion of Identity* (1990). "Through [the] horizontal trajectory of adjectives," Butler writes of diversity feminism (1990, p. 143), "these positions strive to encompass a situated subject, but invariably fail to be complete . . . . This is a sign of exhaustion as well as of the illimitable process of signification itself." Butler's (1995a) denial of the presituated "voluntaristic" subject has produced intense and varied responses in current feminist (and queer) theory. More generally, the project of undermining any notion of a prediscursive subjectivity or a free agent has been addressed under the label of feminism's relation to (and anxieties concerning) post-modernism (Lovibond 1989, Bordo 1990, Fraser & Nicholson 1990, Nicholson 1990, Flax 1990, Hekman 1990, Singer 1992, Walby 1992, Benhabib et al. 1995, Nicholson 1999, MacKinnon 2000), poststructuralism (Alcoff 1988, Fraser 1995), and postmodernity (Brown 1995). Although the sometimes pejorative designation "postmodernism" became a staple of theoretical negotiations in the 1980s and 1990s between feminism and post-Enlightenment deconstructive critiques, it is too vague and covers too many divergent thinkers to provide adequate purchase on the specific theoretical issues in these debates (see Butler 1995a).

Nevertheless, Benhabib (1995a, pp. 18–21), for example, draws on the work of Flax (1990), for example, to locate in the "postmodern position" the three theses of "the death of Man, the death of History, and the death of Metaphysics" and finds affinities between postmodern and feminist claims. Benhabib recommends a feminist "skepticism" in relation to postmodern orientations, lest "female emancipation" founder within post-Enlightenment paradigms that embrace uncertainty, flux, instability, and indeterminateness and forego a "regulative principle" on agency, autonomy, and selfhood. Benhabib's (1995a) conclusion, that feminism and postmodernism are not conceptual political allies, is emphatically shared by MacKinnon (2000) (who problematically allies postmodernism with multiculturalism); but these views have earned responses from theorists who see complementarities between feminism and various deconstructive or poststructural critiques (e.g., Butler 1995a,b; Brown 1995; Carver 1996; Fraser 1997; Scott 1988b; Webster 2000). This controversy remains one of the most vitriolic of current theoretical feminist debates.

What really seems to be at stake in the feminism/postmodernism confrontation is (*a*) the deconstruction of the subject in the category of women in feminist theory and (*b*) the formulation of a post-foundational feminist politics that shifts from the concept of an autonomous agent to the theorization of discursive relations of power, language games, significations, subversions, and performances. On these matters, the work of Butler is central, if not absolutely definitive (see also Riley 1988; Spivak 1988; Cornell 1991, 1992; Scott 1992; Grosz 1994; Brown 1995, 1997; Deutscher 1997; Zerilli 1998a).

The political focus of Butler's theoretical project is to submit notions of the subject, the body, sex, gender, sexuality, and materiality to "a deconstructive critique" geared toward displacing them "from the contexts in which they have been deployed as instruments of oppressive power." The unavoidable accompaniment to this project is the "loss of epistemological certainty" or of a strongly secured ontological identity as the source of agency, matters especially pertinent, as we have seen, to difference and diversity feminisms and to feminist politics (Butler 1995a, p. 51). Butler starts with certain key elements of Foucault's writings and moves beyond them to explore how the sexed-gendered subject is produced and concealed in feminism within a "heterosexual matrix" that perpetuates exclusionary practices, paradoxically undermining feminist goals (1990, pp. 5–6). This exploration, which Butler calls a "*feminist genealogy* of the category of women," involves a complex set of text interpretations ranging across the writings of Freud, Beauvoir, Rubin, Foucault, Lacan, Kristeva, Wittig, and Irigaray. From it we can distill at least three critical points that decisively position Butler's variant of deconstruction feminism (1990, p. 5).

The first point holds that there are no prediscursive, prior, or "natural" sites or foundations for either sex or gender on which to rest identity. In effect, "'sex' is as culturally constructed as gender" and hence is itself a "gendered category" (Butler 1990, p. 7; 1993). Second, gender is inflected with power and regulated through the institution of "a compulsory and naturalized heterosexuality," under the hierarchical and oppressive binary relation of masculine:feminine (1990, pp. 22–23). Yet, third, the political regulations and disciplinary practices that produce gender (as heterosexual difference) can be "displaced from view" through the "play of signifying absences" that are sustained through "corporeal signs and other discursive means" (1990, p. 136). This latter claim initiates Butler's most original insight: Gender is "performative," an intentional act or "strategy" that suggests a "dramatic and contingent construction of meaning" (1990, p. 139). Performativity, as Butler articulates it, "is the discursive mode by which ontological effects are installed" (1996, p. 112) through subversive speech acts of parody, repetition, and recitation, as for example in the cultural practices of "drag," cross-dressing, and the "sexual stylization of butch/femme identities" (1990, p. 137). These practices took on more paradigmatic significance in subsequent literatures than Butler initially intended (1996).

What counts here, for purposes of feminist theory, is the deconstruction that Butler's concept of the discursive "performativity of gender" (1990, p. 139) effects on the subject, the body, and the category of sex, all of which, under these terms, are no longer construed (as they are among social difference and some diversity feminists) as entities prior to practices of signification. Rather, body, sex, desire, and the subject are effects of signification and discursive ordering, "under context, up for grabs," circumscribed as political issues and productions of power (1995a, p. 54). Butler insists, however, that this radical reconceptualization of identity as an effect actually opens up possibilities of agency that are foreclosed by positions that underwrite the heterosexual matrix and "take identity categories as foundational and fixed" (1990, p. 147; 1995b, 1997a). And in her more recent writings, in a psychoanalytic turn, Butler (1997a, 2000a) endeavors to theorize identity as a complex disposition, figured through loss and ambivalence, melancholy and finitude. These moves have not, however, inoculated her critical genealogy against a wide range of friendly and unfriendly criticisms from feminist theorists who view the deconstructive project, and some (if not all) aspects of postmodernism more generally, as undermining the feminist commitment to women's agency (e.g., Benhabib 1995a, Weeks 1998), identity and sense of selfhood (e.g., Di Stefano 1990, Hartsock 1990, Moya 1997, Kruks 2001), liberation (e.g., Fraser 1995), social reality (MacKinnon 2000), and social justice (Nussbaum 1999b). At this level, Butlerian deconstructive feminism, even once inflected with an affirmative gesture toward subjectivity and agency (Butler 1997, 2000a), remains a terrain of contestation, and the "subject" in feminism—whether under the gaze of difference, diversity, or deconstruction—persists as a seemingly ineradicable, perpetually problematic specter haunting feminist thought.

THEORIZING FEMINIST POLITICS

The essential problem and the *idée fixe* of feminist theory remains, to date, the problem of epistemic identification—locating or dislocating the subject, fixing or deconstructing the category "women," discerning or dismantling the meaning of the feminist "we," and theorizing or displacing "identities." Thus, it is not surprising that feminist theories of politics, action, and the public sphere, their considerable variations notwithstanding, tend to map the epistemological/identification controversies concerning the self, the subject, and subjectivity that frame feminist theory writ large. Young (1997b, p. 18) implicitly captures this situation when she states, "Feminist politics evaporates . . . without some conception of women as a social collective." It is a short step from there to Hekman's (1997, p. 142) claim that "feminist politics are necessarily epistemological," an understanding that is shared by many feminist political theorists but not endorsed by those who do not understand theory as geared toward the articulation of philosophical certainties or an epistemological a priori, including philosophically verifiable claims that assert a prior identity of the female subject (Mouffe 1992; Brown 1995; Fraser 1997; Zerilli 1998b, 2000; Heyes 2000; Dietz 2002). Political theorists of the latter type tend to understand identity not formally or philosophically, as prior, for example, to history, economy, culture, or society, but rather as interpretable only through this complex of elements and in relation to human practices and the effects of power. Nevertheless, within current feminist theories of politics, we can indeed see the epistemic problem defining the boundaries and circumscribing the contours of some of the issues at hand. The epistemological debate over "difference" and "diversity" has translated into an extensive literature concerning feminist conceptions of citizenship and ethics, the politics of group difference, representation, and multiculturalism, and the norms of democratic discourse.

One of the most salient features of contemporary feminist theories of politics is their shared commitment, in principle, to the concept of democracy, despite the historical and political reality of women's subjection, subordination, underrepresentation, and disenfranchisement as citizens within modern democratic polities (Pateman 1989; Mendus 1992; Phillips 1991, 1993, 1995). Insofar as feminist theorizing understands itself not only as an interpretive project but also as a project of emancipation, it has sought to articulate problems of democracy with a view toward strategies of representation and participation, collective agency and freedom, that are cognizant of feminist principles and goals. As Pateman argues (1989, p. 223), "a 'democratic' theory and practice that is not at the same time feminist merely serves to maintain a fundamental form of domination and so makes a mockery of the ideals and values that democracy is held to embody." As we have seen, however, the crucial conceptual coordinate "feminist" that Pateman advances is contentious, and so are the theoretical projects that appropriate and deploy it within the current context of feminist democratic political theory. The contestations roughly follow the epistemic terms of difference, diversity, and deconstruction, only now they are translated into the theorizing of citizenship, representation, multiculturalism, democratic discourse, and political action.

Citizenship as Gender(ed) Difference: Women in the Public Sphere

Insofar as social difference feminism is a politics as well as an epistemology, it challenges conventional liberal-egalitarian feminist theories, predominant in the 1970s, that locate women's political emancipation in gender "equity," or in the elimination of invidious gender distinctions between men and women and hence in the minimizing of gender difference itself (e.g., Okin 1989a). On the other side of what came to be known as the debate over "equality versus difference" (e.g., Okin 1989a, Young 1990, Phillips 1991, Bock & James 1992, Mendus 1992, Lister 1997), social difference feminists thematize women's identity and female relationality as the sources of a truly civil society and genuinely democratic citizenship. Like many liberal-egalitarian theorists, social difference feminists assume that persons are preeminently male or female, but instead of underwriting a concept of gender neutrality (a liberal "abstract" universal that they unmask as, in reality, a particular norm from the point of view of masculine domination), they challenge the "patriarchal conception of civil society" (Pateman 1989, p. 52). The alternative to masculinist citizenship is a sexually differentiated but equality-based conception of citizenship that would recognize women as women, valorize the female body, and privilege certain presumptively female social capacities (e.g., intimacy, attentiveness, connectedness, relational self-definition, reciprocity) and social practices (e.g., mothering, care taking, peace making). Jones (1990, p. 18; 1988) calls for a polity "that is friendly to women and the multiplicity of their interests," a polity that contests the allegedly masculine liberal concepts of justice and the male terms of citizenship, as already uncovered in feminist critical theory (e.g., Pateman 1988, 1989; Shanley & Pateman 1990; Okin 1989b; Lister 1997).

In its most programmatic political theoretical form, social difference feminism (like symbolic difference feminism) confronts the "repression of female sexual difference" (Cavarero 1992, p. 40) in an effort to assert the ethical and political value of the feminine against the masculine, the private against the public, and the ethos of care against the ethos of justice. However, social difference feminism emphasizes women's (socially constructed) practices, experiences, and ways of being and knowing, particularly in the realm of mothering, motherhood, and maternal thinking. Accordingly, women's roles in the private realm of the family and intimate relationships, especially that of the mother and child, are advanced as the source for a new public, political morality (Elshtain 1981, 1982; Noddings 1984; Ruddick 1989; Held 1990), a revitalized public sphere (Elshtain 1981, Hartsock 1987), or feminist democratic discourse and action (Elshtain 1982, Jones 1990, Boling 1996). By claiming the "private woman" for the purpose of reinventing the public realm, difference feminism attempts to reverse the normative relation that it identifies in patriarchal Western thought, where the private domain of the feminine is subordinate to the public domain of the masculine. In social difference feminism, then, the "male public" is "womanized" by way of importing putative female virtues into the political realm. Within this project, however, the original conceptual duality of public/private is not itself displaced but remains relatively stable, spatial, and fixed. Thus, social feminism may privilege female virtue, connectedness, and peace in order to challenge the hegemony of the autonomous and violent male warrior in the state-as-public-sphere (Elshtain 1987, Tickner 1992); but at the conceptual level, it dismantles neither the gender binary of male/female nor the spatial binary of public/private. In many respects, the social difference approach to gendered citizenship, with its indebtedness to Gilligan (1982, Gilligan et al. 1988) and its emphasis on women's unitary identity and values, the priority of the family, the private realm as the source of female political values, the care for children, the uniqueness of women's voice and relational connections, and the concern for community, remains the dominant element in much Anglo-American academic feminism as well as in everyday feminist political discourse, including the discourse of electoral and institutional politics in the United States (E. Goodman 2002, unpublished speech).

Within the context of academic feminist political theory, however, social difference feminism has met with a variety of criticisms, perhaps most importantly from Tronto (1987, 1989, 1993). Tronto complicates the ethic of care sociologically, along the lines of race and class, and politically situates care in relation (not opposition) to justice and democratic citizenship, thereby dismantling the social feminist gendering of justice as male and care as female (see also Bubeck 1995, Sevenhuijsen 1998). Difference feminism is also vulnerable to criticism from feminists who theorize more complex accounts of practices of responsibility (Smiley 1992) and women's self-understandings and social lives (Walker 1998), contest social feminism's reliance on the public/private distinction to conceptualize politics (Dietz 1987), and reject maternal thinking and the mother/child dyad as adequate models for democratic, non-hierarchical, citizen politics and action (Dietz 1985, 1987, 2002; Phillips 1991; Mouffe 1992). Of course, social difference feminism's homogenizing, generalizing, and sometimes communitarian impulses are also subject to critique from diversity feminists, who are "suspicious of the univocal concepts of power" (Acklesberg 1997, p. 170) that reside within any unitary or gender-specific concepts of citizenship, community, and politics that do not recognize social and cultural differences among women or formulate axes of identity beyond gender.

Citizenship in Contestation: Universal Feminism and the Clash of Cultures

The tension between equality and difference, and the attendant issue of gender neutrality versus gender specificity, remain fundamental features of feminist theorizing, perhaps most notably in Anglo-American law and legal studies (e.g., Rohde 1989, Minow 1990), theories of justice (Okin 1986, 1989a, Young 1990), and welfare (Fraser 1997; also Young 1997b). However, at the level of theorizing a politics of citizenship, the equality/difference debates reached an impasse in the 1980s, as new theoretical issues altered feminist theories of citizenship. Foremost among these problems is the thematizing of diversity, or how political society, broadly construed, constructs persons and groups along multiple lines of identity, including gender, race, color, sexuality, class, religion, ethnicity, and nationality. The recognition of group differences and cultural diversity poses both local and global dilemmas for feminism that harken back to the movement's opposition to hierarchical forms of domination and its abiding concern for sex equality: how to theorize a conception of justice (or equality of rights) that applies to all persons while still maintaining the integrity of and respect for particular, diverse groups and cultural collectives? The problem, in other words, is how to acknowledge pluralism as group rights or cultural identities without allowing the well-being or interests of any one group or subgroup to be secured unjustly at the expense of another's. Can universality be reconciled with differences? Can truth, rights, and moral equality be defined or theorized in a way to produce a universally, cross-culturally accepted point of view?

Within this context, some feminist theorists have begun to charge cultural rights theorists, or "multiculturalism" in general, with ignoring the rights of women and "inequalities between the sexes" (Okin 1999, p. 23), even as they forward the rights of groups or cultures, thus reinscribing the very structures of masculine domination that feminism resolutely opposes (Okin 1995, 1998; Nussbaum 1995, 1999a; MacKinnon 2000). Among the "perils of multicultural accommodation" (Shachar 1998, p. 287; see also Spinner-Halev 2001), these scholars argue, is acquiescence to the continuing subordination, exploitation, and oppression of women within all spheres of culture and society. Thus a recent book title asks, "Is multiculturalism bad for women?" (Okin 1999). At issue is not only the analysis of cultural or religious practices that the critics of multicultural accommodation deem oppressive of women's and girls' individual rights, dignity, and freedom (e.g., head scarves, veiling, clitoridectomy, polygamy), but also the position of women within cultures and groups. Also at stake is the larger, political philosophical matter of whether (and, if so, how) a modern feminist universalism, attentive to cultures but also committed to abstract principles of justice and rights, can be articulated in the name of women (Benhabib 1995b). Feminist theorists who answer in the affirmative (e.g., Chen 1995; Okin 1995, 1998, 1999; Nussbaum 1995, 1999a, 2000; Benhabib 1995b, 2002; Jaggar 1998; Ackerly & Okin 1999; MacKinnon 2000) do not necessarily agree on the foundations or suppositions that might inform such a project. (Nussbaum, for example, formulates a modified Aristotelian humanism, Okin defends a modified Rawlsian liberalism, and Benhabib offers a modified Habermasian discourse ethics of interaction.) But they all seem to share an orientation that envisions the possibility of a "global dialogical moral community" (Benhabib 1995b, p. 237; 2002) that addresses questions of justice and injustice in the cultural and political conditions of women's lives, especially the lives of poor women in local Second and Third World cultures. Thus, the universal feminist claims about the conditions and rights of women rest on substantive conceptions of the social and public good that are binding insofar as they are subject to rational justification and are practiced concretely.

Yet it is precisely the notion of a "qualified defence of essentialism" (Okin 1995, p. 275), and a global ethical discourse grounded in principles of justice and rights for women *qua* women, that other feminist theorists of local and global cultures wish to counter (e.g., Lazreg 1988, Spivak 1988, Moghadam 1989, Trinh 1990, Mohanty 1991, al-Hibri 1999, Honig 1999, Euben 2001, Butler 2000b). At the very least, these "culture" scholars raise interpretive, methodological, and political concerns about what constitutes an adequate representation of women *qua* women, or a justifiable understanding of cultural practices different from one's own, or an appreciation of context, especially with regard to women of the Second and Third Worlds. The very terms that create an opposition between "women" and "multiculturalism," or reduce multitudes of cultures to a single "-ism," are also matters of concern (Norton 2001). Putnam (1995, p. 311), for example, argues that some feminist universalist projects are vulnerable to charges of "substitutionalism," or, in Alarcón's words (1990, p. 356), a "logic of identi-fication," whereby First World (Anglo-American, middle-class, female) feminist scholars perpetuate the bias of Western theories of justice in the name of all women, especially those not of the West. Correspondingly, other critics charge that uni-versal feminism does not confront "the parochial character of its own norms" or "consider the way in which feminism works in full complicity with U.S. colo-nial aims in imposing norms of civility" on Second and Third World cultures (Butler 2000b, p. 35; see also Ahmed 1992, Smolin 1995–1996, Sassen 1998, al-Hibri 1999).

These responses vividly replay some aspects of the difference/diversity femi-nism debates over the subject, now transferred into the politics of culture and post-colonial theory. In an extension of philosophical discussions of the relation between universalism and particularism, cultural feminists emphasize the importance of dif-ferentiating, along historical and cultural lines, social practices within and across cultures, including oppressive cultural efforts that cut across gender difference (e.g., efforts to control male sexuality) (Honig 1995). A critical feminist theory geared toward emancipation must, these feminists argue, be willing to get its hands dirty by creating concrete historical genealogies. For the universalists who wish to defend the gender binary as a category of analysis and identify inequality between the sexes as the principal aim of "most cultures" (Okin 1999, p. 13), however, these directives toward contextual specificity and respect for cultural differences threaten to slide into relativisms that claim "all cultures are equally valid" (MacKinnon 2000, p. 699) or to converge "with the positions of reaction, oppression, and sex-ism" (Nussbaum 1995, p. 66; 2000).

In sum, despite efforts to the contrary (Okin 1999), the universalist tendency to interpret the cultural feminist suspicion of regulative normative ideals as the equivalent of a nihilistic, radical relativism, and the culturalist tendency to interpret the universalist appeal to abstract moral principles as the replay of Western hegemonic imperialism, have not eased the tension between feminism and multiculturalism in theory or in practice. Although this controversy between universalist and cultural feminists may appear to be headed toward a version of the equality/difference impasse, newly emerging projects within feminist theory seek to restage the concept of the universal (e.g., Zerilli 1998a, Butler 2000b) and explore the paradoxical aspects of the discourse of rights (Scott 1996, Brown 2000) in poststructuralist terms that neither simply reinscribe nor completely abandon Western discourses of modernity. Some of these projects recognize the complexity and discursive ambiguity that constitute the political struggles occurring within the gap between ideal consensus and nihilism, or between "recalcitrant cultural practices and abstract moral principles" (Euben 2001, p. 891). Hence, the aim of this dimension of critical feminist theory is to investigate how concrete, historical struggles employ both universal and cultural discursive strategies with a view toward social justice and freedom.

DEBATING DEMOCRATIC DISCOURSES

In recent years, political theorists have been engaged in debates about what it might mean to conceptualize a feminist political praxis that is aligned with democracy but does not begin from the binary of gender. Along these lines, Mouffe (1992, pp. 376, 378; 1993), for example, proposes a feminist conception of democratic citizenship that would render sexual difference "effectively nonpertinent." Perhaps the most salient feature of such conceptions is the turn toward plurality, which posits democratic society as a field of interaction where multiple axes of difference, identity, and subordination politicize and intersect (e.g., Phelan 1994; Young 1990, 1997b, 2000; Benhabib 1992; Honig 1992; Ferguson 1993; Phillips 1993, 1995; Mouffe 1993; Yeatman 1994, 1998; Bickford 1996; Dean 1996; Fraser 1997; Nash 1998; Heyes 2000; McAfee 2000). Although these theorists tend to share a conception of democratic politics that begins with the reality of adversarial interaction and conflict, they nevertheless exhibit considerable divergences in outlook when it comes to theorizing democratic politics. At issue in each of these outlooks, however, is not so much the legal-juridical question of how to safeguard differences or the institutional question of how to represent them (but see Phillips 1995, Young 2000), but rather the question of what it means to actualize public spaces and enact democratic politics.

Feminist theorists of democratic plurality roughly differentiate along two lines of concern. The associational approaches (see Dietz 2002, pp. 136–37) are closer to the epistemological project of diversity feminism, since they tend to begin from "politicized identity" (Brown 1995, p. 69) and then theorize (democratic) politics in terms of the proliferation, negotiation, and coordination of multiple, intersecting identities, selves, or groups. Associational projects are especially interested in the "politics of recognition" (Fraser 1997) and the conditions necessary to achieve truly democratic discourse, communicative interaction, and solidarity (Fraser 1986; Young 1990, 1997b; Phillips 1995; Benhabib 1996; Bickford 1996; McAfee 2000). From this position, they contribute importantly to the expanding literatures concerning democratic deliberation.

In contrast, agonistic approaches reject identity-based formulations and are more closely related to projects of deconstruction. They theorize politics as a persistently constitutive antagonism that is disruptive and potentially subversive; thus, singular identities such as "women," or even multiple identities such as "*la mestiza*," are never pre-articulated but rather are the productions of speech and articulation, constantly vulnerable to contestation, transformation, and destabilizing maneuvers as performativity (Honig 1992; Mouffe 1992, 1993; Brown 1995; Butler 1997b,c; Zerilli 1998b). Thus, the category of women "is the empty signifier"—not the subject that precedes its claim, but the "articulation of a political identity" (Zerilli 1998a, p. 19). Although they theorize speech, discourse, and language as sites of signification, power, and performance, agonistic approaches do not thematize conditions for political deliberation or coalition politics, nor do they advance theoretical arguments concerning agreement, consensus, or even communicative competence within the field of democratic politics. Instead, they emphasize the dynamics of "democratic equivalence" (Mouffe 1992, p. 381) and "performative freedom" (Honig 1992, p. 226; 1993) that, through action, agonistically generate new and unpredictable identities. [Indicative of the interpretive elasticity of some political theory texts is the fact that both associational and agonistic theorists draw inspiration from Arendt (see Honig 1995, Dietz 2002), even as the former also exhibit affinities with Habermas whereas the latter acknowledge debts to Foucault, and sometimes to Wittgenstein (Mouffe 1992, Zerilli 1998b, Heyes 2000).]

Among the associational theorists, Young (1990, pp. 10, 167, 184) is best known for formulating "the politics of group assertion," and the concepts of "group differentiated citizenship" and the "heterogeneous public," all of which she mobilizes to call for political mechanisms that will provide effective recognition and representation within the public sphere of constituent groups that are disadvantaged, marginalized, or oppressed. Young's political thought is perhaps the paradigmatic example of the effort to theorize (and stabilize) group difference and representation. However, it has been criticized by feminist democratic theorists of plurality who question the very effort to totalize, unify, or essentialize a "social group" (Phillips 1993, Mouffe 1993, Bickford 1996, Narayan 1997, Yuval-Davis 1997), particularly in ways that suppress differences within groups (Lister 1997) or do not adequately distinguish between identity and social position (Bickford 1999) or between cultural and economic concerns (Fraser 1997), or ways that threaten simply to recapitulate interest-group pluralism rather than political solidarity (Mouffe 1992, also Dean 1996). (For a social difference feminist critique of identity group politics, see Elshtain 1995.) At issue in these critiques of group identity or differentiation and the claims that emerge from them is a question of central importance to any theory that, in the wake of late twentieth-century social movements, considers itself committed to a democratic project: Exactly what distinguishes a truly emancipatory struggle for identity or recognition and distinguishes it from a useless distraction, a bourgeois mystification, a solipsistic celebration, or a "wounded attachment" (Brown 1995, p. 52)? This question (and even the legitimacy of asking it) presses particularly hard both among and between associational and agonistic feminist theorists, who often disagree vehemently not only about what constitutes an adequate formulation of identitarian claims to justice or freedom but also about the very priority, centrality, and connectedness of some struggles of resistance in relation to others. How systematically to theorize this matter is also subject to dispute. Fraser (1997), for example, argues that the cultural politics of "recognition" has eclipsed the economic politics of "redistribution," and she seeks to realign the balance between them. Both Young (1997a) and Butler (1997c) criticize Fraser's distinction as overly schematized and inadequately attentive to the political potentiality of identity-based struggles as well as to culture as a key site of resistance.

Whatever the efficacy of a concept of group difference or the priority of a politics of recognition, a turn to models of a heterogeneous public, subaltern counterpublics, or a dispersed network of many publics (Benhabib 1996, p. 83; Fraser 1997) has moved feminist associational projects of democracy directly onto the broad "publicist" terrain of deliberative democracy and discourse ethics. Here, debates about what constitutes emancipatory, communicative interaction, democratic "talk," and, more specifically, adequate processes and procedures for adjudicating rights, needs, and beliefs have galvanized the attention of theorists of democracy, multiculturalism, nationalism, and postcolonialism. Always alert to the ways in which seemingly egalitarian structures and practices can mask or legitimate domination and exclusion, feminist democratic theory brings a critical eye to the deliberative and discursive public sphere (Mansbridge 1990, Lara 1998, Lugones 2000). The contributions of Benhabib (1992) and Fraser (1989, 1992) are noteworthy because both, despite important theoretical differences (see Benhabib et al. 1995), have advanced critiques of liberal models of the bourgeois public in favor of discourse or dialogic models that envision democratic and feminist possibilities. Other associational theorists seek to counter the domination embedded within certain modes of (theorizing) communication by augmenting discursive intersubjectivity with complementary forms of dialogic interaction, including greeting, rhetoric, and storytelling (Young 1997b, Lara 1998), testimony (Sanders 1997), and listening (Bickford 1996). In this mode, some associational democratic feminists incline to theorize political discourse in an interpretive frame that recalls diversity feminism's attention to relational subjectivity (McAfee 2000), as well as personal life narratives, experiential storytelling, and the partial critical perspectives of minority or Third World women (Lara 1998, Ackerly 2000). Others advance models of discourse that forward deliberative reasoning, argumentation, critical scrutiny, and the exercise of political judgment (Benhabib 1996, McAfee 2000). Hence, the necessary discursive and procedural elements within the democratic public sphere, if not the normative priority of communicative over strategic action, remain matters of discussion and disagreement among associational democratic feminists.

The issues that perhaps loom largest between associational and agonistic theories of politics, however, involve the emancipatory quality of language or discourse as politics (nearly all of the associational and agonistic theorists eschew the psychosymbolic structural models of language that inform French feminism; see Fraser 1992). Butler (1997b), whose deconstruction feminism surfaces in other texts as agonistic democratic political theory, distances her own speech-act approach from the procedural and modified Habermasian conception of public sphere deliberative politics favored by Benhabib (1996; also see Kohn 2000, Webster 2000) and amended by Young (2000). As "agonists," Butler (1997b) and Mouffe (2000) believe that the formation of subject positions necessarily takes place within complex webs of power relations that also mark permanent diversity within the semantic field. In this agonistic view (which does not begin by aligning politics with a public communicative space of interaction), politics is essentially a practice of creation, reproduction, transformation, and articulation (not coalition), wherein the rules of the game, as well as the players, are never fully explicit, stable, or fixed; and they are always constituted through acts of power (Mouffe 2000). The agonistic position asserts that the main question for democratic politics is not how to eliminate power or aspire to undistorted communication, but rather "how to constitute forms of power more compatible with democratic values" (Mouffe 2000, p. 100). Thus, agonists eschew projects that analyze the conditions surrounding and the procedures embodied in participatory communicative contexts, on the grounds that these projects misconstrue language and evade rather than confront the constitutive nature of power. Finally, within this account of power, the agonist locates the subject "neither as a ground nor a product, but the permanent possibility of a certain resignifying process" (Butler 1995a, p. 47). Simply put, associational feminists scrutinize the conditions of exclusion in order to theorize the emancipation of the subject in the public sphere of communicative interaction; agonistic feminists deconstruct emancipatory procedures to disclose how the subject is both produced through political exclusions and positioned against them.

This contrast in democratic theorizing brings us back to the central issue of contemporary feminist political theory: the status of the subject as a point of departure for feminist political theorizing. We return, that is, to the question of whether it is possible or desirable to determine a ground of the subject in feminism. And although one political theorist has suggested that it is time "to break the spell" that this epistemic picture holds over feminist theory and feminist politics (Zerilli 1998b, p. 455), this release is unlikely to occur anytime soon. Can feminist theory abandon its fixation on settling (and unsettling) the subject without giving up on feminism as an emancipatory political movement? Can feminism live without an ideal theory that provides regulative criteria for interpretation and political action? For now, responses to these questions exist only within the contestations that are the reality, and the vitality, of contemporary theories of feminism.

The *Annual Review of Political Science* is online at
http://polisci.annualreviews.org

LITERATURE CITED

Ackerly BA. 2000. *Political Theory and Feminist Social Criticism.* Cambridge, UK: Cambridge Univ. Press

Ackerly BA, Okin S. 1999. Feminist social criticism and the international movement for women's rights as human rights. In *Democracy's Edges*, ed. I Shapiro, C Hacker-Cordón, pp. 134–62. Cambridge, UK: Cambridge Univ. Press

Acklesberg M. 1997. Rethinking anarchism/rethinking power: a contemporary feminist perspective. See Shanley & Narayan 1997, pp. 158–77

Adams P, Minson J. 1990. The "subject" of feminism. In *The Woman in Question*, ed. P Adams, E Cowie, pp. 81–101. Cambridge, MA: MIT Press

Ahmed L. 1992. *Women and Gender in Islam: Historical Roots of a Modern Debate.* New Haven, CT: Yale Univ. Press

Alarcon N. 1990. The theoretical subject(s) of *This Bridge Called My Back* and Anglo-American feminism. See Anzaldúa 1990, pp. 356–69

Alcoff L. 1988. Cultural feminism versus post-structuralism: the identity crisis in feminist theory. *Signs J. Women Culture Soc.* 13:405–36

Alcoff L, Potter E, eds. 1993. *Feminist Epistemologies.* New York/London: Routledge

Alexander MJ, Mohanty CT. 1997. *Feminist Genealogies, Colonial Legacies, Democratic Futures.* New York/London: Routledge

al-Hibri A. 1999. Is western patriarchal feminism good for third world/minority women? See Okin 1999, pp. 4146

Anzaldúa GE. 1987. *Borderlands/La Frontera.* San Francisco: Aunt Lute Books

Anzaldúa GE, ed. 1990. *Making Face, Making Soul/Haciendo Caras.* San Francisco: Aunt Lute Fdn.

Anzaldúa GE, Keating A, eds. 2002. *This Bridge We Call Home: Radical Visions for Transformation.* New York: Routledge

Arneil B. 1999. *Politics and Feminism.* Oxford, UK: Blackwell

Benhabib S. 1992. *Situating the Self: Gender, Community and Postmodernism in Contemporary Ethics.* New York: Routledge

Benhabib S. 1995a. Feminism and postmodernism: an uneasy alliance. See Benhabib et al. 1995, pp. 17–34

Benhabib S. 1995b. Cultural complexity, moral interdependence, and the global dialogical community. See Nussbaum & Glover 1995, pp. 235–55

Benhabib S. 1996. Toward a deliberative model of democratic legitimacy. In *Democracy and Difference: Contesting the Boundaries of the Political*, ed. S Benhabib, pp. 67–94. Princeton, NJ: Princeton Univ. Press

Benhabib S. 2002. *The Claims of Culture: Equality and Diversity in the Global Era.* Princeton, NJ: Princeton Univ. Press

Benhabib S, Butler J, Cornell D, Fraser N. 1995. *Feminist Contentions: a Philosophical Exchange.* New York: Routledge

Berger A-E. 1998. The newly veiled woman: Irigaray, specularity and the Islamic veil. *diacritics* 28:93–119

Bickford S. 1996. *The Dissonance of Democracy: Listening, Conflict, and Citizenship.* Ithaca, NY: Cornell Univ. Press

Bickford S. 1999. Reconfiguring pluralism: identity and institutions in the inequalitarian polity. *Am. J. Polit. Sci.* 43:86–108

Bock G, James S, eds. 1992. *Beyond Equality and Difference.* London: Routledge

Boling P. 1996. *Privacy and the Politics of Intimate Life.* Ithaca, NY: Cornell Univ. Press

Bordo S. 1990. Feminism, postmodernism, and gender-scepticism. See Nicholson 1990, pp. 133–56

Braidotti R. 1991. *Patterns of Dissonance:*

a *Study of Women in Contemporary Philosophy.* Transl. E Guild. New York: Routledge

Braidotti R. 1994. *Nomadic Subjects: Embodiment and Sexual Difference in Contemporary Feminist Theory.* New York: Columbia Univ. Press

Brennan T, ed. 1989. *Between Feminism and Psychoanalysis.* London: Routledge

Brown W. 1988. *Manhood and Politics: a Feminist Reading in Political Theory.* Totowa, NJ: Rowman & Allenheld

Brown W. 1995. *States of Injury.* Princeton, NJ: Princeton Univ. Press

Brown W. 1997. The impossibility of women's studies. *Differences* 9:79–101

Brown W. 2000. Rights as paradoxes. *Constellations* 7:230–41

Bubeck D. 1995. *Care, Gender, and Justice.* Oxford, UK: Clarendon

Burke C. 1981. Irigaray through the looking glass. *Fem. Stud.* 7:288–306

Burke C, Schor N, Whitford M, ed. 1994. *Engaging with Irigaray.* New York: Columbia Univ. Press

Butler J. 1986. Sex and gender in Simone de Beauvoir's *Second Sex. Yale Fr. Stud.* 72:35–49

Butler J. 1987. Variations on sex and gender: Beauvoir, Wittig, and Foucault. In *Feminism as Critique: on the Politics of Gender,* ed. S Benhabib, D Cornell, pp. 128–42. Minneapolis: Univ. Minn. Press

Butler J. 1990. *Gender Trouble: Feminism and the Subversion of Identity.* New York: Routledge

Butler J. 1991. Imitation and gender insubordination. In *Inside/Out: Lesbian Theories, Gay Theories,* ed. D Fuss, pp. 13–31. New York: Routledge

Butler J. 1993. *Bodies That Matter: on the Discursive Limits of "Sex."* New York: Routledge

Butler J. 1994. Against proper objects. *Differences* 6:1–26

Butler J. 1995a. Contingent foundations: feminism and the question of "postmodernism." See Benhabib et al. 1995, pp. 35–58

Butler J. 1995b. For a careful reading. See Benhabib et al. 1995, pp. 127–44

Butler J. 1996. Gender as performance. In *A Critical Sense: Interviews with Intellectuals,* ed. P Osborne, pp. 109–26. London/New York: Routledge

Butler J. 1997a. *The Psychic Life of Power: Theories in Subjection.* Stanford, CA: Stanford Univ. Press

Butler J. 1997b. *Excitable Speech: a Politics of the Performative.* New York: Routledge

Butler J. 1997c. Merely cultural. *Soc. Text* 52–53:279–89

Butler J. 2000a. *Antigone's Claim: Kinship Between Life and Death.* New York: Columbia Univ. Press

Butler J. 2000b. Restaging the universal: hegemony and the limits of formalism. In *Contingency, Hegemony, Universality: Contemporary Dialogues on the Left,* ed. J Butler, E Laclau, S Žižek, pp. 11–43. London: Verso

Butler J, Scott JW, eds. 1992. *Feminists Theorize the Political.* New York: Routledge

Campbell R. 1998. *Illusions of Paradox: a Feminist Epistemology.* Lanham, MD: Rowman & Littlefield

Carby H. 1987. *Reconstructing Womanhood: the Emergence of the Afro-American Woman Novelist.* Oxford, UK: Oxford Univ. Press

Card C. 1995. *Lesbian Choices.* New York: Columbia Univ. Press

Carver T. 1996. *Gender is Not a Synonym for Women.* Boulder/London: Lynne Rienner

Cavarero A. 1992. Equality and sexual difference: amnesia in political thought. See Bock & James 1992, pp. 32–47

Cheah P, Grosz E. 1998. The future of sexual difference: an interview with Judith Butler and Drucilla Cornell. *diacritics* 28:19–42

Chen M. 1995. A matter of survival: women's right to employment in India and Bangladesh. See Nussbaum & Glover 1995, pp. 37–57

Chodorow N. 1978. *The Reproduction of Mothering.* Berkeley: Univ. Calif. Press

Christian B. 1988. The race for theory. *Fem. Stud.* 14:67–79

Cixous H. 1976. The laugh of the Medusa.

Transl. K Cohen, P. Cohen. *Signs* 1:875–93

Clough P. 1994. *Feminist Thought: Desire, Power, and Academic Discourse.* Oxford, UK: Blackwell

Code L. 1991. *What Can She Know? Feminist Theory and the Construction of Knowledge.* New York: Routledge

Collins PH. 1991. *Black Feminist Thought: Knowledge, Consciousness and the Politics of Empowerment.* New York: Routledge

Collins PH. 1997. Comment on Hekman's 'Truth and method:feminist standpoint theory revisited': truth of justice? *Signs* 22:375–81

Coole DH. 1993. *Women in Political Theory: from Ancient Misogyny to Contemporary Feminism.* Boulder, CO: Lynne Rienner; Brighton, UK: Harvester/Wheatsheaf. 2nd ed.

Coole DH. 1994. Whither feminisms? *Polit. Stud.* 42:128–34

Cornell D. 1991. *Beyond Accommodation: Ethical Feminism, Deconstruction and the Law.* New York: Routledge

Cornell D. 1992. Gender, sex, and equivalent rights. See Butler & Scott 1992, pp. 280–96

Cornell D. 1995. *The Imaginary Domain: Abortion, Pornography and Sexual Harassment.* New York: Routledge

Cott N. 1986. Feminist theory and feminist movements: the past before us. In *What is Feminism: a Re-Examination*, ed. J Mitchell, A Oakley, pp. 49–62. New York: Pantheon Books

Daly M. 1978. *Gyn/Ecology: the Metaethics of Radical Feminism.* Boston: Beacon

de Beauvoir S. 1949. *The Second Sex.* Transl. H Parshley, 1953. New York: Knopf

de Lauretis T. 1987. *Technologies of Gender: Essays on Theory, Film, and Fiction.* Bloomington/Indianapolis: Indiana Univ. Press

de Lauretis T. 1990. Eccentric subjects: feminist theory and historical consciousness. *Fem. Stud.* 16:115–50

Dean J. 1996. *Solidarity of Strangers.* Berkeley: Univ. Calif. Press

Delphy C. 1984. *Close to Home: a Materialist Analysis of Women's Oppression.* Transl. D. Leonard. London: Hutchinson

Deutscher P. 1997. *Yielding Gender: Feminism, Deconstruction and the History of Philosophy.* London: Routledge

Dietz MG. 1985. Citizenship with a feminist face: the problem with maternal thinking. *Polit. Theory* 13:19–38

Dietz MG. 1987. Context is all: feminism and theories of citizenship. *Daedalus* 116:1–24

Dietz MG. 2002. *Turning Operations: Feminism, Arendt, and Politics.* New York: Routledge

Di Stefano C. 1990. Dilemmas of difference: feminism, modernity and postmodernism. See Nicholson 1990, pp. 63–82

Di Stefano C. 1991. *Configurations of Masculinity: a Feminist Perspective on Modern Political Theory.* Ithaca, NY: Cornell Univ. Press

Echols A. 1983. The new feminism of yin and yang. In *Powers of Desire: the Politics of Sexuality*, ed. A Snitow, C Stansell, S Thompson, pp. 439–59. New York: Monthly Review

Eisenstein H, Jardine A, eds. 1980. *The Future of Difference.* New Brunswick, NJ: Rutgers Univ. Press

Elshtain JB. 1981. *Public Man, Private Woman: Women in Social and Political Thought.* Princeton, NJ: Princeton Univ. Press

Elshtain JB. 1982. Antigone's daughters. *Democracy* 2:46–59

Elshtain JB. 1987. *Women and War.* New York: Basic Books

Elshtain JB. 1995. *Democracy on Trial.* New York: Basic Books

Euben R. 2001. Review essay on Mamdani and Ackerly. *Polit. Theory* 19:888–95

Fausto-Sterling A. 1985. *Myths of Gender: Biological Theories About Women and Men.* New York: Basic Books

Ferguson K. 1984. *The Feminist Case Against Bureaucracy.* Philadelphia: Temple Univ. Press

Ferguson K. 1993. *The Man Question: Visions of Subjectivity in Feminist Theory.* Berkeley/Los Angeles/Oxford: Univ. Calif. Press

Fermon N. 1998. Women on the global market:

Irigaray and the democratic state. *diacritics* 28:120–37

Flax J. 1980. Mother-daughter relationships: psychodynamics, politics and philosophy. See Eisenstein & Jardine 1980, pp. 20–40

Flax J. 1990. *Thinking Fragments: Psychoanalysis, Feminism and Postmodernism in the Contemporary West.* Berkeley: Univ. Calif. Press

Fraser N. 1986. Toward a discourse ethic of solidarity. *Praxis Int.* 5:425–29

Fraser N. 1989. *Unruly Practices: Power, Discourse and Gender in Contemporary Social Theory.* Minneapolis, MN: Univ. Minn. Press

Fraser N. 1992. The uses and abuses of French discourse theories for feminist politics. See Fraser & Bartky 1992, pp. 177–94

Fraser N. 1995. False antitheses. See Benhabib et al. 1995, pp. 59–74

Fraser N. 1997. *Justice Interruptus: Critical Reflections on the "Postsocialist" Condition.* New York/London: Routledge

Fraser N, Bartky SL, eds. 1992. *Revaluing French Feminism: Critical Essays on Difference, Agency, & Culture.* Bloomington/Indianapolis: Indiana Univ. Press

Fraser N, Nicholson L. 1990. Social criticism without philosophy: an encounter between feminism and postmodernism. See Nicholson 1990, pp. 19–38

Friedan B. 1963. *The Feminine Mystique.* Harmondsworth, UK: Penguin

Fuss D. 1989. *Essentially Speaking: Feminism, Nature, and Difference.* New York: Routledge

Fuss D. 1992. "Essentially speaking": Luce Irigaray's language of essence. See Fraser & Bartky 1992, pp. 94–112

Gallop J. 1982. *The Daughter's Seduction: Feminism and Psychoanalysis.* Ithaca, NY: Cornell Univ. Press

Gilligan C. 1982. *In a Different Voice: Psychological Theory and Women's Development.* Cambridge, MA: Harvard Univ. Press

Gilligan C, Ward JV, Taylor JM, with Bardige B, eds. 1988. *Mapping the Moral Domain: a Contribution of Women's Thinking to Psychology and Education.* Cambridge, MA: Harvard Univ. Grad. School Educ.

Grant J. 1993. *Fundamental Feminism.* New York/London: Routledge

Grosz E. 1989. *Sexual Subversions: Three French Feminists.* Sydney: Allen & Unwin

Grosz E. 1994. *Volatile Bodies: Toward a Corporeal Feminism.* Bloomington: Indiana Univ. Press

Gunew S. 1991. *A Reader in Feminist Knowledge.* New York: Routledge

Haraway D. 1988. Situated knowledges: the science question in feminism and the privilege of partial perspective. *Fem. Stud.* 14:575–99

Haraway D. 1990. A manifesto for cyborgs: science, technology and socialist feminism in the 1980s. See Nicholson 1990, pp. 190–233

Haraway D. 1991. *Simians, Cyborgs and Women: the Reinvention of Nature.* New York: Routledge

Harding S. 1986. *The Science Question in Feminism.* Ithaca, NY: Cornell Univ. Press

Harding S. 1987a. The instability of analytical categories in feminist theory. *Signs* 11:645–64

Harding S, ed. 1987b. *Feminism and Methodology.* Bloomington: Indiana Univ. Press

Harding S. 1991. *Whose Science? Whose Knowledge? Thinking from Women's Lives.* Ithaca, NY: Cornell Univ. Press

Hartsock N. 1983. *Money, Sex and Power.* London: Longman

Hartsock N. 1987. The feminist standpoint: developing the ground for a specifically feminist historical materialism. See Harding 1987b, pp. 157–80

Hartsock N. 1990. Foucault on power: a theory for women? See Nicholson 1994, pp. 157–75

Hartsock N. 1997. Comment on Hekman's "Truth and Method: Feminist Standpoint Theory Revisited": truth or justice? *Signs* 22:367–74

Hartsock N. 1998. *The Feminist Standpoint Revisited and Other Essays.* Oxford, UK: Westview

Hawkesworth M. 1989. Knowers, knowing, known: feminist theory and claims of truth. *Signs* (14):533–57

Hekman SJ. 1990. *Gender and Knowledge: Elements of a Postmodern Feminism.* Boston: Northeastern Univ. Press

Hekman SJ. 1997. Truth and method: feminist standpoint theory revisited. *Signs* 22:341–65

Hekman SJ. 1999. *The Future of Differences: Truth and Method in Feminist Theory.* Cambridge, UK: Polity

Held V. 1990. Mothering v. contract. In *Beyond Self-Interest*, ed. J Mansbridge, pp. 287–304. Chicago: Univ. Chicago Press

Heyes CJ. 2000. *Line Drawings: Defining Women Through Feminist Practice.* Ithaca/London: Cornell Univ. Press

Hirschmann NJ. 1992. *Rethinking Obligation: a Feminist Method for Political Theory.* Ithaca/London: Cornell Univ. Press

Honig B. 1992. Toward an agonistic feminism: Hannah Arendt and the politics of identity. See Butler & Scott 1992, pp. 215–35

Honig B. 1993. *Political Theory and the Displacement of Politics.* Ithaca, NY: Cornell Univ. Press

Honig B, ed. 1995. *Feminist Interpretations of Hannah Arendt.* University Park: Penn. State Univ. Press

Honig B. 1999. "My culture made me do it." See Okin 1999, pp. 35–40

hooks b. 1981. *Ain't I a Woman? Black Women and Feminism.* Boston: South End

hooks b. 1984. *Feminist Theory from Margin to Center.* Boston: South End

hooks b. 1989. *Talking Back: Thinking Feminist, Thinking Black.* Boston: South End

hooks b. 1990. *Yearning: Race, Gender and Cultural Politics.* Boston: South End

Hull GT, Scott PB, Smith B, ed. 1982. *All the Women Are White, All the Blacks Are Men, But Some of Us Are Brave: Black Women's Studies.* Old Westbury, NY: Feminist

Irigaray L. 1985a. *Speculum of the Other Woman.* Transl. G Gill. Ithaca, NY: Cornell Univ. Press

Irigaray L. 1985b. *This Sex Which is Not One.* Transl. C Porter. Ithaca, NY: Cornell Univ. Press

Irigaray L. 1993. *An Ethics of Sexual Differ-*

ence. Transl. G Gill, C Burke. Ithaca, NY: Cornell Univ. Press

Irigaray L. 1994. *Thinking the Difference: for a Peaceful Revolution.* Transl. K Montin. New York: Routledge

Irigaray L. 1996. *I Love to You: Sketch of a Possible Felicity in History.* Transl. A Martin. New York: Routledge

Jaggar A. 1983. *Feminist Politics and Human Nature.* Brighton, UK: Harvester

Jaggar A. 1998. Globalizing feminist ethics. *Hypatia* 13:7–31

Jaggar A, Bordo S. 1989. *Gender/Body/Knowledge: Feminist Reconstructions of Being and Knowing.* New Brunswick, NJ/London: Rutgers Univ. Press

Jones KB. 1988. Towards the revision of politics. In *The Political Interests of Gender*, ed. KB Jones, AG Jonasdottir, pp. 11–32. Chicago: Sage

Jones KB. 1990. Citizenship in a woman-friendly polity. *Signs* 15:781–812

Keller EF. 1984. *Reflections on Gender and Science.* New Haven, CT: Yale Univ. Press

Klein E. 1986. *Gender Politics: from Consciousness to Mass Politics.* Cambridge, MA: Harvard Univ. Press

Kohn M. 2000. Language, power, and persuasion: toward a critique of deliberative democracy. *Constellations* 7:408–29

Kristeva J. 1980. *Desire in Language: a Semiotic Approach to Art and Literature.* Transl. L Roudiez. New York: Columbia Univ. Press

Kristeva J. 1982. *Powers of Horror: an Essay on Abjection.* Transl. L Roudiez. New York: Columbia Univ. Press

Kristeva J. 1984. *Revolution in Poetic Language.* Transl. M Waller. New York: Columbia Univ. Press

Kristeva J. 1986. Women's time. In *The Kristeva Reader,* ed. T Moi, pp. 187–213. New York: Columbia Univ. Press

Kruks S. 2001. *Retrieving Experience: Subjectivity and Recognition in Feminist Politics.* Ithaca, NY: Cornell Univ. Press

Laquer T. 1990. *Making Sex: Body and Gender from the Greeks to Freud.* Cambridge, MA: Harvard Univ. Press

Lara MP. 1998. *Moral Textures: Feminist Narratives in the Public Sphere.* Cambridge, UK: Cambridge Univ. Press

Lazreg M. 1988. Feminism and difference: the perils of writing as a woman on women in Algeria. *Fem. Issues* 14:81–107

Le Doeuff M. 1989. *The Philosophical Imaginary.* Transl. C Gordon. London: Athlone

Leland D. 1992. Lacanian psychoanalysis and French feminism: toward an adequate political psychology. See Fraser & Bartky 1992, pp. 113–35

Lister R. 1997. *Citizenship: Feminist Perspectives.* Basingstoke, UK: Macmillan

Lloyd G. 1993. *The Man of Reason: 'Male' and 'Female' in Western Philosophy.* London: Routledge

Lorde A. 1984. *Sister/Outsider.* Freedom, CA: Crossing

Lovenduski J. 1998. Gendering research in political science. *Annu. Rev. Polit. Sci.* 1:333–56

Lovibond S. 1989. Feminism and postmodernism. *New Left Rev.* 178:5–28

Lugones MC. 2000. Multiculturalism and publicity. *Hypatia* 15:175–81

Lugones MC, Spelman E. 1983. Have we got a theory for you! Feminist theory, cultural imperialism, and the demand for the women's voice. *Women's Stud. Int. Forum* 6.6:573–81

MacKinnon CA. 1983. Feminism, Marxism, method and the state: an agenda for theory. In *Signs Reader: Women, Gender and Scholarship*, ed. E Abel, EK Abel, pp. 277–56. Chicago: Univ. Chicago Press

MacKinnon CA. 1987. *Feminism Unmodified: Discourses on Life and Law.* Cambridge, MA: Harvard Univ. Press

MacKinnon CA. 1989. *The Feminist Theory of the State.* Cambridge, MA: Harvard Univ. Press

MacKinnon CA. 2000. Points against postmodernism. *Chicago Kent Law Rev.* 75:687–712

Mansbridge J. 1990. Feminism and democracy. *Am. Prospect* 1:117–31

Marks E, de Courtivron I, eds. 1980. *New French Feminisms.* Amherst: Univ. Mass. Press

McAfee N. 2000. *Habermas, Kristeva, and Citizenship.* Ithaca/London: Cornell Univ. Press

Mendus S. 1992. Losing the faith: feminism and democracy. In *Democracy: the Unfinished Journey 508 BC to AD 1993*, ed. J Dunn, pp. 207–19. Oxford, UK: Oxford Univ. Press

Meyers D. 1992. The subversion of women's agency in psychoanalytic feminism: Chodorow, Flax, Kristeva. See Fraser & Bartkey 1992, pp. 136–60

Miller JB. 1976. *Towards a New Psychology of Women.* Boston: Beacon

Millet K. 1970. *Sexual Politics.* New York: Doubleday

Minow M. 1990. *Making All the Difference.* Ithaca, NY: Cornell Univ. Press

Mitchell J. 1973. *Woman's Estate.* Harmondsworth, UK: Penguin

Moghadam V. 1989. Against eurocentrism and nativism. *Soc. Democr.* f/w:81–104

Mohanty CT. 1991. Under western eyes: feminist scholarship and colonial discourses. See Mohanty et al. 1991, pp. 51–80

Mohanty CT, Russo A, Torres L. 1991. *Third World Women and the Politics of Feminism.* Bloomington/Indianapolis: Indiana Univ. Press

Moi T. 1985. *Sexual/Textual Politics.* New York: Methuen

Moi T, ed. 1987. *French Feminist Thought.* Oxford: Blackwell

Moraga C, Anzaldúa G, eds. 1983. *This Bridge Called My Back: Writings by Radical Women of Color.* New York: Kitchen Table, Women of Color Press

Mouffe C. 1992. Feminism, citizenship, and radical democratic politics. See Butler & Scott 1992, pp. 369–84

Mouffe C. 1993. *The Return of the Political.* London: Verso

Mouffe C. 2000. *The Democratic Paradox.* London: Verso

Moya P. 1997. Postmodernism, "realism," and the politics of identity: Cherrie Moraga and Chicana feminsm. See Alexander & Mohanty 1997, pp. 125–50

Narayan U. 1997. Towards a feminist vision of citizenship: rethinking the implications of dignity, political participation and nationality. See Shanley & Narayan 1997, pp. 48–67

Nash K. 1998. Beyond liberalism? Feminist theories of democracy. In *Gender, Politics and the State*, ed. V Randall, G Waylen, pp. 45–57. London/New York: Routledge

Nicholson L, ed. 1990. *Feminism/Postmodernism*. New York: Routledge

Nicholson L. 1994. Interpreting gender. *Signs* 20(1):79–105

Noddings N. 1984. *Caring: a Feminine Approach to Ethics and Moral Education*. Berkeley/Los Angeles: Univ. Calif. Press

Norton A. 2001. Review essay on Euben, Okin, and Nussbaum. *Polit. Theory* 29:736–49

Nussbaum MC. 1995. Human capabilities, female human beings. In *Women, Culture, and Development: a Study of Human Capabilities*, ed. M Nussbaum, J Glover, pp. 61–104. Oxford, UK: Clarendon

Nussbaum MC. 1999a. *Sex and Social Justice*. Oxford, UK: Oxford Univ. Press

Nussbaum MC. 1999b. The professor of parody. *New Repub.* 2/22:37–45

Nussbaum MC. 2000. *Women and Human Development: the Capabilities Approach*. Cambridge, UK: Cambridge Univ. Press

O'Brien M. 1981. *The Politics of Reproduction*. London: Routledge, Kegan & Paul

Okin SM. 1978. *Women in Western Political Thought*. Princeton, NJ: Princeton Univ. Press

Okin SM. 1986. Are our theories of justice gender-neutral? In *The Moral Foundations of Civil Rights,* ed. R Fullinwider, C Mills, pp. 125–43. Totowa, NJ: Rowman & Littlefield

Okin SM. 1998. Feminism, women's human rights, and cultural differences. *Hypatia* 13:32–52

Okin SM. 1989a. *Justice, Gender, and the Family*. New York: Basic Books

Okin SM. 1989b. Reason and feeling in thinking about justice. *Ethics* 99:229–49

Okin SM. 1995. Inequalities between the sexes in different cultural contexts. See Nussbaum & Glover 1995, pp. 274–97

Okin SM. 1999. *Is Multiculturalism Bad for Women?* Princeton, NJ: Princeton Univ. Press

Pateman C. 1988. *The Sexual Contract*. Oxford, UK: Polity

Pateman C. 1989. *The Disorder of Women: Democracy, Feminism and Political Theory*. Stanford, CA: Stanford Univ. Press

Phelan S. 1989. *Identity Politics*. Philadelphia: Temple Univ. Press

Phelan S. 1994. *Getting Specific: Postmodern Lesbian Politics*. Minneapolis, MN: Univ. Minn. Press

Phillips A. 1991. *Engendering Democracy*. University Park, PA: Penn. State Univ. Press

Phillips A. 1993. *Democracy and Difference*. University Park, PA: Penn. State Univ. Press

Phillips A. 1995. *The Politics of Presence*. Oxford, UK: Clarendon

Pitkin H. 1984. *Fortune is a Woman: Gender and Politics in the Thought of Niccolo Machiavelli*. Berkeley/Los Angeles: Univ. Calif. Press

Plaza M. 1978. "Phallomorphic power" and the psychology of "woman." *Ideol. Conscious.* 4:57–76

Putnam R. 1995. Why not a feminist theory of justice? In Nussbaum & Glover 1995, pp. 298–331

Rich A. 1976. *Of Woman Born: Motherhood as Experience and Institution*. New York: Norton

Rich A. 1983. Compulsory heterosexuality and lesbian existence. In *The Signs Reader: Women, Gender and Scholarship*, ed. E Abel, EK Abel, pp. 139–68. Chicago: Univ. Chicago Press

Riley D. 1988. *"Am I That Name?" Feminism and the Category of "Women" in History*. Minneapolis: Univ. Minn. Press

Rohde D. 1989. *Justice and Gender*. Cambridge, MA: Harvard Univ. Press

Rose H. 1983. Hand, brain and heart: a feminist epistemology for the natural sciences. *Signs* 9:73–90

Rowbotham S. 1992. *Woman's Consciousness: Man's World*. Harmondsworth, UK: Penguin

Rubin G. 1975. The traffic in women: notes on

the "political economy" of sex. In *Toward an Anthropology of Women*, ed. R Reiter, pp. 157–210. New York: Monthly Review

Ruddick S. 1989. *Maternal Thinking: Towards a Politics of Peace*. Boston: Beacon

Sandoval C. 1991. US third world feminism: the theory and method of oppositional consciousness in the postmodern world. *Genders* 10:1–24

Sanders L. 1997. Against deliberation. *Polit. Theory* 25:347–76

Sassen S. 1998. *Globalization and Its Discontents*. New York: New

Scheman N. 1993. *Engenderings: Constructions of Knowledge, Authority, and Privilege*. New York/London: Routledge

Schiebinger LL. 1989. *The Mind Has No Sex? Women in the Origins of Modern Science*. Cambridge, MA: Harvard Univ. Press

Schwab G. 1998. Sexual difference as model: an ethics for the global future. *diacritics* 28:76–92

Scott J. 1988a. Gender: a useful category of historical analysis. In *Gender and the Politics of History*, ed. J Scott, pp. 28–52. New York: Columbia Univ. Press

Scott J. 1988b. Deconstructing equality-versus-difference: or the uses of poststructuralist theory for feminism. *Fem. Stud.* 14:33–50

Scott J. 1992. Experience. See Butler & Scott 1992, pp. 22–40

Scott J. 1996. *Only Paradoxes to Offer: French Feminists and the Rights of Man*. Cambridge, MA: Harvard Univ. Press

Sevenhuijsen S. 1998. Paradoxes of gender: ethical and epistemological perspectives on care in feminist political theory. *Acta Polit.* 28:139–49

Shachar A. 1998. Group identity and women's rights in family law: the perils of multicultural accommodation. *J. Polit. Phil.* 6:285–305

Shanley ML, Pateman C, eds. 1990. *Feminist Interpretations and Political Theory*. Cambridge, MA: Polity

Shanley M, Narayan U, eds. 1997. *Reconstructing Political Theory: Feminist Perspectives*. University Park: Penn. State Univ. Press

Smiley M. 1992. *Moral Responsibility and the Boundaries of Community*. Chicago: Univ. Chicago Press

Smith B, ed. 1983. *Home Girls: a Black Feminist Anthology*. New York: Kitchen Table, Women of Color Press

Smith D. 1987. *The Everyday World as Problematic: a Feminist Sociology*. Boston: Northeastern Univ. Press

Smolin D. 1995–1996. Will international human rights be used as a tool of cultural genocide? The interaction of human rights norms, religion, culture and gender. *J. Law Relig.* 12:143–71

Snitow A. 1989. Pages from a gender diary: basic divisions in feminism. *Dissent* 36:205–224

Spelman EV. 1989. *Inessential Woman: Problems of Exclusion in Feminist Thought*. Boston: Beacon

Spinner-Halev J. 2001. Feminism, multiculturalism, oppression, and the state. *Ethics* 112:84–113

Spivak GC. 1988. *In Other Worlds: Essays in Cultural Politics*. New York: Routledge

Tickner A. 1992. *Gender in IR: Feminist Perspectives on Achieving Global Security*. New York: Columbia Univ. Press

Trinh TMh. 1989. *Woman, Native, Other: Writing Postcoloniality and Feminism*. Bloomington: Indiana Univ. Press

Trinh TMh. 1990. Not you/like you: postcolonial women and the interlocking questions of identity and difference. See Anzaldua 1990, pp. 371–75

Tong R. 1989. *Feminist Thought: a Comprehensive Introduction*. Boulder, CO: Westview

Tronto JC. 1987. Beyond gender difference to a theory of care. *Signs* 12:644–63

Tronto JC. 1989. Women and caring: What can feminists learn about morality from caring? See Jaggar & Bordo 1989, pp. 172–87

Tronto JC. 1993. *Moral Boundaries: a Political Argument for an Ethic of Care*. New York/London: Routledge

Walker MU. 1998. *Moral Understandings: a Feminist Study in Ethics*. New York/London: Routledge

Webster F. 2000. The politics of sex and gender: Benhabib and Butler debate subjectivity. *Hypatia* 15:1–22

Weeks K. 1998. *Constituting Feminist Subjects.* Ithaca, NY: Cornell Univ. Press

Whitford M. 1991. *Luce Irigaray: Philosophy in the Feminine.* London: Routledge

Wittig M. 1976. *The Lesbian Body.* Transl. P Owen. New York: Avon

Wittig M. 1980. The straight mind. *Fem. Issues* 1:47–54

Yeatman A. 1994. *Postmodern Revisions of the Political.* New York: Routledge

Yeatman A. 1998. Feminism and citizenship. In *Cultural Citizenship*, ed. N Stevenson, pp. 138–52. New York/London: Routledge

Young IM. 1981. Beyond the unhappy marriage: a critique of the dual systems theory. In *Women and Revolution: a Discussion of the Unhappy Marriage of Marxism and Feminism,* ed. L Sargent, pp. 43–69. Montreal: Black Rose Books

Young IM. 1990. *Justice and the Politics of Difference.* Princeton, NJ: Princeton Univ. Press

Young IM. 1997a. Unruly categories: a critique of Nancy Fraser's dual systems theory. *New Left Rev.* 222:147–60

Young IM. 1997b. *Intersecting Voices: Dilemmas of Gender, Political Philosophy and Policy.* Princeton, NJ: Princeton Univ. Press

Young IM. 2000. *Inclusion and Democracy.* Oxford, UK: Oxford Univ. Press

Yuval-Davis N. 1997. *Gender and Nation.* London: Sage

Zakin E. 2000. Bridging the social and the symbolic: toward a feminist politics of sexual difference. *Hypatia* 15:19–44

Zerilli LMG. 1994. *Signifying Woman: Culture and Chaos in Rousseau, Burke and Mill.* Ithaca, NY: Cornell Univ. Press

Zerilli LMG. 1998a. This universalism which is not one. *diacritics* 28:3–20

Zerilli LMG. 1998b. Doing without knowing: feminism's politics of the ordinary. *Polit. Theory* 26:435–58

Zerilli LMG. 2000. Feminism's flight from the ordinary. In *Vocations of Political Theory*, ed. J Frank, J Tambornino, pp. 166–86. Minneapolis/London: Univ. Minn. Press

Annu. Rev. Polit. Sci. 2003. 6:433–71
doi: 10.1146/annurev.polisci.6.121901.085659
Copyright © 2003 by Annual Reviews. All rights reserved
First published online as a Review in Advance on Mar. 6, 2003

HERBERT A. SIMON: Political Scientist

Jonathan Bendor

*Graduate School of Business, Stanford University, Stanford, California 94305;
email: bendor_jonathan@gsb.stanford.edu*

Key Words   bounded rationality, research program, heuristics

■ **Abstract**   Although Herbert Simon's work is often cited by political scientists, it
has not generated a large research program in the discipline. This is a waste of a major
intellectual resource. The main challenge to the rational choice research program—
now the most important research program in political science—can be developed by
building on Simon's ideas on bounded rationality. The essay defends this assertion
by examining how the work of both the early Simon (primarily satisficing-and-search
models) and the later Simon (on problem solving) can shed light on important topics
in our discipline such as budgeting, turnout, and party competition.

INTRODUCTION

This chapter's title should end with a question mark. We would naturally like to
believe that, taken as a statement, it accurately describes Herbert Simon's career.
But it doesn't. For the last 40-plus years of his amazingly productive life, he was
a cognitive scientist. All the evidence, both objective and subjective, points to
this conclusion. The vast bulk of his publications from 1960 on were on topics
in cognitive science, as a quick check of his c.v. shows. (For a complete bibliography, see http://www.psy.cmu.edu/psy/faculty/hsimon/hsimon.html.) And it is
not merely the quantitative evidence that reveals the pattern; his original research
from 1960 on was clearly in cognitive science. [Indeed, he continued to work
on original cognitive science projects in the hospital just before he died (J. Hilf,
personal communication).] In contrast, his political science papers published in
this long period were usually responses to external stimuli, such as winning the
Madison or Gaus awards from the American Political Science Association. Although the Madison and Gaus lectures provide useful overviews of the implications of his research for political science, they do not report ongoing research.
Regarding his self-identity, though he remained fond of his roots in political
science (J. Hilf, personal communication), in his autobiography he stated flatly
that by 1956 he had been transformed "professionally into a cognitive psychologist and computer scientist, almost abandoning my earlier professional identity"
(Simon 1991, p. 189). The combination of this objective and subjective evidence
is compelling. Much as we might like to believe the lovely title of Dubnick's

(2002) salute to Simon—"Once a political scientist, always ..."—after 1960 he wasn't.[1] And since Simon was famous for his ferocious dedication to the truth—no epistemological relativist, one can hear him saying, "If this be positivism, let us make the most of it!"—he would be upset if we deluded ourselves. Facts are facts.

Yet, although Simon was not a political scientist for most of his career, his work remains relevant to our discipline. Indeed, it offers far more than has thus far been used. The main point of this essay is to convince readers that this claim is true—and that it applies to his post-1960 period as well as his earlier and more familiar work. The best is yet to come.

Because most of the essay is an attempt to convince readers of this, the following sketch must suffice for now. Although rational choice (RC) theories constitute the most important research program in political science today, there is abundant evidence that decision makers fall well short of perfect rationality in more than a few political situations. [For an overview of violations of expected utility theory, see Camerer (1994); for violations of game theoretic predictions, see Camerer (2003).] However, a series of disconfirming studies is not a theoretical alternative, and a prudent research strategy (Shepsle 1996, p. 217) is to use "The First Law of Wing Walking: 'Don't let go of something unless you have something else to hold onto.'" Enter Simon: There are intellectual resources in the body of work collectively labeled "bounded rationality" that could create an alternative to the RC program. This will take considerable effort, as such a program is not fully developed in Simon's own work. (It would be remarkable if it were.) Part of the essay develops this point: Too much of the potential in Simon's work has gone untapped. We have often waved a magic wand, labeled either "bounded rationality" or "satisficing," but such wands by themselves do little scientific work. It is, however, possible to build an alternative research program.

It is also desirable. Hegemony, put more neutrally, is monopoly—the absence of competition. And as more than a few scholars (Landau in political science; Lakatos and Feyerabend in philosophy; Merton in sociology) have argued, competition among both theories and research programs has many benign scientific effects.

The rest of the paper is organized as follows. The second section offers a short overview of the research program. This is followed by a section that describes the program's two main branches in our discipline: Simon's and the Tversky-Kahneman (T-K) branch. The fourth section briefly examines the somewhat puzzling pattern of the Simonian branch's impact on political science. The fifth section turns to some applications within political science of Simon's early (pre-1960) phase. The sixth section reviews some untapped potential in his later work. The seventh concludes.

----

[1]Of course, as social scientists know, identity can be multifaceted. So it is not surprising that when asked to choose between being considered an economist or a political scientist, Simon easily picked the latter (1999a, p. 112). But this is much weaker evidence than what he worked on or how he saw his own professional identity.

BOUNDED RATIONALITY: WHAT IT ISN'T AND WHAT IT IS

A common misconception is to confuse the general idea of bounded rationality (BR) with the much more specific idea of satisficing. (Much of this is taken from Bendor 2001.) This is sometimes done dismissively, as in the following hallway-syllogism: (*a*) BR "boils down to" satisficing; (*b*) satisficing is simply a theory of search-for-alternatives that takes the costs of computation into account; (*c*) hence, far from being a major rival to the RC program, it is just a minor tweak on optimal search theory.

This is a major error that produces a serious underestimation of the program's content. Confusing BR with satisficing conflates three different types of symbolic formulations: research programs, theories, and specific formal models of those theories. Research programs typically contain many different theories; for instance, RC contains Downsian theories of party competition, theories of collective action, and so on. Some of these theories conflict, whereas others are simply about different phenomena. And many of these theories are formalized as models; for example, Downs's basic theory has given birth to scores of formal models. So to conflate BR with, say, Simon's specific *model* of satisficing (1955) is a methodological howler. Because the BR research program focuses on individual decision making, and because the postulated mechanisms can appear in many different contexts, its empirical domain is vast—it is no less imperialistic than RC—and so its set of possible theories is also very large.

To identify the program's central ideas, one should start with Simon's formulation: "the capacity of the human mind for formulating and solving complex problems is very small compared with the size of the problems whose solution is required for objectively rational behavior in the real world—or even for a reasonable approximation to such objective rationality" (1957, p. 198). Crucially, in this statement BR is a *relation* between a decision maker's mental abilities and the complexity of the problem she or he faces. It is *not* a claim about the brilliance or stupidity of human beings, independent of their task environments. It is common in the literature to miss this central point, and to reify the notion of BR into an assertion about the absolute capacities of human beings (as in the summary that one sometimes gets from students: "Simon thinks people are dumb"). The fundamental notion here is that of cognitive limits, and, as is true of any constraint, if cognitive constraints do not bind in a particular choice situation, then they do not matter; they will not affect the outcome. And whether they bind depends vitally on the demands placed on decision makers by the problem at hand. More vividly, Simon has referred to the joint effects of "the structure of task environments and the computational capabilities of the actor" as "a scissors [with] two blades" (1990, p. 7): Theories of BR have cutting power—especially relative to RC theories—only when both blades operate. Thus any analysis that purports to fall into this research program yet focuses only on the agent's properties is incomplete.

Since this is the program's foundation, it is worthwhile to explore its implications via an example. Consider a group of adults of normal intelligence, randomly paired up to play either chess or tic-tac-toe. A pair can either play the game they were assigned to or they can stipulate a particular outcome, take their money for participating in the experiment, and leave. The intuitive prediction is that more people assigned to tic-tac-toe would stipulate an outcome (a draw); after all, that game is trivial (for normal adults).

But so is chess, in a sense (Rubinstein 1998, p. 130). Zermelo proved long ago that there exists an optimal way to play chess, and if it is played optimally, then—as in tic-tac-toe—the same outcome always occurs: Either white wins or black does or they draw. Indeed, for classical game theory, which ignores cognitive constraints, chess and tic-tac-toe belong to the same class: They are zero-sum, finite games of perfect information. Hence they are game theoretically equivalent.

In the real world, of course, these two games are not equivalent. Normal adults do not play tic-tac-toe; it is pointless. But they do play chess. Indeed, some take it up as a profession, spending thousands of hours on it.

In our thought experiment, people were randomly assigned to the two games, so their different reactions could not be imputed to differences in their cognitive capacities. Instead, they must have been due to the huge differences in the complexity of the games. The point is simple but essential: The mental abilities of normal adults are a binding constraint in chess but not in tic-tac-toe. Accordingly, BR and RC theories make observationally equivalent predictions about the latter but not the former. Hence BR theories have cutting power in chess—knowing the players' cognitive limits gives us predictive leverage—but not in tic-tac-toe.

The example provides a more subtle point. Chess becomes simpler in the endgame, but the players' basic cognitive capacities remain the same. Since the task's demands are falling while mental resources stay fixed, at some point those resources may no longer be a binding constraint. If that happens, the players will play optimally, and so a standard RC theory will accurately predict their behavior from that point onward. And indeed this is so. A chess master suffering from a significant material disadvantage in the endgame will resign, because he knows that his opponent will win and nothing can be done about it. Once it is clear to the players what the optimal strategies are, play becomes completely predictable, hence continuing the game is as pointless as playing tic-tac-toe.

This example reveals the subtlety of the contest between BR and RC theories. Theories from these two research programs make different predictions about behavior in chess only when the game is sufficiently complex as to make players' mental capacities binding constraints. For expert players, this condition holds early in the game but not at the end. Thus the two types of theories make observationally equivalent predictions about the *endgame* behavior of experts. Further, note that novices, not realizing that being up a pawn at the end can be decisive, will often play the game out to the bitter end. Thus a BR theory would predict that the "crossing point"—when cognitive capacities cease to bind—occurs much later, if at all, for novices than for experts. Accordingly, the predictions of the two types of theories will differ more for novices than for experts.

The idea that BR's significance turns on the *difference* between cognitive resources and task demands, not on cognition's absolute levels, implies what might be called a scaling principle of modeling: What matters in a model is not so much how sophisticated the agents are assumed to be or how hard the problems are, but rather the difference between the two. Typically, real humans are more sophisticated than agents in BR models, but real problems are also harder; both are scaled up. And as long as both are scaled up symmetrically, the model in question may be plausible, even though the agents are rather "dumb."

Essential Properties of Humans as Information Processors

What, then, are the essential properties of humans as information processors? That is, what properties should be on any political scientist's "short list" of cognitive features to consider when constructing behaviorally plausible theories of political decision making?[2] (For a much more thorough examination of these and related properties of human information processing, see Jones 2001, pp. 3–127.)

Synthesizing Hogarth (1987), Simon (1990), and Lodge (1995) gives us the following list of attributes:

1. Selective perception of information. There is always far more information in our objective environments than we can perceive or attend to. Thus, perceptions must be strongly guided by anticipations. The main point here is not necessarily bias but "top-down processing"—perception is influenced by schemas and other mental constructs.

2. High-order information processing, especially conscious thinking and attention, is largely serial in nature.[3] This has significant implications for the real-time behavior of busy operators, managers, and executives [to use Wilson's (1989) trichotomy of public officials].

3. Compared with modern computers, humans process many kinds of information slowly. This is partly because of physiological limits; neurons transmit impulses much more slowly than do electrical circuits.

4. People are not strong at calculation, compared with computers or even calculators.

5. Memory is not photographic; it is actively reconstructive. It therefore lacks photographic fidelity.

6. Although there is no known limit to long-term memory, short-term or working memory is very small (Miller 1956). Thus, because everything that enters the former goes through the latter (Miller 1989, p. 151), the working memory is a key bottleneck in information processing.

---

[2]The emphasis here is on a short list of essential properties. Relative to psychology, political science is a complex macro-field. Hence, to keep their theories tractable and reasonably general, political scientists should be ruthless about micro-assumptions, postulating only the most important information-processing properties of individuals. (This strategy parallels the early approach taken by scholars such as Newell and Simon, who advocated that cognitive scientists should concentrate on the information-processing level and take into account only the most fundamental properties of *their* micro-field, neurophysiology.)

[3]The connectionists' claim that lower-order processes (e.g., perception) involve a significant amount of parallelism is taken seriously in the literature.

THEORETICAL IMPLICATIONS FOR POLITICAL SCIENCE: A CAVEAT   It is important for political scientists—properly concerned with much more aggregate phenomena than cognitive psychologists are—to understand the theoretical implications of the above properties for social scientists. For a political scientist interested in modeling a large-scale phenomenon such as voting, it is not necessary that the model explicitly represent the above constraints. Instead, what is fundamental is that the postulated decisional capacities of agents be consistent with these limits. For example, something is wrong if a model assumes that decision makers have perfect recall of the complete history of a long and complicated game (see constraint 5); something is *seriously* wrong if the model's implications depend sensitively (i.e., in a knife-edge way) on such an assumption. On the other hand, if a specialist on public agencies wanted to model the behavior of a single official—an air traffic controller or a general—then it seems appropriate to model these mental limits explicitly.

BOUNDED RATIONALITY'S MAIN BRANCHES IN POLITICAL SCIENCE

There are two main orientations toward BR that are used in political science. The first orientation sees the glass as half full, emphasizing that people manage to do "reasonably well" despite their cognitive limitations, even in complex tasks. In this camp I would put Simon's work and also Lindblom's theory of incrementalism (Lindblom 1959, Braybrooke & Lindblom 1963, Bendor 1995). In the second orientation the glass is half empty: The emphasis tends to be on how people make mistakes even in simple tasks. Here belongs the Tversky-Kahneman (T-K) research tradition on heuristics and biases (e.g., Tversky & Kahneman 1974; for a superb overview see Dawes 1998). Although the distinction is partly one of framing—the two branches agree about much and the T-K tradition has acknowledged its ties to the Simonian program[4]—it is nonetheless significant and warrants elaboration. [For a cogent analysis of the intellectual antecedents of the T-K branch, especially regarding its focus on human error, see Hammond (1990). For a valuable recent overview, see Gilovich & Griffin (2002).]

The Glass is Half Full

As noted above, one of Simon's key premises is that a decision maker's "inner environment"—her cognitive constraints—will only "show through" when the

---

[4]For example, in their well-known (1986) paper, Tversky & Kahneman say, "The present results and analysis—particularly the role of transparency and the significance of framing—are consistent with the conception of bounded rationality originally presented by Herbert Simon (see, e.g., Simon 1955, 1978; March 1978; Nelson and Winter 1982)" (pp. 272–73). Further, they recognize the importance of Simon's scissors: "Perhaps the major finding of the present article is that the axioms of rational choice are generally satisfied in transparent situations and often violated in nontransparent ones" (Tversky & Kahneman 1986, p. 272). Establishing which problem representations are transparent—i.e., cognitively obvious—and which are opaque has been important throughout the T-K line of work.

decision problem is "sufficiently" difficult (Simon 1996). (Exactly what is sufficiently difficult turns out to be more subtle than the Simonian branch had perhaps appreciated. More on this shortly.) When these constraints do not bind, agents will optimize, adapting completely to the demands of the outer environment and revealing only their preferences in the process.[5] This idea naturally suggests that one should study people facing hard problems, for it is in such circumstances that one will empirically discover the important types of mental limits, e.g., on short-term memory (Simon & Chase 1973). Thus it is no accident that chess was a fertile topic for this branch of BR. Its combinatorial explosion ensures that no one (and no thing) can play chess optimally, and so information-processing constraints must show through.

But studying chess revealed more than mental limits. An interesting (though possibly unintended) consequence of studying this game and similar hard problems was the generation of new questions for the Simonian line, especially about performance. In these domains people's performance varies tremendously; a few are Grand Masters, many are duffers. This natural variation cries out for explanation. Thus a new research focus emerges: How do some decision makers do so well, given that presumably they labor under similar cognitive constraints (Simon & Simon 1962)? Thus, this branch came to see that the glass is at least half full: In some undeniably hard domains, some human beings do indeed perform "reasonably well" in terms of an empirically sensible aspiration level.[6] (The theoretically defined aspiration level of optimal play is irrelevant for an empirical theory of chess, since everyone, from Kasparov and Deep Blue on down,

---

[5]Lindblom seems to share this perspective, although it is less explicit in his work. See Braybrooke & Lindblom (1963, pp. 41–57, 66–79) for a discussion of the relation between cognitive capacities and task complexity.

[6]Another empirically based aspiration level for cognitively demanding problems arises from comparing the performance of humans to that of computers. Although the latter are artificial, they are real information-processing systems, not a theoretical benchmark as is the fully rational decision maker of RC. Hence it is interesting that cognitive scientists who have actually tried to build artificial systems that perceive three-dimensional objects, understand natural language, or use (so-called) common sense are greatly impressed by our facility at these and related tasks [see, e.g., Pinker's paean to human abilities in these three tasks (1997, ch. 1)]. Although we take such abilities for granted, it turns out to be hard to construct artificial systems that do these things at all, much less at our level: "the first step we must take in knowing ourselves [is to] appreciat[e] the fantastically complex design behind feats of mental life we take for granted. The reason there are no humanlike robots is not that the very idea of a mechanical mind is misguided. It is that the engineering problems that we humans solve as we see and walk and plan and make it through the day are far more challenging than landing on the moon or sequencing the human genome" (Pinker 1997, p. 4). Again, a comparison to some real entity provides a realistic aspiration level about information processing. A third approach that easily leads to a positive assessment of human information processing is that taken by developmental psychologists who try to figure out how babies grapple with the "booming, buzzing confusion" of their new worlds (see, e.g., Gopnik et al. 1999).

flunks this test. Hence using this criterion produces no variation in the dependent variable of performance.)

What has happened, then, is that researchers in the Simonian branch have in a sense come to take BR for granted—not in the sense of thinking it unimportant, but in believing that it need not be established. There is simply no doubt that mental constraints bind in the problems subjects work on in this branch; the exploding decision trees preclude objective optimization. So what is interesting is not whether the behavior of subjects is fully rational—we know it isn't—but how relatively competent agents work around their (indisputable) cognitive limitations.[7]

In public administration, certain jobs—for example, those of air traffic controllers on busy days or generals in the fog of battle—are clearly hard. It is in such roles that cognitive constraints should show through; yet, human performance varies substantially. Thus the general lessons from the study of chess (not, of course, the detailed conclusions about domain-specific heuristics) are applicable to such roles studied by our discipline.

The Glass is Half Empty

Ward Edwards, a pioneer of behavioral decision theory, once remarked, "A research focus on systematic errors and inferential biases can lead those who read the research with an uncritical eye to the notion that such errors and biases characterize all human decision making" (von Winterfeldt & Edwards 1986, p. 530). Although Edwards went on to say that "a sense of the inevitability of specific kinds of intellectual errors has been more widely disseminated than, we believe, the literature proposes or justifies" (p. 531), his remark is still an accurate description of how many social scientists perceive the heuristics and biases branch of BR (Christensen-Szalanski & Beach 1984).[8] This was probably not Tversky & Kahneman's intention. Their idea was to map the subtle processes of mental

---

[7]This naturally spawns the question, what makes certain problems mentally difficult (Kotovsky et al. 1985)? The answer for chess is obvious: combinatorial explosion. But as the T-K branch has shown, sometimes the answer may turn on subtle issues of framing and mental representations, and so is much less obvious. (On this topic see Kotovsky et al. 1985 and Simon 1979b, part 7.)

[8]Not without some justification, it should be added. The literature has devoted most of its space to documenting "a long list of human judgmental biases, deficiencies, and cognitive illusions" (Einhorn & Hogarth 1981, p. 54); "the logical approach [comparing people to optimal baseline models] triggered an explosion of research on inferential error, and the list of illusions, foibles, flops, and bloopers to which ordinary people were apparently prone became rather long . . . soon, if there was a mistake to be made, someone was making it in the presence of a social psychologist" (Gilbert 1998, p. 121). Thus the impression conveyed by the literature, perhaps not only to the "uncritical eye," is that of decision makers who foul things up. [Christensen-Szalanski & Beach (1984) provide intriguing evidence that this impression is partly due to a citation bias: "evidence for poor performance is cited more frequently than is evidence for good performance" (p. 75)—in fact, six times as often (p. 76).] After reading many of these studies, the glass probably does look half empty—or worse.

framing that can cause cognitive illusions, similar to the study of perceptual illusions. "In the persistence of their appeal, framing effects resemble visual illusion more than computational errors" (Tversky & Kahneman 1986, p. 260). This project's results are more striking if they can be shown to occur even in simple tasks, just as perceptual illusions are more striking if they can be demonstrated with simple stimuli; it is more striking still if one shows that even experts are vulnerable to these cognitive illusions. Thus this branch of BR went down a markedly different path: In its prototypical experiment, experimenters show that even highly trained subjects answering simple questions perform suboptimally—a sharp contrast to the Simonian program's emphasis on "good" performance in difficult domains.

These differences indicate that in one respect the T-K branch has set for itself a more ambitious research agenda. Obviously, it should be harder to demonstrate that our cognitive limits show through on simple problems than on hard ones. Thus the T-K program has worked on pushing out the boundaries of BR by showing that even quite subtle problem representations ("framing") can induce suboptimal performance.[9] One need not go all the way to chess to uncover our mental limitations; it turns out that humans are sufficiently sensitive (hence vulnerable) to framing that judgmental or decisional imperfections will appear even when a task exhibits no combinatorial explosion at all. Thus, one of the main findings of the T-K program is that the empirical domain of the BR program—where it has predictive bite—is larger than we had believed it to be.

Naturally, if one is pushing the boundaries of an idea or hypothesis, one is more likely to step over the line, which in this case means overestimating the boundaries of BR. Unsurprisingly, there has been a scholarly backlash, attempting to show that humans are better decision makers than the T-K program makes us out to be (e.g., Gigerenzer 1991; for a reply see Kahneman & Tversky 1996). Unfortunately, this debate has been clouded by a misunderstanding of Tversky & Kahneman's original intention, which was not to show that *Homo sapiens* are dolts but rather to uncover fundamental cognitive mechanisms that leave their imprint nearly everywhere.[10]

It must be acknowledged, however, that some of the responsibility for this clouding falls on some of the scholars who work in this tradition. Their "gotcha" approach to their subjects and to experimental design gives the impression that the

---

[9]A key axiom of RC theories—so basic that it is often unstated—is description invariance: Decision makers should be unaffected by different yet instrumentally equivalent descriptions of a problem. (For a discussion of this postulate, see Shafir & Tversky 1995, p. 84.) The work on framing and problem representation is theoretically important because it shows that humans often violate this key axiom.

[10]Gigerenzer also misunderstood the importance of transparency in Tversky & Kahneman's work. They have consistently maintained the following variant of Simon's main principle: When normative axioms are transparent (cognitively obvious), people tend to accept them.

goal is to show that humans are, in fact, inept decision makers (for a critique along these lines, see Lopes 1981).

This tendency has been exacerbated by the fact that specialists working in the T-K branch have shown little interest in performance variation. There has been little in this line of work equivalent to the study of chess masters.[11] As noted, this made sense, given the primary objective of demonstrating the nearly ubiquitous character of certain mental processes. But it did have the unfortunate side effect of making the program largely—not completely—indifferent to natural variations in performance.[12] Instead, the evaluations are usually based on dichotomous theoretical standards—do people make choices in accord with the axioms of expected utility theory? Do they revise beliefs in a Bayesian manner? The answers—generally no, they don't—are less informative than would be answers based on a quantitative scale that measured degrees of sophistication, even if the best empirical performance falls far short of the theoretical ideal.

Finally, it is worth noting that the intellectual differences between the two branches are reflected in and reinforced by differences in citations, publication patterns, and other aspects of scholarly practice. Work in the Simonian tradition on problem solving in difficult tasks rarely cites T-K studies. Conversely, beyond brief mentions of Simon's classical articles on bounded rationality of the mid-1950s, T-K studies of human error in simple tasks rarely cite work in the Simonian tradition.[13] It is strange: Simon, known for his pioneering work on behavioral theories of choice, is now rarely cited in surveys on behavioral decision theory. [For two exceptions to this pattern, see Abelson & Levi (1985) and Slovic et al. (1988). Both devote a nontrivial amount of space to the Simonian program.] By "decision making" the literature apparently means behavior in *simple* choice environments. If the task is complex, it is given over to the field of problem solving. Yet this division is artificial; in reality, problem solving and choice are closely connected. Treating them as though they were unrelated does not "cut nature at the joints."

---

[11]For example, Dawes' recent (1998) survey of behavioral decision theory mentions virtually no studies of the performance of experts—except for work in the Meehl tradition, which shows convincingly that experts are out-performed by simple linear models in many choice contexts. Hence even this exception exemplifies the contrast between the two BR branches. The Simonian tradition studies experts to find out how and why they out-perform nonexperts. When the T-K branch studies experts, it is primarily to show either that (*a*) they make the same errors as everyone else or (*b*) they are worse than explicit algorithms.

[12]The literature on calibration of probabilities, which has studied the superior performance of some experts (weather forecasters are superbly calibrated), is an exception to this tendency (Lichtenstein et al. 1982, Koehler et al. 2002).

[13]For a striking example of this, see the articles by Slovic (1990) on "Choice" and Holyoak (1990) on "Problem Solving." Though side by side in the same volume, their citations are almost disjoint sets. The former mentions the Simonian branch infrequently, and the latter does not cite a single work from the T-K branch! Evidently choice and problem solving have little to do with each other.

THE SIMONIAN BRANCH'S IMPACT ON
POLITICAL SCIENCE

The Simonian branch has had a peculiar pattern of impacts. Four facts stand out.

1. By now it has had a bigger impact on theorizing in economics than in Simon's own field of political science.
2. Even this impact took decades, however.
3. Political scientists, now preoccupied with developing the RC program, which originated in economics, are largely unaware of how intensely high-brow economic and game theorists are working on BR models.
4. Simon's biggest impact was on a field that did not exist before he started: the cognitive sciences.

I elaborate on points 1–3 below.

The Simonian program has had a relatively modest impact on political science. True, Simon himself has been extensively cited by political scientists, especially by specialists in public administration. It is also true that his reputation in the discipline is very high. Yet if we inspect the literature in political science for work that either tests his ideas empirically or develops them theoretically, the pickings are lean.

The clearest indication of the lack of theoretical development can be found in the discipline's approach to Simon's most famous idea, satisficing. As set out in his famous 1955 paper, the early theory of satisficing was not applicable to many problems in politics. The reason was simple: Whereas the theory analyzed a single, isolated decision maker, political science focuses on multiperson situations. There was nothing wrong with the initial formulation being decision theoretic; indeed, one could make a good case, based on an incremental strategy of scientific progress, that it was exactly the right first step in developing a behaviorally realistic theory of choice. The problem was the discipline's reaction. Instead of treating the theory and its formalizations (Simon 1955, 1956) as work in progress, the first in what should have been a long series of steps, the discipline largely treated it as a finished product. Hence few political scientists in the following decades constructed theories of satisficing more appropriate to political contexts. Worse, even some thoughtful scholars saw "the Simon-March tradition [as having] been . . . thoroughly nonpolitical in its design and development" (Moe 1991, p. 111).[14] Given that many saw the formulation as a finished product not requiring active work, while others saw it as apolitical, it is perhaps not surprising that the Simonian program stagnated in political science.

The reaction in economics was different, although it too produced a lag. Because economics already had a well-established research program, built on the twin foundations of individual optimization and market equilibrium, and because

---

[14]Moe was careful to add that this was not an in-principle limitation of the research program, but others came to hastier conclusions.

Simon's program challenged a core postulate of RC, the initial reaction of most economists was hostility or, at best, indifference. Cyert & March's significant work, *A Behavioral Theory of the Firm* (1963), was designed to show economists what the new research program could do, but it too failed to generate much interest. There were a few exceptions to this pattern (notably Nelson & Winter 1982), which tended to come from elite economists, but these were just that—exceptions.

Eventually, however, elite opinion had its way. Prominent economists (Arrow 1974) and game theorists (Selten 1989) came to believe that cognitive constraints had to be incorporated in theories of choice. Following them, we see a spate of modeling papers in the past decade, some directly influenced by Simon (the citations are usually to 1955 or 1956), others more indirectly.[15] Today, we see explicit titles such as *Modeling Bounded Rationality*, by a top game theorist, Ariel Rubinstein. So after a long lag, Simon has finally had a big impact on economics. (For a thoughtful overview, see Conlisk 1996.)

Why is Simon's program, and more broadly BR, finally flourishing in economics but not in political science? A sociology-of-science factor has already been alluded to: persuasion by elite economists. This combines with another sociological property: The status hierarchy in economics is clearer than it is in political science, so the opinions of a few elite economists matter a lot. Finally, there is a crucial difference in human capital between economics and political science. Economics had many highly trained formal theorists who, in the 1980s and 1990s, saw how to construct mathematical models of BR—and how to use these in models of strategic interaction. (For a good recent bibliography, see Rubinstein 1998.) Simon himself was not too keen on this line of work (Rubinstein 1998, pp. 188–90), regarding it as insufficiently grounded in our empirical understanding of cognitive constraints, but it is nonetheless clear that this ability to develop mathematical models of BR has made working on the program much more attractive to economic theorists than it otherwise would have been.

This burst of activity has gone largely unnoticed by political scientists. This is ironic. While Simon, trained as a political scientist, is finally having an impact in economics, theoretically oriented political scientists are borrowing RC ideas from economics!

SOME APPLICATIONS OF THE EARLY SIMON

A research program can make serious scientific headway only by demonstrating that it has problem-solving power (Laudan 1977). There are two kinds of such demonstrations. The first is a hurdle: A new program must show that it can handle already-solved problems, e.g., account for an empirical regularity already explained by other programs. The second kind involves novelty: The program shows

---

[15]For example, the literature on learning, now very extensive in theoretical economics, clearly belongs to the general BR program even though few of these models build on the specific theory of satisficing.

that it can handle an unsolved problem. Ideally (Lakatos 1970), a theory of a new research program solves all of the problems handled by the incumbent program plus some new ones. The challenging program would then dominate the incumbent in terms of problem-solving power. Not surprisingly, such clear victories are rare (Laudan et al. 1988).

The following topics are organized roughly chronologically, by the date of the first contribution on the topic.

The Politics of Budgeting

For a long time the study of budgeting was an intellectual backwater in political science. Then Aaron Wildavsky went to graduate school at Yale, was influenced by Lindblom's ideas, and the rest—including *The Politics of the Budgetary Process*—is history.

This is not an inaccurate summary of how it all began, but it is misleading about the ending. For as Green & Thompson (2001) show, the path of this subfield is a curious one. The line of work on budgetary politics spawned by Lindblom and Simon was, by many scientific criteria, quite successful. Yet recently it has not flourished. This subsection describes how the BR research program bore fruit, but the rest of the discipline has not responded with the enthusiasm that one might have expected. (For a more thorough account of this story, see Green & Thompson 2001.)

The study of budgeting has been tied to the BR program since its inception. As Simon recalled in his autobiography (1991, p. 370), his experience studying budgeting in Milwaukee was a formative experience:

> [T]he budget process . . . involved the division of funds between playground maintenance, administered by one organization, and playground activity leadership, administered by another. How was this division (which was a frequent subject of dispute) arrived at? My previous study of economics provided me with a ready hypothesis: Divide the funds so that the next dollar spent for maintenance will produce the same return as the next dollar spent for leaders' salaries. I saw no evidence that anyone was viewing the decision in this way. Was I surprised at their ignoring accepted economic theory? Perhaps, initially, but on reflection, I didn't see how it could be done. How were the values of better activity leadership to be weighed against the values of more attractive and better-maintained neighborhood playgrounds.
>
> Now I had a new research problem: How do human beings reason when the conditions for rationality postulated by neoclassical economics are not met?

Although this experience evidently had a major impact on Simon's thinking about BR in general, it was not applied to budgeting in depth until Wildavsky turned his hand to the topic. (This much of the above bald summary is true.) Since Wildavsky used Lindblom's "The Science of 'Muddling Through'" (1959), we must first briefly examine that famous paper. Lindblom and Simon had clearly been thinking on parallel tracks throughout the 1950s (see Dahl & Lindblom

1953, pp. 82–86; C. Lindblom, personal communication 2002). Both believed that the classical model of rationality was often inaccurate as a descriptive theory of choice. But because there are many ways to think about how cognitively constrained decision makers might go about their business—there are many ways of being imperfectly rational—it is not surprising that their positive alternatives differed in significant ways. In particular, although both maintained that human beings must resort to heuristics in order to cope with a complex, confusing world, they focused on different kinds of heuristics. [Indeed, it is reasonable to view Lindblom's verbal theory as (*a*) a set of claims about why perfect rationality is infeasible for complex problems and (*b*) a collection of heuristics and a set of claims about their performance. See Lindblom (1968) for a formulation that most supports this interpretation. The list on pp. 24–27 is essentially a set of heuristics.] Although Lindblom did not concentrate on one heuristic as much as Simon did on satisficing, perhaps his best-known one was incrementalism—the idea that people would search for solutions in the "neighborhood" of the current policy.

"Incrementalism" became, of course, the name for Wildavsky's theory of budgeting. There were good reasons for this. Wildavsky himself emphasized the incremental nature of budgeting in the United States, both in the above process sense and in an outcome sense (budgets in one year differing only marginally from those of the previous year). And in the quantitative models that Wildavsky developed with Dempster and Davis (DDW), incrementalism occupied center stage (Davis et al. 1966, 1974). But when one inspects the verbal theory of *The Politics of the Budgetary Process*, one sees that the early Wildavsky was, like Lindblom, more a fox than a hedgehog, in Isaiah Berlin's terms. True, like any good BR scholar, Wildavsky recognized two big related facts: the complexity of the task environment he was studying [e.g., "life is incredibly complicated and there is very little theory that would enable people to predict how programs will turn out if they are at all new" (Wildavsky 1979 [1964], p. 9)] and decision makers' ensuing need for "aids to calculation: . . . mechanisms, however imperfect, for helping [them] make decisions that are in some sense meaningful in a complicated world" (p. 11). But after noting these two important facts, Wildavsky turned with gusto to describing the heuristics themselves (pp. 11–62). And here the fox appeared. No elegant axiomatic theory was present. Instead, he provided, as did Lindblom, a list of techniques that make allocation decisions manageable. (Notably, he included satisficing.) And although he did single out incrementalism, calling it "the major aid for calculating budgets" (p. 13), he covered a broad range of mechanisms. (Interestingly, he included one—role specialization, including the budgetary advocacy of program chiefs—that Simon had described long ago in his Milwaukee study.) Thus at this point Wildavsky's verbal theory was more committed to the premise that decision makers needed *some* aids to calculation than it was to the empirical generalization that incrementalism was usually the heuristic of choice in mid-twentieth-century American budgeting. [In this regard, it is worth noting that he introduced the topic of incrementalism by remarking, "It is against a background of the enormous burden of calculation that the ensuing description . . . of incrementalism should be understood" (p. 13).] Thus, as of 1964, Wildavsky was a hedgehog about the underlying theory but a fox about heuristics—and most of his book examined the latter.

Later, however, the stance of *The Politics of the Budgetary Process* was obscured. Wildavsky's budgetary theory became *identified* with incrementalism. This was partly because of polemics: Much of the critical attention focused on this part of the argument. (The more careful critics did, however, note the distinction between process and outcome incrementalism.) But part of the blame falls on Wildavsky himself. When he and his coauthors developed a quantitative model of incrementalism (Davis et al. 1966, 1974), much of the richness of the verbal theory was lost.[16] This is a necessary price of any formalization, but in this case the price was steep: DDW's quantitative models reinforced the perception that the empirical generalization about local search, or worse, local outcomes, was the theory's central claim. Thus Wildavsky, a brilliant fox, was turned by critics—and by some of his own replies to criticism—into an apparent hedgehog.

Fortunately, other scholars working on budgeting recognized that formal BR theories of budgeting needed to be rescued from incrementalism's dominance. Two of the most important efforts in this regard were those of J.P. Crecine (1969) and his student, John Padgett (1980, 1981).[17]

Crecine brought Simon's problem—how do cognitively constrained human beings deal with the complexities of budgeting?—back to the center of the formal theory of public resource allocation. And he did so in a novel way: He emphasized the hierarchical nature of budgeting. He meant "hierarchy" not only in the sense of authority, but also in Simon's sense (1962) of nearly decomposable systems. The idea was straightforward. An exceptionally common heuristic is to break a complex problem into a set of smaller, simpler ones, hoping that if we solve the smaller ones, we will in effect have solved the original big one. In federal budgeting, this heuristic is realized both by the formal process—different governmental departments are given budgets, as are their subunits, and so on down the hierarchy—and by how decision makers think about resource allocation. Unlike the normative decision rules of public finance that lurked in Simon's mind when he studied Milwaukee budgeting, marginal value comparisons between disparate programs rarely occur in Crecine's descriptive theory. Such comparisons are precluded by hierarchical decomposition. In this theory, decision makers do compare spending on "guns

---

[16]The DDW papers, however, contained more than the quantitative models. For example, the 1966 paper included extensive discussions of the verbal theory of boundedly rational budgetary officials facing a very complex task. In particular, the authors clearly continued to regard incremental behavior as significant owing to its properties as "an aid to calculation," i.e., as a heuristic. Thus the underlying cognitive theory's thrust remained intact.

[17]This was not a coincidence. The chair of Crecine's dissertation committee was none other than Herbert Simon, and Padgett's other thesis advisors—Michael Cohen and Robert Axelrod—were, like Crecine, well acquainted with the larger BR tradition that had served as the theoretical base for *The Politics of the Budgetary Process*.

versus butter," and within defense spending they compare the Army's allocation to the Navy's. But they do not compare the spending on maintenance for tanks against spending for computers in the Social Security Administration. Such comparisons are just not made.

Crecine also argued that the hierarchical decomposition of budget decisions helped top executives control budgetary totals while remaining aloof from the process's details. This point, and the stress on the usefulness of the decomposition heuristic, was especially important in his later work on defense budgeting (e.g., Crecine 1970, pp. 231–37) and federal budgeting in general (1985, pp. 114–16, 124–27), in which he argued that for reasons of time and related cognitive constraints it was impossible even for workaholics such as President Johnson to know much about the budgets of many programs. But they *could* focus on what Crecine called the "Great Identity" [revenues + deficit (or −surplus) = defense expenditures + nondefense expenditures], and try to impose their preferences on the big macroeconomic issues and the guns-versus-butter trade-offs. Similarly, the Secretary of Defense could try to impose his preferences on big interservice allocation issues, while letting his subordinates worry about intraservice decisions. And so on down the line.

Much of Padgett's model is devoted to how executive branch officials search for and test alternatives. To understand the significance of his analysis, it is important to compare it to incrementalist theories of the search for alternatives, in which officials search in the neighborhood of last year's appropriation. This is only one way of cutting the decision tree down to a manageable size. As both Lindblom and Wildavsky recognized, there are other heuristics that can narrow search. BR implies that search is limited; it need not always be local (incremental).[18] Thus, Padgett's model should be seen as an effort to close the gap between verbal theories of budgeting and their formalizations. He assumes a probabilistic process of search-for-budgetary-alternatives that is consistent with the general premise of BR but does not imply that requests are always incremental modifications of the status quo budget. Thus, his model implies a distribution of budgetary outcomes that has "fatter tails" than DDW's, a prediction that has empirical support. (For another model of boundedly rational budgeting that yields this implication of fatter tails, see Jones 1999.) That is, rather than relying (as do DDW) on assumptions about "random shocks" hitting a system that is basically deterministic, Padgett builds the stochastic features into the heart of the model, i.e., into the search for budgetary alternatives.

Crecine's and Padgett's achievements were impressive. They rescued Wildavsky from himself by creating formal theories of budgeting that were truer to the informal theory of *The Politics of the Budgetary Process* than Wildavsky's

---

[18]After Pearl Harbor, George Marshall had to decide which integer multiple of the War Department's 1941 appropriation he should request. Although he probably thought of only a few alternatives, it is unlikely that he considered anything in the neighborhood of the pre–December 7 status quo.

own attempts were. Moreover, their models generated quantitative predictions, and by social science standards did so very successfully. Theory, predictions, corroboration—what more could one ask? So as of the early 1980s, one might have predicted a bright future for the behavioral theories of budgeting. Oddly, this did not materialize. Green & Thompson, in their admirable study of this line of work, summarize the current situation as follows: "Mentions of the organizational process model often draws blank stares from students of public budgeting . . . . Bibliographical searches yield only a handful of references or citations. And most contemporary texts entirely overlook the topic" (2001, p. 55).

This is certainly an unusual episode in political science. Rarely in our discipline's history have such successful models been so neglected. (It is rare simply to encounter such successful models, independently of their reception.) Although it is beyond the scope of this chapter to explain this trajectory in detail (the interested reader should see Green & Thompson 2001), three reasons for it are worth mentioning because they pertain to some important themes of this essay:

1. Human capital and tools. Crecine used computer modeling. Very few political scientists were trained in this method. Padgett used analytical stochastic models; even fewer scholars in our discipline understood these techniques.

2. Substance and method. Most political scientists who were mathematically adept were substantively committed to the RC program. In short, the set of people who belonged to the intersection of the two sets (substantive and skills) was very small. Too small, it turned out.

3. Inaccessibility. Crecine published in obscure places (I do not know why). Padgett's work was inaccessible for the above human capital reasons. So for different reasons, two of the best exemplars of this body of work were mostly invisible.

Individual Versus Organizational Rationality

In his first major publication, *Administrative Behavior*, Simon hypothesized—contrary to the American stereotype of bureaucracies as bumbling, mindless systems—that organizations routinely ameliorate the information-processing constraints of individuals. Because the implications of BR for organization have often been misinterpreted, it is worth quoting Simon so readers can see his position for themselves.

> The argument of the present chapter can be stated very simply. It is impossible for the behavior of a single, isolated individual to reach any high degree of rationality. The number of alternatives he must explore is so great, the information he would need to evaluate them so vast that even an approximation to objective rationality is hard to conceive.
>
> . . . A higher degree of integration and rationality can, however, be achieved, because the environment of choice itself can be chosen and deliberately

modified. Partly this is an individual matter . . . . To a very large extent, however, it is an organizational matter. One function that organization performs is
to place the organization members in a psychological environment that will
adapt their decisions to the organization objectives, and will provide them
with the information needed to make these decisions correctly.

In the course of this discussion it will begin to appear that organization
permits the individual to approach reasonably near to objective rationality.
(Simon 1947, pp. 79–80)

It is a striking fact of intellectual history that Simon's viewpoint was not only
ignored—it was *inverted* by several important social scientists. Perhaps the most
prominent example of this inversion was in Allison's *Essence of Decision* (1971).
The part on the "Organizational Process Model" summarized the "Carnegie" approach of Simon, March, and Cyert. Unfortunately, however, this summary completely misunderstood Simon's analysis of how organizational properties compensate for the cognitive constraints of individual decision makers. (For a detailed
analysis of this misunderstanding, see Bendor & Hammond 1992, pp. 311–13.)
Instead, it fell back on old, culturally familiar stereotypes about the negative effects
of organizational routines and the stultifying effects of bureaucracy in general.

Simon's position was, however, taken seriously in Landau's (1969) pioneering
work on organizational redundancy. He showed how structural redundancy, far
from being inevitably wasteful, can make organizations more reliable than any of
their subunits (including any member of that organization). Consider, for example,
an agency working on a difficult R&D project. Suppose the probability that a single
team successfully develops a key component is p, where $0 < p < 1$. Given the
component's centrality and the project's significance, p is considered unacceptably
low. But if the agency assigns the problem to n teams working independently in
parallel, then the probability that the *organization* will succeed is $1 - [(1 - p)^n]$,
which rises steadily toward 1 as n increases.[19]

The problem is harder when institutions can make two types of error, e.g., con-
victing an innocent person or freeing a guilty one. Here Condorcet's jury theorem
comes to the rescue. He showed that both types of error could be reduced as juries
grew in size, if they operated by majority rule. (For an accessible introduction to
the jury theorem see Grofman & Feld 1988.) Further, his result holds even if the
judgmental competency of individual jurors barely exceeds that attained by pure
chance (Grofman et al. 1983, Ladha 1992). Thus, owing to a variety of cognitive

---

[19]Here RC and BR models can overlap quite a bit, because the former can always represent
the possibility of error via agents not having all the required information. (This is, for
example, how RC models of Condorcet's jury theorem are constructed.) However, as Simon
frequently pointed out, the cognitive assumption of perfect information processing becomes
even more strained when it is assumed that agents are operating in a stochastic choice
environment. And when one adds in strategic considerations—essential to the recent game
theoretic models of the jury theorem—the assumption of complete rationality becomes still
more dubious.

constraints, individual decision makers may be extremely fallible, yet the overall organization may be very reliable.

For extensions of Condorcet's result to settings involving conflict (e.g., elections), see Miller (1986) and Grofman & Feld (1988). This work shows that, in view of the fallibility of individual voters, majority rule can be justified as a collective choice procedure because of its role in reducing error. However, Kinder (1998, pp. 799–800) points out some reasons to restrain one's optimism about this effect of aggregation.[20]

SATISFICING AND SEARCH MODELS   In most of the other applications of the pre-1960 Simon, the notion of satisficing is central. The heart of satisficing models is the assumption that a decision maker has an internal standard, an aspiration level, which partitions all current payoffs into two sets: satisfactory and unsatisfactory. Although this seems like a modest notion, it is actually a major departure from expected utility theory. Let us see why. In standard expected utility theory, a decision maker has a complete preference ordering over all outcomes, which induces a preference ordering over actions. The important thing to note is that the only thing that matters is how baskets of consequences *compare to each other*. There is no sense of the absolute value of any outcome or of the actions that generate outcomes. (It takes students a while to learn this. In this respect, expected utility theory is not simply a formalization of ordinary intuitions about decision making.) For this reason, adding or subtracting a positive constant to all the outcomes does not fundamentally change the choice situation at all. A theory that posits an aspiration level is a different animal. For example, an agent with unrealistically high aspirations is dissatisfied with anything that happens. Nothing in the classical theory parallels this possibility. The agent's best option is just that—her best option—and that's the end of the matter.

This notion has many implications in different contexts. The original context Simon worked on was a one-shot search problem: A person is looking for a solution to a problem, and (given satisficing) stops the search as soon as she has found one that meets or exceeds her aspirations. But there many others. Indeed, that's the point—this idea can travel to a great many political contexts. In recent years, the domain of elections has received special attention.

Parties in Competitive Elections

One of the most famous of all RC predictions is that of the median voter theorem in two-party races (Downs 1957). In the standard Downsian setting—voters have single-peaked preferences and vote sincerely, candidates are office-seeking,

---

[20]See Ting (2003) for an important advance on the redundancy argument. In his model, agents are cognizant of each other's activities. Because this may induce shirking—I may not work if I know that you are standing by, ready to back me up—a strategic analysis of redundancy shows that the earlier engineering analyses overestimated the value of organizational duplication.

etc.—how would adaptively rational parties behave? (This is a "hurdle" test. Given the standard setting, the logic of converging to the median voter is compelling; hence a new theory should pass this test.)

In a primitive early simulation model, Bendor & Moe (1986) showed that if a party used a simple hill-climbing heuristic, then it would converge to the median voter. In this model, however, only a single party was actively adapting, so the electoral "landscape" was unchanging and the active party's problem was simple. An important set of papers by Kollman, Miller, and Page (KMP) showed that both parties can eventually adapt, although only the challenger adjusts in any given election (Kollman et al. 1992, 1998). (Importantly, the winner satisfices, keeping the platform that got him elected.) The KMP model ambitiously assumed a multidimensional policy space, but when re-run in a standard unidimensional space, the parties converge to the median voter (S. Page, personal communication, 1999).

Since KMP's model is computer-run, they had to assume that the challenger used a specific search heuristic (hill-climbing, random search, or an artificial intelligence heuristic called the genetic algorithm). But their result for the unidimensional space generalizes to a large class of heuristics. Bendor et al. (2001) explored this issue analytically. Consider the following model-sketch. Suppose there are N platforms, arranged left to right. As in the KMP model, incumbents satisfice while challengers search. Apart from the assumption that the number of platforms is finite, the electoral environment is standard Downsian. In this setting, what are some general assumptions about the challenger's search that still imply convergence to the median? The following spare conditions do most of what we want, i.e., they ensure that eventually the winner's position, hence governmental policy, converges to the median: So long as in every period there is some chance that the challenger will experiment—i.e., take up a platform that she has never espoused before—the trajectory of winning platforms must converge to the median voter's ideal point (proposition 4, Bendor et al. 2001).

Apart from this rather weak condition about the possibility of experimentation, one can assume anything at all about search. For example, search could be blind—the challenger could be equally likely to propose any of the N platforms. Or, following incrementalism (Lindblom 1959), search could be "local," confined to the platforms closest to the challenger's current position, with a hill-climbing heuristic guiding her adjustment. And so on. Under these conditions, eventually at least one party will be at the median voter's ideal; the loser may wander around, but it too will find its way back to the median eventually. Thus the KMP unidimensional result can be generalized significantly. And a key part of Downs's median voter theorem can be recovered even if the candidates are very unsophisticated.

Why does even *blind* search by challengers, plus satisficing by incumbents, suffice? To see why, let us break the process down into two phases: generate and test (Simon 1964). In these models, candidates generate alternatives (platforms) and voters test them. Because citizens always vote for the platform they prefer, the test phase is perfect; for any pair of competing platforms, the winner must be (weakly) preferred by the median voter. Hence elections cannot hurt the median voter. The worst that can happen in an election is that the challenger fails to find an alternative that the median prefers to the incumbent's position. Hence all that is required of search by challengers is that *eventually* a challenger must be able to find a winning platform. For this, completely blind generation suffices.

The KMP models and their analytical generalizations are a useful illustration of how Simon's early decision-theoretic model of satisficing can be extended to a quintessentially political context yet remain tractable. The modeling "trick" is to allow the satisficing decision rule to freeze one of the actors—the incumbent— in a natural way. A winning platform ain't broke, so why fix it? Then, although the *context* retains its strategic character (each party's vote share depends on the other's position as well as its own), the *analysis* in any given period can focus on a single agent's actions and so is quite manageable.

These results tell us that the task environment of two office-seeking candidates in unidimensional policy spaces is sufficiently simple, and the feedback sufficiently clear, so that few of the decision makers' cognitive constraints "show through" (Simon 1996) in the long run. The only one that does, because the models allow search to be blind and memory impoverished, concerns the speed of adaptation.[21] At any given time, the electoral landscape has "nice" properties; the left party's vote share increases monotonically as it moves toward the right party's position (provided it doesn't overshoot) and decreases monotonically as it moves away. These properties ensure clear feedback. And even if the challenger ignores this feedback, the decisiveness of the median voter ensures that incorrect adaptations cannot take hold. So the overall system has enough rationality to ensure a sensible policy outcome eventually.[22]

Similarly, work in economics on markets with "zero-intelligence traders" shows that in certain kinds of markets (especially double auction markets), the disciplining effect of markets and market rules suffices to generate aggregate allocative efficiency; individual optimization is not necessary. Put more quantitatively, "In its first-order magnitude, allocative efficiency seems to be a characteristic of the market structure and the environment; rationality of individual traders accounts for a relatively small fraction (second- or third-order magnitude) of the efficiency" (Gode & Sunder 1993, p. 120). [Given his emphasis on the interaction between a decision maker's task environment and her problem-solving capacity, it is not surprising that Simon saw this point. In *The Sciences of the Artificial* (1996, pp. 32–33), he explains how the market environment can shape the behavior of even quite "stupid" buyers and sellers, per the Gode-Sunder study.]

A multidimensional policy space rarely has a median voter. This means, under standard game theoretic assumptions, that there is no Nash equilibrium in pure strategies; for any position adopted by one party, there always exists another

---

[21]However, experiments (McKelvey & Ordeshook 1990) indicate that subjects can take a long time to converge to the median when they are uncertain about voters' preferences. And real parties rarely converge fully (Stokes 1999, p. 258).

[22]This closely parallels Lindblom's argument in *The Intelligence of Democracy* (1965).

platform that could beat it. The lack of a median voter implies a cognitively more difficult task environment (Kotovsky et al. 1985).[23] Simon's basic argument (1996) implies that more of the agents' adaptive properties should show through in this environment, which is what KMP found (Kollman et al. 1992, 1998). Heuristics such as hill-climbing tend to hang candidates up on local optima, where platforms are better than others in their neighborhood but inferior to a more distant position.

This naturally raises several questions (which collectively form a miniature research agenda). First, what factors create more local optima, thus making electoral landscapes more difficult for adaptive agents to handle? KMP identified one property: Local optima are most common when voters' intensities on different issue dimensions are statistically independent of the location of their ideal points (Kollman et al. 1998, pp. 145, 152). This is a genuine discovery: finding it without their model would have been difficult. Second, what internal features of parties make it more difficult for the party to adapt to the "shape" of its electoral environment? A clear example of such a constraint is a strong ideological commitment to one's platform—the British Labour party under Michael Foot comes to mind. Of course, this is not a purely cognitive constraint in the same way that limits on working memory are for individual decision makers, but it certainly does make it harder for the party to mold itself to the task environment. Further, ideology can become a set of blinders (Lippmann 1922), and so it does have a strong cognitive component.

Boundedly Rational Voters and the "Paradox of Voting"

The preceding application of the early Simon to competing parties, though important, is almost too easy. It is intuitively clear that in a "nice" (unidimensional) Downsian environment, hill-climbing and other plausible heuristics will lead parties toward the median voter.[24] A much harder problem is the so-called "paradox of voting." Why do citizens bother to vote? Though not a true paradox, it is a major anomaly for the RC program; as Fiorina once asked, "Is this the paradox that ate rational choice theory?" (1990, p. 334).

The core of the problem is straightforward. In large electorates, it is very unlikely that any one voter will be pivotal. Therefore, if voting is costly, it is not rational to turn out; the costs will exceed the expected gains. (The expected gains equal the chance that one's vote will cause one's preferred party to win times the value of that victory.) Hence, rational citizens will not participate in elections. Yet turnout in stable democracies is substantial; ergo, an anomaly. (Although this statement of

---

[23]Because they examine equilibria produced by optimizing agents, RC analyses of party competition have systematically ignored the cognitive difficulty of the agent's choice problem.

[24]When the author presented "Adaptive Political Parties and Downsian Competition" (Bendor et al. 2001) at a Stanford seminar, Dave Baron asked, "Why don't you try this apparatus on a hard problem?" When asked for an example of a hard problem, Baron replied, "Turnout."

the problem is decision theoretic, careful game theoretic models of participation show that essentially the same anomaly plagues strategic models as well—see, e.g., Palfrey & Rosenthal 1985.) Furthermore, the difference between the models' predictions and the data is huge. No fancy statistical tests are needed; the discrepancy passes the "ocular test"—one only needs to look at them to see that RC models of turnout, whether decision or game theoretic, are not even in the ballpark.

There is, of course, a way to rescue the RC approach in this domain: Simply assume that some people have a taste for voting. A well-known example of this move is Riker & Ordeshook's (1968) hypothesis that citizens have internalized a duty to vote, which makes staying home costly. There is undoubtedly something to this; for example, most political scientists are probably "political junkies" who enjoy participating in elections. But for sound methodological reasons, many scholars who work in the RC program are uncomfortable with this explanation. It is well known that one can predict virtually any behavior (thus making RC theories unfalsifiable) if one adjusts the agents' utility functions at will, so there is a craft norm of being disciplined about preference assumptions.

Bendor et al. (2003) leave preferences alone—voting remains costly in their model—and instead tackle the problem by assuming that voters are boundedly rational. Their view is that RC models of turnout go wrong because they assume that citizens optimize, thus focusing on whether they are pivotal. (In game theoretic models, this also implies that citizens solve extremely complicated strategic problems: Person A must worry about the possible turnout of B, C, etc., anticipating that his peers do likewise. This boggles the mind.) An alternative way of thinking about this choice is that people learn habits (Simon 1947, p. 88), both in politics and in life in general. Habits, in turn, are influenced by a person's prior choices—what seemed to work and what did not.

Thus, in this context, certain people learn to vote while others develop different propensities. In the model of Bendor et al. (2003) citizens learn by trial and error, repeating satisfactory actions and avoiding unsatisfactory ones. This is aspiration-based adaptation. A "satisfactory" action is one that generates satisfactory outcomes, and the latter are determined by comparing payoffs to one's aspiration level, in the typical way. (In the Bendor et al. model, aspirations are endogenous, themselves adjusting to experience.)

The main finding of Bendor et al. (2003) is that agents who adapt via aspiration-based trial and error turn out in substantial numbers. In most runs of the computational model, turnout averages about 50%, even in electorates as large as 1,000,000. The explanation for this effect is somewhat involved, but an important part of it is that in competitive districts, aspirations typically fall into an intermediate range, so that losing is dissatisfying and winning is gratifying regardless of one's individual action. Hence, losing nonvoters and winning voters become more likely to vote in the next election, because the shirkers' action is inhibited and the voters' action is reinforced. Political demography does the rest. In competitive districts there are many losing shirkers and winning voters. Hence turnout stabilizes at substantial levels.

UNFINISHED BUSINESS: THE EMPIRICAL
CONTENT OF SATISFICING MODELS

Most of this chapter examines the potential in Simon's work, largely untapped because of a certain kind of neglect. But neglect causes a second problem: Shortcomings in a work can go undiscovered. And no matter how brilliant the pioneer, shortcomings always exist. The real question is, how long will it take to find them?

An important problem regarding satisficing theory is that under certain specifications it has little empirical content. Consider, for example, two people repeatedly playing a game such as the Prisoner's Dilemma. If an action yields a satisfactory outcome for player A in period t then A satisfices, i.e., uses the same action in $t + 1$. If the current payoff is below A's aspiration, then with some positive probability the agent searches for a new action. Player B adapts via the same rules. Suppose both players begin with a low aspiration, below the sucker's payoff of S. However, in period 1, A happens to choose cooperation whereas B defects. Given the players' low initial aspirations, each one is satisfied with the payoff (S for A and the temptation payoff of T for B). So, satisficing implies that both will use the same action in period 2, both will continue to be satisfied, and so on indefinitely. Thus, even the extreme outcome of constant exploitation is self-reinforcing, given the satisficing-and-search assumptions and the low initial aspiration levels.

Further, this problem does not go away if aspiration levels are endogenized. Suppose, for example, they adjust via the standard weighted average rule: Tomorrow's aspirations are a weighted average of today's aspiration and today's payoff. In the above example, player A's aspiration will converge to S and B's to T. But at every finite date, A's aspiration will be below S and B's will be below T, so getting exploited will be acceptable for A and exploiting will be fine for B. Thus aspirations, behavior, outcomes, and feedback form one large self-reinforcing system.

Bendor et al. (2002, theorem 4) prove that the above holds for a very large class of games, if payoffs are deterministic (the typical assumption in game theoretic models in political science). Bendor et al. also show how to restore empirical content to satisficing models, either by letting players experiment randomly (precluded by classical satisficing) or by letting them obtain vicarious experience by making their aspirations depend partly on other people's experience (payoffs). The latter method involves building the venerable sociological idea of reference groups into these models. (Classical satisficing theory is asocial.)

The Later Simon: Mostly Unused

All of the preceding lines of research relied on work that Simon had completed by the early 1960s, and most of it on work that had been completed by the late 1950s. But although Simon's earlier publications are better known to political scientists than are his later ones, the latter also have significant implications for our discipline. In this section we look at the later Simon. (For an intriguing and unusual effort to apply the later Simon, see Hammond 2002.) His work in this period is different in method as well as substance. It is more empirical (even experimental), and the models are usually solved computationally rather than analytically. I suspect that if/when political scientists begin to apply this later work, these orientations might reappear in the applications. Indeed, much of what I examine in this section takes the form of verbal theory, knit together partly by empirical generalizations (e.g., of how expert problem solvers perform so well). The author of spare mathematical models of satisficing, as in "A Behavioral Model of Rational Choice" (Simon 1955), moved to much thicker formulations after 1960.

The Study of Problem Solving

The bulk of Simon's work in cognitive science was on how humans and computers solve problems. Although decision making is part of problem solving—typically an agent selects a solution to a given problem and so makes a choice—the terminological shift reflects a change in focus. Studies of problem solving spend more time on how agents think about problems than on what choice rule (maximizing expected utility, satisficing, minmax regret, etc.) is used at the end of the process, when a solution is finally selected.

Relatedly, behavioral decision theory usually examines behavior in relatively simple contexts, whereas the problem-solving literature often studies subjects facing complex tasks. Further, scholars studying problem solving have spent much more time trying to understand performance variation in given problem domains (e.g., chess) and to explain how certain people (experts) become proficient at solving problems in certain domains. The work of Simon and his longtime collaborator, Allen Newell, greatly influenced all these patterns, and all these emphases in the study of problem solving have significance for political science.

THE NEWELL-SIMON PICTURE IN BRIEF   The satisficing agent of *Models of Man* (Simon 1957) has a spare psychology. Indeed, the only feature that identifies this construction as belonging to the cognitive revolution rather than the earlier behaviorism (which, by eschewing mentalistic concepts, generated psychological theories that were extremely stark) is the concept of aspiration levels. As a standard that is internal to an organism, an aspiration level is clearly a mentalistic notion, so it would be avoided by good behaviorists. But the more Simon became a cognitive scientist, the more he became convinced that the depiction in *Models of Man* was too spare to answer the questions he had become interested in. To posit that humans satisfice, when they confront hard problems, tells us how they behave in the search process, i.e., when they will stop searching and make a choice. This is useful (and indeed Simon retained the idea in his later, more psychologically detailed work). But it says nothing about how agents think about problems in the first place or how they generate candidate solutions.

To address these questions, a more detailed picture is required. The following summary is a crude synthesis of *Human Problem Solving* (Newell & Simon 1972) and some of Simon's later work. (The interested reader is urged to look at the summary chapter of Newell & Simon 1972; Simon 1990, 1996; and Simon's entries in *The MIT Encyclopedia of the Cognitive Sciences*, e.g., 1999b.) Figure 1 is a simple representation of this summary. Simon's verbal summary is worth quoting:

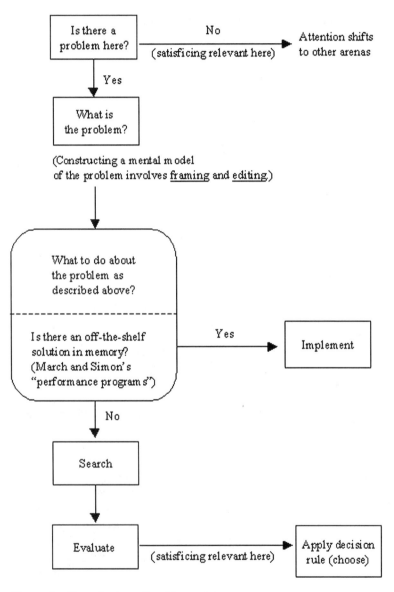

Figure 1   Simon's view of problem solving.

> To solve a problem, a *representation* must be generated, or a preexisting representation accessed. A representation includes (1) a *description* of the given situation, (2) *operators* or actions for changing the situation, and (3) *tests* to determine whether the goal has been achieved. Applying operators creates new situations, and potential applications of all permissible operators define a branching tree of achievable situations, the *problem space*. Problem solving amounts to searching through the problem space for a situation that satisfies the tests for a solution. (Simon 1999b, p. 674; original emphasis)

Note that cognitive constraints can enter anywhere in the above process. The question that students tend to focus on, "Do people optimize [i.e., at the end of the process]?", reflects a misunderstanding of the role and significance of these constraints. As Simon remarked (1979a, p. 498), a scholar often has a choice. If she assumes that the decision maker's model of his task is reasonably complex, then it is empirically plausible to assume that at the end of the process, the agent satisfices or uses some other nonoptimizing rule. Alternatively, she can assume that the decision maker optimizes at the end, but then empirical plausibility will usually require assuming that the agent's problem representation is simple. The overarching hypothesis is that when problems are hard, cognitive constraints will pop up somewhere in the problem-solving process.

Processes that help humans, especially experts, work around these constraints Simon has labeled mechanisms for procedural rationality (1990, 1996). Three are worth noting:

1. Recognition processes. After many years of experience, experts have stored a great deal of information about their task environments in long-term memory, about both situational patterns ("this is situation type X") and actions ("in situation X, do Y"). A fundamental trick, for familiar problems, is to substitute recognition for search. It is this—not superhuman calculation or superhuman search speeds—that enables a Grand Master to play 50 duffers at once.

2. Heuristic search. When recognition fails, experienced decision makers fall back on search. For reasonably complex problems, search is invariably heuristic. There is no guarantee of optimality. Instead, heuristics make complicated problems manageable. They cut them down to human size and, in the hands of experts, often yield "good" solutions. There are two types of heuristics. If the task is highly (and recognizably) structured, experts will use powerful task-specific heuristics, "drawing upon the structural information to guide search directly to the goal" (1990, p. 9). If these are unavailable, then decision makers use general (but weak) heuristics such as satisficing.[25]

---

[25]Note the place of satisficing in this overall view. Far from being the heart of BR, it is merely one of several general-but-weak heuristics.

3. Heuristic search occurs in problem spaces: mental representations of the task at hand. Experts learn to use economical and sometimes powerful problem representations.

Although the above describes a solitary agent, it is straightforward to use this description to develop models of interacting (and conflicting) agents (see, e.g., the work on chess). Indeed, much of Simon's work on procedural rationality sprang directly from his study of chess.

Voters and Jurors, Engineers and Air Traffic Controllers: Hard Problems and Expert Performance

Based only on a reading of the early Simon—in particular, his work on satisficing— one might not have guessed that the later Simon would spend much time studying expertise. In our discipline, a common impression of Simon's approach to decision making is that he stressed that agents "merely" satisfice rather than optimize, which somehow seems to have suggested that he focused on mediocre performance. But this is wrong, and significantly so. As the scissors metaphor makes clear, Simon's view of BR was not that human beings are dumb but that their problems are often hard.

In difficult task environments, people's performance can vary enormously. In chess, for example, a few people are Grand Masters and can pull off amazing feats, such as playing as many as 50 opponents almost simultaneously and beating almost all of them, whereas the rest of us are duffers. This natural variation cries out for explanation. Thus, starting in the 1960s, a new research focus emerged for Simon: How do some decision makers do so well even though they too labor under cognitive constraints (Simon & Simon 1962)? Kasparov may indeed satisfice, but he does not "merely" satisfice. How does he do it?

Before we inspect Simon's answer, it is important to note that in his studies of expertise he selected domains that had two key properties: (*a*) Performance is easy to measure, and (*b*) there are large differences in problem-solving performance among people. [Given (*a*), it is easy to establish (*b*).] Chess fits these criteria beautifully. There is simply no doubt, for example, that Kasparov is a far better chess player than the author of this chapter. It is thus no accident that chess became the "Drosophila" of investigations into expertise. That there is a phenomenon to be explained—some people play chess much better than other people—is indisputable.

When we think of using Simon's ideas in political science, it is important to think about these properties of the task environment. Do we have good measures of performance? And if so, is there a big variation in performance? Consider, for example, the study of voting. More than most scholars who apply Simon's work, Sniderman has been attentive to the "glass half full" aspect of this work. In several publications (e.g., Sniderman 2000, p. 70) he has referred to "Simon's puzzle": How do voters make "approximately rational" decisions in informationally complicated environments? But it is harder to apply the "glass half full" reasoning here than it is in chess. Voters do not compete directly against each other as they do in chess, so we lack a clear performance metric. (For a discussion of the problem of assessing voter competence, see Kuklinski & Quirk 2002.) Or consider foreign policy makers (Axelrod 1976). Although it is clear that Axelrod's subjects *knew* more about foreign policy issues than does the average citizen, this domain lacks chess's compelling performance data. Indeed, in one study of foreign policy making, "Across all seven scenarios, experts were only slightly more accurate than one would expect from chance"(Tetlock 1999, p. 351).

Consequently, in some of these contexts, it is an open question whether there are any real experts at all. (Note that I am implicitly defining expertise in terms of problem-solving performance, not knowledge "in the head.") Indeed, debunking the claims of "experts" to be experts is a longstanding tradition in social science, including Meehl's classic work (for an overview see Dawes et al. 1989). Meehl and his colleagues have established beyond a reasonable doubt that, in some problem domains, simple linear decision rules work better than the judgment of specialists. Who knows? Perhaps a Meehlian analysis of foreign policy making might yield similar results. After all, we don't know whether there truly are experts in that field. Or in voting.

Some readers may object: Surely there is demonstrable expertise in some aspects of politics and government. Of course there is, but not in obvious places. (That is, these places may not be obvious to some political scientists, but readers of *Administrative Behavior* would not find them surprising.) Consider specialists in the Army Corps of Engineers or the California Department of Transportation. It is a good bet that civil and structural engineers in those agencies have demonstrable problem-solving expertise. (Living in earthquake country, I take that bet seriously!) Remarkably, the 1989 Loma Prieta earthquake killed fewer than 100 people, despite its magnitude (about 7.0 on the Richter scale) and its occurring in a metropolitan area with millions of people. A statue honoring these genuine experts, many of whom work in public agencies, should have been erected after Loma Prieta to acknowledge their contribution in helping to avert a catastrophe. (Not long before Loma Prieta, a smaller quake in a much less populated part of Armenia killed thousands. The difference was, I suspect, largely the quality of engineering embodied in buildings in the two sites.) Or consider cryptographers in the CIA, biostatisticians in the Centers for Disease Control, fighter pilots (especially those landing on carriers at night; see Wilson 1989), or air traffic controllers all over the nation. These roles are much less glamorous than that of, say, the National Security Advisor, but from a research perspective they offer the benefit of exhibiting demonstrable expertise. Political scientists have a tendency, perhaps even a systematic bias, to study the exciting and to eschew the mundane. We can learn much from Simon's scientific judgment in this regard. Chess isn't politics. But Drosophila aren't human beings, and geneticists have learned an enormous amount by patiently studying the chromosomes of fruit flies.

Let us briefly examine, then, three very different domains regarding expert performance. (This list is not exhaustive.) In domain 1, all normal human beings perform amazingly well relative to artificial systems. Language acquisition is the paradigmatic example. Despite the "poverty of the stimulus," to use the psycholinguist's phrase, all normal children learn their native language swiftly and easily. Specialists in artificial intelligence are a long way from duplicating this feat. The universality of this performance clearly indicates the operation of powerful evolutionary forces and a resulting hardwired ability. (So Chomsky's "nativist" hypothesis is correct.) In domain 2, after years of "focused practice" (this term is explicated below), a few human beings develop demonstrable expertise. Chess is the paradigmatic example. The huge performance variation suggests that natural selection did not play a direct role; there may be a "language module" in our brains, but there is no "chess module," and probably none for engineering, doing biostatistics competently, or solving cryptographic problems. (Of course, selective forces were undoubtedly important in providing sufficient general intelligence so that ordinary humans can learn to do any of those things. But they require years of concentrated study; learning one's native language does not.) In domain 3, assessing expertise is difficult. Indeed, it is unclear whether any genuine experts exist in this domain (e.g., foreign policy-making). *Claims* to expertise may, of course, abound. Since the explanandum has not been established, there is no point in trying to explain what may not be there. Instead, debunking may be in order. (Naturally, assigning a particular role—voter, engineer, politician—to a domain is an empirical matter.)

Consider domain 2, in which there are people with demonstrable expertise. How do they do it? Recall that Simon's explanation has two main components. First, after years of practice, people specializing in a particular task environment learn to recognize and remember patterns of stimuli—configurations that repeatedly occur. Second, specialists learn and remember action rules that are effective for given patterns. Thus, rather than carrying out time-consuming heuristic search, experts simply *recognize* the solution to a given problem. A key implication of these hypotheses is that experts—even the very best, such as chess Grand Masters—need not have unusual general cognitive capacities such as an exceptionally good long-term memory. Instead, they have accumulated very large and well-organized mental libraries of situations and corresponding actions for specific domains. It is these specialized libraries that enable them to perform their impressive feats.

A beautiful experiment (Simon & Chase 1973) provides compelling evidence for this claim. Many chess masters seem to have formidable memories; the most spectacular examples are those who can successfully play multiple games blindfolded. Because duffers cannot remember a single game blindfolded, much less many of them, one might hypothesize that chess experts have much better memories than does the average human. Simon & Chase tested this hypothesis versus the competing "mental libraries" hypothesis by comparing the performance of masters and novices in two conditions. First they gave the subjects a game, played part way through, to study and memorize. The subjects were shown such boards for 30 seconds and then asked to reconstruct them. Experts made far fewer errors. But then subjects were shown boards on which pieces had been *randomly* arranged—and the error rates of experts and novices converged. Evidently specialists learn to recognize chunks: groupings of pieces that often appear in real games. The "magic number seven" (Miller 1956) does indeed constrain the working memory of chess masters as well as novices, but the masters do not see or try to remember 27 distinct pieces; they only see 6 familiar chunks (patterns). This illustrates Simon's theme perfectly. Instead of eliminating these fundamental limitations on information processing, experts finesse them. Grand Masters remain boundedly rational, but they have learned how to perform superbly within these constraints.

Naturally, this takes time. Simon has estimated that a Grand Master has 50 *thousand* chess chunks stored in long-term memory, and learning this many patterns requires playing and practicing for many years—about 10, it seems. Simon and other researchers have suggested that there is a robust empirical regularity here: To perform at a top-notch level in an informationally intensive field—physics, composing music, chess—usually takes about 10 years. (This claim is meaningful in domain 2, where demonstrable expertise exists, but not in domain 3.)

With this view of expertise in mind, let us now revisit voting. A major controversy in the field is, just how competent *are* voters (e.g., Converse 1975, Sniderman et al. 1991, Kinder 1998)? But before we try to answer Simon's puzzle, it may be sensible to figure out what kind of problem-domain voting belongs to. It is clearly not in domain 1. If it were, specialists would not disagree so vehemently about the competence issue. (Psycholinguists do not disagree about our ability to learn our native tongues; this isn't a "stylized" fact but a plain old-fashioned one.) Further, as Kuklinski & Quirk (2000) argue, it seems unlikely that selective forces present in our species' evolutionary history put a premium on abilities related to voting in large electorates. Voting might belong to domain 2, but it is less clearly a member of this set than, say, chess is. Another possible performance standard is what fully rational citizens would do, but this one raises the awkward issue that perfectly rational people with strictly positive costs of voting would rarely vote at all. As with chess, it is desirable to use empirically relevant performance standards rather than one derived from game theory. So we are left with real, interpersonal comparisons. One might use the (feasible) benchmark of how sophisticated citizens—political scientists, say—with preferences like those of unsophisticated citizens would vote. This, however, may beg a key question: Just how able are sophisticated voters? In other words, although it is empirically clear that some citizens have much more political information than others, and this information is organized in more complex ways, do they exhibit demonstrable expertise in the act of voting?

A similar question can be asked about other political roles that, like voting, are necessarily executed by people who do not specialize in that role—for example, jurors. (For a fascinating experimental study of how well jurors carry out their tasks, see Sunstein et al. 2002.) A comparison of the mental processes of jurors and voters, and of cognitive demands imposed by their roles, would be quite enlightening. Although voters and jurors belong to different subfields in political science (work in one area rarely cites work in the other), in Simon's theory of problem solving they belong to the same category—amateurs trying to solve cognitively hard problems—and so the theory predicts qualitatively similar behaviors. This is an example of how a new research program can reorganize our conceptual landscape and possibly even our academic division of labor.

Finally, it is an open question whether Simon's scissors can be fruitfully deployed on voting, especially in the final election of two-party races, where sophisticated voting is not an issue. Although the decision to *participate* in elections in large jurisdictions is clearly a hard problem, when viewed through game theory's demanding standard, whom one should vote for in the final stage of a two-party race is not. Because voting in primaries or in multi-party races can be significantly more complicated—should I vote sincerely (for my top pick who has no chance) or strategically (for my #2 choice who has a chance)?—Simon's scissors might cut more sharply in those contexts. We may find out that such voting does indeed belong to domain 2: After some training and practice, some citizens do learn to vote strategically, while many others, like duffers in chess, do not display this level of expertise.

This conclusion, by leaving us open to charges of elitism, may make us uncomfortable. But such charges would be based on a misunderstanding of modern theories of expertise, especially those influenced by Simon's work. These theories emphasize that expertise is always domain specific. No one is a "general expert"; such beings do not exist. (Clearly, if becoming a first-class expert in information-intensive fields takes about 10 years, it is impossible over the course of a normal lifetime for anyone to become proficient in more than a few areas.) Thus this perspective differs sharply from the eighteenth-century elitism of, for example, the founding fathers, not only because it is meritocratic in an effort-based sense (rather than assuming that some people are born more gifted) but also because, in the traditional view, problem-solving ability was an attribute of a *person*; it traveled with him (and the person was always male) from situation to situation. In the modern, domain-specific view, everyone is an amateur in most aspects of life. Nisbett & Ross put it eloquently in their book on human inference, in answering a critic who asked, "If we're so dumb, how come we made it to the moon?"

> Getting to the moon was a joint project, if not of *idiot savants*, at least of savants whose individual areas of expertise were extremely limited—one savant who knew a great deal about the propellant properties of solid fuels but little about the guidance capabilities of small computers, ... and so forth. Finally, those savants included people who believed that redheads are hot-tempered [and] who bought their last car on the cocktail-party advice of an acquaintance's brother-in-law .... (Nisbett & Ross 1980, p. 250)

CONCLUSIONS

Whether the work of the early or the late Simon will be more useful for political science in the long run is uncertain. The early Simon is ahead now, and I suspect this trend will continue for some time. His pre-1960 work enjoys significant advantages. In particular, its theoretical structure is much simpler, as a comparison of Simon (1955) versus Newell & Simon (1972) quickly reveals. Hence, his early formulations are easier to use in formal models of political processes such as elections. In contrast, his subsequent works in cognitive science are like Persian miniatures. The computational models in *Human Problem Solving* are detailed even by the standards of psychology, a field that is more micro than our discipline and that naturally studies individual problem-solving and choice in a more fine-grained way.

But these issues are complex. They involve trade-offs between scientifically valued attributes, for example, between the theoretical coherence of our discipline and the verisimilitude of particular theories. Scholars who put great weight on theoretical coherence prefer research programs whose theories have a simple axiomatic structure and which can unify different empirical domains, even at the cost of some predictive accuracy. Scholars who greatly value verisimilitude are willing to sacrifice theoretical simplicity and generality if predictive accuracy is obtained in return.

Simon himself exhibited different positions on this trade-off over his career. The author of *Models of Man* (1957) evidently placed great store on axiomatically simple formulations, often represented by mathematical models with closed-form solutions. But over time he seemed to put increasing weight on verisimilitude and less on simplicity.[26] Indeed, toward the end of his life he had become impatient with mathematical economists who were developing models of BR with what he viewed as insufficient attention to the empirical foundations of their premises. His position is clearly expressed in a fascinating exchange with the distinguished game theorist Ariel Rubenstein, who had written a book on formal models of BR and had graciously published parts of Simon's critical letter in an appendix to the book. Simon criticized what he saw as Rubinstein's neglect of empirics:

> Aside from the use you make of the Tversky-Kahneman experiments, for which I applaud you and them, almost the only reference to empirical matters that I detect in your pages is an occasional statement like "a casual observation" and "the phenomenon exhibited here is quite."
>
> My training in science has installed in me a knee-jerk response to such statements. I ask automatically: 'How do you know'? 'What evidence can you provide to show that this is true'? Long experience in the natural sciences . . . has shown that casual empiricism does not provide a firm foundation for the theories that fit the facts of the real world. Facts do not come from

---

[26]To be fair to Simon, this debate encompasses two very different senses of simplification. One involves ignoring most of what we know about a micro level. This he endorsed. The second involves idealization: making assumptions that we know to be counterfactual in order to make our theories tractable, i.e., simple enough so that we can work out implications via closed-form mathematics. The later Simon increasingly objected to this. (But it seemed that he also objected to idealization-type simplifications even when these are not known to be counterfactual but are merely not grounded empirically.)

the armchair, but from careful observation and experimentation. (quoted in Rubinstein 1998, p. 188)

In the only face-to-face conversation that I ever had with Simon, a few months before his death, I suggested that political science, as a field with much more macro concerns than cognitive science, had to be ruthless about the level of detail of its micro assumptions. I was fortunate to have encountered the elderly Simon; if the stories are true, the younger man would have gone at me with hammer and tongs, intellectually speaking. Having mellowed, he was gentle. Still, he disagreed firmly and repeated the view that he had articulated in the letter to Rubinstein and in many other places: What is the scientific value of theories that are empirically inaccurate? I muttered something about trade-offs that varied continuously, rather than being either-or choices, and dropped the matter. Arguing with one's hero is awkward.

But hero worship should not hamper serious thinking about how to design strategies that make sense in one's field. I think that Simon, genius though he was, got it wrong: Macro fields such as political science *must* be more ruthless than corresponding micro fields, such as cognitive science, about micro assumptions. The former simply face tougher trade-offs than the latter. At the end of the day we are interested in elections, democratic transitions, war and peace—phenomena involving interactions among thousands or even millions of people. Theories of such phenomena that are based on individual decision making cannot look like the models in *Human Problem Solving*; the micro details would overwhelm us.

Simon should have understood this. The author of "The Architecture of Complexity" should have realized—and in other contexts, did realize—that when boundedly rational observers of systems aggregate from the micro to the macro, micro detail must inevitably be lost. And political scientists are just as boundedly rational as other observers.

Curiously, however, another part of his work—that on expertise—helps to explain why he didn't remember this point when he scolded social scientists who build formal models of BR. As I argued in the beginning of this essay, for the last 40 years of his life he was a cognitive scientist. The axiom of serial processing implies that since he was thinking hard and long about issues in that field, he was *not* thinking very much about issues in other fields, such as political science. And so he lost touch with his first specialty. As he emphasized in his work with Chase, expertise is domain specific, developed *and maintained* by intense practice and thoughtful reflections about that practice. He had, in short, mostly forgotten what it meant to be a political scientist—a natural consequence of cognitive processes that he himself had studied.

This is an irony. In cognitive science, Newell & Simon were famous for their declaration, which they defended throughout their careers, that information processing was quasi-independent of the neighboring micro-field of neurophysiology. As in-principle reductionists but pragmatic holists, they argued that cognitive science could progress rapidly if cognitive scientists temporarily ignored how the brain implements mental processes (Newell & Simon 1972, pp. 875–76). And they had good reason to be worried that their new field could get bogged down in neurophysiological details. At that level, the human brain is fantastically complicated (billions of neurons, each connected to thousands of other neurons), and understanding the physical mechanisms could easily divert researchers from studying higher-order processes such as problem solving.

Of course, Newell & Simon recognized that *eventually* cognitive science would require neuroscientific foundations. But in 1955 they thought that their infant field would benefit from temporarily waving a flag of quasi-independence.[27] Much the same is true of the relation between cognitive and political science. Of course scholars who use psychologically spare models of decision making, such as satisficing-and-search, recognize that *eventually* these models need the detailed foundations that only more fine-grained cognitive theories can provide. But temporarily asserting quasi-independence might be a smart research heuristic. What matters in the macro models of interest to political scientists are only a few properties of human problem solving and choice (Simon 1987), such as seriality in high-order mental processes.

Exactly how those properties are produced, and why humans have them, is something that we might want to set aside for now—along with the detailed information-processing models that would provide the answers. If we are lucky, this academic division of labor will work as well for us as the Newell-Simon structure worked for cognitive science.

ACKNOWLEDGMENTS

I would like to thank David Braybrooke, John Conlisk, Robyn Dawes, Persi Diaconis, Daniel Diermeier, Baruch Fischhoff, Elizabeth Gerber, Mark Green, Dale Griffin, Thomas Hammond, John Jost, Daniel Kahneman, Rod Kramer, David Laitin, Charles Lindblom, Elijah Millgram, John Padgett, Nelson Polsby, Ken Shotts, Herbert Simon, Neil Smelser, Joel Sobel, Philip Tetlock, and Fred Thompson for their helpful comments on earlier drafts. All errors are my own.

The *Annual Review of Political Science* is online at
http://polisci.annualreviews.org

LITERATURE CITED

Abelson R, Levi A. 1985. Decision making and decision theory. In *The Handbook of Social Psychology*, ed. G Lindzey, E Aronson, 1:231–309. New York: Random House

Allison G. 1971. *Essence of Decision*. Boston: Little, Brown

Arrow K. 1974. *The Limits of Organization*. New York: Norton

---

[27]Although this was a useful research strategy for a long time, it now seems to be breaking down—but for benign reasons. Neuroscience is presently generating so many tempting research opportunities that the Newell-Simon strategy is now regarded as too costly.

Axelrod R. 1976. *Structure of Decision*. Princeton, NJ: Princeton Univ. Press

Bendor J. 1995. A model of muddling through. *Am. Polit. Sci. Rev.* 89:819–40

Bendor J. 2001. Bounded rationality in political science. In *International Encyclopedia of the Social and Behavioral Sciences*, ed. N Smelser, P Baltes, pp. 1303–7. Amsterdam: Elsevier

Bendor J, Diermeier D, Ting M. 2002. *The empirical content of behavioral models of adaptation*. Presented at UCLA Conf. Comput. Models in Soc. Sci. Lake Arrowhead, CA

Bendor J, Diermeier D, Ting M. 2003. A behavioral model of turnout. *Am. Polit. Sci. Rev.* In press

Bendor J, Hammond T. 1992. Rethinking Allison's models. *Am. Polit. Sci. Rev.* 86:301–22

Bendor J, Moe T. 1986. Agenda control, committee capture, and the dynamics of institutional politics. *Am. Polit. Sci. Rev.* 80:1187–1207

Bendor J, Mookherjee D, Ray D. 2001. *Adaptive political parties and Downsian competition*. Presented at Annu. Meet. Am. Polit. Sci. Assoc. San Francisco, CA

Braybrooke D, Lindblom C. 1963. *A Strategy of Decision*. New York: Free

Camerer C. 1994. Individual decision making. In *Handbook of Experimental Economics*, ed. J Kagel, A Roth, pp. 587–703. Princeton, NJ: Princeton Univ. Press

Camerer C. 2003. *Behavioral Game Theory*. Princeton, NJ: Princeton Univ. Press.

Christensen-Szalanski J, Beach L. 1984. The citation bias: fad and fashion in the judgment and decision literature. *Am. Psychologist* 39:75–78

Conlisk J. 1996. Why bounded rationality? *J. Econ. Lit.* 34:669–700

Converse P. 1975. Public opinion and voting behavior. In *Handbook of Political Science*, ed. F Greenstein, NW Polsby, 4:75–169. Reading, MA: Addison-Wesley

Crecine J. 1969. *Governmental Problem-Solving*. Chicago: Rand McNally

Crecine J. 1970. *Defense budgeting: organizational adaptation to environmental constraints*. Monogr. RM-6121-PR. Santa Monica, CA: Rand

Crecine J. 1985. A positive theory of public spending. In *Advances in Information Processing in Organizations*, ed. L Sproull, P Larkey, 2:99–154. Greenwich, CT: JAI

Cyert R, March J. 1963. *A Behavioral Theory of the Firm*. Englewood Cliffs, NJ: Prentice-Hall

Dahl R, Lindblom C. 1953. *Politics, Economics, and Welfare*. New York: Harper & Row

Davis O, Dempster M, Wildavsky A. 1966. A theory of the budget process. *Am. Polit. Sci. Rev.* 60:529–47

Davis O, Dempster M, Wildavsky A. 1974. Towards a predictive theory of government expenditure. *Br. J. Polit. Sci.* 4:419–52

Dawes R. 1998. Behavioral decision making and judgment. In *The Handbook of Social Psychology*, ed. D Gilbert, S Fiske, G Lindzey, 1:497–548. Boston: McGraw-Hill

Dawes R, Faust D, Meehl P. 1989. Clinical versus actuarial judgment. *Science* 243:1668–74

Downs A. 1957. *An Economic Theory of Democracy*. New York: Harper

Dubnick M. 2002. Once a political scientist, always . . . . In *Remembering a Giant: a Tribute to Herbert A. Simon*. Washington, DC: Am. Polit. Sci. Assoc.

Einhorn H, Hogarth R. 1981. Behavioral decision theory. *Annu. Rev. Psychol.* 32:53–88

Fiorina M. 1990. Information and rationality in elections. In *Information and Democratic Processes*, ed. J Ferejohn, J Kuklinski, pp. 329–42. Urbana: Univ. Ill. Press

Gigerenzer G. 1991. How to make cognitive illusions disappear: beyond heuristics and biases. *Eur. Rev. Soc. Psychol.* 2:83–115

Gilbert D. 1998. Ordinary personology. In *The Handbook of Social Psychology*, ed. D Gilbert, S Fiske, G Lindzey, 2:89–150. Boston: McGraw-Hill

Gilovich T, Griffin D. 2002. Introduction—heuristics and biases: then and now. In *Heuristics and Biases: the Psychology of*

Intuitive Judgment, ed. T Gilovich, D Griffin, D Kahneman, pp. 1–18. Cambridge, UK: Cambridge Univ. Press

Gode D, Sunder S. 1993. Allocative efficiency of markets with zero-intelligence traders: markets as a partial substitute for individual rationality. *J. Polit. Econ.* 101:119–37

Gopnik A, Meltzoff A, Kuhl P. 1999. *The Scientist in the Crib: Minds, Brains, and How Children Learn*. New York: William Morrow

Green M, Thompson F. 2001. Organizational process models of budgeting. In *Evolving Theories of Public Budgeting*, ed. J Bartle, pp. 55–81. Amsterdam: Elsevier

Grofman B, Feld S. 1988. Rousseau's general will: a Condorcetian perspective. *Am. Polit. Sci. Rev.* 82:567–76

Grofman B, Owen G, Feld S. 1983. Thirteen theorems in search of the truth. *Theory Decis.* 15:261–78

Hammond K. 1990. Functionalism and illusionism: Can integration be usefully achieved? In *Insight in Decision Making*, ed. R Hogarth, pp. 227–61. Chicago: Univ. Chicago Press

Hammond T. 2002. *Heuristic search and the power of hierarchy*. Presented at Herbert A. Simon Award ceremony, Midwest Polit. Sci. Assoc. Meet., Chicago

Hogarth R. 1987. *Judgement and Choice*. New York: Wiley. 2nd ed.

Holyoak K. 1990. Problem solving. In *An Invitation to Cognitive Science*, ed. D Osherson, E Smith, 3:117–46. Cambridge, MA: MIT Press

Jones B. 1999. Bounded rationality. *Annu. Rev. Polit. Sci.* 2:297–321

Jones B. 2001. *Politics and the Architecture of Choice*. Chicago: Univ. Chicago Press

Kahneman D, Tversky A. 1996. On the reality of cognitive illusions: a reply to Gigerenzer's critique. *Psychol. Rev.* 103:582–91

Kinder D. 1998. Opinion and action in the realm of politics. In *The Handbook of Social Psychology*, ed. D Gilbert, S Fiske, G Lindzey, 2:778–867. Boston: McGraw-Hill

Koehler D, Brenner L, Griffin D. 2002. The calibration of expert judgment: heuristics and biases beyond the laboratory. In *Heuristics and*

Biases: the Psychology of Intuitive Judgment, ed. T Gilovich, D Griffin, D Kahneman, pp. 686–715. Cambridge, UK: Cambridge Univ. Press

Kollman K, Miller J, Page S. 1992. Adaptive parties in spatial elections. *Am. Polit. Sci. Rev.* 86:929–38

Kollman K, Miller J, Page S. 1998. Political parties and electoral landscapes. *Br. J. Polit. Sci.* 28:139–58

Kotovsky K, Hayes J, Simon H. 1985. Why are some problems hard? *Cogn. Psychol.* 17:248–94

Kuklinski J, Quirk P. 2000. Reconsidering the rational public: cognition, heuristics, and mass opinion. In *Elements of Reason*, ed. A Lupia, M McCubbins, S Popkin, pp. 153–82. New York: Cambridge Univ. Press

Kuklinski J, Quirk P. 2002. Conceptual foundations of citizen competence. *Polit. Behav.* 23:285–311

Ladha K. 1992. The Condorcet Jury Theorem, free speech, and correlated votes. *Am. J. Polit. Sci.* 36:617–34

Lakatos I. 1970. Falsification and the methodology of scientific research programmes. In *Criticism and the Growth of Knowledge*, ed. I Lakatos, A Musgrave, pp. 91–195. Cambridge, UK: Cambridge Univ. Press

Landau M. 1969. Redundancy, rationality, and the problem of duplication and overlap. *Public Admin. Rev.* 29:346–58

Laudan L. 1977. *Progress and Its Problems: Toward a Theory of Scientific Growth*. Berkeley: Univ. Calif. Press

Laudan R, Laudan L, Donovan A. 1988. Testing theories of scientific change. In *Scrutinizing Science*, ed. A Donovan, L Laudan, R Laudan, pp. 3–44. Dordrecht: Kluwer

Lichtenstein S, Fischhoff B, Phillips L. 1982. Calibration of probabilities. In *Judgment Under Uncertainty: Heuristics and Biases*, ed. D Kahneman, P Slovic, A Tversky, pp. 306–34. Cambridge, UK: Cambridge Univ. Press

Lindblom C. 1959. The science of 'muddling through'. *Pub. Admin. Rev.* 19:79–88

Lindblom C. 1965. *The Intelligence of Democracy*. New York: Free

Lindblom C. 1968. *The Policy-Making Process*. Englewood Cliffs, NJ: Prentice-Hall

Lippmann W. 1922. *Public Opinion*. New York: Macmillan

Lodge M. 1995. Toward a procedural model of candidate evaluation. In *Political Judgment*, ed. M Lodge, K McGraw, pp. 11–140. Ann Arbor: Univ. Mich. Press

Lopes L. 1981. Performing competently. *Behav. Brain Sci.* 4:343–44

McKelvey R, Ordeshook P. 1990. Information and elections: retrospective voting and rational expectations. In *Information and Democratic Processes*, ed. J Ferejohn, J Kuklinski, pp. 281–312. Champaign-Urbana: Univ. Ill. Press

Miller G. 1956. The magic number seven, plus or minus two. *Psychol. Rev.* 63:81–97

Miller G. 1989. Scientists of the artificial. In *Complex Information Processing: the Impact of Herbert A. Simon*, ed. D Klahr, K Kotovsky, pp. 145–61. Hillsdale, NJ: Lawrence Erlbaum

Miller N. 1986. Information, electorates, and democracy: some extensions and interpretations of the Condorcet jury theorem. In *Information Pooling and Group Decision Making*, ed. B Grofman, G Owen, pp. 173–92. Greenwich, CT: JAI

Moe T. 1991. Politics and the theory of organization. *J. Law Econ. Org.* 7:106–29

Nelson R, Winter S. 1982. *An Evolutionary Theory of Economic Change*. Cambridge, MA: Harvard Univ. Press

Newell A, Simon H. 1972. *Human Problem Solving*. Englewood Cliffs, NJ: Prentice-Hall

Nisbett R, Ross L. 1980. *Human Inference*. Englewood Cliffs, NJ: Prentice-Hall

Padgett J. 1980. Bounded rationality in budgetary research. *Am. Polit. Sci. Rev.* 74:354–72

Padgett J. 1981. Hierarchy and ecological control in federal budgetary decision making. *Am. J. Sociol.* 87:75–128

Palfrey T, Rosenthal H. 1985. Voter participation and strategic uncertainty. *Am. Polit. Sci. Rev.* 29:62–78

Pinker S. 1997. *How the Mind Works*. New York: Norton

Riker W, Ordeshook P. 1968. A theory of the calculus of voting. *Am. Polit. Sci. Rev.* 62:25–42

Rubinstein A. 1998. *Modeling Bounded Rationality*. Cambridge, MA: MIT Press

Selten R. 1989. Evolution, learning, and economic behavior. *Games Econ. Behav.* 3:3–24

Shafir E, Tversky A. 1995. Decision making. In *An Invitation to Cognitive Science*, ed. E Smith, D Osherson, 3:77–100. Cambridge, MA: MIT Press

Shepsle K. 1996. Statistical political philosophy and positive political theory. In *The Rational Choice Controversy*, ed. J Friedman, pp. 213–22. New Haven, CT: Yale Univ. Press

Simon H. 1947. *Administrative Behavior*. New York: Free

Simon H. 1955. A behavioral model of rational choice. *Q. J. Econ.* 69:99–118

Simon H. 1956. Rational choice and the structure of the environment. *Psychol. Rev.* 63:129–38

Simon H. 1957. *Models of Man*. New York: Wiley

Simon H. 1962. The architecture of complexity. *Proc. Am. Phil. Soc.* 106:467–82

Simon H. 1964. The concept of organizational goal. *Admin. Sci. Q.* 9:1–22

Simon H. 1979a. Rational decision making in business organizations. *Am. Econ. Rev.* 69:493–513

Simon H. 1979b. *Models of Thought*, Vol. I. New Haven, CT: Yale Univ. Press

Simon H. 1987. Politics as information processing. *London School Econ. Q.* 1:345–70

Simon H. 1990. Invariants of human behavior. *Annu. Rev. Psychol.* 41:1–19

Simon H. 1991. *Models of My Life*. New York: Basic Books

Simon H. 1996. *The Sciences of the Artificial*. Cambridge, MA: MIT Press. 3rd ed.

Simon H. 1999a. The potlatch between economics and political science. In *Competition and Cooperation*, ed. J Alt, M Levi,

E Ostrom, pp. 112–19. New York: Russell Sage

Simon H. 1999b. Problem solving. In *The MIT Encyclopedia of the Cognitive Sciences*, ed. R Wilson, F Keil, pp. 674–76. Cambridge, MA: MIT Press

Simon H, Chase W. 1973. Skill in chess. *Am. Scientist* 61(July–Aug.):394–403

Simon H, Simon P. 1962. Trial and error search in solving difficult problems. *Behav. Sci.* 7:425–29

Slovic P. 1990. Choice. In *Invitation to Cognitive Science*, ed. D Osherson, E Smith, 3:89–116. Cambridge, MA: MIT Press

Slovic P, Lichtenstein S, Fischoff B. 1988. Decision making. In *Stevens' Handbook of Experimental Psychology*, ed. R Atkinson, R Herrnstein, G Lindzey, R Luce, pp. 673–738. New York: Wiley. 2nd ed.

Sniderman P, Brody R, Tetlock P. 1991. *Reasoning and Choice: Explorations in Political Psychology*. New York: Cambridge Univ. Press

Sniderman P. 2000. Taking sides: a fixed choice theory of political reasoning. In *Elements of Reason*, ed. A Lupia, M McCubbins, S Pop-

kin, pp. 67–84. Cambridge, UK: Cambridge Univ. Press

Stokes S. 1999. Political parties and democracy. *Annu. Rev. Polit. Sci.* 2:243–67

Sunstein C, Hastie R, Payne J, Schkade D, Viscusi V. 2002. *Punitive Damages*. Chicago: Univ. Chicago Press

Tetlock P. 1999. Theory-driven reasoning about possible pasts and probable futures in world politics: Are we prisoners of our preconceptions? *Am. J. Polit. Sci.* 43:335–66

Ting M. 2003. A strategic theory of bureaucratic redundancy. *Am. J. Polit. Sci.* In press

Tversky A, Kahneman D. 1974. Judgment under uncertainty. *Science* 185:1124–31

Tversky A, Kahneman D. 1986. Rational choice and the framing of decisions. *J. Bus.* 59:S251–78

von Winterfeldt D, Edwards W. 1986. *Decision Analysis and Behavioral Research*. Cambridge, UK: Cambridge Univ. Press

Wildavsky A. 1979 (1964). *The Politics of the Budgetary Process*. Boston: Little, Brown. 3rd ed.

Wilson J. 1989. *Bureaucracy*. New York: Basic

Annu. Rev. Polit. Sci. 2003. 6:473–507
doi: 10.1146/annurev.polisci.6.121901.085601

TERRORIST DECISION MAKING

Gordon H. McCormick

*Department of Defense Analysis, Naval Postgraduate School, Monterey,
California 93943; email: gmccormick@nps.navy.mil*

Key Words   terrorism, political violence, irregular warfare, levels of analysis

■ **Abstract**   How do terrorists and terrorist groups make decisions? And what influence do terrorist decision-making styles have on the course of a terrorist campaign? Efforts to answer these questions have centered on three sets of theories. In order of generality, these are (*a*) strategic theories, in which the decision to employ terrorism and related forms of political violence is considered to be an instrumental choice; (*b*) organizational theories, in which the sources of violence are found in the internal dynamics of the terrorist group itself; and (*c*) psychological theories, in which the decision to employ terrorism is explained within the framework of individual psychology. Most observers agree that these lines of inquiry are not mutually exclusive, but each offers a distinctive approach to terrorist decision making. This essay examines each of these theoretical approaches in turn. It concludes with a brief discussion of the decision-making constraints that help shape terrorist life cycles.

INTRODUCTION

Terrorism has a long and diverse history. The systematic study of terrorism, however, is of much more recent origin. Scholarly interest in the subject did not begin in earnest until the early 1970s, spurred by the sharp increase in terrorist actions carried out in the previous decade. Prior to this time, the study of terrorism—notably, oppositional terrorism—was largely a practical pursuit. Many of the questions that interest scholars today were debated by terrorism's advocates and critics over 150 years ago. How should terrorism be defined? What can it be expected to accomplish? Under what circumstances is it employed? What are its unintended consequences? What forms can it take? What are its ethical implications? What is its relationship to other forms of political resistance? With a few notable exceptions, the interest of these early theorists was tactical rather than intellectual. They were out to win. They were less interested in explaining terrorism as a political and social phenomenon than in building a better bomb and refining their theory of victory.

The goals of modern research have changed, but terrorism has remained a contentious field of inquiry. One of the more controversial aspects of the subject involves its definition. The word itself has become a term of rhetoric. When used in this capacity, its purpose is not to define but to defame. Although most observers are prepared to agree that terrorism is what the enemy does, there are clearly differences of opinion, in any particular case, on who the enemy actually is. Terrorism, in this respect, is not only an instrument of politics; the term itself is an instrument of political debate. Those who hold power often find it advantageous to define any act of violence by their political opponents as an act of terrorism. Those who are attempting to seize power, for their part, often find it expedient to claim that they are the victims of terrorist violence on the part of the state (Jenkins 1981). Where one stands is often a matter of political opinion.

Even among scholars, however, a common analytical definition has proven elusive. Schmid & Jongman (1988) identified over 100 separate definitions of terrorism in 1988, and the situation has not improved much since. Definitional differences persist over a range of important issues, including the line of division between terrorism and other forms of political violence; whether the concept of terrorism should distinguish between the nature of the act and the nature of the perpetrator; the substantive distinction—if any—between state terrorism "from above" and oppositional terrorism "from below"; whether terrorism should be defined as a criminal or a political act; whether the distinction between terrorism and other forms of political violence is a qualitative one (and if so, the criteria that define terrorism's specific characteristics); whether terrorism must always involve violence or the threat of violence; and the definition of a terrorist group or terrorist organization, in contrast to a group or organization that sometimes employs terrorism.

It is neither possible nor necessary to resolve this debate here. Scholarly (and associated policy) differences over the nature and scope of terrorism will be the norm for the foreseeable future. In the discussion that follows, "terrorism" refers to the deliberate use of symbolic violence or the threat of violence against non-combatants for political purposes. This view follows closely from the now classic definition of terrorism advanced by Thornton (1964). Terrorism, in this case, is defined not by the status of the perpetrator but by the nature of the act. Its symbolic quality, which distinguishes it from conventional forms of violence, is due to its indirect and psychological character. Terrorist actions are ultimately designed to influence one target by attacking another. The nature of both target sets varies over time and across cases, depending on the goals and capabilities of the group in question and the circumstances under which it is operating. Terrorism is a purposeful activity, carried out in the name of a larger political objective, regardless of the individual motives or group dynamics that may help explain why a particular action was carried out at a particular time. (See also Hoffman 1998; Rapoport 1992, 1999.)

My purpose here is to review the literature on terrorist decision making. Terrorism is always a choice among alternatives. What factors influence this choice? How do terrorist groups explain and justify their actions? What do they expect to accomplish? What is the nature of terrorist belief systems? Are terrorist actions motivated by a group's external goals or by its internal dynamics? What role does individual psychology play in the decision to employ violence? To what degree and with what effect do the exogenous and endogenous factors that influence group behavior change over time? How, in short, do terrorist groups make decisions? And what impact do their decision-making styles have on the rise and fall of terrorist campaigns? These and related questions have occupied scholars for the past 30 years.

I begin with a brief overview of the behavioral foundations of modern terrorism. This is followed by a discussion of the primary theoretical frames that are used to evaluate terrorist decision-making processes. Finally, I address the subject of terrorist life cycles and examine some of the fundamental tradeoffs that confront terrorist decision makers over time.

RATIONALISTS AND EXPRESSIONISTS

The first systematic justification for terrorism was formulated by the radical German publicist Karl Heinzen (1809–1880) in a two-part essay entitled *Der Mord* (*Murder*), published in January and February 1849 (Heinzen 1978).[1] Heinzen's essay went to press a year after the *Communist Manifesto* and in the midst of the revolutionary outbreak that swept through Europe between 1848 and 1849. (For a discussion of Heinzen and his times, see Wittke 1945, Carlson 1972, Laqueur 1987.) The killing of another human being, Heinzen argued passionately, was immoral. What was immoral in a moral context, however, could be transformed into an act of legitimate self-defense when directed against a murderous tyranny. When confronted by murderers, he wrote, men of principle are bound to act, for neither party under these circumstances can "escape either murdering or being murdered" (Heinzen 1978, p. 53). To show any conscience and to hesitate to kill, in such cases, is itself "unprincipled" (p. 59). "We do not desire *any* killing, *any* murder," Heinzen claimed, "but if our enemies are not of the same mind, if they can justify murder, even going so far as to claim a special privilege in the matter, then necessity compels us to challenge this privilege. . . ." It is "no great step," he went on, "to condemn hundreds of thousands to the scaffold in the interests of humanity" (pp. 54–55).

Murder, Heinzen declared, must be turned into a science. The revolutionary cannot depend on his moral authority alone. The state, he explained, enters the struggle with a significant material advantage in "organization," "training," "numbers," and the "means of destruction" (Heinzen 1978, p. 61). To prevail, revolutionaries must turn their weakness into a political strength by pursuing an offsetting strategy of high-profile violence. Their immediate objective "must be to eliminate the superiority of the barbarian party through the invention of new methods of killing. . . ." Heinzen wondered whether it was possible "to invent instruments

---

[1]Heinzen's essay was originally published in the revolutionary periodical, *Die Evolution*. (For a discussion, see Wittke 1945, Carlson 1972). All quotations are taken from the English translation of selections of *Der Mord* in Laqueur (1978).

which can be made without being seen, be transported without attracting notice, be operated without any great effort, and which are, in sum, no less effective than big guns?" Presaging the threat posed today by the possible terrorist use of weapons of mass destruction, his answer was to create "instruments of destruction which are of little use to the great masses of the barbarians when they are fighting a few lone individuals, but which give a few lone individuals the terrifying power to threaten the safety . . . of whole masses of barbarians" (pp. 62–63).

To prevail in such a contest, revolutionaries must devote themselves "to the study of murder and refine the art of killing to the highest possible degree." The goal of these efforts, Heinzen wrote, was to create an environment in which "the barbarians are afraid for their lives every hour of the day or night." The regime and its supporters, he went on, must be forced into the position where they "think that every drink of water, every mouthful of food, every bed, every bush, every paving stone, every bundle of straw, every pipe bowl, every stick, every pin may be a killer." Every revolutionary action must be designed to create this state of fear. "Murder is their motto," Heinzen argued, "so let murder be their answer, murder is their need, so let murder be their payment, murder is their argument, so let murder be their refutation." The path to a higher "Humanity," he concluded, must "pass through the zenith of Barbarity." The enemies of humanity "have made this principle a law of politics and we shall either have to observe this 'law', follow this 'constitutional path', or be buried, and our freedom with us" (Heinzen 1978, p. 64).

Heinzen's work was an indicator of things to come. His clarion call to "murder the murderers" was followed by similar calls to action by a succession of radical theorists over the next 50 years, including Peter Zaichnevski (1842–1896), Paul Brousse (1844–1912), Michael Bakunin (1814–1876), Sergei Nechaev (1847–1882), Sergei Kravchinski (1852–1895), Nicoli Morozov (1854–1946), Lev Tikhomirov (1852–1923), Johann Most (1846–1906), Elisée Recluse (1830–1905), and Gerasim Romanenko (1858–1927). (For an overview, see Venturi 1960; Avrich 1967; Pomper 1979, 1995; Joll 1980; Laqueur 1987; Miller 1995.) These commentators developed the modern doctrine of terrorism. Central to this doctrine was the concept of "propaganda by the deed," a metaphor for high-profile violence that seems to have been first introduced by the French revolutionary democrat Carlo Piscane in the 1850s. The concept was subsequently extended and popularized by the Italian anarchists Carlo Cafiero and Errico Malatesta in their declaration to the Anarchist International in 1876. The "insurrectionary deed," they declared, was "the most efficient means of propaganda . . . the one most capable of breaking through to the deepest social strata," and the best way "of attracting the most vital forces of humanity to the struggle of the Internationale" (Iviansky 1977). Actions spoke louder than words.

Terrorism during this period was accelerated by two sets of developments. The first was the invention of dynamite in 1866. Dynamite, it was said, was the ultimate democratic weapon. It was "the great equalizer" that would finally allow revolutionaries to realize Heinzen's dream of harnessing the "instruments of science" to overcome the superior power of the state (Avrich 1984, Laqueur 1987). The second set of developments involved the invention of the rotary press, the introduction of the telegraph, and the dramatic increase in public literacy that occurred in the second half of the nineteenth century (Schmid & de Graaf 1982). Actions carried out in one location could now be quickly communicated to another. A single, militant event could now be "witnessed" by a nation-wide constituency. As the early French anarchist Leon Lehautier once observed, "if my protest does not attract a scandal which forcibly attracts attention to my grievances, it is as if I am not complaining at all" (Leites 1979, p. 3). Dynamite ensured that terrorists, with relative ease, could now "attract a scandal." The development of the media ensured that their "grievances" would now be heard by an ever larger audience.

Two competing philosophies of terrorism developed during these formative years that continue to define terrorist behavior to this day. The first was a philosophy of rationalism. To the rational terrorist, violence was a means to an end. Among the first modern groups to systematically employ terrorism in an instrumental way were the "disorganization squads" of the Russian "Land and Freedom" movement, which evolved into the People's Will (*Narodnaya Volya*) (1879–1882). While many *narodniki* were clearly captivated by the heroic mystique of revolutionary violence, the group as a whole pursued its goal with a grim but practical determination. Terrorism, in their view, was an instrument of political mobilization, which, in the words of Nikolai Bukh, could be employed to "stir up the masses, force the people out of their age old sleep, [and] show them clearly that there exists a force which is fighting against their enemies and protecting their interests" (quoted in Hardy 1987). This would be achieved by a campaign of violence designed "to break down the prestige of [the] government, to furnish continuous proof of the possibility of pursuing a contest with the government, to raise in that way the revolutionary spirit of the people, and finally, to form a body suited to and accustomed to warfare" ("Program of the People's Will", in Iviansky 1977).

Coexisting and competing with this utilitarian perspective was the view that terrorism was a means of individual expression. Terrorism, according to this line of argument, was a redemptive act, or, as Bakunin put it, an act of "redemptive destruction." Apart from its political function, it also served the individual and collective psychological needs of the terrorists themselves. The resort to terrorism was an existential choice. The willingness to kill and, if necessary, die for one's political ideals constituted a personal leap of faith. There could be no meaning without commitment, and no form of commitment was more irrevocable than violence. Carrying out a "threatening or murderous act" became "a Nietzchean or Sorelian assertion of will" (Miller 1995, p. 61). Whereas groups like the People's Will and their successors in the Combat Organization (*Boevaia Organizatsiia*) of the Russian Socialist Revolutionary Party sought to ground their actions in reason, others, such as the Black Banner (*Chernoe Znamia*) and Without Authority (*Beznachalie*), effectively turned to terrorism as a substitute for reason (Avrich 1966). As the French intellectual Laurent Tailhade asked rhetorically in 1893, "What do the victims matter if the gesture is beautiful?" (quoted in Hacker 1976, p. 297).

These two philosophies of violence took on an increasingly ideological cast during the latter part of the nineteenth century. "Rationalists" tended to be attracted to the developing doctrine of revolutionary socialism. Socialist theory, in turn, promoted the rational use of violence. Although individual motivations for engaging in terrorism could vary widely, socialist theory as a whole—where it justified the use of violence—considered terrorist actions to be a subordinate but potentially significant political instrument in its larger revolutionary program. "Expressionists," by contrast, tended to be attracted to the doctrine of anarchism. Anarchist theory, in turn, found terrorism attractive because it was "spontaneous, reckless, and in a sense, irrational" (Carter 1978, p. 339). Emotive acts of terrorism, in this view, were the "archetypal form of human resistance . . . and the medium through which heroic values can most fully be expressed" (Carter 1978, p. 339). In the words of one of anarchism's later proponents, "an idea must not be left to pure understanding . . . . Only feeling, passion, and desire have moved and will move men to acts of heroism and self-sacrifice; only in the realm of passionate life, the life of feeling, do heroes and martyrs draw their strength" (Avrich 1966, p. 381). (See also Carr 1961, 1964; Woodcock 1962; Avrich 1967; Miller 1976, 1995; Hobsbawm 2001).

These two schools of thought, not surprisingly, gave rise to two distinct models of terrorist organization. The rationalists, as might be expected, were better organized. Terrorism, in their view, was a collective enterprise that required a high level of organization and careful planning to succeed. One of the first to make this point, paradoxically, was Bakunin. Despite his belief in "instinct," "spontaneity," and the "heroic act," Bakunin argued that anyone who was serious about bringing down the state must be able to build a closed, disciplined, and tightly knit party apparatus. Bakunin's vision, which was never fully realized in his own day, resembles the (networked) terrorist organizations we see today. Imagine a "secret organization," he wrote, "which has scattered its members in small groups over the whole territory of the Empire, but is nevertheless, firmly united, inspired by a common ideal, and a common aim . . . an organization that acts everywhere according to a common plan" (Bakunin 1974 [1870]). The model for such an organization, in his mind, was the Jesuit Order, with its emphasis on secrecy, hierarchy, and discipline on the one hand, and its success at creating an enduring base of international influence on the other (Avrich 1970, Ivianski 1988).

Mainstream "organization" within the anarchist movement evolved in a very different direction. At a philosophical level, the idea of subjecting individuals to the discipline of a hierarchical organization, even for a revolutionary purpose, was antithetical to the movement's libertarian principles. In this respect, at least, the ends did not justify the means. This idea was also at odds with the movement's theory of victory. Regime collapse, according to most anarchist thinkers, could be achieved only by spontaneous combustion. It could not be realized by constructing a counter-organization to challenge the organization of the state. Any attempt to do so would retard rather than promote the individual acts of self-assertion that were needed to trigger and then catalyze a spontaneous popular uprising. Terrorism was an individualized activity designed to facilitate a "creative spirit of insurrection" (Carter 1978). Efficiency was less important than nobility. Working alone or in loose collectives, individual terrorists would shape the future through the power of their example. This, in turn, would inspire others to strike out in their own way. Once set in motion, exemplary violence would take on a dynamism of its own, feeding off itself until society became ungovernable and the state was swept away in an outpouring of popular revulsion.

Both competing schools of thought shared the conviction that advances in science and technology would gradually enhance the dramatic power of the deed. A faith in the power of technology lay at the heart of Heinzen's early argument that the competitive advantage was beginning to shift from the state to the revolutionary opposition. A similar view was expressed in the Nechaev-Bakunin *Revolutionary Catechism*, which called on terrorists to develop a new "science of destruction," for which they should be studying "mechanics, physics, chemistry, [and] perhaps medicine" (translated in Pomper 1979). Through the turn of the century, terrorists experimented with a wide range of different weapons technologies, from enhanced explosives, nitroglycerine grenades—the particular specialty of the brilliant young Russian bomb designer, N.I. Kibalchich—to various kinds of poisons, incendiary devices, fuses and detonating mechanisms, and new and improved means of delivery. As the anarchist Johann Most argued in the opening sentences of his self-published "users guide," *Science of Revolutionary Warfare*,[2] "the importance of explosives as an instrument for carrying out revolutions . . . is obvious. Anyone can see that these materials will be the decisive factor in the next period of world history" (Most, n.d., p. 1).

These themes continue to characterize terrorism today. Although many of the goals and forms of terrorist behavior have changed with the times, the structure and functions of terrorism remain strongly consistent with the past. As in Heinzen's day, terrorists operate in the shadows from a position of relative weakness. Offsetting this disadvantage requires them to carry out terrorist "spectaculars," which command the attention of the media and, through the magnification effect of media exposure, generate a political impact that is greater than the investment required to carry out the attacks in the first place. As Frederick Hacker has suggested, terrorist "events become socially effective and important through their reproduced image. Often they take place only for the sake of the image; they are produced in order to be reproduced" (quoted in Cook 1982, p. 157). The exposure (and associated

---

[2]Today's counterpart to Most's "how to" manual for the do-it-yourself revolutionary is *The Anarchist Cookbook* (Powell 1971) and similar follow-on publications. Like recent reproductions of Most's instructional pamphlet, the "Cookbook" warns readers against trying its "recipes" at home. A more serious example of the same thing is al Qaeda's 11-volume *Encyclopedia of Jihad*, which includes instructional material on everything from physical training, first aid, knife fighting, interrogation techniques, reconnaissance, and the anatomy and history of tanks and other armored vehicles, to the use and manufacture of explosives, mines, and a wide variety of light and heavy weapons.

political attention) that a group receives is directly related to the shock effects of its attacks. To achieve these effects, terrorists continue to look for an edge, tactically and technically, that will allow them to create the theatrical kind of event they desire. In the late nineteenth century it was dynamite; between the 1960s and 1980s it was aircraft hijackings, political kidnappings, and embassy takeovers. Today it is car bombs, suicide attacks, and, for selected groups, the quest for weapons of mass destruction.

It remains useful to distinguish between rationalists and expressionists: between those who employ terrorism on behalf of an external goal and those whose goal is to carry out acts of terror. Terrorist groups, in this respect—as in many others—are not created equal. Nor is their behavior necessarily consistent over the course of their operational life. Some (otherwise distinctive) groups, such as the contemporary Irish Republican Army (IRA), al Qaeda, Hamas, and the Tamil Tigers, have largely managed to subordinate their actions to their political objectives. Like their predecessors in the People's Will, the Socialist Revolutionary Party, or the early Fenian movement, they employ violence largely as a means to an end. Others, such as the late November 17, the Popular Forces of 25 April (FP-25), the Justice Commandos of the Armenian Genocide, or any number of today's "amateur" terrorists, have effectively subordinated their political objectives to their need to act. As for their predecessors in the early anarchist movement or the more recent Japanese Red Army, Baader-Meinhof Gang, or Weather Underground, violence is an instrument of expression rather than an instrument of political change. The decision dynamics associated with each of these two sets of cases are distinct.

THEORIES OF TERRORIST DECISION MAKING

Terrorism cannot be explained in a vacuum. Its attractiveness "depends in part on the effectiveness of alternative forms of dissent, as well as the other criteria used by radical leaders to choose among competing strategies" (DeNardo 1985, p. 242). It also depends on the circumstances or environmental context in which the decision to resort to terrorism is made. Some early efforts to examine the contextual sources of terrorism (and other forms of insurrectionary violence) made a useful distinction between the "preconditions" that lay the groundwork for terrorist activity and the "precipitating" factors that help explain the actual outbreak of violence (e.g., Eckstein 1965, Johnson 1966). Building on this distinction, Crenshaw (1981) suggested that terrorist groups also depend critically on "enabling" or "permissive" factors to create the tactical opportunity they require to conduct operations (see also Weinberg & Davis 1989). Together, these conditions define the strategic space in which terrorist organizations emerge, evolve, and devolve over time.

Within this context, terrorism is a choice. How, why, and in what form this choice is ultimately made, however, remains a matter of discussion. In general, theoretical work in this area can be divided along three levels of analysis depending on the nature of the (primary) independent variable that is used to explain terrorist behavior. Each, arguably, explains a part of the puzzle. In order of generality, these are (*a*) strategic theories, in which the decision to employ terrorism and related forms of political violence is an instrumental choice made by a rational organization attempting to achieve a defined set of external objectives, (*b*) organizational theories, in which the sources of violence are found in the internal dynamics of the terrorist group itself, apart from its stated goals, and (*c*) psychological theories, in which the decision to resort to terrorism is explained within the framework of individual psychology. Although most observers agree that these lines of inquiry are not mutually exclusive, each constitutes a distinctive approach to terrorist decision making. I briefly examine each in turn.

The Strategic Frame

As Schelling once observed, the most important division among students of conflict lies between those who approach the problem "as a pathological state and seek its causes and treatment," and those "who take conflict for granted" and study it sources and effects. Among this second group, he points out, there is a further division between those who consider conflict to be influenced at least partly by nonrational and unconscious considerations, and those who consider it a calculated course of action, a conscious and deliberate choice designed to achieve a defined objective. The parties in the conflict, in the latter case, are considered adaptive strategic agents, who enter a fight in the same way they would approach a "contest" or "game." The object of the game is to win (Schelling 1963, p. 3). The challenge is to find the best way to win given the circumstances of the game and the counter-strategies of the other players.

The strategic frame has been readily adapted to the study of terrorist decision making. Terrorism, in this view, is an instrumental activity designed to achieve or help achieve a specified set of long-run and short-run objectives (e.g., Tullock 1974, Hacker 1976, Price 1977, Corsi 1981, Waterman 1981, Sandler et al. 1983, Waugh 1983, Muller & Opp 1986, Sandler & Lapan 1988, Crenshaw 1990, Lapan & Sandler 1993, Enders & Sandler 1995). Like any such strategy, it is forward-looking and "consequential," in the sense that the decision to use terrorism and the nature of the terrorism that is used are based on the anticipated consequences of current actions. It is also "preference-based," in the sense that alternative courses of action are evaluated in terms of their respective impact on terrorist objectives. The decision to act (or not act), in this view, depends on the answers to four questions (March 1994): What alternative courses of action are available? What are the expected effects of each of these alternatives? How are these expected effects likely to influence group objectives? What decision rule will be employed to decide among the alternatives? Stripped down to its essentials, the terrorist decision-making process, in the strategic view, is one of constrained optimization. Terrorist organizations attempt to either maximize their expected political returns for any given level of effort or minimize the expected costs necessary to achieve a specified set of political objectives.

One important feature of this approach is the assumption that the various players in the game coexist in a reciprocal operational relationship (Schelling 1978). A competitor's best move, in this case, is a function of the prior and anticipated moves of his opponents and allies, and it varies accordingly. This assumption distinguishes games of strategy from games of chance (Schelling 1963). Whereas decision makers, in the latter case, are playing the odds, in the case of a strategic competition they are playing each other. What this implies, for our purposes, is that a terrorist group's decision to act (or not act)—a decision that includes its choice of targets, tactics, and timing—is influenced by the decisions of its opponents, of its political constituency, and of any other actors that influence its strategic environment. As the French geographer Vidal de la Blache observed in 1926, an organization's environment imposes permissive and limiting conditions that shape its incentives, its opportunities, and the short- and long-run consequences of its actions (Vidal de la Blache 1926). As these conditions vary, terrorist behavior can be expected to vary as well. (For examples, see Gutmann 1979, Dowling 1986, Ross & Gurr 1989, Gurr 1990, Kellen 1990.)

A second feature of the strategic model is the simplifying assumption that terrorist groups act with a "collective rationality" (Waterman 1981, Crenshaw 1990). A terrorist group, in this view, is not considered to be a collection of potentially discordant views of the world or opinions about ends and means; it is assumed to be a unitary actor, defined by a single, stable, and ordered set of preferences, that is able to identify, evaluate, and decide among competing options with a single mind. The model of strategic decision making can be said to come in "strong" and "weak" variants, depending on the assumptions that are made about a group's computational powers and its knowledge of its operating environment. The strong or "substantive" theory of strategic decision making, drawn directly from the idealized model developed in neoclassical economics, makes no distinction between the world as it is and the terrorist's world view. It also assumes that terrorist groups can anticipate the consequences of their actions (Simon 1997). Interpreting and predicting terrorist behavior, in this case, is relatively easy. One has only to identify an organization's goals and operating constraints and then choose the available course of action that offers the highest expected return.

The "procedural" theory of strategic decision making, by contrast, assumes that although terrorist groups may act rationally according to their beliefs about the world around them, these beliefs are incomplete reflections of reality (Simon 1997). Decisions, consequently, often prove to be suboptimal, even if they were considered to be the best course of action at the time. Several sets of objective factors can account for this variance, including information limitations, information costs, computational constraints, and time pressures, which can force a group to choose a course of action before they are ready. Sometimes the problem is not one of too little information but too much. In such cases the organization is forced to employ simplifying rules, which may filter, frame, and ultimately distort its perceptions of reality. These and similar constraints can significantly "bound" or condition a group's strategic processes, even if its decision-making procedures are otherwise rational. (For further discussions, see Newell & Simon 1972, Simon 1976, Cyert & March 1992, March & Simon 1993.) Interpreting and predicting terrorist behavior in these circumstances is more complicated, requiring the analyst to "walk in the enemy's shoes" before he can evaluate what a group is likely to do (and not do) under the circumstances.

For analytical purposes, the link between a terrorist action and its (intended and unintended) consequences can be broken down into a series of steps. In step 1, an action is carried out against a specified target. In step 2, the action is interpreted, packaged, and retransmitted by the media. In step 3, the "mediated" message is received and interpreted by the group's target audience(s). In step 4, it is hoped, the target(s) of influence respond in a way that advances group interests. The relationship between an action and its behavioral impact is clearly indirect. Although the terrorist group gets to choose what, how, and when it attacks, it has little control over how the media interprets its actions (the operation's first-order effects), how its actions are received and interpreted by the group's target(s) of influence (the operation's second-order effects), and what, if any, effect they have on audience behavior (the operation's third-order effects). "Strategic" terrorism, in this respect, has a paradoxical quality. On the one hand, as noted above, terrorist attacks typically have a political impact that is greater than the material investment that was needed to carry them out. The nature of this impact and its behavioral implications, however, are often beyond the ability of a terrorist group to control or even accurately predict.[3]

One important way in which these models have been applied is to explain why a political opposition group will find it advantageous to resort to terrorism in the first place. The decision to adopt terrorist tactics, in this view, is a constrained choice, imposed by the absence of alternative options (e.g., Crenshaw 1981, Gurr 1990, Braungart & Braungart 1992, Ross 1993). This constraint is typically due to one of two considerations. The first is a lack of popular support for the group's political agenda in an otherwise permissive *security* environment. Individuals do not back the political opposition, in this case, not because they can't but because they won't. The second is the coercive reputation of the state in an otherwise permissive *political* environment. The opposition's lack of effective support, in this case, is due not to a lack of popular sympathy but to the absence of effective avenues of political expression. In either case, terrorism is a tactic of the weak. It is a "forcing measure," designed to offset an opposition group's opening material disadvantages and place it on a more equal footing with the state.

---

[3]As Hoffman (2002) has observed, a growing number of groups, such as Hamas, the Tamil Tigers, Hizbollah, and many others, have sought to further clarify their message by delivering it directly to their consumers via the internet. Al Qaeda has supplemented such web-based efforts by producing its own packaged video for follow-on broadcast on the Arabic language news network, al Jazeera. Hizbollah has taken this another step further by creating its own television station, which produces well-polished productions on the group's operational activities. (See also Whine 1999, Denning 2001, Zanini & Edwards 2001.) For a good discussion of the relationship between terrorism and the media, see Nacos (1994, 2001), Schmid & de Graaf (1982), Crelinsten (1987), and Wilkinson (1997).

Terrorism in these cases can be an immediate, inexpensive, and effective means of focusing political attention on the opposition and its cause. Such actions can be referred to as "identification moves" (Oberschall 1973). They are designed to define the terms of the struggle, raise popular consciousness, and begin to generate popular support for the terrorists' political agenda. This motivation for engaging in terrorism, as noted above, has a long pedigree. Writing in 1880, Kropotkin argued that high-profile actions "compel general attention." A single incident, he suggested, "may in a few days make more propaganda than thousands of pamphlets" (Kropotkin 1968). Similar views were expressed some 80 years later when Menacham Begin reflected on his years as the leader of the *Irgun*. The *Irgun* was never able to gain a political voice, Begin observed, until it proved that it was willing and able to kill British soldiers to command British attention. Once it had demonstrated that it was prepared to act, he wrote, "we were loved or hated—but no longer jeered at." Any underground group, Begin concluded, "that passes beyond the stage of the inevitable initial ridicule has gone halfway—perhaps the more difficult half of the way to its goal" (Begin 1972, p. 121).

Terrorism, as Begin well understood, can also be employed to provoke. Terrorists, as a general rule, begin the game with the ability to see their opponents but a limited ability to attack what they see. The state, by contrast, begins the game with a much greater ability to attack what it sees but a limited ability to see what it wishes to attack. Terrorist groups enjoy an information advantage; the state enjoys a force advantage. This simple asymmetry is a defining feature of any contest between a state and an underground competitor. A strategy of provocation is designed to take advantage of the underground's information advantage and turn the state's force advantage against it by provoking the regime to strike out indiscriminately at targets it cannot see. Rapoport (1977) has aptly characterized this strategy as "the politics of atrocity." Terrorist atrocities, in this case, "are deliberately calculated to produce counter-atrocities rebounding to the advantage of the original assailant" (Rapoport 1992, p. 1064). Even the perception of such a response can serve terrorist purposes by undermining popular support for the state and generating sympathy for the opposition. The political value of the terrorist's action, in this case, "derives not from its popularity, but from the unpopularity of the ensuing repression" (Leites 1979, p. 22). (See also Price 1977, Rapoport 1977, Waugh 1983, Hoffman 1998, Gurr 1990, Sprinzak 1990).

Even when the population may be sympathetic to the resistance, terrorism can play an important role in transforming passive sympathy into active support. Every violent political contest is defined by a "hard core" element on each side, whose members are prepared to "stick to their guns" regardless of which side is ahead. The (effective) support of the majority of the population, by contrast, typically depends on their subjective estimates of each side's prospects.[4] This poses an

---

[4]I distinguish here between "pure" and "assisted" preferences (Leites & Wolf 1970). Individuals' pure preferences are what they would choose to do if they were making their choices in the absence of constraints. Their assisted preferences are the choices they make under the circumstances that actually confront them at the time.

early mobilization challenge for the opposition, which must overcome its opening image of weakness to effectively exploit its potential base of support. High-profile violence can be a means of reshaping popular perceptions about "who's on top." This, in turn, has two effects on mobilization: to boost popular confidence in the opposition and to diminish popular confidence in the state. All other things being equal, each of these effects can be expected to result in a greater level of active support for the resistance. The larger purpose of this strategy is to create a self-confirming image of group success in an effort to stimulate popular activism, "jump start" the mobilization process, and achieve a sustainable rate of growth (McCormick & Owen 1996, Overgaard 1994).

For similar reasons, the strategic rationale for conducting terrorist attacks typically evolves during the course of the fight. Thornton (1964), for example, suggested that actions designed to accelerate mobilization tend to diminish once this process is under way and the correlation of forces has begun to shift in favor of the rebels. "Agitational terror," he suggested, is particularly attractive (for the reasons we have just discussed) during the initial period of the conflict, when the opposition is trying to establish its *bona fides*. The primary function of violence at this stage is to provoke, disorient, raise popular consciousness, and eliminate or contain the terrorist group's (internal and external) political rivals (Thornton 1964, Rapoport 1977). If all goes according to plan, the importance of these tactics can be expected to decline as the conflict takes on the characteristics of a force-on-force competition between the state and an increasingly regularized opposition.[5] Terrorism can again become important during the final phase of the fight, when the opposition often finds it useful to employ "enforcement terror" to help control its growing territorial base. Assuming an opposition win, these efforts can continue and even grow during the period of consolidation. Terrorism "from below," in this case, transforms itself into terrorism "from above."

In the end, the strategic approach to terrorist decision making offers what Schelling (1984) once called a "cheap theory." Analyzing a group's likely course of action, as noted above, only requires putting ourselves in its place, defining its objectives and operating constraints, and then choosing as it would choose to maximize its expected political return. The simplicity of this approach is both its strength and its weakness. It can certainly provide a useful and easily applied point of departure for analysis, but it does not fully capture the processes by which real decisions are made within a terrorist group or any other organization. Can this be overlooked? Can terrorists be thought of as "proximate" strategic planners? Is it enough to argue that terrorist groups may not always make the best choices but that they at least attempt to do so? The answer to these questions is typically "no."

---

[5]If all does not go according to plan, which is typically the case, the group in question may never succeed in evolving beyond its use of agitational terrorism. Although terrorist groups often open their campaigns with the intention of transforming themselves into broad-based insurgencies, their inability to do so will leave them with no alternative but to either give up the game or escalate, in a final effort to achieve a political breakthrough. Terrorist groups often begin to lose their strategic direction at this point.

There are other variables at work, internal to terrorist groups themselves, that can have an important bearing on group behavior. These factors often push terrorists in very different directions from the ones they would pursue if they always performed as neoclassical optimizers. With this in mind, the literature has moved beyond strategic theory to examine the organizational and psychological variables that can condition terrorist group decision making.

The Organizational Frame

In contrast to the rational choice model, which argues that terrorism represents a calculated and instrumental attempt to achieve an external set of political objectives, the organizational model suggests that much of what terrorists do on the outside can only be understood by looking inside the group itself. A terrorist organization is not a black box but a living system, subject to a range of influences that may be only tangentially related to its stated strategic objectives. This approach to organizational decision making, needless to say, is not unique to the study of terrorism. The argument has a significant foundation across a wide range of disciplines from anthropology to systems engineering. What is of particular interest in this case is that terrorist groups, as violent "underground" organizations,[6] possess certain structural features that make the organizational line of analysis especially productive. To the degree this is true, the reasoning process that lies behind terrorist behavior is not always as clear cut as the strategic model would suggest.

This approach begins with the observation that terrorist groups, for reasons of survival, are clandestine organizations. This clandestine requirement, furthermore, is a hard constraint (Erikson 1981). The effectiveness and long-run survival of the group "depends not only on having a secret, but keeping the fact you have a secret a secret" (McCormick & Owen 2000, p. 175). Groups that ignore this rule are typically not around long enough to matter. The implications of this constraint vary across cases, but as a general rule, the need for secrecy has the effect of isolating terrorist organizations from their larger social and political surroundings (Crenshaw 1985). It also distinguishes them from their "open," nonviolent political counterparts. All other things being equal, the degree to which a group must insulate itself from its societal roots varies directly with changes in its security environment. This, in turn, can be expected to vary directly with the level and nature of its attacks. What this means, as a practical matter, is that the more successful a group becomes at carrying out terrorist attacks, the more pressure it will be under to separate itself from its social and political base.

As terrorists go deeper underground, group decision making can become an increasingly closed, rigid, and inward-looking process (Simmel 1950). This can tend to reinforce a group's preexisting interpretation of its environment and, in doing so, interfere with its ability to adapt. Even under the best of circumstances,

---

[6]I define the "underground" in a manner similar to Molnar (1966) as a covert or clandestine group that is attempting to replace an existing authority.

organizations use simplifying mechanisms to establish priorities, offset deficiencies in information, explain and resolve informational inconsistencies, interpret what is going on around them, and define and evaluate the consequences of their actions (Cyert & March 1992, March 1994). Terrorists, it has been argued, take this to an extreme. The variegated texture of the outside world is gradually replaced by a stark, black and white image of "dichotomous confrontation" (Gerlach & Hine 1970; Post 1984, 1987, 1990; Crenshaw 1988; della Porta 1992). In the process, terrorists can lose their sense of reality, "constructing images that are increasingly remote from both their 'dominant' culture and their own subculture" (della Porta 1992, p. 19). Every aspect of the organization's decision process can be affected—its view of the enemy, its view of itself, its perspectives on society, its ability to accurately identify and respond to changes in its operating environment, and its ability to calculate the costs and benefits of alternate courses of action.

Terrorists wage a "fantasy war" (Ferracuti 1990). One common feature of this fantasy is the belief that, as militants, they are acting as soldiers, in a fashion similar to those of their government opponents. Group actions can often be designed to cultivate this self-image, serving a function that Cordes (1988) has called "auto-propaganda." Although such attacks are inevitably carried out in the name of the group's political objectives, they may not have anything to do with its instrumental goals. A second common illusion is the belief that their actions are defensive (Rapoport 1977). Terrorists almost always "claim to act in defense of a larger community whose integrity and well-being [are] at risk" (Gurr 1990, p. 90; see also Kellen 1982). They avoid responsibility for their actions by blaming their opponents. Their own use of violence is merely a response in kind. These views tend to be reinforced over time in the face of government countermeasures. Government excesses, both real and imagined, are typically used to justify a terrorist group's initial use of violence and rationalize any future decision to escalate.

The problem this poses for strategic decision making is often compounded by a bias toward action (e.g., Kellen 1979; Crenshaw 1985, 1994; Laqueur 1987; Post 1990; Hoffman 1998). The need to act, "to escape the words" (Leites 1979), has been a defining feature of terrorist behavior since the 1870s. Terrorist groups operate with a high time discount—they are impatient for results. The decision to go underground, furthermore, is generally made with the deliberate intention of leaving the "non-violent path" behind. Having made this decision, it is argued, terrorist groups are under a continuous pressure to act. Some groups, such as the early "disorganization" branch of Land and Freedom, the "Combat Cells" of the Russian Socialist Revolutionary Party, or the militant wings of the contemporary IRA and Basque ETA (*Euzkadi ta Askatasuna*), have sought (for a time) to have it both ways by attempting to maintain an open connection to their parent political movements. These relationships, in virtually every case, have proven impossible to sustain. In the end, the militants go their own way, disavowing or redefining their relationship with the center. Once this transition occurs, as Andreas Baader once noted, their "only language is action" (quoted in Seufert 1978).

It is also evident that terrorist organizations often inherit or adopt a preexisting "script" or theory of victory rather than design a program that is tailored to their specific requirements or operational and strategic objectives. Many terrorists, in this respect, belong to "a tradition of historical action" (Dunn 1972). The (interpreted) experiences of their predecessors not only demonstrate that action is possible but can also provide terrorists with a set of procedures, tactics, and rules of thumb for carrying out their own campaigns (Johnson 1973, McCormick 1993). Historical precedents can be attractive guides. For those who wish to replace an incumbent regime but have no prior experience overthrowing governments, which is typically the case, an historical model can provide an immediate (if prepackaged) recipe for action. The problem this poses for rational decision making is not that such precedents are used as strategic aids, per se, but that they are often adopted uncritically. To the degree this is true, a group's concept of operations is less a product of a strategic calculus than of a historical legacy, which may or may not be appropriate to the circumstances at hand. (For a discussion on the imitative nature of terrorism, see Redlick 1979; Heyman 1980; Heyman & Mickolus 1980, 1981; Midlarsky et al. 1980; Hacker 1981; Hamilton & Hamilton 1983; Oots 1986b; Hoffman 1993, 1998.)

Terrorist behavior can also be influenced by interorganizational competition (Jenkins 1981, Crenshaw 1985, DeNardo 1985, Laqueur 1987, McCauley & Segal 1987). Terrorist organizations, in this view, act as political interest groups (Oots 1986a). They frequently compete with each other in radical rivalries for political market share. The currency of this competition is violence, as rival groups jockey for media time and the attention of a more or less fixed base of potential constituents. Examples are numerous, including the historic rivalries between the IRA and the Irish National Liberation Army (INLA) and between the Palestine Liberation Organization (PLO) and the Popular Front for the Liberation of Palestine (PFLP); internecine conflict between various elements within the larger Basque nationalist movement; competition between the Shining Path and the Tupac Amaru Revolutionary Movement (MRTA) in Peru; the three-way competition for public attention that once existed between the Revolutionary Armed Forces of Colombia (FARC), the National Liberation Army (ELN), and the April 19 Movement (M-19); and the ongoing confrontation between such groups as Hamas and Islamic Jihad. In these and other cases, terrorism is not merely an instrument of competition with the state, but a means of crowding out one's political rivals.

This action bias, coupled with the "hothouse" internal environment of terrorist groups, also encourages risk taking (Unseem 1972, Crenshaw 1985). This argument is supported by the broader literature on the social psychology of small groups (e.g., Marquis 1962; Wallach et al. 1962, 1964; Collins & Guetzkow 1964; Wallach & Kogan 1965; Janis 1972; Douglas & Wildavsky 1982; McGrath 1984). This point has been argued convincingly by Janis & Mann (1977), who have shown that decision making within highly insulated organizations, such as terrorist groups, is vulnerable to "groupthink," which can significantly degrade a group's strategic effectiveness. The effects of groupthink, they suggest, include "an illusion of invulnerability," which "encourages taking extreme risks"; a collective effort "to rationalize in order to discount warnings that might lead the members [of the group] to reconsider their assumptions before they recommit themselves to their past policy decisions"; an "unquestioned belief in the group's inherent morality," which can have the effect of "inclining members to ignore the ethical and moral implications of their decisions"; and a "stereotyped" view of the enemy, which is considered to be "too evil to warrant genuine attempts to negotiate" or "too weak or stupid to counter whatever risky attempts are made to defeat their purposes" (Janis & Mann 1977, p. 130). More recently, Whyte (1989) and Elmes & Gemmill (1990) have elaborated on these themes.

The problem of "group think" can be easily reinforced by the tendency toward self-censorship and consensus building that occurs naturally in closed, "primary" collectives (e.g., Shaw 1981). Terrorists everywhere share a strong group dependency (for discussion, see Wilson 1973; Zawodny 1978, 1983; Post 1984, 1986, 1987; Crenshaw 1985, 1992, 2000; McCauly & Segal 1987; della Porta 1992). This bond can be further solidified over time by the hazards and liabilities of a clandestine existence (e.g., Becker 1960, Janis 1968, Wasmund 1983, McAdam 1986). As the organization gradually distances itself from mainstream society, the importance of group solidarity grows. One effect of this is to suppress internal dissent and homogenize the group's decision-making process (e.g., Bion 1961; Verba 1961; Cartwright & Zander 1968; Keniston 1968; Rioch 1978; Knutson 1980; Post 1987, 1990). Questioning the direction or decisions of the group, or any other aspect of its collective perspective, can be interpreted as an act of disloyalty and a threat to the organization's existence (Janis & Mann 1977, Crenshaw 1985, Post 1990). This, in turn, is a threat to its membership. To avoid dissent and possible censure, a dangerous prospect in more ways than one,[7] the members of the underground often go along to get along, which gradually undermines their ability to react to changes in their environment in a calculating manner.

Drawing on Collins & Guetzkow (1964), Crenshaw (1985) has argued that it is often the "inter-personal" rewards of group membership, rather than the "task-environmental" rewards associated with a terrorist group's political mission, that draw individuals to the close quarters of underground life. The value of this payoff, furthermore, can easily grow with time, as the group moves deeper underground and its members sever their remaining ties with the outside world

---

[7]In an attempt to preserve the integrity of the group, terrorists are always on the alert for backsliders. When discovered, they are inevitably treated harshly. An instructive case in point is offered by the Japanese Red Army, which killed roughly one third of its own membership (they were said to have "died of defeatism") between December 1971 and February 1972 (Steinhoff 1989, Farrell 1990). At least 12 members of the group were killed, some reportedly by being buried alive. Of particular note, as well, was the Abu Nidal Organization, which over the course of its operational life was responsible for killing a significant percentage of its own membership (Seale 1992).

(see also O'Toole 1975; Kellen 1979, 1982; Post 1984, 1986, 1987, 1990; della Porta 1992, 1995a; della Porta & Diani 1999). The net effect of this process, once again, is arguably detrimental to deliberative decision making. The survival of the group is no longer a means to an end but an end in itself. Over time, it is suggested, the need to preserve the group can actually begin to supplant its political mission altogether (e.g., Crenshaw 1985, 1987, 1988; Weinberg & Eubank 1990). This process will not always be apparent to outside observers. It may not even be clear to the members of the terrorist group itself, who are likely to continue to fight on in the name of its original ideological objectives. At such time as it occurs, however, terrorist behavior will have become effectively disconnected from the group's original strategic purpose.

These and similar dynamics can undermine a terrorist group's ability to sustain itself over time. Individuals typically enter the underground through preexisting social networks (Zald & Ash 1966; Wilson 1973; Snow et al. 1980; Jäger et al. 1981; Reynaud 1984; Clark 1983, 1984; Snow & Machalek 1983; Wasmund 1983, 1986; Klandermans 1984; Crenshaw 1986). As a group moves deeper into the shadows, its remaining societal connections are gradually abandoned and replaced by stronger interpersonal bonds within the group itself. This often has the positive effect of increasing intraorganizational cohesion. It can also have the negative effect, however, of reducing the organization's effective pool of recruits. The group cannot recruit outsiders it does not know, and it will know fewer outsiders over time. Terrorists can soon find themselves on the horns of a dilemma. The absolute requirement to operate clandestinely in order to survive eventually undermines their ability to replace their losses. Their inability to replace their losses, in turn, begins to interfere with their ability to survive. Terrorist groups typically attempt to break out of this trap through escalation, a response which can easily send them into a self-reinforcing cycle of decline.

The Psychological Frame

The psychological study of terrorist decision making has focused on the role of cognitive and affective distortions in shaping terrorist behavior. (This has been true of political psychology in general; see Mandel 1986.) "Cognitive distortions," in this case, are perceptual deviations that can be attributed to the simplifying models that individuals use to interpret the world. "Affective distortions," by contrast, are emotional factors or other personality characteristics that undermine an individual's ability to see things as they really are. In both cases, the study of terrorist psychology is interested not only in how such distortions influence decision making, but the processes through which this occurs. Within this context, there is an interest in understanding how the psychology of the individual and of the group can help shape group behavior, as well as the ways in which environmental stimuli (to include the behavior of other actors) can influence the psychology of the individual. It is generally recognized that each of these sets of factors can influence the other in reciprocal ways.

Research in this area has largely clustered around four lines of inquiry. The first of these efforts, not surprisingly, attempted to uncover any psychological traits that terrorists might share in common (e.g., Hubbard 1975; Gutmann 1979; Knutson 1980, 1981; Bollinger 1981; Kaplan 1978; Clarke 1982; Jenkins 1982; Russell & Miller 1983; Billig 1985; Oots & Weigele 1985; Rubinstein 1987). The hope at the time, now largely discounted, was that researchers might be able to define a specific terrorist personality or profile that would explain why some individuals, and not others under similar circumstances, take up terrorist activities (for an overview, see Crenshaw 1986). With a number of exceptions (e.g., Feuer 1969), most observers agree that although latent personality traits can certainly contribute to the decision to turn to violence, there is no single set of psychic attributes that explains terrorist behavior (e.g., Liebert 1971, Ross 1996). Terrorists manifest a range of often quite different personality traits and come from a wide variety of backgrounds. It is also generally agreed that most terrorist activity is not due to mental pathologies (e.g., Rasch 1979; Heskin 1980, 1984; Corrado 1981; Ferracuti & Bruno 1981; Jäger et al. 1981; Süllwold 1985; McCauley & Segal 1987; Ferracuti 1990; Reich 1990a; Silke 1998). Although some researchers have suggested that terrorists are abnormal "in more subtle ways" (Crenshaw 2000, p. 407), most observers believe that terrorists are "disturbingly normal" (Hoffman 1998, p. 7).

A second line of analysis has focused on the relationship between frustration and aggression. In its simplest form, the "frustration-aggression" hypothesis posits that (individual and collective) violence is often the result of a discrepancy between individual expectation and achievement. This discrepancy, it is argued, can result in high levels of individual frustration that is often externalized through violence. This argument was first advanced over 60 years ago (Dollard et al. 1939) and was subsequently extended to the problem of political violence and terrorism (e.g., Davies 1962, 1969; Feierabend & Feierabend 1966, 1972; Gurr 1968; Feierabend et al. 1969; Margolin 1977; Gurney & Tierney 1982). Frustration-aggression theory was brought squarely into the realm of individual psychology with Gurr's concept of "relative deprivation" (1970a,b). Individual feelings of deprivation, in Gurr's view, are subjectively derived and need have no real basis in fact. "An individual's point of reference may be his own past condition, an abstract ideal, or the standards articulated by a leader as well as a 'reference group'" (Gurr 1970a, p. 25). The frustrations associated with these feelings, he argued, are "as fundamental to understanding civil strife as the law of gravity is to atmospheric physics" (Gurr 1970b). If individual (political) frustrations are allowed to continue to develop unchecked, they will eventually result in an outbreak of violence and the possible resort to terrorism (Margolin 1977).

A parallel set of efforts to explain the psychological sources of terrorist behavior has employed "narcissism-aggression" models of violence. The possible linkage between narcissism and terrorism was first advanced by Morf (1970) and subsequently discussed by Lasch (1979), Crayton (1983), Haynal et al. (1983), Post (1984, 1986, 1990), and Pearlstein (1991). Pearlstein defines narcissistically motivated violence as "an internal, intrapsychic regulatory tool that enables the individual to defend the self from damage and harm" (1991, p. 7). Acts of terrorism, by extension, are often (unconsciously) motivated by narcissistic injury, defined as "profound [and] permanent damage to an individual's self-image or self-esteem." Terrorism can serve as an auto-defense mechanism for restabilizing an individual's self-esteem and restoring a sense of self-worth. This perspective is supported by the work of Post (1990), who has suggested that narcissistically affected personalities are typically subject to "splitting" and "externalization." In these processes, negative self-images are split away and projected onto an external enemy, who is then subject to attack. While recognizing that other factors typically play an important role in shaping an individual's decision to turn to terrorism, this school of thought argues that preexisting narcissistic injury is an important source of terrorist behavior.

A fourth important body of work on terrorist psychology has approached the subject as an interactive and developmental problem. The "developmental" argument has been advanced, in various forms, by a wide range of commentators (e.g., Knutson 1981; Jenkins 1982; Braungart & Braungart 1983, 1989, 1992; Sayari 1985; Crenshaw 1986; Bandura 1990; Sprinzak 1990, 1991, 1995; Friedland 1992; della Porta 1992, 1995a,b; Passerini 1992; della Porta & Diani 1999). Terrorism, in this view, is not the product of a single decision but the end result of a dialectical process that gradually pushes an individual toward a commitment to violence over time. The process takes place within a larger political environment involving the state, the terrorist group, and the group's self-designated political constituency. The interaction of these variables in a group setting is used to explain why individuals turn to violence and can eventually justify terrorist actions. One of the attractive features of this approach is that it does not depend on explaining terrorism in psychopathological terms ("subtly" or otherwise). Neither, however, does it deny the potential significance of personality factors in contributing to one's subsequent political development. The individual's preexisting psychological state is a point of departure in his or her evolution toward terrorism. A person can ultimately arrive at this end state from a number of different starting points.

An important variant of this approach has been developed by Bandura (1973, 1986, 1990), who has sought to explain how terrorists justify their actions through a process of "moral disengagement" over time. "Self-sanction," Bandura suggests, "plays a central role in the regulation of human conduct." Individuals "refrain from behaving in ways that violate their moral standards because such behavior would bring self-condemnation" (Bandura 1990, p. 161). An individual's moral constraints, however, are subject to change. The "internalized control" mechanisms that regulate individual behavior can be selectively "disengaged" and reconstructed. One can achieve this by redefining one's actions in moral terms, by deflecting or shifting personal responsibility for otherwise immoral behavior, by obscuring or misrepresenting the consequences of one's actions, or by blaming or dehumanizing the victim. This disengagement and reshaping process, Bandura argues, occurs in a social setting and is particularly important in the case of violence that is deliberately designed to target innocent third parties, in contrast to actions directed against the "guilty." Once this process is completed, the individual's regulatory framework is effectively reversed. Actions that were once morally reprehensible take on the character of a moral imperative.

A related developmental model has been advanced by Sprinzak (1990, 1991, 1995). The process of radicalization that pushes some individuals toward violence (and leaves others behind), in Sprinzak's view, is a psychological one that occurs over time in a sequential manner. This conversion, he argues, involves a cognitive transformation that unfolds in three stages: through (*a*) a "crisis of confidence," (*b*) a "conflict of legitimacy," and (*c*) a "crisis of legitimacy" (Sprinzak 1990, p. 79). Each stage represents a particular individual (and group) psychopolitical identity at a different point in time. Individuals begin this cognitive evolution with the belief that the existing political order can be reformed from within. They end the process convinced that reform is impossible and that the system can only be changed by force from without. During this transformation, a new collective identity is forged among those who share this conviction, distinguishing them (and distancing them) from those who do not. For these individuals, the world is increasingly cast in black and white. Actions—notably the resort to terrorism—that were once unthinkable are now justified by a new moral logic.

One unifying theme that underlies the psychological study of terrorism is the important behavioral role that is attributed to the individual's belief system (see Kellen 1979, 1982; Cordes 1988; Crenshaw 1988, 1992; Hoffman 1998). As suggested above, terrorists view themselves and the enemy in stereotypical ways. They consider themselves to be a political elite fighting for a righteous cause. Those who oppose them do so because they are evil. This bifurcated view of the world is often extended to associated third parties, who are divided into two categories: those who are prepared to support the resistance and those who are part of the problem. Despite considerable debate among psychological analysts concerning how and why this belief system is formed, there is common agreement that it exists. Once in place, furthermore, it is resistant to change. As noted above, this is due in part to the insular nature of the underground, which tends to restrict and recast any new information that might challenge the individual's premises about himself, his opponents, or his political mission. It is also, arguably, due to a natural tendency toward "defensive avoidance" (Janis & Mann 1977) once the threshold of terrorism has been crossed. Having made a commitment to terrorism, the individual psychological costs of calling one's prior actions into question are potentially significant. An individual's belief system, in this regard, can become increasingly rigid in an attempt to justify earlier terrorist attacks.

As suggested above, it is also commonly agreed that terrorist belief systems are influenced significantly by intragroup dynamics (e.g., Kaplan 1978; Ferracuti & Bruno 1981; Wolfgang & Ferracuti 1982; Post 1984, 1986, 1990; Crenshaw 1985, 1990, 1992; Ferracuti 1990; Sprinzak 1990, 1991; della Porta 1992, 1995a). While an individual must share something in common with a political collective to become affiliated in the first place, once this affiliation has occurred, any remaining differences between the individual and the group are subject to the unifying forces of group psychology (Post 1987). Weinberg & Davis (1989) identify two distinct dynamics at work in this process. Would-be members of the underground are "pushed" toward a particular group because of their preexisting cognitive or affective attributes and are "pulled" into the group (and resocialized) by forces in play within the collective itself. Once inside, individuals make the final decision to resort to terrorism together, rather than independently. After that, the internal cognitive restructuring that takes place within the closed environment of the underground can often make it difficult for a terrorist group to let newcomers into the club. This is not merely an issue of security; it is also due to the group's increasingly idiosyncratic world view, which can distance it—and lead it to distance itself—from those who might otherwise be sympathetic to its cause.

It is difficult to generalize about psychological models of terrorist decision making. Many "are replete with explanations that ignore or blur the variety and complexity of terrorism" (Reich 1990a, p. 262). Similarly, much of this work effectively ignores the significant differences that exist between the cultural and social environments from which individual terrorists and terrorism evolve. It is reasonable to ask whether the individual psychology of terrorism can be separated from its larger cultural and social context. If not, is it reasonable to expect to find a psychological common denominator that links, in more than a casual way, individual terrorists from such radically disparate environments as Northern Ireland, northern Idaho, and the Northwest Frontier Province of Pakistan? Indeed, even a quick look at a list of historic terrorist personalities, from bin Laden to Bernadine Dorn, suggests that the individual's path to terrorism can not only vary significantly between cultures at different points in time, it often differs significantly within the same cultural setting at the same time. Complicating our efforts to uncover the psychological frames that lead otherwise normal individuals to carry out heinous acts of violence is the fact that we must often make our "diagnosis at a distance" (for this critique, see Silke 1998).

In the end, however, psychological research into the sources of terrorist behavior is based on a central assumption that is impossible to disprove and difficult to argue with, namely that the roots of terrorist activity lie in the mind. Although opinion on this issue is divided, as noted above, most observers agree that terrorists (with exceptions) are nonpathological personalities. Although there is reason to believe that particular personality disorders may play a role in attracting certain individuals to violent underground organizations, they are neither a necessary nor sufficient condition for becoming a terrorist. What distinguishes terrorists psychologically from the general population is their belief system, which places them at the center of a Manichean struggle between good and evil. The process leading up to this mental state is an interactive one that often displays features of a self-fulfilling prophecy (Merton 1957). Once a negative image of one's political adversary has taken hold, it can be easily reinforced by eliciting a reaction from the adversary that confirms what the individual (and his or her reference group) believed to be true in the first place. The "specious validity" of this self-confirming cycle "perpetuates a reign of error" that can become increasingly polarizing over time (Deutsch & Shichman 1986, p. 231). (See also Gurr 1990, Crenshaw 1992, Braungart & Braungart 1992).

The study of terrorist psychology has advanced significantly in the past two decades, but much more needs to be done to develop a true psychology of terrorist decision making. The majority of work to date has focused on explaining the individual's decision to resort to terrorism in the first place. Much less attention has been given to the subsequent psychological development of individuals who have already made the transition to terrorism. Of particular interest, in this respect, is the psychological basis of group factionalism, the psychology of escalation and de-escalation, and the cognitive evolution that can lead an individual to eventually leave the faith and renounce terrorism altogether. Similarly, although there is growing interest in how the social psychology of the group can influence the individual, much less attention has been given to how the psychology of the individual can influence the group. This is of particular importance in the case of underground organizations such as the Baader-Meinhof Gang, the Shining Path, al Qaeda, and the Abu Nidal Organization, to name just a few, which have been constructed around defining personalities. This is more common than is commonly assumed, particularly in the initial stages of a terrorist group's development. The individual psychology of a handful of individuals, in such cases, can often provide significant insights into group behavior in the face of changing circumstances.

TERRORIST LIFE CYCLES

Terrorist groups, it is generally agreed, emerge out of larger radical social movements (e.g., Sprinzak 1990, Klandermans 1997, della Porta & Diani 1999). Such movements are typically diverse collectives and are often subject to considerable internal differences over strategy and objectives. According to DeNardo (1985), disagreements over strategy tend to occur between patient "base builders" on the one hand, who believe that the best way to achieve their goals is to systematically construct a broad base of popular support, and impatient "advocates of violence" on the other, who are driven by a need to act. Disagreements over movement goals, in contrast, tend to occur between movement "pragmatists," who are willing to accept a piece of the pie if they are able to reach a compromise settlement with the state, and movement "purists," who will accept nothing less than the whole pie and the state's unconditional defeat. These two lines of division, DeNardo suggests, are among the "principal axes of factional cleavage in radical politics" (1985, p. 244). If left unresolved, they tend to result in an ever-deepening schism within the movement over time, culminating in the formation of a breakaway faction of violent purists who are often prepared to resort to terrorism to achieve their goals. (For a further discussion of the dynamics of group formation, see Braungart & Braungart 1992, Weinberg & Eubank 1987.)

Once a group has made the transition to terrorism, it must navigate between two objective constraints if it is going to stay in the game. The first is a security constraint. Terrorist groups must be able to maintain a minimum level of internal security (by maintaining a critical level of invisibility) to keep from being hunted down and broken up, or otherwise destroyed. Should the group's rate of attrition rise above its capacity to replace its losses, it will eventually cease to exist. The second constraint is an influence constraint. Terrorists must maintain a minimum "violent presence" to remain effective. This is important not only to their ability to achieve their stated objectives but also to their (long-run) ability to continue to operate at all. In a political sense, at least, terrorists begin to disappear when they drop off the headlines. This will gradually undermine their ability to mobilize support, continue to grow the organization, and sustain themselves over time. To hold their audience, they must continue to act, and by acting command political attention (see, for example, McCormick & Owen 2000, Bell 1998, Molnar 1966).

The influence and security of a group depends in part on its choice of targets, tactics, and timing,[8] but in competing ways. Group security, for its part, is inversely related to the scale and dramatic quality of its attacks. The more frequently a terrorist group operates (and the "noisier" its preparations are), the easier it is to identify and localize. Similarly, the more dramatic and politically disruptive its operations become, the harder its opponents can be expected to look for it and the sooner it is likely to be found. The only real defense that terrorist groups enjoy is their invisibility. Should the state succeed in penetrating their veil of anonymity, eliminating them is relatively easy. When it comes to security, in this respect, "smaller" is better. By contrast, the level of influence a group can be expected to achieve is directly related to its operating profile. All other things being equal, the more frequently it is able to capture the headlines, the more political leverage it can be expected to enjoy. This is not only a question of the frequency of the group's attacks but also of the degree to which those attacks succeed in capturing the attention of its target audience. When it comes to influence-building, "bigger" is often better.[9]

As we can see, a fundamental tension exists between terrorist influence objectives and their basic security requirements. All other things being equal, the relationship between a group's operating profile and its level of influence and security vary independently with changes in its environment. As shown in Figure 1, each of these relationships can be thought of as monotonic functions that can be expected to change more or less continuously over time. For purposes of illustration, we assume that the minimum levels of influence and security that a group must maintain to stay in the game are given by α and β, respectively. For any given strategic environment, these minimum values establish threshold limits within which the group must continue to operate in order to survive. The resulting security

---

[8]A terrorist group's choices of targets, tactics, and timing represent its three degrees of freedom. It can choose what targets it will attack and how and when it will do so. Together, these choices define a group's "operating profile."

[9]This is true up to a point. As Gurr (1990) and others have noted, operational excesses can result in a "backlash" on the part of a group's own constituents that can reduce its net base of support. The outer limits of a group's operating profile can sometimes be constrained by its own political supporters.

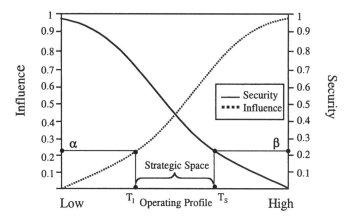

Figure 1   Terrorist strategic space.

threshold is T_S and the influence threshold by T_I. The operating range between T_S and T_I defines the group's "strategic space" at a given time. As long as $T_S–T_I > 0$, which is to say, as long as this space is positive, the group has the room for maneuver it needs to continue to operate. Should this space disappear, i.e., should $T_S–T_I$ ever become ≤ 0, the group will eventually be "squeezed" out of business, either because it will be rolled up by its opponents or because it will have gone to ground to avoid being uncovered and destroyed.

A terrorist group's room for maneuver, as noted above, is likely to be subject to wide variations over time. For any strategic space $T_S–T_I > 0$, however, there exists a critical operating point T^* at any time (t) that provides the group with the best subjective tradeoff between influence and security. This point is determined by the particular characteristics of the group's operating environment, as well as a host of other idiosyncratic factors, such the nature of its objectives, its risk preference, its expectations for the future, and its time discount. As these and other related considerations change, the group's best tradeoff between influence and security can be expected to change in turn. The set of all optimal operating points over a given time period defines its "tactical path." A terrorist group, by definition, cannot improve its performance as long as it can identify and stay on its tactical path. Any effort to improve its political position by increasing its operating profile, at this point, will be more than offset by a loss in security. Similarly, any effort to increase security by reducing its operating profile will be more than offset by a loss of influence (McCormick 2002).

Considered in these terms, the terrorist decision-making process can be evaluated abstractly as a "feedback control system" that attempts to identify and execute the best course of action given the group's competing influence and security objectives on the one hand, and the nature of its operating environment on the other. Two factors that influence this process are (*a*) the degree to which terrorist decision makers believe that the operational choices they make in the short run can help shape their range of strategic options over time, and (*b*) the degree to which they are willing to forego current gains in an effort to improve the group's future position and thereby increase its expected long-run returns. At any particular point in time, as I have said, a terrorist group's strategic space defines the left and right limits within which it must operate to stay in the game. In the long run, however, the actions it carries out in one time period can often improve (or restrict) its strategic room for maneuver in the next. Groups with a high time discount operate with a short time horizon. Groups with a low time discount operate with an eye on the future.

As a practical matter, of course, identifying and maintaining a "best" course of action in the face of a changing strategic environment is effectively impossible. A group's ability to even approach this ideal, furthermore, is a function of its information base and particular decision-making style. The inverse relationship between influence and security is a fact of life for violent underground organizations, but their ability to read and adapt to changes in their environment and, therefore, changes in their tactical path depends on the speed, accuracy, and instrumental rationality of their decision processes. Their performance will vary accordingly. Terrorist decision making, in this respect, can be thought of as an iterative cycle of consecutive steps. A group must first establish a stable set of preferences. It must then develop an accurate understanding of its strategic environment, identify its range of tactical options, accurately evaluate the payoffs associated with these options, select and carry out the course of action that promises to deliver the highest expected return given its preference structure, compare its actual and expected achievements, and, finally, adjust its operating profile (and/or assumptions) to improve its performance.

The more rapidly and accurately a group moves through this cycle, the more closely its actual performance can be expected to follow its tactical path. Conversely, group performance can be expected to deteriorate to the degree its decision cycle is slowed or distorted by unstable preferences, information constraints, uncertainties concerning its strategic environment, structural barriers in the decision process, interpretive differences over questions of strategy and tactics, or any of the other organizational and psychological dynamics discussed above. Obstacles of this nature, of course, are impediments to progress for any organization. The problems they can pose for underground organizations, however, are particularly severe. First, active terrorist groups operate in an unusually dynamic environment. Their security situation, in particular, can fluctuate rapidly depending on the initiative of their opponents. The ability to recognize and adapt to such changes is critical to group survival. Second, terrorist groups typically operate with very little margin for error. They are seldom more than a few steps away from either dropping off the political horizon or making a fatal operational slip that results in their exposure and destruction.

Examining terrorist decision making as a "system control" problem can provide a number of insights into the underlying dynamics of terrorist life cycles. In the long run, a group's operating profile is constrained by its strategic environment.

For any given set of security and influence requirements, this environment defines the minimum and maximum operating profile the group must maintain to continue to play the game. If a group drops below its minimum and stays there, it will gradually disappear as a political force. If it exceeds its maximum and stays there, it will gradually be exposed and eliminated as a physical force. Changes in a group's strategic environment result in corresponding variations in its security threshold, its influence threshold, or some combination of the two. Should a group's strategic environment become more permissive over time, its room for maneuver will expand. Should it become more restrictive, its strategic space (and, hence, its margin for error) will contract. The dynamic nature of most terrorist environments places a premium on a group's ability to identify and adjust to changes in its effective operating thresholds. Any failure to adapt in the face of an increasingly permissive environment will result in a loss of opportunity. A similar failure in an increasingly restrictive environment can force it out of business.

In summary, a terrorist group's life cycle is shaped by its changing environmental constraints and by the degree to which it is able to continue to operate within these fluctuating constraints. Over the long run, the terrorist group's strategic space $(T_S–T_I)$ defines the limits of the possible. Its principal decision problem, in this respect, is to identify its available room for maneuver, consider how it might increase its room for maneuver down the road, and design and execute an operational plan that offers the highest expected return. All other things being equal, the more closely the group's decision processes resemble the neoclassical ideal discussed above, the longer it will be able to play the game. The rational terrorist group with good situational awareness can identify and adapt to changes in its environment until its strategic space contracts to the point that it finally runs out of options. Anything that interferes with the group's capacity to operate rationally or distorts its cognitive processes is likely to shorten its life span. Groups thus hindered cannot effectively adapt to changes in their environments and will drive themselves out of business over time.

CONCLUSIONS

Terrorist decision-making processes vary widely. At one extreme, terrorists can be thought of as adaptive strategic agents. Terrorism, in this view, is a means to an end. The "strong" variant of this theory assumes that a terrorist group's strategic and tactical decisions are based on an accurate and informed worldview. The "weak" variant assumes that the decision process itself is rational but that decision makers work with incomplete information and, hence, a conditional or bounded view of their operating environment. At the other end of the spectrum, terrorist decision making is subject to an internal logic that is effectively divorced from a group's external objectives. Terrorism, in this view, is not an instrumental activity but the product of a wide range of possible organizational and individual psychological factors within the group itself. The worldview and belief system that frame terrorist group decision making may have little or nothing to do with reality. Evaluating and predicting the behavior of any particular terrorist group over time will almost always require an integrated analytical approach.

The organizational and psychological approaches to terrorist decision making do not generally suggest that terrorist groups cannot operate with strategic intent, only that the strategic model is incomplete. Other, nonrational considerations, it is argued, can and regularly do influence the choices terrorist groups make behind the scenes. These factors can have a wide range of effects on terrorist decision making, from introducing small perturbations into an otherwise rational process of choosing among alternatives, to effectively supplanting this process altogether. The net result can be a pattern of terrorist activity that sometimes looks quite different from what we would expect to see if the group were operating as an unconditional strategic actor. Whenever possible, deviations of this type need to be addressed systematically. As Schelling (1984) has suggested, nonrational variables can be factored into the analysis of terrorist group decision making as long as they occur in identifiable, regularized, and hence predictable ways. The strategic frame, in such cases, can be used to establish a baseline assessment of expected behavior. Once established, this baseline can then be modified as necessary to develop a customized model of group decision making.

The *Annual Review of Political Science* is online at
http://polisci.annualreviews.org

LITERATURE CITED

Alexander Y, Gleason JM, eds. 1981. *Behavioral and Quantitative Perspectives on Terrorism*. New York: Pergamon

Avrich P. 1966. Anarchism and anti-intellectualism in Russia. *J. Hist. Ideas* 27:381–90

Avrich P. 1967. *The Russian Anarchists*. Princeton, NJ: Princeton Univ. Press. 303 pp.

Avrich P. 1970. The legacy of Bakunin. *Russian Rev.* 29:129–42

Avrich P. 1984. *The Haymarket Tragedy*. Princeton, NJ: Princeton Univ. Press. 535 pp.

Bakunin M. 1974 (1870). M. Bakunin to Sergei Nechayev, 2 June 1870 (letter). In *Daughter of a Revolutionary*, ed. M Confino, pp. 238–39. London: Alcove

Bandura A. 1973. *Aggression: a Social Learning Analysis*. Englewood Cliffs, NJ: Prentice Hall. 390 pp.

Bandura A. 1986. *Social Foundations of Thought and Action: a Social Cognitive Theory*. Englewood Cliffs, NJ: Prentice Hall. 617 pp.

Bandura A. 1990. Mechanisms of moral disengagement. See Reich 1990b, pp. 161–91

Becker HS. 1960. Notes on the concept of commitment. *Am. J. Sociol.* 66:32–40

Begin M. 1972. *The Revolt*. Los Angeles: Nash. 386 pp.

Bell JB. 1998. *The Dynamics of the Armed Struggle*. London: Frank Cass. 287 pp.

Billig O. 1985. The lawyer terrorist and his comrades. *Polit. Psychol.* 6:29–46

Bion W. 1961. *Experiences in Groups*. London: Tavistock. 198 pp.

Bollinger L. 1981. Die Entwicklung zu terroristichem Handeln als psychosozialer Prozess: Begegnungen mit Beteiligten. In *Analysen zum Terrorismus*, ed. H Jager, G Schmidtechen, L Süllwold, Vol. 2. Oplanden, Ger.: Westdeutscher Verlag

Braungart RG, Braungart MM. 1983. Terrorism. In *Prevention and Control of Aggression*, ed. Cent. Res. Aggression, Syracuse Univ., pp. 299–337. New York: Pergamon

Braungart RG, Braungart MM. 1989. Political generations. In *Research in Political Sociology*, ed. RG Braungart, MM Braungart, 5:281–319. Greenwich, CT: JAI

Braungart RG, Braungart MM. 1992. From protest to terrorism: the case of SDS and the Weathermen. In *Social Movements and Violence: Participation in Underground Organizations*, ed. D della Porta, pp. 45–78. Greenwich, CT: JAI

Carlson AR. 1972. *Anarchism in Germany*. Metuchen, NJ: Scarecrow. 448 pp.

Carr EH. 1961. *Michael Bakunin*. New York: Vintage Books. 501 pp.

Carr EH. 1964. *Studies in Revolution*. New York: Grosset & Dunlop. 228 pp.

Carter A. 1978. Anarchism and violence. In *Anarchism*, ed. JR Pennock, JW Chapman, pp. 320–40. New York: New York Univ. Press

Cartwright D, Zander A. 1968. *Group Dynamics: Research and Theory*. New York: Harper & Row. 580 pp.

Clark RP. 1983. Patterns in the lives of ETA members. *Terrorism* 6:423–54

Clark RP. 1984. *The Basque Insurgents: ETA, 1952–1980*. Madison, WI: Univ. Wisc. Press. 328 pp.

Clarke JW. 1982. *American Assassins: the Darker Side of Politics*. Princeton, NJ: Princeton Univ. Press. 321 pp.

Collins BE, Guetzkow H. 1964. *The Social Psychology of Group Processes for Decision-Making*. New York: Wiley. 254 pp.

Cook S. 1982. Germany: from protest to terrorism. In *Terrorism in Europe*, ed. Y Alexander & KA Meyers, pp. 154–78. New York: St. Martin's

Cordes B. 1988. When terrorists do the talking: reflections on terrorist literature. See Rapoport 1988, pp. 150–73

Corrado RR. 1981. A critique of the mental disorder perspective of political terrorism. *Int. J. Law Psychiatry* 4:1–17

Corsi JR. 1981. Terrorism as a desperate game. *J. Confl. Resolut.* 25:47–85

Crayton JW. 1983. Terrorism and the psychology of the self. See Freedman & Alexander 1983, pp. 33–41

Crelinsten RD. 1987. Terrorism as political communication: the relationship between the controller and the controlled. In *Contemporary Research on Terrorism*, ed. P Wilkinson, AM Stewart, pp. 3–23. Aberdeen, Scotland: Aberdeen Univ. Press

Crenshaw M. 1981. The causes of terrorism. *Comp. Polit.* XIII:379–99

Crenshaw M. 1985. An organizational approach to the analysis of political terrorism. *Orbis* XXXIX:19–21

Crenshaw M. 1986. The psychology of political terrorism. In *Political Psychology*, ed. MG Hermann, pp. 379–413. San Francisco: Jossey-Bass

Crenshaw M. 1987. Theories of terrorism: instrumental and organizational approaches. *J. Strat. Stud.* 10:13–31

Crenshaw M. 1988. The subjective reality of the terrorist: ideological and psychological factors in terrorism. In *Current Perspectives on International Terrorism*, ed. RO Slater, M Stohl, pp. 12–46. New York: St. Martin's

Crenshaw M. 1990. The logic of terrorism: terrorist behavior as a product of strategic choice. See Reich 1990b, pp. 7–24

Crenshaw M. 1992. Decisions to use terrorism: psychological constraints on instrumental reasoning. In *Social Movements and Violence: Participation in Underground Organizations*, ed. D della Porta, pp. 29–44. Greenwich, CT: JAI

Crenshaw M. 1994. How terrorists think: What psychology can contribute to understanding terrorism. In *Terrorism: Roots, Impact, Response*, ed. L Howard, pp. 71–80. New York: Praeger

Crenshaw M. 1995. *Terrorism in Context*. University Park, PA: Penn. State Univ. Press

Crenshaw M. 2000. The psychology of terrorism: an agenda for the 21st century. *Polit. Psychol.* 21:405–20

Cyert RM, March JG. 1992. *A Behavioral*

Theory of the Firm. Oxford, UK: Blackwell. 252 pp. 2nd ed.

Davies J. 1962. Toward a theory of revolution. *Am. Sociol. Rev.* 27:5–9

Davies JC. 1969. The J-curve of rising and declining satisfactions as a cause of some great revolutions and a contained rebellion. In *Violence in America: Historical and Comparative Perspectives*, ed. HD Graham, TR Gurr, pp. 690–730. New York: Praeger

della Porta D. 1992. Introduction: on individual motivations in underground political organizations. In *Social Movements and Violence: Participation in Underground Organizations*, pp. 3–28. Greenwich, CT: JAI

della Porta D. 1995a. *Social Movements, Political Violence, and the State.* Cambridge, UK: Cambridge Univ. Press. 270 pp.

della Porta D. 1995b. Left wing terrorism in Italy. See Crenshaw 1995, pp. 105–59

della Porta D, Diani M. 1999. *Social Movements: an Introduction.* Oxford, UK: Blackwell. 326 pp.

DeNardo J. 1985. *Power in Numbers: the Political Strategy of Protest and Rebellion.* Princeton, NJ: Princeton Univ. Press. 267 pp.

Denning DE. 2001. Activism, hacktivism, and cyberterrorism: the internet as a tool for influencing foreign policy. In *Networks and Netwars*, ed. J Arquilla, D Ronfeldt, pp. 239–88. Santa Monica, CA: RAND

Deutsch M, Shichman S. 1986. Conflict: a social psychological perspective. In *Political Psychology*, ed. MG Hermann, pp. 219–50. San Francisco: Jossey-Bass

Dollard J, Doob LW, Miller NE, Mowrer OH, Sears RR. 1939. *Frustration and Aggression.* New Haven, CT: Yale Univ. Press. 209 pp.

Douglas M, Wildavsky AB. 1982. *Risk and Culture.* Berkeley: Univ. Calif. Press. 221 pp.

Dowling RE. 1986. Terrorism and the media: a rhetorical genre. *J. Commun.* 36:12–24

Dunn J. 1972. *Modern Revolutions; an Introduction to the Analysis of a Political Phenomenon.* Cambridge, UK: Cambridge Univ. Press. 346 pp.

Eckstein H. 1965. On the etiology of internal wars. *Hist. Theory* 4:133–63

Elmes MB, Gemmill G. 1990. The psychodynamics of mindlessness and dissent in small groups. *Small Group Res.* 21:28–44

Enders W, Sandler T. 1995. Terrorism: theory and applications. In *Handbook of Defense Economics*, ed. K Hartley, T Sandler, pp. 129–48. Amsterdam: Elsevier

Erickson BH. 1981. Secret societies and social structures. *Soc. Forces* 60:188–210

Farrell WR. 1990. *Blood and Rage: the Story of the Japanese Red Army.* Lexington, MA: Lexington Books. 265 pp.

Feierabend IK, Feierabend RL. 1966. Aggressive behaviors within polities, 1948–1962: a cross-national study. *J. Confl. Resolut.* 10: 249–71

Feierabend IK, Feierabend RL. 1972. The relationship of systematic frustration, political coercion, and political stability. In *Macro-Quantitative Analysis: Conflict, Development, and Democratization*, ed. JV Gillespie, BA Nesvold, pp. 417–40. Beverly Hills, CA: Sage

Feierabend IK, Feierabend RL, Nesvold BA. 1969. Social change and political violence: cross-national patterns. In *Violence in America: Historical and Comparative Perspectives*, ed. HD Graham, TR Gurr, pp. 632–87. New York: Praeger

Ferracuti F. 1990. Ideology and repentance: terrorism in Italy. See Reich 1990b, pp. 59–64

Ferracuti F, Bruno F. 1981. Psychiatric aspects of terrorism in Italy. In *The Mad, the Bad, and the Different*, ed. IL Barak-Glantz, CR Huff, pp.199–213. Lexington, MA: Lexington Books

Feuer GL. 1969. *The Conflict of Generations.* New York: Basic Books. 543 pp.

Freedman LZ, Alexander Y. 1983. *Perspectives on Terrorism.* Wilmington, DE: Scholarly Resour.

Friedland N. 1992. Becoming a terrorist: social and individual antecedents. In *Terrorism: Roots, Impacts, Responses*, ed. L Howard, pp. 81–94. New York: Praeger

Gerlach LP, Hine V. 1970. *People, Power, Change: Movements of Social Transformation.* New York: Bobbs-Merrill. 257 pp.

Gurney JN, Tierney KJ. 1982. Relative deprivation and social movements: a critical look at twenty years of theory and research. *Sociol. Q.* 23:33–47

Gurr TR. 1968. A causal model of civil strife: a comparative analysis using new indices. *Am. Polit. Sci. Rev.* 62:1104–24

Gurr TR. 1970a. *Why Men Rebel.* Princeton, NJ: Princeton Univ. Press. 421 pp.

Gurr TR. 1970b. Sources of rebellion in western societies: some quantitative evidence. *Ann. Am. Acad. Polit. Soc. Sci.* 391:128–44

Gurr TR. 1990. Terrorism in democracies: its social and political bases. See Reich 1990b, pp. 86–102

Gutmann D. 1979. Killers and consumers: the terrorist and his audience. *Soc. Res.* 46:516–26

Hacker FJ. 1976. *Crusaders, Criminals, Crazies: Terror and Terrorism in Our Time.* New York: Norton. 335 pp.

Hacker FJ. 1981. Contagion and attraction of terror and terrorism. See Alexander & Gleason 1981, pp. 73–85

Hamilton LC, Hamilton JD. 1983. Dynamics of terrorism. *Int. Stud. Q.* 27:39–54

Hardy D. 1987. *Land and Freedom: the Origins of Russian Terrorism, 1876–1879.* Westport, CT: Greenwood. 212 pp.

Haynal A, Molnar M, De Puymege G. 1983. *Fanaticism: a Historical and Psychoanalytical Study.* New York: Schocken. 282 pp.

Heinzen K. 1978. Murder. In *The Terrorism Reader*, ed. W Laqueur, pp. 53–64. Philadelphia, PA: Temple Univ. Press

Heskin K. 1980. *Northern Ireland: a Psychological Analysis.* New York: Columbia Univ. Press. 174 pp.

Heskin K. 1984. The psychology of terrorism in Ireland. In *Terrorism in Ireland*, ed. Y Alexander, A O'Day, pp. 88–105. New York: St. Martin's

Heyman E. 1980. The diffusion of transnational terrorism. In *Responding to the Terrorist Threat: Security and Crisis Management*, ed. R Shultz, S Sloan, pp. 190–244. New York: Pergamon

Heyman E, Mickolus EF. 1980. Observations on why violence spreads. *Int. Stud. Q.* 24:299–305

Heyman E, Mickolus EF. 1981. Imitation by terrorists: quantitative approaches to the study of diffusion patterns in transnational terrorism. See Alexander & Gleason 1981, pp. 175–228

Hobsbawm E. 2001. *Revolutionaries.* New York: New. 326 pp.

Hoffman B. 1993. Terrorist targeting: tactics, trends, and potentialities. In *Technology and Terrorism*, ed. P Wilkinson, pp. 1–11. London: Frank Cass

Hoffman B. 1998. *Inside Terrorism.* New York: Columbia Univ. Press. 288 pp.

Hoffman B. 2002. *Underground voices: insurgent terrorist communication in the 21st century.* Mimeo. Santa Monica, CA: RAND. 32 pp.

Hubbard DG. 1975. A glimmer of hope: a psychiatric perspective. In *International Terrorism and Political Crimes*, ed. MC Bassiouni, pp. 27–32. Springfield, IL: Charles C. Thomas

Iviansky Z. 1977. Individual terror: concept and typology. *J. Contemp. Hist.* 12:43–63

Iviansky Z. 1988. Sources of inspiration for revolutionary terrorism: the Bakunin-Nechayev alliance. *Confl. Q.* 8:49–68

Jäger H, Schmidtchen G, Süllwold L. 1981. *Analysen zum Terrorismus*, vol. 2. *Lebenslauf-Analysen.* Opladen, Ger.: Westdeutscher Verlag. 243 pp.

Janis IL. 1968. Group identification under conditions of external danger. In *Group Dynamics: Research and Theory*, ed. D Cartwright, A Zander, pp. 80–90. New York: Harper & Row

Janis IL. 1972. *Victims of Groupthink.* Boston, MA: Houghton Mifflin. 277 pp.

Janis IL, Mann L. 1977. *Decision Making: a Psychological Analysis of Conflict, Choice, and Commitment.* New York: Free. 488 pp.

Jenkins BM. 1981. The study of terrorism: definitional problems. See Alexander & Gleason 1981, pp. 3–10

Jenkins BM. 1982. *Terrorism and Beyond: an*

International Conference on Terrorism and Low Level Conflict. Santa Monica: RAND

Johnson C. 1966. *Revolutionary Change.* Boston, MA: Little, Brown. 191 pp.

Johnson C. 1973. *Autopsy on People's War.* Berkeley, CA: Univ. Calif. Press. 118 pp.

Joll J. 1980. *The Anarchists.* Cambridge, MA: Harvard Univ. Press. 299 pp.

Kaplan A. 1978. The psychodynamics of terrorism. *Terrorism* 1:237–54

Kellen K. 1979. *Terrorists—What are They Like? How Some Terrorists Describe Their World and Actions.* N-1300-SL. Santa Monica, CA: RAND. 67 pp.

Kellen K. 1982. *On terrorists and terrorism.* N-1942-RC. Santa Monica, CA: RAND. 54 pp.

Kellen K. 1990. Ideology and rebellion: terrorism in West Germany. See Reich 1990b, pp. 43–58

Keniston K. 1968. *Young Radicals: Notes on Committed Youth.* New York: Harcourt, Brace & World. 368 pp.

Klandermans B. 1997. *The Social Psychology of Protest.* Oxford, UK: Blackwell. 257 pp.

Klandermans BG. 1984. Mobilization and participation in social movements: a social-psychological expansion on resource mobilization theory. *Am. Sociol. Rev.* 49:583–600

Knutson JN. 1980. The terrorists' dilemma: some implicit rules of the game. *Terrorism* 4: 195–222

Knutson JN. 1981. Social and psychodynamic pressures toward a negative identity: the case of an American revolutionary terrorist. See Alexander & Gleason 1981, pp. 105–52

Kropotkin P. 1968. The spirit of revolt. In *Revolutionary Pamphlets*, ed. P Kropotkin, pp. 35–43. New York: Dover

Lapan HE, Sandler T. 1993. Terrorism and signalling. *Eur. J. Polit. Econ.* 9:383–97

Laqueur W. 1978. *The Terrorism Reader.* Philadelphia: Temple Univ. Press. 291 pp.

Laqueur W. 1987. *The Age of Terrorism.* Boston, MA: Little, Brown. 385 pp.

Lasch C. 1979. *The Culture of Narcissism: American Life in the Age of Diminishing Expectations.* New York: Norton. 447 pp.

Leites N. 1979. Understanding the next act. *Terrorism* 3:1–46

Leites N, Wolf C Jr. 1970. *Rebellion and Authority: an Analytic Essay on Insurgent Conflicts.* R-462-ARPA. Santa Monica, CA: RAND

Liebert R. 1971. *Radical and Militant Youth: a Psychoanalytic Inquiry.* New York: Praeger. 257 pp.

Mandel R. 1986. Psychological approaches to international relations. In *Political Psychology*, ed. MG Hermann, pp. 251–78. San Francisco: Jossey-Bass

March JG. 1994. *A Primer on Decision Making.* New York: Free. 289 pp.

March JG, Simon HA. 1993. *Organizations.* Oxford, UK: Blackwell. 287 pp. 2nd ed.

Margolin J. 1977. Psychological perspectives in terrorism. In *Terrorism: Interdisciplinary Perspectives*, ed. Y Alexander, SM Finger, pp. 377. New York: John Jay

Marquis DG. 1962. Individual responsibility and group decisions involving risk. *Ind. Manage. Rev.* 3:8–23

McAdam D. 1986. Recruitment to high risk activism: the case of Freedom Summer. *Am. J. Sociol.* 92:64–90

McCauley CR, Segal ME. 1987. Social psychology of terrorist groups. *Group Processes and Inter-group Relations*, ed. C Hendrick, pp. 231–56. Newbury Park, CA: Sage

McCormick GH. 1993. *Sharp Dressed Men: Peru's Tupac Amaru Revolutionary Movement.* Santa Monica, CA: RAND

McCormick GH. 2002. *A "system control" model of terrorist decisionmaking.* Occ. Pap., Dep. Defense Analysis. Monterey, CA: Naval Postgrad. School. 21 pp.

McCormick GH, Owen G. 2000. Security and coordination in a clandestine organization. *Math. Comput. Model.* 31:175–92

McCormick GH, Owen G. 1996. Revolutionary origins and conditional mobilization. *Eur. J. Polit. Econ.* 12:377–402

McGrath JE. 1984. *Groups: Interaction and Performance.* Englewood Cliffs, NJ: Prentice Hall. 287 pp.

Merton RK. 1957. *Social Theory and Social Structure*. New York: Free. 645 pp.

Midlarsky MI, Crenshaw M, Yoshida F. 1980. Why violence spreads: the contagion of international terrorism. *Int. Stud. Q.* 24:262–98

Miller MA. 1976. *Kropotkin*. Chicago: Univ. Chicago Press. 342 pp.

Miller MA. 1995. The intellectual origins of modern terrorism in Europe. See Crenshaw 1995, pp. 27–62

Molnar A. 1966. *Human Factors Considerations of Underground Insurgencies*. Washington, DC: Am. Univ. 291 pp.

Morf G. 1970. *Terror in Quebec*. Toronto: Clarke, Irwin. 185 pp.

Most J. n.d. *Science of Revolutionary Warfare*. Oakland, CA: AK Press Dist. 74 pp.

Muller EN, Opp KD. 1986. Rational choice and rebellious collective action. *Am. Polit. Sci. Rev.* 80: 471–88

Nacos BL. 1994. *Terrorism and the Media*. New York: Columbia Univ. Press. 214 pp.

Nacos BL. 2001. Accomplice or witness? The media's role in terrorism. *Curr. Hist.* 99:174–78

Newell A, Simon HA. 1972. *Human Problem Solving*. Englewood Cliffs, NJ: Prentice Hall. 920 pp.

Oberschall A. 1973. *Social Conflict and Social Movements*. Englewood Cliffs, NJ: Prentice Hall. 371 pp.

Oots KL. 1986a. *A Political Organization Approach to Transnational Terrorism*. New York: Greenwood. 174 pp.

Oots KL. 1986b. An individual-level model of terrorist contagion. *The 1986 Annual on Terrorism*, ed. Y Alexander, pp. 109–25. Dordrecht: Martinus Nijhoff

Oots KL, Wiegele TC. 1985. Terrorist and victim: psychiatric and physiological approaches from a social science perspective. *Terrorism* 8:1–32

O'Toole R. 1975. Sectarianism in politics: case studies of Maoists and Leninists. In *Sectarianism: Analysis of Religious and Non-Religious Sects*, ed. R Wallis, pp. 162–89. New York: Wiley

Overgaard PB. 1994. Terrorist attacks as a signal of resources. *J. Confl. Resolut.* 38:452–78

Passerini L. 1992. Lacerations in the memory: women in the Italian underground organizations. In *Social Movements and Violence: Participation in Underground Organizations*, ed. D della Porta, pp. 161–212. Greenwich, CT: JAI

Pearlstein RM. 1991. *The Mind of the Political Terrorist*. Wilmington, DE: Scholarly Resour. 237 pp.

Pomper P. 1979. *Sergei Nechaev*. New Brunswick, NJ: Rutgers Univ. Press. 273 pp.

Pomper P. 1995. Russian revolutionary terrorism. See Crenshaw 1995, pp. 63–101

Post JM. 1984. Notes on a psychodynamic theory of terrorist behavior. *Terrorism* 8:241–57

Post JM. 1986. Hostilité, conformité, fraternité: the group dynamics of terrorist behavior. *Int. J. Group Psychother.* 36:211–24

Post JM. 1987. Rewarding fire with fire: effects of retaliation on terrorist group dynamics. *Terrorism* 10:23–36

Post JM. 1990. Terrorist psycho-logic: terrorist behavior as a product of psychological forces. See Reich 1990b, pp. 25–42

Powell W. 1971. *The Anarchist Cookbook*. Secaucus, NJ: Lyle Stuart. 160 pp.

Price EH Jr. 1977. The strategy and tactics of revolutionary terrorism. *Comp. Stud. Soc. Hist.* 19:52–66

Rapoport DC. 1977. The politics of atrocity. In *Terrorism: Interdisciplinary Perspectives*, ed. DC Rapoport, Y Alexander, pp. 127–216. New York: Pergamon

Rapoport DC. 1988. *Inside Terrorist Organizations*. London: Frank Cass. 259 pp.

Rapoport DC. 1992. Terrorism. In *Routledge Encyclopedia of Government and Politics*, ed. M Hawkesworth, M Kogan, 2:1061–79. London: Routledge

Rapoport DC. 1999. Terrorism. In *Encyclopedia of Violence, Peace, and Conflict*, 3:497–509. London: Academic

Rasch W. 1979. Psychological dimensions of political terrorism in the FRG. *Int. J. Law Psychiatry* 2:79–85

Redlick AS. 1979. The transnational flow of

information as a cause of terrorism. In *Terrorism: Theory and Practice*, ed. Y Alexander, D Carlton, P Wilkinson, pp. 73–95. Boulder, CO: Westview

Reich W. 1990a. Understanding terrorist behavior: the limits and opportunities of psychological inquiry. See Reich 1990b, pp. 261–81

Reich W. 1990b. *Origins of Terrorism*. Cambridge, UK: Cambridge Univ. Press

Reynaud E. 1982. Identités collectives et changement social: les cultures collectives comme dynamique d'action. *Sociol. Travail* 2:159–77

Rioch M. 1978. The work of Wilfred Bion on groups. *Psychiatry* 33:55–66

Ross JI. 1993. Structural causes of oppositional political terrorism: toward a causal model. *J. Peace Res.* 30:317–29

Ross JI. 1996. A model of the psychological causes of oppositional political terrorism. *Peace Confl. J. Peace Psychol.* 2:129–41

Ross JI, Gurr TR. 1989. Why terrorism subsides: a comparative study of trends and groups in terrorism in Canada and the United States. *Comp. Polit.* 21:405–26

Russell CA, Miller BH. 1983. Profile of a terrorist. See Freedman & Alexander 1983, pp. 45–60

Sandler T, Lapan HE. 1988. The calculus of dissent: an analysis of terrorists' choice of targets. *Synthese* 76:245–61

Sandler T, Tschirhart JT, Cauley J. 1983. A theoretical analysis of transnational terrorism. *Am. Polit. Sci. Rev.* 77:36–54

Sayari S. 1985. *Generational Change in Terrorist Movements: the Turkish Case*. Santa Monica, CA: RAND

Schelling TC. 1963. *The Strategy of Conflict*. New York: Oxford Univ. Press. 309 pp.

Schelling TC. 1978. *Micromotives and Macrobehavior*. New York: Norton. 252 pp.

Schelling TC. 1984. *Choice and Consequence*. Cambridge, MA: Harvard Univ. Press. 363 pp.

Schmid AP, de Graaf J. 1982. *Violence and Communication: Insurgent Terrorism and the Western News Media*. London: Sage. 282 pp.

Schmid AP, Jongman AJ. 1988. *Political Terrorism: a New Guide to Actors, Authors, Concepts, Data Bases, Theories and Literature*. Amsterdam: North-Holland. 700 pp.

Seale P. 1992. *Abu Nidal: a Gun for Hire*. New York: Random House. 339 pp.

Seufert M. 1978. Dissension among the terrorists: Killing people is wrong. *Encounter* 51:84–85

Shaw ME. 1981. *Group Dynamics: the Psychology of Small Group Behavior*. New York: McGraw-Hill. 531 pp. 3rd ed.

Silke A. 1998. Cheshire-cat logic: the recurring theme of terrorist abnormality in psychological research. *Psychol. Crime Law* 4:51–69

Simmel G. 1950. The secret and the secret societies. In *The Sociology of George Simmel*, ed. KH Wolff, pp. 345–76. New York: Free

Simon H. 1976. From substantive to procedural rationality. In *Method and Appraisal in Economics*, ed. SJ Latsis, pp. 129–48. Cambridge, UK: Cambridge Univ. Press

Simon HA. 1997. Rationality in psychology and economics. In *Models of Bounded Rationality*, HA Simon, 3:367–86. Cambridge, MA: MIT Press

Snow DA, Machalek R. 1983. The convert as a social type. In *Sociological Theory*, ed. R Collins, pp. 259–89. San Francisco: Jossey-Bass

Snow DA, Zurcher LA, Ekland-Olson S. 1980. Social networks and social movements: a microstructural approach to differential recruitment. *Am. Sociol. Rev.* 45:787–801

Sprinzak E. 1990. The psychological formation of extreme left terrorism in a democracy. See Reich 1990b, pp. 65–85

Sprinzak E. 1991. The process of delegitimization: towards a linkage theory of political terrorism. *Terrorism Polit. Violence* 3:50–68

Sprinzak E. 1995. Right-wing terrorism in a comparative perspective: the case of split delegitimization. *Terrorism Polit. Violence* 7:17–43

Steinhoff PG. 1989. Hijackers, bombers, and bank robbers: managerial style in the Japanese Red Army. *J. Asian Stud.* 48:724–40

Süllwold L. 1985. Biographical features of

terrorists. In *Psychiatry: the State of the Art,* ed. P Pichot, P Berner, R Wolf, K Thau, 6:407–8. New York: Plenum

Thornton TP. 1964. Terror as a weapon of political agitation. In *Internal War*, ed. H Eckstein, pp. 71–99. New York: Free

Tullock G. 1974. *The Social Dilemma: the Economics of War and Revolution.* Blacksburg, VA: Univ. Publ. 143 pp.

Unseem M. 1972. Ideological and interpersonal change in the radical protest movement. *Soc. Prob.* 19:451–69

Venturi F. 1960. *Roots of Revolution.* New York: Knopf. 850 pp.

Verba S. 1961. *Small Groups and Political Behavior: a Study of Leadership.* Princeton, NJ: Princeton Univ. Press. 273 pp.

Vidal de la Blache PMJ. 1926. *Principles of Human Geography.* New York: Holt. 511 pp.

Wallach MA, Kogan N. 1965. The roles of information, discussion, and consensus in group risk taking. *J. Exp. Soc. Psychol.* 1:1–19

Wallach MA, Kogan N, Bem DJ. 1962. Group influences on individual risk taking. *J. Abnorm. Psychol.* 65:75–86

Wallach MA, Kogan N, Bem DJ. 1964. Diffusion of responsibility and level of responsibility in groups. *J. Abnorm. Psychol.* 68:263–74

Wasmund K. 1983. The political socialization of terrorist groups in West Germany. *J. Polit. Milit. Sociol.* 11:195–222

Wasmund K. 1986. The political socialization of West German terrorists. In *Political Violence and Terror*, ed. PH Merkl, pp. 191–228. Berkeley, CA: Univ. Calif. Press

Waterman H. 1981. Reasons and reason: collective political activity in comparative and historical perspective. *World Polit.* 33:554–89

Waugh WL Jr. 1983. The values in violence: organizational and political objectives of terrorist groups. *Confl. Q.* 3:5–19

Weinberg L, Davis PB. 1989. *Introduction to Political Terrorism.* New York: McGraw-Hill. 234 pp.

Weinberg L, Eubank WL. 1987. *The Rise and Fall of Italian Terrorism.* Boulder, CO: Westview. 155 pp.

Weinberg L, Eubank W. 1990. Political parties and the formation of terrorist groups. *Terrorism Polit. Violence* 2:125–44

Whine M. 1999. Islamist organizations on the internet. *Terrorism Polit. Violence* 11:123–32

Whyte G. 1989. Groupthink reconsidered. *Acad. Manage. Rev.* 14:40–56

Wilkinson P. 1997. The media and terrorism: a reassessment. *Terrorism Polit. Violence* 9:51–64

Wilson JQ. 1973. *Political Organizations.* New York: Basic Books. 359 pp.

Wittke C. 1945. *Against the Current: the Life of Carl Heinzen.* Chicago: Univ. Chicago Press. 342 pp.

Wolfgang M, Ferracuti F. 1982. *The Subculture of Violence.* London: Tavistock. 387 pp.

Woodcock G. 1962. *Anarchism.* Cleveland, OH: World. 504 pp.

Zald M, Ash R. 1966. Social movement organizations: growth, decay, and change. *Soc. Forces* 44:327–41

Zanini M, Edwards SJA. 2001. The networking of terror in the Information Age. In *Networks and Netwars*, ed. J Arquilla, D Ronfeldt, pp. 29–60. Santa Monica: RAND

Zawodny JK. 1978. Internal organizational problems and the sources of tensions of terrorist movements as catalysts of violence. *Terrorism* 1:277–85

Zawodny JK. 1983. Infrastructures of terrorist organizations. See Freedman & Alexander 1983, pp. 61–70

Annu. Rev. Polit. Sci. 2003. 6:509–31
doi: 10.1146/annurev.polisci.6.121901.085642
First published online as a Review in Advance on Mar. 6, 2003

WHAT ROLE DOES PREJUDICE PLAY IN ETHNIC CONFLICT?

Donald P. Green and Rachel L. Seher

*Department of Political Science, Yale University, 77 Prospect Street, New Haven,
Connecticut 06520; email: donald.green@yale.edu*

Key Words prejudice, ethnic conflict, racism, genocide, propaganda

■ **Abstract** The extensive literatures on prejudice and ethnic conflict exist largely in isolation from one another. This essay attempts to bridge the gap between the social-psychological study of prejudice and macropolitical explanations of ethnic conflict. We argue that social-psychological inquiry could be strengthened by cross-national field research. Macro-level investigation of ethnic conflict would profit from more systematic research design, particularly where authors seek to establish the influence of micro-level mechanisms, such as persuasion by the mass media.

INTRODUCTION

For sheer size and scope, few social science literatures rival the corpus of work on the subject of prejudice. From their inception, the social sciences have been engaged in the investigation, and sometimes the justification, of intergroup differences. Long before survey research came into vogue as a social science enterprise, psychologists and sociologists conducted interviews to learn how various minority groups were perceived by others (Garth 1931, Keith 1931). Some of the earliest studies involving participant-observation and unobtrusive measurement techniques are classic studies of discrimination (La Piere 1934). The study of prejudice is one of the few topics that continues to spark vigorous discussion in such diverse disciplines as political science, anthropology, economics, and psychology. The anthropologist seeks to understand the cultural context in which group differences are perceived; the political scientist aims to understand how prejudices are formed and expressed within the polity; the economist considers how discriminatory market outcomes persist amid market pressures; the psychologist examines how prejudiced beliefs and feelings develop and the manner in which they are elicited.

To survey such an immense literature, even within the confines of a single discipline, is a daunting task. Political scientists approach the study of prejudice and discrimination from two very different vantage points. Behavioral research focuses on individual-level phenomena. Why do some people harbor negative beliefs about certain groups? How do these beliefs develop over the course of the life-cycle? Under what conditions do these views manifest themselves in political opinions and behavior? In contrast to the behavioral approach, scholars who study the politics of ethnic violence focus on aggregate patterns. To what extent and in what ways do political entrepreneurs create and manipulate out-group prejudices? What is the role of the state in maintaining group hierarchies and ideologies of group difference? Under what conditions do these ideologies lead to violence or the disruption of the political system?

The divide between the behavioral and macropolitical literatures runs so deep that few reviews attempt to traverse it. Brubaker & Laitin (1998) and Williams (1994) consider the political, social, and economic bases for ethnic conflict and violence but say almost nothing about the specific role of prejudice. Conversely, Fiske (1998) and Krysan (2000), in their reviews of prejudice, discrimination, and political attitudes, say almost nothing about ethnic violence. The disjuncture between these two literatures provides the occasion for a different type of review, one that focuses on research questions that have languished owing to the methodological and disciplinary separation between behavioral and macropolitical scholarship.

The unanswered questions are many, but none is more important than the issue of whether and to what extent political elites create and mobilize prejudices so as to encourage activities ranging from petty discrimination to genocide. Both literatures, we argue, may be blamed for the lack of systematic inquiry on this point. The behavioral literature has tended to become a form of cognitive science that is increasingly detached from the behavioral outcomes that inspired the study of prejudice in the first place. Rarely do researchers in this literature attempt to link their attitudinal measures to conduct outside the laboratory, such as workplace discrimination, hate crime, or participation in exclusionary organizations. As the behavioral literature becomes more detached from political action, its conceptual debates wander away from issues central to macropolitical analyses of ethnic violence.

The macropolitics literature may be faulted as well. Studies of ethnic violence are often vague about the psychological processes that underlie individual action. When tracing the causes of genocide or ethnic civil war, scholars tend to refer obliquely to longstanding hatreds, nationalist ideologies, or animus generated by propaganda campaigns. Rarely do these studies attempt to measure these constructs or demonstrate individual-level relationships between attitudes and actions. Equally rare are systematic attempts to demonstrate that state communications or programs of indoctrination in fact create, amplify, or mobilize prejudice.

The synthesis we recommend involves refocusing behavioral studies on comparative political outcomes while encouraging macropolitical analysts to attend more to the micro-level mechanisms by which prejudices evolve and express themselves. This essay is organized as follows. We begin by describing certain core issues in the study of prejudice, particularly the responsiveness of prejudice to mass communication and other short-term influences. Next, we provide an overview of the main currents of research in both behavioral and macropolitical studies of prejudice, arguing that they have diverged increasingly over time. The final section suggests ways to strengthen and unify these two literatures by making the systematic study of regional or temporal variation characteristic of behavioral research a more prominent feature of macropolitical inquiry.

DEFINITIONS AND CORE ISSUES

Ethnic Conflict and Ethnic Violence

"Ethnic conflict" refers to confrontation between members of two or more ethnic groups.[1] It generally involves a public action of two or more people that articulates a distinctly ethnic or racial claim, expresses a grievance, or attacks members of another ethnic group or their property. The target of a conflict may be the state or state representatives, or it may be another ethnic population that is involved either symbolically or as participants in the confrontation. Ethnic conflict can take various forms, including (*a*) intrastate collective action such as demonstrations, protests, strikes, and communal rioting; (*b*) internal wars such as secessionism and irredentism, civil wars, and coups; or (*c*) interstate wars, terrorism, annexation, and genocide (see Brubaker & Laitin 1998; Olzak 1992, pp. 8–9; Williams 1994, p. 54).

The term ethnic violence refers to "violence perpetrated across ethnic lines, in which at least one party is not a state (or representative of a state), and in which the putative ethnic difference is integral rather than incidental to that violence, that is in which the violence is meaningfully oriented in some way to the different ethnicity of the target" (Brubaker & Laitin 1998, p. 428).[2]

Prejudice and Attitude Change

Prejudice is conventionally defined as hostility toward groups predicated on false, simplistic, overgeneralized, or unconscious beliefs. Allport's (1954, p. 9)

---

[1]"Ethnicity" or "ethnic identity" is a social boundary that partitions a group of people on the basis of ascriptive characteristics, such as language, religion, phenotypical markers, dress, custom, culture, or historical experiences. Members of ethnic groups often attribute these commonalities to birth and blood and describe their ethnic affiliation in terms of kinship or familial ties. "Race" is a specific instance of ethnicity in which membership is based on what are assumed to be inherited phenotypical characteristics (see Horowitz 1985, ch. 2; Barth 1969, Introduction; Olzak 1992).

[2]"Ethnic competition" is an ethnically based struggle between individuals or groups over scarce resources. It differs from ethnic conflict in two key ways. First, it is impersonal, in that the competing individuals or groups are not necessarily in direct communication or contact with one another. Second, it generally takes place under rules, which are designed to limit the damage that competitors can inflict on each other (Olzak 1992, pp. 24–31; Williams 1994, p. 54).

often-cited definition holds that "Ethnic prejudice is an antipathy based upon a faulty and inflexible generalization. It may be felt or expressed. It may be directed toward a group as a whole, or toward an individual because he is a member of that group." Note that by these definitions, ethnic violence and prejudice need not intersect. Ethnic violence may arise from, say, economic competition rather than animus rooted in faulty generalization (see Blumer 1958). Whether prejudice is in fact implicated in ethnic violence is an interesting and open empirical question.

Etiology of Prejudice

This perspective naturally leads to an investigation of where prejudice originates. A longstanding and still vigorous line of argument traces it to mass communication. A small sampling of these arguments shows their range, even within the topic of anti-black prejudice in the United States. The racial prejudices of antebellum whites were shaped by pro-slavery narratives of racial uprisings (Menand 2001); racist literature and the immensely popular film *Birth of a Nation* diffused beliefs about racial hierarchy (Wade 1987); race-baiting propaganda by Southern planter interests prevented the formation of a class-based coalition of poor blacks and whites (Cox 1948); the media's portrayal of poor people as disproportionately black altered whites' beliefs about who is needy and undercut their support for the welfare state (Gilens 1999); the specter of black criminality raised by the notorious Willie Horton ad run by the Bush campaign during 1988 turned white opinion against a liberal presidential candidate (Mendelberg 2001). Many of the recent behavioral works on visual priming of racial attitudes during political commercials or news coverage (Gilliam & Iyengar 2000) grow out of a tradition of tracing political conduct to mass communication.

Although behavioral studies such as those of Gilens (1999) and Mendelberg (2001) demonstrate a link between media messages and specific policy views or voting intentions, studies have rarely demonstrated a link between propaganda and general attitudes. Attitudes are typically defined as enduring evaluative orientations toward certain stimuli (Jahoda & Warren 1966). One may, for example, harbor a favorable or hostile attitude toward Jews that is elicited when one is presented with a picture of a Jewish star, a song from the musical *Fiddler on the Roof*, or anything else that calls Jews to mind. One indication that enduring evaluative predispositions exist comes from studies of preconscious exposure to attitude objects. Showing a white subject a picture of a black person's face changes the speed with which the subject draws a connection between two positively valenced objects (Dasgupta et al. 2000). Another indication is that attitudes are sometimes very slow to change, even when circumstances have caused them to become outdated (Sears & Funk 1999). The claim that mass communication shapes the salience of particular policy concerns is politically important, but much less so than the more forceful claim that communication creates or strengthens attitudes.

Conceptualization and Measurement of Prejudice

Many spirited debates among students of prejudice revolve around the conceptualization and measurement of these attitudes. At the broadest level are conceptualizations that treat attitudes as manifestations of personality types or the underlying drives that give rise to personality configurations. The most famous construct of this type is authoritarianism (Adorno 1950, Altemeyer 1981). Developed originally from extensive interviews with and psychometric assessments of former Nazis, this theoretical perspective attracted enormous attention during the 1950s and waned thereafter, but recently returned to prominence through the work of Altemeyer (1981). In brief, this theory contends that individuals with authoritarian tendencies harbor a deep ambivalence toward authority as a result of their harsh treatment at the hands of loved authority figures during childhood. They resolve this ambivalence by venerating those above them in the social hierarchy while suppressing those below, over whom they have authority. Other personality constructs thought to contribute to prejudiced attitudes include tough-mindedness (Eysenck 1954) and closed-mindedness (Rokeach 1960). In each instance, prejudice is treated as a by-product of the way that people with certain personality types negotiate their environment.

At a somewhat lower level of generality are conceptualizations that focus on certain attitude syndromes. Ethnocentrism (Levine & Campbell 1972) manifests itself in a complex of attitudes including positive identification with one's own group (see Brewer 1999) and xenophobia expressed in varying degrees to outside groups. Social dominance orientations (Sidanius & Pratto 1999) describe the extent to which a person endorses social hierarchies. In both instances, prejudices directed at specific groups are treated as manifestations of more basic psychological orientations.

Prejudice, Racism, and Issues of Validity

In recent decades, the use of the term prejudice has receded, and expressions of prejudice are increasingly described using the unfortunate terminology of racism— "old-fashioned" racism, aversive racism (see Dovidio 2001), or, most prominently, symbolic or new racism (Sears 1988). We think this unfortunate because racism is ordinarily understood as a doctrine rather than a description of a psychological orientation. Just as doctrines such as liberalism and conservatism may bear only an incidental connection to the policy views held by ordinary voters (Converse 1964), racist ideologies as expressed by their proponents are neither explicitly endorsed nor strongly reflected in the views of all but a small segment of the public. The noun equivalent to "people who are prejudiced" is "racist," which implies a much stronger set of beliefs. Problematic though prejudice may be in societies throughout the world, it would be difficult to name a polity in which appreciable segments of the mass public nowadays subscribe to classic racist doctrines of hierarchy, destiny, and revenge. Although Converse (1964) intimated that racial attitudes are more structured and enduring than other political orientations of Americans, his penetrating analysis showing the disjuncture between ideological doctrines and the equivocal liberalism-conservatism expressed by the public applies as well to racist doctrines.[3]

How Malleable is Prejudice?

Regardless of one's preferences regarding the terms racism and prejudice, and regardless of which syndrome of prejudiced attitudes one chooses to consider, the fact remains that the empirical link between mass communications and attitudes toward out-groups remains uncertain. The modern literature on propaganda, which arose in response to Josef Goebbels' extraordinary efforts to convey Nazi ideology to the German masses during Hitler's reign, was singularly unsuccessful in its initial attempts to demonstrate the influence of propaganda. The brilliant studies of World War II propaganda films by Hovland et al. (1949), which still stand as the most compelling field experiments ever conducted in this area, found propaganda to have negligible effects. Allied films designed to justify the war effort imparted information to soldiers but did little to change their opinions about the war or more basic attitudes such as patriotism. These findings eventually led to Hovland's (1959) famous "minimal effects" thesis, in which he argued that the causative influence of propaganda is typically overstated. When the message conveyed through propaganda is clear, often repeated, and reinforced by people in one's small-group environment, mass communication may prompt political action—but these conditions are seldom met in practice.

This argument, coupled with theories about the difficulty of achieving the conditions necessary for reducing prejudice through equal-status contact between groups (Allport 1954, Pettigrew 1998), led social scientists to explain the origins of prejudice with reference to long-term causes. One of the most important recurrent themes in the literature on prejudice is that invidious distinctions between groups are learned early in childhood and persist with great tenacity during an individual's life (Sears 1988). By this account, the cause of ameliorating prejudice progresses one funeral at a time.

Somewhere between the two positions is the view that a person's prejudices change gradually over time. Those who have tracked racial attitudes in the United

---

[3]The problem is particularly acute in the case of symbolic racism, the subject of extensive debate dating back to the 1970s (Sears et al. 1979, Sniderman & Tetlock 1985). Unlike old-fashioned racism, which asserts the biological inferiority of non-Aryan stock, symbolic racism holds that racial/ethnic minorities violate norms of self-reliance and deserve no remedial attention from government (e.g., affirmative action). Symbolic racism finds expression in a less clearly identifiable doctrine or social movement. One can readily imagine setting up a criterion group of certified racists to validate a psychological inventory of this type of prejudice; indeed, the author of *The Authoritarian Personality* made a gesture in precisely this direction (see also Green et al. 1999). But what is the criterion group for symbolic racism, and what social movement do they populate?

States (Hyman & Sheatsley 1964, Schuman et al. 1985) have found that public opinion evolved rapidly from the 1940s to the 1970s, with all generational cohorts moving away from the view that whites should have priority on public conveyances or when applying for jobs. Schuman et al. also point out, however, that policy views regarding whether and how government should reduce racial inequality remain ambivalent over time, and it is this disjuncture between declining support for segregation and stable lukewarm attitudes toward remedial policies that opened the door to symbolic racism theories. Old-fashioned race prejudice died out, but anti-black affect continued to be expressed through opposition to special favors for minorities.

In recent years, the minimal-effects thesis has come under increasing attack from political scientists studying the media, reopening the question of whether prejudices can be manipulated in the short term. In a series of influential experiments using newscasts and political advertising, Iyengar, Kinder, and their colleagues have demonstrated that even if news stories do not change policy views on particular topics, they do increase the political salience of those topics; moreover, the tone of political advertisements may influence a person's inclination to vote (Iyengar et al. 1982, Iyengar & Kinder 1987, Ansolabehere & Iyengar 1995). Gilliam & Iyengar (2000) show that exposure to local television news, with its customary focus on nonwhite perpetrators of crime, increases whites' support for punitive anti-crime policies (see also Mendelberg 1997).

Moreover, in an important departure from the usual findings, which show only priming or issue-specific effects, Gilliam & Iyengar (2000) contend that exposure to crime stories about nonwhite perpetrators increases the prevalence of negative attitudes about nonwhites among whites. Note that the television news is far from a government-sanctioned outlet for propaganda. The newsreaders, for example, do not editorialize on or even mention the perpetrator's race.

The detached stance of newsreaders is important to consider in light of more nuanced theories about the conditions that make messages more persuasive. The important work of Zaller (1992), which builds on that of Converse (1962) and McGuire (1968), distinguishes between contested and uncontested messages. Zaller argues that mass communication has special influence when endorsed by leaders from across the political spectrum (see also Brody & Shapiro 1991 on rally-round-the-flag effects). Myrdal's (1944, pp. 1372–73) account of pre–World War II news coverage of African-Americans, particularly in the South, suggests that it overwhelmingly portrayed this group in a negative light. And during ethnic conflicts in the Balkans, Rwanda, and Southeast Asia, which we discuss below, governments monopolized the airwaves and filled them with stridently nationalist propaganda that played on the listeners' acute sense of fear and uncertainty. If uncontested messages have special force, this propaganda may explain how populations may be mobilized to carry out genocide.

However, one may wonder whether a monopoly of airtime amounts to a monopoly of discourse. The famous Asch (1958) experiment, which demonstrated how individuals succumb to the pressure to conform to the views expressed by others, also shows that this pressure dissipates when the monopoly of public opinion is broken by even a single dissenter. Many narratives of ethnic violence emphasize the steady drumbeat of government propaganda that preceded it, but the literature on agricultural societies challenges the notion that the general population accepts whatever state authorities tell it (Scott 1985). As we point out below, narrative accounts of ethnic violence seldom look closely or systematically at small-group environments (e.g., families, workplaces) to gauge the extent to which government messages are endorsed or dissent expressed.

One reason why propaganda may lack influence is that government and its spokespeople often lack credibility. Research on persuasion emphasizes that messages are discounted when the speaker seems to have an interest in persuading the listener; disinterested speakers are generally more influential. On the other hand, it may be that the messages put out by the central government gain credibility when endorsed and echoed by local leaders, who in the case of Rwanda played an integral role in carrying out genocide.

Disentangling Communication's Effects from its Causes

The startling fact remains that more than half a century after the Hovland et al. (1949) experiments on propaganda, scarcely any research demonstrates rigorously that such government-sponsored campaigns advocating interethnic violence actually influence the attitudes and conduct of those exposed to them. Although this lack of evidence does not mean that no such relationship exists, it is possible that propaganda is used in much the same way as campaign advertising, not so much to persuade as to signal the government's position to its potential supporters. If leaders sense widespread ethnic tension among large segments of the population, they have an incentive to express these concerns in ways that encourage public support.

A similar argument may be made with respect to the interparty politics that lie beneath the surface of government action. One of the central themes in the propaganda campaigns used in Nazi Germany, Rwanda, and Serbia is that the enemy must be destroyed before they destroy those native to the country. This message not only identifies and demonizes an external enemy but also warns that any dissent from government policies is part of a plot to collaborate with that enemy. Thus, even if propaganda does nothing to augment ethnic prejudices, it might still be in the interest of the regime, which seeks to defend its grip on power against other factions.

Paradox of Collective Action

One peculiar feature of mass participation in ethnic violence is that it seems to fly in the face of the collective-action problem (Olson 1965), which is that individuals in large groups shirk political action and shift its costs onto others on the grounds that their own participation will not unilaterally determine the outcome of a group effort. If this is true, why would Serbians volunteer for dangerous and unpleasant military service? Why would Hutu participate day after day in the slaughter of their Tutsi neighbors? One possibility is coercion by the state, which in the case of Rwanda terrorized local leaders who refused to carry out the ruling party's genocidal policies. In this context, propaganda may serve to remind citizens not only of what the state demands of them but also of the state's determination to let no one stand in its path. A related possibility is that even in the absence of outright coercion, people often defer to authority (Milgram 1974), at least in the short run. Finally, individuals might participate in ethnic violence in anticipation of extracting resources from the victims. Plunder and rape are recurrent themes in accounts of Serbian and Rwandan massacres (Glenny 1996, pp. 203–9; Gourevitch 1998, pp. 114–15).

Often, however, it is difficult to trace specific acts of ethnic violence to any discernible "selective incentive," be it coercion or material reward. In such cases, it is tempting to speak of psychic selective benefits of participation resulting from feelings of solidarity with others, stature within one's peer group, or the intrinsic satisfaction of expressing one's prejudiced convictions (Chong 1991). The latter is often used by narrators of ethnic violence to explain acts of gratuitous violence, particularly among those who believe themselves to be throwing off the shackles of a repressive out-group. The expressive dimension of violence is not inconsistent with Horowitz's (1985, 2001) and Kalyvas's (1999) important observation that what may appear to be pell-mell violence is often highly structured, with assailants taking pains to differentiate between legitimate and illegitimate targets. The satisfaction of expressing one's animus toward an out-group in part requires that the victims be selected with care.

In sum, the phenomenon of ethnic violence and the politics within which it occurs seem to call out for an assessment of how the state enjoins the support and participation of the public. Yet basic questions about the public's motivation and the state's role in fostering public support remain unanswered. In the next section, we describe how the behavioral literature on prejudice has drifted away from these questions and, indeed, from real-world settings more generally. This trend, unfortunately, diminishes the prominence of social-psychological explanations in the literature on ethnic violence. The net effect is a psychological literature that has tenuous connections to explanations of real-world ethnic conflict and an ethnic-conflict literature that is unstructured by research questions arising from the behavioral literature on prejudice.

TRENDS IN BEHAVIORAL STUDIES OF PREJUDICE

Behavioral studies may be grouped into four broad categories: ecological studies, field experiments, laboratory experiments, and survey analysis.

Ecological Studies

Ecological studies grow out of the tradition established by Hovland & Sears (1940). These authors showed that lynchings rose during periods of retrenchment in cotton prices, a fact that supported their theory that whites expressed the frustrations associated with economic downturn by "displacing" their aggression against a vulnerable out-group, African-Americans. Although this literature has from time to time examined the relationship between economic conditions and hate crime (Green et al. 1998a), between authoritarianism and support for punitive policies (Doty et al. 1991), and between other aggregate phenomena related to prejudice (Green et al. 1998b, Krueger & Pischke 1997), it remains small.

Field Experiments

Somewhat larger but less vigorous of late is the literature on field experiments. The 1970s saw a range of "unobtrusive" studies (reviewed in Crosby et al. 1980) that measured prejudice by observing subjects' conduct rather than asking them survey questions. In several field experiments, intergroup contact in schools and other locations was randomly manipulated in an effort to study its effects on racial prejudice (Aronson et al. 1978, DeVries et al. 1978; see Brewer & Miller 1988, Pettigrew 1998). After 1980, these experimental efforts largely subsided, although "audit studies," in which individuals with identical characteristics but different skin colors attempt to secure loans, buy cars, or obtain jobs, remain a common technique used to establish the prevalence of discrimination (e.g., Yinger 1995). Unfortunately, audit studies rarely assess the link between prejudiced attitudes and discriminatory behavior, leaving open the question of whether discrimination results from ethnic hostility or from the incentive systems in which bank loan officers or car dealers work. (For an attempt to blend audit research and laboratory experimentation, see Hodson et al. 2002.)

Laboratory Experiments

A large and increasing number of laboratory studies examine the causes and expression of prejudice within controlled environments. A large body of research examines subjects' proclivity to form group identities and discriminate against out-groups (Brewer 1999). These works call to mind Blumer's (1958) argument that individual-level prejudice is of secondary importance; what matters, from the standpoint of understanding the perpetuation of hierarchies, is each group's sense of social position in relation to the others. In some sense, many of the key social-psychological experiments, such as those by Haney et al. (1973) or Milgram (1974), may be read as implicit critiques of the prejudice literature, as they suggest that organizational roles and obedience may be sufficient to produce violence against out-groups even in the absence of hostility (see Arendt 1963).

A more recent line of laboratory research explores the distinction between conscious and unconscious prejudices. A rapidly growing list of studies attempts to show that individuals' reactions to subliminal racial primes reflect attitudes that are beyond their awareness and control (Fazio et al. 1995), although some individuals who harbor negative stereotypes seem able to monitor their views and make conscious decisions to override them (Devine 1989, Devine et al. 2002). Some studies purport to show a link between implicit prejudice and social behavior (Dovidio et al. 2002), but it is unclear whether unconscious attitudes manifest themselves in political conduct. For that matter, it is unclear what small-group laboratory studies imply about real-world manifestations of prejudice (Sears 1986). Given the artificiality of the laboratory setting and the practice of experimenting on undergraduate subjects, it is troubling that laboratory research has largely supplanted field experimentation in social psychology.

Survey Analysis

The other dominant research method in the study of prejudice is survey analysis. This enormous literature may be grouped into three categories. The smallest category comprises surveys that track opinion before, during, and after a political event in an effort to gauge its effects on public opinion. For example, Sears & Allen (1984) and Taylor (1986) tracked opinion prior to and immediately after the implementation of court-ordered school desegregation. When panel data are used to track respondents over time, this type of study is analogous to a before-after experiment. Unfortunately, relatively few studies fall into this category, and of these, only a handful attempt to predict behavior other than voting for a particular candidate (see Green & Cowden 1992).

The second category encompasses correlational studies that attempt to measure one or more dimensions of prejudice and relate them to some type of policy or candidate preference. Some of the more noteworthy examples of this type of study are Sears et al.'s (1979, 1980) attempts to show that racial attitudes, but not measures of economic self-interest, predict preferences toward policies such as affirmative action or school desegregation and Bobo's (1988) analysis suggesting that the collective interests of whites predict their policy stances even if their individual self-interests do not (see also Ignatiev 1995). Many of the essays in this category constitute measurement exercises of one form or another. Katz & Hass (1988), for example, argue that positive attitudes toward blacks are empirically distinct from negative attitudes, a claim that Green & Citrin (1994) reject as a measurement artifact. Sniderman & Tetlock (1986) critique the conceptual and empirical validity of symbolic racism, which Sears & Kinder (1985) and Kinder & Sanders (1996) defend. This category properly includes as well surveys that use depth interviews rather than standardized questionnaires (e.g., Wellman 1993).

The final category consists of survey experiments, in which respondents are randomly assigned to treatment groups, each of which is presented with a somewhat different questionnaire. By randomly manipulating the content, context, and order of the questions, researchers seek to uncover both the prevalence and structure of prejudice. For example, Kuklinski et al. (1997) employ a clever list experiment to detect racial grievances among the public in a way that avoids the problem of extracting truthful answers from respondents who might otherwise conceal their prejudiced attitudes. The authors present two groups of respondents with different lists of possible grievances and ask them to simply report the number of items on the list that they find objectionable. The two lists are identical except that the second list also contains a racial grievance. By comparing the average number of grievances reported by the two groups, Kuklinski et al. gauge the level of prejudice in the population. Other examples of experimental survey methodology in this area may be found in the works of Sniderman & Piazza (1993), Sniderman & Carmines (1997), Hurwitz & Peffley (1998), and Kinder & Sanders (1990).

Although survey experiments have attracted a great deal of interest among prejudice researchers, they have been confined to relatively narrow questions about how public opinion responds in the short term to various manipulations in questionnaire content. Survey experiments, like surveys more generally, have seldom been used to study behavioral outcomes. An important exception is Glaser (2002), which shows that racially charged voting on school-bond referenda can be influenced by the way that ballot choices are presented to voters. Of course, this correspondence is not altogether surprising, since voting is similar in many respects to expressing a preference on a survey, and public-opinion research can be expected to provide useful insights into the factors that shape, for example, ethnic voting. Less certain is what surveys, randomized or not, tell us about more costly and ongoing behaviors, such as taking up arms against another ethnic group.

ETHNIC CONFLICT AND VIOLENCE

The literature on ethnic conflict and violence is large and diffuse, ranging across a variety of geographic regions and historical eras. Recent years have witnessed important attempts to integrate the large corpus of studies of particular conflicts (Horowitz 1985), to create and analyze comparative data bases (Sambanis 2000), and to bring theoretical coherence to a vast and methodologically disparate literature (Fearon & Laitin 1996). Currently, theoretical perspectives on ethnic violence fall into three categories (see discussions in Jones-Luong 2002,[4] Varshney 2002).

Theoretical Perspectives

PRIMORDIALIST THEORIES   Primordialist theories contend that ethnic and racial identities are fundamental and immutable, arising from congruities of blood, speech, and custom. Human beings do not actively choose their ethnic identities. Rather, they inherit them when born into communities that speak certain languages, practice particular religions, and follow specific social customs. People are bound to their kinsman "*ipso facto*; as a result not merely of personal affection, practical necessity, common interest, or incurred obligation, but at least in great part by virtue of some unaccountable absolute import attributed to the very tie itself" (Geertz 1963, pp. 109–10). This "natural—some would say spiritual—affinity" serves as the basis for ethnic and racial conflict. Political mobilization along ethnic

---

[4]Jones-Luong P. 2002. The Soviet legacy in Central Asia: explaining the origins of regional ethno-political cleavages. Chapter in unpublished manuscript.

and racial lines occurs when people mobilize to defend, sustain, or propagate their own kinship group, culture, and way of life. The implication of this perspective is that ethnic conflict is inevitable; it is the "natural outlet" for primordial attachments (see Eller & Coughlan 1993, Grosby 1994, Van den Berghe 1995).

INSTRUMENTALIST THEORIES   In sharp contrast to primordialist theories, instrumentalist theories portray ethnic identification and ethnic conflict as the result of rational decision making. Ethnic identities, according to this view, are strategically chosen. Although ethnic groups may exhibit common social, religious, or linguistic traits, the bond between group members is not natural or given. Rather, it is a malleable and fluid bond based on common interest. Individuals choose to associate with an ethnic group because they believe that they will somehow benefit from doing so.

By extension, instrumentalists view ethnic conflict as the product of the individual pursuit of private interests. Individuals choose to take part in ethnically based political movements in order to acquire material or political goods. A prominent variant of this argument concerns the role of political elites or "ethnic entrepreneurs" in ethnic mobilization. These entrepreneurs capitalize on differences between groups, such as language, physical appearance, or religion, in order to establish ethnically based political movements aimed at increasing the economic and political well-being of their group or region. They do so by making individuals aware of the connection between private interest and political action (see Barth 1969; Bates 1983; Waters 1990; Hardin 1992, 1995; Fearon & Laitin 1996).

CONSTRUCTIVIST THEORIES   Constructivists see ethnic identities and ethnic conflict as the product of concrete historical processes. Ethnic identities, according to constructivists, are not social givens but are produced through processes of socialization and acculturation. Neither primordial ties nor common interest hold ethnic groups together. Rather, ethnic groups are social constructs generated and maintained by specific historical processes such as the distribution of official identity cards. Although ethnic identities are actually produced by historical processes, they are not necessarily perceived in this way. Over time, ethnic identities gain widespread social acceptance. Individuals come to perceive ethnic identities as immutable social facts and have difficulty separating their personal identities from those of the groups to which they belong.

A particular understanding of ethnic conflict and ethnic mobilization stems from this conceptualization of ethnicity. Unlike primordialists and instrumentalists, who continually refer to emotions or strategic calculations, constructivists concentrate on external processes in explaining the politicization of ethnic identities. They devote particular attention to the external forces that increase or decrease the likelihood of ethnic mobilization. These often include general historical processes such as modernization, decolonization, the structuring of colonial states, and the weakening of central political institutions (see Vail 1989, Comaroff & Comaroff 1992, Ignatieff 1994, Wilmer 1997).

Application of Theory to Studies of Ethnic Violence

One of the leading themes of this literature is the debate over the relative significance of short-, medium-, and long-term causes. Do ethnic conflicts arise from
primordial group attachments, which in turn arise from the cultural or phenotypic
distinctiveness of groups and the social boundaries that separate them? Do ethnic
conflicts instead reflect the ways that states and group ideologues have historically
categorized groups and characterized group differences? Or do they reflect the
strategic behavior of elites, who use nationalist appeals and ethnic violence as a
means of consolidating power or pursuing ideological objectives?

For any given ethnic conflict, one finds proponents of each of these interpretations. Consider, for example, analyses of the Rwandan genocide. Journalists and
policy makers, in particular, tend to emphasize the longstanding hatreds between
Hutu and Tutsis. This journalistic comparison of the conflicts in Burundi and
Rwanda illustrates this type of narrative (Michaels 1994, p. 56):

> Local people call their country "the Burundi cocktail." Its volatile ethnic
> mixture seems ready to explode at any time. Rwanda's next-door neighbor
> to the south is virtually a mirror image of that devastated country, threatened
> by the same passionate hatreds. As in Rwanda, Burundi's dense population is
> divided between two tribes, 85% Hutu and 15% Tutsi. As in Rwanda, Belgian
> colonialization hoisted the status of the Tutsi, who after independence slowly
> lost power to the majority Hutu. And as in Rwanda, the potential for ethnic
> violence has risen to the surface in the political vacuum left by the assassination
> of the Presidents of both countries last April. Now "every Hutu goes to sleep
> afraid he will be killed by a Tutsi," says Sicaire Ndikymana, a taxi driver in
> Bujumbura, the capital. "Every Tutsi goes to sleep afraid he will be killed by
> a Hutu."

By contrast, the constructivist accounts offered by Mamdani (2001) and others
emphasize the medium-term origins of the Hutu-Tutsi conflict, noting that colonial
powers hardened the boundaries between these two formerly fluid groups and
supplied an ideology stressing the racial superiority of the putatively "Hamitic"
Tutsi. The hierarchy created by colonial rulers inevitably caused the Hutu majority
to resent the arrogant Tutsi "foreigners" in their midst. Notice that these arguments
about the primordial or socially constructed origins of ethnic conflict are broadly
analogous to the behavioral argument that prejudices are formed early in life and
transmitted by parental and peer influences.

Short-term strategic maneuvering by elites is emphasized in many accounts
of the events leading up to the Rwandan genocide. Both Gourevitch (1998) and
Des Forges (1999) note that the Hutu leader Habyarimana consolidated power and
outflanked his Hutu competitors by pursuing an increasingly strident anti-Tutsi
program. Although vulnerable to charges of incompetence and corruption, his
regime proved adept at using the simmering border war with Tutsi-led insurgents
as a pretext for suppressing opposition. In the months leading up to the genocide,

government radio messages became increasingly shrill and bellicose, eventually calling for a self-defensive genocide: "You cockroaches must know you are made of flesh. We won't let you kill. We will kill you" (quoted in Gourevitch 1998, p. 114).

Parallel arguments arise in the analysis of other ethnic conflicts, with most authors using primordialist interpretations as a foil for arguments that emphasize short-term influences. For example, Bennett's (1996, p. viii) account of the outbreak of war in Yugoslavia downplays the role of ancient hatreds, emphasizing instead the "very modern nationalist hysteria which was deliberately generated in the media ... Yugoslavia's disintegration is largely a testimony to the power of the media in the modern world." Woodward's (1995, p. 335) analysis of this process places less emphasis on the role of the media than on the progression of events; in her view, the escalation of violence resulted from an interaction between nationalist sentiments and feelings of extreme insecurity in an environment where competing nationalist factions produced a power vacuum. Cigar (1995) ascribes the genocide of Muslims in Bosnia-Herzegovina to a "rational policy" whereby the Serbian elite fomented intergroup conflict in order to consolidate power and expand Serbian influence over the region. Silber & Little (1995) blame Serbian leader Slobodan Milosevic himself, whose nationalist appeals propelled him to power by mobilizing the Serbian public while undercutting his Serbian political adversaries.

Whether one believes that short-term maneuvers by elites are foreordained by ancient hatreds or instead represent contingent acts that reflect the immediate strategic circumstances, the mechanisms by which a government's program of "ethnic cleansing" are actually carried out by individuals remain mysterious. In the case of the Rwandan or Balkan genocides, it is unclear how much mass support existed for these efforts or how the level of support changed over time. Were the participants taught to fear and despise the opposition, or did the government's blandishments make salient and mobilize longstanding hatreds? Or did mass participation reflect a strategic decision to obey orders, thereby relieving the assailants of moral responsibility and fear of state reprisal?

In part, this gap reflects an inherent historiographic bias in accounts that emphasize elite maneuvering over the harder-to-measure dynamics in mass opinion and behavior. Since survey data are often nonexistent, it may be necessary to turn to other indicators, such as regional and temporal patterns of defection from the army (Bearman 1991, Levi 1997), party membership (Brustein 1996), or other administrative records that might provide an indirect measure of regime support. Occasionally, analysts have gathered retrospective accounts of participants and victims (Straus 2002), but seldom are these accounts gathered according to a systematic sampling procedure that attends to regional or temporal variation.

The focus on elite politics and broad-gauged historical trends reflects not only the availability of data but also the disjuncture between this literature and the behavioral study of prejudice. The bibliographic references of most studies are almost entirely innocent of social psychology. It is not just that key works go uncited; there is little indication that the analysis of ethnic violence is inspired or informed by the behavioral literature. Even Brubaker & Laitin (1998), who devote special attention to instrumental theories and asymmetries of information among elites, do not address the question of how the collective-action problem is overcome in this form of mass political action.

In part, this oversight reflects a tendency to analyze political events rather than the micro-level processes that underlie them. One typical example of the genre is Bew et al. (1995), which, in discussing the roots of Catholic mobilization in Northern Ireland's ethnic violence, refers to alienation and the structural factors that give rise to it but does not analyze individual-level processes. Even accounts of this crisis that rely on depth interviews and eyewitness reports (Bell 1993, White 1993) make no systematic attempts to measure prejudice, gauge the ways in which it varies spatially or over time, or relate this variation to patterns of violence.

The absence of systematic psychological inquiry from the study of ethnic violence is particularly striking given the importance of fear in the etiology of ethnic violence. For example, one common strand linking the Nazi murder of Jews, Serbian murder of Muslims, and Hutu murder of Tutsi was the apparently widespread belief that the two parties in each conflict were locked in mortal combat that could end only in the expulsion or elimination of one side. In the case of Rwanda, this fear was amplified both by the massacre of Hutu by Tutsi in neighboring Burundi and by the ongoing border war between Hutu and Tutsi forces. The role of fear in undercutting tolerance has been debated extensively in behavioral research (Stouffer 1955, Rogin 1967, Sullivan et al. 1982), but it does appear that a public perception of crisis encourages public support of extreme state actions and emboldens officeholders who might otherwise shy away from such policies.

Similarly, ethnic violence often occurs within the special psychological environment created by the breakdown of state authority. The disappearance of conventional political authority gives license to mob violence and creates an atmosphere of uncertainty that is itself terrorizing.

> The wholesale extermination of Tutsis got underway. ... Following the militia's example, Hutus young and old rose to the task. Neighbors hacked neighbors to death in their homes, and colleagues hacked colleagues to death in their workplaces. Doctors killed their patients and schoolteachers killed their pupils. Within days, the Tutsi populations of many villages were all but eliminated. ... Throughout Rwanda, mass rape and looting accompanied the slaughter. Drunken militia bands...were bused from massacre to massacre. (Gourevitch 1998, pp. 114–15)

Indeed, even in situations where state authority remains intact throughout much of the country, the strategic withdrawal of political authority from a given region may unleash a torrent of ethnic violence (see Van Dyke 1996). Again a parallel literature exists in psychology on the momentum that unpunished lawlessness accumulates. Zimbardo's (1969) famous illustration of how an abandoned car becomes the object of increasingly destructive acts of vandalism presaged the "broken windows" literature in criminology (Wilson & Kelling 1982), which suggests that criminals look for signs that the state has ceded its authority over a particular target area. Presumably, the ebb and flow of authority in the context of ethnic unrest provides a useful laboratory for understanding the dynamics of fear and violence. A similar point may be made with respect to other social-psychological processes, such as conformity to social norms, obedience to authority, or the gradual breakdown of inhibitions in the wake of deviant behavior.

Finally, although several studies take pains to analyze mass communications, such as official government programming or the editorials of leading newspapers, seldom is there an effort to link the timing of these communications to shifts in mass opinion or violent conduct. And, as noted above, there is no direct micro-level evidence that exposure to these messages changes attitudes or measurably increases individuals' propensity to act violently or in support of violence by the regime.

In sum, the ethnic-violence literature has yet to explore systematically the micro-foundations of mass involvement, particularly in light of the usual impediments to mass participation in political action. This oversight has impeded the theoretical development of the literature. Analyses of ethnic violence and genocide that emphasize the role of strategic manipulation by elites are generally vague about psychological and small-group mechanisms by which mass compliance is achieved. This literature tells us why elites might be motivated to precipitate ethnic violence but not why they find it in their interests to carry out such a program given the vagaries of implementation.

PREJUDICE AND ETHNIC VIOLENCE: THE POTENTIAL FOR SYNTHESIS

Both the literature on ethnic violence and that on the social psychology of prejudice have important strengths. Works on ethnic violence provide gripping accounts of how ordinary politics sidles into the extraordinary—how through a series of small steps regimes embark on campaigns of routinized mass slaughter. These accounts suggest many provocative hypotheses about how demonization of out-groups allows demagogues to consolidate power against their in-group rivals and how historical memories are manufactured and made salient by political entrepreneurs. For its part, the prejudice literature is resolutely systematic in its approach, carefully debating each nuance of measurement and conceptualization. The behavioral literature on prejudice offers clear accounts of what the independent and dependent variables are in a given study, what hypotheses are being tested, and what kinds of statistical criteria will be used to assess them.

Yet both literatures are in certain respects intellectually and methodologically myopic. The prejudice literature focuses to an extraordinary degree on the narrow politics of the United States, often from the even narrower perspective of college undergraduates. Extraordinary political action, such as hate crime or support for extreme movements, is seldom studied directly (see Green et al. 2001). Indeed, with the exception of electoral support, the same may be said for political action more generally. The behavioral literature on prejudice has told us more about ambient levels of prejudice (variously defined) than about the conditions under which prejudice manifests itself in violence.

One can readily imagine a synthesis of the two approaches that could benefit both. The study of ethnic violence in the field would lend external validity to psychological scholarship that has increasingly focused on the structure of thought rather than on the links between thought and action. By the same token, the integration of psychological research methods into the study of ethnic violence would encourage more systematic evaluation of causal hypotheses.

A few examples illustrate what forms this fusion might take. At present, scholarship on ethnic violence tends not to investigate research questions that capitalize on regional or temporal variation in economic, political, or social circumstances. It is said, for example, that the extraordinary swiftness of the Rwandan genocide (remarkable even by Nazi standards) reflects the extensiveness of the multilayered administrative state (Des Forges 1999). If true, one should observe different rates of bloodshed among villages within Rwanda with varying degrees of administrative capacity. Similarly, it is argued that government radio broadcasts spurred assailants to action. Were there significant regional variations in reception of government broadcasts or exposure to competing communications from other sources? If so, were these variations related to rates of rank-and-file participation in bloodshed?

One barrier to the systematic analysis of cross-regional or cross-temporal variation is simply the lack of data. This problem, it should be noted, is not confined to developing countries. The anti-immigrant violence that followed German unification largely escaped systematic measurement (see Krueger & Pischke 1997), despite plentiful social science expertise nearby. The same may be said for the paucity of individual-level data, especially panel data that track respondents over time. Rarely have social scientists endeavored to observe a set of people as their life circumstances change radically because of unfolding events (Jennings & Niemi 1981, McFalls 1995) and never to our knowledge in the context of ethnic violence. When scholars in this area have used individual-level data, they have tended to rely on retrospective accounts or participant interviews; neither of these is inherently unreliable, but the absence of sampling procedures or methods for cross-validation raises concerns about whether these data can support unbiased inference. Whether the collection of reliable ecological or individual data represents an insurmountable hurdle in the study of ethnic violence's micro-foundations remains unclear. It appears that this type of research design, which links variation in preconditions to variation in behavioral outcomes, has rarely structured inquiry on the topic of ethnic violence.

This argument should not be taken to imply that the narratives that focus primarily on elite politics are unimportant. Rather the point is that aspects of ethnic violence that could inform broader questions about collective action and other kindred topics of interest to students of political behavior and social science have eluded systematic inquiry. Some scholars have made important initial steps toward systematic data collection. Giuliano (2000), for instance, in her discussion of Tartastan ethnic mobilization, moves toward analyzing the individual psychological processes that underlie ethnic conflict. She argues that "ethnic group preferences do not preexist in some essential latent form prepared for mobilization in support of nationalist programs." Instead, she says, "voters' preferences are constructed through multilayered interactions among politicians' framing of issues, the competitive rhetorics of parties, and voters' preexisting beliefs" (Giuliano 2000, p. 299). Although Giuliano uses qualitative historical evidence, as opposed to survey data, she treats ethnic-group preferences as an object of analysis rather than taking them as given. The next step in this line of research is to approach the study of ethnic violence with an eye toward linking it to temporal or spatial variation in social-psychological circumstances.

ACKNOWLEDGMENTS

We are grateful to Pauline Jones-Luong, who provided many useful suggestions on an earlier draft. The project was funded by a grant from the Institution for Social and Policy Studies at Yale University.

The *Annual Review of Political Science* is online at
http://polisci.annualreviews.org

LITERATURE CITED

Adorno TW. 1950. *The Authoritarian Personality*. New York: Norton

Allport GW. 1954. *The Nature of Prejudice*. Cambridge, MA: Addison-Wesley

Altemeyer RA. 1981. *Right-wing Authoritarianism*. Winnipeg, Can.: Univ. Manitoba Press

Ansolabehere S, Iyengar S. 1995. *Going Negative: How Attack Ads Shrink and Polarize the Electorate*. New York: Free

Arendt H. 1963. *Eichmann in Jerusalem: a Report on the Banality of Evil*. New York: Viking

Aronson E, Stephan C, Sikes J, Blaney N, Snapp M. 1978. *The Jigsaw Classroom*. Beverly Hills, CA: Sage

Asch SE. 1958. Effects of group pressure upon the modification and distortion of judgments. In *Readings in Social Psychology*, ed. EE Macoby, TM Newcomb, EL Hartley, pp. 174–83. New York: Holt, Rinehart & Winston. 3rd ed.

Barth F. 1969. *Ethnic Groups and Boundaries*. Boston: Little Brown

Bates R. 1983. Modernization, ethnic competition, and the rationality of politics in contemporary Africa. In *States versus Ethnic Claims: African Policy Dilemmas*, ed. D Rothchild, VA Olorunsola. Boulder, CO: Westview

Bearman PS. 1991. Desertion as localism: army unit solidarity and group norms in the United States Civil War. *Soc. Forces* 70:321–42

Bell JB. 1993. *Irish Troubles: A Generation of Violence, 1967–1992*. New York: St. Martin's

Bennett C. 1996. *Yugoslavia's Bloody Collapse: Causes, Course and Consequences*. London: Hurst

Bew P, Gibbon P, Patterson H. 1995. *Northern Ireland: 1921–1994: Political Forces and Social Classes*. London: Serif

Blumer H. 1958. Race prejudice as a sense of group position. *Pac. Soc. Rev.* 1:3–6

Bobo L. 1988. Group conflict, prejudice and the paradox of racial attitudes. See Katz & Taylor 1988, pp. 85–114

Brewer MB, Miller N. 1988. Contact and co-operation: When do they work? See Katz & Taylor 1988, pp. 315–26

Brewer MB. 1999. The psychology of prejudice: ingroup love or outgroup hate? *J. Soc. Issues* 55:429–44

Brody RA, Shapiro CR. 1991. The rally phenomenon in public opinion. In *Assessing the President: The Media, Elite Opinion, and Public Support*, ed. RA Brody. Stanford: Stanford Univ. Press.

Brubaker R, Laitin DD. 1998. Ethnic and nationalist violence. *Annu. Rev. Sociol.* 24:423–52

Brustein W. 1996. *Logic of Evil: the Social Origins of the Nazi Party, 1925 to 1933.* New Haven, CT: Yale Univ. Press

Chong D. 1991. *Collective Action and the Civil Rights Movement.* Chicago: Univ. Chicago Press

Cigar N. 1995. *Genocide in Bosnia: The Policy of "Ethnic Cleansing."* College Station, TX: Texas A&M Univ. Press

Comaroff J, Comaroff J. 1992. *Ethnography and the Historical Imagination.* Boulder, CO: Westview

Converse PE. 1962. Information flow and the stability of partisan attitudes. *Public Opin. Q.* 26:578–99

Converse PE. 1964. The nature of belief systems in mass publics. In *Ideology and Discontent*, ed. DE Apter, pp. 206–61. New York: Free

Cox CO. 1948. *Caste, Class and Race.* New York: Doubleday

Crosby F, Bromley S, Saxe L. 1980. Recent unobtrusive studies of black and white discrimination and prejudice: a literature-review. *Psychol. Bull.* 87:546–63

Dasgupta N, McGhee DE, Greenwald AG, Banaji MR. 2000. Automatic preference for white Americans. *J. Exp. Soc. Psychol.* 36:316–28

Des Forges A. 1999. *Leave None to Tell the Story: Genocide in Rwanda.* New York: Human Rights Watch

Devine PG. 1989. Stereotypes and prejudice: their automatic and controlled components. *J. Pers. Soc. Psychol.* 56:5–18

Devine PG, Plant EA, Amodio DM, Harmon-Jones E, Vance SL. 2002. The regulation of explicit and implicit race bias: the role of motivations to respond without prejudice. *J. Pers. Soc. Psychol.* 82:835–48

DeVries DL, Edwards KJ, Slavin RE. 1978. Biracial learning teams and race relations in the classroom: four field experiments on Teams-Games-Tournament. *J. Educ. Psychol.* 70:356–62

Doty RM, Peterson BE, Winter DG. 1991. Threat and authoritarianism in the United States, 1978–1987. *J. Pers. Soc. Psychol.* 61:629–40

Dovidio JF. 2001. On the nature of contemporary prejudice: the third wave. *J. Soc. Iss.* 57:829–49

Dovidio JF, Kawakami K, Gaertner SL. 2002. Implicit and explicit prejudice and interracial interaction. *J. Pers. Soc. Psychol.* 82:62–68

Eller JD, Coughlan RM. 1993. The poverty of primordialism: the demystification of ethnic attachments. *Ethn. Racial Stud.* 16:183–203

Eysenck HJ. 1954. *Psychology of Politics.* London: Routledge

Fazio RH, Jackson JR, Dunton BC. 1995. Variability in automatic activation as an unobtrusive measure of racial attitudes: a bona fide pipeline? *J. Pers. Soc. Psychol.* 69:1013–27

Fearon JD, Laitin DD. 1996. Explaining interethnic cooperation. *Am. Polit. Sci. Rev.* 90:715–35

Fiske ST. 1998. Stereotyping, prejudice and discrimination. In *The Handbook of Social Psychology*, ed. DT Gilbert, S Fiske, G Lindzey, 2:357–414. New York: McGraw-Hill. 4th ed.

Garth TR. 1931. *Race Psychology.* New York: McGraw-Hill

Geertz C. 1963. *Old Societies and New States: The Quest for Modernity in Asia and Africa.* New York: Free

Gilens M. 1999. *Why Americans Hate Welfare:*

Race, Media, and the Politics of Antipoverty Policy. Chicago: Univ. Chicago Press

Gilliam FD, Iyengar S. 2000. Prime suspects: the influence of local television on the viewing public. *Am. J. Polit. Sci.* 44:560–73

Giuliano E. 2000. Who determines the self in the politics of self-determination: identity and preference formation in Tartastan's Nationalist Mobilization. *Comp. Polit.* 32:295–316

Glaser JM. 2002. White voters, black schools: structuring racial choices with a checklist ballot. *Am. J. Polit. Sci.* 46:35–46

Glenny M. 1996. *The Fall of Yugoslavia: the Third Balkan War*. New York: Penguin Books

Gourevitch P. 1998. *We Wish to Inform You That Tomorrow We Will Be Killed with Our Families: Stories from Rwanda*. New York: Farrar, Straus & Giroux

Green DP, Citrin J. 1994. Measurement error and the structure of attitudes: Are positive and negative judgments opposites? *Am. J. Polit. Sci.* 38:256–81

Green DP, Cowden JA. 1992. Who protests: self-interest and white opposition to busing. *J. Polit.* 54:471–96

Green DP, Glaser J, Rich A. 1998a. From lynching to gay-bashing: the elusive connection between economic conditions and hate crime. *J. Pers. Soc. Psychol.* 75:82–92

Green DP, McFalls LH, Smith JK. 2001. Hate crime. *Annu. Rev. Sociol.* 27:479–504

Green DP, Strolovitch DZ, Wong JS. 1998b. Defended neighborhoods, integration, and racially-motivated crime. *Am. J. Sociol.* 104:372–403

Grosby S. 1994. The verdict of history: the inexpungeable tie of primordiality—a response to Eller and Coughlan. *Ethn. Racial Stud.* 17:164–72

Haney C, Banks WC, Zimbardo PG. 1973. Interpersonal dynamics in a simulated prison. *Int. J. Crim. Pen.* 1:69–97

Hardin R. 1992. *One for All: the Logic of Group Conflict*. Princeton, NJ: Princeton Univ. Press

Hardin R. 1995. Self-interest, group identity. In *Nationalism and Rationality*, ed. A Breton, G

Galeotti, P Salmon, R Wintrobe. Cambridge, UK: Cambridge Univ. Press

Hodson G, Dovido JF, Gaertner SL. 2002. Processes in racial discrimination: differential weighting of conflicting information. *Pers. Soc. Psychol. Bull.* 28:460–71

Horowitz D. 1985. *Ethnic Groups in Conflict*. Berkeley: Univ. Calif. Press

Horowitz D. 2001. *Deadly Ethnic Riot*. Berkeley: Univ. Calif. Press

Hovland CI. 1959. Reconciling conflicting results derived from experimental and survey studies of attitude change. *Am. Psychol.* 14:8–17

Hovland CI, Lumsdaine AA, Sheffield FD. 1949. *Experiments on Mass Communication*. Princeton, NJ: Princeton Univ. Press

Hovland CI, Sears RR. 1940. Minor studies in aggression: VI. Correlation of lynching with economic indices. *J. Psychol.* 9:301–10

Hurwitz J, Peffley M, ed. 1998. *Perception and Prejudice*. New Haven, CT: Yale Univ. Press

Hyman HH, Sheatsley PB. 1964. Attitudes toward desegregation. *Sci. Am.* 211:16–23

Ignatieff M. 1994. *Blood and Belonging: Journeys in the New Nationalism*. New York: Farrar, Straus & Giroux

Ignatiev N. 1995. *How the Irish Became White*. New York: Routledge

Iyengar S, Kinder DR. 1987. *News that Matters: Television and American Opinion*. Chicago: Univ. Chicago Press

Iyengar S, Peters MD, Kinder DR. 1982. Experimental demonstrations of the not-so-minimal consequences of television-news programs. *Am. Polit. Sci. Rev.* 76:848–58

Jahoda M, Warren N. 1966. *Attitudes*. Baltimore, MD: Penguin Books

Jennings MK, Niemi RG. 1981. *Generations and Politics: a Panel Study of Young Adults and Their Parents*. Princeton, NJ: Princeton Univ. Press

Kalyvas S. 1999. Wanton and senseless? The logic of massacres in Algeria. *Ration. Soc.* 11(3):243–285

Katz I, Hass RG. 1988. Racial ambivalence and American value conflict: correlation and priming studies of dual cognitive structures. *J. Pers. Soc. Psychol.* 55(6):893–905

Katz PA, Taylor DA. 1988. *Eliminating Racism.* New York: Plenum

Keith A. 1931. *The Place of Prejudice in Modern Civilization.* New York: John Day

Kinder DR, Sanders LM. 1990. Mimicking political debate with survey questions: the case of white opinion on affirmative action for blacks. *Soc. Cogn.* 8:73–103

Kinder DR, Sanders LM. 1996. *Divided by Color: Racial Politics and Democratic Ideals.* Chicago: Univ. Chicago Press

Krueger AB, Pischke JS. 1997. A statistical analysis of crime against foreigners in unified Germany. *J. Hum. Resour.* 32:182–209

Krysan M. 2000. Prejudice, politics, and public opinion: understanding the sources of racial policy attitudes. *Annu. Rev. Sociol.* 26:135–68

Kuklinski JH, Cobb MD, Gilens M. 1997. Racial attitudes and the "New South." *J. Polit.* 59:323–49

LaPiere RT. 1934. Attitudes vs. actions. *Soc. Forces* 13:230–37

Levi M. 1997. *Consent, Dissent, and Patriotism.* Cambridge/New York: Cambridge Univ. Press

Levine RA, Campbell DT. 1972. *Ethnocentrism: Theories of Conflict, Ethnic Attitudes, and Group Behavior.* New York: Wiley

Mamdani M. 2001. *When Victims Become Killers: Colonialism, Nativism, and the Genocide in Rwanda.* Princeton, NJ: Princeton Univ. Press

McFalls LH. 1995. *Communism's Collapse, Democracy's Demise?: The Culture Consequences of the East German Revolution.* London, UK: Macmillan

McGuire WJ. 1968. Personality and susceptibility to social influence. In *Handbook of Personality Theory and Research,* ed. EF Borgatta, WW Lambert, pp. 1130–87. Chicago: Rand-McNally

Menand L. 2001. *Metaphysical Club.* New York: Farrar, Straus & Giroux

Mendelberg T. 1997. Executing Hortons: racial

crime in the 1988 presidential campaign. *Public Opin. Q.* 61:134–57

Mendelberg T. 2001. *The Race Card: Campaign Strategy, Implicit Messages, and the Norm of Equality.* Princeton, NJ: Princeton Univ. Press

Michaels M. 1994. Hell postponed: Burundi's balance of fear. *Time* 144(9):56–57

Milgram S. 1974. *Obedience to Authority.* New York: Harper

Myrdal G. 1944. *American Dilemma.* New York: Harper

Olson M. 1965. *Logic of Collective Action.* Cambridge, MA: Harvard Univ. Press

Olzak S. 1992. *The Dynamics of Ethnic Competition and Conflict.* Stanford, CA: Stanford Univ. Press

Pettigrew TF. 1998. Intergroup contact theory. *Annu. Rev. Psychol.* 49:65–86

Rokeach M. 1960. *Open and Closed Mind: Investigations into the Nature of Belief Systems and Personality Systems.* New York: Basic Books

Rogin MP. 1967. *The Intellectuals and McCarthy: the Radical Specter.* Cambridge, MA: MIT Press

Sambanis N. 2000. The psychology of prejudice: ingroup love or outgroup hate? *J. Soc. Iss.* 55:429–44

Schuman H, Steeh C, Bobo L. 1985. *Racial Attitudes in America.* Cambridge, MA: Harvard Univ. Press

Scott JC. 1985. *Weapons of the Weak: Everyday Forms of Peasant Resistance.* New Haven, CT: Yale Univ. Press

Sears DO. 1986. College sophomores in the laboratory: influences of a narrow database on social psychology view of human nature. *J. Pers. Soc. Psychol.* 51:515–30

Sears DO. 1988. Symbolic racism. See Katz & Taylor 1988, pp. 53–84

Sears DO, Allen HM. 1984. The trajectory of local desegregation controversies and whites' opposition to busing. In *Groups in Contact: The Psychology of Desegregation,* ed. M Miller, M Brewster, pp. 123–51. New York: Academia

Sears DO, Funk CL. 1999. Evidence of the

long-term persistence of adults' political predispositions. *J. Polit.* 61:1–28

Sears DO, Hensler CP, Speer LK. 1979. Whites' opposition to busing: self-interest or symbolic politics. *Am. Polit. Sci. Rev.* 73:369–84

Sears DO, Kinder DR. 1985. Whites' opposition to busing: on conceptualizing and operationalizing group conflict. *J. Pers. Soc. Psychol.* 48:1141–47

Sears DO, Lau RR, Tyler TR, Allen HM. 1980. Self-interest vs symbolic policy attitudes and presidential voting. *Am. Polit. Sci. Rev.* 74:670–84

Sidanius J, Pratto F. 1999. *Social Dominance: an Intergroup Theory of Social Hierarchy and Oppression.* Cambridge, UK: Cambridge Univ. Press

Silber L, Little A. 1995. *The Death of Yugoslavia.* New York: Penguin Books

Sniderman PM, Carmines EG. 1997. *Reaching beyond Race.* Cambridge, MA: Harvard Univ. Press

Sniderman PM, Piazza T. 1993. *The Scar of Race.* Cambridge, MA: Harvard Univ. Press

Sniderman PM, Tetlock PE. 1986. Symbolic racism: problems of motive attribution in political analysis. *J. Soc. Iss.* 42:129–50

Stouffer SA. 1955. *Communism, Conformity, and Civil Liberties: a Cross-section of the Nation Speaks Its Mind.* Garden City, NY: Doubleday

Straus S. 2002. *Rwanda's converted executioners: motivation and mobilization in the 1994 genocide.* Presented at Annu. Meet. Am. Polit. Sci. Assoc., Boston, MA

Sullivan JL, Pierson J, Marcus GE. 1982. *Political Tolerance and American Democracy.* Chicago: Univ. Chicago Press

Taylor DG. 1986. *Public Opinion and Collective Action: the Boston School Desegregation Conflict.* Chicago: Univ. Chicago Press

Vail L, ed. 1989. *Creation of Tribalism in South Africa.* Berkeley: Univ. Calif. Press

Van den Berghe P. 1995. Does race matter? *Nations Natl.* 1(3):359–68

Van Dyke V. 1996. The anti-Sikh riots of 1984 in Delhi: politicians, criminals, and the discourse of communalism. In *Riots and Pogroms,* ed. PR Brass, pp. 201–20. New York: NY Univ. Press

Varshney A. 2002. *Ethnic Conflict and Civic Life: Hindus and Muslims in India.* New Haven, CT: Yale Univ. Press

Wade WC. 1987. *The Fiery Cross: the Ku Klux Klan in America.* New York: Simon & Schuster

Waters M. 1990. *Ethnic Options: Choosing Identities in America.* Berkeley: Univ. Calif. Press

Wellman DT. 1993. *Portraits of White Racism.* New York: Cambridge Univ. Press

White RW. 1993. *Provisional Irish Republicans: an Oral and Interpretive History.* London: Greenwood

Williams RM. 1994. The sociology of ethnic conflicts: comparative international perspectives. *Annu. Rev. Sociol.* 20:49–79

Wilmer F. 1997. Identity, culture and historicity: the social construction of ethnicity in the Balkans. *World Aff.* 160:3–16

Wilson JQ, Kelling GL. 1982. Broken windows: the police and neighborhood safety. *Atl. Month.* 249(Mar.):29–38

Woodward SL. 1995. *Balkan Tragedy: Chaos and Dissolution after the Cold War.* Washington, DC: Brookings Inst.

Yinger J. 1995. *Closed Doors, Opportunities Lost: the Continuing Costs of Housing Discrimination.* New York: Russell Sage Fdn.

Zaller JR. 1992. *Nature and Origins of Mass Opinion.* Cambridge, UK: Cambridge Univ. Press

Zimbardo PG. 1969. The human choice: individuation, reason, and order versus deindividuation, impulse, and chaos. *Nebr. Symp. Motiv.* 17:237–307

SUBJECT INDEX

533

CUMULATIVE INDEXES

CONTRIBUTING AUTHORS, VOLUMES 1–6

CHAPTER TITLES, VOLUMES 2–6

Volume 2 (1999)

Volume 3 (2000)

Volume 4 (2001)

Volume 5 (2002)

Volume 6 (2003)